The International Trading System, Globalization
and History
Volume I

Critical Perspectives on the Global Trading System and the WTO

Series Editors: Kym Anderson
Professor of Economics and Executive Director,
Centre for International Economic Studies
University of Adelaide, Australia
and Lead Economist, Development Research Group
World Bank, USA
Bernard Hoekman
Research Manager, International Trade
World Bank, USA

1. The WTO, Intellectual Property Rights and the Knowledge Economy
   Keith E. Maskus

2. The WTO and Agriculture (Volumes I and II)
   Kym Anderson and Tim Josling

3. The WTO and International Trade Law/Dispute Settlement
   Petros C. Mavroidis and Alan O. Sykes

4. The WTO and Technical Barriers to Trade
   Spencer Henson and John S. Wilson

5. The WTO, Trade and the Environment
   Gary Sampson and John Whalley

6. The International Trading System, Globalization and History (Volumes I and II)
   Kevin H. O'Rourke

Future titles will include:

The WTO and Anti-Dumping
Douglas R. Nelson and Hylke Vandenbussche

The WTO's Core Rules and Disciplines
Kym Anderson and Bernard Hoekman

The WTO and Government Procurement
Simon J. Evenett and Bernard Hoekman

Wherever possible, the articles in these volumes have been reproduced as originally published using facsimile reproduction, inclusive of footnotes and pagination to facilitate ease of reference.

For a list of all Edward Elgar published titles visit our site on the World Wide Web at
www.e-elgar.com

The International Trading System, Globalization and History
Volume I

Edited by

Kevin H. O'Rourke

Professor of Economics
Trinity College Dublin, Ireland

CRITICAL PERSPECTIVES ON THE GLOBAL TRADING SYSTEM AND THE WTO

An Elgar Reference Collection
Cheltenham, UK • Northampton, MA, USA

Published by
Edward Elgar Publishing Limited
Glensanda House
Montpellier Parade
Cheltenham
Glos GL50 1UA
UK

Edward Elgar Publishing, Inc.
136 West Street
Suite 202
Northampton
Massachusetts 01060
USA

A catalogue record for this book is available from the British Library

ISBN   1 84376 427 X (2 volume set)

Printed and bound in Great Britain by MPG Books Ltd, Bodmin, Cornwall

Contents

Acknowledgements

The editor and publishers wish to thank the authors and the following publishers who have kindly given permission for the use of copyright material.

American Economic Association for article: Jeffrey G. Williamson (1998), 'Globalization, Labor Markets and Policy Backlash in the Past', *Journal of Economic Perspectives*, **12** (4), Fall, 51–72.

American Historical Association for article: Paul W. Schroeder (1993), 'Economic Integration and the European International System in the Era of World War I', *American Historical Review*, **98** (4), October, 1130–37.

Cambridge University Press for articles and excerpts: François Crouzet (1964), 'Wars, Blockade, and Economic Change in Europe, 1792–1815', *Journal of Economic History*, **24** (4), December, 567–88; C.P. Kindleberger (1975), 'The Rise of Free Trade in Western Europe, 1820–1875', *Journal of Economic History*, **35** (1), March, 20–55; Charles P. Kindleberger (1989), 'Commercial Policy between the Wars', in Peter Mathias and Sidney Pollard (eds), *The Cambridge Economic History of Europe*, Volume VIII: The Industrial Economies: The Development of Economic and Social Policies, Chapter II, 161–96, 1153–5; Douglas A. Irwin (1995), 'The GATT's Contribution to Economic Recovery in Post-War Western Europe', in Barry Eichengreen (ed.), *Europe's Post-War Recovery*, Chapter 5, 127–50; Kevin H. O'Rourke (1997), 'The European Grain Invasion, 1870–1913', *Journal of Economic History*, **57** (4), December, 775–801.

Johns Hopkins University Press for article: Paul W. Schroeder (1986), 'The 19th-Century International System: Changes in the Structure', *World Politics*, **39** (1), October, 1–26.

Oxford University Press for excerpt: Charles H. Feinstein, Peter Temin and Gianni Toniolo (1997), 'The Legacy of the First World War', in *The European Economy between the Wars*, Chapter 2, 18–37, references.

Kari Polanyi Levitt for excerpts: Karl Polanyi (1944), 'The Hundred Years' Peace' and 'Conservative Twenties, Revolutionary Thirties', in *The Great Transformation*, Chapters 1 and 2, 3–19, 20–30.

Population Council for article: Ashley S. Timmer and Jeffrey G. Williamson (1998), 'Immigration Policy Prior to the 1930s: Labor Markets, Policy Interactions, and Globalization Backlash', *Population and Development Review*, **24** (4), December, 739–71.

David Rockefeller Center for Latin American Studies for excerpt: John H. Coatsworth and Jeffrey G. Williamson (2004), 'The Roots of Latin American Protectionism: Looking before the Great Depression', in Antoni Estevadeordal, Dani Rodrik, Alan M. Taylor and Andrés Velasco (eds), *Integrating the Americas: FTAA and Beyond*, Chapter 2, 37–73.

Carl Strikwerda for his own articles: Carl Strikwerda (1993), 'The Troubled Origins of European Economic Integration: International Iron and Steel and Labor Migration in the Era of World War I', *American Historical Review*, **98** (4), October, 1106–29; Carl Strikwerda (1993), 'Response to "Economic Integration and the European International System in the Era of World War I"', *American Historical Review*, **98** (4), October, 1138–42.

Taylor and Francis Books Ltd for excerpt: Alan Milward (1981), 'Tariffs as Constitutions', in Susan Strange and Roger Tooze (eds), *The International Politics of Surplus Capacity: Competition for Market Shares in the World Recession*, Chapter 5, 57–66.

Taylor and Francis Books Ltd and Martin Gilbert for map included in the following article: Charles H. Feinstein, Peter Temin and Gianni Toniolo (1997), 'The Legacy of the First World War', in *The European Economy between the Wars*, Chapter 2, 18–37, references.

United Nations for excerpt: League of Nations (1942), 'An Analysis of the Reasons for the Success or Failure of International Proposals', in *Commercial Policy in the Interwar Period: International Proposals and National Policies*, Part II, 101–64.

University of Chicago Press for article: C.P. Kindleberger (1951), 'Group Behavior and International Trade', *Journal of Political Economy*, **59** (1), February, 30–46.

Every effort has been made to trace all the copyright holders but if any have been inadvertently overlooked the publishers will be pleased to make the necessary arrangement at the first opportunity.

In addition the publishers wish to thank the Library of the University of Warwick and the Library of Indiana University at Bloomington, USA for their assistance in obtaining these articles.

Introduction

Kevin H. O'Rourke

The establishment of a multilateral international trading regime, underpinned by institutions like the GATT (General Agreement on Trade and Tariffs) and WTO (World Trade Organization), is one of the great achievements of post-World War II international diplomacy. Public debate today properly focuses on the many flaws in the system – for example, on the failure to liberalize trade sufficiently in areas of particular concern to developing countries, such as agriculture and textiles. Nonetheless, the contrast between the widespread cooperation of today and the complete failure of the interwar period to achieve a durable trade liberalization is striking.

Despite the recent emergence of an 'anti-globalization' movement, it is tempting to conclude that the international economy is now set on an irreversible course towards ever-greater levels of integration. History cautions against any such an assumption, however. The world has gone through previous eras of international integration, and all have been followed by disintegration, typically associated with war: the record clearly shows that globalization is not irreversible. Moreover, during the interwar period the international community erected a number of international institutions which were supposed to help facilitate supranational responses to common economic problems: for example, the League of Nations, the Bank for International Settlements, and the International Labour Organization. Numerous international conferences tried to promote trade liberalization; but all these efforts came to nothing. The mere existence of international organizations, and a multilateral approach to tariff reduction, cannot guarantee an open trading system.

If history cannot offer us guarantees or false reassurances, maybe it can help us to think more rigorously about what is required for an open international trading system to be established and maintained. There is a vast literature on the determinants of international trade policy, and all the usual suspects are represented in these volumes: ideas (Volume I, Chapters 1, 8, 17; Volume II, Chapter 5); the economic interests of sectors or classes within society (Volume I, Chapters 6, 13, 14, 16); a variety of state-level explanations (Volume I, Chapter 7; Volume II, Chapters 1–8, 16, 17); technical issues regarding the ways in which trade treaties are constructed (Volume II, Chapters 8–10); and miscellaneous but nonetheless important considerations such as the needs of states for revenue (Volume I, Chapter 3; Volume II, Chapter 15), and the important symbolic role which tariffs can play in debates about the distribution of power within societies (Volume I, Chapter 2). It is this diversity of possible explanations that makes this field so intellectually fascinating; at the same time, it makes generalizations about the 'lessons of history' difficult.

These volumes' main focus is the history of the international trading system over the past two centuries, from the turmoil associated with the Anglo-French wars of 1793–1815, to the post-1945 liberalization under the auspices of the GATT. Broadly speaking, the period can be divided into three epochs. The nineteenth century (1815–1914), and especially the late nineteenth century (1870–1914), was a period of impressive globalization: trade shares expanded rapidly, price gaps between markets shrank, and inter-continental flows of both capital and labour boomed (O'Rourke and Williamson 1999). On the other hand, the period encompassing the two world wars (1914–1945) was one of protectionism, barriers to migration, and widespread default associated with a drying up of international lending. Finally, the period since 1945 has seen the gradual recovery of the international economic system to pre-1914 levels of integration, with a sharp acceleration in several measures of globalization during the 1990s.

Both price and quantity data clearly show a U-shaped pattern of international economic integration, with high levels of integration in 1914 being followed by interwar disintegration and post-1945 re-integration. This U-shape can be documented for international capital and labour markets, as well as for international commodity trade (Obstfeld and Taylor 1998; O'Rourke 2002). A cursory reading of the historical record might lead to the assumption that these trends can entirely be explained by policy: nineteenth-century liberalism, followed by interwar autarky and post-1945 US-led liberalism. While the focus of these volumes is on the causes of international trade policy, rather than on its consequences, it is important to note that such an account would be much too simplistic. The primary cause of nineteenth-century globalization was technological change: railroads and steamships dramatically cut transport costs, facilitating the movement of goods and people, while the telegraph was crucial in integrating international capital markets. To be sure, politics played an important supporting role in this process. In the half century following Waterloo, many countries gradually abandoned the severe restrictions that had been associated with the Napoleonic Wars, and several, notably the UK, moved towards substantial trade liberalization (Kindleberger, Volume I, Chapter 1). Trade wars remained the exception rather than the rule in the late nineteenth century, in sharp contrast with previous epochs (the classic exception being the Franco-Italian trade war of 1887–1898) (Volume II, Chapters 16, 17). However, the late nineteenth century was never the free-trading *Belle Epoque* that it is sometimes portrayed as; tariffs were high in the United States throughout the period, as is well known, but tariffs were also extremely high in Latin America (Volume I, Chapter 3). In much of Europe, tariffs were increased in the 1880s and 1890s in an attempt to offset the distributional impact of the transport revolution (Volume I, Chapters 12, 13).

Nineteenth-century globalization was not primarily caused by declining tariffs; on the other hand, the policy environment was never so restrictive that it overturned the impact of the new transport technologies. The interwar disintegration can however be blamed on commercial policy, since transportation technology clearly did not regress during the period. Kindleberger (Volume I, Chapter 4) gives a concise account of the mostly unsuccessful attempts to undo the damage to the international trading system caused by World War I, which characterized the 1920s, as well as the descent into much deeper levels of protectionism associated with the Great Depression, and the American attempts to reduce tariffs following the signing of the Reciprocal Trade Agreements Act in 1934. Finally, post-1945 integration can largely be explained by trade liberalization; the rate of technological change affecting international transportation was less dramatic in the late twentieth century than it was in the late nineteenth (Hummels 1999; Mohammed and Williamson 2003).

The traditional account of nineteenth- and twentieth-century trade policy stressed the conversion of the UK to free trade, and the gradual spread of free trade principles to the European Continent in the middle decades of the century (Volume I, Chapter 1). The 1860s and 1870s represented a high water mark for international economic liberalism according to this account, with the period from 1880 onwards marking a gradual return to protectionism, nationalism and imperialism. This trend was greatly reinforced by World War I, and the interwar period saw a wholesale reversion to autarky. Finally, after 1945 institutions such as the GATT and the European Payments Union oversaw a return to a more liberal trading environment. Several readings in these volumes dispute the clear divisions between periods implicit in this familiar narrative. As already mentioned, there was no free trading golden age in nineteenth-century Latin America (or in the New World more generally), although accounts of the economic history of that continent during the interwar period often implicitly assume that there had been. Similarly, Milward (Volume I, Chapter 2) downplays the contrast between European trade policy before and after 1880, pointing out that many of the larger states, such as Russia and the Habsburg Empire, had not liberalized their economies at all in the earlier period, or only barely so: the nineteenth century was according to him a predominantly protectionist one. Gallagher and Robinson (Volume II, Chapter 6) argue that there was no dramatic shift towards imperialism on the part of the British after 1880; rather, British imperial policy was consistent throughout the mid and late nineteenth century, aiming at securing trade by informal means when possible, and by formal annexation only when strictly necessary. (This claim has been the subject of some dispute, and Platt (Volume II, Chapter 7) gives a flavour of the debate.)

Despite these caveats, most of the readings in these volumes implicitly accept the traditional account, and speak to some or all of the following questions: Why was the nineteenth century more liberal than the centuries which preceded it, and than the 1914–1945 period which was to follow? What explains the widespread European liberalization of the mid nineteenth century, and the higher tariffs of the 1880s and 1890s? Why were the international institutions and multilateral conferences of the interwar period so ineffectual in their attempts to restore an open international trading environment, and what changed after 1945?

One crucial reason why the nineteenth century was more liberal than earlier centuries is simply that it was more peaceful. Geopolitics are a crucial determinant of the openness of the international trading regime, and insecurity and warfare had been major impediments to international trade in centuries past. For example, commodity price gaps between Amsterdam and Southeast Asia clearly reveal disintegration during the 1650s and 1660s, coinciding with the first and second Anglo-Dutch Wars; during the 1750s, coinciding with the Seven Years War (1756–1763); and during the 1790s, coinciding with the outbreak of the French and Napoleonic Wars (1793–1815) (O'Rourke and Williamson 2002). Crouzet (Volume I, Chapter 6) shows that the disruption associated with the last of these wars was both extensive and long-lived. Blockades and embargoes had large relative price effects, the volume of trade declined sharply, and import-substitution was everywhere encouraged. This last effect is the primary reason why wars (or Great Depressions) have such long-lasting effects: industries which have grown up under such hothouse conditions tend to require protection to survive, and whenever wars end they leave powerful protectionist coalitions in their wake (Findlay and O'Rourke 2001). Thus, according to Crouzet the trade embargoes and blockades associated with the wars of 1793–1815 replaced French industry's traditional Atlantic orientation with an inward-looking and defensive one, and help explain France's abiding suspicion of the international marketplace; while Jefferson's Embargo Act (1807–9) arguably had similar effects in the Northern USA. In exactly the same manner, World War I led to peacetime demands for industrial protection in countries such as India, Australia and Argentina; more seriously, it led to wartime expansions of grain production in regions such as North America, to cope with Allied demand, which in turn provoked a postwar crisis of agricultural over-supply which was a key source of interwar trade tensions, and helped provoke the American Smoot-Hawley tariff (Volume I, Chapters 11, 15 and 17).

Wars and openness are fundamentally incompatible. It is therefore an important fact that the ratio of battlefield deaths to population in Europe was between seven and eight times higher in the eighteenth century than in the nineteenth (not counting the wars of 1793–1815). Viewed in this context, a key institutional innovation which ushered in the long nineteenth century, and helped make it the canonical period of globalization, was the international system instituted by the Congress of Vienna, which marked the end of an unusually bloody, lengthy, and worldwide conflict (Schroeder, Volume I, Chapter 7). In Paul Schroeder's view, the political equilibrium which ensued arose from 'a mutual consensus on norms and rules, respect for law, and an overall balance among the various actors in terms of rights, security, status, claims, duties and satisfactions rather than power' (Schroeder 1992, p. 694). Rather than relying on an unattainable balance of power, the Congress implicitly recognized British and Russian hegemony in their respective spheres of influence (the wider globe, and Eastern Europe and much of Asia respectively); but the hegemony was relatively benign, and the entire system relied on 'the restoration of the rule of law, beginning with its foundation, the security and legitimacy of all thrones' (Schroeder 1992, p. 696).

Ultimately, of course, the Vienna system was unable to withstand the rise of Germany, which simultaneously challenged British dominance overseas, Russian dominance in Eastern Europe, and British economic dominance in Western Europe. Nonetheless, the fact remains that European wars were less important during this canonical globalization period than they have been before or since; and this is surely no coincidence. While some Marxists have argued that World War I was an inevitable consequence of capitalism's scramble for overseas territories to exploit, others have argued that self-interest made business a powerful advocate for peace during the nineteenth century, a position harking back to the very old argument that trade fosters peace. Polanyi (Volume I, Chapter 17) argues that financiers were a key anti-war constituency during the nineteenth century, while Strikwerda (Volume I, Chapter 8; see also Chapters 9 and 10) argues that the growth of multinational business, especially in the coal and iron industries, might have helped prevent a European war had not the less rational impulses of nationalism intervened.

Whether it was inevitable or not, clearly World War I had a devastating, long-run impact on the international economy, as had previous conflicts. Economic historians seeking to understand long-run patterns of integration and disintegration have much to learn from scholars working in other fields, notably political and military history, and international relations. On the other hand, warfare was not the only threat facing the late-nineteenth-century international economy. Standard Heckscher–Ohlin trade theory predicts that globalization will have distributional consequences, and if the losers from trade or international factor flows are sufficiently powerful, they may be able to lobby politicians successfully for a variety of defensive measures. This was the case in much of Europe from the 1880s, as landowners saw their rents and asset values threatened by an invasion of cheap grain from the New World and Russia; while some countries such as Denmark overhauled their agricultural structures in response to this shock, a more common response was agricultural tariffs (Kindleberger, Volume I, Chapter 12). Moreover, the extent to which countries responded via tariffs can be related to the quantitative impact which cheap grain would have had on their land rents or real wages (O'Rourke, Volume I, Chapter 13): these tariffs can be thought of as an endogenous response to a globalization shock. In much the same way, the countries of the New World began erecting immigration restrictions during this period, in response to the impact which large unskilled labour flows were having on inequality levels there (Timmer and Williamson, Volume I, Chapter 14). The nineteenth-century experience shows that if left unmanaged, globalization can undermine itself.

This is not to deny the importance of World War I in destroying the liberal economy of the pre-1914 era: it was an enormous shock which had long-run as well as short-run consequences for international economic integration. Indeed, the imbalances to which it gave rise were, as already stated, one of the key causes of the interwar descent into autarky. So was the complete failure of the League of Nations in its attempts to revive world trade; although it hardly seems fair to blame that organization for the shortcomings of its member states. The League itself surveyed its own record in 1942 (Volume I, Chapter 16), and blamed a number of factors which are echoed in other readings: the concern of interwar governments about balance of payments problems, particularly in the context of faltering international capital markets (Volume I, Chapter 16; Volume II, Chapters 1 and 8); the difficulties which the most-favoured nation (MFN) principle implied for negotiating trade agreements (Volume II, Chapter 8); the role of ideas, and in particular a belief that autarky offered important advantages to nations (Volume I, Chapter 17); and political insecurity, which made economic cooperation much more difficult. In a classic contribution, Kindleberger (Volume II, Chapter 1) offered a more systemic explanation for the interwar debacle: it lacked a dominant or hegemonic power which would provide public goods to the rest of the world and thus facilitate the smooth functioning of the international economic system. Such a hegemon would maintain capital flows to other countries, especially in times of distress; and it would pursue open trading policies, ensuring that others would always be able to export there. Whereas the British had stuck to unilateral free trade after 1846, and provided large amounts of liquidity to the rest of the world, the United States failed to provide liquidity to other countries during the Great Depression, and imposed the infamous Smoot-Hawley tariff of 1930, which triggered a wave of retaliation.

This thesis is so plausible that it has triggered an enormous literature. Several of the readings in Volume II (in particular Chapters 2 and 4) dispute the empirical validity of the argument as it applies to the nineteenth century: for example, the western European trade liberalization of the 1860s appears to have had nothing to do with British pressure; furthermore, Britain was more hegemonic in 1815 than in 1860, so why did it take so long for an open system to emerge? Others (Volume II, Chapters 3, 5) point out that by maintaining an open system, the hegemon may undermine its own relative position, as other countries converge on it in terms of their economic development. This may lead some in the leader country to question its continued adherence to free-trade principles, especially in a situation where others are not abiding by the same principles: calls for 'fair trade' rather than free trade were a feature of economic debate in the early twentieth century in Britain, and in the United States during the 1980s (Volume II, Chapter 11). O'Brien and Pigman (Volume II, Chapter 5) argue that by ignoring such pleas, and naively adhering to a rigid unilateral free-trade ideology, British politicians undermined British interests. On the other hand, British policies were rigorously self-interested in the developing world during this period, and were indeed aimed at opening markets for trade: it is in the British Empire that the hegemonic argument works best in a nineteenth-century context (Volume II, Chapters 6 and 7).

David Lazer (Volume II, Chapter 9) provides a quite different, but still systemic, account of why the mid nineteenth century saw such a burst of tariff cutting in western Europe. According to him, bilateral trade deals such as the Cobden–Chevalier Treaty of 1860 between the United

Kingdom and France gave other countries a strong incentive to push for such deals themselves, since otherwise they faced being squeezed out of what amounted to preferential trading areas. France and Belgium signed a treaty in 1861; a Franco-Prussian treaty was signed in 1862; Italy entered the 'network of Cobden–Chevalier treaties' in 1863 (Bairoch 1989, p. 40); Switzerland in 1864; Sweden, Norway, Spain, the Netherlands and the Hanseatic towns in 1865; and Austria in 1866. The argument that the Cobden–Chevalier Treaty was so successful in sparking further liberalization because it was discriminatory is ironic, since it embodied the MFN clause, and the many trade treaties to which it gave rise also incorporated the non-discrimination principle. In Irwin's words, the nineteenth-century trade treaties were examples of 'progressive bilateralism' (Irwin, Volume II, Chapter 8), which held out the possibility that countries not initially involved in the treaty making could subsequently engage in the process, and which gave them every incentive to do so.

By contrast, the MFN clause proved to be an obstacle to tariff cutting in the interwar period, since it not only made it more difficult for regional arrangements such as customs unions or free-trade areas to get off the ground, but also gave individual countries an incentive to free ride, by waiting to reap the benefits of other parties' agreements, while refusing to lower tariffs themselves. The principle of non-discrimination makes a lot of sense in terms of economic efficiency and after the heavily managed trade of 1914–1918, restoring the MFN principle was a major priority for policy makers (Van V. Fay, Volume II, Chapter 10). Indeed, the interwar period saw many examples of 'pernicious bilateralism' which justified this conventional wisdom, with countries imposing exchange controls and entering into a range of exclusionary, and often coercive, bilateral deals. However, whereas in the 1860s the MFN clause ensured that tariff concessions, once granted, were rapidly generalized to all, in the interwar period, and again at the Torquay GATT Round of 1950–1951, it proved an obstacle to reaching agreement on tariff cuts in the first place (Volume I, Chapters 5, 16; Volume II, Chapter 8). Moving from bilateral to multilateral trade negotiations was how the international community overcame these free-rider problems from the 1960s onwards, albeit at the cost of ever-more complicated negotiations.

The classic exception to the MFN principle, and the one explicitly allowed under GATT and WTO rules, is the customs union; of which the two classic examples are the German Zollverein of 1834–1871, and the European Economic Community which was founded in 1957. Today's Europhiles might like this juxtaposition of examples, since the Zollverein culminated in German unity; and indeed both organizations have faced similar practical problems, such as the difficulty of reaching decisions when these are subject to national vetoes (Henderson, Volume II, Chapter 14). On the other hand, there is little evidence that the Zollverein per se fostered a German spirit of unity, since most of its members fought with Austria against Prussia in the war of 1866 (Volume II, Chapter 13); nor is there much evidence that the German customs union was founded in order to achieve static or dynamic gains from trade, or that it was the dominant cause of nineteenth-century German industrialization (Volume II, Chapters 14, 16). Whether the European project, as well as the many other current moves towards regional free-trade arrangements, constitute progressive or pernicious bilateralism remains to be seen. History suggests that this will be one crucial factor determining whether the international trading regime remains relatively open in the years ahead.

References

Bairoch, Paul (1989), 'European trade policy, 1815–1914', in Peter Mathias and Sidney Pollard (eds), *The Cambridge Economic History of Europe*, Vol. VIII. Cambridge: Cambridge University Press.

Findlay, Ronald and Kevin H. O'Rourke (2001), 'Commodity market integration 1500–2000', *NBER Working Paper* 8579. Cambridge, MA: NBER.

Hummels, David (1999), 'Have international transportation costs declined?' Mimeo, Purdue University.

Mohammed, Saif I. Shah and Jeffrey G. Williamson (2003), 'Freight rates and productivity gains in British tramp shipping 1869–1950', *NBER Working Paper* 9531. Cambridge, MA: NBER.

Obstfeld, Maurice and Alan M. Taylor (1998), 'The Great Depression as a watershed: international capital mobility in the long run', in Michael D. Bordo, Claudia D. Goldin and Eugene N. White (eds), *The Defining Moment: The Great Depression and the American Economy in the Twentieth Century.* Chicago: University of Chicago Press.

O'Rourke, Kevin H. (2002), 'Europe and the causes of globalization, 1790–2000', in Henryk Kierzkowski (ed.), *From Europeanization of the Globe to the Globalization of Europe.* London: Palgrave.

O'Rourke, Kevin H. and Jeffrey G. Williamson (1999), *Globalization and History: The Evolution of a Nineteenth-Century Atlantic Economy.* Cambridge, MA: MIT Press.

O'Rourke, Kevin H. and Jeffrey G. Williamson (2002), 'When did globalization begin?' *European Review of Economic History*, **6**, 23–50.

Schroeder, Paul W. (1992), 'Did the Vienna Settlement rest on a balance of power?' *American Historical Review*, **97**, 683–706.

Part I
Overviews

[1]

The Rise of Free Trade in Western Europe, 1820-1875

I

THE textbook theory of tariffs, and their converse, the movement to freer trade, has more elements than we need for the nineteenth century, but also lacks some. In the usual comparative statics, a tariff may be said to have ten effects: on price, trade, production (the protective effect), consumption, revenue, terms of trade, internal income distribution, monopoly, employment and the balance of payments.

For present purposes we can dispense with the employment effect. The terms-of-trade effect arises only in connection with export taxes; and the monopoly effect must be converted to dynamic form, that increased imports stimulate growth by forcing competition and responsive innovation.

We may illustrate the bulk of the needed effects with the simplest of partial-equilibrium diagrams of a familiar sort. In Figure 1, an import tariff, t, raises the domestic price P_t above the world price P_w (assumed to be unaffected by the tariff), reduces trade from MM to M'M', expands production by MM' and reduces consumption by M'M. An increase in rent to producers consists of the quadrilateral a; revenue accruing to the government is represented by b. Removal of the tariff reverses all movements. An export tax in Figure 2 reduces price and trade, cuts down on producers' rent, increases consumption, reduces production and earns governmental revenue. Conversely, removal of an export tax raises price, production and producers' rent, enlarges trade, reduces domestic consumption, loses revenue. In the nineteenth century when direct taxation was limited, the revenue effect could not be disregarded as it is today. Prohibition of exports or imports had in varying degree all other effects on price, trade, production, consumption, redistribution, monopoly, but wiped out revenue (and the terms of trade). This assumed that the prohibition or prohibitive tax was not undermined by smuggling.

Static theory needs two further elements. The first is a theory of incidence. With more than two factors, are rents retained by the

20

Rise of Free Trade   21

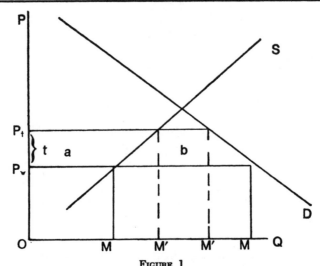

FIGURE 1
IMPORT TAX IN PARTIAL EQUILIBRIUM
Source: see text.

initial recipient or are they competed away in bidding for still
more scarce resources? The second is another factor, or institutional
interest, beyond the normal agriculture and manufacturing, that is,
the merchant, with whom may be included shipping. The merchant

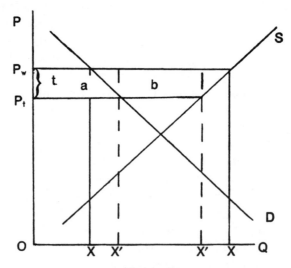

FIGURE 2
EXPORT TAX IN PARTIAL EQUILIBRIUM
Source: see text.

is interested in maximizing trade not for its impact on production or consumption, but to increase turnover, on which, provided national merchants and ships are used, he earns a return. For trade, any goods will do, including those of foreigners which have no impact on domestic production or consumption of the goods in question. (Shipping interests of course insist on the use of national-flag vessels.)

Such is the economic model. Political and sociological elements will be added as required and will include: the view (for example, of Cobden) that free trade leads to peace; trade treaties as foreign treaties in general, desired for reasons of foreign policy, balance of power and the like; ideology, bandwagon effects, and the need of most men to be consistent. It is especially necessary to indicate the relationships between economic interest and political power.

In his interesting study of the formation of the United States tariff of 1824, Jonathan Pincus asserts that tariff-making can be explained by the success or failure of various interests in obtaining rents, the quadrilateral *a* in Figure 1. In this view, the tariff is a collective good, passage of which requires limited numbers of concentrated producers: if the interested parties are diffuse, the fallacy of composition takes over as each element seeks to become a "free rider," leaving the transactions costs of engineering the tariff change to others. This is a theory applicable to representative democracies, and leaves little room for executive leadership.[1] Nor does it make allowance for intermediate goods.

That diffuse interests are less well served than concentrated ones in the legislative process is widely accepted in the theory of tariff formation in comparing producers and final consumers. Households count for little in tariff-making since the interest of any one is too small to stir it to the political effort and financial cost necessary to achieve results. With intermediate goods however, the consumption effect cannot be disregarded, as industries which rely on a given

---

[1] See Jonathan Pincus, "A Positive Theory of Tariff Formation Applied to Nineteenth-Century United States," Ph.D. dissertation, Stanford University, 1972. For the theory of collective goods, see M. Olson, Jr., *The Logic of Collective Action: Public Goods and the Theory of Groups* (Cambridge, Mass.: Harvard University Press, 1965; rev. ed., 1971); Albert Breton, *The Economic Theory of Representative Democracy* (Chicago: Aldine, 1974); and, introducing leadership, N. Frohlich, J. A. Oppenheimer and O. R. Young, *Political Leadership and Collective Goods* (Princeton: Princeton University Press, 1971). Frohlich, Oppenheimer and Young view leaders as political entrepreneurs, interested in maximizing their "surplus" or profit in providing collective goods against taxes, extortions, donations or purchases.

import, or on a product exported by another industry, may be as effectively concentrated as producers of final goods.

On the Pincus theory, the movement toward free trade in Western Europe would have to be based on the dominance of the interests of consumers of intermediate imports over those of their producers, and of producers of exports over consumers of exported intermediates. A variety of other general explanations have been offered.

In Bastiat's view, the rise of free trade was the result of the spread of democracy.[2] Free trade has also been regarded as the interest of the bourgeois class in England and the landed aristocracy on the Continent, while protection has been sought by the aristocracy in England and the bourgeois manufacturing classes on the Continent.[3]

Somewhat more dynamically, Johnson asserts that countries whose competitiveness in world markets is improving tend to move in the free-trade direction while countries whose competitiveness is deteriorating tend to move to increasing protection. A footnote states "Outstanding examples are the adoption of free trade by Britain in the 19th century . . . the espousal of freer trade by the United States and Canada in the period after the Second World War."[4]

In what follows we shall find these views insufficiently detailed.

II

The beginnings of free trade internationally go back to the eighteenth century. French Physiocratic theory enunciated the slogan *laisser faire, laisser passer* to reduce export prohibitions on agricultural products. Pride of place in practice, however, goes to Tuscany, which permitted free export of the corn of Sienese Maremma in 1737, after the Grand Duke Francis had read Sallustio Bandini's *Economical Discourse*.[5] Beset by famine in 1764, Tuscany gradually opened its market to imported grain well before the Vergennes Treaty of 1786 between France and Britain put French Physiocratic doctrine into practice. Grain exports in Tuscany had been restricted

[2] Cited by Alexander Gerschenkron, *Bread and Democracy in Germany* (Berkeley: University of California Press, 1943), p. 65.

[3] Karl F. Helleiner, *Free Trade and Frustration, Anglo-Austrian Negotiations, 1860-70* (Toronto: Toronto University Press, 1973), p. 63.

[4] Harry G. Johnson, "Economic Theory of Protectionism, Tariff Bargaining and the Formation of Customs Unions," *Journal of Political Economy*, LXXIII (1965), 256-83.

[5] James Montgomery Stuart, *The History of Free Trade in Tuscany* (London: Cassell, Potter & Galpin, 1876), p. 24.

24   *Kindleberger*

under the "policy of supply," or "provisioning," or "abundance," under which the city-states of Italy limited exports from the surrounding countryside in order to assure food to the urban populace. Bandini and Pompeo Neri pointed out the ill effects this had on investment and productivity in agriculture.

The policy of supply was not limited to food. In the eighteenth and early nineteenth century exports were restricted in, among others, wool and coal (Britain), ashes, rags, sand for glass and firewood (Germany), ship timbers (Austria), rose madder (the Netherlands), and silk cocoons (Italy). The restrictions on exports of ashes and timber from Germany had conservation overtones. The industrial revolution in Britain led further to prohibitions on export of machinery and on emigration of artisans, partly to increase the supply for local use, but also to prevent the diffusion of technology on the Continent. We return to this below.

What was left in the policy of supply after the Napoleonic War quickly ran down. Prohibition of export of raw silk was withdrawn in Piedmont, Lombardy and Venetia in the 1830's, freedom to export coal from Britain enacted in the 1840's. Details of the relaxation of restrictions are recorded for Baden[6] as part of the movement to occupational freedom. The guild system gradually collapsed under the weight of increasing complexity of regulations by firms seeking exceptions for themselves and objecting to exceptions for others. A number of prohibitions and export taxes lasted to the 1850's—as industrial consumers held out against producers, or in some cases, like rags, the collectors of waste products. Reduction of the export tax on rags in Piedmont in 1851 produced a long drawn-out struggle between Cavour and the industry which had to close up thirteen plants when the tax was reduced.[7] To Cavour salvation of the industry lay in machinery and the substitution of other materials, not in restricting export through Leghorn and Messina to Britain and North America.

Elimination of export taxes and prohibitions in nineteenth-century Europe raises doubt about the universal validity of the theory of the tariff as a collective good, imposed by a concentrated interest at

[6] Wolfram Fischer, *Der Staat und die Anfänge der Industrialisierung in Baden, 1800-1850* (Berlin: Duncker u. Humblot, 1962).

[7] Luigi Bulferetti and Claudio Costantini, *Industria e Commercio in Liguria nell'età del Risorgimento (1700-1861)* (Milan: Banca Commerciale Italiana, 1966), pp. 495-501.

the expense of the diffuse. The interest of groups producing inputs for other industries are normally more deeply affected than those of the consuming industries, but it is hardly possible that the consuming is always less concentrated than the producing industry.

III

The question of export duties sought by domestic manufacturers on their raw materials, and of import duties on outputs demanded by producers for the domestic market was settled in the Netherlands in the eighteenth century in favor of mercantile interests.[8] These were divided into the First Hand, merchants, shipowners and bankers; the Second Hand, which carried on the work of sorting and packing in staple markets, and wholesaling on the Continent; and the Third Hand, concerned with distribution in the hinterland. Dutch staple trade was based partly on mercantile skills and partly on the pivotal location of Amsterdam, Rotterdam, and other staple towns dedicated to trade in particular commodities, largely perishable, non-standardized and best suited to short voyages. The First Hand dominated Dutch social and political life and opposed all tariffs on export or import goods, above a minimum for revenue, in order to maximize trade and minimize formalities. From 1815 to 1830 when Holland and Belgium were united as the Low Countries, the clash between the Dutch First Hand and Belgian producers in search of import protection from British manufactures was continuous and heated.

The First Hand objected to taxes for revenue on coffee, tea, tobacco, rice, sugar, and so on, and urged their replacement by excises on flour, meat, horses and servants.[9] Tariffs for revenue must be held down to prevent smuggling and to sustain turnover. The safe maximum was given variously as three percent,[10] five percent,[11] and on transit even as one-half percent. Transit in bond, and transit with duty-cum-drawback were thought too cumbersome. The Dutch made a mistake in failing to emulate London which in 1803 adopted

---

[8] H. R. C. Wright, *Free Trade and Protection in the Netherlands, 1816-30: A Study of the First Benelux* (Cambridge: Cambridge University Press, 1955), pp. 58-59.

[9] Ibid., p. 112.

[10] Ibid., p. 139.

[11] Ibid., p. 113.

26   *Kindleberger*

a convenient entrepôt dock with bonding.[12] Loss of colonies and of overseas connections in the Napoleonic Wars made it impossible from early in the period to compete with Britain in trade. Equally threatening was Hamburg which supplied British and colonial goods to Central Europe in transit for one-half percent revenue duty maximum,[13] many products free, and all so after 1839.[14] More serious, however, was the rise of direct selling as transport efficiency increased. Early signs of direct selling can be detected at the end of the seventeenth century when Venice and Genoa lost their role as intermediary in traffic between Italy and the West.[15] By the first half of the nineteenth century, they were abundant. "By the improved intercourse of our time (1840), the seller is brought more immediately into contact with the producer."[16] Twenty years earlier, the Belgian members of a Dutch Belgian fiscal commission argued that "there was no hope of restoring Holland's general trade. Owing to the spread of civilization, all European countries could now provide for themselves in direct trading."[17]

It is a mistake to think of merchants as all alike. As indicated, First, Second and Third Hands of the Netherlands had different functions, status and power. In Germany, republican merchants of Hamburg differed sharply from those of the Imperial city, Frankfurt, and held out fifty years longer against the Zollverein.[18] Within Frankfurt there were two groups, the English-goods party associated with the bankers, and the majority, which triumphed in 1836, interested in transit, forwarding, retail and domestic trade within the Zollverein. In Britain a brilliant picture had been drawn of a pragmatic free trader, John Gladstone, father of William, opposed to timber preferences for Canada, enemy of the East India Company

---

[12] G. R. Porter, *The Progress of the Nation* (New ed., London: John Murray, 1847), chapter 16.

[13] Joachim F. E. Bläsing, *Das goldene Delta und sein eisernes Hinterland, 1815-1841, von niederländisch-preuschischen zu deutschniederländischen Wirtschaftsbeziehungen* (Leiden: H. E. Stenfert Kroese, 1973), p. 85.

[14] John MacGregor, *Germany, Her Resources, Government, Union of Customs and Power under Frederick William IV* (London: Whittaker and Co., 1948), p. 246.

[15] Luigi Bulferetti and Claudio Costanti, *Industria e Commercio in Liguria,* Chapter 2.

[16] John Bowring, "Report on the Prussian Commercial Union, 1840," *Parliamentary Papers,* 1840, Volume XXI, pp. 38.

[17] H. R. C. Wright, *Free Trade and Protection,* p. 124.

[18] Helmut Böhme, *Frankfurt und Hamburg: Des Deutsches Reiches Silber- und Gold-loch und die Allerenglishte Stadt des Kontinents* (Frankfurt-am-Main: Europäische Verlagsanstalt, 1968), Chapter 1.

Rise of Free Trade   27

monopoly on trade with China and India, but supportive of imperial preference in cotton and sugar, and approving of the Corn Laws on the ground of support for the aristocracy he hoped his children could enter via politics.[19] The doctrinaire free traders of Britain were the cotton manufacturers like Gladstone's friend, Kirman Finlay, who regarded shipowners and corn growers as the two great monopolists.

The doctrinaire free trade of the Dutch merchants led to economic sclerosis,[20] or economic sickness.[21] Hamburg stayed in trade and finance and did not move into industry. In Britain, merchants were ignorant of industry, but were saved by the coming of the railroad and limited liability which provided an outlet for their surplus as direct trading squeezed profits from stapling. The economic point is simple: free trade may stimulate, but again it may lead to fossilization.

IV

The movement toward freer trade in Britain began gross in the eighteenth century, net only after the Napoleonic Wars. In the initial stages, there was little problem for a man like Wedgewood advocating free trade for exports of manufactures under the Treaty of Vergennes with France, but prohibitions on the export of machinery and emigrations of artisans.[22] Even in the 1820's and 1830's, a number of the political economists—Torrens, Baring, Peel, Nassau Senior —favored repeal of the Corn Laws but opposed export of machinery.[23] The nineteenth century is seen by Brebner not as a steady march to *laisser-faire* but as a counterpoint between Smithian *laisser-faire* in trade matters and, after the Reform Bill, Benthamic intervention of 1832 which produced the Factory, Mines, Ten Hours and similar acts from 1833 to 1847.[24]

---

[19] S. G. Checkland, *The Gladstones, A Family Biography, 1764-1851* (Cambridge: Cambridge University Press, 1971), pp. 139, 333.

[20] Francois Crouzet, "Western Europe and Great Britain: 'Catching Up' in the First Half of the Nineteenth Century," in A. J. Youngson, ed., *Economic Development in the Long Run* (London: Allen & Unwin, 1972), p. 120.

[21] Joachim F. E. Bläsing, *Das goldene Delta*, p. 83.

[22] Herbert Heaton, *Economic History of Europe* (New York: Harper & Bros., 1936), pp. 398-99.

[23] Bernard Semmel, *The Rise of Free Trade Imperialism: Classical Political Economy, The Empire of Free Trade and Imperialism, 1750-1850* (Cambridge: Cambridge University Press, 1970), pp. 181 ff.

[24] J. Bartlett Brebner, "Laissez-Faire and State Intervention in Nineteenth Century Britain," in E. M. Carus-Wilson, ed., *Essays in Economic History*, Vol. 3 (London: Edward Arnold, 1962), pp. 254-256.

First came the revenue aspect, which was critical to the movement to freer trade under Huskisson in the 1820's, Peel in the 1840's, and Gladstone in the 1850's. Huskisson and Gladstone used the argument that the bulk of revenue was produced by taxes on a few items—largely colonial products such as tea, coffee, sugar, tobacco, and wine and spirits—and that others produced too little revenue to be worth the trouble. Many were redundant (for example, import duties on products which Britain exported). Others were so high as to be prohibitory or encouraged smuggling and reduced revenue. When Peel was converted to free trade, it was necessary to reintroduce the income tax before he could proceed with repeal of 605 duties between 1841 and 1846, and reductions in 1035 others. The title of Sir Henry Parnell's treatise on freer trade (1830) was *Financial Reform*.

But Huskisson was a free trader, if a cautious one. He spoke of benefits to be derived from the removal of "vexatious restraints and meddling interference in the concerns of internal industry and foreign commerce."[25] Especially he thought that imports stimulated efficiency in import-competing industry. In 1824 the prohibition on silk imports had been converted to a duty of thirty percent regarded as the upper limit of discouragement to smuggling. In a speech on March 24, 1826, said by Canning to be the finest he had heard in the House of Commons, Huskisson observed that Macclesfield and Spitalfield had reorganized the industry under the spur of enlarged imports, and expanded the scale of output.[26] Both Michel Chevalier[27] and Count Cavour[28] referred to this positive and dynamic response to increased imports in England.

Restrictions on export of machinery and emigration of artisans went back, as indicated, to the industrial revolution. Prohibition of export of stocking frames was enacted as early as 1696. Beginning in 1774 there was a succession of restrictions on tools and utensils for the cotton and linen trades and on the emigration of skilled artisans. The basis was partly the policy of supply, partly naked maintenance of monopoly. Freedom had been granted to the emi-

[25] *William Huskisson, (The Speeches of the Right Honorable)* (London: John Murray, 1832), II, p. 328.
[26] Ibid., pp. 503-05.
[27] Pierre Labracherie, *Michel Chevalier et ses idées économiques* (Paris: Picart, 1929), p. 131.
[28] A. J. White, *Early Life and Letters of Cavour, 1810-1848* (London: Oxford University Press, 1925), ŋ. 131 (*sic*).

gration of workmen in 1824. After the depression of the late 1830's, pressure for removal of the prohibition came from all machinery manufacturers. Following further investigation by a Select Committee of Parliament, the export prohibition was withdrawn.

The main arguments against prohibition of the export of machinery and emigration of artisans were three: they were ineffective, unnecessary, and harmful. Ineffectuality was attested to by much detail in the Select Committee reports on the efficiency of smuggling. Machinery for which licenses could not be obtained could be dispatched illegally in one of a number of ways—by another port, hidden in cotton bales, in baggage or mixed with permitted machinery and in a matter of hours. Guaranteed and insured shipments could be arranged in London or Paris for premia up to thirty percent.

That prohibition was unnecessary was justified first by the inability of foreigners, even with English machinery and English workmen, to rival English manufacturers. Britain has minerals, railways, canals, rivers, better division of labor, "trained workmen habituated to all industrious employments."[29] "Even when the Belgians employed English machines and skilled workers, they failed to import the English spirit of enterprise, and secured only disappointing results."[30] In 1825, the Select Committee concluded it was safe to export machinery, since seven-year-old machinery in Manchester was already obsolete.[31]

In the third place it was dangerous. Restriction on emigration of artisans failed to prevent their departure, but did inhibit their return.[32] Restriction of machinery, moreover, raised the price abroad through the cost of smuggling, and stimulated production on the Continent. Improvement in the terms of trade through restriction of exports (but failure to cut them off altogether) was deleterious for its protective effect abroad.

Greater coherence of the Manchester cotton spinners over the machinery makers spread over Manchester, Birmingham and London may account for the delay from 1825 to 1841 in freeing up ma-

[29] Report of the Select Committee on the Laws Relating to the Export of Tools and Machinery, 30 June 1825, in *Parliamentary Papers, Reports of Committee,* (1825), Vol. V, p. 12.
[30] H. R. C. Wright, *Free Trade and Protection,* p. 130.
[31] *Report of the Select Committee,* p. 44.
[32] Charles Babbage, *The Economy of Machinery and Manufactures* (London: Charles Knight, 4th ed., 1835), p. 363.

Kindleberger

chinery, and support Pincus' theory on the need of concentrated interests. But the argument of consistency was telling. In 1800 the Manchester manufacturers of cloth had demanded a law forbidding export of yarn, but did not obtain it.[33] The 1841 Second Report concluded that machinery making should be put on the same footing as other departments of British industry.[34] It is noted that Nottingham manufacturers approved free trade but claim an exception in regard to machinery used in their own manufacture.[35] Babbage observed that machinery makers are more intelligent than their users, to whose imagined benefits their interests are sacrificed, and referred to the "impolicy of interfering between two classes."[36] In the end, the Manchester Chamber of Commerce became troubled by the inconsistency and divided; the issue of prohibition of machinery was subsumed into the general attack on the Corn Laws.[37] In the 1840's, moreover, the sentiment spread that Britain should become the Workshop of the World, which implied the production of heavy goods as well as cotton cloth and yarn.[38]

Rivers of ink have been spilled on the repeal of the Corn Laws, and the present paper can do little but summarize the issues and indicate a position. The questions relate to the Stolper-Samuelson distribution argument, combined with the Reform Bill of 1832 and the shift of political power from the landed aristocracy to the bourgeois; incidence of the Corn Laws and of their repeal, within both farming and manufacturing sectors; the potential for a dynamic response of farming to lower prices from competition; and the relation of repeal to economic development on the Continent, and especially whether industrialization could be halted by expanded and assured outlets for agricultural produce, a point of view characterized by Gallagher and Robinson[39] as "free-trade imperialism." A number of lesser issues may be touched upon incidentally: inter-

[33] Karl Polanyi, *The Great Transformation* (New York: Farrar & Rinehart, 1944), p. 136.

[34] Second Report of the Select Committee on Exportation of Michinery, 1841, in *Parliamentary Papers*, (1841), Vol. VII, p. xx.

[35] Ibid., p. xiv.

[36] Charles Babbage, *The Economy of Machinery*, p. 364.

[37] A. E. Musson, "The 'Manchester School' and Exportation of Machinery," *Business History*, XIV (January 1972), 49.

[38] J. D. Chambers, *The Workshop of the World British Economic History, 1820-1880* (London: Oxford University Press, 2nd ed., 1968), Chapter I.

[39] J. Gallagher and R. Robinson, "The Imperialism of Free Trade," *Economic History Review*, 2nd ser., VI (1953), 1-15.

action between the Corn Laws and the Zollverein, and its tariff changes in the 1840's; the question of whether repeal of the Corn Laws, and of the Navigation Acts would have been very long delayed had it not been for potato famine in Ireland and on the Continent; and the question of whether the term "free-trade imperialism" is better reserved for Joseph Chamberlain's Empire preference of fifty years later.

In the normal view, the Reform Bill of 1832 shifted power from the land and country to the factory and city, from the aristocratic class to the bourgeois, and inexorably led to changes in trade policies which had favored farming and hurt manufacturing. One can argue that repeal of the Corn Laws represented something less than that and that the Reform Bill was not critical. The movement to free trade had begun earlier in the Huskisson reforms; speeches in Parliament were broadly the same in 1825 when it was dominated by landed aristocrats as in the 1830's and 1840's. Numbers had changed with continued manufacturing expansion, but nothing much more. Or one can reject the class explanation, as Polanyi does, and see something much more ideological. "Not until the 1830s did economic liberalism burst forth as a crusading passion." The liberal creed involved faith in man's secular salvation through a self-regulating market, held with fanaticism and evangelical fervor.[40] French Physiocrats were trying to correct only one inequity, to break out of the policy of supply and permit export of grain. British political economists of the 1830's and 1840's, who won over Tories like Sir Robert Peel and Lord Russell, and ended up in 1846 with many landlords agreeable to repeal of the Corn Laws, represented an ideology.[41] "Mere class interests cannot offer a satisfactory explanation for any long-run social process."[42]

Under a two-sector model, free trade comes when the abundant factor acquires political power and moves to eliminate restrictions imposed in the interest of the scarce factor which has lost power. In reality factors of production are not monolithic. Some confusion in the debate attached to the incidence of the tax on imported corn within both farming and manufacturing. The Anti-Corn Law League of Cobden and Bright regarded it as a tax on food, taking as much

[40] Karl Polanyi, *The Great Transformation*, pp. 133-37.
[41] D. C. Moore, "The Corn Laws and High Farming," *Economic History Review*, 2nd ser., XVIII (December 1965).
[42] Karl Polanyi, *The Great Transformation*, p. 152-53.

32   *Kindleberger*

as twenty percent of the earnings of a hand-loom weaver. Cobden
denied the "fallacy" that wages rose and fell with price of bread.[43]
Benefits, moreover, went to the landlord and not to the farmer or
farm-laborer, as rents on the short leases in practice rose with the
price of corn.[44] There are passages in Cobden which suggest that
hurt of the Corn Laws fell upon the manufacturing and commercial
classes rather than labor[45] but the speeches run mainly in terms of
a higher standard of living for the laborer who would spend his
"surplus of earnings on meat, vegetables, butter, milk and cheese,"
rather than on wheaten loaves.[46] The Chartists were interested not
in repeal, but in other amenities for the workers. Peel's conversion
waited on his conclusion that wages did not vary with the price of
provision, and that repeal would benefit the wage earner rather than
line the pockets of the manufacturer.[47]

In any event, with Gladstone's reductions in duties on meat, eggs
and dairy products, with High Farming, and an end to the movement off the farm and out of handwork into the factory real wages
did rise in the 1850's, but so did profits on manufacturing. As so
often in economic debates between two alternatives, history provides
the answer which economists abhor, both. Nor did repeal bring a
reduction in incomes to landlords—at least not for thirty years—as
the farm response to repeal, and to high prices of food produced by
the potato famine, was more High Farming.

Cobden may have only been scoring debating points rather than
speaking from conviction when on a number of occasions he argued
that the repeal would stimulate landlords "to employ their capital
and their intelligence as other classes are forced to do in other pursuits" rather than "in sluggish indolence," and to double the quantity
of grain, or butter, or cheese, which the land is capable of providing,[48] with "longer leases, draining, extending the length of fields,
knocking down hedgerows, clearing away trees which now shield

[43] Richard Cobden, *Speeches on Questions of Public Policy*, John Bright and James
E. Thorold Rogers, ed., Vol. I (London: Macmillan, 1870), pp. 4, 18.
[44] Ibid., p. 57.
[45] The Corn Laws "inflict the greatest amount of evil on the manufacturing and
commercial community . . ." (Ibid., p. 57). "Silversmiths and jewellers get orders
not from the Duke of Buckingham but from Manchester, from Glasgow or Liverpool
or some other emporium of manufactures," (Ibid., p. 90).
[46] Ibid., p. 106.
[47] J. D. Chambers, *The Workshop*, p. 71.
[48] Richard Cobden, *Speeches*, p. 70.

the corn"[49] and to provide more agricultural employment by activity to "grub up hedges, grub up thorns, drain, ditch."[50] Sir James Caird insisted that High Farming was the answer to the repeal of the Corn Laws[51] and many shared his view.[52] The fact is, moreover, that the 1850's were the Golden Age of British farming, with rapid technical progress through the decade though it slowed thereafter. Repeal of the Corn Laws may not have stimulated increased efficiency in agriculture, but they did not set it back immediately, and only after the 1870's did increases in productivity run down.

The political economists in the Board of Trade—Bowring, Jacob, MacGregor—sought free trade as a means of slowing down the development of manufacturing on the Continent. They regarded the Zollverein as a reply to the imposition of the Corn Laws, and thought that with its repeal Europe, but especially the Zollverein under the leadership of Prussia, could be diverted to invest more heavily in agriculture and to retard the march to manufacturing. There were inconsistencies between this position and other facts they adduced: Bowring recognized that Germany had advantages over Great Britain for the development of manufacturing, and that Swiss spinning had made progress without protection.[53] The 1818 Prussian tariff which formed the basis for that of the Zollverein was the lowest in Europe when it was enacted—though the levying of tariffs on cloth and yarn by weight gave high effective rates of protection despite low nominal duties to the cheaper constructions and counts. Jacob noted that the export supply elasticity of Prussian grain must be low, given poor transport.[54] "To export machinery, we must import corn,"[55] but imports of corn were intended to prevent the development of manufacturers abroad, whereas the export of machinery assisted it. The rise and progress of German manufacturing was attributed to restrictions on the admission of German agricultural products and wood, imposed by France and England, but also

---

[49] Ibid., p. 100.
[50] Ibid., p. 103.
[51] Sir James Caird, *High Farming . . . The Best Substitute for Protection*, pamphlet, 1848, in Lord Ernle, *English Farming Past and Present* (London: Longmans Green, 4th ed., 1937), p. 374.
[52] D. C. Moore, "The Corn Laws and High Farming."
[53] John Bowring, *Report on the Prussian Commercial Union*, p. 55.
[54] Lucy Brown, *The Board of Trade and the Free-Trade Movement, 1830-1842* (Oxford: Clarendon Press, 1958), pp. 135, 171 ff.
[55] Testimony of Thomas Ashton, in *First Report of the Select Committee*, para. 235.

34   *Kindleberger*

to "the natural advantages of the several states for manufacturing industry, the genius and laborious character and the necessities of the German people, and . . . especially the unexampled duration of peace, and internal tranquility which all Germany enjoyed."[56]

The clearest statements are those of John Bowring. In a letter of August 28, 1839 to Lord Palmerston he asserted that the manufacturing interest in the Zollverein "is greatly strengthened and will become stronger from year to year unless counteracted by a system of concessions, conditional upon the gradual lowering of tariffs. The present state of things will not be tenable. The tariffs will be elevated under the growing demands and increasing power of the manufacturing states, or they will be lowered by calling into action, and bringing over to an alliance, the agricultural and commercial interests."[57] In his testimony before the Select Committee on Import Duties in 1840 he went further: "I believe we have created an unnecessary rivalry by our vicious legislation; that many of these countries never would have been dreamed of being manufacturers."[58]

On this showing, the repeal of the Corn Laws was motivated by "free trade imperialism," the desire to gain a monopoly of trade with the world in manufactured goods. Zollverein in the 1830's merely indicated the need for haste.[59] Torrens and James Deacon Hume, among others, had been pushing for importing corn to expand exports in the 1820's, before Zollverein was a threat.

Reciprocity had been a part of British commercial policy in the Treaty of Vergennes in 1786, in treaties reducing the impact of the Navigation Laws in the 1820's and 1830's. The French were suspicious, fearing that they had been out-traded in 1786. They evaded Huskisson's negotiations in 1828. But reciprocity was unnecessary, given David Hume's law. Unilateral reduction of import duties increased exports.[60] Restored into the British diplomatic armory in 1860, reciprocity later became heresy in the eyes of political economists, and of the manufacturing interest as well.

The view that ascribes repeal of the Corn Laws to free-trade imperialism, however, fails adequately to take account of the ideology of the political economists, who believed in buying in the cheapest

[56] John MacGregor, *Germany, Her Resources*, p. 68.
[57] John Bowring, *Report on the Prussian Commercial Union*, p. 287.
[58] *Minutes Evidence*, p. 59, para. 782.
[59] Bernard Semmel, *The Rise of Free Trade Imperialism*, p. 149.
[60] D. C. M. Platt, *Finance, Trade and Politics in British Foreign Policy, 1815-1914* (Oxford: Clarendon Press, 1968), p. 87.

Rise of Free Trade   35

market and selling in the dearest, or of the short-run nature of the interests of the Manchester merchants themselves. It was evident after the 1840's that industrialization on the Continent could not be stopped, and likely that it could not be slowed down. The Navigation Acts were too complex; they had best be eliminated.[61] The Corn Laws were doomed, even before the Irish potato famine, though that hastened the end of both Corn Laws and Navigation Acts, along with its demonstration of the limitation of market solutions under some circumstances.[62]

"A good cause seldom triumphs unless someone's interest is bound up with it."[63] Free trade is the hypocrisy of the export interest, the clever device of the climber who kicks the ladder away when he has attained the summit of greatness.[64] But in the English case it was more a view of the world at peace, with cosmopolitan interests served as well as national.

It is difficult in this to find clearcut support for any of the theories of tariff formation set forth earlier. Free trade as an export-interest collective good, sought in a representative democracy by concentrated interests to escape the free rider would seem to require a simple and direct connection between the removal of the tariff and the increase in rents. In the repeal of the Corn Laws, and the earlier tariff reductions of Huskisson and Peel, the connection was roundabout—through Hume's law, which meant that increased imports would lead to increased prices or quantities (or both) exported on the one hand, and/or through reduced wages, or higher real incomes from lower food prices on the other. Each chain of reasoning had several links.

Johnson's view that free trade is adopted by countries with improving competitiveness is contradictory to the free-trade-imperialism explanation, that free trade is adopted in an effort to undermine foreign gains in manufacturing when competitiveness has begun to decline. The former might better account in timing for Adam Smith's advocacy of free trade seventy years earlier—though that

---

[61] J. H. Clapham ,"The Last Years of the Navigation Acts," in E. M. Carus-Wilson, ed., *Essays in Economic History*, p. 161.

[62] Cecil Woodham-Smith, *The Great Hunger: Ireland, 1845-1849* (New York: Harper & Row, 1962).

[63] Mill, cited by Bernard Semmel, *The Rise of Free Trade Imperialism*, p. 207.

[64] List, cited by Kenneth Fielden, "The Rise and Fall of Free Trade," in C. J. Bartlett, ed., *Britain Pre-eminent: Studies in British World Influence in the Nineteenth Century* (London: Macmillan, 1969), p. 85.

Kindleberger

had large elements of French Physiocratic thought—or apply to the
1820's when British productivity was still improving, before the
Continent had started to catch up. In turn, free-trade imperialism is
a better explanation for the 1830's than for the end of the 1840's,
since by 1846 it was already too late to slow, much less to halt, the
advance of manufacturing on the Continent.

Vested interests competing for rents in a representative democracy, thrusting manufacturers seeking to expand markets, or faltering innovators, trying as a last resort to force exports on shrinking
markets—rather like the stage of foreign direct investment in Vernon's product cycle when diffusion of technology has been accomplished—none of these explanations seems free of difficulties as
compared with an ideological explanation based on the intellectual
triumph of the political economists, their doctrines modified to incorporate consistency. The argument took many forms: static, dynamic,
with implicit reliance on one incidence or another, direct or indirect
in its use of Hume's law. But the Manchester School, based on the
political economists, represented a rapidly rising ideology of freedom for industry to buy in the cheapest and sell in the dearest market. It overwhelmed the Tories when it did not convert them.
Britain in the nineteenth century, and only to a slightly lesser extent
the Continent, were characterized by a "strong, widely-shared conviction that the teachings of contemporary orthodox economists,
including Free Traders, were scientifically exact, universally applicable, and demanded assent."[65] In the implicit debate between
Thurman Arnold who regarded economic theorists (and lawyers)
as high priests who rationalize and sprinkle holy water on contemporary practice, and Keynes who thought of practical men as responding unconsciously to the preaching of dead theorists, the
British movement to free trade is a vote, aided by the potato famine,
for the view of Keynes.

V

France after 1815 was a high-tariff country which conformed to
the Pincus model for a representative democracy with tariffs for
various interests, except that (a) there were tariffs for all, and
(b) it was not a democracy. The Physiocratic doctrine of *laisser-
faire* for agricultural exports had been discredited in its reciprocal
form by the disaster wreaked by imports up to 1789 under the Treaty

---

[65] Ibid., p. 78.

of Vergennes. The Continental system, moreover, provided strong protection to hothouse industries which was continued in the tariff of 1816, and elaborated in 1820 and 1822. To the principles of Turgot, that there should be freedom of grain trade inside France but no imports except in period of drought, were added two more: protection of the consumer by regulating the right of export of wheat—a step back from Physiocratic doctrine—and protecting the rights of producers by import tariffs.[66] In introducing the tariff of 1822 for manufactures, Saint-Cricq defended prohibitions, attacked the view that an industry which could not survive with a duty of twenty percent should perish, saying that the government intended to protect all branches together: "agriculture, industry, internal commerce, colonial production, navigation, foreign commerce finally, both of land and of sea."[67]

It was not long, however, before pressures for lower duties manifested themselves. Industries complained of the burden of the tariff on their purchases of inputs, and especially of the excess protection accorded to iron. It was calculated that protection against English iron cost industrial consumers fifty million francs a year and had increased the price of wood—used for charcoal, and owned by the many noble *maîtres de forges*—by thirty percent on the average and in some places fifty percent.[68] Commissions of inquiry in 1828 and 1834 recommended modifications in duties, especially to enlarge supplies which local industry was not in a position to provide, and to convert prohibitions into tariffs. A tumult of conflict broke out in the Chamber among the export interests of the ports, the textile interests of Alsace and Normandy, the *maîtres de forges* and the consumers of iron, with no regard, says the protectionist Gouraud, for the national interest. The Chambers were then dissolved by the cabinet, and tariffs adjusted downward, in coal, iron, copper, nitrates, machinery, horses. Reductions of the 1830's were followed in the peaks of business by similar pressure for reductions in prosperous phases of the cycle of the 1840's and 1850's.[69]

A troubling question that involved conflicting interests in this

[66] Charles Gouraud, *Histoire de la politique commerciale de la France et son influence sur le progrès de la richesse publique depuis le moyen age jusqu'à nos jours,* I, II (Paris: Auguste Durand, 1854), p. 198.
[67] Ibid., p. 208.
[68] Léon Amé, *Etudes sur les tariffs de douanes et sur les traités de commerce,* I, II (Paris: Imprimerie Nationale, 1876), pp. 170-74.
[69] Maurice Lévy-Leboyer, *Histoire économique et sociale de la France depuis 1848* (Paris: Cours de Droit, Institut d'études politiques, 1951-52), p. 96.

Kindleberger

period was presented by sugar, for which it was impossible to find a solution agreeable at the same time to colonial planters, ship-owners, port refiners, consumers and the treasury. Colonial supply was high cost and a 55 francs per 100 kilograms duty on foreign supplies was needed to keep the sugar ports content. This, however, made it economical to expand beet-sugar production, begun during the Continental blockade, and the sugar ports turned to taxing this domestic production, less heavily at first, but with full equality in 1843. By this time it was too late, and with the freeing of the slaves in 1848, French colonial sugar production no longer counted.

The free-trade movement in France had its support in Bordeaux, the wine-exporting region; Lyon, interested in silk; and Paris, producer of so-called Paris article for sale abroad (cabinet ware, perfumes, imitation jewelry, toys, and so on). Later Norman agricultural interests in the export of butter and eggs to London teamed up with Bordeaux in wine to resist the attempts by textile interests to enlist agriculture in favor of higher tariffs.[70]

Intellectual support to free trade led by Bastiat from Bordeaux, and with Michel Chevalier as its most prestigious member, is dismissed by Lévy-Leboyer[71] as unimportant. Nonetheless, Chevalier had an important part in the negotiation of the treaty, and in persuading Napoleon III to impose it on France in the face of the united opposition of the Chamber of Deputies. Some attention to his thought is required.

The prime interest of the *Société d'Economie Politique* and of Chevalier was growth.[72] His two-year visit to the United States in 1833-1835 impressed him with the contribution of transport to economic growth and contributed to his 1838 major work on *The Material Interests of France in Roads, Canals and Railroads*. American protectionist doctrine of Henry Carey seems not to have affected him. Polytechnician, graduate of the *Ecole des Mines*, Chevalier's first interest in freer trade came from a project to establish woolen production in the Midi, and to obtain cheaper wool.[73] Much of his later reasoning was in terms of the penalty to industry from expensive materials: Charging 35 francs for a quintal of iron

[70] Michel Augé-Laribé, *La politique agricole de la France de 1880 à 1940* (Paris: Presses Universitaires de France, 1950), p. 66.

[71] Maurice Lévy-Leboyer, *Histoire économique et sociale*, p. 92.

[72] Michel Lutfalla, "Aux origines du libéralisme économique de la France," *Revue d'histoire économique et sociale*, L (1972), 500, 515, 517.

[73] Maurice Levy-Leboyer, *Histoire economique et sociale*, p. 95.

Rise of Free Trade   **39**

worth 20 imposes on industry "the labor of Sisyphus and the work of Penelope."[74] His major argument, at the *Collège de France,* and in his *Examen du Système Commercial,* cited the success of Spital-field and Macclesfield when Huskisson permitted competition of imports; and the experience of the manufacturers of cotton and woolen textiles in Saxony who were worried by the enactment of Zollverein but sufficiently stimulated by import competition so that in two or three years their industry was flourishing.[75] The letter of Napoleon III to Fould[76] talks in specifics of the need to abolish all duties on raw materials essential to industry to encourage production, and to reduce by stages the duties on goods which are consumed on a large scale. In the more general introduction it states that "lack of competition causes industry to stagnate," echoing the Chevalier view. Chevalier himself was one of the judges of the Universal Exposition of 1855 in Paris and noted that France received so many prizes that no one dared confess to being a protectionist.[77]

There were economic purposes behind the Anglo-French treaty, as evidenced by the proposal in France in 1851 for tariffs of twenty percent, ten percent and a duty-free on wholly manufactured goods, semi-finished manufactures and raw materials[78]; by actual reductions in duties on coal, iron and steel in 1852 as the railroad boom picked up; and by the legislative proposal designed by Napoleon III in 1855, but not put forward until after the Crimean War, to admit 241 items duty free, reduce tariffs on 19 others, remove all prohibitions and set a top limit of thirty percent. This last was turned down by the Chamber and Napoleon promised not to submit a new tariff proposal before 1861.

Economic interests were involved, and the theories of great men like Cobden and Chevalier. However, there was more: Napoleon III was starting to engage on foreign adventure. He wanted to rid Italy of Austrian rule by use of arms. The British opposed his military measures, despite their recent use of force in Crimea. The treaty was

---

[74] Michel Chevalier, *Cours d'economie politique, Fait au Collège de France,* I, II, III (2nd ed., Paris: no publisher stated, 1855), p. 538.

[75] Pierre Labracherie, *Michel Chevalier,* pp. 130-31.

[76] S. Pollard and C. Holmes, *Documents of European Economic History. Vol. I: The Process of Industrialization, 1750-1870* (New York: St. Martin's Press, 1968), pp. 384-86.

[77] Michel Chevalier, *Cours d'economie politique,* p. 521.

[78] A. A. Illasu, "The Cobden Chevalier Commercial Treaty of 1860," *The Historical Journal,* XIV (March 1971), 80.

40   *Kindleberger*

used to hold British neutrality, as much as or more than to stimulate growth in France. Moreover, it did not need to be submitted to the Chamber. Under the Constitution of 1851, the Emperor had the sole power to make treaties, and such treaties encompassed those dealing with trade.

The move was successful both politically and economically. With the help of the French armies, Italy was unified under the leadership of Piedmont, and French growth never faltered under the impetus of increased imports. French industries met competition successfully and checked the growth of imports after two years.[79] While its effects are intermingled with those of the spread of the French railroad network, it "helped to bring about the full development of the industrial revolution in France."[80]

Further, it added impetus to the free-trade movement in Europe. This was under way in the early 1850's, following repeal of the Corn Laws. The Swiss constitution of 1848 had called for a tariff for revenue only and protective duties were reduced progressively from 1851 to 1885. The Netherlands removed a tariff on ship imports and a prohibition against nationalization of foreign ships. Belgium plugged gap after gap in its protective system in the early 1850's, only to turn around at the end of the decade and adopt free trade down the line. Piedmont, as we shall see, and Spain, Portugal, Norway and Sweden (after 1857) undertook to dismantle their protective and prohibitive restrictions.[81] With the Anglo-French treaty the trickle became a flood. France, Germany, Italy and Britain engaged in negotiating reciprocal trade treaties with the most-favored nation clause.[82]

[79] Marcel Rist, "Une experience française de liberation des échanges au dix-neuvième siècle: le traité de 1860," *Revue d'Economie Politique*, 66 annèe (novembre-decembre 1956), p. 937.

[80] Arthur L. Dunham, *The Anglo-French Treaty of Commerce of 1850 and the Progress of the Industrial Revolution in France* (Ann Arbor: University of Michigan Press, 1930), p. 179.

[81] Hans Rosenberg, *Die Weltwirtschaftskrise von 1857-1859* (Stuttgart-Berlin: Verlag von W. Kohlhammer, 1934), pp. 24-26.

[82] Most lists are given separately by country. For an overview, see Sidney Pollard, *European Economic Integration, 1815-1870* (New York: Harcourt, Brace and Jovanovich, Inc., 1974), p. 117. The impact of repeal of the timber duties and the Navigation Acts in stimulating export-led growth in Scandinavia is treated by Victor D. Norman, "Trade Liberalization and Industrial Growth: The Impact of British Trade Liberalization in the 1840s on Industrialization in the Scandinavian Countries," (MIT, unpublished, December 1970), p. 82. The stimulus to shipping in Norway and to timber exports in Sweden led via linkages to industrialization which the free trade imperialists were seeking to avoid.

Following French defeat at Sedan in 1870 and the abdication of Louis Napoleon, the Third Republic brought in the protectionist Thiers. The Cobden treaty was denounced in 1872. Reversal of policy waited upon the repeal of the Le Chapelier law of 1791, taken in the heat of the French revolution against associations, which forbade economic interests from organizing. Dunham claims that a country with leadership would have accepted a moderate tariff in 1875, but that the free traders had neither organization nor conviction, that is, too many free riders.[83]

The French movement to free trade was taken against the weight of the separate interests,[84] in the absence of strong export interests, with an admixture of economic theory of a dynamic kind, and imposed from above. The motivation of that imposition was partly economic, partly, perhaps even mainly, political. Moreover, it had a bandwagon effect in spreading freer trade.

In the French case, the leadership overwhelmed the concentrated economic interests. That leadership earned its surplus to use Frohlich, Oppenheimer and Young's expression, in a coin different than economic, that is, in freedom to maneuver in foreign policy. It may be possible to subsume increases in leadership surplus in this form into an "economic theory of national decision-making" with costs to vested interests accepted in exchange for political benefits to a national leader, ruling by an imposed constitution, the legitimacy of which is not questioned. The effort seems tortured.

VI

As mentioned earlier, the Prussian tariff of 1818 was regarded when it was enacted as the lowest in Europe.[85] But the duties on coarse yarns and textiles were effectively high, since the tariff was levied by weight. Jacob in 1819 noted that the "system of the Prussian government has always been of manufacturing at home every-

---

[83] Arthur L. Durham, *The Anglo-French Treaty of Commerce*, p. 333.

[84] Apart from consumers of imported materials and machinery. But see the view of Lhomme that the State adopted free trade because it loved the *grande bourgeoisie* and knew their interests better than they did; that the *grande bourgeoisie* recognized this fact and agreed with the tariff reductions except for a few intransigent protectionists like Pouyer-Quartier. See Jean Lhomme, *La Grande Bourgeoisie au Pouvoir, 183-1880* (Paris: Presses Universitaires de France, 1960), p. 179. It is, however, impossible to accept this rationalization.

[85] S. Pollard, *European Economic Integration*, p. 112; William Huskisson, *The Speeches of* —, III, p. 131.

42   *Kindleberger*

thing consumed within the Kingdom; of buying from others, nothing that can be dispensed with," adding "As scarcely any competition exists, but with their own countrymen, there is little inducement to adopt the inventions of other countries, or to exercise their facilities in perfecting their fabrics; none of these have kept pace. . . ."[86] Baden, on joining the Zollverein which adopted the Prussian tariff for the totality, believed itself to be raising its tariff level when it joined.[87] What Baden did, however, was to acquire enforcement: its long border had previously been effectively open.

The Prussian tariff dominated that of the Zollverein, organized in the years from 1828 to 1833, primarily because Prussia took a very liberal view of tariff revenues. Most goods by sea entered the German states via Prussia, directly or by way of the Netherlands, but the text of the Zollverein treaty of 1833 provided that the revenues from the duties after deduction of expenses would be divided among the contracting states according to population.[88] Prussia thus received 55 percent, Bavaria 17 percent, Saxony 6.36 percent, Wurtemberg 5.5 percent, and so on, and was said in 1848 to have sacrificed about two million thalers a year, exclusive of the fiscal loss sustained by smuggling along the Rhine and Lake Constance.[89] This can be regarded as a side-payment made by the beneficiary of income-distribution under Pareto-optimal conditions to gain its policy, or as the disproportionate share of overhead costs of the collective good saddled on the party that most wanted it.[90]

Despite adjustments made in Prussian customs duties between 1819 and 1833, the tariff remained low by British standards. Junker grain growers were hopeful of importing British manufactures in order to sell Britain more grain. Junker bureaucrats, brought up on

[86] William Jacob, *A View of the Agriculture, Manufactures, Statistics and Society in the State of Germany and Parts of Holland and France* (London: John Murray, 1820), pp. 201-02.

[87] Wolfram Fischer, *Der Staat und die Anfänge der Industrialisierung*, p. 128, 134.

[88] S. Pollard and C. Holmes, *Documents of Economic History*, I, p. 374.

[89] John MacGregor, *Germany, Her Resources*, p. 6.

[90] Mancur Olson, Jr. and Richard Zeckhauser, "An Economic Theory of Alliances," *Review of Economics and Statistics*, XLVIII (August 1966). For a view emphasizing the revenue aspects of the Zollverein, and especially saving in the costs of collection and the reduction in smuggling, see Rolf H. Dumke, "The Political Economy of Economic Integration, The Case of the Zollverein of 1834," (Queen's University *Discussion Paper*, 153, presented to the Canadian Economics Association, June 5, 1974). Revenues available from the Zollverein permitted the petty princes to maintain their rule without democratic concessions to bourgeois interests.

Rise of Free Trade   43

Adam Smith and free trade by instinct, were fearful that highly protective rates would reduce the revenue yield.[91]

Outside of Prussia plus Hamburg and Frankfort and the other
grain-growing states of Mecklenburg, Pomerania, and so on, there
was interest in higher tariffs, but apart from the Rhineland, little
in the way of organized interests. Von Delbrück comments that
Prussia and Pomerania had free trade interests and shipping interests, but that outside the Rhineland, which had organized Chambers
of Commerce under the French occupation, there were few bureaucrats, or organs with views on questions of trade and industry. Nor
did the Prussian government see a need to develop them.[92]

Saxony was sufficiently protected by its interior location so as not
to feel threatened by low tariffs, which, as mentioned, were not
really low on coarse cloths. On joining the Zollverein, Baden was
concerned over raising its tariff, and worried lest it be cut off from
its traditional trading areas of Switzerland and Alsace. It fought
with the Zollverein authorities over exemptions for imported capital
equipment, but gradually evolved into a source of pressure, with
Bavaria and Wurtemberg, for higher tariffs on cotton yarns and
iron. Fischer points out that the request for lifting the duty on cotton
yarns from two talers per centner to five was resisted by the weav-
ers of Prussia (the Rhineland) and Silesia.[93]

Cotton yarns and iron were the critical items. Shortly after the
formation of Zollverein, a trend toward protection was seen to be
under way.[94] The Leipsig consul reported a new duty on iron to the
Board of Trade in February 1837 and observed that the switch from
imports of cotton cloth to imports of yarn pointed in the direction
of ultimate exclusion of both.[95] Bowring's letter of August 1839
noted that the manufacturing interest was growing stronger, that
the existing position was untenable, and that tariffs would be raised
under the growing demands and increasing power of the manufacturing states, or would be lowered by an alliance between the agricultural and commercial interests.[96]

[91] *European Economic Integration*, p. 112.
[92] Rudolph von Delbrück, *Lebenserinnerungen*, I (Leipsig: Duncker u. Humblot,
1905), pp. 142-44.
[93] Wolfram Fischer, *Der Staat und die Anfänge der Industrialisierung*, p. 136.
[94] William H. Dawson, *Protection in Germany: A History of German Fiscal Policy
during the Nineteenth Century* (London: P. S. King and Son, 1904), p. 20.
[95] Lucy Brown, *The Board of Trade*, p. 113.
[96] John Bowring, *Report on the Prussian Commercial Union*, p. 287.

44   *Kindleberger*

Open agitation for protection began two and one-half years after the formation of the Zollverein when the South pushed for duties on cotton yarns. Linen yarns and cloth went on the agenda in 1839 and iron, protection for which was sought by Silesian and west German ironwork owners, beginning in 1842.[97] But these groups lacked decisive power. The Prussian landed nobility covered their position by citing the interests of the consumers,[98] and Prince Smith, the expatriate leader of the doctrinaire free traders, in turn tried to identify free trade and low tariffs with the international free-trade movement rather than with the export-interests of the Junkers.[99] The tariff on iron was raised in 1844, those on cotton yarns and linen yarns in 1846. Von Delbrück presents in detail the background of the latter increases, starting with the bureaucratic investigations into linen, cotton, wool, and soda, with their negative recommendation, continuing through the negotiations, in which Prussia was ranged against any increase and all the others in favor, and concluding that the Prussian plenipotentiary to the Zollverein conference was right in not vetoing the increases, as he could have done, operating on the theory that a compromise was more important than the rationally correct measure of this or that tariff.[100] The head of the Prussian Handelsamt was not satisfied with the outcome of the conference but had to accept it.

From 1846 on, the direction of Zollverein tariffs was downward, aided first by the repeal of the Corn Laws and secondly by the Cobden-Chevalier treaty. With the increases of the 1840's and English reductions, the Zollverein tariff from one of the lowest in Europe had become relatively high. Von Delbrück was one of the doctrinaire free traders in the Prussian civil service and notes that in 1863 he had been trying for a reduction on the tariff in pig iron for seven years, since the tariff reform of 1856, which reordered but did not lower duty schedules. He also wanted a reduction in the tariff on cotton cloth; duties on woolens were no longer needed. The opportunity came with the announcement of the Anglo-French treaty. He noted that Austria had gone from prohibitions to tariffs,

[97] Rudolph von Delbrück, *Lebenserinnerungen,* p. 147.

[98] Hans Rosenberg, *Die Weltwirtschaftskrise,* p. 207.

[99] W. O. Henderson, "Prince Smith and Free Trade in Germany," chapter 7 in W. O. Henderson, *Britain and Industrial Europe, 1750-1870: Studies in British Influence on the Industrial Revolution in Western Europe* (Liverpool: Liverpool University Press, 1954), p. 171.

[100] Rudolph von Delbrück, *Lebenserinnerungen,* pp. 162-64.

that the Netherlands had reformed its tariffs with a five percent maximum on industrial production, and that the levels of Italian duties were lower than those in Germany. "Could we stay away from this movement? We could not."[101]

Bismarck was no barrier to the Junker bureaucracy. His view about tariff negotiations was expressed in 1879 in the question: "Who got the better of the bargain?" Trade treaties, he believed, were nothing in themselves but an expression of friendship. His economic conscience at this time, he said later, was in the hands of others.[102] Moreover, he had two political ends which a trade treaty with France might serve: to gain her friendship in the Danish question, and to isolate Austria which was bidding for a role in the German Confederation.[103] Austrian tariffs were high. The lower the levels of the Zollverein the more difficulty she would have in joining it and bidding against Prussia for influence. The Zollverein followed the 1863 treaty with France with a series of others.

Exports of grain from Prussia, Pomerania, and Mecklenberg to London as a percentage of total English imports hit a peak in 1862 at the time of the Civil War[104] and proceeded down thereafter as American supplies took over. The free-trade movement nonetheless continued. Only hesitation prevented a move to complete free trade at the peak of the boom in 1873.[105] There is debate whether the crash later in the year triggered off the return to protection in 1879 or not. Victory in 1871 had enlarged competition in iron and cotton textiles by including Alsace and Lorraine in the new German Empire. Radical free traders and large farmers achieved the reduction in duties on raw iron in 1873 and passed legislative provision for their complete removal in 1877.[106] But Lambi notes that *Gewerbefreiheit* (freedom of occupation) had caused dissatisfaction and in some versions subsumed free trade.[107] By 1875 the iron interests are

---

[101] Ibid., p. 200.

[102] William H. Dawson, *Protection in Germany*, p. 21.

[103] Ivo Nikolai Lambi, *Free Trade and Protection in Germany, 1868-1879* (Wiesbaden: Franz Steiner Verlag, 1963), p. 5.

[104] Wolfgang Zorn, "Wirtschafts- und socialgeschichtliche Zusammenhänge der deutschen Reichsgründungszeit, 1859-1879," in Helmut Böhme, ed., *Probleme der Reichsgrundungszeit, 1848-1879* (Cologne-Berlin: Kipenheur & Witsch, 1968), p. 296.

[105] Kenneth D. Barkin, *The Controversy over German Industrialization, 1890-1902* (Chicago: University of Chicago Press, 1970), p. 33.

[106] Ibid.

[107] Ivo Nikolai Lambi, *Free Trade and Protection*, pp. 83, 113.

organizing to resist the scheduled elimination of iron duties in 1877.

The difference between the 1873 depression which led to tariffs, and the 1857 crisis which did not, lay in (a) the fact that the interests were not cohesive in the earlier period, and (b) that Britain did not keep on lowering duties in the later period as it had in the first.[108] On the first score the Verein Deutscher Eisen- und Stahl Industrielle was formed in 1873 after vertical integration of steel back to iron mining had removed the opposition between the producers and consumers of iron. This much supports the view of the effectiveness of concentrated interests achieving their tariff goals when scattered interests will not—though again it has nothing to do with representative democracy. On the other hand, the free traders also organized; in 1868 the Kongress Nord-Deutscher Landwirte was organized, and in 1871 it was broadened to cover all Germany. In 1872, a Deutsche Landwirtschaftsrat was formed.[109] Many of these organizations and the once free-trade Congress of German Economists were subverted and converted to protection after 1875, but a new Union for the Promotion of Free Trade was formed in September 1876.[110] German economic interests as a whole became organized, and the struggle was among interests concentrated on both sides.

Abandonment of the opposition of the landed interests is perhaps critical. Consumers of iron in machinery, they opposed tariffs on iron up to 1875, but with the decline in the price of grain and the threat of imports, their opposition collapsed. It might have been possible to support tariffs for grain and free trade for iron, but inconsistency is open to attack. After von Delbrück's resignation or discharge in April 1876, Bismarck forged the alliance of bread and iron. As widely recounted, he had strong domestic political motives for higher tariffs on this occasion, as contrasted with his international political gains from lower tariffs up to 1875.

In general, however, the German case conforms to the Stolper-Samuelson explanation: the abundant factor wants free trade; when it becomes relatively scarce, through a gain in manufacturing at home and an expansion of agriculture abroad, it shifts to wanting tariffs. Doctrine was largely on the side of free trade. List's advocacy of national economy had little or no political force. His ultimate goal was always free trade, and his early proposal of ten percent

108 Hans Rosenberg, *Die Weltwirtschaftskrise,* p. 195.
109 Ivo Nikolai Lambi, *Free Trade and Protection,* p. 57.
110 Ibid., p. 191.

duties on colonial goods, fifteen percent on Continental and fifty percent on British was more anti-British than national.[111] In the 1840's he was regarded in Germany, or at least by the Prussians, as a polemicist whose views were offered for sale.[112] Bismarck is often regarded as the arch-villain of the 1879 reversal of Zollverein low tariffs, but it is hard to see that his role was a major one.   .

VII

Italian moves in the direction of free trade prior to 1850 were tentative and scattered. The abandonment of the policy of supply in Tuscany in the eighteenth century has been mentioned earlier, as well as the removal of prohibitions on the export of raw silk in Piedmont, Lombardy and Veneto. Lombard and Venetian tariff policies were largely imposed by Austria, which was perhaps not wholly indifferent to local interests and to the promotion of industry.[113] Piedmont concluded a series of trade treaties with the larger states, especially France and Britain, and in 1847-48, explored a tariff union with Tuscany and the Papal states.[114] But the major initiatives were taken after Cavour became Minister of Agriculture, Industry and Commerce, when Minister of Finance (1851) and then Prime Minister (1852). The low tariffs which Cavour achieved for the Kingdom of Sardinia, were subsequently extended to Italy as a whole after its unification in 1860 under Cavour's leadership, and followed by a series of trade agreements lowering import duties still further.

As a young man Cavour had visited France and Britain, once in 1833-1835 and again in 1842-1843. Like Chevalier, whose lectures he attended in the second visit, he was interested in growth, through banks, public works, and especially market forces encouraged by freedom of trade. He knew Babbage, Nassau Senior, Cobden, de Tocqueville, Sismondi, Cherbuliez, Michalet, Pellegrino Rossi (an

[111] Judith Blow Williams, *British Commercial Policy and Trade Expansion, 1750-1850* (London: Oxford University Press, 1973), p. 199.
[112] Werner Thiedig, *Englands Uebergang zum Freihandel und die deutsche Handelspolitik, 1840-1856* (Giessen: no publisher stated, 1927; 40-page summary of a thesis), pp. 31-32.
[113] Kent Roberts Greenfield, *Economics and Liberalism in the Risorgimento, A Study of Nationalism in Lombardy, 1814-1848* (Baltimore: Johns Hopkins University Press, rev ed., 1965), p. 113.
[114] Shepherd B. Clough, *The Economic History of Modern Italy* (New York: Columbia University Press, 1964), p. 27.

Kindleberger

Italian free-trader, resident in Paris), Chevalier, and Faucher, wrote long papers on English Poor Laws, the Irish question and the Corn Laws.

Cavour was attacked as a doctrinaire who deserted a tried and effective system to follow an abstract theory,[115] but has been defended by biographers as having "a genius for the opportune."[116] His fifty-two speeches on the tariff question as Finance Minister had high educational quality, says Thayer, and achieved an economic revolution. There are views that Cavour's successful pressure for free trade represented economic interests. He was a large landowner and the low tariff has been said to "reflect clearly the interests of the large landowners."[117] Piedmont agriculture was related to western European markets for rice, silks, wine and hides.[118] The application of Piedmont's low tariff to all of Italy has been said to assure the interests of the ruling classes of Britain and France.[119]

For the most part, however, it seems evident that in following low tariff policies in the Kingdom of Sardinia in the early 1850's and in Italy after unification in 1860, Cavour was operating on the basis of a theory. His views were widely shared. Prodi notes that the liberal faith in freedom through the market in 1860 not only triumphed but remained sure and irrefutable. There were some like Cappellarsi who wanted to reduce tariffs slowly as industry was getting ready to export, as in England, and Martullo who was conscious of the differences between Italy and England, and elastic in his application of Adam Smith to Italy.[120] For the most part, however, the tariff problem was ignored in Italy until the inquiry of 1870. Industrialists, led by the wool manufacturer Rossi, disliked the Piedmont low tariff and especially the twenty or more trade treaties which followed. Limited transport over land meant, however, that there was no unified domestic market for local manufacturers to exploit.

[115] A. J. Whyte, *The Political Life and Letters of Cavour, 1848-1861* (London: Oxford University Press, 1930), p. 73.
[116] William Roscoe Thayer, *The Life and Times of Cavour* (Boston: Houghton Mifflin, 1921), p. 133.
[117] Antonino Pedone, "La Politica del Commercio Estere," in Giorgio Fua, ed., *Le Sviluppo Economico in Italia*, Vol. II, Gli Aspetti generali (Milan: Franco Agnelli Editore, 1969), p. 242.
[118] Valerio Castronovo, *Economia e societa in Piemonte dell' unità al 1914*, (Milan: Banca Commerciale Italiana, 1969), p. 16.
[119] Mori, quoted by Gino Luzzato, *L'economia italiana dal 181 al 1914*, Vol. I (1861-1894), (Milan: Banca Commerciale Italiana, 1963), p. 28n.
[120] Romano Prodi, "Il protezionismo nella politica e nell' industria italiana dall' unificazione al 1886," *Nuova Rivista Storica*, L fasc. I-II, 1966, pp. 1-10.

Clough[121] observes that the advantages which were supposed to devolve automatically from the free movement of goods in international commerce did not seem to accrue to Italy. For one thing, loss of custom revenues upset the finances of first Sardinia and then Italy, despite a vigorous expansion of trade.[122] Customs duties had provided 14.7 million lire out of a total revenue of 69.4 million.[123] Secondly, the balance of payments turned adverse, partly, perhaps mainly, as a result of Cavour's and his successors' programs of public works. Piedmont ran up a large debt which later developed on the Kingdom of Italy. In 1866 it became necessary to halt redemption of the lira in gold and the depreciation of the currency during the *corso forzoso* (forced circulation) alleviated some of the effects of competitive imports. But the spread of the railroad in the 1860's and the low tariff policies proved ruinous to industry, especially in the South. The Sardinian tariff schedule was by and large at the same level as those of Modena, Parma and Tuscany, well below that of Lombardy in most goods, though higher in others, but far below the levels of the Papal States and especially of the Kingdom of the Two Sicilies (Naples).[124] After a long period when the country was "strangely deaf" to the troubles caused by the low tariff,[125] the Commission of Inquiry was launched in 1870, the tariff was raised in 1878, and a new system of high tariffs on industry, modified by trade agreements favoring agriculture, was instituted in its place.[126]

IX

My first conclusion reached from this survey was that free trade in Europe in the period from 1820 to 1875 had many different causes. Whereas after 1879, various countries reacted quite differently to the single stimulus of the fall in the price of wheat—England liquidating its agriculture, France and Germany imposing tariffs,

[121] Shepherd B. Clough, *The Economic History of Modern Italy*, p. 114.

[122] Isidore Sachs, *L'Italie, ses finances et son développement économique depuis l'unification du royaume, 1859-1884, d'après des documents officiels* (Paris: Librairie Guillaumin, 1885), p. 748.

[123] Paolo Norsa and Mario Pozzo, *Imposte e tasse in Piemonte durante il periodo cavouriano* (Turin: Museo Nazionale del Risorgimento, 1961), pp. 16, 17.

[124] Giannino Parravicina, *La politica fiscale e le entrate effective del Regno d'Italia* (Archivo Economico dell'Unificazione Italiana, Turin: ILTE, 1958), p. 326.

[125] Gino Luzzato, *L'economia italiana*, p. 28.

[126] Frank J. Coppa, "The Italian Tariff and the Conflict Between Agriculture and Industry: The Commercial Policy of Liberal Italy, 1860-1922," THE JOURNAL OF ECONOMIC HISTORY, XXX (December 1970), 742-69.

50   *Kindleberger*

though for different political and sociological reasons, Italy emigrating (in violation of the assumptions of classical economics), and Denmark transforming from producing grain for export to importing it as an input in the production of dairy products, bacon and eggs[127] —before that the countries of Europe all responded to different stimuli in the same way. Free trade was part of a general response to the breakdown of the manor and guild system. This was especially true of the removal of restrictions on exports and export taxes, which limited freedom of producers. As more and conflicting interests came into contention, the task of sorting them out became too complex for government (as shown in *Gewerbeförderung* in Baden, and the refinement of the Navigation Laws in England), and it became desirable to sweep them all away.

Part of the stimulus came from the direct self-interest of particular dominant groups, illustrated particularly by the First Hand in the Netherlands. In Britain, free trade emerged as a doctrine from the political economists, with a variety of rationalizations to sustain it in particular applications: anti-monopoly, increases to real wages, higher profits, increased allocative efficiency, increased productivity through innovation required by import competition. In France, the lead in the direction of free trade came less from the export interests than from industrial interests using imported materials and equipment as inputs, though the drive to free trade after 1846 required the overcoming of the weight of the vested interests by strong governmental leadership, motivated by political gain in international politics. The German case was more straightforward: free trade was in the interest of the exporting grain and timber-producing classes, who were politically dominant in Prussia and who partly bought off and partly overwhelmed the rest of the country. The Italian case seems to be one in which doctrines developed abroad which were dominant in England and in a minority position in France, were imported by strong political leadership and imposed on a relatively disorganized political body.

Second thoughts raise questions. The movement to free trade in the 1850's in the Netherlands, Belgium, Spain, Portugal, Denmark, Norway and Sweden, along with the countries discussed in detail, suggests the possibility that Europe as a whole was motivated by

[127] C. P. Kindleberger, "Group Behavior and International Trade," *Journal of Political Economy*, LIX (February 1951), 30-47.

Rise of Free Trade   51

ideological considerations rather than economic interests. That Louis Napoleon and Bismarck would use trade treaties to gain ends in foreign policy suggests that free trade was valued for itself, and that moves toward it would earn approval. Viewed in one perspective, the countries of Europe in this period should not be considered an independent economies whose reactions to various phenomena can properly be compared, but rather as a single entity which moved to free trade for ideological or perhaps better doctrinal reasons. Manchester and the English political economists persuaded Britain which persuaded Europe, by precept and example. Economic theories of representative democracy, or constitutional monarchy, or even absolute monarchy may explain some cases of tariff changes. They are little help in Western Europe between the Napoleonic Wars and the Great Depression.

C. P. KINDLEBERGER, *Massachusetts Institute of Technology*

APPENDIX

REFERENCES

Amé, Leon. *Etudes sur les tariffs de douanes et sur les traités de commerce*, I, II. Paris: Imprimerie nationale, 1876.

Augé-Laribé, Michel. *La Politique agricole de la France de 1880 a 1940.* Paris: Presses Universitaires de la France, 1950.

Babbage, Charles. *The Economy of Machinery and Manufactures.* London, 4th ed.: Charles Knight, 1835.

Barkin, Kenneth D. *The Controversy over German Industrialization, 1890-1902.* Chicago: University of Chicago Press, 1970.

Benaerts, Pierre. *Les origines de la grande industrie allemande.* Paris: Turot, 1933.

Bläsing, Joachim F. E. *Das goldene Delta und sein eisernes Hinterland, 1815-1841. von niederländisch-preuschischen zu deutschneiderländischen Wirtschaftsbeziehungen.* Leiden: H. E. Stenfert Kroese, 1973.

Böhme, Helmut. *Frankfurt und Hamburg: Des Deutsches Reiches Silberund Goldloch und die Allerenglishte Stadt des Kontinents.* Frankfurtam-Main: Europäische Verlagsanstalt, 1968.

Bowring, John. "Report on the Prussian Commercial Union, 1840," *Parliamentary Papers*, 1840, Volume XXI, p. 200.

Brebner, J. Bartlett. "Laissez-faire and State Intervention in Nineteenth-Century Britain," in E. M. Carus-Wilson, ed., *Essays in Economic History*, Vol. 3. London: Edward Arnold, 1962, pp. 252-262.

Breton, Albert. *The Economic Theory of Representative Democracy.* Chicago: Aldine, 1974.

Brown, Lucy. *The Board of Trade and the Free-Trade Movement, 1830-1842*. Oxford: Clarendon Press, 1958.

Bulferetti, Luigi and Claudio Costanti. *Industria e Commerciio in Liguria nell'età del Risorgimento (1700-1861)*. Milan: Banca Commerciale Italiana, 1966.

Caird, Sir James. *High Farming . . . The Best Substitute for Protection*, pamphlet, 1848, cited in Lord Ernle, *English Farming Past and Present*. London: Longmans Green, 4th ed., 1937, p. 374.

Castronovo, Valerio. *Economia e societa in Piemonte dell' unità al 1914*. Milan: Banca Commerciale Italiana, 1969.

Chambers, J. D. *The Workshop of the World British Economic History, 1820-1880*. London: Oxford University Press, 2nd ed., 1968.

Checkland, S. G. *The Gladstones, A Family Biography, 1764-1851*. Cambridge: Cambridge University Press, 1971.

Chevalier, Michel. *Cours d'économie politique*. Fait au Collège de France, I, II, III, 2nd ed. no publisher stated, 1855.

Clapham, J. H. "The Last Years of the Navigation Acts," in E. M. Carus-Wilson, ed., *Essays in Economic History*. London: Edward Arnold, 1962, pp. 144-78.

Clough, Shepherd B. *The Economic History of Modern Italy*. New York: Columbia University Press, 1964.

Cobden, Richard. *Speeches on Questions of Public Policy*. Edited by John Bright and James E. Thorold Rogers. Vol. I. London: Macmillan, 1870.

Coppa, Frank J. "The Italian Tariff and the Conflict between Agriculture and Industry: The Commercial Policy of Liberal Italy, 1860-1922," THE JOURNAL OF ECONOMIC HISTORY, XXX (December 1970), 742-69.

Crouzet, François. "Western Europe and Great Britain: 'Catching Up' in the First Half of the Nineteenth Century," in A. J. Youngson, ed., *Economic Development in the Long Run*. London: Allen & Unwin, 1972, pp. 98-125.

Dawson, William H. *Protection in Germany: A History of German Fiscal Policy during the Nineteenth Century*. London: P. S. King and Son, 1904.

von Delbrück, Rudolph. *Lebenserinnerungen*, I, II. Leipsig: Duncker u. Humblot, 1905.

Dumke, Rolf H. "The Political Economy of Economic Integration: The Case of the Zollverein of 1834." Queens University *Discussion Paper*, No. 153, presented to the Canadian Economics Association, June 5, 1974.

Dunham, Arthur L. *The Anglo-French Treaty of Commerce of 1850 and the Progress of the Industrial Revolution in France*. Ann Arbor: University of Michigan Press, 1930.

Fielden, Kenneth. "The Rise and Fall of Free Trade," in C. J. Bartlett, ed., *Britain Pre-eminent: Studies in British World Influence in the Nineteenth Century*. London: Macmillan, 1969, pp. 76-100.

Fischer, Wolfram. *Der Staat und die Anfänge der Industrialisierung in Baden, 1800-1850.* Berlin: Duncker u. Humblot, 1962.

Frolich, N., J. A. Oppenheimer, and O. R. Young. *Political Leadership and Collective Goods.* Princeton: Princeton University Press, 1971.

Gallagher, J. and R. Robinson. "The Imperialism of Free Trade." *Economic History Review,* 2nd ser., VI (1953), 1-15.

Gerschenkron, Alexander. *Bread and Democracy in Germany.* Berkeley: University of California Press, 1943.

Gouraud, Charles. *Histoire de la politique commerciale de la France et son influence sur le progrès de la richesse publique depuis les moyens ages jusquà nos jours,* I, II. Paris: August Durand, 1854.

Greenfield, Kent Roberts. *Economics and Liberalism in the Risorgimento: A Study of Nationalism in Lombardy, 1814-1848,* rev. ed. Baltimore: Johns Hopkins University Press, 1965.

Heaton, Herbert. *Economic History of Europe.* New York: Harper & Bros., 1936.

Helleiner, Karl F. *Free Trade and Frustration: Anglo-Austrian Negotiations, 1860-70.* Toronto: University of Toronto Press, 1973.

Henderson, W. O. "Prince Smith and Free Trade in Germany." Ch. 7 in W. O. Henderson, *Britain and Industrial Europe, 1750-1870: Studies in British Influence on the Industrial Revolution in Western Europe.* Liverpool: Liverpool University Press, 1954.

The Speeches of the Right Honourable William Huskisson. London: John Murray, 1832.

Illasu, A. A. "The Cobden Chevalier Commercial Treaty of 1860." *The Historical Journal,* XIV (March 1971), 67-98.

Johnson, Harry G. "Economic Theory of Protectionism, Tariff Bargaining and the Formation of Customs Unions." *Journal of Political Economy,* LXXIII (1965), 256-83, reproduced in P. Robson, ed., *International Economic Integration.* Harmondsworth: Penguin, 1972, pp. 99-142.

Keynes, John Maynard. *The General Theory of Employment, Interest and Money.* New York: Harcourt, Brace and Co., 1936.

Kindleberger, C. P. "Group Behavior and International Trade." *Journal of Political Economy,* LIX (February 1951), 30-47.

Labracherie, Pierre. *Michel Chevalier et ses idées économiques.* Paris: Picart, 1929.

Lambi, Ivo Nikolai. *Free Trade and Protection in Germany, 1868-1879.* Wiesbaden: Franz Steiner Verlag, 1963.

Lévy-Leboyer, Maurice. *Histoire économique et sociale de la France depuis 1848.* Paris: Les Cours de Droit, Institut d'études politiques, 1951-52.

Lhomme, Jean. *La Grande Bourgeoisie au Pouvoir, 1830-1880.* Paris: Presses Universitaire de France, 1960.

Lutfalla, Michel. "Aux origines de la libéralisme économique de la France." *Revue d'histoire économique et sociale,* L (1972), 494-517.

54   *Kindleberger*

Luzzato, Gino. *L'economia italiana dal 1861 al 1914,* Vol. I (1861-1894). Milan: Banca Commerciale Italiana, 1963.

MacGregor, John. *Germany, Her Resources, Government, Union of Customs and Power under Frederick William IV.* London: Whittaker and Co., 1948.

McCord, Norman. *Free Trade: Theory and Practice from Adam Smith to Keynes.* London: Newton Abbot, David & Charles, 1970.

Moore, D. C. "The Corn Laws and High Farming." *Economic History Review,* 2nd series, XVIII (December 1965), 544-61.

Musson, A. E. "The 'Manchester School' and Exportation of Machinery." *Business History,* XIV (January 1972), 17-50.

Norman, Victor D. "Trade Liberalization and Industrial Growth: The Impact of British Trade Liberalization in the 1840s on Industrialization in the Scandinavian Countries." Unpublished paper, M.I.T., December 1970.

Norsa, Paolo and Mario Pozzo. *Imposte e tasse in Piemonte durante il periodo cavouriano.* Turin: Mueso nazionale del Risorgimento, 1961.

Olson, M., Jr. *The Logic of Collective Action: Public Goods and the Theory of Groups.* Cambridge, Mass.: Harvard University Press, 1965, rev. ed., 1971.

Olson, Mancur, Jr., and Richard Zeckhauser. "An Economic Theory of Alliances." *Review of Economics and Statistics,* XLVIII (August 1966), 266-79.

Parravicina, Giannino. *La Politia fiscale e le entrate effective del Regno d'Italia.* Archivo Economico dell' Unificazione Italiana. Turin: ILTE, 1958.

Pedone, Antonino. "La Politica del commercio estere," in Giorgio Fua, ed., *Le Sviluppo Economico in Italia,* vol. II, Gli aspetti generali. Milan: Franco Angelli Editore, 1969.

Pincus, Jonathan J. "A Positive Theory of Tariff Formation Applied to Nineteenth Century United States." Dissertation for the Ph.D., Stanford University, 1972.

Platt, D. C. M. *Finance, Trade and Politics in British Foreign Policy, 1815-1914.* Oxford: Clarendon Press, 1968.

Polanyi, Karl. *The Great Transformation.* New York: Farrar & Rinehart, 1944.

Pollard, Sidney. *European Economic Integration, 1815-1870.* New York: Harcourt Brace Jovanovitch, Inc., 1974.

Pollard, S. and C. Holmes. *Documents of European Economic History. Vol. 1: The Process of Industrialization, 1750-1870.* New York: St. Martin's Press, 1968.

Porter, G. R. *The Progress of the Nation.* New ed., London: John Murray, 1847.

Prodi, Romano. "Il protezionismo nella politica e nell' industria italiana dall' unificazione al 1886." *Nuova Rivista Storica,* L. Fasc. I-II, 1966, pp. 1-74.

Rise of Free Trade   55

Rist, Marcel. "Une experience française de liberation des échanges au dixneuvième siècle: le traité de 1860." *Revue d'Economie Politique,* 66 annee (novembre-decembre 1956), pp. 908-61.

Robinson, Moncure. *Obituary Notice of Michel Chevalier, 1806-1879.* Read to the American Philosophical Society, May 7, 1880.

Rosenberg, Hans. *Die Weltwirtschaftskrise von 1857-1859.* Stuttgart-Berlin: Verlag von W. Kohlhammer, 1934.

Sachs, Isidore. *L'Italie, ses finances et son developpement économique depuis l'unification du royaume, 1859-1884,* d'après des documents officiels, Paris: Librairie Guillaumin, 1885.

Second Report of the Select Committee on Exportation of Machinery, 1841 (11 June 1841), *Parliamentary Papers,* 1841, Vol.` VII.

Semmel, Bernard. *The Rise of Free Trade Imperialism: Classical Political Economy, The Empire of Free Trade and Imperialism, 1750-1850.* Cambridge: Cambridge University Press, 1970.

Stuart, James Montgomery. *The History of Free Trade in Tuscany, with Remarks on its Progress in the Rest of Italy.* London: Cassell, Potter & Galpin, 1876.

Thayer, William Roscoe. *The Life and Times of Cavour.* Boston: Houghton Mifflin, 1921.

Thiedig, Werner. *Englands Übergang zum Freihandel und die deutsche Handels-politik, 1840-1856.* Giessen: no publisher stated, 1927 (40-page summary of a thesis).

Whyte, A. J. *Early Life and Letters of Cavour, 1810-1848.* London: Oxford University Press, 1925.

Whyte, A. J. *The Political Life and Letters of Cavour, 1848-1861.* London: Oxford University Press, 1930.

Woodham-Smith, Cecil. *The Great Hunger: Ireland, 1845-1849.* New York: Harper & Row, 1962.

Wright, H. R. C. *Free Trade and Protection in the Netherlands, 1816-30: A Study of the First Benelux.* Cambridge: Cambridge University Press, 1955.

Zorn, Wolfgang. "Wirtschafts- und sozialgeschichtliche Zusammenhänge der deutschen Reichsgründungszeit, 1859-1879," in Helmut Böhme, ed., *Probleme der Reichsgrundungszeit, 1848-1879.* Cologne-Berlin: Kipenheuer & Witsch, 1968.

[2]

Tariffs as Constitutions

ALAN MILWARD

Could mid-nineteenth-century free trade economists see the grip they still had on our historical understanding they would surely be well pleased. Their position is not unmerited; they formulated a theory so simple and powerful linking international trade and political evolution that it still provides the only intellectual context in which the history of the economics and politics of international trade can be comprehended in a unified system. Otherwise we are forced to catalogue it as a series of disjointed historical events, tending sometimes in one direction and sometimes in another, swayed by the winds of chance, jolted by wars and revolutions, propelled by merely technological innovations and always at the mercy of the fluctuations of international goodwill.

The prevailing interpretation of international trade in history owes almost everything to their perception. In the early nineteenth century, it is usually assumed, countries were highly protectionist as they always had been, seeking advantages from international trade at the expense of others. As the extent to which the process of international development depended on mutually beneficial international exchanges was comprehended under the forceful influence of the industrial revolution in Western Europe, so were European tariffs increasingly modified to a point in mid-century where goods and factors flowed across frontiers with relative ease, at least until they reached Russia. It is still quite commonplace to discover the highly romanticised and entirely inaccurate image of the traveller of the 1860s setting forth across Europe, probably by the new international express trains, with no passport and no need of any other medium of exchange than gold francs or sovereigns. By the 1880s this image of peace and progress has dimmed. The world is explained as having slipped back to protectionism and its inevitable concomitants — nationalism, imperialism and militarism. In the interwar period this protectionism did not at first diminish and after 1929 reached new levels which made war inevitable. The United States Department of State based much of its planning for peace during the Second World War on the assumption that a peaceful world could not long endure the sorts of trading policies practised by Nazi Germany. The link between low tariffs, multilateralism and international peace thus received the most powerful of all official blessings. From 1958 onwards these goals were increasingly achieved, to the enormous economic and political benefit of much of the world, but the failure to cleave firmly enough to those policies threatens again to bring all the inevitable political disasters of protectionism in its train. 'We are now', argued a long anonymous article in *Le Matin* in January 1979, 'in 1932.' The article was headed 'Demain, la guerre?'.

Set against the historical record this is no more than a crass popular simplification. That is by no means to say that it is entirely or even mostly wrong. But it does not always match the accurate historical record, where we have that record, and there are important areas where we do not have that record. It rests therefore on some errors and on much ignorance, as well as on some accurate perceptions. This is not much of a foundation for so sweeping an interpretation and it certainly encourages the search for a more sensitive theory of the relations between international trade and political evolution. The one offered here really amounts to no more than a different perception of these events which necessarily implies a different perception of what is happening now. Before any interpretation can be accepted as having any real validity, however, it would be necessary for historians to concern themselves much more with the history of nineteenth-century tariffs and their meaning than they have so far done. One reason they have avoided the issue so much is probably because tariffs are extraordinarily uninteresting things unless related to the political events which give them meaning. The economic historian knows full well that there are always other far more important influences on the flow of trade and that the most important obstacles to that flow were very seldom tariffs but almost always non-tariff barriers. Other historians seldom work up sufficient interest in the humdrum detail of tariff setting and bargaining to be able to say what such bargains effectively represent in terms of social and political interests. None the less a more accurate historical account of the long-run development of tariffs than the foregoing is possible, even though it still leaves much obscure.

The trend towards lower tariffs and towards the reduction of non-tariff barriers to trade only obtained real momentum in 1860. The unilateral lowering of tariffs by Britain before that date and the reduction of the Belgian tariffs in the 1850s was certainly the start of this process, as is always pointed out. But it would probably turn out, were someone to make the calculations involved, that the lower tariffs which began to emerge before 1860 were offset by the impact of falling prices of many manufactured goods on specific tariff rates, even though there was a brief period in the 1850s when average prices seemed to have risen again. The Anglo-French commercial treaty of 1860 was the real starting point of trade liberalisation, because it was signed between the two greatest international traders and because it embodied for the first time the most-favoured-nation clause. Similar clauses were included in the network of trade treaties signed in the immediately ensuing period between all the more developed Western European countries.

One reason for the ease with which this process was accomplished was that the developing economies of early nineteenth-century Europe, the NICs of that period, had already developed favourable trade balances with protected Britain, the largest industrial producer and exporter. Their judgement of the situation in the short term was an accurate one – the balances remained in their favour even when they reduced their own levels of protection. The judgement was perhaps drawn from the previous symbiosis between the two largest producers and traders, Britain and France, still between themselves responsible for 60 per cent of world trade in the 1870s. Between them tariff reduction was a relatively painless affair. France had been the biggest market in most years for British manufactured exports and Britain always the biggest market for French manufactured exports. It was the extent of French trade surpluses with Britain which permitted the increasing imports into France of raw materials from elsewhere in Europe and the increasing outward flow of foreign investment which often financed their production. As for Britain, its deficits on commodity account with France were insignificant compared with the size of its total export surpluses. Europe was still in the 1860s the major supplier of food and raw materials to the eager British and French markets, and the European NICs of that period such as the Zollverein or Sweden had large intra-European primary export trades.

Bairoch's figures show rates of expansion of international trade for some countries in the 1860s which were never surpassed – 6·4 per cent for Belgium, 5·7 per cent for France and 7·3 per cent for Sweden. Of course these are rates of expansion starting from relatively low levels and represent a lower absolute growth in trade than the lower percentage rates recorded in the protectionist 1890s. None the less, as far as a limited area of industrialising north-western Europe was concerned, trade liberalisation proved painless and rewarding, although it did not by any means bring peace to the region. The inherent limitations on the whole process, however, should also be considered.

The larger territorial units were scarcely touched. Russia and the United States did not take part. The Habsburg Empire did enter the network for a few years but its tariffs had so high a starting point and its absolute and per capita levels of international trade were so low that its brief moment of trade liberalisation made little difference. Secondly, a major question remained unanswered in this period: what would be the response to the emergence of a larger international trader than Britain or France? It was not a hypothetical question. The situation was drawing nearer rapidly and came into existence after 1880 when German exports suddenly appeared in much greater quantities on world

60   *The International Politics of Surplus Capacity*

markets at the same time as both the British and French economies began a decade of virtual stagnation. Thirdly, how would the liberalised European trade system cope with the arrival of cheaper food and raw materials from outside Europe on European markets?

As German exports relentlessly displaced those of Britain and France from European markets, and then after 1900 began to compete effectively with them on extra-European markets, the frailty of the agreements of the 1860s became very clear. There were popular agitations against imports from Germany and claims of unfair trading practices by Germany strikingly reminiscent of those now made against Japan. Furthermore the period of tariff liberalisation had made no worthwhile concessions other than those which Britain had already made before 1860 to opening trade with colonies and it made no worthwhile concessions to other primary exporters. In one way the close preservation of colonial markets was fortunate – without India's surpluses on trade with continental Europe and the United States the multilateral payments system that accidentally evolved and that we have come to call the 'gold standard' would have been deprived of one of its main pillars. The British colonial system was relatively liberal but every sort of non-tariff barrier from the most specific to the most nebulous guaranteed that the lion's share of India's manufactured imports would come from Britain.

Other colonial powers had more rigidly exclusive rules. Algeria was incorporated into the French tariff in 1884. The 1892 French tariff incorporated all other French colonies which were considered 'developed' enough to stand the shock, that is to say all those that made any significant contribution to the French export trade: Martinique, Guadeloupe, South-East Asia, Gabon and Réunion. The French African colonies were usually governed by highly profitable and exclusive shipping and trading companies – the Société Commerciale de l'Ouest Africain and the Compagnie Française de l'Afrique Occidentale. The valuable Cuban market remained closed to all but Spain until the Spanish-American War. As the pressure from German, and other European, exporters mounted, the share of British and French exports going to colonies and dominions increased. Between 1890 and 1900, 9 per cent of French exports went to the colonies, and between 1906 and 1912, 15 per cent. Algeria became as much the instrument of preservation of the French cotton goods export trade as India did of that of Britain. Food and raw material exports from 'colonial' markets, however, competed all over developed and developing Europe.

In spite, therefore, of the advent of protection in the later 1870s and its rapid development in the 1880s, about which so much critical ink has been used, the contrast between the mid- and late nineteenth century was more apparent than real and the tariff history of the late nineteenth century in some ways an easily forecastable result of the seemingly more hopeful developments of the 1860s. In another way, too, the contrast was much less than most writers suggest. The higher nominal tariffs between the developed Western European states continued to be modified by conventional agreements. Indeed, like the French tariff of 1892 – the Méline tariff, usually regarded as the wickedest of them all before 1914 – they were designed expressly for that purpose. The Méline tariff embodied two separate sets of rates on each article, the lower intended for all conventional partners. Nominal tariff rates, or in the French case after 1892, the higher stipulated rate, were applied only to those who were outside the charmed circle and had always been outside it. In so far as the chief sufferers were the fresh generation of next-to-be-industrialised countries the situation had changed dramatically, if not surprisingly; in so far as they were LDCs it had not changed at all. When the existence of fixed nominal tariffs as bargaining points led to tariff wars these were, with only one exception, launched against NICs or LDCs. The most vicious was that waged by France against Italy from 1888 to 1896 when the Italian government tried to join the club by abandoning low tariffs and legislating its own high nominal rates. The French government simply refused to negotiate and applied its highest rates to all Italian exports – one reason for the virtual cessation of economic growth in Italy in those years. Compare this with the consequences of the British refusal to sign any tariff convention based on the French rates of 1892. They were simply that Britain and France continued through third parties to apply most-favoured-nation treatment to each other's exports. The weaker the primary exporter, the more susceptible to victimisation by tariff warfare. The bogus veterinary restrictions applied by Austria-Hungary to Serbia's main export – cattle – was a glaring example, for 70 per cent of Serbia's exports went to the Austro-Hungarian market.

In so far as the 'Third World' entered significantly into international trade before 1914 it was preponderantly a European 'Third World'. On the eve of the First World War half of the world trade in foodstuffs and 61 per cent of that in cereals still originated in Europe. Somewhere between one-quarter and one-third of world trade in wheat originated in Russia. The eruption of North American grain surpluses and South American and Australasian meat surpluses into Europe markets, which began on a significant scale at the end of the 1870s, was not the signal for a dramatic return to protectionism which it is always represented to have been – it was only an exacerbation of the problem. In the simpler framework of the previous three decades countries like Germany, Sweden and Italy had themselves had a comparative advantage in agricultural exports. Industrialisation and development had taken place there accompanied by a growing prosperity in the agricultural sector to which exports made an important contribution. But the next wave of NICs were in no position to suppose that the

62   *The International Politics of Surplus Capacity*

admission of manufactured goods at low tariffs would sustain a similar pattern of development. They were more backward, politically weaker, faced with far more competition and themselves the victims of fiercely unfair practices. It was not merely that adherence to the multilateral payments pattern of the gold standard hurt them more than the developed countries. This it did because in the periodic deflations necessary to bring payments into equilibrium the developed countries cut back sharply on primary imports and the underdeveloped economies simply did not have access to the short-term international capital market (which might have cushioned these blows) on the same terms as the developed countries. Argentina and Russia both provide excellent examples of the traumatic consequences which moderate recessions in the developed world could produce in the developing world. But any country without the political power to prevent it was likely to have the conditions for its imports laid down by direct intervention by the developed countries, for which the immediate excuse was usually the need to guarantee the flow of interest payments on earlier capital borrowing. Turkey, Greece, Bulgaria, Egypt and China were among those who lost complete tariff autonomy for periods in this way.

If the mid-nineteenth-century period of trade liberalisation was but a brief moment when the self-interest of the developed economies temporarily suggested mutual tariff reductions at the expense of others, and if, as I am arguing here, the things that would soon bring that policy to an end were already apparent, and if the later protectionist period was merely pursuing the economic logic of the earlier liberal period, the contrast between the two periods was even less marked because of the global inadequacy of protectionism of this kind to serve its purpose. The tax-rebate certificates which German rye exporters received when traded to German grain importers served to stimulate the great surge of Russian barley exports, established the Russian barley trade and thus cheapened the price of imported feedstuffs into Denmark; and in so doing reduced in turn the cost of the breakfast of a skilled British workman making much the same things as his German counterpart.

The nineteenth century was in fact a highly protectionist century and the mid-twentieth-century period of trade liberalisation was not, in spite of much neat academic comparison, a rediscovery of the true path from which the developed world had been diverted by various domestic vested interests and pressure groups after 1875. The pattern is not one of progress after 1850, regression during the late nineteenth century, the inevitable punishment for this in the first half of our century, and the rediscovery in the 1950s of the connection between human progress and that virtuous purple twilight through which Tennyson a hundred years previously had imagined future aerial argosies dropping with bales. Indeed those bales arrived on other shares with remarkable persistence as nominal tariffs increased. Higher tariffs may have slowed down the rate of growth of imports of manufactures in the 1880s, but once manufacturers had adjusted to the increase manufactured imports rose at roughly the same ratio to industrial production that they had shown in mid-century.

As for 1931–3, with the failure of the London Conference, the cry of *sauve qui peut* and the arrival of the Nazis we must beware of allowing it to acquire the same layers of bogus interpretation that have so long clung to 1873 and the mythical Great Depression which followed the stock-markets crash of that year. The sterling area and the Reichsmark bloc certainly provided better terms for their primary goods exporters than the multilateral arrangements of 1925-30 and in each case they covered a very important proportion of world trade. That the Nazi government was an exceptionally cruel and threatening regime does not mean that its international trading arrangements deserved the moral approbrium heaped on them by Cordell Hull and the United States Department of State. Those arrangements were in any case more the result of external economic weakness than economic strength. The resolute attack of the United States administration after 1945 on the sterling area in the name of a return to trade liberalisation was likely to do far more harm than good to the growth of international trade and to the less developed economies. If the early rounds of GATT amounted to very little that was because American policy there, as at Dumbarton Oaks and Bretton Woods, was based on a liberal interpretation of the history of international trade which was entirely unjustified historically.

Protectionism seems in reality not to have been simply the consequence of certain economic pressure groups acquiring enough power within the body politic at particular moments so as to distort tariffs and trade policy in their favour but rather to have had deeper political implications and more integral connections with the long-run process of political development. It might be closer to the truth to portray it as a set of stages in the widening participation of different groups in that body politic. In this sense the transition from mid-nineteenth-century liberalisation of trade to late nineteenth-century protectionism was not a regressive, atavistic response by conservative agrarian pressure groups but a progression in democratic political participation.

The French tariff of 1892 was won because its best-known proponent, Jules Méline, who gave his name to it, stumped the country and in mass meetings brought peasants back into the political life of France with real vigour and in common pursuit of a cause for the first time since they had triumphantly bowed out of it in 1793. The cause was not purely economic, it was in the deepest sense one of political participation. The campaign was against the 'arbitrary treaties', as the conditions imposed by the most-favoured-nation clauses were called. It was against the right of the Chamber to determine, by the incorporation of

64   *The International Politics of Surplus Capacity*

such clauses in treaties, tariff policy up to two decades ahead. The campaign was mounted to take effect before the common date of expiry and presumed renewal of the major treaties and to prevent the Chamber from including most-favoured-nation clauses in these future treaties. The level of tariffs, it was argued, must be left open to repeated public redetermination within the democratic assembly. The original Franco-British treaty of 1860 had been the work of a small coterie around the autocrat Napoleon III. The agricultural sector still employed about 9,700,000 people in France in 1890 and its most valuable product was that most threatened by external competition – wheat. This is not to say that the preservation of so large an uncompetitive sector in the French economy represented a rational economic choice. But the political cause was neither ignoble nor retrogressive. The dissemination of economic development, and the opening of the prairies and of the Russian hinterland to international commerce, brought the largest group in the French population into active struggle for the defence of a position which they had long held with little sign of disturbance.

The same political point may be made about the return to higher tariffs in Germany. The demand for agricultural protection offered Bismarck the chance to base the new Reich on a more solid foundation of political support, and to achieve the constitutional compromise between essentially authoritarian government and popular support which he had sought since 1848. He was able for the first time to give certain manufacturing interests good economic reasons for continuing to support his regime, rather than having to rely on the sporadic enthusiasm generated by nationalist successes which in themselves had been very limited. Aspiring groups of businessmen and manufacturers no longer needed to espouse the cause of liberal constitutionalism in their own interest. More important, he could unite such groups in one alliance of real interest for the first time with their traditional opponents – the landowners and farmers – and cement it with the little touch of intellectual glue provided by the miscellaneous group of economists and other writers who wished to preserve something of the old German society which they saw changing too quickly under the pressures of industrialisation and foreign influence. The tariff became an alternative to the constitution, as well it might for the constitution demonstrated that the existence of assemblies elected by universal suffrage did not necessarily mean the existence of an effective forum where real economic interests could be brought to a compromise in a popularly influenced government policy. Subsequent debates over tariff policy, as at the time of Caprivi's chancellorship, were more crucial to people's real interests and generated more intense political interest than any other issues until 1917. The industrial and commercial groups who had briefly glimpsed their desire for political participation turn into reality in 1848 and then seen those hopes removed were thus brought into the active political arena on quite different terms at the end of the 1870s and in safe conjunction with an agrarian interest as large as in France. It was only the initial stages of the campaign for agricultural protection, which were financed and organised by the established rural elites. The campaign soon proved almost as popular as Méline was to make it in France.

If we ask why the movement towards trade liberalisation in the 1860s was politically as painless as it was economically, the answer again is that it represented an earlier step towards wider participation in the political nation. In Britain the repeal of the Corn Laws was the first significant permanent stake in national policy which urban and manufacturing interests were able to obtain – the stake that had been denied them by the 1832 Reform Bill. Similarly the victory of Frere Orban in Belgium in the 1850s represented the arrival to full political participation there of the same interests. There was a substantial body of manufacturing support for Napoleon's tariff *coup de main* in 1860. The tariff was conceived and presented as a step in modernisation and for its industrial opponents it was sweetened by an extensive system of grants for modernising equipment and machinery. It was one more stage in the Emperor's attempts to base his rule on what he regarded as the more modern and progress elements in the nation. Delbrück's lowering of the tariff in the foundation years of the new German Reich was likewise a political concession to gain support from the same groups.

The imperfect mechanisms of incomplete democracies made the tariff books seem as important an expression of the political balance of the nation as the constitution. They represented written compromises on real tests of political as well as economic strength. Hence the extraordinary importance of tariffs in public argument when non-tariff barriers were probably, as now, much more important in regulating and obstructing international trade. They were regarded as a written expression of what the economic and social balance of the nation should be. Like the frontier on which it was levied, the tariff was a visible expression of national unity and as that unity increasingly had to include deeper strata in the nation the tariff became the instrument of their inclusion.

The significance of such an interpretation, which corresponds more closely to the historical record than the prevailing one, lies for the present in the question whether that process of widening political participation has reached its end. The growth of all Western European economies, except possibly Britain's, between 1951 and 1974 represented a virtuous circle in which a surge of exports stimulated and maintained high rates of growth in total output. The higher the proportion of manufactured goods exported, the higher the average level of productivity in industry, the higher the level of presumed future com-

66   *The International Politics of Surplus Capacity*

petitiveness on international markets and the higher the rate of growth of GNP per capita. All that has come to an end. Is the renewed demand for protectionism a retrogressive move, a short-sighted defensive policy error, or is it a further stage in political participation in Western democracies, an important and necessary step in political change and adaptation? Agreement between managers and workers in British Leyland to exclude those driving foreign cars from the car parks may be the only agreement they can achieve, but what would be the influence of genuine 'industrial democracy' in the mixed economy on tariffs and trade? If liberal trade regulations no longer convince entrepreneurs, they have practically never convinced their employees. But they have rarely anywhere been able to express their views on equal terms even in labour and socialist parties whose leadership in Western Europe, presumably under the heavy influence of history, has frequently (for reasons of greater political participation) been nearer to a free trade position than their conservative opponents. As the organs of nineteenth-century political democracy become less and less adequate and responsive to the popular will it is hard to imagine that lower-level assemblies, regional parliaments, elected factory councils (or perhaps some more genuinely democratic version of the corporate state than that with which reactionaries of the interwar period toyed) would not bring to fruition another wave of protectionist agitation. This might well represent a significant step forward in democratic politics, even though it might well be bad economics. The consolation, if one is needed, is to be found, of course, in the likelihood that it may cause no more of a break in the trend of international trade from the 1950s and 1960s than existed, in reality, between the late and mid-nineteenth century. In retrospect it might, as in the nineteenth century, be an issue of much political importance but, economically, no great matter.

[3]

The Roots of Latin American Protectionism: Looking before the Great Depression

John H. Coatsworth and Jeffrey G. Williamson

Introduction

This chapter uncovers a fact that has not been well appreciated: Tariffs in Latin America were far higher than anywhere else in the world from the 1860s to World War I, long before the Great Depression. Indeed, they were even *rising* in the decades before the 1890s, a period that was part of what has been called the first global century (O'Rourke and Williamson 1999). This fact is surprising for three reasons: first, because this region has been said to have exploited globalization forces better than most during the pre-1914 *belle époque;* second, because standard economic histories say so little about it; and third, because most of us have been taught to view the Great Depression as *the* critical turning point when the region is said to have turned toward protection and de-linked itself from the world economy for the first time.

After establishing this fact, this chapter shows that its explanation cannot lie with some perceived GDP per capita gains from protection, since, while such gains were certainly present in industrial Europe and its non-Latin offshoots (Clemens and Williamson 2001), they most definitely were *not* present in Latin America. On the contrary, those countries with the highest tariff rates in Latin America grew slowest, and those who had the lowest tariff rates grew fastest. The chapter then explores Latin American tariffs as a revenue source, as a reaction to deindustrialization fears, as a strategic response to trading partners tariffs, as a redistributive device for special interests, and as a consequence of other political economy struggles. While the exploration is mostly qualitative for the first half-century of independence, it is quite quantitative for the period 1870–1950, using annual data for a sample of eight Latin American countries treated both as a panel and with fixed effects.

Belle Époque Latin America Was the World's Most Protectionist Region!

There is a well-developed literature that debates the measurement of economic openness (e.g., Anderson and Neary 1994; Sachs and Warner 1995; Anderson 1998). That literature makes it clear that trade shares are poor measures of openness since they are endogenous. Among the explicit policy measures of openness available, the average tariff rate is by far the most homogenous protection measure and the easiest to collect across countries and over time,[1] and it is most effective prior to the 1930s before the introduction of widespread non-tariff barriers. This chapter uses the computed average tariff rate to explore the policy experience of eight Latin American countries compared with twenty-seven others around the world between 1865 and World War II: the United States; three members of the European industrial core (France, Germany, United Kingdom); three non-Latin European offshoots (Australia, Canada, New Zealand); ten from the European periphery (Austria-Hungary, Denmark, Greece, Italy, Norway, Portugal, Russia, Serbia, Spain, Sweden); ten from Asia and the Mideast (Burma, Ceylon, China, Egypt, India, Indonesia, Japan, the Philippines, Siam, Turkey), and eight from Latin America (Argentina, Brazil, Chile, Cuba, Colombia, Mexico, Peru, Uruguay).[2]

Figure 2.1 plots average world tariffs before World War II (unweighted and weighted by export shares in world markets), and Figure 2.2 plots them for some regional clubs.[3] Figure 2.2 plots six regions—the United States, the European core, the European periphery, European non-Latin offshoots, Asia, and Latin America—the country members of which were identified above. Four important observations can be drawn from these figures.

First, Figure 2.1 documents a steady climb in tariff rates worldwide between 1870 and the 1890s, although qualitative evidence surveyed elsewhere (Coatsworth and Williamson forthcoming) suggests that the climb started much earlier. Was this a globalization backlash or was it driven by other forces? In any case, the climb marked a slow but steady retreat from the liberal and pro–global trade positions in the mid-century (Williamson 1998). The interwar surge to world protection is, of course, better known.

Figure 2.1   Average World Tariffs before World War II

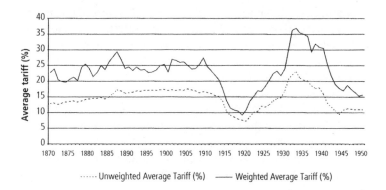

······ Unweighted Average Tariff (%)   —— Weighted Average Tariff (%)

Figure 2.2   Unweighted Average of Regional Tariffs before World War II

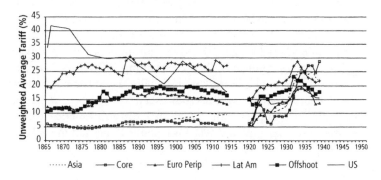

······ Asia   —□— Core   —▲— Euro Perip   —+— Lat Am   —■— Offshoot   —— US

Second, note the enormous variance in levels of protection between the regional club averages. The richer new-world European offshoots had levels of protection more than twice that of the European core around the turn of the last century. When the United States is shifted to the rich European offshoot club, the ratio of tariffs between European offshoot and core jumps to more than three times. To take additional examples, in 1925 the European periphery had tariffs 2.4 times higher than those in the European part of the industrial core. And in 1885 the poor but independent parts of Latin America (Brazil, Colombia, Mexico, and Peru) had tariffs 4.6 times higher than those in the poor and dependent parts of Asia (Burma, Ceylon, China, Egypt, India, Indonesia, and the Philippines).

Third, there was also great variance *within* these regional clubs. In 1905, tariffs in Uruguay (the most protectionist land-abundant and labor-scarce country; see Figure 2.4) were about 2.5 times those in Canada (the least protectionist land-abundant and labor-scarce country). In the same year, tariffs in Brazil and Colombia (the most protectionist of Latin American countries) were almost ten times those in China and India (the least protectionist in Asia). The same high-low range appeared among the industrial core countries (the United States five times the United Kingdom) and the European periphery (Russia six times Austria-Hungary). Thus, explaining differences between countries before 1940 is at least as challenging as explaining changes in tariff policy over the eight decades after 1865—perhaps more so. This observation applies with special force to Latin America, where the range just prior to World War I was about 17 percent in Chile to about 48 percent in Columbia (Figure 2.4).

Finally, note the most critical fact that motivates this chapter. With notable exceptions, historical accounts argue that the reluctance of Latin American countries to open in the late-twentieth century was the product of the Great Depression and the de-linking import-substitution strategies that arose to deal with it (Diaz-Alejandro 1984; Corbo 1992; Taylor 1998). Yet, nineteenth-century Latin America— whether our poor four (Brazil, Colombia, Mexico, Peru), our rich three in the southern cone (Argentina, Chile, Uruguay), or even Cuba—already had *by far* the highest tariffs in the world (Figure 2.4). With the exception of the United States, Latin American tariffs were the highest in the world by 1865. At the crescendo of the *belle époque*, Latin American tariffs were at their peak, and still soaring above the rest of the world. Furthermore, the rise in Latin America's tariffs from

Figure 2.3 Gap Between Latin American Tariffs and World Average

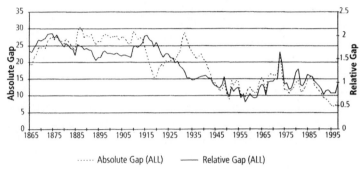

.... Absolute Gap (ALL)   ——— Relative Gap (ALL)

the late 1860s to the turn of the century was much steeper than in Europe, including France and Germany about which so much tariff history has been written.

Apparently, the famous export-led growth spurt in Latin America was consistent with extremely high tariffs (even though the region might have done even better without them). Latin American tariffs were still the world's highest in the 1920s, although the gap between Latin America and the rest of the world had shrunk considerably (Figure 2.3). Oddly enough, it was in the 1930s that the rest of the world (the European Core and Asia) finally surpassed Latin America in securing the dubious distinction of being the most protectionist. By the 1950s, and when import-substitution industrialization (ISI) policies were flourishing, Latin American tariffs were actually *lower* than those in Asia and the European periphery.[4] Thus, whatever explanations are offered for the Latin American commitment to protection, we must search for its origin well before the Great Depression.

There are some surprises in these tariff data that have not been noticed by those who have concentrated on one epoch, one region, or even just one country. This chapter stresses the first big Latin American surprise: Latin America had the highest tariffs in the world as early as 1865, a position it held until the 1930s. The second big Latin America surprise is this: The traditional literature written by European economic historians has made much of the tariff backlash on the continent after the 1870s (Kindleberger 1951; Bairoch 1989; O'Rourke and Williamson 1999). Yet, this heavily researched continental move to protection is relatively minor when compared with the rise in tariff rates over the same period in our four poor Latin American countries (up 6.9 percentage points to 34 percent), and this for a region that has been said to have exploited the pre-1914 globalization boom so well.

In the interwar decades, tariffs worldwide took two big leaps upward. The first leap was in the 1920s, which might be interpreted as a policy effort to return to 1914 levels. It might also have been due to postwar deflation. Inflations and deflations seem to have influenced tariff rates in the 1910s, the 1920s, and at some other times, a phenomenon labeled "specific-duty-inflation effect," to which we will return later in this chapter. The second interwar leap in tariff rates was, of course, in the 1930s, with aggressive beggar-my-neighbor policies reinforced by the specific-duty-inflation effect. Except for the two countries with the highest prewar tariffs, Colombia and Uruguay, tariffs rose everywhere in Latin America. But note that for most Latin American countries, tariff rates rose to levels in the late 1930s that were no higher than they had been in the *belle époque* (Figure 2.4).[5]

So, what was the political economy that determined Latin American protection in the century before the end of the Great Depression?

Protection Did *Not* Foster Economic Growth in Latin America

Does protection help or hinder growth? We need to answer this question first to see whether anything in the experience of the Latin Amer-

Figure 2.4 Own Tariffs in Latin America before World War II

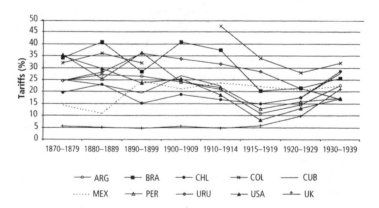

ican countries could have persuaded policy makers in the ninteenth century to adopt or persist in maintaining high levels of protection.[6] Let us start with the familiar late-twentieth century evidence. It is unambiguous on the issue, and can be found in four kinds of studies.[7]

First, the authors of a large National Bureau of Economic Research project assessed trade and exchange-control regimes in the 1960s and 1970s by calculating deadweight losses (Bhagwati and Krueger 1973–76). They concluded that the barriers imposed significant costs in all but one case. However, these standard welfare calculations have been criticized by those who have pointed out that such studies fail to allow protection a chance to lower long-run cost curves, as in the traditional infant-industry case, or to foster industrialization and thus growth, as in those modern growth theories in which industry is the carrier of technological change and capital deepening. Thus, economists have had to look for more late-twentieth-century proof to support the openness-fosters-growth hypothesis.

Second, analysts have contrasted the growth performance of relatively open economies with that of relatively closed economies. The World Bank has conducted such studies for forty-one countries going back before the first oil shock. The correlation between trade openness and growth is abundantly clear in these studies (Lindert and Williamson 2001: Table 3), but the analysis is vulnerable to the criticism that the effect of trade policies alone cannot be isolated since other policies usually change at the same time. Thus, countries that liberalized their trade also liberalized their domestic factor markets, liberalized their domestic commodity markets, and set up better property-rights enforcement. The appearance of these domestic policies may deserve more credit for raising income, while the simultaneous appearance of more liberal trade policies may deserve less.

Third, there are country event studies in which the focus is on periods when trade policy regimes change dramatically enough to see their effect on growth. Growth improved where there was a move toward liberalization in the 1960s (Krueger 1983, 1984). More recently, David Dollar and Aart Kraay (2000) examined the trade liberalizations in the 1980s and 1990s, finding, once again, the positive correlation between freer trade and faster growth. Of course, these reform episodes may have changed more than just global participation, so that an independent trade effect may not have been isolated.

Fourth, macroeconometric analysis has been used in an attempt to resolve the doubts left by the simpler historical correlations revealed by the other three kinds of studies. This macroeconometric literature shows that free trade policies have been associated with fast growth in the late-twentieth century, especially with many other relevant influences held constant. The most famous study is by Jeffrey Sachs and Andrew Warner (1995), but many others have also confirmed the openness-fosters-growth hypothesis for the late-twentieth century (e.g., Dollar 1992; Edwards 1993; Bloom and Williamson 1998; Dollar and Kraay 2000). While this recent macroeconometric literature is not without its critics (Rodriguez and Rodrik 2001), it is certainly consistent with forty years of previous research.

If free trade has been associated with fast growth since World War II, why was it associated with slow growth before then? About thirty years ago, Paul Bairoch (1972) argued that protectionist countries grew *faster* in the nineteenth century, not slower as every economist has found for the late-twentieth century. Bairoch's sample was mainly from the European industrial core, it looked at pre-1914 experience only, and controlled for no other factors. Like the second group of modern studies listed above, it simply compared growth rates of major European countries in protectionist and free trade episodes. More recently, Kevin O'Rourke (2000) got the Bairoch finding again, this time using macroeconometric conditional analysis on a ten-country sample drawn from the pre-1914 Atlantic economy. In short, these two scholars were not able to find *any* evidence before World War I supporting the openness-fosters-growth hypothesis.

These pioneering historical studies suggest that a tariff-growth paradox took the form of a regime switch somewhere between the start of World War I and the end of World War II: before the switch, protection was associated with growth; after the switch, free trade was associated with growth. Was Latin America part of this paradox, or was it only an attribute of the industrial core? Recent work by Clemens and Williamson (2001) has shown that protection *was* associated with fast growth in the industrial core before World War II, but that it was *not* associated with fast growth in most of the periphery. Table 2.1 offers a revised version of the Clemens-Williamson result, where the model estimated is of the convergence variety, but is conditioned only by the country's own tariff rate and regional club dummies. The tariff rate and GDP per capita level are both measured at year *t*, while the subsequent GDP per capita growth rate is measured over the half decade following. The two world wars are ignored (but they are not ignored in the rest of the chapter).

Table 2.1 Tariff Impact on GDP per Capita Growth by Region

Dependent Variable	5-Year Overlapping Average Growth Rate			
	(1)	(2)	(3)	(4)
Included countries	ALL	ALL	ALL	ALL
Years per period	1	1	1	1
Time interval	1875–1908	1875–1908	1924–1934	1924–1934
ln GDP/capita	0.18	0.12	−1.01	−0.86
	1.88	*1.23*	*−3.52*	*−3.03*
ln own tariff	0.09	0.36	−0.04	1.45
	1.06	*2.28*	*−0.13*	*2.93*
(European periphery dummy) × (ln tariff rate)		−0.53		−2.23
		−2.48		*−3.38*
(Latin America dummy) × (ln tariff rate)		−1.04		0.37
		−3.22		*0.33*
(Asia dummy) × (ln tariff rate)		0.20		−2.41
		0.79		*−3.56*
European periphery dummy	−0.18	1.12	−0.37	5.63
	−1.36	*2.05*	*−0.93*	*3.14*
Latin America dummy	0.25	3.36	−0.91	−2.51
	1.54	*3.39*	*−2.12*	*−0.74*
Asia dummy	−0.31	−0.50	−2.32	4.18
	−1.77	*−0.95*	*−4.27*	*2.25*
Constant	−0.24	−0.43	9.50	4.21
	−0.32	*−0.54*	*3.47*	*1.41*
Country dummies?	No	No	No	No
Time dummies?	No	No	No	No
N	1,180	1,180	372	372
R^2	0.0359	0.0516	0.0618	0.1091
Adjusted R^2	0.0318	0.0451	0.0490	0.0894

Note: t-statistics are in italics.

The tariff-growth paradox is stunningly clear in Table 2.1. In columns 2 and 4, the estimated coefficient on log of the tariff rate is 0.36 for 1875–1908 and 1.45 for 1924–34, and both are highly significant. Thus, and in contrast with late-twentieth century evidence, tariffs were associated with fast growth before 1939. But was this true the world around, or was there instead an asymmetry between industrial economies in the core and primary producers in the periphery? Presumably, the protecting country has to have a big domestic market, and has to be ready for industrialization, accumulation, and human capital deepening if the long-run, tariff-induced dynamic effects are to offset the short-run gains from trade given up. Table 2.1 tests for asymmetry in columns 2 and 4, and the asymmetry hypothesis wins— in the Latin American case especially if we focus on the pre-World War I decades. That is, protection was associated with faster growth in the European core and their English-speaking offshoots (again, the coefficient on own tariff 1875–1908 is 0.36 and highly significant), but it was *not* associated with fast growth in the European or Latin American periphery (the negative coefficient on the interaction term exceeds the positive coefficient on the tariff rate alone), nor was it associated with fast growth in interwar Asia. Most important, note that before World War I protection in Latin America was associated significantly and powerfully with *slow* growth (0.36 + (–)1.04 = –0.68).

The moral of the story is that while Latin American policy makers may have been aware of the pro-protectionist infant-industry argument[8] offered for *Zollverein* Germany by Frederich List and for federalist United States by Alexander Hamilton, there is absolutely no evidence after the 1860s that would have supported those arguments for Latin America. We must look elsewhere for plausible explanations for the exceptionally high tariffs in Latin America long before the Great Depression. As a signal of things to come, one place to look for alternative explanations is to note that the causation in Table 2.1 could have gone the other way round in Latin America. That is, countries achieving rapid GDP per capita growth would also have undergone faster growth in imports and in other parts of the tax base, thus reducing the need for high tariff *rates*. And countries suffering slow growth would have had to keep high tariff rates to ensure adequate revenues.

The Political Economy of Latin American Tariffs: War, Insurrection, and Revenue

The "Protectionist" Stage Is Set: The First Half-Century of Independence

In young, recently independent economies with low or even declining capacity to tax, few bureaucratic resources to implement efficient collection, and limited access to foreign capital markets, customs duties are an easy-to-collect revenue source essential to support central government expenditures on infrastructure and defense.[9] This was certainly true of the newly independent United States. It was even more true for a Latin America beset in the first half of the nineteenth century with the end "of the de facto customs union, capital flight, … the collapse of the colonial fiscal system," civil wars, and violent border disputes (Prados de la Escosura 2002: 2). Nor did Latin America gain access to European capital markets until later in the century, an event which would have eased the need for tax revenues in the short run. The average share of customs duties in total revenues across eleven Latin American republics was 57.8 percent between 1820 and 1890 (Centeno 1997: Table 1).[10] Customs revenues were even more important for federal governments (65.6 percent), since local and state governments who form a union typically are reluctant to give up their limited tax weapons. Furthermore, customs revenues are especially important for land-abundant countries with federal governments since they do not have the population and tax-payer density to make other forms of tax collection efficient. Now add to these conditions the huge revenue needed to fight wars and we get the high U.S. Civil War tariffs in the early 1860s and the high (and rising) tariffs in a newly independent Latin America that experienced almost continuous war and civil strife between the 1820s and the 1870s.

Mares (2001) reports ten major Latin American wars between 1825 and 1879, but limits his data to conflicts that produced at least one thousand battlefield deaths. Centeno (1997) has counted thirty-three major international and civil wars between 1819 and 1880, but his data exclude Cuba altogether as well as numerous small- and medium-scale internal conflicts and a number of costly international wars. Of the eight countries for which we have data on levels of protection, all fought at least two major wars between independence and 1880. Only Brazil and Chile (after 1830) avoided violent military coups. All eight experienced episodes of massive and prolonged civil strife. In six countries, internal civil wars raged more or less continuously for decades after independence.

The universal preoccupation with national defense and internal security pushed the newly independent Latin American countries toward higher revenue-maximizing tariffs. Military expenditures quickly rose to consume over 70 and often more than 90 percent of all revenues (Centeno 1997). Weak governments, under attack from within and without, abandoned internal taxes that required an extensive and loyal bureaucracy, and concentrated tax collection efforts instead on a few ports and mines. The ratio of tariff revenues to imports, and thus levels of protection, rose in every country for which there are data, as did customs revenues as a percentage of national government revenues. Policymakers were not seeking to protect local producers but rather to keep troops in the field against foreign and domestic enemies. The fiscal imperative of the region's endemic military conflicts swamped all other preoccupations.

Revenue Targets and Optimal Tariffs for Revenue Maximization

Were the newly independent Latin American nations searching for some optimal tariff? Maybe or maybe not, but as Douglas Irwin (1997: 8–12) has pointed out for the United States and Victor Bulmer-Thomas (1994: 141) for Latin America, the revenue-maximizing tariff hinges crucially on the price elasticity of import demand. Tariff revenue can be expressed as

$$R = tpM \tag{1}$$

where R is revenue, t is the average ad valorem tariff rate, p is the average price of imports and M is the volume of imports. Totally differentiating (1) with respect to the tariff, and assuming that the typical nineteenth-century Latin American country was a price taker for manufacturing imports, yields

$$dR/dt = pM + (tp)dM/dt. \tag{2}$$

The revenue-maximizing tariff rate, t^*, is found by setting $dR/dt = 0$, in which case

$$t^* = -1/(1 + \eta) \tag{3}$$

where η is the price elasticity of demand for imports. Irwin (1997: 14) estimates the price elasticity to have been about –2.6 for the United States between 1869 and 1913. Since the import mix was similar for the United States and Latin America, suppose the price elasticity for the latter was about –3. Under those conditions, the average tariff in Latin America would have been very high indeed, 50 percent.[11]

Suppose instead that some Latin America government during the *belle époque*—riding on an export boom between the 1870s and World War I—had in mind some target revenue share in GDP ($R/Y = r$) and could not rely on foreign capital inflows to balance the current account (so $pM = X$). Then

$$r = tpM/Y = tX/Y. \tag{4}$$

Clearly, if foreign-exchange earnings from exports (spent on imports) were booming (an event which could even be caused by a terms-of-trade boom, denoted here by a fall in p, the relative price of imports), the target revenue share, r, could have been achieved at lower tariff rates, *t*. The bigger the export boom and the higher the resulting export share (X/Y), the lower the tariff rate.

So, did Latin American governments act as if they were meeting revenue targets? Ceteris paribus, did they lower tariff rates during world primary product booms when export shares were high and rising, and did they raise them during world primary product slumps?

The Political Economy of Latin American Tariffs: What Else Might Have Mattered?

The Specific-Duty-Inflation Effect

It has been argued that inflations and deflations have had a powerful influence on average tariff rates in the past. Import duties were typically *specific* until modern times, quoted as pesos per bale, yen per yard, or dollars per bag.[12] Under specific duties abrupt changes in price levels would change import values in the denominator, but not the legislated duty in the numerator, thus producing big equivalent ad valorem or percentage rate changes. Ad valorem rates are more common today, so that equivalent tariff rates are less affected by inflation and deflation. The impact of inflations during the two world wars was quite spectacular, and had nothing to do with policy. Thus, actual tariff *rates* fell sharply in all regions between 1914 and 1919, and again between 1939 and 1947 (Figure 2.1). Similarly, part of the rise in tariff rates immediately after World War I was due to postwar deflation. Price deflation after 1929 was even more spectacular, and it too served to raise tariff rates at least on imports still subject to specific duties. The process was repeated during the World War II inflation, but, in contrast, there was no return to the very high prewar rates of the 1930s.

This argument assumes, of course, that changing the legislated tariff structure is politically expensive, and thus is only infrequently changed by new legislation. We are certainly not the first to notice this specific-duty-inflation effect. Douglas Irwin has made the same point in accounting for the U.S. tariff experience between the Civil War and the Great Depression (Irwin 1998: 1017), and Graciela Márquez Colin has made it for prerevolutionary Mexico (Márquez 2002: 307), but, as far as we know, it has not been explored for a larger sample.

Strategic Trade Policy, the Terms of Trade and Tariffs

A well-developed theoretical literature on strategic trade policy predicts that nations have an incentive to inflate their own terms of trade

Figure 2.5 Unweighted Regional Average of Principal Trading Partners' Tariffs

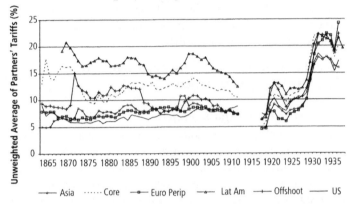

with high tariffs, thereby lowering global welfare.[13] In as much as favorable terms of trade translate into better economic performance, we might expect a country's own tariffs to depend at least in part upon the country's external tariff environment. Thus, Figure 2.5 plots a principal-trading-partners-tariff index for the same regional clubs. It is calculated in this way: first, we identify the major trading partners for each country (up to five); second, we calculate exports going to each major trading partner as a share of total country exports going to all major trading partners; third, we use these shares as weights by which to construct the average tariff faced by each country; finally, we construct an unweighted average for each region.

Figures 2.2 and 2.5 tell us that in the two decades before World War I, every region except the industrial core faced lower tariff rates in their main export markets than they themselves erected against competitors in their own markets. The explanation, of course, is that the main export markets were located in the core, where tariffs were much lower. Thus, the periphery faced lower tariffs than did the core (for the European periphery this was true throughout, but for the rest of the periphery it was true only up to just before 1900, when the United States replaced Britain as a major export market for them). During the interwar, every club faced very similar and high tariff rates in export markets, but those rates were rising very steeply outside the core as the core itself made the biggest policy switch—compared with the other clubs—from free trade to protection.

Figure 2.5 also tells us that Latin America faced *far* higher tariffs than anyone else since they traded with heavily protected countries such as the United States and each other. So, did this "hostile" policy environment abroad trigger a like response at home?

Deindustrialization Fears

If Latin Americans feared that globalization might inhibit industrialization or even induce local deindustrialization, they would have paid close attention to the competitive position of manufacturing at home relative to that abroad. The best indicator of foreign manufacturing's competitiveness would be its ability to drive down the relative price of manufactures in world markets through productivity advance. Thus, deindustrialization fears ought to have been manifested by a rise in Latin American tariff rates when the relative price of manufactures fell in world markets. Figure 2.6 suggests that there was, in fact, little to fear since, relative to the price of Latin America's key primary-product exports, the price of manufactures *rose* in world markets. Another way of saying the same thing is that the price of Latin American primary products fell in world markets relative to manufactures.[14] Of course, booms and busts may have mattered more to policy formation than long-run trends (which, after all, may simply have reflected long-run relative quality improvements in manufactured goods). In any case, if

Figure 2.6 Trend in Latin America's Relative Price of Export Products 1870–1950

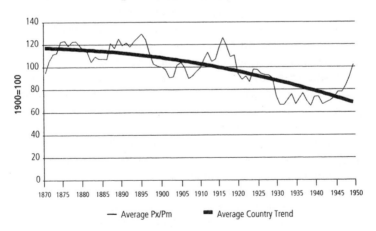

— Average Px/Pm   ■ Average Country Trend

the qualitative literature is correct in identifying a switch in the motivation behind *belle époque* tariffs from revenue to industrial-protection goals late in the century, then we should see evidence of the switch in the terms-of-trade effect as well.

The Tariff-Transport Cost Trade Off

Whatever the arguments for protection of manufacturing, high transport costs on imports from one's trading partner are just as effective as high tariffs. And when transport costs fall dramatically, the winds of competition thus created give powerful incentive to import-competing industries to lobby for more protection. Since there certainly *was* a nineteenth-century transport revolution (O'Rourke and Williamson 1999: Ch. 3), manufacturing interests in the periphery must have been given plenty of incentive to lobby for protection as the natural barriers afforded by transport costs melted away. This connection was confirmed long ago for "the invasion of grains" into Europe from Russia and the New World (O'Rourke and Williamson 1999: Ch. 6). But what about Latin America and the "invasion of European manufactures"? There are two reasons to doubt that the tariff-transport cost trade-off, at least along sea lanes, prevailed with the same power in Latin America as in Europe. First, while overseas freight rates along the northward routes to Europe from the coasts of Latin America followed world trends by collapsing after the 1840s, they fell much less along the southward leg (Stemmer 1989: 24). The northward leg was for bulky Latin American staple exports such as beef, wheat, and guano, the high-volume, low-value primary products whose trade gained so much by the transport revolution along sea lanes. The southward leg was for Latin American imports such as textiles and machines, the high-value, low-volume manufactures whose trade gained much less from the transport revolution. Second, overseas freight costs were a much smaller share of the CIF price (cost, insurance, and freight) of traded manufacturers than was true of traded primary products in the 1860s (Stemmer 1989: 25). However, transport costs into the Latin American interior were much more important protective barriers for local manufacturers—except for Buenos Aires, Montevideo, and Rio de Janeiro—than were overseas transport costs. In 1842, the cost of moving a ton of goods from England to Latin American capital cities was (in pounds sterling): Buenos Aires and Montevideo 2, Lima 5.12, Santiago 6.58, Caracas 7.76, Mexico City 17.9, Quito 21.3, Sucre or Chuquisca 25.56, and Bogotá 52.9 (Brading 1969: 243–4).

Thus, transport revolutions along the sea lanes connecting Latin America to Europe probably had far less to do with tariff responses than did investment in railroads at home. Where railroads integrated the Latin American interior with the world economy, we should see a protectionist response to the extent that import-competing industries were successful in lobbying for protection from these new winds of competition.

The Stolper-Samuelson Theorem and Latin American Capitalists

Even if the motivation for Latin American tariffs lay with revenues or some other source, they were still protective. After all, tariffs served to twist relative prices in favor of import-competing sectors, thus suppressing growth in the export sector and stimulating urban-based manufacturing. But was protection of manufacturing a *central* motivation for high tariffs in Latin America, especially after the export-led boom filled treasuries with new revenues that reduced debt service to manageable dimensions?

Ronald Rogowski (1989) has used the Stolper-Samuelson theorem to search for a political economy explanation for those extraordinarily high tariffs during the *belle époque*. Though their economies certainly varied in labor scarcity, every Latin American country faced relative capital scarcity and relative natural resource abundance. Thus, according to Stolper-Samuelson thinking, Latin American capitalists should have been looking to form protectionist coalitions as soon as *belle époque* peace and growth began to threaten them with freer trade. In most cases, they did not have to look far, either because they managed to dominate oligarchic regimes that excluded other interests, or because they readily found coalition partners willing to help, or both.

Peace, political stability, and economic growth after the 1870s did not produce democratic inclusion. Most Latin American countries limited the franchise to a small minority of adult men until well into the twentieth century. Literacy and wealth requirements excluded most potential voters in virtually every country (Engerman and Sokoloff 2001). Of course, nonvoters found other (more violent) ways to express their political interests, but except for Argentina (after 1912), independent Cuba, postrevolutionary Mexico (after 1917), and Uruguay, restrictions on the adult male franchise did not fall until after 1930 when the votes of scarce labor began to count.

Throughout Latin America, potentially pro–free trade agrarian interests were politically underrepresented. Large landowners certainly dominated local politics in rural areas, but at the national level urban capitalists—linked to external trade and finance—played a dominant role.

Rogowski has argued to the contrary that unlike the United States, Canada, New Zealand, and other frontier regions, free-trading landowners seized control in nineteenth-century Latin America (Rogowski 1989: 47). Rogowski appears to have gotten both the politics and tariff policy outcome wrong. Four of the five Latin American agricultural exporters examined here (Argentina, Brazil, Colombia, and Uruguay) expanded export production in the late-nineteenth century by putting new lands to the plough or modernizing and extending pastoral production (cattle and wool) for export. In backward economies with high land-labor ratios, Rogowski argued that expanding trade should produce assertive free-trading landed interests pitted against defensive populist alliances of capitalists and workers. In all four of these frontier nations, however, tariff rates were substantially higher than in other world regions. Either export producing landowners had less political clout or had weaker free trade preferences than this account suggests—or both.

Free-trading mineral export interests usually had less direct leverage in governmental decision making, despite the size and significance of their investments. This is because modern mining enterprises tended to be foreign owned and concerned more with controlling labor agitation and keeping taxes low. In the case of the three mineral exporters (Mexico, Chile, and Peru), mining interests could have allied themselves with powerful regional agricultural interests to lobby against protection. Yet, this did not happen, nor were agricultural exporters very effective in forging free trade coalitions with other interests. Perhaps one reason it did not happen is that they feared even more likely alternatives to tariff revenues, such as higher taxes on mineral production or new taxes on land (Bulmer-Thomas 1994: 140).

In short, urban capitalists secured explicitly protectionist tariffs for existing and new industries beginning in the 1890s. They did so against weak opposition and in close collaboration with modernizing political elites. They did not yet need the populist coalitions that emerged in the interwar decades.

Policy Packages and Real Exchange Rate Trade-Offs

Few policies are decided in isolation from others. Indeed, there were other ways that Latin American governments could have improved the competitive position of import-competing industries if such protection was their goal, and they explored many of these alternatives in the 1930s and in the ISI years that followed. One powerful tool was manipulating the real exchange rate. If governments chose to go on the gold standard or to peg to a core currency, they got more stable real exchange rates in return. However, protection via real exchange rate manipulation was forgone, or so the argument goes. Was this true for Latin America even before the 1930s?

The Political Economy of Latin American Tariffs 1870s–1950s: Looking at All Factors in Conjunction

Empirical Strategy

Of course, the potential explanations for Latin American protectionism discussed above are not necessarily competing: each may have played a role between independence and the Great Depression. But even if we can show this to be true, we would still like to know which played the biggest roles in accounting for the fact that Latin America was so protectionist for the century before the 1930s. We would also like to know whether things were different before and after World War I.

Table 2.2 is an econometric attack on the problem in four ways: first, it treats the Latin American eight-country historical experience as a pooled OLS panel, 1870–1950; second, it treats the experience as comparative Latin American economic history by using country-fixed effects (TS); third, it explores the cross-section variance across these Latin American countries by using time-fixed effects (CS); and finally, it uses fixed effects for both (FE). Although Table 2.2 presents all four of these regression estimates, we prefer the comparative history (TS) in the second column and the fixed effects (FE) in the last column, primarily because we think the random effects (RE) and OLS results are suspect for three reasons. First, RE is best used when we think the estimated effects are based on a randomly drawn sample from a large population. Our Latin American sample is small, so randomness is doubtful. Second, RE is typically more efficient and unbiased when the unobserved explanatory variables are uncorrelated with the observed explanatory variables. In our case, we think it is likely that the unob-

Table 2.2 Comparative Regressions of Endogenous Tariff Determinants, 1870–1950

	ln (Own Tariff)			
	(1)	(2)	(3)	(4)
Dependent Variable	OLS	TS	CS	FE
ln(lagged exports/GDP)	−0.13	−0.07	−0.04	−0.10
	−3.34	*−1.42*	*−1.12*	*−1.90*
	−0.21	**−0.12**	**−0.08**	**−0.17**
ln(GDP/capita)	−0.21	−0.07	0.01	0.06
	−3.36	*−1.02*	*0.14*	*0.76*
	−0.26	**−0.09**	**0.01**	**0.08**
ln(population)	−0.12	−0.76	0.26	−0.66
	−2.99	*−10.23*	*4.79*	*−5.27*
	−0.31	**−1.91**	**0.67**	**−1.66**
ln(lagged partner tariffs)	0.24	0.22	0.19	−0.02
	5.55	*5.31*	*3.49*	*−0.37*
	0.25	**0.23**	**0.20**	**−0.03**
ln(effective distance)	0.07	−0.01	0.07	−0.12
	2.56	*−0.52*	*1.93*	*−1.71*
	0.12	**−0.03**	**0.13**	**−0.21**
ln(km railways)	0.05	0.37	−0.18	0.17
	1.58	*10.03*	*−5.28*	*2.70*
	0.15	**1.22**	**−0.60**	**0.57**
ln(primary school enrollment)	−0.29	0.07	−0.14	−0.01
	−5.02	*1.22*	*−2.09*	*−0.17*
	−0.43	**0.10**	**−0.20**	**−0.02**
Inflation	−0.006	−0.005	−0.004	−0.004
	−3.79	*−3.94*	*−2.40*	*−3.01*
	−0.17	**−0.15**	**−0.11**	**−0.12**
Inflation^2	0.00011	0.00014	0.00013	0.00015
	2.02	*3.08*	*2.47*	*3.26*
	0.09	**0.12**	**0.11**	**0.13**
Federal system	−0.03	−0.20	−0.16	−0.19
	−0.87	*−4.62*	*−3.60*	*−4.17*
	−0.04	**−0.23**	**−0.18**	**−0.22**
ln(% population urban)	0.15	−0.61	0.27	−0.39
	2.45	*−7.41*	*4.31*	*−3.99*
	0.22	**−0.92**	**0.40**	**−0.59**
ln(lagged Px/Pm)	−0.16	−0.33	−0.45	−0.26
	−2.39	*−5.35*	*−5.30*	*−3.28*
	−0.10	**−0.21**	**−0.29**	**−0.17**
Gold standard	0.30	0.15	0.22	0.12
	8.68	*4.94*	*5.40*	*3.04*
	0.36	**0.18**	**0.26**	**0.14**

Continued on next page

Table 2.2 Comparative Regressions of Endogenous Tariff Determinants, 1870–1950, continued

	ln (Own Tariff)			
	(1)	(2)	(3)	(4)
Dependent Variable	OLS	TS	CS	FE
Constant	5.86	10.91	2.49	11.05
	8.60	*15.82*	*3.03*	*8.82*
Country ($N = 8$) dummies?	No	Yes	No	Yes
Year ($T = 81$) dummies	No	No	Yes	Yes
R^2	0.3487	0.5801	0.5413	0.6546
Adjusted R^2	0.3323	0.5636	0.4497	0.5789
Number of observations	530	530	530	530
Fixed effects comments				n/t
F-stat, H_0: all coeff's $= 0$	21.25	35.15	5.91	8.66
F-stat, H_0: all dummies $= 0$	40.06	2.47	20.33/1.25	
Number of groups		8	76	8/76
Average obs. per group		66.3	7	66.3/7.0
Hausman test statistic		404	185	156/31

Notes: t-statistics are in italics. Beta values are in bold.

served time and country-fixed effects are correlated with the observed right-hand side variables in Table 2.2. Third, econometric tests indicate that the FE results appear to be more efficient and unbiased than the RE results. This is confirmed by the Hausman test, which essentially compares the RE and FE results to see if they are significantly different. The high test statistic reported in Table 2.2 indicates that they *are* substantially different, and that the RE results should be discarded.

Having revealed our bias in favor of FE, we must confess that it contains eighty-seven dummy variables, a big number that makes us nervous about the efficiency of the FE estimates. Our expositional strategy will be to focus on the TS results in column 2 and the FE results in column 4 of Table 2.2, but we shall note (the infrequent cases) where the time series (TS) and cross sections (CS) sharply differ.

The right-hand side variables used throughout are the following (all but dummies in logs):

Lagged Exports/GDP, a measure of export boom. We expect booms in the previous year to diminish the need for high tariff rates in the current year—if government revenues are the goal as the qualitative literature suggests—thus yielding negative coefficients in the regression;

GDP/capita and Primary School Enrollment, the latter a rate. We take both of these variables as proxies for skill endowments, with the expectation that the more abundant the skills, the more competitive the industrial sector, and the less the need for protection, thus yielding a negative coefficient in the regression;

Population. Large countries have bigger domestic markets in which it is easier for local firms to find a spatial niche. Alternatively, bigger populations imply higher density, and higher density implies more efficient internal tax administration and less need for revenue tariffs. Thus, the demand for high tariffs should be lower in larger countries, and the regression should produce a negative coefficient;

Lagged Partner Tariffs, measured as a weighted average of the tariff rates in the trading countries' markets, the weight being trade volumes, lagged. Strategic tariff policy suggests that Latin American countries should have imposed higher tariffs in the current year if they faced high tariffs in their main markets abroad in the prior year;

Effective Distance, the distance from each Latin American country to either the United States or the United Kingdom (depending on trade volume), that distance adjusted by seaborne freight rates specific to that route. If protection was the goal, effective distance should have been viewed as a substitute for tariffs, so the regression should yield a negative coefficient;

km Railways, railway mileage added in kilometers. Poor overland transport connections to interior markets serves as a protective device. Railroads reduce that protection, requiring higher tariffs to offset the effect. Thus, the regression should yield a positive coefficient;

Inflation and Inflation Squared, the rates in home markets. To the extent that Latin America used specific duties, we expect inflation to lower tariff rates, thus yielding a negative coefficient. However, very rapid inflation might well have triggered a speedier legislative reaction with increases in specific duties, thus yielding a positive and offsetting coefficient on the squared term in the regression;

Federal System, a dummy variable; if a federal system = 1, if centralized = 0. Federal governments had a stronger need for customs duties, while centralized governments could better exploit internal revenue sources. Thus, the regression should report a positive coefficient;

Percent Population Urban, taken as share of population in cities and towns greater than 20,000. We take this urbanization statistic to be a proxy for the lobbying power of urban capitalists and artisans, thus yielding a positive coefficient in the regression;

Lagged Px/Pm. This terms of trade variable measures the price of each *j*th Latin American country's primary product exports (Px_j) relative to the price of import products (Pm) in world markets. There are two possible results here, and they will help discriminate between two hypotheses: While the export-share variable includes the combined effect of both price and quantity booms, the terms-of-trade variable here could also have a separate influence if the revenue motivation was dominant. This implies a negative coefficient since a boom in Px implies a boom in imports and in tariff revenues, thus diminishing the need for high tariff rates. Alternatively, if deindustrialization fears were dominant, a positive coefficient should appear. That is, as productivity growth achieved by industrial trading partners lowered the relative cost of manufactures in the long run (thus raising Px/Pm), a greater threat to import-competing industries in Latin America would be generated (e.g., inviting deindustrialization), encouraging a protective tariff response. In short, price shocks in world markets that were good for Latin American export sectors were bad for import-competing sectors. Thus, the sign on ln(lagged Px/Pm) should tell us whether revenue motivations dominated deindustrialization fears;

Capital inflows. This variable measures annual British capital exports to the Latin American country in question. It is expected that countries favored by British lending would have less need for tariff revenues and thus would have lower tariffs.

Gold Standard. A dummy variable that takes on a value of one when the country is on the gold standard or pegged to a core currency. It is expected that countries that give up some control over the real exchange rate will raise tariffs to help protect the now more exposed import-competing industries.

The Determinants of Latin American Tariffs, 1870–1950

Table 2.2 suggests that the regression model does quite well in accounting for almost a century of Latin American tariff policy. Furthermore, the *t*-statistics on all these variables are typically high enough to pass conventional significance tests. Most importantly, almost everything seems to be of right sign (taken from the TS column in Table 2.2). The results are organized around nine issues:

1. Revenue Goals

Consistent with government revenue motivation, the coefficient on ln(lagged exports/GDP) is negative (–0.07). While the estimate does not pass conventional significance tests for TS (t-statistic –1.42), it does for FE (–1.90). Thus, export booms were correlated with lower tariff rates (but perhaps even higher tariff revenues). Symmetrically, export slumps were correlated with higher tariff rates (to extract higher tariff revenues). Furthermore, this revenue effect was fairly big, as measured by the beta coefficient (–0.12 in TS and –0.17 in FE) entered in bold in the row under the t-statistic.[15] Furthermore, we shall see in a moment that revenue motivation is also confirmed by the coefficient on the terms of trade variable. In combination, these two variables tell us that revenue goals were one of the more important motivations driving Latin American tariffs to such lofty heights over the eighty years before 1950. Note, however, that the Federal System dummy has the wrong sign in both the TS and FE results, and the result is highly significant. Our expectation was that federalist governments, prior to the interwar rise in the welfare state, would have had more difficulty securing local taxes, and thus would have had to rely more heavily on customs duties. While this may have been the case during the first half-century of independence, it was not the case after 1870. The coefficient on Federal System is negative in TS (–0.20), not positive, and significant. It is negative everywhere in Table 2.2 and significant everywhere but in the OLS version. This result suggests to us that in a Latin America with a turbulent past, member states wanted to keep their federal governments weak.

2. Relative Price of Manufactures in World Markets

If there were deindustrialization fears in Latin America, they should have been reflected by changes in the relative price of manufactures. Table 2.2 explores the inverse of the relative price of manufactures (*Px/Pm*), namely the price of Latin American primary-product exports divided by the price of manufactures, both quoted in British or U.S. markets. *Pm* is a weighted average of the commodities imported by each Latin American country, and *Px* is a weighted average of the prices of the main primary products exported by each Latin American country. When the relative price of manufactures (*Pm*) fell in world markets—reflecting relatively fast productivity advance in European or North American industry, the threat of an invasion of manufactures should, according to the deindustrialization-fears prediction, have triggered a powerful protectionist response in Latin America, but it did not. Indeed, the coefficient on ln(lagged Px/Pm) is *negative* and highly significant (−0.33 in the TS). We interpret this result to mean that revenue goals dominated protectionist goals. When the relative price of manufactures fell in world markets, the relative price of Latin American export goods rose, increasing foreign exchange earnings, generating an import boom, and creating a tariff revenue glut. With a revenue glut, high tariff rates could be reduced. Symmetrically, a decline in the relative price of Latin American exports put upward pressure on tariff rates, helping account for the observed "globalization backlash" during the Latin America *belle époque* as well as during the interwar years. But the backlash in Latin America was not driven by fear that the penetration of lower-priced foreign imports would destroy domestic industry, but rather by a fall of export prices eroding government revenue.[16] These results are consistent with those on ln(lagged exports/GDP). Revenue goals were central in driving Latin American tariff rates.

3. Protectionist Policy

While revenue motivations may have dominated tariff policy, that fact does not necessarily mean that protectionist forces were absent. After controlling for everything else, were these Latin American countries acting as if they had the protection of local manufacturing in mind when they set tariffs? The answer is yes. Consider the coefficients on two variables. The variable ln(effective distance) has the predicted negative coefficient (−0.01), but it does not pass conventional significance tests: countries that were protected by higher transport costs along the sea lanes connecting European and local Latin American ports, had lower tariffs, but the effect was weak. However, the variable ln(km Railways) has a positive and highly significant coefficient (0.37): countries that developed better internal railroad networks also raised tariffs, presumably to protect domestic producers from foreign penetration of their internal domestic markets. We also note that the beta coefficient on ln(km railways) is *much* bigger than that on ln(effective distance), and the second biggest in Table 2.2, fully consistent with our predictions that overcoming the hostile geography of Latin America was a much more important contributor to globalization forces than were productivity changes along the sea lanes. The combined effect of these two variables suggests that high Latin American tariffs were in part driven by protectionist goals. This does not mean, of course, that protectionist goals dominated revenue goals. Indeed, we have already seen that the response of tariff policy to terms-of-trade movements in world markets was dominated by revenue needs, not deindustrialization fears. They may have had those fears, but they did not dominate. Finally, note that the positive and significant coefficient on the Gold Standard dummy is also consistent with an explicit protectionist policy favoring import-competing industries. When Latin American countries pegged their exchange rates by going on the gold standard (or pegging to a core currency), they gave up much of their ability to manipulate the real exchange rate in favor of those industries. It appears that they increased tariffs as an offset.

4. Market Size and Density

Big countries, as measured by population size, had lower tariff rates (–0.76), a result consistent with the view that big domestic markets were more friendly to foreign imports since local firms would have found it easier to carve out regional and product niches, or since internal tax revenues would have been easier to collect in more densely populated countries, or both. Producers in countries with relatively small markets—such as Chile, Cuba, and Uruguay in our sample—would have found it harder to hide in spatial niches, thus lobbying for higher tariffs, and the low efficiency in internal tax collection may have favored their efforts. The beta coefficient (–1.91) is the biggest in Table 2.2.

5. Strategic Tariff Policy

These eight Latin American economies also seem to reveal strategic tariff policy behavior to the extent that the coefficient on ln(lagged partner tariffs) is positive (0.22) and significant: countries trading with high tariff partners (mainly the United States) adopted high tariffs themselves; countries trading with low tariff partners (mainly the United Kingdom) adopted low tariffs themselves. Still, the beta coefficient in TS (0.23) suggests that it was not a central determinant of Latin American tariff policy, at least prior to World War I, and the absence of any the effect in FE is consistent with that conclusion.

6. Education, Skills, and Industrial Competitiveness

The ln (Primary School Enrollment) variable is a proxy for skilled labor endowment, and thus for capacity to compete with imported foreign manufactures. The coefficients estimated here do not offer powerful support for the hypothesis: in the CS and OLS, higher skill endowment was associated with lower tariffs (on manufactured goods, of course); however, it was associated with higher tariffs in TS (0.07), and insignificant in FE. The negative coefficient on ln(GDP/capita) in CS is consistent with the result that richer countries—who get that way by being more productive and investing more in human and physical capital per capita—had lower tariff rates (−0.21), but none of the other coefficients are significant.

7. Stolper-Samuelson Political Economy

It appears that classic Stolper-Samuelson forces receive only mixed support from Latin American history, at least when we control for other factors. Urban interests should have favored protection in Latin America. The negative coefficient on ln(% population urban) does not support this assertion in TS (−0.61), but we note that it is *strongly* supported in the CS results (0.27) and highly significant. What was true in the cross section was not true in the time series, and we need to learn more about why.

8. Inflation and Specific Duties

Inflation had exactly the predicted effect during an epoch when specific duties were so much more common than ad valorem duties, although, as predicted, very rapid inflation rates apparently triggered faster adjustment. Thus, tariff rates were lower during inflationary episodes, as long as the inflations weren't too spectacular. However, judging by the beta coefficients, this inflation effect had a pretty modest influence on tariffs compared to other forces at work.

9. External Finance

Latin American countries that were successful in getting external finance would have had less reason to use high tariffs to augment revenues for short-run expenditure needs. Elsewhere, we have explored this idea using data on British capital exports before World War I (Coatsworth and Williamson forthcoming). While these data do not cover all sources of capital nor all years, we found a negative coefficient on the variable, in other words more foreign capital was associated with lower tariffs, a result consistent with revenue motivation.

Were the Determinants of Tariffs Different after the Belle Époque?

One would think that the determinants of tariffs might change over time. For example, Márquez (2002: Ch. 3) documents that after 1887 the increase in internal tax collections and better access to international credit markets made it possible to redirect Mexican tariff policy toward the goals of industrial growth. Were these forces ubiquitous across Latin America?

Table 2.3 reports an attempt to test the null hypothesis that the years after *belle époque* were the same as those before, at least in the way that tariffs were determined. The third column under each of the four estimation procedures, "All," covers the full 1870–1950 period, and it repeats Table 2.2. The other two columns report the estimation for the period up to 1913 (the *belle époque*) and after 1914 (the post–*belle époque* interwar dark ages). The comparison is not without problems, since the data base for the earlier period is probably not as good; indeed, the *belle époque* is missing many country-year observations. Nonetheless, we predict the tariff levels for both periods, and then perform a *t*-test to see if the means are the same in the two periods. The *t*-test is performed three times each for both the OLS and the time series: 1870–1913 versus 1870–1950 (was the *belle époque* the same as the full period?); 1914–50 versus 1870–1950 (was the post–*belle époque* the same as the full period?); and 1870–1913 versus 1914–50 (were the *belle époque* and the post–*belle époque* the same?). In all cases, we can reject the null hypothesis that the predicted levels are the same.

So, not only were tariffs very high in the *belle époque*, but the determinants of tariff policy were different then too. How were they different? Consider the time series results in Table 2.3 (where country dummies = country fixed effects). Some of the tariff determinants remain unchanged on either side of 1913, such as population size, railways, effective distance, and urbanization (our Stolper-Samuelson proxy). Two remain unchanged in sign, but change in magnitude: the impact of inflation on tariff rates was much more powerful after 1913 than before, and being on the gold standard served to raise tariffs much more (and more significantly) after 1913 than before. Another underwent no change in sign or magnitude when we might reasonably have expected the opposite: the impact of ln(lagged *Px/Pm*) was pretty much the same before and after World War I, implying that revenue needs dominated deindustrialization fears even after the *belle époque*. The remaining five explanatory variables *did* undergo change. Consider three. First, strategic tariff policy as reflected by ln(Lagged Partner Tariffs) was not only more powerful after 1913, but was not present at all in the *belle époque*. The rise of strategic tariff policy in Latin

Table 2.3 Were Tariff Policy Determinants Different after the *Belle Époque*?

	(1)	(2)	(3)	(4)	(5)	(6)
		ln(Own Tariff)				
	Pooled OLS			Time Series		
Dependent Variable	1870–1913	1914–1950	All	1870–1913	1914–1950	All
ln(lagged exports /GDP)	0.13	−0.55	−0.13	0.01	−0.36	−0.07
	2.47	*−9.46*	*−3.34*	*0.13*	*−4.66*	*−1.42*
	0.29	**−0.78**	**−0.21**	**0.02**	**−0.52**	**−0.12**
ln(GDP/capita)	0.27	−0.83	−0.21	0.09	−0.51	−0.07
	3.19	*−8.75*	*−3.36*	*0.84*	*−3.05*	*−1.02*
	0.38	**−1.01**	**−0.26**	**0.13**	**−0.62**	**−0.09**
ln(population)	0.36	−0.71	−0.12	−0.35	−1.12	−0.76
	6.05	*−9.09*	*−2.99*	*−2.36*	*−5.47*	*−10.23*
	1.07	**−1.52**	**−0.31**	**−1.06**	**−2.40**	**−1.91**
ln(lagged partner tariffs)	0.44	0.22	0.24	−0.01	0.24	0.22
	7.00	*3.68*	*5.55*	*−0.14*	*3.77*	*5.31*
	0.59	**0.21**	**0.25**	**−0.01**	**0.23**	**0.23**
ln(effective distance)	0.30	0.06	0.07	0.02	0.01	−0.01
	6.58	*1.83*	*2.56*	*0.03*	*0.88*	*−0.52*
	0.54	**0.12**	**0.12**	**0.03**	**0.01**	**−0.03**
ln(km railways)	−0.20	0.32	0.05	0.20	0.49	0.37
	−5.67	*6.04*	*1.58*	*4.40*	*3.38*	*10.03*
	−0.80	**0.83**	**0.15**	**0.82**	**1.27**	**1.22**
ln(primary school enrollment)	−0.08	−0.22	−0.29	−0.20	0.06	0.07
	−0.87	*−2.41*	*−5.02*	*−2.61*	*0.58*	*1.22*
	−0.12	**−0.25**	**−0.43**	**−0.31**	**0.07**	**0.10**
Inflation	−0.0022	−0.0084	−0.006	−0.0019	−0.0064	−0.005
	−1.29	*−3.61*	*−3.79*	*−2.61*	*−2.83*	*−3.94*
	−0.07	**−0.24**	**−0.17**	**−0.06**	**−0.18**	**−0.15**
Inflation^2	0.00008	0.00012	0.00011	0.00009	0.00013	0.00014
	1.33	*1.74*	*2.02*	*1.96*	*1.83*	*3.08*
	0.08	**0.11**	**0.09**	**0.08**	**0.12**	**0.12**
Federal system	−0.15	0.17	−0.03	−0.15	0.02	−0.20
	−3.07	*2.17*	*−0.87*	*−2.75*	*0.27*	*−4.62*
	−0.22	**0.17**	**−0.04**	**−0.23**	**0.02**	**−0.23**
ln(% population urban)	0.03	0.34	0.15	−0.01	−0.28	−0.61
	0.38	*4.17*	*2.45*	*−0.01*	*−1.42*	*−7.41*
	0.06	**0.46**	**0.22**	**0.00**	**−0.38**	**−0.92**
ln(lagged Px/Pm)	−0.39	−0.23	−0.16	−0.38	−0.42	−0.33
	−4.01	*−2.37*	*−2.39*	*−5.03*	*−3.91*	*−5.35*
	−0.24	**−0.14**	**−0.10**	**−0.23**	**−0.26**	**−0.21**

Continued on next page

Table 2.3 Were Tariff Policy Determinants Different after the *Belle Époque?*, continued

	ln(Own Tariff)					
	(1)	(2)	(3)	(4)	(5)	(6)
	Pooled OLS			Time Series		
Dependent	1870–	1914–		1870–	1914–	
Variable	1913	1950	All	1913	1950	All
Gold standard	0.28	0.28	0.30	0.04	0.18	0.15
	6.96	*5.16*	*8.68*	*1.07*	*3.22*	*4.94*
	0.41	**0.31**	**0.36**	**0.06**	**0.20**	**0.18**
Constant	−1.43	11.39	5.86	6.91	14.16	10.91
	−1.43	*10.85*	*8.60*	*5.89*	*7.99*	*15.82*
Country dummies?	No	No	No	Yes	Yes	Yes
Year dummies	No	No	No	No	No	No
R^2	0.3796	0.4709	0.3487	0.6917	0.5945	0.5801
Adjusted R^2	0.3501	0.4420	0.3323	0.6687	0.5578	0.5636
Number of observations	288	242	530	288	242	530
t-Tests on ln (predicted tariffs):						
1870–1913 = 1870–1950			−14.8133			−10.1379
1914–1950 = 1870–1950			−3.615			−3.6715
1870–1913 = 1914–1950			6.6729			5.198

Notes: t-statistics are in italics. Beta values are in bold.

America during the years when the global economy was disintegrating is certainly consistent with the traditional literature and with other recent quantitative work (Clemens and Williamson 2001). Second, and much to our surprise, the revenue effects as measured by ln(lagged exports/GDP)—export booms being associated with lower tariffs and export slumps with higher tariffs—was entirely a *post*-1913 phenomenon: when we control for everything else, the effect of Exports/GDP was absent from the *belle époque*, a result completely at odds with the "unconditional" qualitative literature. Third, the negative association between tariff height and Federal System was entirely a pre-1913 phenomenon, a result consistent with the view that after the nation-building chaos between the 1820s and the 1870s members were suspicious of federal authority and kept them weak, but that this suspicion had evaporated by World War I.

Concluding Remarks and an Agenda
on Historical Persistence

This chapter started by uncovering a fact that has not been well appreciated. Tariffs in Latin America were far higher than anywhere else
from the 1860s to World War I, long before the Great Depression. Indeed, tariff rates in Latin America were even on the rise in the decades
before 1914, a period that has been called the first globalization boom
for the world economy and the *belle époque* for Latin America. To repeat our introductory remarks, this fact is surprising because: this region has been said to have exploited globalization forces better than
most during the pre-1914 *belle époque*; standard economic histories
say so little about it; most of us have always been taught to view the
Great Depression as *the* critical turning point when the region is said
to have turned toward protection and de-linked from the world economy for the first time.

High tariffs should have favored the domestic import-competing
industry, and that was manufacturing in Latin America. It also should
have taken some of the steam out of the export-led boom during the
belle époque. But was it protection and deindustrialization-from-glob-
alization fears that motivated those high tariffs?

This chapter showed that the explanation for high tariffs in Latin
America since independence almost two centuries ago cannot lie with
some perceived GDP per capita gains from protection, since such gains
were never present in Latin America. On the contrary, those countries
with the highest tariff rates in Latin America grew the slowest, and
those with the lowest tariff rates grew fastest. The chapter then explored the motivation for Latin American tariffs as a revenue source, as
a response to deindustrialization fears, as a strategic policy response to
trading partners tariffs, as a redistributive device for special interests,
and as a consequence of other political economy struggles.

The bottom line is that tariff formation in Latin America was complex and that *all* the forces suggested by the new literature on the political economy of tariffs were present. But revenue needs were always the
key to those exceptionally high tariffs, and this motivation had its roots
in the exceptional levels of military conflict in the region for a half-century or more when the rest of the world was enjoying Pax Britannica.

While the chapter concludes by showing exactly how *belle époque*
tariff determination differed from the period after 1913, it does not
report whether the same pro-protection conditions that existed more
than a century ago also exist today. Surely, that should be the next item

on any agenda that intends to explore the political economy of protection in Latin America. Even if generated by conditions and motivations long since erased by time, high tariffs in the distant past can remain high in the present as a result of institutional and political habit.

References

Anderson, James E. 1998. "Trade Restrictiveness Benchmarks." *Economic Journal* 108 (July): 1111–25.

Anderson, James E., and J. Peter Neary. 1994. "Measuring the Restrictiveness of Trade Policy." *The World Bank Economic Review* 8 (May): 151–69.

Bagwell, Kyle W., and Robert W. Staiger. 2000. "GATT-Think." National Bureau of Economic Research Working Paper 8005, Cambridge, MA.

Bairoch, Paul. 1972. "Free Trade and European Economic Development in the Nineteenth Century." *European Economic Review* 3 (November): 211–45.

Bairoch, Paul. 1989. "European Trade Policy, 1815–1914." In *The Cambridge Economic History of Europe*, vol. III, edited by P. Mathias and S. Pollard. Cambridge: Cambridge University Press.

Beatty, E. 2001. *Institutions and Investment: The Political Basis of Industrialization Before 1911*. Stanford: Stanford University Press.

Bhagwati, Jagdish, and Anne O. Krueger, eds. 1973–1976. *Foreign Trade Regimes and Economic Development*. 9 vols. New York: Columbia University Press.

Blattman, Christopher, Michael A. Clemens, and Jeffrey G. Williamson. 2002. "Who Protected and Why?: Tariffs the World Around 1870–1937." Paper presented to the Conference on the Political Economy of Globalization, Trinity College, Dublin, August 29–31.

Bloom, David E., and Jeffrey G. Williamson. 1998. "Demographic Transitions and Economic Miracles in Emerging Asia." *World Bank Economic Review* 12 (September): 419–55.

Brading, C. W. 1969. "Un analisis comparativo del costo de la vida en diversas capitales de hispanoamerica." *Boletin Historico de la Fundacion John Boulton* 20 (March): 229–63.

Bulmer-Thomas, Victor. 1994. *The Economic History of Latin America Since Independence*. Cambridge: Cambridge University Press.

Centeno, M. A. 1997. "Blood and Debt: War and Taxation in Nineteenth-Century Latin America." *American Journal of Sociology* 102 (May): 1565–605.

Cleary, D. 1998. "'Lost Altogether to the Civilized World': Race and the Cabanagem in Northern Brazil, 1750–1850." *Comparative Studies in Society and History* 401 (January): 109–35.

Clemens, Michael A., and Jeffrey G. Williamson. 2001. "A Tariff-Growth Paradox? Protection's Impact the World Around 1875–1997." National Bureau of Economic Research Working Paper 8459 (September), Cambridge, MA.

Clemens, Michael A., and Jeffrey G. Williamson. 2002. "Closed Jaguar, Open Dragon: Comparing Tariffs in Latin America and Asia before World War II." Paper presented to the Latin American and Caribbean Economic Association Meetings, Madrid, October 11–13.

Coatsworth, John H. 1988. "Patterns of Rural Rebellion in Latin America: Mexico in Comparative Perspective." In *Riot, Rebellion, and Revolution: Rural Social Conflict in Mexico,* edited by F. Katz. Princeton: Princeton University Press.

Coatsworth, John H., and Jeffrey G. Williamson. 2002a. "The Roots of Latin American Protectionism: Looking Before the Great Depression." National Bureau of Economic Research Working Paper no. 8999 (June), Cambridge, MA.

Coatsworth, John H., and Jeffrey G. Williamson. Forthcoming. "Always Protectionist? Latin American Tariffs from Independence to Great Depression." *Journal of Latin American Studies.*

Corbo, Vittorio. 1992. "Development Strategies and Policies in Latin America: A Historical Perspective." International Center for Economic Growth Occasional Paper No. 22 (April): 16–48. San Francisco.

Diaz-Alejandro, Carlos. 1984. "Latin America in the 1930s." In *Latin America in the 1930s,* edited by R. Thorpe. New York: Macmillan.

Dixit, Avinash K. 1987. "Strategic Aspects of Trade Policy." In *Advances in Economic Theory: Fifth World Congress,* edited by T. F. Bewley. New York: Cambridge University Press.

Dollar, David. 1992. "Outward-Oriented Developing Economies Really Do Grow More Rapidly: Evidence from 95 LDCs, 1976–1985." *Economic Development and Cultural Change* 40 (April): 523–44.

Dollar, David, and Aart Kraay. 2000. "Trade, Growth, and Poverty." World Bank, Washington, DC (October). Photocopy.

Drake, Paul W. 1989. *The Money Doctor in the Andes: The Kemmerer Missions 1923–1933.* Durham, NC: Duke University Press.

Edwards, Sebastian. 1993. "Openness, Trade Liberalization, and Growth in Developing Countries." *Journal of Economic Literature* 31 (September): 1358–94.

Engerman, Stanley L., and Kenneth L. Sokoloff. 2001. "The Evolution of Suffrage in the New World: A Preliminary Examination." Paper presented to the 2001 Cliometrics Conference, Tuscon, AZ, May 18–20.

Irwin, Douglas A. 1997. "Higher Tariffs, Lower Revenues? Analyzing the Fiscal Aspects of the Great Tariff Debate of 1888." National Bureau of Economic Research Working Paper no. 6239 (October), Cambridge, MA.

Irwin, Douglas A. 1998. "Changes in U.S. Tariffs: The Role of Import Prices and Commercial Policies?" *American Economic Review* 88 (September): 1015–26.

Irwin, Douglas A. 2001. "The Optimal Tax on Antebellum U.S. Cotton Exports." National Bureau of Economic Research Working Paper no. 8689 (December), Cambridge, MA.

Kindleberger, Charles P. 1951. "Group Behavior and International Trade." *Journal of Political Economy* 59 (February): 30–46.

Krueger, Anne O. 1983. "The Effects of Trade Strategies on Growth." *Finance and Development* 20 (June): 6–8.

———. 1984. "Trade Policies in Developing Countries." In *Handbook of International Economics*, vol. 1, edited by R. Jones and P. Kenan. Amsterdam: North-Holland.

Leff, Nathaniel H. 1982. *Underdevelopment and Development in Brazil.* Vol. 1, *Economic Structure and Change, 1822–1947* and vol. 2, *Reassessing the Obstacles to Economic Underdevelopment.* London: Allen & Unwin.

Lindert, Peter H., and Jeffrey G. Williamson. 2001. "Does Globalization Make the World More Unequal?" National Bureau of Economic Research Working Paper 8228 (April), Cambridge, MA.

Mares, D. 2001. *Violent Peace: Militarized Interstate Bargaining in Latin America.* New York. Columbia University Press.

Márquez Colin, Graciela. 1998. "Tariff Protection in México, 1892–1909: *Ad Valorem* Tariff Rates and Sources of Variation." In *Latin America and the World Economy Since 1800*, edited by J. H. Coatsworth and A. M. Taylor. Cambridge, MA: Harvard University Press.

———. 2002. "The Political Economy of Mexican Protectionism, 1868–1911." Ph.D. dissertation, Harvard University (March).

McGreevey, W. P. 1971. *An Economic History of Colombia, 1845–1930.* Cambridge: Cambridge University Press.

O'Rourke, Kevin H. 2000. "Tariffs and Growth in the Late Nineteenth Century." *Economic Journal* 110 (April): 456–83.

O'Rourke, Kevin H., and Jeffrey G. Williamson. 1999. *Globalization and History.* Cambridge, MA: MIT Press.

Prados de la Escosura, Leandro. 2002. "The Economic Consequences of Independence in Latin America." Universidad Carlos III, Madrid. Photocopy.

Prebisch, Raúl. 1950. "The Economic Development of Latin America and Its Principal Problems." Reprinted in *Economic Bulletin for Latin America* 7 (1962): 1–22.

Pritchett, Lant. 1997. "Divergence, Big Time." *Journal of Economic Perspectives* 11 (Summer): 3–18.

Rodriguez, Francisco, and Dani Rodrik. 2001. "Trade Policy and Economic Growth: A Skeptic's Guide to the Cross-National Evidence." In *NBER Macroeconomics Annual 2000*, vol. 15, edited by B. S. Bernake and K. Rogoff. Cambridge, MA: MIT Press.

Rogowski, Ronald. 1989. *Commerce and Coalitions: How Trade Affects Domestic Political Alignments.* Princeton, NJ: Princeton University Press.

Sachs, Jeffrey D., and Andrew Warner. 1995. "Economic Reform and the Process of Global Integration." Brookings Institution Papers on Economic Activity no. 1, Washington, DC.

Singer, Hans W. 1950. "The Distribution of Gains between Investing and Borrowing Countries." *American Economic Review* 40: 473–85.

Stemmer, Juan E. Oribe. 1989. "Freight Rates in the Trade between Europe and South America." *Journal of Latin American Studies* 21, (1) (February): 22–59.

Taylor, Alan M. 1998. "On the Costs of Inward-Looking Development: Price Distortions, Growth, and Divergence in Latin America." *Journal of Economic History* 58 (March): 1–28.

Williamson, Jeffrey G. 1998. "Globalization, Labor Markets and Policy Backlash in the Past." *Journal of Economic Perspectives* 12 (Fall): 51–72.

Notes

A data appendix for this chapter is available upon request from Williamson. The tariff data have been taken from collaboration between Jeffrey Williamson and Michael Clemens (2001), and we are grateful to the latter for allowing us to use that data here too. We have also received superb research assistance from Chris Blattman, David Clingingsmith, and István Zöllei. In addition, we have benefited from conversations with Graciela Márquez, Richard Cooper, Alan Dye, Toni Estevadeordal, Ron Findlay, Jeff Frieden, Steve Haber, Elhanan Helpman, Doug Irwin, Leandro Prados, Dani Rodrik, Dick Salvucci, Ken Sokoloff, Alan Taylor, and participants at joint development, international, and history workshops at Copenhagen, Harvard, and Yale, the Harvard Workshop on Political Economy, the Conference on the Political Economy of Globalization (Dublin, August 29–31, 2002), and the FTAA and Beyond conference meetings at Cambridge (May 31–June 1, 2002) and Punta del Este

(December 15–16, 2002). Williamson acknowledges with pleasure financial support from the National Science Foundation SES-0001362.

1   The average tariff rate is measured here as customs revenues (import duties only) as a share of total import values.

2   This chapter is part of an ongoing series of papers. In another, the present authors explore the qualitative evidence and the pre-1870 period in Latin America much more extensively (Coatsworth and Williamson forthcoming). In addition, Clemens and Williamson (2002) have explored the differences between Asia and Latin America. Finally, Blattman, Clemens, and Williamson (2002) have recently used the full tariff sample to explore many of the same issues raised in this paper.

3   As in Figure 2.1, we have calculated (but do not report) weighted tariff averages for the regional clubs in Figure 2.2, where weights are the country's total export share in regional exports or its GDP share. However, we prefer to treat countries as independent policy units regardless of size.

4   This finding—higher levels of protection in Asia than in Latin America before the 1970s—is confirmed by Alan Taylor (1998: Table 2, p. 7) even when more comprehensive measures of protection and openness are employed that include nontariff barriers.

5   Of course, quotas, exchange-rate management, and other non-tariff policy instruments served to augment the protectionist impact of tariff barriers far more in the 1930s than in the *belle époque*, when nontariff barriers were far less common.

6   Policy makers of that time didn't have the models, methods, and evidence that we exploit in Table 2.1, but they certainly had the intuition.

7   This section draws on a recent survey paper by Peter Lindert and Jeffrey Williamson (2001) and some new work on the impact of tariffs on growth before 1950 (Clemens and Williamson 2001).

8   And *late*-nineteenth century Latin American policy makers were certainly aware (Bulmer-Thomas 1994: 140). However, it is important to stress *late* since the use of protection specifically and consciously to foster industry does not appear to occur until well after the 1860s, e.g., Argentina with the 1876 tariff, Mexico by the early 1890s, Chile with its new tariff in 1897, Brazil in the 1890s, and Colombia in early 1900s (influenced by Mexican experience). True, Mexico saw some precocious efforts in the late 1830s and 1840s to promote modern industry, but these lapsed with renewed local and international warfare. So, the qualitative evidence suggests that domestic industry protection becomes a motivation for Latin American tariffs only in the late-nineteenth century.

9   A century later, things had changed, at least with the appearance of the

"money doctor," Princeton Professor Edwin Kemmerer, and his team of young economists (including Kossuth M. Williamson; see Drake 1989).

10   In the words of Bulmer-Thomas (1994: 140), the tariff "was the main source of government income in all [Latin] countries and virtually the only source in a few republics." It was still true of the late-nineteenth century, at least in Mexico where import duties between 1884–85 and 1890–91 were on average 46.1 percent of total revenue (Márquez 2002: 160). The big change in that share took place in the 1880s (Márquez 2002: 203).

11   We should note that for the *antebellum* United States Irwin (2001) also reports that the optimal export tax would have been about 50 percent at a time when U.S. cotton was King in world markets. In simple trade models, an export tax and an import tariff can be equivalent.

12   They were also specific in nineteenth-century Latin America (Bulmer-Thomas 1994: 141).

13   Exemplified by Dixit (1987) and recently surveyed in Bagwell and Staiger (2000).

14   Figure 2.6 is consistent, of course, with the initial findings of the great terms of trade debate launched by Prebisch and Singer a half century ago. Furthermore, and although we do not show it in Figure 2.6, all of that average downward trend is for six Latin American countries— Brazil, Chile, Columbia, Cuba, Mexico, and Peru—and none of it is for Argentina and Uruguay. In addition, the downward slide appears to start in the mid 1890s.

15   The beta coefficient is defined as the estimate of the coefficient on the explanatory variable in question multiplied by the ratio of the standard deviation of the underlying explanatory variable to that of the dependent variable. The beta coefficient is one indicator of the relative importance of different regressors; it is the number of standard deviations of the regressand explained by one standard deviation of the regressor.

16   This result appears whether the Px/Pm variable is measured as deviation from trend (e.g., Table 2.2) or as the actual Px/Pm, or even as trend and deviation component together. The result also appears to have been equally strong on either side of 1913.

[4]

Commercial policy between the wars*

I.   War and post-war reconstruction

The First World War marked the end of an era in the history of commercial relations among countries. New boundaries set in the peace treaties, especially with Austria and Hungary, converted pre-1914 internal trade to international trade. Trade relations interrupted by war could not always be restored. Extended fighting and disruption of peacetime economic intercourse produced substantial changes in the economic capacities and interests of major trading nations. Monetary disturbance evoked responses in trade policy, especially increases in tariffs, to offset effects of exchange depreciation abroad. A loosely concerted attempt was made after the war to patch up the fabric of trade relationships, but with nothing like the fervour exhibited after the Second World War. There was virtually no planning of post-war trade policies, despite President Wilson's third of the fourteen points that called for 'removal, as far as possible, of all economic barriers and the establishment of an equality of trade conditions among all nations consenting to the peace and associating themselves with its maintenance'.

Exigencies of war led to changes in commercial policy. The McKenna budget in Britain in 1915 imposed duties of $33\frac{1}{3}$ per cent on motor cars and parts, musical instruments, clocks, watches, and cinematographic film in an effort to reduce imports of luxuries and to save shipping space – although the point has been made that the shipping space taken by watches is minimal (Kreider, 1943, p. 13). Unlike previous luxury taxes in Britain, these duties on imports were not matched by domestic excises to eliminate the protective effect. The tariffs, moreover, made it possible for the United Kingdom to discriminate in trade in favour of the British Empire, something it could not do under the regime of free trade which had prevailed since the 1850s. Canada had granted preferential tariff treatment to Britain on a unilateral and non-reciprocal basis since 1898 – Britain assenting to the extent that it denounced the trade treaties with Germany and Belgium going back to the 1860s under which those

* I am grateful for the comments on the original draft of Barry Eichengreen, Jonathan Hughes, and Donald Moggridge.

countries had the right to claim concessions made by one part of the Empire to another on a most-favoured-nation basis. The Finance Act of 1919 further reduced excise taxes on Empire tea, cocoa, coffee, chicory, currants, and certain dried fruits by one-sixth, and on Empire wines by one-third. The Key Industries Act of 1919 designed to strengthen defence industries equally contained preferences for the Empire, as did the Safeguarding of Industries Act of 1921. If the McKenna duties were designed to economize shipping and foreign exchange, the Finance Act of 1919 to raise revenue, and the Key Industries Act of 1919 to serve national defence, the Safeguarding of Industries Act levying tariffs on imports of gloves, domestic glassware, gas mantles – a list extended in 1925 to include leather, lace, cutlery, pottery, packing paper, and enamelled hollow ware – represented straightforward protection of industries hurt by foreign competition.

A number of countries increased tariff coverage and raised rates to gain revenue. French minimum tariff rates had been raised by 1918 from 5 to 20 per cent, and maximum rates from 10 to 40 per cent. The use of import quotas in France dates from 1919, rather than the depression in 1930, although export and import prohibitions were a widespread feature of Colbert's mercantilism two and a half centuries earlier. In countries where the principal fiscal instrument was the tariff, such as Canada, tariff duties were increased early after the outbreak of war.

Fitful attention was given to commodity problems by Britain. Long concerned about the prospect of interruption of cotton supplies from the Southern United States as a result either of boll weevil or black rebellion, she had contemplated an Empire scheme for producing cotton. The planting of Gezira in the Sudan was started in 1914 with the decision to irrigate 300,000 acres, but the Empire Cotton Growing Corporation was not chartered until November 1921, sometime after the acute shortage of cotton fibre during the war and early post-war period. An Empire Resources Development Committee proposed in 1915 a scheme for producing palm kernel in West Africa and processing it in the United Kingdom, foreshadowing the East African groundnut scheme after the Second World War. The technique envisaged was an export tax of £2 per ton to be continued for five years after the war, but that was to be rebated in favour of British processors. The scheme was started in October 1919 but met sharp Gold Coast resistance. When the price of palm kernel fell, the project became untenable and the duty was withdrawn in July 1922 (Hancock, 1940, pp. 113–18).

Limited as it was, post-war planning took place along lines of military alliance. France took the lead in an Allied economic conference in June 1916 that produced a resolution committing the Allies to take first temporary and then permanent steps to make themselves independent of enemy countries in matters of raw-material supply, essential manufactures, and the organization of trade, finance and shipping (Drummond, 1972, p. 56). Neutral reaction, including that of the United States neutral at that time, was hostile. When the United States entered the war, the notion was dropped despite French efforts to revive it at Versailles (Viner, 1950, pp. 24–5). On the other side, Germany and Austria concluded a treaty before the Armistice in 1918, providing for customs union after the war; the arrangement was not for complete free trade within the union, but permitted Austria–Hungary to retain protection at a preferential level in certain weak industries (*ibid.*, pp. 105–6). In defeat it proved academic, except perhaps as a precedent to the 1931 proposal for *Zollunion* (customs union) between Austria and Germany, and the 1937 *Anschluss*.

Commercial-policy features of the treaties ending the First World War were minimal. Germany was required to agree to apply the tariff nomenclature worked out at The Hague in 1913 (as well as to accept the international conventions of 1904 and 1910 suppressing the white slave trade, the conventions of 16 and 19 November 1885 regarding the establishment of a concert pitch (the wavelength of the musical note of A) and a host of others). The principal effect of these measures seems to have been to stiffen German resistance to subscribing to the agreements. More significantly, Germany was required by the treaty of Versailles to grant the Allies unilateral and unconditional most-favoured-nation treatment for five years. On 10 January 1925 when the five years elapsed and Germany was free to negotiate trade agreements on her own, the post-war period of reconstruction may be said to have come to an end – at least in the area of trade. The lapse of these provisions helped Germany but posed a problem for France which now had to negotiate to obtain outlets for Alsatian textiles and Lorraine minette iron ore which earlier had been marketed in Germany without payment of duties (Schuker, 1976, pp. 219–27).

These five years, however, constituted a period of considerable disorder in fluctuations of business and of exchange rates, and, in consequence, in policies relating to international trade. Anti-dumping legislation was enacted in Japan in 1920, in Australia, Britain, New Zealand and the United States in 1921, when also earlier legislation dating from 1904 in Canada was amended; the anti-dumping provisions of the Fordney–McCumber tariff took effect in 1922 (Viner, 1923, repr. 1966, pp. 192, 219, 227, 231, 246, 258). The United Kingdom further authorized $33\frac{1}{3}$ per cent duties against countries devaluing their currencies, although these were never imposed and were allowed to lapse in 1930. With the franc free to fluctuate, France initiated a system of tariff coefficients which could be adjusted to compensate for inflation at home or revaluations of the exchange rate. The Fordney–McCumber Act of 1922 in the United States not only extended anti-dumping provisions but raised tariffs on a variety of materials which had fallen in price in the sharp recession of 1920–1. Insult was added to injury from this and from the wartime enactment of Prohibition in the United States that cut off imports of wine, beer, and spirits, when the United States took sanitary measures against Spanish grapes and oranges to limit the danger of entry of fruit flies, without giving consideration to the possibility of refrigeration which kills the fruit fly (Jones, 1934, p. 35).

In Eastern Europe, new countries struggled with inflation, depreciation and inadequate sources of revenue, and were forced to levy heavy taxes on trade in a vain effort to restore financial balance. Export taxes were imposed along with import duties, despite a variety of international resolutions urging strongly against prohibitions of exports, and taxation, on the basis of equal access to materials (Bergsten, 1974, pp. 23–4). The finances of Austria and Hungary were supervized by experts under programmes of the Finance Committee of the League of Nations – Austria in 1922, Hungary in 1924 – which experts exerted strenuous efforts to liberalize trade.

As the world economy slowly settled down, the pre-war system of trade treaties was resumed, with extension of the principle of high legislative tariffs – so-called 'bargaining' or 'fighting' tariffs – which would be reduced through mutual tariff concessions agreed in bilateral treaties, and extended through the most-favoured-nation clause. To a degree, the initial increases in tariff rates succeeded better than the subsequent reduction through negotiation, especially as not all countries were prepared to subscribe to the unconditional version of the most-favoured-nation clause (League of Nations (W. T. Page), 1927). The United States especially, with its high Fordney–McCumber tariff, stood aloof from the system. Except in the period from 1890 to 1909 the United States Administration was not empowered to enter into tariff treaties; under the Dingley tariff from 1897 to 1919, no tariff treaties came into force since Senate approval was required but not forthcoming. The Fordney–McCumber tariff of 1922, however, changed United States policy from conditional most-favoured-nation to unconditional treatment. Under the conditional version, concessions offered to one country were made available to others only in exchange for a reciprocal concession. The Tariff Act of 1922's provision for retaliation by the United States against countries which discriminated against American exports was judged to require the more general form of the non-discrimination clause (US Department of State, *Foreign Relations of the United States*, 1923, I, pp. 131–3). Exceptions to the unconditional most-favoured-nation clause were recognized for specific countries, such as Cuba and the

Philippines insofar as the United States was concerned, and regional arrangements, in which 'propinquity' was a usual characteristic (Viner, 1950, p. 19). The British position, opposed by the United States, was that a further exception could be based on 'historical associations, such as were generally recognized'. This referred to Empire preference.

As a policy, Empire preference meant more the relations of the United Kingdom with the Dominions than those with the colonies, including India. 'Tariff reformers' at the turn of the century would have welcomed an imperial *Zollverein*, eliminating all tariffs between the mother country and the rest of the Empire. This was opposed not only by British free traders, who viewed free-trade areas and preferences both as disguises for protectionism, but also by the Dominions that regarded tariffs as a symbol of sovereignty and were unwilling to remove all vestiges of protection for their manufactures against British products. Preferences in the Dominions meant largely tariffs to be levied in Britain against non-Empire foodstuffs, and higher domestic tariffs on foreign manufactures, rather than reductions in existing duties on British goods. Resistance to Empire preference in Britain came not only from free traders, but from those who wanted to hold down the price of food on the one hand, and on the other, those who sought protection against Empire as well as against foreign food producers.

The slogan of Empire visionaries in Britain and the Dominions after the war was 'men, money, and markets'. 'Men' meant assisted settlement of British workers in the Dominions; 'money' help for Empire borrowers in various ways, ranging from preferences in the queue to guaranteed interest; 'markets' referred to Empire preference, to a considerable degree in new products that especially Australia wished to have produced for export by immigrants settled on new farms – particularly dried fruit and frozen beef – rather than the traditional wheat, butter, wool, apples, bacon, cheese.

The Imperial Economic Conference of 1923 made little progress toward tariff preferences: the election called by Stanley Baldwin in 1924 to provide tariffs that could be used for the purpose ended in a Labour victory and even repeal of the McKenna duties and the preferences granted under them. The return of Baldwin to power eleven months later restored the McKenna duties, with lorries added to motor cars, but the Conservatives stopped short of extending tariff discrimination. Feeble efforts were made to undertake non-tariff discrimination through an Empire Marketing Board which was to perform research and promotion. Empire settlement fizzled gently. Empire preference was postponed.

The reconstruction period to 1925 or so was characterized by instability. Rapidly changing exchange rates required rapidly changing tariffs through countervailing charges, or the application of coefficients. Trade agreements were frequently contracted for only three months. Where changes in tariff rates did not occur, administrative regulation was applied. The League of Nations Economic Committee worked to improve the position through such actions as the International Convention Relating to the Simplification of Custom Formalities of 1923, although this soon proved inadequate as far as worst practices were concerned (Winslow, 1936, p. 182).

II.   *Normalization of world trade*

The end of the reconstruction period about the middle of the decade was marked by the opening up of capital markets, following the success of the Dawes Loan in 1924 that primed the resumption of German reparations after the hyperinflation of 1923, by the restoration of the pound sterling to par on the gold standard in 1925, or perhaps by the expiration of the Versailles restriction on Germany's right to conclude commercial treaties, and with it the rapid extension of trade agreements in Europe. Whatever the event, it marked the initiation of increased efforts for trade normalization. A minor effort was represented by the International Convention for the Protection of Industrial Property of 1925 (Brown, 1950, p. 34). Of greater weight were the convention for the Abolition of Import and Export Prohibitions and Restrictions, with which was associated a special agreement on hides, skins and bones, and a World Economic Conference on trade expansion, all in 1927. In 1929 a special conference produced a convention calling for national treatment for foreign nationals and enterprises. A modernized tariff nomenclature to replace the 1913 Hague list was started in the 1920s, produced a first draft in 1931, and a final one in 1937 (League of Nations, 1942, p. 45).

A number of these conventions failed to be ratified. That on the treatment of foreign nationals fell through because some states were unwilling to liberalize, and the liberal states were unwilling to sign an agreement which would have weakened the force of the principle of national treatment (League of Nations, 1942, p. 27). The Convention on Imports and Exports prohibitions finally lapsed when the Poles refused to sign, because of an exception made for Germany, which reduced the value of the treaty in their eyes. Agreement on a tariff truce and subsequent reductions in rates was reached at the 1927 World Economic Conference, but this meeting was attended by delegations in their individual capacities and did not bind governments. Governments agreed on the necessity of reducing tariffs but did nothing about it. The League of Nations review of commercial policies in the inter-war period called it a striking paradox that conferences unanimously adopted recommendations, and governments proclaimed their intentions to lower tariffs, but did nothing (League of Nations, 1942, p. 101), asking why governments made such recommendations if they did not propose to carry them out (*ibid.*, p. 109). The answer furnished by one economist who had served on the economic secretariat of the League was that 'the pseudo-internationalism of the nineteenth century was clearly an outgrowth of British financial leadership and trading enterprise, backed by the economic supremacy of London and by the British Navy' (Condliffe, 1940, p. 118). With British hegemony lost and nothing to take its place, international relations lapsed into anarchy. Britain lost the will and lacked the power to enforce international cooperation as she had done in the nineteenth century (*ibid.*, p. 145).

Discouragement over the failure of tariffs to come down despite agreement to lower them led to an attempt at a commodity-by-commodity approach, foreshadowing the free trade for iron and steel undertaken in the European Coal and Steel Community on Robert Schuman's initiative in May 1950. The Economic Committee of the League of Nations reported in March 1928 that there was no prospect of a general tariff reduction by means of standard cuts or the setting of a maximum scale of duties. Cement and aluminium were chosen for a case-by-case approach. A year of negotiation, however, produced no result. The League's account of the attempt cites as reasons (1) that reductions in duties in single products would upset national industrial structures; (2) that it would increase the protection of finished goods – implying the so-called effective-rate-of-protection argument which was more fully developed in the 1960s; and (3) that among the limited groups of commodities and countries concerned, compensatory reductions were hard to find (League of Nations, 1942, pp. 128–9).

While governments were agreeing to the necessity to lower tariffs but doing nothing about it, action was taken directly on a number of commodity fronts. Most conspicuous was the Stevenson rubber plan of 1923–4 which raised the price of rubber by 1926 to almost four times its 1923 level. To American protests, the British replied that it was 'impossible to argue that the present high price is attributable solely or even mainly to the operation of the rubber restriction scheme. It is due to the great expansion of the demand for rubber. Only one half of the supply comes from the restricted area' (*Foreign Relations of the United States*, 1926, vol. II, p. 359). The fact that the other half – the Netherlands East Indies – had been left out of the scheme contributed to its early breakdown (Knorr, 1946).

More cartels were formed in a variety of commodities, that Mason divides into three groups: (1) industrial raw materials and foodstuffs, like tin, oil, wheat, sugar, etc.; (2) standardized processed and semi-fabricated goods such as steel rails, cement, tinplate, plate glass, dyes, etc.; and (3) highly fabricated, specialized, and frequently patented items such as electrical equipment, pharmaceuticals, glass, etc. (Mason, 1946, p. 16). Mason notes that the Soviet Union was a party to at least three international control schemes and eight cartel arrangements, despite its hostility to capitalism (*ibid.*, p. 14n.). Most of the commodity agreements begun in the 1920s broke down in the depression of the 1930s. The rubber scheme collapsed in 1928. Prices of agricultural commodities levelled off in 1925 and declined thereafter, faster after 1928, as European reconstruction crowded the extra-European supplies expanded to fill the gap left by war and post-war shortages, and demand shrank with such changes as the replacement of oats for horses by gasoline for motor cars.

Two of the most durable agreements were in oil: the As-Is Agreement concluded at Achnacarry, Scotland in 1928 between Sir Henry Detering of the Shell Oil Company and Walter Teagle of the Standard Oil Company of New Jersey, that provided that no oil company would seek to penetrate into markets where it was not already distributing, so that everything would stay 'as is'; and in the same year the Red-Line Agreement, among members of the Turkish Petroleum Company, that drew a line across the Middle East (through what is now Kuwait) and limited exploration by partners below that line, thereby ultimately making it possible for the Standard Oil Company of California, which was not a partner, to discover oil in Saudi Arabia (Federal Trade Commission, 1952, pp. 199ff., 63).

National programmes further affected world markets in wheat and sugar. The Italian 'battle for grain' begun by Mussolini in 1925 was of limited economic significance, since Italy could not escape dependence on foreign supplies, but provided a disturbing symptom of the troubles of the 1930s. Great Britain expanded production of beet sugar through a bounty; Japan undertook sugar production in Formosa (Taiwan) and ceased to buy from Java. As the price of wheat declined, Germany raised tariffs in 1928 to slow down the movement of labour off the farm. From 1927 to 1931, German tariffs on foodstuffs were broadly doubled. France raised tariffs in 1928 and 1929 before resorting to quotas. Mixing provisions, under which foreign grain had to be mixed with domestic, were undertaken from 1929 on, patterned after the practice in motion pictures which allowed exhibitors to show foreign films only in fixed proportions to those domestically produced. In the United States, help for agriculture took the form of proposals for export subsidies, but President Coolidge's veto of the McNary–Haugen bill in 1928 led presidential candidate Herbert Hoover to seek other means of agricultural relief, and to promise help for farmers in his campaign speeches in the summer and autumn of that year. The League of Nations commented in 1942 that 'before the end of 1928 it was evident that the United States tariff was going to be raised above the formidable level of 1922' (League of Nations, 1942, p. 126).

Grain exporters of Eastern Europe were especially affected by the world decline in price and sought solutions in meetings at Warsaw in August 1930, Bucharest in October 1930, Belgrade in November 1930, and Warsaw again in the same month. They tried on the one hand to limit exports of grain to improve the terms of trade, and on the other to obtain preferences in import markets of Western Europe. The first proposal was never adopted. After the 1932 Stresa meeting, some reciprocal preferences were worked out between Austria and Hungary on one side and Italy on the other, but with poor results.

A strenuous effort was made to halt tariff increases. The World Economic Conference of 1927 recognized that general demobilization of tariffs would be slow, and the Economic Committee of the League of Nations in March 1928 saw no prospect of general reduction. The September 1929 General Assembly of the League moved from attempts at reduction to an effort to halt increases. It called for a conference to stabilize rates for two or three years and then to lower them. The Preliminary Conference with a View to Concerted Action met in February 1930, but too late. It proposed extending existing agreements to 1 April 1931 and to provide opportunities for negotiation before tariffs were raised. By this time, however, retaliation against the forthcoming Hawley–Smoot tariff bill was far along. A second Conference with a View to Concerted Economic Action in November 1930 failed equally. The Netherlands, which, along with Britain, had pressed for the tariff truce, turned to a smaller group and organized the Oslo group. On 22 December, Norway, Sweden, Holland, and Belgium signed an agreement undertaking not to raise tariffs without giving notice to other members. It was a brave example without much impact.

Quite unrelated to the fortunes of world incomes, prices, or trade, a highly original argument for tariffs emerged in Australia at the end of the prosperity of the 1920s. It bore resemblance to an earlier argument put forward by Alvin S. Johnson in 1908 that tariffs could add to capital formation by reallocating income from spenders to savers – an argument which went unnoticed until Harvey Leibenstein introduced similar notions into the discussion of economic growth in the 1960s. J. B. Brigden published an article in the *Economic Record* of November 1925 on 'The Australian Tariff and the Standard of Living'. He concluded that whereas the tariff on wheat in Britain favoured the landed classes, that on manufactured goods in Australia would redound to the standard of living of wage-earners, and increase the population of the country. Subsequently the Australian government appointed a committee of experts, including Brigden, D. B. Copland, E. C. Dyason, L. F. Giblin, and Wickens, which in 1929 produced *The Australian Tariff: An Economic Enquiry* that supported Brigden's conclusion. The analysis remained to be worked out by W. F. Stolper and P. A. Samuelson in their classic article of 1941, 'Protection and Real Wages', and was to be rediscovered for Canada in the post-war period by C. L. Barber. It was heatedly debated during the 1930s both in Australia and in Anglo-Saxon economic literature. What was clear, however, was that Australia chose not to be guided by the neo-classical static maximizing calculus of foreign-trade theory, but rather to introduce into the discussion dynamic considerations of economic growth, migration, as well as income redistribution.

III. *The disintegration of world trade*

A. THE HAWLEY–SMOOT TARIFF

The origins of the Hawley-Smoot tariff, as already noted, reach back to the autumn of 1928 when Herbert Hoover, campaigning for the presidency, promised to do something to help farmers suffering under the weight of declining agricultural prices. A special session of the Congress was called in January 1929, long in advance of the stock-market crash of October of that year, and began to prepare a tariff bill. Its scope was widened from agriculture to include industry; Democrats joined Republicans in their support for tariffs for all who sought them; and both Republicans and Democrats were ultimately pushed from the committee room as lobbyists took over the task of setting the rates (Schattschneider, 1935). A groundswell of resentment spread around the world and quickly led to retaliation. Italy objected to duties on hats and bonnets of straw, wool-felt hats, and olive oil; Spain reacted sharply to increases on cork and onions; Canada took umbrage at increases on maple sugar and syrup, potatoes, cream, butter, buttermilk, and skimmed milk. Switzerland was moved to boycott American typewriters, fountain pens, motor cars, and films because of increased duties on watches, clocks, embroidery, cheese, and shoes (Jones, 1934). Retaliation was begun long before the bill was enacted into law in June 1930. As it passed the House of Representatives in May 1929, boycotts broke out and foreign governments moved to raise rates against United States products, even though rates could be moved up or down in the Senate or by the conference committee. In all, 34 formal protests were lodged with the Department of State from foreign countries. One thousand and twenty-eight economists in the United States, organized by Paul Douglas, Irving Fisher, Frank Graham, Ernest Patterson, Henry Seager, Frank Taussig, and Clair Wilcox, and representing the 'Who's Who' of the profession, asked

President Hoover to veto the legislation (*New York Times*, 5 May 1930). A weak defence was offered contemporaneously by President Hoover as he signed the bill, saying 'No tariff act is perfect' (Hoover, 1952, p. 291), and another 45 years later by Joseph S. Davis, who claimed that the Senate got out of hand, but that Hoover had won two key points: inclusion of the flexible provisions permitting the Tariff Commission to consider complaints and recommend to the president higher or lower rates, and exclusion of an export-debenture plan along the lines of the McNary–Haugen bill (Davis, 1975, p. 239). Both views were in the minority.

The high tariffs of 1921, 1922, and *a fortiori* 1930 were generally attacked on the grounds that the United States was a creditor nation, and that creditor nations were required to maintain low tariffs or free trade in order that their debtors might earn the foreign exchange to pay their debt service. This view is now regarded as fallacious since the macro-economic impacts effects of tariffs on the balance of payments are typically reversed, wholly or in large part, by the income changes which they generate. Under the post-Second World War General Agreement on Tariffs and Trade, balance of payments considerations are ignored in settling on tariff reductions in bilateral or multilateral bargaining. In addition, a careful study for the Department of Commerce by Hal. B. Lary states that the effect of the tariff increases of 1922 and 1930, and those of the reductions after 1930, cannot be detected in the import statistics. This was partly perhaps because tariffs were already close to prohibitive and early reductions were minimal, but mainly for the reason that wide fluctuations in world economic activity and prices overwhelmed any lasting impact of tariffs on trade (Lary, 1943, pp. 53–4).

The significance of the Hawley–Smoot tariff goes far beyond its effect on American imports and the balance of payments to the core of the question of the stability of the world economy. President Hoover let Congress get out of hand and failed to govern (Schattschneider, 1935, p. 293); by taking national action and continuing on its own course through the early stages of the depression, the United States served notice on the world that it was unwilling to take responsibility for world economic stability. Sir Arthur Salter's view (1932, pp. 172–3) that Hawley–Smoot marked a turning point in world history is excessive if it was meant in causal terms, apposite if taken symbolically.

Retaliation and business decline wound down the volume and value of world trade. The earliest retaliations were taken by France and Italy in 1929. In Canada the Liberal government kept parliament in session during the final days when the conference committee was completing the bill, and then put through increases in tariff rates affecting one-quarter of Canadian imports from the United States. Despite this resistance to its neighbour, the government lost the August 1930 election to the Conservatives, who then raised tariffs in September 1930, June 1931, and again in connection with the 1932 Ottawa agreements (McDiarmid, 1946, p. 273). The action in May under the Liberal, W. L. Mackenzie King involved both increases and decreases in duties, with Empire preference extended through raising and lowering about one-half each of general and intermediate rates, but lowering the bulk of those applicable to Empire goods. Subsequent measures typically raised Empire rates, but general and intermediate rates more. In September 1930, anti-dumping rates were increased from 15 to 50 per cent.

B. DEEPENING DEPRESSION

The Hawley–Smoot tariff began as a response to the decline in agricultural prices and was signed into law as the decline in business picked up speed. For a time during the second quarter of 1930, it looked as though the world economy might recover from the deflationary shock of the New York stock-market crash in October 1929, which had come on the heels of the failure in London of the Clarence Hatry conglomerate after the discovery of fraudulent collateral used to support bank loans in September and the failure of the Frankfurt Insurance Company in Germany in August. This is not the place to set forth the causes of the depression in agricultural overproduction, the halt to foreign lending by the United States in 1928, the end of the housing boom, the stock-market crash, frightened short-term capital movements, United States monetary policy and the like. It is sufficient to observe that the chance of recovery was seen to fade at the end of June 1930 with the signing of the Hawley–Smoot tariff, the outbreak of retaliatory cuts in international trade, and the near-failure of the Young loan (to reprime German reparations) in international capital markets. Events thereafter were uniformly depressing from Nazi gains in German elections in September 1930, the collapse of the Creditanstalt in Vienna in May 1931, the run on German banks in June and July, until the Standstill Agreement that blocked repayment of all German bank credits shifted the attack to sterling, which went off the gold standard in September 1931, followed by the yen in December.

One item of commercial policy contributed to the spreading deflation. In the autumn of 1930, Austria and Germany announced an intention to form a customs union. The proposal had its proximate origin in a working paper prepared by the German Foreign Ministry for the World Economic Conference in 1927. It was discussed on the side by Austrian and German Foreign Ministers at the August 1929 meeting on the Young Plan at The Hague. Germany took it up seriously, however, only after the September 1930 elections which recorded alarming gains for the National Socialists, and Brüning, the Chancellor, felt a strong need for a foreign-policy success. The French immediately objected on the grounds that customs union between Austria and Germany violated the provision of the treaty of Trianon which required Austria to uphold her political independence. France took the case to the International Court of Justice at The Hague for an interpretation of the treaty. Other French and British and Czechoslovak objections on the grounds of violation of the most-favoured-nation clause were laid before the League of Nations Council (Viner, 1950, p. 10). The International Court ultimately ruled in favour of the French position in the summer of 1931. By this time, however, the Austrian Creditanstalt had collapsed – barely possible because of French action in pulling credits out of Austria, though the evidence is scanty – the Austrian government responsible for the proposal of customs union had long since fallen, and the run against banks and currencies had moved on from Austria to Germany and Britain.

In the autumn of 1931, appreciation of the mark, the dollar and the gold-bloc currencies as a consequence of the depreciation of sterling and the currencies associated with it, applied strenuous deflation to Germany, the United States and to Western Europe from September 1931 to June 1932. Depreciation of the yen in December 1931 marked the start of a drive of Japanese exports into British and Dutch colonies in Asia and Africa, and of colonial and metropolitan steps to hold them down. June 1932 was the bottom of the depression for most of the world. The United States economy registered a double bottom, in June 1932 and again in March 1933, when spreading collapse of the system of many small separate banks climaxed in the closing of all banks for a time, and recovery thereafter. German recovery started in 1932 after the resignation of Brüning, who had hoped to throw off reparations by deflation to demonstrate the impossibility of paying them, the succession of von Papen as Chancellor, and finally the takeover of the chancellorship by Hitler in February 1933. The gold-bloc countries remained depressed until they abandoned the gold parities of the 1920s, first Belgium in 1935, and the remaining countries in September 1936.

In these circumstances, there was little if any room for expansive commercial policy. Virtually every step taken was restrictive.

C.   OTTAWA

The Hawley–Smoot Tariff Act occupied most of the time of the Congress for a year and a half (Smith, 1936, p. 177). Empire preference was the major issue in Canadian politics for more than half a century (Drummond, 1975, p. 378). The Imperial Economic Policy Cabinet worried more about tariffs than about any other issue (*ibid.*, p. 426), though much of it dealt with objectively insignificant goods (Drummond, 1972, p. 25). Drummond several times expresses the opinion that the Ottawa discussions in the summer of 1932 should have abandoned the question of tariff preferences and focused on monetary policy, and especially exchange rate policy. In fact Prime Minister Bennett of Canada sought to raise the issue of the sterling exchange rate prior to Ottawa only to be rebuffed by Neville Chamberlain with the statement that the Treasury could not admit the Dominions to the management of sterling. Canada did succeed in getting exchange rates put on the Ottawa agenda, but the Treasury insisted that the question was minor and nothing came of it (Drummond, 1975, pp. 214–16).

Monetary policy and tariff policy were occasionally complements, occasionally substitutes. The Macmillan Committee report contained an addendum, no. 1, by Ernest Bevin, J. M. Keynes, R. McKenna and three others recommending import duties, and, insofar as existing treaties permitted, a bounty on exports, the combination being put forward as a substitute for devaluation of sterling (Committee on Finance and Industry, 1931). In the event, Britain undertook both depreciation of sterling and the imposition of import duties.

Sterling left the gold standard on 21 September 1931 and depreciated rapidly from $4.86 to a low of $3.25 in December, a depreciation of 30 per cent. Canada and South Africa adopted anti-dumping duties against British goods. On its side, Britain enacted an Abnormal Importations Act on 20 November 1931 that gave the Board of Trade the right to impose duties up to 100 per cent as a means of stopping a short-run scramble to ship goods to Britain before the exchange rate depreciated further. While 100 per cent tariffs were authorized, only 50 per cent were imposed. This act was followed in a few weeks by a similar Horticultural Products Act. Both the Abnormal Importations Act and the Horticultural Products Act exempted the Empire from their provisions (Kreider, 1943, p. 20).

In the Christmas recess of parliament, Lord Runciman, President of the Board of Trade, persuaded Chamberlain to take up protection as a long-run policy, as had been recommended by Keynes and the Macmillan Committee, prior to the September depreciation, and opposed by Beveridge (1931), since without tariffs, Britain had nothing to exchange with the Dominions for preferences in their markets. The resultant Import Duties Act of February 1932 established a 10 per cent duty on a wide number of imported products – but not copper, wheat, or meat – and created an Import Duties Advisory board, charged with recommending increases in particular duties above the flat 10 per cent level. At the last minute a concession was made to the Dominions and colonies.

The latter were entirely exempted from the increase, and the former were granted exemption until November 1932, by which time it was expected that mutually satisfactory arrangements for preferences would have been reached. Eighteen countries responded to the Import Duties Act by asking Britain to undertake negotiations for mutual reductions. The reply was universally negative on the grounds that it was first necessary to arrive at understandings with the Empire (Condliffe, 1940, pp. 300–8). In the spring of 1932, the Import Duties Advisory Board was hard at work raising duties above the 10 per cent level, with the notable increase in iron and steel products to $33\frac{1}{3}$ per cent. Three years later in March 1935 the iron and steel duties were increased to 50 per cent in order to assist the British industry in negotiating a satisfactory basis with the European iron and steel cartel (Hexner, 1946, p. 118).

Imperial economic conferences held in 1923, 1926, and 1930 had all broken down on the failure of Britain to raise tariffs which would have put her in a position to extend preferences to the Empire. Substitute assistance in the form of arrangements for Empire settlement or Empire marketing boards failed to produce significant effects on either migration or trade. British bulk-purchase schemes sought especially by Australia had been halted as early as 1922 and had not been resumed. Hopes were high for the Imperial Economic Conference of 1932 in Ottawa which now had British tariffs to work with.

Canada cared about wheat, butter, cheese, bacon, lamb, and apples; Australia about wheat, chilled meat, butter, cheese, currants, dried fruits, canned fruits; South Africa about wine and dried and canned fruits; New Zealand, butter and mutton. The position differed in those commodities that the Dominions produced in greater amounts than Britain could absorb, like wheat, in which diversion of Dominion supplies to Britain from third markets would produce an offsetting increase in non-Dominion sales in non-British markets, and leave Dominion export prices overall unchanged, from those in which Britain depended upon both Dominion and foreign sources of supply, among the latter notably Argentina in meat, Denmark in butter, Greece in dried currants and raisins, and, it would like to think, the United States in apples. Trade diversion from foreign to Dominion sources was possible in this latter group, but only at some cost in British goodwill in the indicated import markets. On this score, the United Kingdom was obliged to negotiate at Ottawa with an uneasy glance over its shoulder.

A significant Dominion manufacture, as opposed to agricultural product, which had earlier received preference in the British market, in 1919 under the McKenna duties, was motor cars. This preference had led to the establishment of tariff factories in Canada, owned and operated by United States manufacturers. Its extension in the Ottawa agreement led to the unhappy necessity of defining more precisely what a Canadian manufactured motor car consisted of, and whether United States-made motor parts merely assembled in Canada qualified as Canadian motor cars.

In exchange for concessions in primary products in the British market, the United Kingdom expected to get reductions in Dominion duties on her manufactures. But it proved impossible at Ottawa to fix levels of Dominion tariffs on British goods. Instead, the Dominions undertook to instruct their respective tariff boards to adjust the British preference tariff to that level which would make British producers competitive with domestic industry. Resting on the notion of horizontal supply curves, rather than the more usually hypothesized and far more realistic upward-sloping curves, the concept was clearly unworkable and gave rise to unending contention. It was abandoned in 1936.

Argentina, Denmark, Greece, Norway, and Sweden were not content to yield their positions in the British market without a struggle. Even before the Import Duties Act had taken effect, Denmark in January 1932 legislated preferences favouring Britain, and on raw materials used in manufactured exports. By June 1932, total imports had been reduced 30 to 40 per cent, but import permits issued for British goods allowed for a 15 per cent increase (Gordon, 1941, p. 80). In similar fashion Uruguay undertook to discriminate in the allocation of import licences in favour of countries that bought from her. The threat to discriminate against Britain was clear. Quickly after Ottawa British customers pressed to take up negotiations postponed from early 1932 and to settle the extent to which Ottawa would be allowed to squeeze them out of the British market.

In the Roca–Runciman Agreement of 1 May 1933, Britain agreed not to cut back imports of chilled beef from Argentina by more than 10 per cent of the volume imported in the year ended 30 June 1932, unless at the same time it reduced imports from the Dominions below 90 per cent of the same base year. This was disagreeable to Australia which was seeking through the Ottawa agreements to break into the chilled-beef market in Britain in which it had previously not been strong (Drummond, 1975, p. 310). Three-year agreements with Denmark, Norway, and Sweden, running from various dates of ratification about mid-1933, provided minimum butter quotas to Denmark and (much smaller) to Sweden, a minimum bacon quota to Denmark amounting to 62 per cent of the market, and agreement not to regulate the small and irregular shipments of bacon, ham, butter, and cheese by Norway. But guarantees to these producers left it necessary, if domestic British producers of, say, butter were to be protected, to go back on the Ottawa agreements which guaranteed unlimited free entry into the British market. The position was complicated by New Zealand's backward-bending supply curve which increased butter production and shipments as the price declined, and Australian policy, which evoked the most profound distrust from New Zealand, of subsidizing the export of butter to solve a domestic disposal problem (Drummond, 1975, pp. 320ff., 475). The problems of the Dominions and of the major foreign suppliers of the British markets for foodstuffs compounded the difficulties of British agriculture. In defence of the lost interest, the British agricultural authorities developed a levy-subsidy scheme under which tariffs imposed on imports were segregated to create a fund to be used to provide subsidies to domestic producers. The levy-subsidy scheme was first applied in Britain on wheat in 1932; strong voices inside the British cabinet urged its application to beef, dairy products, and bacon and ham. Wrangling over these proposals went on between British and Commonwealth negotiators for the next several years as Britain tried to modify the Ottawa agreements, with Dominion and foreign-supplier consent, in order to limit imports. In the background, dispute deepened within the British cabinet between the Agricultural Minister, Walter Elliott, who wanted subsidies, and the Chancellor of the Exchequer, Neville Chamberlain, who feared their effect on the budget and consistently favoured raising prices and farm incomes, in Britain and abroad, by cutting production and limiting imports.

In its agreements in Scandinavia, Britain sought to bind its trading partners to give preferences to British exports, and especially to guarantee a percentage share of the market to British suppliers in that sorely afflicted export industry, coal. In eight trade agreements, British coal exporters were guaranteed generally the major share of import volume, with quotas as follows: Denmark, 90 per cent; Estonia, 85 per cent; Lithuania, 80 per cent; Iceland, 77 per cent; Finland, 75 per cent; Norway, 70 per cent; Sweden, 47 per cent. In addition, Denmark agreed that all bacon and ham exported to the United Kingdom should be wrapped in jute cloth woven in the United Kingdom from jute yarn spun in the United Kingdom (Kreider, 1943, pp. 61–2). The Danish government gave British firms a 10 per cent preference for government purchases, and undertook to urge private Danish firms to buy their iron and steel in the United Kingdom wherever possible. Kreider notes that these agreements constrained British trade into a bilateral mode: British agreements with Finland lifted the unfavourable import balance from 1 to 5 against Britain in 1931 to 1 to 2 in 1935. The agreement with Russia called for the import/export ratio to go from 1 to 1.7 against Britain in 1934 to 1 to 1.5 in 1935, 1 to 1.4 in 1936 and 1 to 1.2 in 1937 and thereafter. Argentina agreed to allocate the sterling earned by its exports to Britain to purchases from Britain.

The Ottawa agreement dominated British commercial policy from 1932 to the Anglo-American Commercial Agreement of 1938, and to a lesser extent thereafter. It was continuously under attack from foreign suppliers other than the United States that entered into trade and financial agreements with the United Kingdom, and from the United States which undertook to attack it as early as the World Economic Conference of 1933. But at no time could the agreement have been regarded as a great success for the Empire. It produced endless discussion, frequently bitter in character, and dissatisfaction on both sides that each felt they had given too much and gained too little. By 1936 and 1937, there was a general disposition to give up the attempt, or at least to· downgrade its priority.

D.   THE NETHERLANDS

The United Kingdom embraced free trade, broadly speaking, with the repeal of the Corn Laws in 1846, and gave it up with the McKenna duties in 1916. The Netherlands' support goes back at least to the sixteenth century, and lasted until 1931. A faithful supporter of attempts to spread freer trade throughout the world from the World Economic Conference in 1927 until the Convention on Import and Export Prohibitions and the Conference with a View to Concerted Economic Action, The Netherlands ultimately turned to the smaller arena of the Oslo agreement of Scandinavia and the Low Countries. The pressure from declining wheat prices, however, proved too severe. In 1931 The Netherlands undertook to regulate farm prices and marketing. The Wheat Act of 1931 set the domestic price at 12 florins per 100 kg at a time when the world price had fallen to 5 florins, necessitating the first major break with the policy of free trade in nearly three centuries. There followed in 1932 as a response to the depreciation of sterling, first an emergency fiscal measure establishing 25 per cent duties generally, and then in agriculture the Dairy Crisis Act and the Hog Crisis Act, which were generalized in the following year as the Agricultural Crisis Act of 1933 (Gordon, 1941, p. 307). The freer-trade tradition of the Oslo group continued, however. At the depth of the depression in June 1932, the Oslo group concluded an agreement to reduce tariffs among themselves on a mutual basis by 10 per cent per annum for five years. Though it was already blocking out the discrimination to be achieved at Ottawa two months later, the United Kingdom objected on the grounds that the arrangement would violate the most-favoured-nation clause. After dissolution of the gold bloc in 1936, the Oslo group resumed its example-setting work in reducing trade barriers, agreeing first to impose no new tariffs and then to eliminate quotas applied to one another's trade on a mutual basis. Since

THE DISINTEGRATION OF WORLD TRADE   179

the most-favoured-nation clause applied only to tariffs and not to quotas, there was no basis for an objection or to claim extension of the concession.

During the period of restricted trade, The Netherlands licensed not only imports, but in some cases exports. The latter practice was followed where quotas in foreign import markets left open the question whether the difference between the domestic price and the world price would go to importers or exporters. A law of 24 December 1931 established a system of licensing exports in instances of foreign import quotas, with permits distributed among exporters in accordance with the volumes of some historical base period. Licence fees were then imposed, in the amount of 70–100 per cent of the difference between the world price and the domestic price in the import market, with the collected proceeds distributed to Dutch producers. The purpose of the fees was to divert the scarcity rents available from import restriction, first to the exporting country as a whole, and then, within the exporting country, from exporting firms to agricultural producers (Gordon, 1941, p. 356).

E.   FRANCE

The French are often given the credit in commercial policy between the wars for the invention of the quota, a protective device which was to flourish until well into the 1950s, and even then to experience revival in various forms in the 1970s. While its origins go well back in time, the proximate causes of the quota in 1930 were the limitation on France's freedom of action imposed by the network of trade treaties it had fashioned, beginning with that with Germany in 1927, and the difficulty of ensuring a restriction of imports sufficient to raise domestic prices – the object of the exercise – in the face of inelastic excess supplies abroad. Like the Hawley–Smoot tariff increases in committee, quotas spread from agricultural produce to goods in general.

Under an old law of December 1897 – the so-called *loi de cadenas* – the French government had authority in emergency to change the rate of duty on any one of 46 agricultural items. The emergency of falling agricultural prices after 1928 caused the laws of 1929 and 1931 which extended the list. With especially wheat in excess supply overseas in regions of recent settlement like Australia and Canada, the French decided that raising the tariff under their authority would not only pose questions about their obligations under trade treaties, but might well not limit imports, serving only to reduce world prices and improve the terms of trade. Australia, in particular, lacked adequate storage capacity for its wheat and had no choice but to sell, no matter how high the price obstacles erected abroad. The decision was accordingly taken to restrict quantity rather than to levy a customs duty (Haight, 1941, p. 145). The device was effective. As the depression deepened, and as imports grew with the overvaluation of the franc, it was extended to industrial goods. Other countries followed suit, especially Germany with its foreign exchange control. In 1931, Brüning and Pierre Laval, the then French premier reached an agreement establishing industrial understandings to coordinate production and trade between German and French industries. One such understanding in electrical materials developed into a cartel. The rest were concerned primarily with restricting German exports to France. When they failed to do so, they were replaced by French quotas (Hexner, 1946, pp. 119, 136). After a time, the French undertook bilateral bargaining over quotas, which led in time to reducing quotas below desired limits in order to have room to make concessions during negotiations.

F.   GERMANY

Less by design than by a series of evolutionary steps, Germany developed the most elaborate and thorough-going system of control of foreign trade and payments. Foreign claims on Germany were blocked on 15 July 1931, when Germany could no longer pay out gold and foreign exchange to meet the demands of foreign lenders withdrawing funds. This default was followed by a negotiated Standstill Agreement between creditors and Germany, involving a six-month moratorium on withdrawals, subsequently renewed. The decision not to adjust the value of the Reichsmark after the depreciation of sterling in September 1931 made it necessary to establish foreign exchange control, and to prevent the free purchase and sale of foreign currencies in the private market. The proceeds of exports were collected and allocated to claimants of foreign exchange seeking to purchase imports. Clearing agreements developed under which German importers paid Reichsmarks into special accounts at the Reichsbank in favour of foreign central banks, which then allocated them to their national importers of German goods. The foreign central bank faced a particular problem whether or not to pay out local currency to the exporter in advance of its receipts of local currency from national importers of German goods. Some central banks did pay off local exporters against claims on the German clearing, following what was later called the 'payments principle', and experienced inflation through the resultant credit expansion. Other central banks made their exporters wait for payment which both avoided monetary expansion and held down the incentive to export to Germany (Andersen, 1946).

A number of countries with large financial claims on Germany, such as Switzerland, insisted that the proceeds of German exports be used in part to pay off creditors abroad, thus converting 'clearing' into 'payments' agreements. These payments agreements were also used in a few cases to require Germany to continue spending on non-essential imports of importance to the exporter, such as tourism in Austria.

Germany set limits on the use of foreign-owned marks within Germany as well as against their conversion into foreign exchange. They were not permitted to be used for many classes of exports, capable of earning new foreign exchange, but only for incremental exports which could be sold only at implicit depreciated exchange rates, for travel within Germany – the so-called Reisemark – and under certain limitations for investment in Germany. Foreshadowing some post-war limitations on foreign direct investment, permission was granted for investment by foreigners in Germany with outstanding mark balances only when the investment was considered generally beneficial to the German economy, was made for at least five years, did not involve a foreign controlling interest in a German enterprise, and did not exceed a stipulated rate of interest (Gordon, 1941, pp. 92–3).

In August 1934, the New Plan was adopted under the leadership of the German Minister for Economics, Hjalmar Schacht. In the words of Emil Puhl, an associate of Dr Schacht's at the Reichsbank, it provided totalitarian control over commodities and foreign exchange, with stringent controls on imports and on foreign travel, administered through supervisory boards for a long list of commodities and foreign exchange boards in the Reichsbank (Office of the Chief Council for Prosecution of Nazi Criminality, *Nazi Conspiracy and Aggression*, vol. VII, 1946, p. 496). Along with trade and clearing agreements, designed especially to ensure German access to food and raw materials, and to promote exports, the Reichsbank developed a series of special marks for particular purposes. In addition to the Reisemarks for travel, there were special-account (*Auslands-Sonder-Konto*, or 'Aski') marks which came into existence through imports of raw materials, especially from Latin America, and which were sold by the recipients at a discount and used by the buyers on a bilateral basis for purchases of incremental German goods. The incremental aspect of the exports was of course difficult to police. Because Aski-marks would be sold only at a discount, the raw-material supplies against them tended to raise their prices in the bilateral trade (Gordon, 1941, p. 180). On the German side, Schacht established a price-control agency in 1935 in each export group – amounting to 25 in all – to prevent German exporters from competing with one another for export orders and to assure that all exporters sold at the highest possible price (*Nazi Conspiracy*, vol. VII, 1946, p. 383).

Beginning in 1934, German foreign-trade plans were intended particularly to ensure access to imported food and raw materials. The New

Plan, and especially the Four Year Plan which succeeded it in the fall of 1936, were designed to produce synthetic materials, especially Buna-S (synthetic rubber) and gasoline from coal, where foreign supplies for wartime needs could not be assured. Particular problems were encountered in non-ferrous metals, in iron ore, for which the low-grade Salzgitter project was developed in the Four Year Plan, and in synthetic fertilizer required for self-sufficiency in food. Schacht at the Reichsbank, Goering as Schacht's successor in the Economics Ministry and as the head of the Four Year Plan, the War and Food Ministries wrangled among themselves over policies, including especially whether to export wheat against foreign exchange following the bumper crops of 1933 and 1934 or conserve it as a war reserve; whether to hoard Germany's meagre free foreign exchange reserves or to spend them for crucially short raw materials; the mobilization of privately owned foreign securities and their conversion to cash for buying materials; the pricing of exports; the purchase of unnecessary imports like frozen meat from Argentina, for lack of which Schacht was unable to conclude a favourable trade treaty, etc. (*Nazi Conspiracy*, vol. VII, 1946). The documents published by the prosecution at the Nuremberg post-war trials reveal considerable internal dissension, especially in the exchanges between Schacht and Goering that lasted through 1937 and ended in Schacht's defeat and resignation.

German sentiment had continuously decried the loss of the country's African colonies in the Versailles treaty. Schacht continuously referred to the loss in Young Plan discussions of the late 1920s and was still harping on the issue in an article in *Foreign Affairs* in 1937. In a conversation with the American ambassador, Bullitt, in the autumn of 1937, Goering noted that Germany's demand for a return of the German colonies which had been taken away by the Versailles treaty was just, adding immediately that Germany had no right to demand anything but these colonies. Particularly sought were the Cameroons which could be developed by German energy (*Nazi Conspiracy*, vol. VII, 1946, pp. 890, 898). Three weeks earlier, however, in a private conference, Hitler had stated that it made more sense for Germany to seek material-producing territory adjoining the Reich and not overseas (*ibid.*, vol. I, 1946, p. 380). And at a final war-preparatory briefing in May 1939, he went further to explain the need for living space in the East to secure Germany's food supplies. It was necessary to beware of gifts of colonial territory which did not solve the food problem: 'Remember blockade' (*ibid.*, vol. I, 1946, p. 392). The directive to the Economic Staff Group on 23 May 1941 just before the attack on the Soviet Union stated that the offensive was designed to produce food in the East on a permanent basis.

It was widely claimed that Germany squeezed the countries of Southeast Europe through charging high prices for non-essential exports, while not permitting them to purchase the goods they needed, at the same time delaying payment for imports through piling up large debit balances in clearing arrangements. In a speech at Königsberg in August 1935, Schacht expressed regret that Germany had defaulted on debts to numerous pro-German peoples abroad, indicated confidence that Germany could obtain the raw materials it needed, acknowledged that the trade relations of Germany with different countries had changed a great deal, but insisted that these new relations had created for a number of countries new possibilities of exporting to Germany which had helped relieve them from the rigours of the world depression (*Nazi Conspiracy*, vol. VII, 1946, p. 486). In a polemical exchange in 1941, Einzig insisted that Benham was in error in holding that South-east European countries had improved their terms of trade in dealing with Germany, which paid higher prices than Western Europe was able to pay, and sold German goods competitively in the area. A post-war analysis of the matter tended to show that Benham and Schacht had been right (Kindleberger, 1956, pp. 120ff.).

An intellectual defence of the Benham–Schacht position had been offered in a somewhat different context as early as 1931 by Manoilesco who expressed the view that the theory of comparative advantage had to be qualified if the alternative to tariff protection for an industry were either unemployment, or employment at a wage below the going rate. His statement of this position in *The Theory of Protection and International Trade* (1931) was strongly attacked on analytical grounds by the leading international-trade theorists of the day – Habeler, Ohlin, and Viner, each in extended treatment – but was resurrected after the war by Hagen, and then generalized into a second-best argument for interference with free trade, e.g. by tariffs. When the conditions for a first-best solution under free trade do not exist, protection may be superior in welfare for a country to free trade. By the same token, export sales at less than optimal terms of trade may be superior to no exports and unemployment.

G. THE UNION OF SOVIET SOCIALIST REPUBLICS

During the 1920s, commercial policy in the Soviet Union had been the subject of a great debate under the New Economic Plan, between the Right that advocated expansion of agriculture, and of other traditional exports, plus domestic production of manufactured consumer goods to provide incentives for farmers, and the Left that favoured development of domestic heavy industry and the relative neglect of agriculture. Under the proposals of the Right, exports of agricultural products would be expanded to obtain imports of machinery, metals, raw materials, and exotic foodstuffs such as coffee and tea. This was the trade-dependent strategy. The Left, on the other hand, sought to increase trade in order to achieve autarky as rapidly as possible, as it feared dependence on a hostile capitalist world. With Stalin's achievement of power, the Left strategy was adopted in the First and subsequent Five Year Plans. Strong efforts were made to reduce dependence on imports to a minimum. Territorial losses during the First World War, land reform which divided large estates, and the inherent bias of planning which favoured domestic users over foreign markets helped reduce the ratio of exports to national income, which fell from a figure variously estimated within the range of 7–12 per cent in 1913 to 3.5 at the inter-war peak in 1931. Estimates of the volume of Soviet exports vary, depending upon the weights chosen, but on the basis of 1927/8 weights, exports fell from 242 in 1913 to 53 in 1924/5 before recovering to 100 in 1929. Thereafter they rose sharply to 150 in 1930 and 164 in 1931 with disastrous consequences for the Russian peoples (Dohan and Hewett, 1973, p. 24).

In 1930 and 1931, Soviet exports conformed to the model of the backward-bending supply curve in which volume increases, rather than decreases, as price falls. Declines in the prices of grain, timber and oil, starting as early as 1925, had threatened the Soviet Union's capacity to pay for the machinery and materials necessary to complete its Five Year Plans, and threatened as well its capacity to service a small amount of foreign debt contracted in the 1920s. To counter this threat, the Soviet authorities diverted supplies of foodgrains from domestic consumption to export markets, shipping it from grain–surplus areas to export ports and leaving internal grain-deficit areas unsupplied. The result was starvation and death for an unknown number of the Russian people numbering in millions. The world price of wheat fell by half between June 1929 and December 1930, and more than half again by December 1932. So hard did the Soviet Union push exports that supplies of pulp wood, woodpulp, timber, lumber, and even coal, asbestos, and furs threatened to enter the Canadian market, a notable exporter of these products in ordinary times, and led the Canadian government in February 1932 to prohibit the import of these commodities from the Soviet Union (Drummond, 1975, p. 205). Similar discriminatory restrictions were taken in many other markets. The dysfunctional character of forcing exports on the world market became clear and the volume of Soviet exports levelled off and started downward in 1932. As primary-product prices rose after 1936, moreover, the export volume declined sharply below the 1929 level.

H.   JAPAN

Japan had not participated fully in the boom of the 1920s, but the fact that it had restored the yen to par after the First World War as late as January

1930 made it highly vulnerable to the liquidity crisis of 1930 and 1931. It was vulnerable, too, because of heavy dependence on silk, a luxury product, about to experience both a sharp decline in its income–elastic demand and severe competition from rayon and later from nylon. In 1929 silk was responsible for 36 per cent of Japanese exports by value, and produced 20 per cent of Japanese farm income. The price of silk fell by about half from September 1929 to December 1930. With the help of the depreciation of the yen after December 1931, it reached a level of $1.25 a pound in March 1933, compared with $5.20 in September 1929.

The combination of sharp exchange depreciation and the collapse of the American market in silk produced a drastic reorientation in Japanese export trade, away from North America and Europe and toward Asia, Africa, and Latin America. Export drives were especially intense in British and Dutch colonies, and in the so-called 'yen bloc' of Korea, Formosa, Kwantung, and Manchuria. The Japanese share of the Netherlands East Indies market, for example, rose from 10 per cent in the 1920s to 32 per cent in 1934 before restrictive measures were applied under the Crisis Act of 1933. (Furnival, 1939, p. 431; Van Gelderen, 1939, p. 24). Japanese exports to the yen bloc rose from 24 per cent in 1929 to 55 per cent in 1938, with imports rising from 20 to 41 per cent over the same period (Gordon, 1941, p. 473). Within Asia, Japan developed sugar production in Formosa and stopped buying it in Java in the Netherlands East Indies. The British and Dutch Empires imposed quantitative restrictions on Japanese imports, especially in textiles. Foreshadowing a technique extensively used by the United States after the war, at one stage the British asked the Japanese to impose export controls on shipments to India or face abrogation of the Indo-Japanese Commercial Convention of 1904 (Drummond, 1973, p. 133). By 1938 Netherlands East Indies imports from Japan were down to 14 per cent of the total from a high of 30 per cent in 1935 (Van Gelderen, 1935, p. 17). Japanese fear of reprisals led them to amend the Export Association Act of 1925, which had been enacted to promote exports, so as to control exports in accordance with restrictions imposed by importing countries (Gordon, 1941, p. 360).

I.   THE WORLD ECONOMIC CONFERENCE OF 1933

Sir Arthur Salter termed the Hawley–Smoot tariff a turning-point in world history. Lewis Douglas thought the Thomas amendment under which the dollar was devalued in March 1933 marked 'the end of Western civilization as we know it' (Kindleberger, 1973, p. 202). W. Arthur Lewis regarded the failure of the World Economic Conference of 1933 as 'the end of an era' (Lewis, 1950, p. 68). Each characterization contained an element of hyperbole. The World Economic Conference offered only the slightest of chances to reverse the avalanche of restrictions on world trade and to stabilize exchange rates. The reversal in tariffs came the next year with the June 1934 Reciprocal Trade Agreements Act in the United States. More stability in exchange rates took root with the Tripartite Monetary Agreement of September 1936 among, initially, the United Kingdom, France, and the United States.

The inspiration for a new world economic conference after 1927 went back to the early years of deflation and to a suggestion of Chancellor Brüning of Germany to treat disarmament, reparations, war debts and loans as a single package to be settled on a political basis, rather than separately in each case by economic experts. A preparatory commission of economic experts under the auspices of the League of Nations fashioned a package of somewhat different ingredients, in which the United States would lower the Hawley–Smoot tariff, France would reduce quota restrictions, Germany relax foreign exchange control and the United Kingdom would stabilize the pound. War debts were excluded from the agenda by the United States, and consequently reparations by France and Britain. Pending the convening of the conference, delayed first by the November 1932 elections in the United States and then by domestic preoccupations of the newly elected President Roosevelt, Secretary of State Cordell Hull tried to work out a new tariff truce, but ran into blocks. The United States desired new tariffs on farm products subject to processing taxes under the new Agricultural Adjustment Act; Britain had some pending obligations under the Ottawa agreements; France reserved her position until she could see what would happen to United States' prices as a response to the depreciation of the dollar initiated in April 1933. Only eight countries in all finally agreed to a truce on 12 May 1933, many with explicit reservations. In the final preparations for the conference, commercial-policy measures seemed secondary to all but Cordell Hull, as contrasted with the problem of raising international commodity prices and international public-works schemes, for neither of which could general solutions be found. In the end the United States broke up the conference by refusing to stabilize the exchange rate of the dollar (only to reverse its position seven months later in February 1934), the British felt moderately comfortable with their Empire solution in trade with the vast volume of wrangles still to come, and the gold bloc battened down to ride out the storm. The only positive results were an agreement on silver negotiated by Senator Key Pitman of the US delegation, and bases laid for subsequent international agreements in sugar and wheat. Perhaps a negative result was the *de facto* constitution of the sterling bloc with most of the Commonwealth, save Canada and the subsequent withdrawal of the Union of South Africa, plus foreign adherents such as Sweden, Argentina, and a number of countries in the Middle East.

J.   COMMODITY AGREEMENTS

From the decline in commodity prices in the mid-1920s, one after another attempt had been made to devise schemes for raising prices. Some were private, like aluminium, copper, mercury, diamonds, nickel, iron and steel; some were governmental. Of the governmental, some were under the control of a single government – Brazil in coffee, Chile in nitrates, the United States in cotton, the Netherlands East Indies in cinchona bark; others, especially in sugar and wheat, were world-wide. Some of the private/government agreements in iron and steel, petroleum, and aluminium were regional, especially European (Gordon, 1941, pp. 430ff.).

The Chadbourne Plan in sugar was reached in May 1931 among leading export countries – Belgium, Cuba, Czechoslovakia, Germany, Hungary, Java, Peru, and Poland – later joined by Yugoslavia. But British India, France, and United Kingdom, and the United States – important consumers that also maintained substantial production – remained outside the agreement. The United States formulated its own legislation, the Jones–Costigan Act of 1934, which assigned rigid quotas to imports from abroad and discriminated in favour of Cuba. Under the Chadbourne Plan, production declined among the signatories but rose almost as much outside. Particularly hard hit was Java which lost both the Japanese and the Indian markets, the former to Formosan production, the latter to domestic production. Unsold stocks in Java reached $2\frac{1}{2}$ million tons in 1932, and the government took over in January 1933 as the single seller. The failure of the Chadbourne scheme led the World Economic Conference to push for a new agreement, which was finally reached under League of Nations auspices only in May 1937 at the height of the recovery of primary-product prices.

The World Economic Conference was the twentieth international meeting on the subject of wheat after 1928 when the price of wheat started to plummet – two on imperial preference, seven limited to Eastern Europe as already mentioned, and eleven general. The agreement that emerged after the World Economic Conference achieved a system of export quotas for major producers, but no agreement on acreage controls to limit production (Malenbaum, 1953).

Tea was regulated in this period by an international committee which met in London. In March 1931 the four leading producers of tin – Malaya, Bolivia, Nigeria, and the Netherlands East Indies – cooperated in the Joint Tin Committee. In May 1934 nine countries in South-east Asia producing 95 per cent of the world's rubber supply undertook to impose export quotas to reconstitute the Stevenson rubber plan which had broken down in 1928 (Van Gelderen, 1939, pp. 51ff.). Their problem was complicated by sharply differing supply elasticities in the plantation and the native sectors, the latter characterized in many countries by backward-bending responses. As rubber prices rose in the 1936/7 inventory boom, a number of governments sought to tax away the price increase from the producers, but until the price collapse of September 1937 succeeded mainly in raising the price to buyers in a sellers' market. With the eventual decline in prices, the incidence of the export taxes shifted back from the foreign consumer to the domestic producer and in most instances they were quickly removed.

K.   SANCTIONS

In December 1934 a border incident occurred between Italian Somalia and Ethiopia. Italy demand an apology; Ethiopia refused. With tension rising, the League of Nations sought to arbitrate but received no help from Italy. After further border clashes, Italian troops invaded Ethiopia on 3 October 1935 without a declaration of war. Later in the month, the League of Nations declared Italy the aggressor and voted sanctions to be applied to her in arms supply, finance, and export–import restrictions. The League did not, however, decree sanctions in the critical item, oil. Germany refused to comply with the League vote; the United States, though not a member of the League of Nations, was strongly sympathetic. Oil sanctions were discussed again in March 1936. At this time an attempt was made to apply them informally through major world oil companies. These companies stopped selling to Italy, but the increase in oil prices thereby brought about encouraged a vast number of small shippers to enter the business for the first time and to deliver oil to Italian troops at Red Sea ports in the full quantities required. With the fall of Addis Ababa, the Italians proclaimed empire over Ethiopia and withdrew from the League. League members continued to apply sanctions with increasing resolution until 15 July 1936 when sanctions were abandoned (Feis, 1946, vol. III).

IV.   *The disintegration of the world economy*

In a few countries – notably France and the United States – foreign trade fell by the same proportion as national income from 1929 to 1938. In others trade fell more than output. Thus the ratio of imports to industrial production declined by 10 per cent in the United Kingdom, nearly 20 per cent in Canada, 30 per cent in Germany, and 40 per cent in Italy. Crop failures in the United States in 1934 and 1936, and in Germany in 1937 and 1938, prevented the decline in the proportion of imports from being wider (League of Nations (Meade), 1939, pp. 107–8). Buy-British and Buy-American campaigns, involving government discrimination

Table 18. *Proportions of world trade balanced bilaterally and multilaterally (in percentage of total)*

	By non-merchandise	Multilaterally	Bilaterally
1928	11.1	21.2	67.7
1938	14.3	16.9	68.8

Source: Thorbecke (1960), p. 82.

against foreign as against domestic suppliers with margins of initially 10 per cent, increased to 25 per cent, in the United States, and 100 per cent for items under $100, were often supported by programmes affecting state governments, and campaigns to persuade the general public to discriminate as well (Bidwell, 1939, pp. 70–1 and Appendix A). The major influences to be sure were higher tariffs, quotas, clearing and payments agreements, and preferential trade agreements.

What trade remained was distorted, as compared with the freer market system of the 1920s, both in commodity and in country terms. The index of German imports for 1937 with a base of 100 in 1929 strongly reflected *Wehrwirtschaft*, and especially rearmament: 'other ores' 153, manganese ore 142, iron ore 122, iron and steel 121, copper 100, cotton 73, wool 62, coal 59, oil seeds 57, timber 28 (League of Nations (Meade), 1938, p. 128). The share of Germany in Turkish, Greek, and Italian imports rose between 1928 and 1939 respectively from 13 to 43 per cent, 8 to 29 per cent, and 10 to 24 per cent; the same percentages of national exports to Germany rose from 13 to 43 per cent, 27 to 39 per cent and 13 to 17 per cent for the same countries in the same order (Thorbecke, 1960, p. 100). By 1937, bilateral clearings amounted to 12 per cent of total world trade and 50 per cent of the trade of Bulgaria, Germany, Greece, Hungary, Romania, Turkey, and Yugoslavia (League of Nations, 1942, p. 70). Pioneering estimates of the shrinkage of multilaterally as opposed to bilaterally balanced trade were made for the League of Nations Economic and Financial Department by Folke Hilgerdt. In 1928, bilateral balancing of export and import values between pairs of countries on the average covered 70 per cent of merchandise trade, with about 5 per cent more covered by exports or imports of services or capital movements, and 25 per cent balanced multilaterally (League of Nations (Hilgerdt), 1941). Hilgerdt's two studies emphasized the shrinkage of the proportion of the trade balanced multilaterally during the depression years, without furnishing a precise estimate for the end of the 1930s (League of Nations (Hilgerdt), 1941 and League of Nations (Hilgerdt), 1942). A post-war study on a somewhat different basis furnished a comparison for 1938 with 1928, shown in Table 18.

Major changes occurred both world-wide and within Europe. On a world basis, the largest change shown in the Hilgerdt analysis derived from the fact that the developing countries of the tropics no longer earned large surpluses in merchandise trade with the United States to pay their interest on debts owed to Europe, and especially to the United Kingdom. Regionally, within Europe, the most important change was the failure of Germany to earn an export surplus in Europe, largely Britain, to enable her to pay for her net imports of raw materials from overseas. Another striking feature was the shift by Britain of procurement from Europe to the sterling area. France, The Netherlands, and especially Britain diverted trade from the rest of Europe to their colonial empires, a trend which would be reversed after the Second World War, and especially after the formation of the European Economic Community in 1957 and Britain's accession to it in 1973. In 1913 22 per cent of British exports went to the Empire. By 1938 the figure had more than doubled to 47 per cent. In imports, the proportion rose over the same period from 22.3 to close to 40 per cent. As noted earlier, the figures might have risen further had it not been for what has been called 'Imperial Insufficiency' (Hancock, 1940, p. 232; see also Drummond, 1972).

V.   *World trading systems*

Recovery of raw-material prices from 1933 to 1937 was followed by some considerable reduction in tariffs, and relaxation of quota restrictions. The renewed, though less far-reaching, decline of these prices in September 1937, outside the fields dominated by European rearmament, set back the movement towards freer trade. The last five years of the inter-war period were most clearly characterized by what have been called disparate 'world trading systems' (Tasca, 1939). At the limits were the system of German trade, locked into a network of bilateral clearing and payments agreements, and practising autarky for the sake of war economy (Petzina, 1968), and at the other extreme, the United States, which stood aloof from all payments and clearing agreements, with few quota restrictions, largely in agriculture, some subsidies to export in agricultural commodities, plus government credit through the Export–Import Bank for export promotion. Within Europe, the Balkan countries were nearer to the German model, the Oslo group to the American. Midway between was the Empire preference scheme of Britain, the Dominions, India, and the dependent colonies. Latin America had been hard hit by declines in raw-material prices and the decline in foreign lending, but was hopeful of trade expansion under the Roosevelt 'Good Neighbor' policy. The Soviet Union went its own way. Anxious to join a system, but largely orphaned outside them were the Middle East and

Japan, the latter of which carved out its own Greater East Asia Co-Prosperity Sphere.

There were limited attempts at achieving a single unified world trading system. The League of Nations Committee for the Study of the Problem of Raw Materials reported in September 1937 at a time when payments difficulties had eased but the position was on the point of reversal (League of Nations (Meade), 1938, p. 162). It found few problems of supply or access to materials, and argued in favour of valorization schemes to raise prices provided that consumers' interests were safeguarded. The report went to the League of Nations Assembly where it was pigeonholed as a consequence of the sharp check to commodity prices and deterioration in payment balances.

Before that time, the British and French governments had asked Paul Van Zeeland, a former Belgian Prime Minister, to prepare a programme for world action in the commercial-policy field. In January 1938, the Van Zeeland report was presented to the public, equally an inopportune time. It called for reciprocal reductions of tariffs, generalized by the most-favoured-nation clause, replacement of industrial quotas by tariffs or by tariff quotas, removal of foreign exchange control, clearing agreements, and the ban on new lending in London; and, as a final step when all else was in operation, six-months agreements on foreign-exchange rates leading ultimately to the establishment of fixed rates under the gold standard (League of Nations (Meade), 1938, p. 159). The report was received with universal agreement that the restoration of trade was needed, but equally universal reluctance on the part of all governments to take any decisive initiative in the matter (Condliffe, 1940, p. 47).

The 1937–9 recession in fact led to increases in tariffs in Belgium, France, Greece, Italy, the Netherlands East Indies, Norway, Sweden, Switzerland, and Yugoslavia in 1938, and in that stronghold of free-trade sentiment, The Netherlands, in March 1939. Rubber and copper quotas which had been freed in 1937 under their commodity schemes were tightened down again. Brazil, Colombia, and Japan extended their foreign exchange restrictions. Germany and Italy introduced the death penalty for violations of foreign exchange regulations in December 1936 and June 1939, respectively. Italy also constituted a Supreme Autarky Commission in October 1937 (League of Nations (Meade), 1939, p. 197). In all, the number of clearing and payments agreements rose from 131 on 1 June 1936 to 171 by 1 January 1939 (Gordon, 1941, p. 131).

Meanwhile some considerable relaxation of commercial policy was underway in the United States, led by Cordell Hull, whom Herbert Feis, his economic adviser in the Department of State, called a monomaniac on the subject of tariff reductions (Feis, 1966, p. 262). Hull had long been a Congressman from eastern Tennessee, which specialized in tobacco for export, before becoming Secretary of State, and had been in opposition to the Fordney–McCumber and Hawley–Smoot tariff increases in 1922 and 1930 as a member of the House of Representatives Committee on Ways and Means. As early as the World Economic Conference of 1927, as a Congressman, he had been thought to believe that the tariff of the United States was the key to the entire world situation (US Department of State, *Foreign Relations of the United States*, vol. I, 1928, p. 239). As Secretary of State and leader of the United States delegation to the World Economic Conference of 1933, he had been frustrated in his attempts to get world tariffs reduced by the repudiation of President Roosevelt which prevented him from encountering the profound disinterest of the other countries. The tariff truce of May 1933 lapsed when the conference failed, but Secretary Hull persevered. At the Seventh Conference of American States at Montevideo in November 1933 – the first having been held in 1889 – he had tariffs put on the agenda for the first time and induced President Roosevelt to offer the Latin American republics tariff reductions (Gordon, 1941, p. 464). The main business accomplished at Montevideo was the strengthening of the most-favoured-nation clause, as Hull had tried to do at London, by government agreement not to invoke the clause in order to prevent the consummation of multilateral tariff reductions in agreements to which a government was not a party. The full agreement provided for no tariff reductions, and was signed by eight countries, though ratified only by the United States and Cuba (Viner, 1950, p. 37).

Upon his return from Montevideo, Secretary Hull found that the President had established an Executive Committee on Commercial Policy under the chairmanship of George Peek, agricultural expert and opponent of trade liberalization, and that the committee had already drafted a bill providing for trade treaties to be subject to Senate ratification. This was unsatisfactory to Hull. The Department of State had already been negotiating with Argentina, Brazil, Colombia, Portugal, and Sweden in the summer of 1933, had signed an agreement only with Colombia, but had not submitted it to the Senate for ratification. In early 1934 new legislation was drawn up that delegated authority from the Congress to the Executive branch of government to conclude reciprocal trade agreements on its own authority. The draft legislation was completed on 24 February, approved by President Roosevelt on 28 February, passed the House of Representatives on 20 March, the Senate on 4 June, and was signed into law on 13 June 1934 as the Reciprocal Trade Agreements Act. The initial delegation of authority was for a period of three years. The legislation was renewed in 1937 and 1940. It provided for mutual bilateral reductions in tariff duties, generalized by the most-favoured-nation clause, limited to 50 per cent of the existing (largely Hawley–Smoot) tariff levels.

Even before the legislation had been drafted, further talks were going forward to reduce tariffs, with Belgium and Denmark in January 1934, and with Canada. Canada and the United States each made official public statements on the subject in February 1934, emphasizing the importance of their mutual trade relations. A request for negotiations was made by the Canadian government in November 1934 and an agreement was achieved a year later to the effect on 1 January 1936. Canada received concessions on 88 items, largely primary products, including along with Hawley–Smoot items the lumber and copper affected by the US Revenue Act of 1932. United States concessions obtained from Canada were largely in manufactured goods.

The first agreement under the Reciprocal Trade Agreements Act, however, was that concluded with Cuba in August 1934. By November 1939, agreements had been reached with twenty countries, eleven of them in Latin America. A second agreement was concluded with Canada in November 1938, but the most important was the British agreement concluded simultaneously with the revision of the Canadian agreement.

In the British and Canadian agreements, the United States hoped to break down Empire preference. This was beginning to happen of its own accord. In a British–Canadian trade agreement of 1937, five years following the Ottawa agreements of 1932, the British persuaded the Canadians to abolish the doctrine of equalizing competition and to substitute fixed tariff rates and fixed preferential margins in the agreements (McDiarmid, 1946, p. 295). New Zealand was ready to abandon the Ottawa agreements, and started to conclude agreements outside them with Sweden (1935), Greece (1936), Germany (1937), and was negotiating a dozen others (Hancock, 1940, p. 278). Britain meanwhile was highly critical of Australian performance under Ottawa, on the ground that Australia had persistently violated its commitments. Australian Tariff Board studies were limited, and even when the Tariff Board recommended reductions on British goods, the government often failed to introduce them in parliament (Drummond, 1975, pp. 392ff.). British and Australian interests were only partly complementary. Accordingly the United Kingdom, Canada, and the other Dominions as well were ready in their agreements with the United States to sacrifice advantages in each other's markets in return for significant compensation in the market in the United States (Hancock, 1940, p. 265).

To an extent, the Anglo-American trade agreement was more symbolic than effective. Two years of hard bargaining went into it, and it lasted only eight months, from 1 January 1939 until British wartime controls were imposed on the outbreak of war with Germany in September 1939. Reductions were agreed on nine items in which trade amounted to no more than $350 per annum. Important concessions, as in cotton textiles, were prevented from being generalized to Japan and other competitors through reclassification. Full 50 per cent reductions in the United States were made on 96 items but the total trade involved was only $14 million. Under all twenty agreements, the unweighted (equal weights) United States *ad valorem* duties were reduced from 57 per cent on products subject to the tariff to 35 per cent, a reduction of 39 per cent, whereas the reduction under the British agreement, from 42 to 30 per cent on the same basis, amounted only to a reduction of 28 per cent. The 35 per cent level achieved on 1 January 1939 was somewhat lower than the Fordney–McCumber average of 38.5 per cent and the Payne–Aldrich tariff (1909) of 40.8 per cent, and well below the Hawley–Smoot average of 51.5 per cent. It was nevertheless still well above the 1913 Underwood level of 27 per cent (Kreider, 1943, pp. 170ff.).

Moreover, the trade agreements applied largely to industrial products and materials. United States opposition to Empire preference had export concerns in view, especially in competition with Canada in pork and apples. The reductions in tariffs under the agreements, however, went side by side with continued US protection against agricultural imports and subsidies on agricultural exports. Protection was required under those domestic programmes which raised prices in the United States and would, without new restrictions, have attracted further supplies from abroad; and subsidies were deemed necessary to offset the price disadvantage this imposed on American producers in their traditional markets. The trade agreements reduced tariffs on a few items, such as maple sugar from Canada, which had been a particular irritant under the Hawley–Smoot Act, and altered the arbitrary valuations on fresh fruits and vegetables early in the season that had hitherto been kept out of Canada by this device. A sanitary agreement between the United States and Argentina on the regulation of foot-and-mouth disease was not ratified by the Congress (Bidwell, 1939, pp. 217–18); and independence for the Philippines was accelerated to push its sugar production outside the tariff borders of the United States. On the whole, the trade agreements marked the beginning of regarding liberal commercial policies as appropriate only for manufactures, and their inputs, and leaving agricultural trade largely to special arrangements.

A small beginning was made by the United States on what was to be a major post-war issue, East–West trade. The United States was unwilling to recognize the government of the Soviet Union all through the 1920s. With President Roosevelt's New Deal, this was changed and recognition was accorded in 1933. In the mid-thirties, the United States and the Soviet Union undertook a series of trade agreements. In 1935, the Soviet Union contracted to purchase at least $30 million worth of US goods in the following year; in return, the United States accorded the Soviet Union most-favoured-nation treatment. In August 1937 under a new pact, the Soviet Union agreed to step up its purchases from the United States to $40 million (Gordon, 1941, p. 407).

British adherence to the more liberal trade policies pursued by Cordell Hull was highly ambiguous. Kreider claims that the British concessions were not spectacular but represented a reversal of policy (1943, p. 240). At the same time, the British government was unwilling to repudiate the principle of Ottawa, despite its effects, as Mackenzie King claimed, in destroying the principle of imperial harmony (Drummond, 1975, p. 316).

Moreover, British ministers were experimenting with a new technique quite at variance with the American professed principle of increased reliance on the international market. Mention was made above of the special tariff assistance given to the iron and steel industry to assist in its negotiations with the International Steel Cartel. At the depth of the depression, in October 1933, the British had encouraged negotiations between Lancashire and Indian cotton-textile mill owners. The resultant Lees–Mody pact of October 1933 provided that India would lower her tariffs on British textiles to 20 per cent while holding those against other (i.e., Japanese) goods at 75, to which they had been raised from $31\frac{1}{2}$ per cent in August 1932 in several steps. As part of the negotiation, involving governments and business groups on both sides, the British agreed to take one and a half million bales of cotton that had piled up as a result of a Japanese retaliatory boycott. At the time Lord Runciman stated, 'The work of the Delegation has gone some way in justifying the Government in their belief that the best approach to the problem of international industrial cooperation is by the method of discussion between industrialists' (Drummond, 1972, p. 316).

In early 1939, immediately after signing the Anglo–American Reciprocal Trade Agreement in November 1938, and as part of an export drive, the British Board of Trade encouraged the visit to Düsseldorf of a delegation of the Federation of British Industry to meet with the Reichsgruppe Industrie, its institutional counterpart, and to fix quantitative relationships between the exports of the two countries in each commodity and market. In prospect, *The Economist* after some qualifications expressed itself as approving (CXXXIV, no. 4585 (February 1939), p. 383). The agreement was concluded on 16 March 1939, one day after the German invasion of Czechoslovakia (text in Hexner, 1946, Appendix III, pp. 402–4). The British government repudiated the agreement on political grounds, but not before *The Economist* had denounced it on the grounds that it involved cartelization of domestic industry as well as of trade, that it would extend Anglo-German subsidies to exports, and that it might involve joint action against competitors who refused to join the arrangement, including possible American firms (March 1939, p. 607).

In Eastern Europe the German bloc was strengthened in ways to guarantee German access to raw materials and foodstuffs in short supply. An agreement with Hungary in 1934 provided for a shift of Hungarian agriculture from wheat to oilseeds with an assured outlet in Germany. German treaties with Romania in March 1935 and again four years later fostered the expansion of Romanian agriculture in oil seeds, feedgrains, vegetable fibres, as well as industrial and financial cooperation, including the development of Romanian transport and petroleum under German–Romanian companies supervized by joint government commissions (Gordon, 1941, pp. 425–6). In 1937, the proportion of German exports sold through clearing agreements amounted to 57 per cent, while 53 per cent of her imports came through clearings. The comparable figures for Turkey were 74 and 72 per cent respectively, for Romania 67 and 75 per cent, for Switzerland 28 and 36 per cent, for Sweden 17 and 24 per cent, and for the United Kingdom 2 and 2 per cent (Gordon, 1941, Table 7, p. 133).

The disintegration of world trade thus proceeded, despite the attempts of the United States, the Oslo group, Premier Van Zeeland under Anglo-French auspices and the economists of the Economic and Financial Department of the League of Nations. With some prescience Condliffe concluded his book written at the outbreak of the Second World War (1940, p. 394), 'If an international system is to be restored, it must be an American-dominated system, based on *Pax Americana*.'

CHAPTER II

Commercial policy between the wars

For a useful, immediately post-war bibliography on international economics generally, with approximately seventeen pages on commercial policy, see American Economic Association (H. S. Ellis and L. Metzler), *Readings in the Theory of International Trade*, Homewood, Ill., 1950, pp. 555ff. and especially pp. 608–25.

Andersen, F. Nyboe. *Bilateral Exchange Clearing Policy*. Copenhagen, 1946.

Arndt, H. W. *The Economic Lessons of the Nineteen-Thirties*. London, 1944.

Australia: Committee on Economics (Brigden, J. B.) *The Australian Tariff, An Economic Enquiry*. Melbourne, Melbourne University Press, 1929.

Benham, Frederic C. *Great Britain under Protection*. New York, 1941.

Bergsten, C. Fred. *Completing the GATT: Toward New International Rules to Govern Export Controls*. No place stated, British–North-American Committee, 1974.

Beveridge, William H. *Tariffs, The Case Examined by a Committee of Economists under the Chairmanship of Sir William Beveridge*. New York, 1931.

Bidwell, Percy W. *The Invisible Tariff. A Study of Control of Imports into the United States*. New York, 1939.

—— *Raw Materials: A Study of American Policy*. New York, 1958.

Brigden, J. L. 'The Australian Tariff and the Standard of Living', *Economic Record*, vol. I, no. I (November 1925), pp. 29–46.

Brown, William Adams, Jr. *The United States and the Restoration of World Trade*. Washington, DC, 1950.

Childs, Frank C. *The Theory and Practice of Exchange Control in Germany*. The Hague, 1958.

Committee on Finance and Industry (United Kingdom, Macmillan Report, Cmd 3897), London, 1931.

Condliffe, J. B. *The Reconstruction of World Trade: A Survey of International Economic Relations*. New York, 1940.

Copland, Douglas B. and James, C. V. *Australian Tariff Policy: A Book of Documents, 1932–1937*. Melbourne, 1937.

Davis, Joseph S. *The World Between the Wars, 1919–1939: An Economist's View*. Baltimore, Md., 1975.

Dohan, Michael and Hewett, Edward. *Two Studies in Soviet Terms of Trade, 1918–1970*. Bloomington, Ind., 1973.

Drummond, Ian M. *British Economic Policy and the Empire, 1919–1939*. London, 1972.

—— *Imperial Economic Policy, 1917–1939: Studies in Expansion and Protection*. Toronto, 1975.

—— *Economist, The*.

Einzig, Paul J. *Bloodless Invasion: German Penetration into the Danube States and the Balkans*. London, 1938.

Elliott, William Y., May, Elizabeth S., Rowe, J. F. W., Skelton, Alex and Wallace, Donald H. *International Control in Non-ferrous Metals*. New York, 1937.

Federal Trade Commission. *The International Petroleum Cartel*, US Senate Select Committee on Small Business, 82nd Congress, Committee Print no. 6. Washington, DC, August 1952.

Feis, Herbert. *Three International Episodes seen from E.A.* New York, 1946.

—— *1933, Characters in Crisis*. Boston, 1966.

Friedman, Philip. *The Impact of Trade Destruction on National Income: A Study of Europe, 1924–38*. Gainesville, Fla., 1974.

Furnivall, J. S. *Netherlands India: A Study of Plural Economy*. Cambridge, 1939.

Gordon, Margaret S. *Barriers to World Trade: A Study of Recent Commercial Policy*. New York, 1941.

Haight, Frank Arnold. *A History of French Commercial Policies*. New York, 1941.

Hancock, W. Keith. *Survey of British Commonwealth Affairs*, vol. II: *Problems of Economic Policy*. London, 1940.

Hexner, Erwin. *International Cartels*. Durham, NC, 1946.

Hoover, Herbert. *The Memoirs of Herbert Hoover*, vol. III, *The Great Depression, 1929–1941*. New York, 1952.

Hull, Cordell. *The Memoirs of Cordell Hull*. New York, 1948.

Johnson, Alvin S. 'Protection and the Formation of Capital', *Political Science Quarterly*, vol. XXIII (June 1908), pp. 220–41.

Johnson, D. Gale. *Trade and Agriculture; A Study of Inconsistent Policies*. New York, 1950.

Jones, Joseph M., Jr. *Tariff Retaliation, Repercussions of the Hawley-Smoot Bill*. Philadelphia, 1934.

Kindleberger, Charles P. *The Terms of Trade: A European Case Study*. New York, 1956.

—— *The World in Depression, 1929–1939*. Berkeley, 1973; revised edn, 1986.

Knorr, Klaus E. *World Rubber and its Regulation*. Stanford, 1946.

Kreider, Carl. *The Anglo-American Trade Agreement: A Study of British and American Commercial Policies, 1934–39*. Princeton, 1943.

Lary, Hal B. (US Department of Commerce, Bureau of Foreign and Domestic Commerce). *The United States in the World Economy*, Economic Series, no. 23. Washington, DC, 1943.

League of Nations. *Enquiry into Clearing Agreements*. Geneva, 1935.

—— *Commercial Policy in the Interwar Period: International Proposals and National Policies*. Geneva, 1942.

—— Economic Committee. *Considerations on the Present Evolution of Agricultural Tariffs*. Geneva, 1935.

—— (Folke Hilgerdt). *Europe's Trade, A Study of the Trade of European Countries with Each Other and with the Rest of the World*. Geneva, 1941.

—— (Folke Hilgerdt). *The Network of World Trade, A Companion Volume to 'Europe's Trade'*. Geneva, 1942.

—— (James E. Meade). *World Economic Survey, 1937/38*. Geneva, 1938.

—— (James E. Meade). *World Economic Survey, 1938/39*. Geneva, 1939.

—— (W. T. Page). *Memorandum on European Bargaining Tariffs*. Geneva, 1927.

—— (Jacob Viner). *Trade Relations between Free-market and Controlled Economies*. Geneva, 1943.

Lewis, Cleona. *Nazi Europe and World Trade*. Washington, DC, 1941.

Lewis, W. Arthur. *Economic Survey, 1919–1939*. Philadelphia, 1950.

Liepmann, H. *Tariff Levels and the Economic Unity of Europe*. London, 1938.

McDiarmid, Orville J. *Commercial Policy in the Canadian Economy*. Cambridge, Mass., 1946.

Malenbaum, Wilfrid. *The World Wheat Economy, 1895–1939*. Cambridge, Mass., 1953.

Manoilesco, Mihail. *The Theory of Protection and International Trade*. London, 1931.

Mason, Edward S. *Controlling World Trade, Cartels and Commodity Agreements*. New York, 1946.

Office of the Chief Counsel for Prosecution of Nazi Criminality. *Nazi Conspiracy and Aggression*, vols. I and VII. Washington, DC, 1946.

Petzina, Dieter. *Autarkiepolitik im dritten Reich, Der national-sozialistiche Vierjahresplan*. Stuttgart, 1968.

Reitsama, A. J. 'Trade and Redistribution of Income: Is There Still an Australian Case?', *Economic Record*, vol. XXIV, no. 68 (August 1958), pp. 172–88.

Richardson, J. H. *British Economic Foreign Policy*. London, 1936.

Roepke, Wilhelm. *German Commercial Policy*. London, 1934.

—— *International Economic Disintegration*. London, 1942.

Rowe, J. W. F. *Markets and Men: A Study of Artificial Control Schemes*. New York, 1936.

Salter, Sir Arthur. *Recovery, the Second Effort*. London and New York, 1932.

Schacht, Hjalmar. 'Germany's Colonial Demand', *Foreign Affairs*, vol. XIV (January 1937), pp. 223–34.

Schattschneider, E. E. *Politics, Pressures and Tariffs: A Study of Free Private Enterprise in Pressure Politics as Shown by the 1929–30 Revision of the Tariff*. New York, 1935.

Schuker, Stephen A. *The End of French Predominance in Europe: The Financial Crisis of 1924 and the Adoption of the Dawes Plan*. Chapel Hill, NC, 1976.

Smith, Mark A. 'The United States Flexible Tariff', in *Explorations in Economics, Notes and Essays Contributed in Honor of F. W. Taussig*. New York, 1936.

Stolper, W. F. and Samuelson, P. A. 'Protection and Real Wages', *Review of Economic Studies*, vol. IX (November 1941), pp. 58–73.

Suetens, M. *Histoire de la politique commerciale de la Belgique jusqu'à nos jours*. Brussels, 1955.

Tasca, Henry J. *The Reciprocal Trade Agreement Policy of the United States: A Study in Trade Philosophy*. Philadelphia, 1938.

Thorbecke, Erik. *The Tendency toward Regionalization in International Trade, 1928–1956*. The Hague, 1960.

United Nations, Department of Economic Affairs. *Customs Union: A League of Nations Contribution to the Study of Custom Union Problems*. Lake Success, NY, 1947.

United States Department of State. *Foreign Relations of the United States*. Washington, DC, various years.

—— Tariff Commission. *Foreign Trade and Exchange Controls*, Report no. 150. Washington, DC, 1942.

Van Gelderen, J. *The Recent Development of Economic Foreign Policy in the Netherlands East Indies*. London, 1939.

Viner, Jacob. *The Customs Union Issue*. New York, 1950.

—— *Dumping: A Problem in International Trade*. 1923, rep. New York, 1966.

Winslow, E. M. 'Administrative Protection: A Problem in Commercial Policy', in *Explorations in Economics: Notes and Essays in Honor of F. W. Taussig*. New York, 1936.

World Trading Systems. Paris, 1939.

[5]
The GATT's contribution to economic recovery in post-war Western Europe

DOUGLAS A. IRWIN

1 Introduction

The contrast between the decade of economic instability in Western Europe after World War I and the economic recovery established in the decade following World War II is nowhere more evident than in the area of international trade relations. Economic reconstruction following World War I lacked any institutional mechanism to facilitate the reduction of trade barriers that had arisen during the war and had become entrenched thereafter. The political weakness of European countries in trade policy was evident when a proposal for "equality of trade conditions" in a draft League of Nations charter was rejected in favor of a weaker provision for "equitable treatment." The World Economic Conference in 1927 still found it necessary to call upon governments to remove wartime controls on trade, which included import quotas, licensing requirements, and foreign exchange controls. A decade after its formation, the League of Nations had yet to sponsor any negotiations on liberalizing world trade from high tariffs, and the onset of the depression vanquished any serious prospect of trade reform in Europe and elsewhere.

Yet during World War II, even in advance of official US participation in the conflict, the United States and the United Kingdom already envisioned a post-war world trading system based on reducing all trade barriers and limiting discriminatory tariff preferences. Just two years after Germany's surrender, twenty-three countries established a General Agreement on Tariffs and Trade (GATT) that set rules to restrict national trade policies and even started to decrease tariffs in binding agreements. Just five years after the end of the war, all major Western European countries had

Financial support was provided by the James S. Kemper Faculty Foundation Research Fund of the Graduate School of Business at the University of Chicago. I wish to thank the Division of International Finance at the Board of Governors of the Federal Reserve System for their hospitality during my stay as a visiting scholar when much of this paper was completed, as well as Barry Eichengreen and J. Michael Finger for helpful comments.

participated in three separate negotiating rounds that had expanded GATT membership and further reduced import tariffs.

The GATT often has been hailed, almost by virtue of its very existence, as a key factor in promoting post-war recovery in Western Europe and in preventing a return to the disasters of the interwar period. By freeing Europe's regional and international trade from government restrictions, the GATT permitted economies to take advantage of specialization along lines of comparative advantage and thereby expand more rapidly and efficiently. While it is exceedingly difficult to quantify the impact of any institution on aggregate economic activity, *prima facie* evidence of the GATT's success arises from the divergence in the behavior of European trade after World War I – when no such institution was in place – and after World War II – when the GATT facilitated the reduction of trade barriers.

Figures 5.1 and 5.2 depict the path of a GNP-weighted average of export volume and real income for five major West European countries – France, Germany, Italy, the Netherlands, and the United Kingdom – after the two wars. By 1929, a dozen years after the war, the export volume of these countries had just barely surpassed its prewar (1913) peak. After World War II, by contrast, exports surpassed their prewar level in about five years, although it is important to note that the prewar (1938) level was perhaps artificially low owing to protectionism and the depression. Still, exports expanded by a factor of eight in the decade after World War II compared with a four-fold increase after World War I. The picture for national income is similar. This favorable outcome cannot clinch the case for the GATT's positive impact in promoting economic recovery after World War II, but the correlation between the dramatic increase in post-war trade and income and the establishment and activities of the GATT negotiations has weighed heavily in the minds of economists and policymakers.

This chapter describes and assesses the contribution of the GATT in fostering economic recovery in Western Europe during the decade from 1947 to 1956. Three questions will be posed for consideration:

(1) What were the origins of the GATT and what did it aim to achieve?
(2) How successful was the GATT in liberalizing Europe's trade?
(3) Was the GATT responsible for the post-war export boom?

To anticipate the chapter's main conclusions, the formation of the GATT does not appear to have stimulated a particularly rapid liberalization of world trade in the decade after 1947. It is therefore difficult to attribute much of a role to the GATT in the dramatic economic recovery during the immediate post-war period beyond that of an effective supporting actor. The principal contribution of the GATT during its first decade of operation

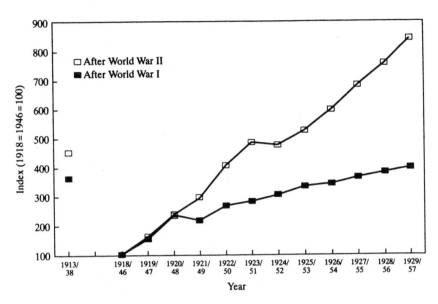

Figure 5.1   Export volume after World Wars I and II (in five West European economies)

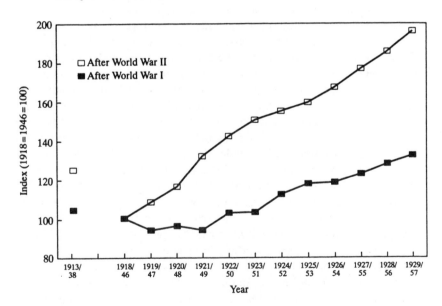

Figure 5.2   Real output after World Wars I and II (in five West European economies)

130   *Douglas A. Irwin*

rests more in securing binding agreements on early tariff reductions, thereby preventing countries from instituting higher tariffs as import quotas and foreign exchange controls were being phased out during the 1950s under the auspices of other international institutions. Yet despite the GATT's weaknesses on several fronts, the institution succeeded in establishing among major countries a fairly credible commitment to an open and stable environment for world trade that fostered the post-war rise in trade and income.

2 The origins and purposes of the GATT

Preparations for a new world trading order began during World War II and date from the Atlantic Charter (August 1941) and the Lend-Lease (February 1942) agreements between the United States and the United Kingdom. In early discussions, both governments endorsed the principles of non-discrimination and free trade in post-war commercial policy. The British War Cabinet proposal on "Commercial Union" (drafted by James Meade) and the US State Department document "Multilateral Convention on Commercial Policy" emerged in September–October 1943 and formed the basis for ongoing bilateral discussions until 1945. In December 1945, the State Department completed a draft multilateral accord on rules for international trade that was acceptable to both governments.

The architects of the post-war international economic order were principally concerned with establishing institutions and promoting policies that would avoid the repetition of the interwar experience. To this end, their first objective was to design a stable international monetary system that would allow for domestic policies to maintain full employment. The reduction of tariffs and elimination of quantitative restrictions on international trade was an important part of the broad objective, but was not seen to be as urgent a priority as restoring monetary stability and achieving full employment. Consequently, while the Articles of Agreement of the International Monetary Fund (IMF) and the International Bank for Reconstruction and Development (IBRD) were formalized at the Bretton Woods Conference in 1944 and took effect shortly thereafter, agreements and institutions on commercial policy materialized more slowly. That trade was placed on this second track was to have important consequences for the types of agreements and institutions that later emerged.

With the completion of a draft charter in 1945, the US proposed opening international negotiations to finalize multilateral agreement on a charter for an International Trade Organization (ITO) that would take a place along side the IMF and IBRD. The ITO was to have wide scope over various aspects of international economic activity, with rules covering not just commercial policy but also employment, commodity agreements, restrictive business practices, and international investment. To hasten efforts at reducing tariff barriers, the US also invited countries to participate in tariff negotiations in concert with the ITO talks. In February 1946, the Economic and Social Council of the United Nations resolved to convene an international conference on trade and employment to negoti- ate an ITO charter, and eighteen countries attended a preparatory meeting in London during October–November 1946. In January–February 1947 at Lake Success, New York, negotiators drafted the technical articles of the charter along with a preliminary general agreement on commercial policy, and by August a subsequent conference in Geneva prepared an ITO draft charter for submission to the UN conference. From November 1947 to March 1948. the UN Conference on Trade and Employment in Havana (composed of fifty-six countries) finalized and ratified the ITO charter. This approval came nearly four years after the Bretton Woods Conference, over two years after the initial US proposal for an ITO, and almost half a year after the first post-war negotiations on reducing tariffs (as will be discussed shortly).

The lack of urgency with which the ITO was created portended its demise as an institution. The Havana Charter languished for an additional three years as the agreement encountered domestic controversy in the United States during efforts to obtain formal approval. Business interests that had supported bilateral tariff negotiations in the 1930s under the Reciprocal Trade Agreements Act of 1934 balked at supporting an international organization with wide-ranging regulatory authority over trade, invest- ment, and business practices. The Executive Committee of the US Council of the International Chamber of Commerce, as quoted in Diebold (1952a, pp. 20–1), denounced the draft ITO charter as a "dangerous document because it accepts practically all of the policies of economic nationalism; because it jeopardizes the free enterprise system by giving priority to a centralized national governmental planning of foreign trade; because it leaves a wide scope to discrimination, accepts the principles of economic insulation, and in effect commits all members of the ITO to state planning for full employment."

Other pressing international concerns also prevented the Truman administration from viewing the ITO as a major priority and from marshalling business support for the agreement; the United States was preoccupied with the Marshall Plan in 1948, with the North Atlantic Treaty Organization in 1949, and with the Korean War in 1950. In the face of continued opposition to the ITO, the Truman administration an- nounced in December 1950 that the ITO would not be submitted for Congressional approval, effectively killing the agreement.

Fortunately, the collapse of the ITO did not extinguish the only means of liberalizing world trade policies. Also at the Geneva meeting in 1947, on a parallel track with the ITO negotiations, twenty-three nations agreed to enact revised versions of the commercial policy articles in the existing ITO draft charter – called the General Agreement on Tariffs and Trade – and agreed to reduce tariffs amongst themselves. The agreement and the tariff reductions were finalized on October 30, 1947 and came into force for most countries on January 1, 1948 – and did not require Congressional approval in the case of the United States. The GATT was viewed as an intermediate measure to implement the commercial policy clauses of the ITO and accelerate the reduction of tariffs on world trade while the ITO was being finalized. The GATT was never designed to exist as an institution itself, but only to serve as a temporary agreement until it could be absorbed into the ITO structure. The GATT immediately became the forum for early trade policy discussions, however, and in the wake of the ITO's failure became the sole body for overseeing international commercial policies.

The Geneva negotiations in 1947 that produced the GATT were undertaken by twenty-three participating countries, listed in table 5.1, who became Contracting Parties. The purpose of the GATT, as stated in its preamble, was to contribute to rising standards of living and full employment by "entering into reciprocal and mutually advantageous arrangements directed to the substantial reduction of tariffs and other barriers to trade and to the elimination of discriminatory treatment in international commerce." Part I of the General Agreement contained two articles, the first mandating unconditional most-favored-nation (MFN) treatment for all Contracting Parties and the second consisting of annexed schedules of all tariff reductions that arose during negotiations. Part II of the Agreement included the main rules on commercial policy but was applied "provisionally," meaning the Contracting Parties were obligated to implement them "to the fullest extent not inconsistent" with existing national legislation. Article XI contained a general prohibition on quantitative restrictions, although Article XII made an exception in the case of balance of payments safeguards. Article XIX described conditions under which a GATT obligation could be nullified or withdrawn with compensation for trading partners. Many of the other articles dealt with mundane issues such as customs valuation, marks of origin, and other technical matters. Part III of the Agreement contained articles on the functioning of the GATT.

3 What did the GATT accomplish?

In light of the protectionist legacy of the 1930s and the deeply entrenched state regulation of economic activity bequeathed by World War II, the

The GATT's contribution to economic recovery   133

Table 5.1. *Participants at GATT negotiating rounds*

Geneva, 1947

Australia, Belgium, Brazil, Burma, Canada, Ceylon, Chile, China, Cuba, Czechoslovakia, France, India, Lebanon, Luxembourg, the Netherlands, New Zealand, Norway, Pakistan, South Africa, Southern Rhodesia, Syria, the United Kingdom, the United States

Annecy, 1949

Above, plus

Colombia, Denmark, Dominican Republic, Finland, Greece, Haiti, Italy, Liberia, Nicaragua, Sweden, Uruguay

Torquay, 1950–1

Above, plus

Austria, Germany, Guatemala, Korea, Peru, Philippines, Turkey

Note: Not all participants became Contracting Parties to the GATT.
Source: Various GATT publications.

GATT's agenda of trade liberalization and constraints on national discretion in trade policy was quite ambitious. The rules set down for the conduct of commercial policy were stringent, particularly unconditional MFN treatment for GATT members and the general prohibition of quantitative restrictions. There was sufficient latitude within the Agreement, however, to accommodate state behavior at variance with a strict interpretation of GATT rules. Colonial tariff preferences in effect in 1947 were not affected by the MFN requirement, quotas for balance of payments purposes were permitted, and import restrictions on agricultural and fisheries products were sanctioned. Gaining fuller adherence to all GATT rules by members was not immediately achieved and could only come with time – indeed, it has yet to be attained even today.

   But the most pressing objective of the GATT was to oversee the reduction of import tariffs, and it was here that the GATT could make an important contribution to European recovery. These reductions took place over a series of negotiating rounds, three of which were held in the crucial, early post-war period.

First round: Geneva, Switzerland, April–October 1947

The Geneva negotiations in advance of the ITO's formation were motivated in part by the expiry of US presidential negotiating authority in June 1948. In 1945, Congress renewed the Reciprocal Trade Agreements Act of 1934 for three additional years and permitted the president to reduce US tariffs up to 50 percent in reciprocal agreements. The pending expiration of this negotiating authority put pressure on international negotiators to conclude a preliminary agreement with the United States on reducing tariffs. Consequently, twenty-three participating countries that accounted for roughly 80 percent of world trade successfully agreed to cut and bind tariffs in negotiations held from April to October 1947, with the tariff reductions designed to enter into effect in January 1948 for most countries.

The first several GATT rounds consisted of *bilateral* tariff negotiations on a product-by-product basis under the principle of "reciprocal mutual advantage" and the principal-supplier rule. In preparation for the negotiations, countries would exchange lists of "requests" for tariff modifications on various products. Each country would consider a request for such a tariff "concession" on a given product only from the "principal supplier" of that product in exchange for a reduction in the principal supplier's tariff on another item of interest to the country. Under the "reciprocal mutual advantage" principle, no country would be forced to make any unilateral concessions. If a bilateral agreement was reached, the tariff reduction would then be "generalized," i.e., applied in an MFN fashion to all other GATT participants. Other countries would thus benefit from the tariff reduction, but it was up to the major supplier to a particular market to ensure that a given tariff in that market would be reduced. Thus, the GATT harnessed export interests in the negotiations to create the impetus for lower tariffs.

In the first Geneva round in 1947, according to the GATT (1949, p. 11), the twenty-three countries made not less than 123 agreements covering 45,000 tariff items that related to approximately one-half of world trade. The tariff reductions were certainly not across the board or applied to import-sensitive sectors, such as agriculture, but concentrated on sectors that lacked the political strength to absolve them from consideration. Unfortunately, there is no convenient data on the precise depth of the tariff cuts of the Contracting Parties. The United States, however, calculated that the average cut in its tariff from existing levels amounted to 35 percent, as discussed in Finger (1979). As it is generally acknowledged that the United States made the deepest tariff cuts, this is probably the upper bound for the overall tariff reductions of European countries. The scaling down of the US tariff was important for Western Europe because greater access to the US market enabled these countries to earn scarce dollar reserves, which could then be used to purchase US capital goods and other imports. To place an order of magnitude on the value of these tariff concessions would be a difficult exercise, but the United States deserves credit for taking the first and largest step on the road to lower tariffs and for providing the leadership that led to the GATT.

The Contracting Parties agreed that the tariff reductions negotiated at Geneva should remain in place for at least three years, until January 1, 1951. Thus the GATT provided some protection or safeguard against the nullification or impairment of these tariff "concessions" made in Geneva. This binding applied only to tariff concessions made in the Geneva negotiations, however, and other tariffs could be adjusted freely.

Second round: Annecy, France, April 1949–October 1949

The primary purpose of the Annecy negotiations was to allow the accession of eleven other countries – listed in table 5.1 – to the GATT as Contracting Parties. The original twenty-three members did not exchange tariff concessions with each other but did negotiate with the eleven new members of the GATT, and these tariff changes were generalized. This widened the geographic scope of GATT membership and provided for a marginal reduction in tariff levels.

Third round: Torquay, England, September 1950–April 1951

The third GATT round saw the original Contracting Parties again exchanging tariff concessions among themselves along with several new members acceding to the GATT, most importantly the Federal Republic of Germany. But the additional tariff reductions emerging from these negotiations were modest, and the round was not considered a success. The official communiqué, cited in Diebold (1952b, p. 229), announced that the agreements were not "of such scope and magnitude as to represent a sufficient contribution to the reduction of existing disparities in the level of European tariffs." And the GATT (1952, p. 9) later stated that "the results of Torquay were not as broad or as extensive as some had hoped," with only 144 agreements reached out of an expected 400. Adding to the impression of failure was the announcement during the negotiations by President Truman that the ITO would not be sent to the Congress, thereby effectively killing the prospective institution.

The Torquay round ran into two problems that accounted for much of this failure: a dispute between the United States and the United Kingdom, and the growing disparity of tariff levels within Europe. The continuing dollar shortage in Europe prompted the United Kingdom to request unilateral tariff cuts by the United States, which the United States rejected on the grounds of the reciprocal mutual benefit criteria. For its part the United States sought elimination or substantial reduction of tariff preferences within the British Commonwealth. After failures to find common ground, the United Kingdom agreed to reduce the preference margin only slightly so both sides could claim success in the negotiations, but neither side compromised significantly and there were no bilateral tariff cuts on US–UK trade. The failure of both countries to agree on tariff concessions meant that others would not benefit indirectly from their generalization. According to Koch (1969, p. 71), "this attitude unfavorably affected countries that would have reaped indirect benefits from such tariff cuts and made them cautious about granting concessions in their own negotiations."

Also during the Torquay negotiations, the Benelux and Scandinavian countries argued that a new negotiating approach on tariffs was needed because the bargaining power of the low-tariff countries was limited and the GATT was not proving effective in reducing the tariffs of the high-tariff countries. The GATT charter stated that "the binding against increases of low duties or of duty-free treatment shall, in principle, be recognized as a concession equivalent in value to the substantial reduction of high duties or the elimination of tariff preferences." But adherence to this statement was not enforceable in practice because of the reciprocal mutual advantage provision.

In September 1951, several countries proposed to drop the bilateral, product-by-product method of GATT in favor of a broader approach to liberalization. The "GATT Plan" – put to the Contracting Parties in 1953 with the support of Belgium, Denmark, France, West Germany, and the Netherlands – called for a 30 percent weighted-average reduction in tariffs to be phased in over three years. Tariffs were divided into product categories – raw materials, food, semi-processed goods, and industrial goods – and tariff rates were capped at mandated ceilings. The plan elicited little enthusiasm from the United States and the United Kingdom, which had both become resistant to further liberalization. The GATT plan as a multilateral approach lay dormant through the 1950s, although it became the method to eliminate tariffs within the European Economic Community and was applied with great success in the Kennedy round of the 1960s.

One positive result from Torquay was that all tariff reductions from the Geneva and Annecy rounds were renewed and extended until 1954 (and later extended again until the end of the 1950s). Before the rebinding of tariffs there was a brief window in which concessions could be moderated or withdrawn, but there were only a few minor instances of countries invoking this provision.

Widespread pessimism and frustration with the GATT process marked the end of the Torquay round. After a fruitful negotiating round in 1947 and a membership expansion in 1949, the GATT's momentum had suddenly stalled very early in the post-war recovery. After the difficulties at Torquay, more than five years elapsed before the next GATT conference, and that one (in Geneva in 1956) produced similarly meager results. GATT membership also stagnated: in January 1952, the GATT had thirty-four Contracting Parties that accounted for over 80 percent of world trade, but from 1952 to 1957, GATT membership increased by only one country on net, with the withdrawal of Liberia being balanced by the accession of Japan and Uruguay. The momentum toward lower tariffs was lost; further progress on reduced trade barriers had stalled.

Intransigence on both sides of the Atlantic accounted for the faltering of the GATT. On the one hand, "an important factor [behind the passivity during this period] was the growing protectionism in the United States . . . there was a feeling that the United States had given away concessions without any real corresponding benefit, as the European countries were slow in eliminating their discrimination against dollar goods," writes Koch (1969, pp. 82, 84). On the European side, the United Kingdom refused to dismantle colonial preferences, and the low-tariff countries were frustrated by their inability to bargain effectively with high-tariff countries.

Thus, by 1951 the GATT was at a crossroads. The multilateral effort to reduce tariffs progressively was locked in a stalemate that continued through much of the 1950s. It is doubtful that an ITO, with its multifaceted agenda, could have expedited this process; indeed, things may have proceeded more slowly under an ITO owing to the greater complexity of the issues it was designed to address. The pause in GATT activity reflected the transatlantic wrangle over the future course of trade negotiations, and a shift toward regional concerns where common objectives and interests were more readily apparent. Consequently, the GATT remained largely inactive in the 1950s while a European program of trade liberalization proceeded under the auspices of the Organization for European Economic Cooperation and the European Economic Community. Not until the Dillon and Kennedy rounds in 1961–2 and 1964–7 did the GATT return as the forum for a significant attempt at world trade liberalization. Thus, if the GATT had an impact on the immediate post-war economic recovery in Europe, it would come as a result of its accomplishments in the late 1940s.

So what were the major GATT achievements and shortcomings?

TARIFF REDUCTIONS
The major achievement of the GATT was the extensive tariff reductions in the first negotiating round in Geneva. Unfortunately, as already noted, the

138   *Douglas A. Irwin*

Table 5.2. *Average tariff levels in select countries (in percent)*

	1913	1925	1927	1931	1952
Belgium	6	7	11	17	n.a.
France	14	9	23	38	19
Germany	12	15	24	40	16
Italy	17	16	27	48	24
Netherlands	2	4	n.a.	n.a.	n.a.
United Kingdom	n.a.	4	n.a.	17	17
United States	32	26	n.a.	n.a.	16

Note: Not all years are comparable.
Sources: Calculations for 1913 and 1925 are from the League of Nations as
reported in GATT (1953), p. 62, also the source for the 1952 GATT
calculation. For 1927 and 1931 tariff data, see Liepmann (1938), p. 415, and
Kitson and Solomou (1990), pp. 65–6, for the United Kingdom in 1932.

extent of these tariff reductions is extremely difficult to quantify. The GATT
itself refused to calculate the actual reductions for fear that they could be
used by import-sensitive business interests to slow the liberalization
process. Table 5.2 presents the sole official GATT calculation of tariff levels
in major Western European countries for the year 1952, along with
estimates from earlier years. The GATT figures did not include a
calculation of tariff levels in 1947, just before the Geneva cuts went into
effect, but a comparison with prewar (i.e., 1925) tariff levels suggest that
tariffs were much lower in the United States and in Scandinavia by 1952 but
remained higher in the United Kingdom, France, and Germany.

What the United States actually conceded in the GATT negotiating
rounds is overstated by this calculation, however, because a significant
amount of trade liberalization took place from 1934 to 1947 under the
Reciprocal Trade Agreements Act. According to Lavergne (1983, pp. 32–3),
these agreements cut tariffs by 44 percent on over 60 percent of US trade (by
value), amounting to a 33.2 percent reduction in duties overall and leaving
duties at 66.8 percent of their level in 1930. The first GATT round in
Geneva reduced duties by 35.0 percent on just over 50 percent of all
dutiable imports, making the overall tariff reduction 21.1 percent and
leaving the US tariff at 52.7 percent of its 1930 level. The Annecy and
Torquay rounds cut tariffs on less than 12 percent of trade and barely made
a mark on US duties overall.

While questions remain about the extent of the tariff cuts among
European countries, there is also considerable uncertainty about the effects
of the tariff cuts on trade. Because quantitative restraints and foreign
exchange restrictions remained in place, it is not clear that the tariff

reductions translated into more open market access in Europe. The US market was demonstrably more open because the country never resorted to quotas on manufactured goods, but European imports from the United States were hampered by dollar restrictions. Even within the European market trade was hampered by exchange controls and other restrictions.

For this reason, the tariff cuts from the Geneva and subsequent negotiations may have had limited effect. One early study of the impact of GATT concessions by Lawrence Krause (1959, p. 555) found that "such tariff reductions as those given by the US at Torquay do not lead to a significant increase in the volume of imports." However, the initial ineffectiveness of the tariff reductions – particularly for European countries – may have diminished over time as other forms of liberalization took place over the 1950s. As the GATT (1952, p. 8, emphasis added) itself recognized, "the cumulative effect of the three post-war tariff conferences will permit an expanding volume of trade at more moderate levels of customs duties, *particularly when quantitative restrictions on imports are removed.*"

Indeed, the Geneva tariff cuts may have been larger than otherwise politically possible because they were viewed as initially neutralized by quantitative and foreign exchange restrictions. As Curzon (1965, p. 70) explains, "countries believing that quantitative restrictions would be a permanent feature of the post-war world gave sham but very substantial reductions on their tariff rates in exchange for real reductions from the only country not to apply quotas on manufactured goods, i.e., the United States." "As quotas and discriminatory use of import licensing fade, ultimately vanish, the concessions exchanged at Geneva . . . will acquire real substance," argued the *Economist* (April 23, 1949, p. 757). In this respect, the initial tariff concessions may have been larger than countries had anticipated, and with time – toward the end of the 1950s – their impact on trade may have become apparent. One could speculate that the GATT cut tariffs so significantly that it hindered efforts to eliminate quantitative and foreign exchange restrictions, but this contention lacks supporting evidence.

TARRIF BINDINGS

Each Contracting Party was bound to the terms of the GATT indefinitely, including any tariff concessions that became embodied in the annexes to Article II. While tariff concessions once given were considered fixed in perpetuity, countries retained the right to invoke Article XXVIII, which allowed them to revoke tariff concessions after negotiating an agreement with the principal supplier or after accepting the withdrawal of equivalent concessions from other countries. This article thus contained a mechanism by which the negotiated tariff cuts could be unraveled by mutual agreements.

To ensure the continuity and integrity of the Geneva cuts and provide for a measure of tariff stability that had been absent in the interwar period, the Contracting Parties at Geneva ruled out the right to invoke Article XXVIII for three years, i.e., until 1951. At the Torquay negotiations this period of "firm validity" was extended through 1954 and was later extended again through 1957. Each time the period of "firm validity" was extended, a short window was offered to countries to modify their tariffs as allowed in Article XXVIII, but only minor withdrawals and modifications were taken by a very few countries. Although reluctant to march toward further trade liberalization, countries at least recognized the gains from preventing an erosion of the early GATT successes. Freezing the right to resort to Article XXVIII ensured that the initial tariff cuts under the GATT would be preserved throughout the 1950s even if no further progress was made in lowering tariffs and even as import quotas were being phased out. This may have been one of the GATT's major contributions to promoting economic recovery in Western Europe – ruling out for an extended period reliance on tariffs to replace other trade barriers that were falling.

NON-DISCRIMINATION

Article I of the GATT makes unconditional most-favored-nation treatment a cornerstone of the Agreement. The major exception was for preferential tariff policies in effect in 1947, which included the United Kingdom (the Commonwealth), the United States (Cuba and the Philippines), and France and the Benelux countries (their colonies), although the Contracting Parties agreed not to increase or establish new preferences. Only British Commonwealth preference persisted as a major issue, and in the first Geneva GATT negotiations the United States and the United Kingdom wrangled over the preferences. The UK adamantly refused to bend to US opposition to these preferences, but a compromise in which preference margins were reduced defused the issue temporarily. The US failure to achieve its long-held goal of eliminating the Commonwealth tariff preferences was never achieved.

Indeed, it soon became clear that a host of discriminatory policies in Europe would exist outside the GATT purview, as Finger (1993) has described. The members of the Organization for European Economic Cooperation (OEEC), for example, began an effort to stimulate intra-European trade by eliminating license, quota, and exchange restrictions as they affected each other. Although this technically violated the GATT's MFN provision, the US not merely acquiesced but encouraged this program as part of its policy to strengthen Europe. Koch (1969, p. 116) notes that "the OEEC policy was tacitly accepted without any waiver being asked for" and, subsequently, the GATT has not posed as a barrier to discriminatory policies of this sort.

QUANTITATIVE RESTRICTIONS

For achievements on the tariff front to be fully realized, they needed to be matched by advances in the removal of quantitative restrictions (QRs). Article XI contains a general commitment of GATT members not to use QRs on trade. Article XIV, however, provides an exception in the case of the "post-war transition period" and Article XII permits the limited use of QRs in the context of short-term balance of payments problems. Their use for this reason came principally under the domain of the IMF and this justification remained viable into the 1950s. QRs were not even the subject of negotiation during the first three GATT rounds and indeed did not come under GATT negotiations until the Dillon round of 1961–2.

In 1950, with the stalled Torquay round in process, the major Western European countries in the Organization for European Economic Cooperation agreed to a Code of Liberalization that set a timetable for the gradual elimination of QRs on intra-European trade. Discrimination continued against hard-currency countries such as the United States, but the OEEC achieved considerable success in freeing Europe's trade from QRs. The OEEC countries originally agreed to remove all quota restrictions on 50 percent of their imports in 1949, and the formal Code established targets of 60 percent in 1950 and 75 percent in 1951. Although some backsliding occurred in Germany in 1951 and in the United Kingdom and France in 1952, owing to balance of payments difficulties and an economic downturn, respectively, table 5.3 shows that this reversal proved temporary.

The OEEC program of progressively eliminating intra-European trade barriers, described in more detail by Boyer and Sallé (1955), provided a distinct boost to European trade. Figure 5.3 illustrates the volume of OEEC exports to OEEC countries and to other countries. Intra-European trade grew in step with Europe's worldwide trade in 1947–9, but with the relaxation of quota restrictions in 1949–50, intra-European export volume jumped significantly above overall export volume. When further headway was made against QRs from 1953, intra-European trade again grew more rapidly than overall trade. The OEEC's great success paved the way for the creation of a Common Market later in the decade.

Thus, significant progress on a key aspect of liberalizing trade came not from the GATT but from other European institutions. According to Koch (1969, p. 144), "The fact cannot be denied that OEEC contributed to a substantial relaxation of controls on intra-European trade in a period when the members of the OEEC felt that there was little prospect of getting results

Table 5.3. *Liberalization of intra-OEEC trade, 1950–5 (percent, by end of year)*

	1950	1951	1952	1953	1954	1955
France	66	76	0	18	65	78
Germany	63	0	81	90	90	91
Italy	76	77	100	100	100	99
Netherlands	66	71	75	87	88	96
United Kingdom	86	61	44	75	83	85

Source: OEEC (1958).

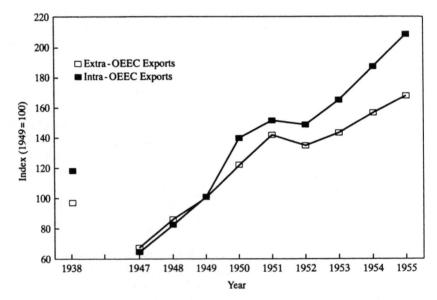

Figure 5.3   Post-war OEEC export volume
Source: OEEC (1956), p. 69.

in the GATT." Yet the GATT was not entirely moot on the QR question. As she also points out (ibid.), "the [GATT] system of consultations led to constant pressure on member countries to motivate and defend their restrictive measures. . . . Even if convertibility and economic expansion had been a contributory factor in the process of dismantling quantitative restrictions on industrial goods, there is no doubt that at a later stage GATT consultations were an important factor."

ASSESSMENT

The impression is often given that the GATT, since its formation, has made consistent and incremental progress on trade liberalization. A re-examination of its first decade illustrates that this progress came quickly in the late 1940s and then languished for some time. Indeed, the GATT experienced many shortcomings during its first decade – tariff cutting was rather limited, preferences and other discriminatory practices were not eradicated, and import quotas were not abolished and fell outside its jurisdiction. In retrospect, the initial achievements of the GATT appear somewhat modest in light of its success in the Kennedy round in the 1960s and thereafter. The GATT diminished tariffs at its founding conference in 1947, but the climate for further substantial reductions was not evident thereafter. In terms of concrete actions, the best that can be said for the GATT after 1947 is that it established non-discrimination as the presumption for the conduct of trade relations and, perhaps more importantly, that it held the line on the temptation for countries to substitute higher tariffs for liberalized quotas under the OEEC program.

The principal, initial effects of the GATT may lie in the important but nebulous areas of credibility and commitment. That is, individuals and firms may be more willing to engage in trade if they suspect that governments are committed to certain tariff rates – a stable trading environment – and the outlook promises further, if uneven, progress on trade liberalization. The GATT gained some measure of credibility by virtue of its early agreement to reduce tariffs and expand membership. In sharp contrast to the frequent government proclamations in favor of freer trade during the interwar period, proclamations that were left hanging with no concrete action whatsoever, negotiators within the GATT actually secured and implemented an agreement to reduce tariffs just two years after the end of World War II. The GATT Contracting Parties demonstrated some commitment to this outcome by not allowing tariff concessions to expire, thereby avoiding the need to renegotiate trade agreements frequently, which had created problems for pre-World War I tariff treaties, described in Irwin (1993). The interwar period was marked by the absence of any credible move toward trade liberalization or any demonstration of commitment to that objective, although the effect of these features of the GATT regime on economic performance cannot be ascertained in a precise way.

4 European trade under the GATT: a comparison with the post-World War I experience

Despite what appears to have been very limited initial achievements, especially in light of subsequent trade liberalization, the GATT did make a firm break with interwar commercial policies and set world trade policies on a new path. And the outcome of the post-World War II period, in terms of recovery in economic activity and international trade, has never been viewed as anything but a great success exactly because in the decade following the war Europe managed to avoid the interwar catastrophe. The fact that this happened under the GATT's stewardship means that the institution itself stands to credit. But a closer comparison of the behavior of European trade and income during these two periods may shed light on what the GATT (and the OEEC) helped to accomplish.

Figures 5.1 and 5.2 depict the evolution of export volume and real income (weighted by GNP) for a sample of five Western European countries – France, Germany, Italy, the Netherlands, and the United Kingdom – using data from appendices A and F of Maddison (1991). Figure 5.1 presents exports in the twelve years after the armistice (1918–29) and after Germany's surrender (1946–57). Figure 5.2 shows real income over the same period. Both figures also indicate the relevant prewar level of exports and income – 1913 before World War I and 1938 before World War II. In the dozen years after World War I, incomes doubled and exports nearly quadrupled. In the dozen years after World War II, incomes almost tripled and exports grew eight-fold. Clearly, the post-World War II expansion was significantly greater than that after World War I. While it took seven years (to 1924) for European incomes after 1918 to match their prewar level, just four years after World War II (to 1949) incomes reached their 1938 level. Exports after World War I matched their prewar peak in eleven years (to 1928), while after World War II it took just six years (to 1951) for exports to surpass their 1938 level.

Yet the tremendous increase in export volume after World War II may reflect nothing other than this more rapid increase in income – owing perhaps to favorable macroeconomic factors rather than the GATT – and the underlying relationship between trade and income could have remained similar during the two periods. But econometric evidence points to substantial differences in the relationship between trade and income in the two post-war periods. Concerns about spurious correlation because of common trends rule out any regression of the levels of export volume and real income variables alone, so consider the following error-correction model which includes the variables in both levels and differenced terms:

$$\Delta x_t = \beta_1 \Delta y_t + (\alpha - 1)\{x_{t-1} - \gamma_1 y_{t-1} - \gamma_0\} + \varepsilon_t,$$

where x_t is the log of export volume and y_t is the log of real income. This equation relates the change in exports to the change in income and a lagged deviation of the long-run association of the two variables. This reflects both the short- and long-run interaction of the variables: the differenced terms capture the short-run impact of a change in income on the change in export volume; the error-correction mechanism, expressed in levels, allows exports to return to their long-run value (because $\alpha - 1 < 0$). The long-run relationship is based on $x_t = v_0 + v_1 y_t + v_2 y_{t-1} + \alpha x_{t-1} + \xi_t$, a structure sufficient to ensure that ξ_t is white noise, and errors from the long-run solution are defined as $z_t = x_t - \gamma_1 y_t - \gamma_0$, where $\gamma_1 = (v_1 + v_2)/(1 - \alpha)$, which is the long-run elasticity of trade with respect to income, and $\gamma_0 = v_0/(1 - \alpha)$. Subtracting x_{t-1} from this equation and noting that $z_t = (1 - \alpha)x_t - (v_1 + v_2)y_t - v_0$ yields the error-correction model.

To ascertain the short- and long-run impact of an increase in income on the volume of exports, the model is estimated using OLS for the periods 1919–29 and 1947–57 with a sample of five major West European economies (France, Germany, Italy, the Netherlands, and the United Kingdom) using Maddison's (1991) data. The estimation yields the following results (standard errors in parenthesis):

1919–29

$$\Delta x_t = 1.94\Delta y_t - 0.66\{x_{t-1} - 1.53 y_{t-1} + 1.52\}$$
$$\quad\;\;(0.73)\qquad(0.30)\qquad\;\;(0.34)\qquad\;(1.59)$$
$$R^2 = 0.88 \qquad F = 30.9 \qquad \sigma = 6.4\% \qquad DW = 3.02$$

1947–57

$$\Delta x_t = 1.40\Delta y_t - 0.63\{x_{t-1} - 2.33 y_{t-1} + 5.49\}$$
$$\quad\;\;(0.66)\qquad(0.10)\qquad\;\;(0.29)\qquad\;(1.54)$$
$$R^2 = 0.90 \qquad F = 34.2 \qquad \sigma = 5.2\% \qquad DW = 2.60.$$

Although they must be interpreted with caution because of the short sample period, the results nonetheless provide some useful insights into the behavior of trade and income over the two post-war periods. The short-run impact of a change in real income was associated with a much larger increase in trade after World War I than after World War II – 1.94 percent as opposed to 1.40 percent. However, the long-run elasticity of trade with respect to income (γ_1) was substantially greater in the post-World War II era (2.33) than in the interwar period (1.53). These long-run relationships are sufficiently distinct from one another to suggest a much greater responsiveness of trade to rising income after World War II than after World War I. Furthermore, the long-run elasticity is greater than the short-run elasticity after World War II, indicating that the effect of income on trade grew with time instead of overshooting and reverting to a lower mean.

Unfortunately, the econometric results are incompletely informative about the underlying source of the difference in the trade and income relationship after the two wars. It could well be that the mere presence of the GATT – in stabilizing tariffs and committing countries to the path of trade liberalization – spurred a more rapid increase in trade than seen after World War I, but alternative hypotheses are also consistent with the evidence and cannot be dismissed. Other post-war institutions aiming at international monetary stability, for example, may have fostered an environment that was conducive to international exchange, or domestic economic policies that were absent after World War I may have triggered the greater trade response.

Another plausible explanation for the greater trade responsiveness to income after World War II was that a catch-up or convergence process in trade-to-GNP ratios was taking place. In the Western economies that later comprised the Organization for Economic Cooperation and Development (OECD), according to Maddison (1989, p. 143), the ratio of merchandise exports to GDP at current prices stood at 21.2 percent in 1913. This ratio fell to 18.9 percent in 1929 as a result of World War I, and fell further to 15.1 percent in 1950 as a result of the depression and wartime disruptions. Consequently, there was ample room for international trade to be restored to a higher share of economic activity as normal, peacetime patterns of trade returned. Indeed, through the 1950s and 1960s the ratio gradually moved back to over 20 percent, where it had been in 1913. In any case, the fact remains that trade grew faster after World War II than after World War I not simply because incomes grew faster, but because the underlying relationship between the two had changed. And trade liberalization under the GATT and the OEEC provides one conceivable explanation for this outcome.

These equations, which suggest that growth in trade arose from increases in real income, raise the related question of whether real income can truly be viewed as the exogenous, driving variable. An obvious alternative hypothesis, suggested by Bhagwati (1988) for example, is that expanding international trade led to higher real income after World War II. These regressions cannot even begin to address such complex, dynamic relationships between trade and income, but Irwin (1992) reports Hausman tests on similar regressions with a larger sample of countries and a longer sample period which indicate that, for econometric purposes, income is not endogenous with respect to trade and that a channel runs more distinctly from income to trade than from trade to income. This should not be interpreted as saying that trade had no effects on economic growth, but that these effects are more subtle than can be identified in annual, aggregate time-series data.

Furthermore, in a stark macroeconomic accounting sense, real net exports were a secondary contributor to rising real income in the early post-war period. Table 5.4 shows that real net exports never accounted for much more than a percentage point of economic growth in the OEEC

Table 5.4. *Sources of growth in OEEC's real national product, 1948–55 (percentage point contribution to change in GNP)*

Year	National expenditure	Net exports	Gross national product
1948	4.2	3.3	7.5
1949	6.1	1.2	7.3
1950	6.1	1.1	7.2
1951	6.2	−0.7	5.5
1952	1.9	1.0	2.9
1953	5.2	0.3	5.5
1954	4.9	−0.2	4.7
1955	6.0	0.0	6.0

Source: Calculated from the OEEC (1957), p. 39.

countries (essentially all of Western Europe) and that domestic demand was the primary source of expansion. Yet the notable exception to this pattern is in 1948, the year in which the GATT tariff cuts first took effect, when net exports amounted to 3.3 percentage points of the 7.5 percent increase in the GNP of the OEEC countries. This may have been just part of the economic recovery from 1946 to 1947, but if the GATT actually made a contribution to this figure then post-war economic growth could have been even more rapid had the movement toward lower tariffs not stalled after about 1950.

5 The GATT's contribution: a tentative assessment

One is left with tremendous uncertainty about the precise role of the GATT in promoting economic recovery in Western Europe in the first decade after the war. Its role was almost surely secondary to sound domestic macro-economic and microeconomic policies. After all, the GATT did not achieve much for an entire decade after the 1947 tariff cuts and the 1949 membership expansion. These initial tariff cuts did not fully take hold until other trade restrictions were eliminated over the course of the 1950s. And the trade liberalization of the 1950s that was of substantial importance took place outside of the GATT. The OEEC program of rolling back quantitative restrictions on intra-European trade, the Treaty of Rome and the elimination of tariffs within the European Economic Community, the unilateral liberalization by several countries – most notably West Germany, which in 1956 and 1957 cut its tariffs by 25 percent each year – all these efforts complemented the GATT's objectives but did not originate from the institution itself.

But a rather modest contribution of the GATT is probably to be found in two subtle but highly useful influences. First, the GATT set standards for state behavior, which – even if far from being met initially – at least created a reference point about the direction in which trade policies should be heading. The architects of the post-war economic system agreed that trade policy should be conducted on an open and non-discriminatory basis; by giving this objective an institutional basis they possibly prevented a drift in economic policy away from the principles embodied in the GATT. Second, while tariff cutting may have had no immediate effect in the immediate post-war environment, as the myriad of quotas and other restrictions on trade were gradually dismantled through the 1950s, the GATT ensured that countries could not substitute higher tariffs for these measures as their economies became more open to world markets.

The GATT, in other words, held the line on tariffs and did not allow them to undermine reforms elsewhere. For an *ad hoc* institution that was never designed to exist on its own, for an institution with no independent power and no financial resources or lending capability to ensure compliance to its rules, this was a notable achievement. This achievement came from a remarkably small organization which was largely dedicated to a single purpose. By concentrating its effort almost exclusively on tariffs, the GATT did not spread its scarce resources or political capital too thinly or lose sight of its main objective. One can speculate that this structure may have enabled it to be more effective than the ITO, whose multifaceted agenda and potentially sprawling bureaucracy might have proved an impediment to real action. The role of Eric Wyndham White, the first director of the GATT, in ensuring the survival of the institution during the dark days of the 1950s so that it could see another, better day, should also not be left unmentioned.

If one is looking for the proximate cause for the economic recovery in Western Europe during the decade or so after 1945, the GATT is probably not the first or even the second place to look. Taking the several decades of post-war economic growth into one's perspective, however, it is hard not to attribute some role to the GATT, conceding at the very least that it served as an effective supporting actor. By setting standards and holding the line on tariffs as other trade restrictions were lifted, the GATT was not geared or positioned to provide a quick boost to GNP but was more akin to a long-term investment with a long-term payoff. This payoff may not have been fully realized until the late 1950s when European currency convertibility had been restored and tariffs as trade barriers again mattered most.

Then the stage was set for a major advance against tariffs which came with the Kennedy round negotiations of 1964–7, when the GATT fulfilled the promise the architects of the post-war economic order had envisioned.

References

Bhagwati, Jagdish (1988), *Protectionism*, Cambridge, Mass.: MIT Press.

Boyer, F. and J.P. Sallé (1955), "The Liberalization of Intra-European Trade in the Framework of the OEEC," *Staff Papers*, 4 (February): 179–216.

Curzon, Gerard (1965), *Multilateral Commercial Diplomacy: The General Agreement on Tariffs and Trade and Its Impact on National Commercial Policies and Techniques*, London: Joseph.

Diebold, William Jr. (1952a), "The End of the ITO," *Essays in International Finance*, no. 16, International Finance Section, Department of Economics, Princeton University.

(1952b), *Trade and Payments in Western Europe: A Study in Economic Cooperation, 1947–51*, New York: Harper and Row.

Finger, J.M. (1979), "Trade Liberalization: A Public Choice Perspective," in Ryan C. Amacher, Gottfried Haberler, and Thomas D. Willett (eds.), *Challenges to a Liberal International Economic Order*, Washington: American Enterprise Institute, pp. 421–453.

(1993), "GATT's Influence on Regional Arrangements," in J. de Melo and A. Panagariya (eds.), *New Dimensions in Regional Integration*, New York: Cambridge University Press, 128–158.

General Agreement on Tariffs and Trade (1949), "The Attack on Trade Barriers," A Progress Report on the Operation of the GATT, January 1948 – August 1949, Geneva.

(1950), "Liberating World Trade," 2nd Report on the Operation of the GATT, Geneva.

(1952), "GATT in Action," 3rd Report on the Operation of the GATT, Geneva.

(1953), "International Trade, 1952," Geneva.

Irwin, Douglas A. (1992), "Long-Run Trends in World Trade and World Output," unpublished manuscript, University of Chicago.

(1993), "Multilateral and Bilateral Trade Liberalization in the World Trading System: An Historical Perspective," in J. de Melo and A. Panagariya (eds.), *New Dimensions in Regional Integration*, New York: Cambridge University Press, pp. 90–118.

Kitson, Michael and Solomos Solomou (1990), *Protectionism and Economic Revival: The British Interwar Economy*, Cambridge University Press.

Koch, Karin (1969), *International Trade Policy and the GATT, 1947–1967*, Stockholm: Almquist and Wiksell.

Krause, Lawrence B. (1959), "United States Imports and the Tariff," *American Economic Review*, 49 (May): 542–51.

Lavergne, Real P. (1983), *The Political Economy of US Tariffs: An Empirical Analysis*, New York: Academic Press.

150   *Douglas A. Irwin*

Liepmann, Heinrich (1938), *Tariff Levels and the Economic Unity of Europe*, New York: Macmillan.

Maddison, Angus (1989), *The World Economy in the 20th Century*, Paris: OECD.
(1991), *Dynamic Forces in Capitalist Development*, New York: Oxford University Press.

Organization for European Economic Co-operation (1956), *Statistical Bulletin*, no. 4, July, Paris.
(1957), *Statistics of National Product and Expenditure*, no. 2, 1938 and 1947–1955, Paris.
(1958), "A Decade of Cooperation: Achievements and Prospects," 9th Annual Report, Paris, April.

Part II
War and Peace

[6]

Wars, Blockade, and Economic Change in Europe, 1792-1815*

THE wars which raged almost continuously from 1792 to 1815 and which are generally, but not quite properly, called in English the Napoleonic wars, are the longest period of warfare which Europe has known since the early eighteenth century, and as they took place at a crucial stage of economic development, when the Industrial Revolution had just taken off in England and when its preliminary stirrings were showing in various places of the Continent, their impact upon the growth of industry in Continental Europe was quite serious. Unlike the twentieth-century world wars, the Napoleonic wars were not marked by large-scale physical destruction; though the productive potential of some towns or districts suffered from military operations or civil disturbances, such destruction was quite limited in space and time. On the other hand, most European countries suffered during the wars from bouts of paper-money inflation, which had undoubtedly serious consequences —especially in France during the Revolution, when the working capital of many merchants and manufacturers was destroyed through the combination of a sharp rise in their costs, of price control under the *maximum*, and of payment of government orders in depreciated *assignats*. Also, the diversion of resources to military purposes and the heavy burden of taxation and exactions must not be underestimated.

However, the impact of the wars upon the long-run development of industry, which this paper will try to investigate, was felt mostly through the dislocations in international trade which were brought about by the twenty-year-long conflict between Britain and France and by the progressive involvement of all other European countries in this bitter struggle in which economic warfare played a prominent part. Those trade dislocations were at work during the whole war period and not only during the Continental blockade—which was, of course, the most dramatic episode of the wars from the economic point of view, but which was also only their high-water mark; in fact most of the developments which are often thought of as charac-

* Due to limitations of space, some footnotes to this article had to be omitted. These may be obtained on request from the writer.

teristic of the blockade years (1806-1813) had started much earlier, so that a longer view is needed to set the problem in its proper perspective.

Three main factors worked during the Napoleonic wars toward disturbing traditional trade relations: maritime blockade by the British, "self-blockade" of the Continent imposed by the French, and lastly the large-scale redrafting of Europe's political map. Each of them had its own pattern of consequences for the Continent's industries.

I

First the British, thanks to their superior sea power, imposed upon the seaborne trade of Continental countries which were at war with them a number of restrictions which caused the decline and eventually the almost complete interruption of their seaborne trade; this led to serious difficulties and even to a complete and lasting collapse of the large sector of Continental industry which was dependent upon overseas trade.

The eighteenth century can be truly called the Atlantic stage of European economic development. Foreign trade, and especially trade with the Americas, was the most dynamic sector of the whole economy (for instance, French colonial trade increased tenfold between 1716 and 1787), and furthermore the demand from overseas markets was stimulating the growth of a wide range of industries as well as increased specialization and division of labor. Owing to the superiority of sea transport over land transport, the eighteenth-century European economy was organized around a number of big seaports, the most prosperous being those with the largest share in the growing colonial trade, such as Bordeaux or Nantes; each of these had, not only its own industries, but also its industrial hinterland in the river basin of which it was the outlet. For instance, Bordeaux had shipbuilding yards, sugar refineries, distilleries, tobacco factories, and glassworks, while along the Garonne and its tributaries were to be found industries such as sail and rope making, foundries making guns for West Indiamen and boilers for sugar mills, manufactures of linens for slaves and woolens for planters, as well as cornmills producing fine flour for export to the West Indies. The seaboard provinces of France were undoubtedly the most industrialized in the eighteenth century, but the influence of the great seaports penetrated far into the interior; for instance,

Wars, Blockade, and Change   **569**

Pierre Léon has shown how much the industries of a landlocked province such as Dauphiné were also interested in the West India trade. And if this "Americanization" of trade and industry was the most pronounced for countries which owned a colonial empire (such as Britain, France, Holland, and Spain), its influence extended also farther to the east, to countries which had no colonies but were able to send goods to America as reexports from the colonial powers, especially through Cadiz; so German linens, cutlery, and hardware reached the West Indian and Spanish-American markets. And the growing demand for colonial produce and for raw materials used for shipbuilding stimulated seaborne trade and production for export along the whole European seaboard. So the eighteenth-century European economy was outward-looking, ocean oriented, and its most dynamic trading and industrial centers were geared to seaborne trade and American markets.

This "Atlantic" sector was of course bound to suffer whenever relations with America were hampered. This had been experienced during the wars of the eighteenth century; but during the Napoleonic wars, the situation was much worse owing to the more complete mastery of the seas which was achieved by the Royal Navy and to the far longer duration of hostilities.

French colonial trade collapsed quite early in the war, owing mostly to the slave revolt in Santo Domingo which completely ruined "the jewel of the Caribbean"; three quarters of French colonial trade had been with Santo Domingo, and the sudden and complete destruction of such a valuable branch of trade dealt to several French ports and industries blows from which they did not recover. During the early years of the war, other maritime countries profited a good deal from the decline in French (and Dutch) trade and shipping, and ports such as Barcelona (up to 1796), Leghorn, Lisbon, Hamburg, Copenhagen, and later Trieste, enjoyed periods of great prosperity; but their trade booms all came to an abrupt end when these ports were occupied by the French or when their governments sided with France against England.[1] Still, up to 1807, most enemy ports were not put by the British under rigorous blockade and they could go on trading under neutral flags; though direct relations between enemy ports and their colonies were forbidden

---

[1] No significant industrial development resulted from such temporary trading booms; and if many merchants, in the Hanseatic towns or Trieste, for instance, made money through smuggling activities or speculation, they used such capital after the wars for resuming their traditional trade and not for industrial investment.

by the British government, neutral ships (mostly American) were allowed to carry on an indirect trade by calling at some United States port on their way. So war with England did not cut at once all relations between Continental countries and the Americas or East Indies, but this trade did in fact decrease a good deal (especially exports of manufactured goods, because American ships often went to England for their return cargoes, and so Continental manufacturers lost ground in their own colonies).[2] Eventually such trade came to a complete stop when the British government decided, partly as a retaliation to the Continental blockade but also in order to placate some pressure groups—the West India and shipping interests—to tighten its blockade. In November 1807, Orders in Council prohibited in fact the indirect trade which neutral ships had been carrying between enemy countries and their colonies; an earlier order of January 1807 had forbidden neutrals to trade between enemy ports, thus destroying most of the active international coasting trade, especially between northern and southern Europe. Moreover, the last French and Dutch colonies were soon to be conquered by the British; and when, in 1808, the Spanish colonies sided with the Spanish insurgents against Napoleon, they fell into the economic orbit of England and their markets were lost to their traditional Continental suppliers of manufactured goods.

So in the later years of the Napoleonic wars, from 1807 onward, Continental countries, nearly all of whom had by then sided willy-nilly against England, were subjected to a drastic sea blockade by the British; they were completely cut off from overseas markets and the most valuable part of their seaborne trade was destroyed. Some coasting trade was of course maintained, and the English permitted—even encouraged—relations with Britain herself; but though they were very active at some periods, they were no helpful substitute for Continental industries, because the Continent could export to England only foodstuffs and raw materials.[3]

It is well known that, as a consequence, the great seaports of the Continent, which had been the hubs of its economic life in the

---

[2] In Barcelona, indirect trade with the colonies through neutrals was in 1806 only a third of the direct trade in 1804. In Nantes, ships entering the port and clearing out had in 1806 a total tonnage of 54,000 as against 80,000 in the peace year of 1802. Moreover, trade through neutral ships did not prevent unemployment of national shipping and depression of shipbuilding.

[3] The only exception was German linens, large quantities of which were imported into Britain (and reexported) in 1809-10; American ships were also able to carry them from Tonningen or ports in the Baltic to Latin America.

eighteenth century, were completely crippled from 1807 onwards. Harbors were deserted, grass was growing in the streets,[4] and in large towns like Amsterdam, Bordeaux, and Marseilles, population did actually decrease. However, the collapse of industrial production in the ports and in their hinterland has not been as much noticed. It resulted from the loss of overseas markets and to a lesser degree from the difficulty in obtaining raw materials. In Marseilles, the value of industrial output fell from 50 million francs in 1789 to 12 in 1813.

Among the victims were, of course, shipbuilding and its ancillary industries, such as sail and rope making (Tonneins, east from Bordeaux, had 700 rope makers in 1783, 200 in 1801, none ten years later). Other industries to suffer were those processing imported colonial produce—especially sugar refining (Amsterdam had 80 refineries in 1796, 3 in 1813; Bordeaux 40 before the Revolution, 8 in 1809), also tobacco factories, and tanneries because of the shortage of hides which had been imported from South America. Also affected were industries which had been preparing foodstuffs for overseas markets or for provisioning ships, such as cornmills, distilleries, breweries (in Holland, and glassworks as a consequence), and those for salting, curing, drying, preserving of fish, vegetables, condiments (Marseilles had many such industries and their output fell very low). In Nantes and Hamburg, cotton printing was almost entirely wiped out. However, the most important casualty was the linen industry, which had been very widespread in several Continental countries in the eighteenth century, specially in western France, Flanders, Holland, and Germany. It was an export industry (in the 1780's, Bas-Maine had been exporting two thirds of its output) with its main markets overseas, in the West Indies and in Spanish America, to which large quantities of French and German linens were reexported through Cadix. During the Revolution, French exports to those markets were almost completely stopped, and in Normandy, Brittany, and Maine, output collapsed, falling by as much as two thirds in some districts; there was little recovery under the Empire, owing to the peninsular war; in 1810, Laval

---

4 On March 26, 1808, the American consul at Bordeaux reported, "From the Baltic to the Archipelago nothing but despair and misery is to be seen. Grass is growing in the streets of this city. Its beautiful port is deserted except by two Marblehead fishing schooners and three or four empty vessels which still swing to the tide" (quoted by F. E. Melvin, *Napoleon's Navigation System: A Study of Trade Control during the Continental Blockade* [New York: Appleton, 1919], p. 48).

François Crouzet

was making 18,000 pieces of linens, as against 36,000 in 1789. In Germany, the situation was not so bad, up to 1806-1807, because exports to America went on and may have increased thanks to the fall in French competition; but after that date German linens also lost their overseas markets, and the linen-making districts of Westphalia, Saxony, and Silesia underwent a serious and lasting crisis; exports of linens from Landshut in the Riesengebirge fell from 174,000 *schock* in 1804 to 29,000 in 1811.

This decline of the linen industry (which can be observed also in Holland, Switzerland, and Italy) was of course in accordance with long-term trends in economic development: it was an archaic industry which was doomed anyway and which had already suffered in the eighteenth century from competition by the fast-rising cotton industry. Still there is no doubt that its decline and decay were greatly accelerated by the loss of overseas markets which it suffered during the Napoleonic wars, and the resulting crisis was so sharp that it made impossible for most centers of the industry any successful effort to adapt or to turn to other activities. In such a domestic manufacture, organized according to the putting-out system and with little fixed capital, the merchant-manufacturers were the key men; once they had lost their working capital, the industry was left in a hopeless condition.

The same remarks apply to the various industries which in the ports and in their hinterlands had been making consumption goods for overseas markets. They were of course small-scale industries, with generally an archaic technology, and at that stage they were not very susceptible to technical improvement and fast expansion. However their decline was unfortunate, as it did decrease opportunities for industrial employment and for accumulation of capital which could have been shifted later to more productive industries.

Moreover the "Atlantic" sector of the European economy was not to recover when peace had been restored in 1815. There was of course a revival of traffic in the ports, but even where a fairly high level was attained, most of them had lost their position as international entrepôts and had become mere regional ports. As for their industries, they were relatively far less active. Such was the case, for instance, of Nantes, Bordeaux, Barcelona (P. Vilar writes that its career as a great colonial and international port was over), and Amsterdam, the "general trade" of which did not revive. This was due to a number of reasons, including having lost touch with interna-

Wars, Blockade, and Change   573

tional trade during a period of rapid change and losing therefore the necessary skills, information, and capital; but including also the long-term decline in the importance of the West Indies in the world economy, the ruin of Santo Domingo, and the fact that the Latin American markets were henceforth, and for nearly a century, monopolized by the British, while the United States market had little demand for most of the Continent's traditional exports. These developments can also be considered as inevitable, owing to the technical advance and therefore lower prices of British industry and to superior British commercial organization; in fact, before the war, British manufactures had been infiltrating the Spanish and even the French colonies, indicating that Continental industries had been dependent upon the maintenance of a high wall of protection under the old colonial system. Still, war conditions greatly helped the British to engross overseas markets and made it impossible for Continental industries to adapt fast enough to resist English competition and to regain a foothold in those markets after the peace.

Because of the permanent injury inflicted on many Continental industries by interruption of overseas trade, the war brought about a lasting deindustrialization or pastoralization of large areas (with, in some parts of France and Holland, a definite shift of capital from trade and industry towards agriculture). Seaboard districts failed generally to attract the new industries which developed during the wars, or when some new activities were attracted (like the wool industry in Denmark), they did not strike deep roots and declined after the peace—largely because those districts were outlying parts of a Continental empire at a time when land transportation was most expensive. Such was the case of nearly the whole French seaboard, especially the western and southwestern provinces, and also Languedoc, on the Mediterranean, which had in the eighteenth century an important woolen industry working mostly for the Levant markets; in 1809, a German traveler commented that this industry was unable to modernize, owing to stagnating production, lost markets, and reduced profits. These provinces have been ever since, and still are, much less industrialized than northern and eastern France, and to my mind their relative underdevelopment has one of its major causes in the collapse of their traditional industries during the Napoleonic wars (of course, one has still to explain why they failed to industrialize again after 1815, but this is another story).

In France, this crisis was partly offset by the rise of new industries, but this did not happen in some other countries, such as Spain. There, industry had revived during the eighteenth century, especially in Catalonia, largely to answer the growing colonial demand; it was prosperous up to 1796, stagnated during the next twelve years, and collapsed in 1808; the loss of the colonial empire—and the devastation during the struggle against Napoleon—destroyed a vital part in the economic mechanism and worked towards a lasting pastoralization of the country. In Portugal, there was some industrial progress up to 1806, mostly to supply the Brazilian market; but this was lost to the British in 1808, and in 1811, over one third of industrial establishments were described as in a state of decay or closed. In Holland, the wars did not promote any significant industrial growth, while not only the "port industries," but the manufacturing of woolens in Leyden, of silks, and of earthenware in Delft was completely ruined. In Norway, war with England did bring about a sharp decline in its only industries—timber sawing and iron making —and the ruin of the business upper-middle class; and recovery after 1815 was hampered because England had turned to Canada for her timber supply, while Norway, annexed by Sweden, lost the Danish market for her iron.

The dislocation and eventual interruption of the Continent's seaborne trade, owing to maritime war and British blockade, brought about undoubtedly a collapse of the "Atlantic sector" in the Continental economy, which had serious and lasting consequences.

II

There was however a second type of trade dislocation, the consequences of which were not so negative. This was the "self-blockade" by Continental countries against British trade and especially their attempts at preventing imports of British manufactured goods. This was of course the purpose of the Berlin Decree and the Continental blockade, but in France and her satellites, this policy was no innovation and had been enforced since the war had started. The self-blockade was never perfectly effective, and, except for short periods, many British goods were smuggled into the Continent; still, serious obstacles were erected against the import of such goods. Although the self-blockade was intended first and foremost as a means to force England into surrender, it acted practically, and from the point of view we are interested in, as a system of extreme protection, and its effect was to foster the growth of the industries which were the most seriously threatened by British competition.

Wars, Blockade, and Change   **575**

The most important example in this respect is the cotton industry, and especially the spectacular rise of machine spinning upon a large scale. The cotton industry had grown quite fast during the eighteenth century in several parts of France, in Switzerland, and in Saxony and was well established there before the wars; but, though jennies had been introduced in France in the 1770's and in Germany in the 1780's and a handful of cotton mills had been built in France before 1793, hand spinning remained overwhelmingly predominant everywhere when the war started. From 1796 onward, however, machine spinning increased a great deal in France, and at the turn of the century cotton mills, using water frames or mules, and some of them driven by waterpower, were established in several other countries. Their simultaneous rise is very striking, as the first mills were built in Bohemia in 1797, in Switzerland (St. Gall) in 1800, in Saxony (Chemnitz), Austria, Belgium (Ghent), and Holland in 1801, in Alsace in 1802. This was an answer to English competition, which during the 1790's had met with few obstructions except in France, and which was threatening with extinction the hand-spinning industries of countries like Saxony and Switzerland; but shortage of labor and difficulties in getting British yarns during the war of the second coalition may have had also some influence. However, during the first years of the nineteenth century, machine spinning spread relatively slowly (in each center of the industry only a handful of mills were built), not only because of teething troubles in the use of the new machinery, but also because British competition was unabated and even stronger owing to a continuous fall in the price of English yarn.

In February 1806, imports of yarn were prohibited or surtaxed in France, and soon the Continental blockade made such imports much more difficult and expensive for most countries than formerly—though they were never completely stopped, especially in Switzerland. Moreover, the simultaneous prohibition of British and of Indian cotton goods greatly increased the demand for locally produced yarns, and in Alsace, for instance, cotton printers were induced to start spinning mills and weaving sheds. There is a definite connection between these prohibitions and the boom in machine spinning which started in 1806 and developed up to 1810, with only one interruption in 1808.

Though in France, owing to an already high protection, progress had been rather fast during the preceding years, there was a sharp upward swing, and many new, relatively large mills were established.

576   *François Crouzet*

The output of machine-spun yarn seems to have doubled from 1806 to 1808 and doubled again at least in the next two years. Lille, Roubaix, and Tourcoing had 32,000 spindles in 1806, 114,000 in 1808, and 177,000 in 1810; towns like Ghent and Mulhouse, where cotton spinning had been almost unknown before 1800, show a fast increase of the same order. However, the 1806 turning point was still more pronounced in Saxony, which before that date had been exposed to British competition and which enjoyed suddenly an unhoped-for prosperity; the number of mule spindles increased from 13,000 in 1806 to 256,000 in 1813. A fast growth took place also in lower Austria and in Switzerland, where the building of new mills went on during the unprosperous years after 1810, owing to increased difficulties in getting English yarn. And on the left bank of the Rhine, where machine spinning had been quite unknown before 1806, it made dramatic progress in the Gladbach-Rheydt district. At the end of the Empire, Continental Europe had built up, within a dozen years, a spinning industry which had, in very rough figures, over one million and a half spindles, of which one million were in France, over 250,000 in Saxony, and 150,000 in Switzerland. (In 1811, Britain had 4,900,000 spindles.) This fast growth was undoubtedly a direct consequence of the Continental blockade, which of course did not create the industry but guaranteed its expansion. It brought about a concomitant decline in hand spinning, which by 1815 had almost entirely disappeared except in some isolated places. And it was accompanied by a good deal of technical progress, and especially by the substitution of the mule for the jenny and the water frame, which allowed the spinning of much finer counts of yarn. The mule was almost unknown in 1800 but became dominant after 1806, its triumph being helped by the crises of 1808 and 1811 which also increased concentration by wiping out the smaller firms and encouraging the creation of large, integrated concerns.

Technical progress took place also in other branches of the cotton industry: the flying shuttle was introduced in Switzerland in 1801, in Ghent shortly after, and in Mulhouse in 1805; cylinder printing started in Paris in 1797 and spread to Alsace and Switzerland around 1805, but was not taken up in Saxony. However, spinning was the only branch to undergo a complete technical revolution, and in others the innovations (including the Berthollet process for bleaching) did not come into general use. As a matter of fact, the sharp progress of machine spinning must not be taken as an index for the cotton industry as a whole.

Wars, Blockade, and Change   577

In France, where the industry enjoyed a continuous protection against English competition, there was undoubtedly an important increase in cotton-goods output. The cotton industry was the only one which did not collapse during the Revolution and even managed to increase its output; though some centers were hurt, especially in printing, which had been working for overseas markets, some others developed fast during the Directory and the early 1800's, particularly Paris and Lille; around 1800, the French consumption of raw cotton was slightly larger than before 1789. Then the boom of the nineteenth century's first decade extended also to weaving and printing, especially in Ghent and around Lille and Mulhouse, and the raw-cotton consumption doubled at least within ten years; despite serious crises in 1808 and 1811, output remained generally at a high level at the end of the Empire.

In other countries, however, the story was rather different. In Saxony, English competition was increasingly dangerous between 1793 and 1806, hurting first the making of muslins, then the coarser goods. The industry was really saved by the Continental blockade, but it seems that overall cotton-cloth production did not rise much during the next few years, an increase in calicoes for printing being offset by a fall in muslins. In Switzerland and Berg, the situation was more unfavorable, because the cotton industries of both countries were heavily dependent upon exports, which were made difficult by the protectionist policy of Napoleon which closed the French and Italian markets. Though the Swiss managed to switch their exports to Germany, the industries of both countries suffered, especially in Berg (which had boomed during the French Revolution) and in the cotton printing and muslin making of Switzerland. However, the situation would probably have been worse if these industries had been exposed to the full blast of English competition, and one may say that the Continental blockade saved the Swiss as well as the Saxon cotton industry.

There is no doubt on the whole that the prohibition of British cotton yarns and goods which was instituted first in France and then in the countries which joined the Continental system gave to the Continental cotton industry a much needed protection, without which it would have been largely wiped out, as well as the opportunity of meeting the demand for cotton goods, which was expanding very fast owing to a shift in tastes and fashions.

On the other hand, one must stress that the balance sheet of the wars period was far from being entirely favorable to the cotton industry. First, the bitter and protracted struggle with England did certainly slow down the introduction of British machinery, production methods, and skilled workers (though it was in the thick of war that Lievin Bauwens smuggled out from England his first mules). Moreover, during the later part of the war period from 1808 onward, the cotton industry labored under a serious difficulty—the shortage and high prices of its raw materials. This was due partly to the Continental blockade but also to the American embargo and to a British Order in Council, of November 1807, which prohibited the carrying of raw cotton into enemy ports. However, except for a few months late in 1808, when many mills had to stand idle, there was never a real cotton famine and the shortage was alleviated by imports from the Levant overland and by cultivation in southern Italy, so that output could be increased again in 1810. Still, after 1807, manufacturers obtained their raw material at much higher prices than did their British competitors—at least twice and even four times higher; and the French were at a special disadvantage, because, owing to a more efficient customs system and to high duties upon raw cotton imposed in August 1810, prices were notably higher in France than in Germany, Austria, or Switzerland. This situation was one of the factors in the crisis which broke out in 1811 and hit the industry very hard, though output recovered the next year. There is no doubt that its expansion was hampered by these high prices of raw materials, and on the whole the cotton industry did not grow as fast on the Continent during the war period as in Britain. British consumption of raw cotton, which can be used as a rough index of output, did increase roughly fourfold between 1790 and 1810; we have no comparable figures for the Continent as a whole, but in France, which had the largest cotton industry, the consumption of raw cotton increased roughly threefold during the same period. Quantitatively, the Continent in fact lost ground to England, while in technology a twenty-year time lag persisted.

This fact has been stressed by various writers, such as Eli Heckscher, who have moreover pointed out that, when peace was restored in 1814 and 1815, the Continental cotton industries were hit very hard by British competition; in France, for instance, some of the largest manufacturers went bankrupt,[5] and prohibitions as

---

[5] In fact, the direct cause of this collapse was the sudden abolition in April 1814 of the high customs duties on cotton wool, which at a stroke depreciated manufacturers' stocks and brought sharply down yarn and cloth prices.

severe as during the Continental blockade had to be reimposed in order to save the industry. This has been seen as a proof of the blockade's futility, since it did not succeed in making the industry competitive with England, and so the Continental cotton industry has been denounced as a typical "hothouse" industry which developed under artificial conditions of wartime extreme protection and which constituted a serious misallocation of resources.

However this line of argument neglects two basic facts of the concrete economic situation in Europe during the late eighteenth and early nineteenth centuries. The first was that war was being waged and that England was using its mastery of the seas to dislocate the Continent's trade and to destroy some of its traditional industries. Though the Continental blockade was intended as offensive economic warfare, it was in fact a defensive reflex by the Continental economy, inasmuch as the war obliged it to labor under unfavorable conditions such as high prices of raw materials, a serious shortage of capital, and high rates of interest. It is most likely that if there had been no war, if relations with England had been maintained, if a moderate protection had been established, economic and technical progress on the Continent would have been faster. But after all, there was a war.

The second basic fact was the absolute ascendancy, the overwhelming superiority, which the British had achieved, so that no Continental industry, except silk, could be competitive with its English rivals—in fact, a full century was to elapse before foreigners were able to compete successfully with Lancashire mills except for some special lines of goods such as fine printed cottons from Alsace. By 1800, Continental Europe was threatened by pastoralization and the fate of India in the nineteenth century. In fact, countries like Spain, Portugal, and Sweden which fell into the economic orbit of England during the wars suffered a crisis or a collapse of their traditional industries without any compensating rise of new ones; and countries where the cotton industry did not develop during the wars, like Italy or Spain, were to miss the first bus of nineteenth-century industrialization. On the other hand, though the Continental blockade did not reduce much the time lag in techniques between England and the Continent and though the development of the cotton industry (and of some others) under protection was a misallocation of resources, it was a necessary one and the only way to introduce the Industrial Revolution. As a matter of fact, the cotton industry was the strategic sector at that stage. It was the only one likely to expand fast, the best suited to machine production, and it required little capital; its development and technical improvement were the best way to introduce the new technology and to train workers and managers in the skills of machine production and the factory system; also they were the only possible basis for a machine-building industry. And truly its hothouse development during the Napoleonic wars did just that: it gave to the Continent its first experience of large-scale, capitalist, integrated, mechanized industry; it created a new group of manufacturers with a progressive (and sometimes adventurous) outlook and a taste for technical advance and for expansion; moreover, jointly with technical change in the woolen industry, it gave birth to a machine-building industry in a few places, such as Paris, Liège, Verviers, Essen, Mulhouse, Zurich, and Chemnitz; it was of course much smaller than in England and not so advanced, but the quality of its mechanics and of its products improved and its rise was a necessary preliminary stage of industrialization.

On the whole, the cotton industry and especially machine spinning had struck rather strong roots in Continental soil during the Napoleonic wars, and so the foundations for further industrialization had been laid.[6] As a matter of fact, the beginnings of the Industrial Revolution on the Continent could be dated from the simultaneous establishment of machine spinning in various countries, around 1800, which has been pointed out earlier. As, moreover, it is not apparent to what other uses capital and labor resources could have been applied at this stage of economic development,[7] I can not think that the growth of the cotton industry was unfortunate from the point of view of economic growth. However, the "bad thing" was that it created vested interests which during the postwar crisis clamored for renewed protection and generally got it (especially in France), while in fact the industry could likely have developed more efficiently, with only a moderate amount of protection.

[6] During the postwar years, some centers of the cotton industry—especially in Germany and Austria—suffered serious difficulties under the impact of renewed British competition but most of them managed to survive and some went on growing.

[7] Improvement of agricultural techniques would have resulted in releasing labor which only industry could employ; moreover, home demand for foodstuffs was inelastic, export markets unstable, and the British market, which had a regular import demand, was largely closed right at the end of the wars by the new Corn Laws. Attempts at renovating archaic manufactures, especially the linen industry, would have led into a blind alley, as they were suffering a secular decline. Luxury industries, like silk, were not likely to expand fast and were unsuited to machine production.

Wars, Blockade, and Change   **581**

As for the Continent's wool industries, the "self-blockade" had upon them an impact which was of the same kind as upon its cotton industry but not as powerful—because they were less in need of protection, because the Continent did not usually buy large quantities of English woolen goods, and because the possibilities of expansion were more limited. In France, the wool industry suffered badly during the Revolutionary period, as it was cut off by the war from its traditional markets in Germany, Spain, and the Levant; in 1795, production had fallen by two thirds as compared with 1789. But a general revival followed, and during the Napoleonic period the prerevolution level of output was exceeded, though some old centers of manufacture went on decaying. However, the most interesting development took place in territories which had been annexed to France and which benefited both from strong protection against the British and from the opening of the large French market, which they could take advantage of, thanks to decisive technical progress. This was especially true in Verviers, which at the turn of the century underwent within a few years (from 1799 to 1804) a true Industrial Revolution; the result was a sudden acceleration of growth, with output increasing at a mean average yearly rate of 6 per cent from 1800 to 1810, and a large increase in fixed capital and productivity. The woolen industry of Aachen also expanded a good deal, the value of its output increasing from 5 million and a half francs in 1786 to 11 million in 1811. But in many of the old French centers of the industry, technical change took place also upon a large scale; machine carding, spinning, and finishing became quite common. Protection through the self-blockade was, moreover, responsible for the taking off of a small woolen industry in Switzerland and in the Dutch district of Tilburg and for expansion of the Moravian wool manufactures. Elsewhere, there was little change.

However, two important industries were not much affected by the closing of the Continent to British competition. The first was the silk industry: far from needing any protection against the British, this was much larger and more efficient.[8] The other was the iron industry:

---

[8] However, different trade dislocations made their impact felt. During the Revolutionary period, the French silk industry underwent a serious crisis owing to a falling demand for luxury goods on the home market and to its being cut off from foreign markets; in 1801, its output was still about half that of 1789. At the same time, the silk manufacturers in Switzerland, Germany, and Austria were quite prosperous, owing to the elimination of French competition. However, the French silk industry recovered under the Empire and launched an export drive, which Napoleon tried to

most centers of production stagnated during most of the war period, the Liège and Düren districts being exceptions, and the overall increase in output of pig iron and iron seems to have been relatively small. As for technical progress, it was very limited—in France to the introduction of rolling mills. In various ironmaking districts (for instance in Berg during the blockade years), experiments were attempted to introduce the new English techniques of coke smelting, puddling, and crucible steelmaking, but nearly all of them failed and were given up. This stagnation may appear puzzling but can be easily explained: British exports of iron products to the Continent had been relatively small before the wars, and their interruption did not create a large vacuum to be filled up by local industries, while several centers of the iron industry (such as Berg) suffered from losing their overseas markets. As for the military demand for iron products, one must be careful not to overestimate it: it certainly helped to keep many ironworks active, but as it guaranteed to ironmasters a stable market for their output it acted, in fact, as a brake upon innovation. On the other hand, prohibition of English goods seems to have stimulated steelmaking and the secondary metal industries, such as the making of hardware, cutlery, tools, buttons, harness pieces, and tinplate articles, but their expansion was not sharp enough to take the primary iron industry out of the doldrums which discouraged technical progress and investment—though the disappearance of many small firms was a forerunner of the post-1815 development.

A complete balance sheet of wartime dislocations would include also a study of the chemical industries, in which the shortage of traditional imported raw materials such as barilla and potashes resulted in drastic technical change and especially in the introduction of the Leblanc process for soda making. Though these new industries expanded fast, they were still relatively small at the end of the war period; but their rise was significant for future growth, just as was that of the machine-building industry. On the other hand, the making of *ersatz* for colonial produce had no importance in the long run; as an example, the beet-sugar industry was wiped out after 1814, not to revive in Europe before the 1830's.

---

help as much as possible. This had unpleasant consequences in Switzerland and Germany, where the makers of ribbons in Basel and Barmen and of silks in Berlin were the main sufferers (but some centers of the industry remained prosperous). In Italy, there was little expansion of output.

III

To the trade dislocations wrought by the maritime and continental blockades must be added those which resulted from the large-scale redrafting of the political map of Europe during the wars, from the annexation to France of large areas, and from the drastic territorial changes which took place in Germany and Italy. These upheavals brought about frequent and important changes in the customs lines which crisscrossed the Continent and therefore, from the point of view of manufacturers, the closing of traditional markets and the opening of new ones.

The most important developments in this respect resulted from the annexation to France of Belgium and the left bank of the Rhine. Succeeding a period during which these districts had been battlefields and had suffered from French exactions, this had at first unfavorable consequences by interrupting traditional trade relations; but quite soon—roughly after 1800—the industries of Belgium and the Roer department expanded very fast and enjoyed a remarkable prosperity under the Imperial Régime. They shifted their sales from their former markets, mostly in Central Europe, toward the French market on which they concentrated. This integration with a huge protected and unified area of 30 million customers was the decisive influence which was responsible first and foremost for the fast expansion of the woolen industries of Verviers, Aachen, and Jülich, of the silk industry of Crefeld, of the metal industries of Liège and Düren, and for the rise of the cotton industry in Ghent and Gladbach. Its impact was especially strong on the left bank of the Rhine, where, from 1806 onwards, the exclusion from France of Berg manufactured goods brought about a massive immigration of manufacturers and workers from Berg. Industry struck strong roots in this district, which had been overwhelmingly agricultural in the eighteenth century; by 1811, the Roer department had 2,500 industrial establishments with 65,000 workers, and, according to H. Kisch, in a recent article, "French domination proved, in its long run effect, a true blessing." The annexation of Mulhouse in 1798 and the integration of Alsace to the French customs area (outside of which it had remained under the Old Régime) had similar effects for this province, which benefited from an immigration of Swiss capital and labor. This expansion of Belgian and Rhineland industries was helped by comparative advantages they enjoyed over those of *l'ancienne France:* they had suffered less from the economic blizzard which struck French industry during the Revolution; their labor costs were cheaper owing to the existence of a destitute urban proletariat; and the woolen manufacturers had the luck that William Cockerill settled in Belgium and supplied them with excellent machinery, which allowed Verviers to achieve a precocious, fast, and perfect Industrial Revolution, without much trial and error.

However, territorial changes had for other industrial centers far less happy consequences, because they were cut off from their traditional markets without enjoying the compensation which Belgium and the left bank of the Rhine found in France. This was aggravated by Napoleon's protectionist policy which closed the markets of France and Italy, not only to the British but to his own vassals and allies, while trying to persuade them to admit French goods. The continuous annexations to France of new territories which were at once closed to their neighbors made things steadily worse. Moreover, many states, especially in Germany, raised their tariff walls mostly for fiscal reasons. So the Continental market was far from unified and was, in fact, bristling with obstacles to trade.

The result was a general dislocation of trade relations and serious difficulties for countries which were exporting manufactured goods upon a large scale. The two main sufferers were Switzerland and Berg, which were both heavily dependent upon the French and Italian markets and which were badly hurt by the ultraprotectionist French tariff of 1806 and, a few months later, by their exclusion from the Kingdom of Italy. Berg exports fell one third from 1807 to 1810. However, the difficulties which the two countries suffered during the Continental blockade have been exaggerated; the growth of their industry was slowed down or stopped, they suffered from stagnation (especially the Swiss cotton, watchmaking, and jewelry industries and the ribbon making of Barmen), but no irreparable damage was done, there was no general deindustrialization except the disappearance of some Swiss centers of cotton printing. And one must not forget that Berg industries had grown fast up to 1806. As for Italy, which Napoleon made a *chasse gardée,* a preserve, an economic colony of France, surrounded by impassable custom walls except on the side of France, its industry survived nonetheless.[9]

9 Grossly overdone are the lamentations and diatribes of B. de Cérenville against Napoleon (whom he charges with having deliberately tried to destroy Swiss industry), although the charges have been endorsed by E. F. Heckscher. See Cérenville, *Le Système continental et la Suisse, 1803-1813* (Lausanne: G. Bridel, 1906), pp. 17, 51,

Wars, Blockade, and Change   585

On the other hand, recurrent and sudden changes in political frontiers and in customs regulations, as well as the violent and brutal methods which Napoleon used to enforce the blockade, did frighten and discourage businessmen, destroy security and confidence, and were baneful to entrepreneurship.

On the whole, there is no doubt that the manifold and serious dislocations which international trade suffered during the Napoleonic wars had an unfavorable and retardative effect upon the growth of Continental industry. In addition to causing the permanent decline of the "maritime" and of the linen industries, they slowed down the progress of many industries as a result of serious and protracted crises either during the French Revolution or in the later years of the Empire. During the 1790's, French industrial output collapsed and, though it recovered from 1796 onward, by 1800 it was at best 60 per cent of its pre-1789 level. The causes of this disaster were many, but the interruption of French foreign trade (not only through the British sea blockade, but also owing to the closing of Continental markets in enemy countries) was one of the most decisive. However, part of the damage was not irreparable; for instance, the wool and silk industries revived sharply under Napoleon, though some old wool centers had been mortally wounded. From 1802 to 1810, there was a powerful outburst of industrialization, but its first effect was only to make good earlier losses, and around 1810, the aggregate volume of industrial production was not much higher than in the 1780's (possibly an increase of 50 per cent).[10] As for other Continental countries, they had benefited from the French collapse during the 1790's, but (except for cotton spinning and for the industries of Belgium and the left bank of the Rhine) there is little evidence of fast growth at the time of the Continental blockade, and some important indus-

---

117, 132, 141, 148 ff., 170, 173 ff., 180, 210-20, 279-81, 321; and Heckscher, *The Continental System. An Economic Interpretation* (Oxford: Clarendon Press, 1922), pp. 307-10. On Berg, see Ch. Schmidt, *Le grand-duché de Berg (1806-1813). Etude sur la domination française en Allemagne sous Napoléon Ier* (Paris: Alcan, 1905), 326-38, 341-43, 354, 382-83, 386, 406-8, 417, 421.

[10] This is a very rough guess. The *Statistique de la France publiée par le ministère de l'agriculture et du commerce. Industrie*, I (Paris, 1847), xv-xvii, gives the value of industrial production for 1812 (and for *l'ancienne France*) as double the 1788 figure; but this seems over optimistic. On the other hand, according to W. Hoffman's index, the volume of British industrial production did less than double between 1792 and 1815; Hoffman, *British Industry, 1700-1950* (Oxford: Basil Blackwell, 1955), table 54.

tries did certainly stagnate. Moreover, in 1810-1811, a sharp crisis, aggravated by various dislocations connected with the Continental blockade (overspeculation on colonial produce, enforcement of the Trianon decree), broke the momentum of the Napoleonic industrialization. The last years of the Empire were of stagnation, and many business firms disappeared in the final collapse of 1813-1814.

The balance sheet of the Napoleonic wars for the Continent as a whole might therefore be something like this: collapse of the "maritime" industries, decay of the linen industry, stagnation of the primary iron industry, modest growth of the wool, silk, and secondary-metal industries, relatively fast progress of the cotton industry, and a modest increase in overall industrial output. This was certainly smaller than the rise which had taken place meanwhile in Britain—though recent research has come to the conclusion that the Napoleonic wars had a retardative effect upon British industrial growth and investment in industry. So on the whole the impact of the wars was more unfavorable to the Continent than to England and made more serious its time lag. However, the rise of the cotton-spinning, machine-building, and chemical industries had laid foundations for future development which was also to be fostered by the reforms which French dominion had introduced into many parts of the Continent, such as freedom of enterprise and abolition of the manorial system and the guilds.

Moreover, some other important developments had taken place within the Continental economy. One was the shift, which was to be permanent, in the location of Continental industries. Many industries located in seaboard districts had declined or collapsed, and moreover such districts, with a few exceptions (mostly between the Seine and the Scheldt), did not benefit from the rise of new industries; even in Holland, industries developed inland, in Tilburg and Enschedé. On the other hand, industrial centers which expanded or maintained their levels of output were as a rule inland, within a large area which extended between the Seine and the Elbe rivers; and some of the most important developments (as well as much accumulation of capital, largely through smuggling activities) took place in the ex-*Lotharingia*, with the fast growth of industries in the *Nord* department of France, in Ghent, Verviers, Liège, around Aachen, and in Alsace. This shows how unfortunate it was for France to be deprived of her "natural frontiers" in 1814. The axis of the Continental economy had now moved from the Atlantic to-

Wars, Blockade, and Change   587

ward the Rhine,[11] and this was of course a forerunner of the growing concentration of European industry in northern and eastern France, Belgium, and northwestern Germany, which was to be so characteristic of the nineteenth and of the early twentieth centuries, and owing to which the so-called Golden Triangle (Paris-Hamburg-Milan) still possesses the largest part of the Common Market's industrial power. There were also some interesting developments along an axis situated farther to the east, in Saxony, Bohemia, Austria, and even Hungary.[12]

This shift of industry from the seaboard to the heartland of western Europe was moreover the sign of another significant change. In the eighteenth century, the European economy had been outward looking and geared to overseas markets; all important industries had been heavily dependent upon the export trade.[13] However, during the Napoleonic wars, and especially at the time of the Continental blockade, export industries had suffered the most and one could well say that the prosperity of each industrial center had been inversely proportional to its dependence upon international trade—as is well shown by the story of the linen-making areas, of Lyons, of Switzerland, and of Berg. Moreover, the British had engrossed overseas markets. So the Napoleonic wars made most European industries inward looking and geared first and foremost to national markets (a typical case was Catalonia which, after the collapse of her colonial trade, turned entirely toward the Spanish home market). This had been encouraged by the formation of larger economic units through the abolition of internal customs barriers. This development had run its full course in France, where the Revolution had created a national market which was relatively quite large, so that manufacturers to whom war and postwar conditions had made access to foreign markets difficult were encouraged to limit their ambitions within their own borders. In Central Europe, the situation

[11] This was helped by the accumulation of capital, through smuggling, in the hands of merchants in Basel, Strasbourg, Frankfort, and Essen, and its subsequent use for investment in industrial ventures.

[12] Industrial growth in these countries was stimulated by the shift toward the east of trade routes across Europe at the time of the blockade and by lower prices of raw materials. On Hungary, see György Mérei, "Ueber einige Fragen der Anfaenge der Kapitalistischen Gewerkentwicklung in Ungarn," *Etudes historiques*, II (Budapest: Académie Hongroise des Sciences, 1960), 753-59.

[13] Because of obstacles to internal trade, high costs of land transport, and low incomes per capita, production upon a large scale could not be based on national or regional demand and had to rely upon export markets.

588   *François Crouzet*

was different because *Kleinstaaterei* maintained many customs barriers; still, larger economic units had been created and there was a
clear tendency of Berg and Saxony industrialists to increase their
sales on the German markets, especially in the eastern parts of Germany. Later on, the creation of large national markets through the
Zollverein and Italian unity was of course to strengthen this trend.
With a few exceptions (like Switzerland or Alsace) and up to the
worldwide economic expansion of Germany in the late nineteenth
century, Continental industries were to work mostly for their own
national markets and for those of the neighboring countries. This
was in sharp contrast with England and her worldwide trading interests—but after all the inward-looking character of the Continental
economy was a consequence of the decisive defeat which it had
suffered in its struggle against British ascendancy. So the trade
dislocations of the Napoleonic wars were responsible for some of
the specific characters of Continental industry and for some of its
differences with British industry—differences which they aggravated
and which have persisted up to our own day. They are not unsig-
nificant in order to understand some current problems of political
economy.

FRANÇOIS CROUZET, *University of Paris*

[7]

THE 19TH-CENTURY INTERNATIONAL SYSTEM:
Changes in the Structure

By PAUL W. SCHROEDER*

I

THE problem to be posed in this essay is a central one in the history of international politics. Having dealt with it intensively in the 19th and early 20th centuries, historians of international politics have long regarded it as basically solved. The question is how to account for the overall peaceful stability of 19th-century European international politics from 1815 on. The phenomenon in question is a familiar one, and the conventional answer is firmly established in the historical literature. In describing in unavoidably oversimplified fashion the phenomenon and the normal explanation, I hope to show that a real question remains and that a different kind of broad answer is more satisfactory.

Most scholars would agree that Europe was more stable from 1815 to 1854 than during any equivalent era in the entire 18th century, and that, taken as a whole, the 19th century was more peaceful than the 18th. Various explanations have been offered: the widespread exhaustion, war-weariness, fear of revolution, and desire for peace produced by a generation of war and upheaval from 1787 to 1815; a moderate peace settlement, a stable balance of power, a system of diplomacy by conference, a Concert of Europe, and other diplomatic devices; the prevalence of monarchial conservative ideology; international cooperation to preserve the existing social order; and prudent, skillful statesmanship. The explanations are complementary rather than conflicting, so that historians can disagree on emphases while tacitly accepting that the phenomenon can be explained adequately by some combination of these factors.

The explanations involve an explicit or implicit denial of any systemic change in international politics in this more peaceful, stable era. They do so in three general ways. First, the 1815 settlement is commonly interpreted as a restoration of an 18th-century-style balance of power, a con-

* This article is an outgrowth of a colloquium paper presented March 19, 1984, at the Woodrow Wilson International Center for Scholars, Washington, DC. I am grateful to Professors Enno Kraehe of the University of Virginia and Peter Krüger of Marburg University for their comments, and to the Wilson Center for the Fellowship that allowed me to work on the study. A different, shortened version containing part of this material was presented on February 21, 1985, at the Consortium for Revolutionary Europe at Baton Rouge, La.

scious return to classical 18th-century political principles.[1] Second, most if not all historians see the post-1815 change in the character of international politics as temporary, with stability and harmony beginning to fade by 1820 and in definite decline by 1830, and normal political competition back in force after 1848.[2] Third, peace and stability are usually explained as volitional and dispositional rather than structural—i.e., a matter of what statesmen chose to do and were inclined to do in international politics, rather than what the prevailing system constrained them from doing or permitted them to do.

On these particular counts, this essay disputes the general consensus. It is not exactly wrong, but it leaves important things out. Nineteenth-century international peace and stability derived mainly from systemic change, reflected in major institutionalized arrangements and practices divergent from the 18th-century norm. The 1815 settlement did not restore an 18th-century-type balance of power or revive 18th-century political practices; the European equilibrium established in 1815 and lasting well into the 19th century differed sharply from so-called balances of power in the 18th. The systemic change, moreover, proved enduring; it lasted into the latter part of the century, despite the upheavals of 1848-1850 and the wars of 1854-1871. Furthermore, 19th-century political patterns of conduct differed from their 18th-century counterparts not so much because of the more pacific, conservative dispositions, aims, and desires of most statesmen—this difference, if it existed, tended to disappear quickly—but because the two prevailing systems afforded different systemic constraints and possibilities for action.

Much of the argument involved in this counter-thesis cannot be presented here, much less demonstrated. To show, for example, how the typical 19th-century conception of the European equilibrium differed from the prevailing 18th-century ideas of balance of power, and how it worked differently, or to explain how new rules and practices of politics emerged in the crucible of the Napoleonic Wars, would require lengthy historical analyses. In this essay, I intend only to present a plausible argument that systemic changes really occurred, and to identify certain ways in which they show up.

---

[1] E.g., Edward V. Gulick, *Europe's Classical Balance of Power* (Ithaca, NY: Cornell University Press, 1955); Peter R. Rohden, *Die klassische Diplomatie von Kaunitz bis Metternich* (Leipzig: Koehler & Amelang, 1939).

[2] F. Roy Bridge and Roger Bullen, *The Great Powers and the European States System 1815-1914* (London: Longman, 1980).

II

To start with, the most impressive aspect of post-1815 European politics is not simply the virtual absence of war. More notable is an array of positive results achieved in international politics in this era, of problems settled and dangers averted by diplomacy. Leaving the remarkable record of the Vienna Congress in this respect aside entirely, a short list of the accomplishments would have to include the following: the speedy evacuation of Allied armies from France and France's quick reintegration into the European Concert; the completion and implementation of the federal constitution of Germany; the suppression of revolutions in Naples, Piedmont, Spain, and the Danubian Principalities by international action, without serious European quarrels; the recognition of Latin American independence; the prevention of war between Russia and Turkey for seven years (1821 to 1828), and a moderate end to that war after it did break out; the creation of an independent Greece; the prompt recognition of a new government in France after the revolution of 1830; the creation of an independent, neutralized Belgium, despite major dangers of war and obstacles to a settlement created mainly by quarrels between the Dutch and the Belgians; the prevention of international conflict in 1830-1832 over revolts in Italy, Germany, and Poland; the managing of civil wars in Spain and Portugal without great-power conflict; and two successful joint European rescue operations for the Ottoman Empire.

One need not accept that all these outcomes represented long-range gains for domestic and international peace and stability in Europe; nor would anyone claim that they were reached without crises, tensions, and crosspurposes. Nonetheless, it remains remarkable that such results could be achieved at all—that 19th-century statesmen could, with a certain minimum of good will and effort, repeatedly reach viable, agreed-upon outcomes to hotly disputed critical problems. The 18th century simply does not record diplomatic achievements of this kind. To the contrary, enormous efforts were repeatedly expended by 18th-century statesmen not so much to solve problems as simply to keep them under control and avert breakdown—usually in vain. Consider, for example, how England and France struggled fruitlessly to control Elizabeth Farnese's Spain, and tried not to get into war with each other in 1739-1741 and 1754-1756; how much useless effort Charles VI put into securing the peaceful accession of Maria Theresa in Austria; how Austria and France unsuccessfully attempted to keep Russia from dominating Poland and the Ottoman Empire or from partitioning them. The list could readily be extended.

Of course, we are told that European statesmen after 1815 were in a different mood. But were they? How much so? Previous European wars, allowing for differences in population and level of economic development, had been almost as costly and exhausting as those of 1792-1815—the Thirty Years' War had probably been worse[3]—and had left behind comparable legacies of war-weariness and fear of revolution. After the conclusion of every great war, in 1648, 1713-1714, 1763, 1783, 1801, 1807, and 1809, there had been statesmen who desperately yearned for peace, wanting not just peace treaties but durable peace settlements. The results achieved in this direction in the early 18th century alone by George I, Stanhope, the Abbé Dubois, Baron Münchhausen, Carteret, Cardinal Fleury, Townshend, Walpole, Bernstorff, and others in no way compare with the will and energy expended, or with the record of 1815-1848. The presence or absence of good will and peaceful intentions clearly does not suffice to explain this phenomenon.[4]

Moreover, the conservative "Holy Alliance" spirit of 1815 cannot mainly account for 19th-century international stability, for this spirit, never universal in Europe, clearly did not survive the revolutions of 1848, while the structural changes in the states system established in 1815 largely did. The upheavals of 1848-1850 affected European international politics in three main ways. First, the revolutions discredited the so-called Metternich system, the attempt to repress liberalism, nationalism, and revolution purely by authoritarian preventive measures. After 1850, even governments that were still basically authoritarian, such as those of Austria, Prussia, and Louis Napoleon's France, tried to deal with national discontent and revolution by active policies of modernization and economic development directed from above; these policies tended to promote rivalry between states, especially in the economic arena.[5] Second, the Holy Alliance between the three Eastern powers was undermined. Prussia and Austria once again became open rivals in Germany, and Russia and Austria were concealed rivals in the Balkans, while France under

[3] Josef V. Polišensky, *War and Society in Europe, 1618-1648* (Cambridge: Cambridge University Press, 1978); Theodore Rabb, *The Struggle for Stability in Early Modern Europe* (New York: Oxford University Press, 1975).
[4] Heinz Duchardt, *Gleichgewicht der Kräfte, Convenance, Europäisches Konzert* (Darmstadt: Wissenschaftliche Buchgesellschaft, 1976); Ragnhild Hatton, *George I, Elector and King* (Cambridge: Harvard University Press, 1978); David B. Horn, *Great Britain and Europe in the Eighteenth Century* (Oxford: Clarendon Press, 1967); Paul Langford, *The Eighteenth Century, 1688-1815* (New York: A. and C. Black, 1976); Derek McKay and Hamish M. Scott, *The Rise of the Great Powers 1648-1815* (London and New York: Longman, 1983); Gaston Zeller, *Les temps modernes*, 2 vols. (Paris: Hachette, 1953-55).
[5] Helmut Böhme, *Deutschlands Weg zur Grossmacht*, 2d ed. (Cologne and Berlin: Kiepenheuer & Witsch, 1972); Harm-Hinrich Brandt, *Der österreichische Neoabsolutismus*, 2 vols. (Göttingen: Vandenhoeck & Ruprecht, 1978).

19th-CENTURY INTERNATIONAL SYSTEM   5

Louis Napoleon and to some extent Britain under Palmerston looked for chances to exploit and widen the rifts. Third, European conservatism itself made long strides away from the pacific, legalistic internationalism of Metternich's generation, and toward its own union with nationalism. The new generation of leaders, though often almost as conservative in domestic politics as Metternich had been, hoped to defend the existing order not so much by preserving international peace and monarchial solidarity as by maintaining a strong army and an active foreign policy that would attach the masses to the regime.

In other words, the events of 1848 generally undermined the old monarchial-conservative spirit of 1815 and liberated new forces of nationalism and liberalism, even in Eastern Europe, thereby changing the tone and character of international politics. With the old motives for a peaceful, stable international system in decline or in disrepute, the system itself should presumably have been overthrown. Yet, despite revolutions in 1848-1850 more widespread than those of 1789-1793 and almost as radical; despite clashes between insurgents and police or armies almost everywhere in Central and Southern Europe, and serious civil conflicts in France, Prussia, Saxony, Southwest Germany, Naples, Lombardy, Venetia, Lower Austria, Bohemia, Hungary, Croatia, Transylvania, and the Rumanian Principalities; despite two wars in strategically vital areas, one in Northern Italy, the other in Schleswig-Holstein, each involving one major power in combat and other major powers in political complications, what actually happened in international politics was that, when everything was over, not one war between Great Powers had broken out, not one international boundary had been altered, and not one treaty had been torn up. In short, though all the factors that were said to have produced peace and stability after 1815 had been suspended or destroyed, peace had been maintained, and the international crises had been managed.

But, the critic will reply, not for long. When the Crimean War (1853-56) broke out, it wrecked the European Concert and paved the way for the greater convulsions of 1859-1871.[6] True enough, but not perhaps the most important truth. A.J.P. Taylor indicates the salient fact, without exactly explaining it, in his essay entitled "Crimea: The War that Would Not Boil."[7] Considering the explosive elements in it, this war should in

[6] Winfried Baumgart, *Der Frieden von Paris 1856* (Munich and Vienna: R. Oldenbourg, 1972); Paul W. Schroeder, *Austria, Great Britain and the Crimean War* (Ithaca, NY, and London: Cornell University Press, 1972); John S. Curtiss, *Russia's Crimean War* (Durham, NC: Duke University Press, 1979); Norman Rich, *Why the Crimean War?* (Hanover, NH, and London: University Press of New England, 1985).

[7] Taylor, *Rumours of Wars* (London: H. Hamilton, 1952), 30-40.

the normal course of events have become a general European conflict. It was the first war between European great powers in 39 years. Britain and Russia, world rivals and the strongest powers in Europe, were pitted against each other. Public opinion, mass passions, and hostile ideologies figured prominently in the outbreak and conduct of the war. It involved the most complicated, persistent, and dangerous question in European politics, the Eastern Question. And above all, two of the major combatants, Britain and France, persistently employed every means at their command to make it a general war by drawing Austria, Prussia, the German Confederation, and other neutrals into it. The leader in that effort, Lord Palmerston, pursued a typical 18th-century war aim, a sweeping reduction of Russia's territory and power, ostensibly to restore the balance of power in Europe.

And what were the results, after two years of costly fighting and unremitting diplomatic pressure? No neutral joined the war except Sardinia-Piedmont, which came in almost as a mercenary auxiliary for reasons of its own.[8] Despite his great energy and popularity in Britain, Palmerston could not even carry his own cabinet along in his extreme war aims; in the end, Britain was persuaded by France, with Austria's help, to end the war and make peace before it wanted to. The war had some profound domestic and international consequences, without a doubt. Russia was humiliated and weakened internally; Austria was left isolated and vulnerable, and the Italian, German, and Balkan questions were thrown open. But France won only a prestige victory, and Britain not even that, while the map of Europe and the treaty system remained almost unchanged. The only real winners, it turned out, were those who could later exploit the war for their individual purposes: Sardinia-Piedmont, Prussia, and the nationalists in the Rumanian Principalities.

To be sure, the wars of Italian and German unification quickly followed, and profoundly altered the map and the treaty system of Europe. They had significant effects upon the European states system, particularly the long-range impact of the so-called unification of Germany.[9] Yet this very period of upheaval in some ways demonstrates the persistent strength of the European system, showing how even in its decline it continued to inhibit conflict and promote international arrangements and stability in a way that could hardly have occurred in the 18th century.

Two striking features of these wars were the difficulties Cavour and

[8] Ennio di Nolfo, *Europa e Italia nel 1855-1856* (Rome: Istituto per la storia del Risorgimento italiano, 1967).
[9] Paul W. Schroeder, "The Lost Intermediaries: The Impact of 1870 on the European System," *International History Review* 6 (February 1984), 1-27.

Bismarck encountered in getting them started under the right conditions, and the relative ease and speed with which they were ended. By 1859, Austria and Sardinia-Piedmont had been waging a cold war for a decade; their diplomatic relations had been suspended for a year, and both powers were poised in armed confrontation; Cavour had concluded a conspiratorial agreement for war with Napoleon III; revolutionary nationalist agitation was rife in Italy and tension was high in Europe; and Austria had almost no friends and many enemies. Despite all this, Cavour was at the point of resigning in despair in April 1859 because his quest for war had been foiled by European diplomacy; at the last moment, Austria rescued him with its fatal ultimatum to Sardinia.[10] When Bismarck became Minister-President of Prussia in 1862, Austria's position was even worse and the prevailing conservative restraints upon the exercise of *Machtpolitik* were still weaker. Bismarck matched or possibly exceeded Cavour in skill, daring, and lack of scruple, and he operated from a far stronger base of power. Yet it took him four years before he could maneuver Austria into war under the right conditions. When he chose to confront France four years later, only a combination of amazing luck and French blunders saved him from political defeat and enabled him to conduct a German national war against France without European interference. In other words, in both 1866 and 1870, despite the undoubted decay of the European system, there remained enough residual resistance to the kind of ruthless 18th-century *Realpolitik* Bismarck frankly espoused to make his task difficult.[11]

Like Palmerston's efforts in the Crimean War, the record of 1866 and 1870 illustrates how 18th-century politics worked when tried in the 19th century. Cavour and Bismarck were in many respects 18th-century-style *Kabinettspolitiker*, pursuing the traditional expansionist policies of the Houses of Brandenburg and Savoy. Their 18th-century predecessors, Frederick the Great and the Dukes of Savoy, had had different problems, however: their wars were easy enough to start, but difficult to control and to end. Historians have often noted the remarkably limited extent, duration, and violence of the wars between 1859 and 1871, considering how

[10] Franco Valsecchi, *L'unificazione italiana e la politica europea* (Milan: Istituto per gli studi di politica internazionale, 1939); Umberto Marcelli, *Cavour, diplomatico 1856-1859* (Bologna: A. Forni, 1961); Adolfo Omodeo, *L'opera politica del conte di Cavour (1848-1857)* (Milan and Naples: R. Ricciardi, 1968); Friedrich Engel-Janosi, "L' 'Ultimatum' austriaco del 1859," *Rassegna storica del Risorgimento* 24 (September and October 1937), 1393-1425, 1565-1600.

[11] Helmut Burckhardt, *Deutschland, England, Frankreich* (Munich: W. Fink, 1970); Richard Millman, *British Foreign Policy and the Coming of the Franco-Prussian War* (Oxford: Clarendon Press, 1965); Dietrich Beyrau, *Russische Orientpolitik und die Entstehung des Deutschen Kaiserreiches 1866 bis 1870/71* (Munich: Osteuropa-Institut, 1974); Heinrich Lutz, *Österreich-Ungarn und die Gründung des Deutschen Reiches* (Frankfurt: Propyläen, 1979).

8   WORLD POLITICS

much was at stake in them, and have often explained this as resulting
from the skill and moderation of Bismarck and Cavour. Leaving aside
the question of whether the aims and tactics of either statesman can be
called moderate (Cavour's almost certainly were not and Bismarck's only
in a limited sense),[12] that kind of explanation is clearly inadequate system-
ically. Cavour did not end the war in 1859; France and Austria did, in
good part because of European pressure. Cavour was not responsible for
the European response to his actions in 1860-1861, and was not even alive
to see Italian unity completed. As for Bismarck, remarkable though his
fertility in expedients was, he clearly was working within a framework
of limits and opportunities set by the European system, and he always
knew it.

Even more surprising than the limited extent and duration of these
wars is the rapid integration of their results into the European system.
Two states that had aggrandized themselves by methods widely condemned in Europe, defeating and humiliating other European great
powers in the process, now sought recognition and acceptance. One
leaped in a decade from last to first place in the European pentarchy; the
other, though still essentially a second-class state, now demanded recognition as a great power. One was widely feared as being militarist and
ruthless, the other generally despised as weak and unreliable. Yet both
were readily accepted into the great-power club and, more important, no
effort was ever made to reverse this outcome. For the other powers, this
involved not merely coming to terms with accomplished facts and present
realities. It meant putting aside deeply rooted traditions and goals, and
incurring real risks. Austria, for example, has been accused of hoping
after 1859 to reverse the outcome in Italy (which is largely true) and, after
1866, of plotting revenge on Prussia for Sadowa (which is almost wholly
false). What needs explanation and ought to catch the attention of historians is instead the astonishing readiness of Austria to come to terms with
the new states of Italy and Germany. It involved seeking good relations
in the south with a state that was bound to be its rival in the Adriatic and
its potential competitor in the Balkans, and that still harbored claims to
Austrian territory. At the same time, Austria sought an actual alliance
with its historic rival to the north, now expanded into a national state that
threatened Austria militarily, jeopardized the loyalty of its most important national group, and undermined its raison d'être as a multinational
state and European great power.

[12] Denis Mack Smith, *Cavour and Garibaldi, 1860* (Cambridge: Cambridge University
Press, 1954), and *Victor Emmanuel, Cavour, and the Risorgimento* (London: Oxford University
Press, 1971); Lothar Gall, *Bismarck der weisse Revolutionär* (Frankfurt: Propyläen, 1980).

In a similarly myopic fashion, historians have concentrated their attention on France's refusal to accept the loss of Alsace-Lorraine in the wake of the Franco-Prussian War, and the fatal effect this is supposed to have had on Franco-German relations.[13] Actually, while the war was still going on, France accepted something that proved to be vastly more dangerous for French security and power than the loss of Alsace-Lorraine—namely, the union of South Germany with the North under Prussian control; now, a militarily superior Germany would directly face France along a greatly extended Franco-German frontier. Russia, in accepting German unification under Prussia, swallowed the loss of its most important security asset, a defensive glacis to the west, the cornerstone of which had always been a federal, divided structure for Germany and a rivalry between Austria and Prussia that Russia could rely upon and exploit.

The question is not whether the European powers were wise in thus accepting the *faits accomplis* presented to them by Sardinia-Piedmont and Prussia. My own view is that in many ways this was a fatal error, and that Italian and German national unification needed at least to be controlled and legalized by Europe in concert, even if after the fact. The important consideration here is that this kind of peaceful accommodation to drastic changes in the system did not happen, and could not have happened, in the 18th century. One only needs to remember, by way of contrast, how long and determinedly Austria resisted the loss of Silesia to Prussia, and France the loss of colonial supremacy to Britain. Some systemic change is required to account for it.

There is another important and general phenomenon of 19th-century international politics; it is suggested in the title of A.J.P. Taylor's *The Struggle for Mastery in Europe 1848-1918*.[14] Actually, for most of the period covered, up to 1890 or 1900 at least, there was no such struggle for mastery in the sense of a conscious drive to achieve preeminent position and dominant power. Although it makes sense to speak of a struggle for mastery in Germany and Italy, no one state ever tried for, much less achieved, such mastery in Europe as a whole, and it is questionable whether any coalition did. Britain enjoyed command of the seas, and for a long while was preeminent in empire, industry, and commerce. But so far as continental Europe is concerned, what Lord Salisbury said was always true and well known: "We are fish." Russia was the strongest member of the Holy Alliance up to the 1850s, but never dominated Europe as

[13] See, for example, George F. Kennan, *The Decline of Bismark's European Order* (Princeton: Princeton University Press, 1979); Allan Mitchell, *Bismarck and the French Nation, 1848-1890* (New York: Pegasus, 1971).
[14] Oxford: Clarendon Press, 1954.

a whole, or even Central Europe; after the Crimean War, it no longer even led the Eastern bloc. The common view that Russia enjoyed an enormous and growing power and prestige in Europe until the Crimean War broke the bubble is a great exaggeration.[15] After 1815, Russia never was the arbiter of Europe or exercised the dominant influence in Germany that Catherine II or Paul I had enjoyed for a time, and the young Alexander I had aspired to. France, Austria, and Italy were never serious candidates for mastery. That leaves only Bismarck's Germany. What it enjoyed (or rather, possessed without really enjoying it) was, in Andreas Hillgruber's phrase, a labile half-hegemony in Europe, an unintended result of Bismarck's policy.[16] Basically, he had not wanted to control Europe, but to disentangle Prussia and Germany from extraneous European quarrels. Instead, as Lothar Gall's excellent biography shows, he became a sorcerer's apprentice, overwhelmed by his own success, compelled to manage and manipulate European problems he had hoped to be able to ignore.[17]

The same thesis applies to 19th-century coalitions and alliances: in contrast to 18th-century ones, they were not bids for mastery in Europe. The dominant coalition of 1815 was strictly a defensive one against France (and tacitly against one of its members, Russia); it quickly broke down. After 1820, the Holy Alliance could not control events in Western Europe, and the Western powers could not control those in Central and Eastern Europe. Near Eastern alignments frequently crossed and shifted. Britain and France could not create a dominant coalition against Russia in the 1850s. Napoleon III toyed with the idea of a dominant Franco-Russian or Franco-Prussian-Italian coalition, but never seriously pursued it. Bismarck's alliance system after 1879 was a reluctant defensive coalition intended to keep France from seeking revenge, and Austria and Italy or Austria and Russia from fighting each other. The rival alliances of the 1890s were basically blocking coalitions in Europe; they were used as bases to compete for world position.

This is not a quarrel over words, or one of those unavoidable but tiresome disputes by historians over periodization or taxonomy. It involves the fundamental nature of the 19th-century international system, and challenges the overall view of the history of international politics expounded by Ludwig Dehio[18] and many others, who saw it as a succession

---

[15] E.g., Georg Stadtmüller, "Die russische Weltmacht und ihr Rückzug (1783-1867)," in Stadtmüller, *Grundfragen der europäischen Geschichte* (Munich and Vienna: R. Oldenbourg, 1965).

[16] Hillgruber, *Bismarcks Aussenpolitik* (Freiburg: Rombach, 1972).

[17] Gall (fn. 12).

[18] Dehio, *The Precarious Balance* (New York: Knopf, 1962), trans. Charles Fullman, from *Gleichgewicht oder Hegemonie* (Krefeld: Scherpe, 1948).

of bids by various powers for hegemony or supremacy, met ultimately by defeat and the restoration of a balance of power. That thesis may fit other eras (though even here one can have serious doubts). It does not suit the 19th century, which contains no Charles V, Philip II, Louis XIV, Chatham, Catherine the Great, Napoleon, Hitler, or Stalin. The reason is not that 19th-century statesmen were wiser or more restrained, but that the 19th-century system inhibited bids for mastery in Europe.

Certainly there was serious competition in 19th-century international politics. It was essentially competition for advantage, like the competition for shares of the market in an oligopolistic industry. The main advantage sought was the ability to profit from the international system at little cost, to enjoy freedom and choices others did not, and to escape burdens and payments that others had to bear. "Being the arbiter of Europe," "having a free hand," and "holding the balance" were code terms for this advantageous situation. The critical consideration, in any case, is that in the 19th century, unlike in others, the competition for advantage went on for a long time without degenerating into a struggle for mastery.

Some evidence even exists to satisfy those who would like quantifiable data to support the supposed qualitative difference between 18th- and 19th-century international politics. This evidence lies in the numbers of battlefield deaths in European wars in the two centuries. It should not be pressed too hard, of course. Statistics are not very reliable, calculations are inexact and hard to interpret in this area, and there are many variables, such as the size of the respective armies, the effects of different weaponry, tactics, and strategy, different standards of hygiene and care of the wounded, and so forth. Nonetheless, the contrast between the two centuries is revealing enough as an indicator of the scale and frequency of warfare to be meaningful even if large margins are allowed for error. If one takes the total number of deaths for 1715-1792 (1,858,000, according to a recent assessment) and compares it to that for 1815-1914 (635,000), and then figures in the growth in the population of Europe between the two centuries (not quite double) and the greater number of years in the 19th-century sample, the ratio of 18th- to 19th-century battlefield deaths per year is somewhere between 7:1 and 8:1.[19]

---

[19] Jack S. Levy, *War in the Modern Great Power System, 1495-1975* (Lexington: University of Kentucky Press, 1983), 88-89. I have omitted the wars of 1792-1815 from the calculations, even though historically they belong to the 18th century, to meet the objection that World War I should then be included for the 19th century. In any case, the discrepancy between the two centuries is no statistical quirk caused by a preponderance of deaths in one particular war or period. Each century shows a comparable pattern of initial stability (1715-40 and 1815-53), followed by upheaval (1740-63 and 1853-71) and a return to relative stability (1763-92 and 1871-1914). In each period the ratio of battlefield deaths is roughly the same.

III

Thus, a prima facie case exists that a profound, durable change occurred in international politics after 1815. Three features introduced into
international politics in 1813-1815, which became constitutive elements of
the system, help to account for this change, and make it systematic in
character. They made it possible for 19th-century statesmen to manage
three central and perennial problems of international politics in the face
of which the 18th century system had been relatively helpless. The three
problems were: how to assure a reasonable amount of mutual security
and status for all the great powers; how to insulate Europe from extra-
European sources of conflict; and how to reconcile the legitimate requirements of smaller states for a secure independence with the equally legitimate and unavoidable quest of great powers for spheres of influence
beyond their frontiers.

The three new elements of international politics that served to meet
these problems were the treaty system of 1815 and the European Concert;
the "fencing off" of the European state system from the extra-European
world; and the establishment of a system of intermediary bodies between
the great powers. I will make no attempt here to show how these elements arose, on what new bases of collective outlook they rested, how
they worked in most individual cases, what led to their gradual breakdown and supersession, and how this affected the system. That sort of
historical exposition must be done if the argument is to hold up in the
long run, but to attempt it here would shatter the bounds of this essay.

The treaty system of 1815 and the European Concert are the best-
known elements, and the easiest to define and illustrate. Beginning with
the Vienna settlement, the 19th-century international system guaranteed
the existence, security, status, and vital interests of all the European great
powers. Between 1813 and 1815, the members of the final coalition
against France worked out Europe's boundaries in a way mutually tolerable to all the important powers, including France, and then guaranteed these territorial arrangements by a series of interlocking treaties and
a general great-power alliance, from which France was initially excluded,
but which it soon joined. A variety of procedures and devices strengthened this network of treaty guarantees, including a system of diplomacy
by conference and some general principles of a European Concert. The
latter protected the rights, interests, and equal status of the great powers
above all, but they also committed these powers to the performance of
certain duties connected with those rights—respect for treaties, noninter-
ference in other states' internal affairs, willingness to participate in the
Concert's decisions and actions, and a general observance of legality and

restraint in their international actions.[20] This system of guarantees for the rights, status, and existence of the great powers, though egregiously violated and badly strained in the mid-century wars, managed to make something of a comeback and to endure after a fashion till the turn of the century.

By contrast, though 18th-century statesmen and theorists had often talked about such a system,[21] the rights, status, vital interests, and very existence of great powers were never safe at that time, and were often deliberately attacked. Attempts to partition the territory of other major powers and to reduce them to second- or third-rank status were a normal part of 18th-century politics[22]—constitutive and necessary features of the system rather than its accidental products.[23] Thus, the total destruction of the European balance during the revolutionary and Napoleonic wars represents merely the climax of a process begun much earlier, rooted in the conviction shared by all great powers and many smaller ones that, in order to preserve their status and security, they not only needed to aggrandize themselves but also to eliminate the threats posed by the existence of their rivals.

The second major element is not as obvious. In the 19th-century system, international politics within Europe was essentially separated from colonial, maritime, and commercial competition between European powers in the non-European world. In Gustav Adolph Rein's phrase, Europe was hedged in, fenced off from the rest of the world.[24] The most striking evidence of this change from the 18th century is what happened to maritime and colonial questions in the peace settlement and after it. Like the major 18th-century wars, the wars of the Revolution and Napoleon were world contests fought around much of the globe. The main stakes in the struggle between France and Britain were maritime and colonial su-

[20] Karl Griewank, *Der Wiener Kongress und die europäische Restauration*, 2d ed. (Leipzig: Koehler & Amelang, 1954); Maurice Bourquin, *Histoire de la Sainte Alliance* (Geneva: Librairie de l'Université Georg, 1954); Richard B. Elrod, "The Concert of Europe: A Fresh Look at an International System," *World Politics* 28 (January 1976), 159-74.

[21] Duchardt (fn. 4).

[22] For good discussions of how and why this happened, with particular reference to the Seven Years' War, see Walther Mediger, *Moskaus Weg nach Europa* (Braunschweig: G. Westermann, 1952); Johannes Kunisch, *Staatsverfassung und Mächtepolitik* (Berlin: Duncker & Humblot, 1979); and Michael G. Müller, "Russland und der Siebenjährige Krieg. Beitrag zu einer Kontroverse," *Jahrbücher für Geschichte Osteuropas* 28 (No. 2, 1980), 198-219.

[23] For example, Klaus Zernack shows how Russia's expansion in its northern wars and the first partition of Poland were in a sense system-preserving actions: "Das Zeitalter der nordischen Kriege von 1558 bis 1809 als frühneuzeitliche Geschichtsepoche," *Zeitschrift für historische Forschung* (No. 1, 1974), 55-79, and "Negative Polenpolitik als Grundlage deutschrussischer Diplomatie in der Mächtepolitik des 18. Jahrhunderts," in *Russland und Deutschland. Festschrift für Georg von Rauch* (Stuttgart: E. Klett, 1974), 144-59.

[24] Rein's comments are quoted in Wolfgang von Groote, ed., *Napoleon I und die Staatenwelt seiner Zeit* (Freiburg: Rombach, 1969), 198-99.

premacy which, after 1807, became almost the only reason for continuing the war. While France's most effective propaganda weapon in Europe was to denounce Britain's tyranny on the seas, Napoleon's attempt to counter British seapower through the Continental System may have done more than anything else to hasten his ultimate downfall. The maritime and colonial conflict had enormous world-historical results. Among other things, it brought the United States into the war and helped confirm its independence, led to the revolutionary liberation of Latin America, and laid the foundations of Britain's territorial empire in India. Moreover, maritime and colonial issues were heavily involved in European international politics; a good part of the diplomacy of the various allied coalitions, including the final one, consisted of efforts by various continental powers to get Britain to make colonial and maritime concessions to France and its allies in the interests of continental peace. Yet before the war was over, this intimate, seemingly indissoluble connection between European and overseas wars and politics had been severed. Britain flatly barred the issue of maritime law from discussion at the peace table and firmly rejected any Russian or allied mediation of its war with the United States. As to the colonial settlement, the British insisted that though they would be generous (and on the whole they were), in principle they would not make colonial concessions in return for France's agreement to continental peace terms. First Britain's major allies, then France, and finally its client Holland accepted the terms Britain offered, and that ended it. The only overseas issue discussed at Vienna concerned the slave trade, which involved morality and prestige more than power or material interests. In other words, Europe accepted British naval and colonial supremacy, choosing to live with it and, so far as strictly European politics was concerned, to ignore it.

Something similar happened with regard to the Ottoman Empire, which had become a major zone of European conflict in the late 18th century and the Napoleonic wars. Proposals were made to include it in the general settlement and its guarantees, but they were not pursued. Russia had unsettled grievances against the Turks which it did not want to submit to European control; Metternich—who viewed the Balkans as part of Asia, and Austria's southeastern border with Turkey as equivalent to a sea frontier—wanted the Ottoman Empire left as it was. Other parts of Asia (India, Persia, the Middle East) also underwent major changes in the Napoleonic wars; some historians have traced the origins of Anglo-Russian world rivalry back to 1815 or earlier.[25] But even if certain roots of the

[25] See, for example, Jacques-Henri Pirenne, *La Sainte-Alliance, organisation européenne de la paix mondiale*, 2 vols. (Neuchâtel: Editions de la Baconnière, 1946-49); Edward Ingram, *Commitment to Empire* (New York: Oxford University Press, 1981).

19th-CENTURY INTERNATIONAL SYSTEM   15

later struggle can be detected at this stage, the British government as a whole did not begin to see Russia as a serious menace to India and the empire until the 1830s; even then, British policy remained Europe-centered overall.[26] The post-Vienna period, in fact, witnessed the abatement of both rivalry and intimacy in Anglo-Russian relations. Before 1815, Catherine II, Paul I, and Alexander I had each at various times been avowed enemies and close allies of Britain. After 1815, the two powers were neither one nor the other—never enemies until 1853, and never close allies, despite the efforts of Nicholas I and his advisers to reach a partnership with England on European and Near Eastern questions.[27] In the typical post-Vienna manner, each power saw the other as a potential rival to be managed by ostensible friendship. In any case, the Eastern powers—especially Austria and Prussia, but Russia as well—did not let extra-European questions seriously affect their policies in Europe.[28]

Nor, in the main, did the English and French. Their rivalry overseas never disappeared entirely after 1815, and flared up on occasion over various issues, such as the slave trade, Britain's right of search, Latin America, Madagascar, Tahiti, and Algeria. But this was more an irritant than a serious danger; it kept the two powers from genuine entente but never threatened the peace. In Europe, Britain and France were able to cooperate in a wary fashion in the Iberian Peninsula, Belgium, Greece, and the Near East. The only serious crisis between them, in 1840, arose over a European Concert issue, the Eastern Question, where a perceived insult to France's honor was deemed more important than any blow to her interests.[29] In a similar way, Britain and the Netherlands remained friends in Europe despite their commercial and colonial rivalries and disputes in the Far East.[30]

To dismiss this shielding of European politics from extra-European quarrels as unimportant, or to attribute it simply to Britain's unchallenged superiority overseas, is to ignore or underrate the sharp contrast between the 18th and 19th centuries in this respect, as well as the change

[26] David Gillard, *The Struggle for Asia 1828-1914* (London: Methuen, 1977); Kenneth Bourne, *Palmerston: The Early Years, 1784-1841* (New York: Macmillan, 1982); Malcolm E. Yapp, *Strategies of British India* (Oxford: Clarendon Press, 1980).

[27] Harold N. Ingle, *Nesselrode and the Russian Rapprochement with Britain, 1836-1843* (Berkeley: University of California Press, 1976).

[28] *Ibid.*; Manfred Kossok, *Im Schatten der Heiligen Allianz* ([East] Berlin: Akademie-Verlag, 1964); Russell H. Bartley, *Imperial Russia and the Struggle for Latin American Independence, 1808-1828* (Austin: Institute for Latin American Studies, University of Texas, 1978).

[29] Roger Bullen, *Palmerston, Guizot and the Collapse of the Entente Cordiale* (London: Athlone, 1974); Raymond Guyot, *La première Entente Cordiale* (Paris: F. Rieder, 1926); Douglas Johnson, *Guizot: Aspects of French History, 1787-1874* (London: Routledge & Keagan Paul, 1963).

[30] Nicholas Tarling, *Anglo-Dutch Rivalry in the Malay World, 1780-1824* (London and New York: Cambridge University Press, 1962), and *Imperial Britain in South-East Asia* (Kuala Lumpur and New York: Oxford University Press, 1975).

in outlook that made it possible. The 18th century was filled with wars in North America, the West Indies, India, and on the high seas, which spilled over into Europe, and vice versa. Eighteenth-century statesmen had often tried, without success, to separate European from extra-European quarrels—witness Walpole's failure in 1739-1740, and Newcastle's in 1754-1756.[31] Nineteenth-century statesmen not only could separate the two if they wished, but found it relatively easy and normal to do so. Europe's acceptance of British maritime and overseas domination does need explanation; it was not automatic. During the latter part of the 18th century and the Napoleonic Wars, British naval practices aroused much resentment of Britain on the continent, as British statesmen were well aware; several major efforts at united action were promoted against them (the Leagues of Armed Neutrality led by Russia in 1780 and 1800-1801, and the Continental System). No such anti-British continental combination was ever contemplated in the 19th century until Russia proposed one during the Boer War, and then it came to nothing. One major reason was that Britain made its maritime and colonial supremacy far more tolerable to other powers, and even advantageous to them in some respects, than it had been in the 18th century. Thus the position advanced by Friedrich von Gentz and other defenders of Britain during the Napleonic wars— that the anti-British arguments about maritime law and neutral rights were spurious and that Britain's control of the seas, though vital to Britain's existence, threatened no one else—was made good in the postwar era. With the gradual transition from a mercantilist to a free-trade empire, British maritime supremacy became at worst only an irritant and a latent threat to others, and in some ways even an asset. British naval vessels cleared out pirates in the Red Sea and the Persian Gulf to the advantage of all nations,[32] guarded sea lanes all could use, and held colonies with whom all could trade. Moreover, while expanding its own empire, Britain did not for most of the century seriously interfere with imperial expansion and consolidation by other states, especially France and the Netherlands. Nineteenth-century Britain is often praised for maintaining peace and the balance of power within Europe, and criticized for greedy imperialism outside it. So far as the European states system is concerned, the verdict could well be reversed. Britain, in my view, did not really

---

[31] John H. Plumb, *Sir Robert Walpole*, 2 vols. (Boston: Houghton-Mifflin, 1956-61); Reed Browning, *The Duke of Newcastle* (New Haven and London: Yale University Press, 1975); Patrice Higgonet, "The Origins of the Seven Years' War," *Journal of Modern History* 40 (March 1968), 57-90; T. R. Clayton, "The Duke of Newcastle, the Earl of Halifax, and the American Origins of the Seven Years' War," *Historical Journal* 24 (September 1981), 571-603.

[32] John B. Kelly, *Britain and the Persian Gulf, 1795-1800* (Oxford: Clarendon Press, 1968); Thomas E. Marston, *Britain's Imperial Role in the Red Sea Area, 1800-1878* (Hamden, CT: Shoestring Press, 1961).

maintain the European balance and more than once endangered the peace of Europe, but the way Britain ran its empire contributed much to making the 19th-century system work.

IV

The third element is the least recognized, but quite possibly the most important. The settlement of 1815 established a broad system of intermediary bodies in Europe: smaller states situated and organized to serve as buffers and spheres of influence. While they separated the great powers, making it more difficult for them to fight, they also linked them by giving them something in common to manage. The importance of intermediary bodies in the 19th-century system has been little recognized—not because the facts about them are unknown, but because these facts have been interpreted in a different framework. The arrangements made concerning smaller powers in the Vienna settlement have traditionally been viewed in terms of balance-of-power politics, or a barrier system designed to contain France, or territorial deals and compensations negotiated to meet rival state and dynastic claims. None of these explanations is wrong. Statesmen thought and acted according to these ideas, as the documents show, though they also talked about intermediary bodies and their uses. But here is where one must distinguish between what the leaders intended to do and what they actually did. The system of intermediary bodies emerging from the Vienna settlement was less a product of deliberate planning than it was the ultimate outcome of arrangements reached mainly for other, more immediate purposes. The most important historic results are often unintentional. Mazzini once said of the Italian *Risorgimento*, "We aimed for ten and achieved two." In 1815, European statesmen aimed for two and achieved six or seven.

The Kingdom of the United Netherlands, formed of the Dutch provinces, Belgium, and Luxemburg, is a good case in point. It was of course designed to be the keystone of the proposed defensive barrier against France. In its actual role and function, however, it was no more simply a barrier state than Poland or Czechoslovakia after World War I were simply part of the French *cordon sanitaire* against Germany and Russia. King William I intended his kingdom to be an independent power playing a meaningful general role in European politics; that is the main reason he fought so stubbornly against the loss of Belgium after 1830.[33] Metternich specifically called the Netherlands an intermediary body linking Austria

[33] Gustaaf J. Renier, *Great Britain and the Establishment of the Kingdom of the Netherlands, 1813-1815* (London: George Allen & Unwin, 1930).

to Britain, through South and West Germany, forming a conservative phalanx to keep the restless powers, Russia and France, from weighing on the European center.[34] Prussia, once its own conflicts with the Dutch were settled, considered the Netherlands a sphere of influence to be shared with England, linking Prussia and Britain. The other German princes looked at William, a member of the German Confederation as Grand Duke of Luxemburg, as their ally in preserving the independence of middle-sized and small states against Austria and Prussia.[35] Even Russia considered its influence in the Netherlands important and for this reason promoted a marriage between the Dutch Crown Prince and a Russian Grand Duchess. In short, the United Netherlands served a number of functions as an intermediary body; most of these survived when its role as a barrier against France disappeared with the Belgian revolt of 1830. Belgium itself became an intermediary body with various important functions aside from that of being a neutral barrier against France.[36]

Scandinavia (Denmark and Sweden-Norway) represents another intermediary body after 1815, but one to which balance-of-power and barrier-system considerations hardly apply at all. Once the territorial struggle between Sweden and Denmark over Norway was settled in 1814, the Baltic was opened to general, peaceful trade. None of the three neighboring great powers, Russia, Prussia, and Britain, tried to dominate it exclusively, but all were anxious to maintain free access through the straits and preserve the status quo. Scandinavia was thus effectively removed from great-power politics, ending the centuries-old Northern Question, which had been a major arena of conflict throughout the 18th century and the Napoleonic wars.[37]

Neutral Switzerland is the clearest and most familiar example of an intermediary body in the peace settlement. It is important to correct an impression fostered by some Swiss historians that, in restoring and neutralizing the Swiss Confederation in the Vienna settlement, the great powers merely reestablished a traditional Swiss arrangement, with the intention of removing Switzerland entirely from European politics. Although the allies certainly based their work on Swiss tradition, the Swiss Confederation of 1815 was distinctly a great-power accomplishment—

[34] Wolf D. Gruner, "Die belgisch-luxemburgische Frage im Spannungsfeld europäischer Politik 1830-1839," *Francia* 5 (1977), 316.

[35] Johan C. Boogman, *Nederland en de Duitse Bond, 1815-1851*, 2 vols. (Groningen: C. Wolters, 1955).

[36] See, for example, Hermann von der Dunk, *Der deutsche Vormärz und Belgien 1830/48* (Wiesbaden: F. Steiner, 1966).

[37] Zernack (fn. 23); Otto Brandt, "Das Problem der 'Ruhe des Nordens' im 18. Jahrhundert," *Historische Zeitschrift* 140 (No. 3, 1929), 550-64; Claude Nordmann, *Grandeur et liberté de la Suède (1660-1792)* (Paris: Béatrice-Nauwelaerts, 1971).

something the cantons themselves, riddled by internal rivalries, could never have achieved on their own.[38] Moreover, in guaranteeing the Swiss federal constitution, the allies were not attempting to remove Switzerland from the European states system, but to ensure that the Swiss played certain important roles within it. An independent, neutral, loosely federated Switzerland was intended to be part of the barrier system, to hold the Alpine passes, to provide a bulwark against revolution, and to afford a safe sphere of influence for its neighbors. Including the Swiss constitution in the Final Act of Vienna did not mean that no power could say anything about Swiss affairs, but that no one power could have an exclusive say; all had the right to hold Switzerland to the performance of its international obligations. From 1815 to 1848, Switzerland's neighbors made considerable use of their right of intervention in Switzerland, sometimes illegitimately, sometimes with good reason.

The German Confederation (*Deutscher Bund*) was an even more important intermediary body than Switzerland. The conventional textbook view is that the *Bund* represented a good way of organizing Germany for external defense against France and Russia without making it a threat to its neighbors. For internal purposes, however, it was considered unsatisfactory, since it kept the German territory divided into many small states dominated by Austria and Prussia, who used their control to repress liberalism, constitutionalism, and nationalism. This liberal-nationalist view contains some truth, but also considerable distortion, as scholars have long recognized. For one thing, the main foreign policy problem of Germany was not the external threat from France or Russia, but the internal rivalry between Austria and Prussia. Their 18th-century conflicts and wars had devastated Germany, destroyed all chances for reform in the old Empire, promoted both French and Russian influence in German affairs, and ultimately led to conquest by the French.[39] The partnership between Austria and Prussia and their joint victory in the War of Liberation and the final campaign against France temporarily overcame this rivalry, but did not itself solve the problem. It remained alive during the Congress of Vienna, reaching a climax in the Polish-Saxon question; in 1814-1815, both French and Russian leaders still entertained ideas about regaining their former influence in German affairs by exploiting Austro-Prussian differences. Thus, from the standpoint of the European system, the main function of the German Confederation was to make the problem of Aus-

[38] William Martin, *La Suisse et l'Europe 1813-1814* (Lausanne: Payot, 1931).
[39] Karl O. von Aretin, *Heiliges Römisches Reich 1776-1806*, 2 vols. (Wiesbaden: F. Steiner, 1967), and *Vom Deutschen Reich zum Deutschen Bund* (Göttingen: Vandenhoeck & Ruprecht, 1980).

tro-Prussian rivalry manageable, which it did for almost half a century— a remarkable achievement. The whole of Germany became an intermediary body for Europe generally and for Austria and Prussia in particular. It was neither divided into separate Austrian and Prussian spheres, as Prussia wanted, nor was the Empire restored under Habsburg leadership. Instead, Germany was united into a princely confederation of independent states which Austria and Prussia had to manage jointly. This same approach served to make Germany's other foreign policy problems, also internal in origin, similarly manageable—it settled rivalries and territorial disputes between various smaller states, between estates and princes, between the beneficiaries and the victims of Napoleonic rule, between Catholics and Protestants, and even between different factions of Catholics and Protestants.[40]

It is equally mistaken to assume that the main forces that the German Confederation of 1815 needed to accommodate, but chose instead to repress, were liberal and nationalist ideas and movements stimulated by the French Revolution and the War of Liberation. These ideas were indeed repressed, especially in 1819-1820 and after; but they had only a narrow following in Germany anyway—among some students, intellectuals, and enlightened state officials. The prevailing political sentiment among rulers and masses alike was much more conservative in 1815 than in 1792. The War of Liberation was fought and won overwhelmingly by regular standing armies; as for the people (i.e., the peasants), they either did not rise at all in 1813 or did so mainly for God, king, and local country—not for a free and united Germany.[41] Therefore the main realities of 1792-1813 in Germany with which allied statesmen had to deal—aside from considerable destruction, residual Francophobia, and a heightened aversion to revolution[42]—were the results of the destruction of the old Empire and Napoleon's Confederation of the Rhine. The princely revolution of 1803 and after, not the French Revolution of 1789 or the German uprising of 1813, represented the dominant political fact of post-Napoleonic Germany. Lacking even the rudimentary bond of the old Empire and its ideal of government based on law rather than power, Germany now included centralized, territorially integrated states, run by new bureaucra-

[40] Ernst R. Huber, *Deutsche Verfassungsgeschichte seit 1789*, I, 2d ed. (Stuttgart: E. Kohlhammer, 1967); Enno E. Kraehe, *Metternich's German Policy*, 2 vols. (Princeton: Princeton University Press, 1963-83).
[41] Rudolf Ibbeken, *Preussen 1807-13* (Cologne: Grote, 1970); Jacques Droz, *L'Allemagne et la Révolution française* (Paris: Presses universitaires de France, 1949).
[42] Timothy C. W. Blanning, *The French Revolution in Germany* (Oxford: Clarendon Press, 1983).

cies and supported by a new state-consciousness. These states had already swallowed up the ecclesiastical principalities, mediatized and absorbed the small semi-independent princes, incorporated most free cities, and were working to uproot old estate, religious, local, and tribal loyalties.[43] This not only cleared the stream bed of German history (as German historians say); it also created divisions more than unity, and promoted state patriotism more than German nationalism, at least in the short run.[44] The main task of German statesmen in 1813-1815, rather than satisfying a popular cry for German unity, lay in bridging conflicts, not merely between states, but especially between the old dispossessed and the new *beati possidentes*.

A further problem: although Germany was intended to be the main component of the defensive system against France, neither Austria nor Prussia wanted that direct responsibility. Both tried to put other states on the front line, distancing themselves from France as much as possible. Witness Austria's refusal to take back its former holdings in the Netherlands, its readiness to shed its old Southwest German territories, and its steady rejection of new territory or obligations on the Rhine; recall also Prussia's effort to annex the whole of Saxony and to compensate the King of Saxony with a new kingdom made up partly of Prussian territory on the Rhine. The rest of Germany, in other words, was supposed to be a buffer and intermediary body between France and Austria and Prussia.

As a result, while the *Bund* was certainly designed to hold France in check, it did not take sensible Frenchmen long to realize that it might be penetrated politically, thereby restoring France's old influence. For years after 1815, French diplomats continued to consider Bavaria as France's natural ally, for example; some leading Bavarians, including the King, agreed with them.[45] To be sure, France failed to exploit the opportunities

---

[43] Karl-Georg Faber, *Die Rheinlande zwischen Restauration und Revolution* (Wiesbaden: F. Steiner, 1966); Elisabeth Fehrenbach, *Traditionelle Gesellschaft und revolutionäres Recht* (Göttingen: Vandenhoeck & Ruprecht, 1978); Eberhard Weis, "Der Einfluss der französischen Revolution und des Empire auf die Reformen in den süddeutschen Staaten" *Francia* 1 (1973), 569-83, and "Bayern und Frankreich in der Zeit des Konsulats und des Ersten Empire (1799-1815)" *Historische Zeitschrift* 237 (December 1983), 559-95.

[44] See, for example, Wolfgang Quint, *Souveränitätsbegriff und Souveränitätspolitik in Bayern* (Berlin: Duncker & Humblot, 1971); Karl O. von Aretin, *Bayerns Weg zum Souveränen Staat* (Munich: Beck, 1976); and Erwin Hölzle, *Württemberg im Zeitalter Napoleons und der deutschen Erhebung* (Stuttgart and Berlin: W. Kohlhammer, 1937). For evidence of a countervailing force, see Mack Walker, *German Home Towns* (Ithaca, NY: Cornell University Press, 1971).

[45] Anton Chroust, ed., *Gesandtschaftsberichte aus München, 1814-1848. Abteilung 1: Die Berichte des französischen Gesandten*, 5 vols. (Munich: Akademie der Wissenschaften, 1935-41); Karl Hammer, *Die französische Diplomatie der Restauration und Deutschland, 1814-1830* (Stuttgart: A. Hiersemann, 1930).

it had, and German public opinion even in formerly pro-French circles turned nationalist and Francophobe, as proved by the crisis of 1840.[46] Yet, even after France lost its chance to regain its former influence and friends, the *Bund* never threatened France, and actually contributed to its security. Certainly it was a safer arrangement than a Germany united under either German great power, or under both of them. If Frenchmen resented the Confederation, it was for the same reasons they resented the whole settlement of 1815: not because it was a danger to France, but because they somehow considered it an insult and a humiliation.

When all this is added up, it becomes clear that the *Bund* really functioned as a great multipurpose intermediary body in Central Europe. It both linked and separated all the parts of Germany, preserving their individual independence while enabling them to exist in the same space. It separated Germany as a whole from the rest of Europe, preventing the sort of outside intervention common in the 18th century, while linking it to Europe in various ways—to the other great powers, guarantors of the federal constitution through the Final Act of Vienna; to the Netherlands and Denmark, who were part of the *Bund* as owners of Luxemburg and Holstein; to Italy (Istria, Trieste, and the South Tyrol were members); and even to the Slav world (Bohemia and Carinthia). The Prussian and Austrian territories that were not part of the historic Reich (East and West Prussia, Posen, Galicia, Hungary, Dalmatia, Illyria, and Lombardy-Venetia) were not included, however, so that Austria's and Prussia's roles as European great powers were consciously separated from their functions as leaders of Germany. The *Bund* did not unify Germany; that would have been impossible in 1815, and dangerous at any time. But it did a reasonable job of providing for Germany, in Metternich's words, "*Einigkeit ohne Einheit*," concord without union.

In three areas of Europe—Italy, the Balkans, and Poland—the intermediary body interpretation of the 1815 settlement does not seem to work. Even here, however, closer examination alters the initial impression. Italy supposedly came under direct Austrian control in 1815. True, Austria gained Lombardy-Venetia and enjoyed strong dynastic and treaty links to much of the rest of Italy. Metternich used all his diplomatic skill, both in 1814-1815 and later, to try to exclude French and Russian influence. At the same time, Italy was deliberately organized to separate France and Austria, and Austria's leading influence never developed into exclusive control. Various attempts by Metternich to make it so (for ex-

[46] Raymond Poidevin and Heinz-Otto Sieburg, eds., *Aspects des relations franco-allemandes 1830-1848* (Metz: Centre de recherches relations internationales de l'Université de Metz, 1978).

ample, his efforts to create a *Lega Italica*, an Austrian-led Italian Confederation) failed in the face of Piedmontese and papal resistance.[47] British influence and naval power remained important. The fact that Austria retained the lead in Italy for two decades after 1815 was due not so much to the peace settlement or Austrian power as to the fact that most Italian governments were even more conservative and fearful of revolution than Austria, and sought Austria's help in time of trouble. France had chances to compete successfully, but threw them away. Had Napoleon not come back from Elba and overthrown Louis XVIII in March 1815, the Bourbons would have been restored at Naples under royal French sponsorship, giving France the lead in southern Italy. In this and other ways, Napoleon's last adventure set back French policy in Italy for a generation. In any case, independent entities such as Sardinia-Piedmont and the Papal States functioned as intermediary bodies, separating France and Austria, making it harder for them to go to war (which was of considerable importance in 1831-32), and giving them common problems that they somehow had to approach jointly. By 1831, France and Austria were involved in an international conference over the Roman question. By the mid-1830s, Metternich was trying to limit French influence rather than to exclude it; and by the mid-1840s, he was actively trying to work with France in Italy.

Although the Ottoman Empire in southeastern Europe was not formally included in the peace settlement, it functioned as an intermediary body between Austria and Russia. It is clear why no formal arrangement was reached: after three generations of growing rivalry in the Balkans[48]—a rivalry that reached its most dangerous stage for Austria in 1809-1812 with Russia's attempt to annex the Rumanian Principalities— both great powers found it wiser to leave the issue alone, since their relations were strained enough by other questions. Besides, any formal arrangement, such as a guarantee of Turkish territory, would run afoul of Russia's residual territorial claims on Turkey, as well as of traditional Russian interests, ambitions, and claims to a protectorate over the Orthodox Church in the Balkans. Moreover, throughout the first half of the 19th century, Russia's position vis-à-vis Turkey was far stronger than Austria's—militarily, strategically, and on ethnic and religious grounds. Thus, the only possible basis for general Austro-Russian cooperation in

[47] Karl Grossman, "Metternichs Plan eines italienischen Bundes," *Historische Blätter* 4 (1931), 37-76; Paul W. Schroeder, *Metternich's Diplomacy at Its Zenith, 1820-1823* (Austin; University of Texas Press, 1962); Alan Reinerman, *Metternich and the Papacy in the Age of Metternich*, I (Washington, DC: Catholic University Press, 1980).

[48] Karl A. Roider, Jr., *Austria's Eastern Question, 1700-1790* (Princeton: Princeton University Press, 1982).

Europe (wanted by both sides) was conservative nonintervention in Turkey. So long as Russia was content to preserve the Ottoman Empire as a weak, inoffensive neighbor (which was most of the time), and to accept Austria as a junior partner in this, the two got along well. Whenever Russia seemed headed toward destroying Turkey or dominating it exclusively, it caused an Austro-Russian breach which, as in 1853-1855, could lead to the brink of war. The Balkans served as an intermediary body for other powers as well. In the new kingdom of Greece after 1830, Britain, France, and Russia competed and cooperated as supervisors,[49] while internal Ottoman crises in the 1830s and 1840s made Turkey the central object of Concert diplomacy.

Poland does not fit the general pattern of 1815, of intermediary bodies separating and linking great powers. It was partitioned in 1772-1795 by Russia, Austria, and Prussia, although these powers knew this would cause trouble by giving them long common frontiers; in 1814-1815, it was re-partitioned in an even more dangerous way, bringing Russia deep into Central Europe. Everyone knew that the partition of Poland violated the rules and made Poland a problem for Europe. Many Austrian leaders admitted privately that the original partition had been a great mistake, and Castlereagh and Talleyrand argued in principle for restoring an independent Poland. But no one really believed in this possibility, and for good reasons. The weaknesses that had promoted Poland's demise in the 18th century had grown worse through war, devastation, and internal divisions. More important still, in 1815 an independent Poland would not have been a barrier to Russian expansion, but an integral part of it, just as an independent Ukraine would have served German imperialism if Germany had won the First World War. The plan Prince Adam Czartoryski presented to Alexander I in 1813 proposed, in fact, to join the kingdom of Poland permanently to Russia and to make it Russia's junior partner in dominating Central Europe.

Poland thus was not restored for much the same reasons as those for which the Holy Roman Empire was not restored: the attempt could not have succeeded, and would have constituted a dangerous power play by one state against the others. What Russia and Prussia actually tried to do in relation to Poland and Saxony was bad enough. The only way the Polish lands could serve intermediary functions after 1815 was the one actually employed: each of the partitioning powers promised to respect Polish nationality and culture and to grant its Polish territories a separate

[49] John A. Petropoulos, *Politics and Statecraft in the Kingdom of Greece, 1833-1843* (Princeton: Princeton University Press, 1968).

administration and institutions. The arrangements made for this purpose were unsatisfactory from the outset, and the situation became worse with time and Polish insurrections. Yet the provisions were not worthless, at least at first, and contributed something to the survival of Polish nationality.[50] So far as international politics was concerned, while Poland represented a European problem and a danger to peace, especially in the revolts of 1830-1831 and 1863, in a curious and tragic way it was also a source of stability—the cement that helped hold the Holy Alliance powers together while simultaneously keeping them potential rivals.

Even apparent exceptions like Poland, then, show how the 1815 settlement involved a network of intermediary bodies in Europe, designed to inhibit great-power conflict and to promote flexible interaction. The system did not make the smaller powers of Europe simply the tools and pawns of the great ones, as some have believed. One of the more striking aspects of the 1813-1815 negotiations is the genuine concern of the allies to ensure the independence of all states, including the smaller ones. The charge of greedy expansionism fits some smaller states (the United Netherlands, Bavaria, Sweden, Sardinia-Piedmont) better than any of the bigger ones. Nor did the European Concert and great-power solidarity, when they existed, mean that the desires and interests of small states could be ignored. Small states could get away with much resistance and obstruction, even in the face of united European pressure. Witness how Bavaria and Württemberg resisted the great powers in 1814-1816 with regard to the *Bund* and territorial questions, and how Holland and Belgium did so from 1831 to 1839. There has never been an era in European history before 1815-1848 or since that time when a small state could feel so confident that it would not be the target of conquest or annexation by some great power. This respect for small-state independence was not based on legitimist dogma, self-denial, or moral sentiments, but on a healthy realism—the recognition that buffers and barriers were needed all round, not just against France, and that the independence of great powers was intertwined with that of lesser states. In the 18th century, by contrast, smaller states had been pawns on the great-power chessboard, continual objects of compensation, exchange, and conquest, while those intermediary bodies that were in existence (the Holy Roman Empire, Scandinavia, Poland, Italy, Turkey) were spongy, riddled with internal weaknesses and rivalries, and thus were vulnerable targets for takeover or arenas of all-out conflict.

[50] Norman Davies, *God's Playground: A History of Poland*, II (New York: Columbia University Press, 1982); Piotr S. Wandycz, *The Lands of Partitioned Poland, 1795-1918* (Seattle: University of Washington Press, 1974).

V

If this essay has succeeded in showing that real systemic change occurred in international politics between the 18th and 19th centuries and in identifying some of its structural elements, it still affords no basis for hard conclusions or sweeping generalizations. Historians and political scientists will undoubtedly want to have many questions answered, challenges met, and details clarified before they accept the *prima facie* case made here. Still, if this thesis adds something to the political scientists' fund of concepts and models for analyzing international politics, and encourages diplomatic historians to concentrate more on systemic factors and systemic change, it will not be useless. Moreover, the central problems with which the 19th-century system had to cope are not unique to its time; they may be irreducible constitutive elements of international politics in any era. How to ensure the security and status of great powers while curbing great-power hegemony and imperialism; how to shield the overall system and its central power-political relationships from shocks emanating from peripheral conflicts; how to reconcile the independence and security of smaller states with the inevitable determination of great powers to exercise influence beyond their borders and to protect their wider interests—these are problems that statesmen still face every day, and presumably always will. More light on the reason for the 19th century's relative success may not be irrelevant to today's concerns.

[8]

AHR Forum
The Troubled Origins of European Economic Integration: International Iron and Steel and Labor Migration in the Era of World War I

CARL STRIKWERDA

TWO WATERSHED YEARS, 1992, the European Community's attempt to achieve total economic integration, and 1989, the dramatic disappearance of the Iron Curtain, have created a new sense of Europe as an economic unit. Rather than orienting themselves to twenty-five individual national economies, business leaders, politicians, and investors have begun to adapt to a truly continental arena. Spain and Hungary compete now for the same investment funds; airlines and insurance companies scramble to find international partners; and professionals, stocks, and credit card information have begun moving across national borders in greater numbers than ever before.

In discussing how economic integration occurred in twentieth-century Europe, historians generally refer to two basic literatures. On the one hand, theoretical perspectives have portrayed integration as the natural, logical outcome of long-term economic trends. Once the industrial revolution made national economies dependent on large-scale imports and exports and financial transfers, it was inevitable that, eventually, business organizations and labor would also flow across borders, along with raw materials, goods, and capital investment.[1] On the other hand, specific studies have discussed how only after World War II, with the creation of the European Coal and Steel Community and Common Market, did meaningful integration in Western Europe take place.[2] The disjuncture between

I would like to acknowledge the financial support of the American Philosophical Society, and of the Office of International Studies and Programs and the General Research Fund, both of the University of Kansas; the generous hospitality of Dr. Ulrich and Frau Irene Knapp of Wellinghofen-Dortmund while doing research in the Ruhr; the permission of Cockerill-Sambre S.A. to use archival documents in the Archives de l'Etat de Liège; the authorization by Franz Haniel & Cie GmbH to consult the Historische Archiv der Gutehoffnungshütte Oberhausen; the special assistance of M. Serge Hoffmann of the Archives de l'Etat de Luxembourg and Dr. Dirk Appelbaum of the Gutehoffnungshütte Archiv; and the useful criticisms of Kenneth Barkin, Gail Bossenga, Geoff Eley, Gerd-Rainer Horn, John McKay, Donald Reid, Joshua Rosenbloom, Hans Schmitt, John Sweets, Cornelis Trompetter, Rutger Van Dijk, and Guy Vanthemsche.

[1] Ali El-Agraa, "The Theory of Economic Integration," in *International Economic Integration*, El-Agraa, ed. (London, 1982); Peter Robson, *The Economics of International Integration* (London, 1980).

[2] Hans Schmitt, *The Path to European Union: From the Marshall Plan to the Common Market* (Baton Rouge, La., 1962); Uwe W. Kitzinger, *The Politics and Economics of European Integration*, 2d edn. (Westport, Conn., 1963); Pierre-Henri Laurent, "Historical Perspectives on Early European Integration," *Journal of European Integration*, 12 (1989): 89–100.

these two literatures is obvious but has rarely been explored. Why, if integration is a natural product of long-term trends created by the industrial revolution, did integration take so long to come about?

One answer, of course, is that integration is not simply the consequence of economic forces but has always been strongly influenced by political decisions. This article will look at both political and economic factors affecting European economic integration in the crucial period surrounding World War I. It will argue that a high degree of economic integration already existed in Western Europe on the eve of the war, a level not achieved again until at least the 1960s. Thus there were indeed economic forces pulling the European economy toward greater unity. World War I and its ripple effects, however, shattered the trend toward increasing integration in ways that we are only recently beginning to realize. The "1992" project by the European Community and the dismantling of the Soviet bloc are in one sense restoring the implicit unity of the pre-1914 world.

The implications of this thesis are four-fold. First, pre-1914 integration raises questions about the economic origins of World War I. Many scholars have portrayed European industry and government, especially in imperial Germany, as close allies.[3] The internationalization of business described below, however, suggests that many business leaders saw peaceful ties between states as the best means to economic growth and were wary of programs for autarky proposed by governments and interest groups.

Second, the high level of economic integration before World War I also raises important questions about interpretive models used by many business and social historians to explain the pace and financial underpinnings of multinational development. Business historians, who hardly discuss World War I, have portrayed multinational corporations as evolving gradually until American leadership spurred their take-off in the 1950s.[4] By contrast, another group of historians, largely though not exclusively Marxist, have argued that the early twentieth century marked a stage of so-called "finance capitalism," in which the great banks controlled industry. The war largely ended this stage of finance capitalism and thereby destroyed a basis for economic unity, which reemerged only under American hegemony.[5] The multinational business ties between heavy industry in different European countries, explored in this article, raise problems with both of these interpretations. The development of European multinational corporations

[3] Fritz Fischer, *War of Illusions: German Policies from 1911 to 1914* (New York, 1975); Hans-Ulrich Wehler, "Der Aufstieg des Organisierten Kapitalismus und Interventionsstaates in Deutschland," in *Organisierter Kapitalismus: Voraussetzungen u. Anfange*, Heinrich August Winkler, ed. (Göttingen, 1974).

[4] John Cantwell, "The Changing Form of Multinational Enterprise in the Twentieth Century," in *Historical Studies in International Corporate Business*, Alice Teichova, Maurice Lévy-Leboyer, and Helga Nussbaum, eds. (Cambridge, 1989); Alfred D. Chandler, "Technological and Organizational Underpinnings of Modern Industrial Multinational Enterprise," in *Multinational Enterprise in Historical Perspective*, Teichova, Lévy-Leboyer, and Nussbaum, eds. (Cambridge, 1986); Richard J. Barnett and Ronald E. Muller, *Global Reach: The Power of the Multinational Corporation* (New York, 1974).

[5] Rudolf Hilferding, *Finance Capital: A Study of the Latest Phase of Capitalist Development* [1910], Tom Bottomore, ed. (London, 1981), has influenced writers from Lenin through Ernest Mandel, *Late Capitalism* (London, 1975), Giovanni Arrighi, *The Geometry of Imperialism: The Limits of Hobson's Paradigm* (London, 1983), esp. 121–48, and Kees van der Pijl, *The Making of an Atlantic Ruling Class* (London, 1984).

            Carl Strikwerda

in heavy industry did not follow a slow, continuous path but expanded rapidly before World War I, only to contract in the 1920s and 1930s. Furthermore, industrial at least as much as finance capitalism created multinational economic ties before World War I. Many historians have overlooked the lead that industrialists in heavy industry increasingly took in foreign investment after 1900. Although severed by two world wars, the earlier international links forged by industrial capitalism provided an important precedent for the post–World War II search for European economic cooperation.

Third, the painful, punctuated quest for European unity shows how powerful a role governments and interest groups play in determining economic integration. Before the Great War, business and labor moved across borders easily because the state generally allowed private powers to act freely; since the early 1950s, Europe has been integrating its economies through deliberate state action.

Fourth, this thesis may help reconceptualize our periodization of twentieth-century history. Historians are professionally averse to prophecy, but other scholars may be forgiven for imagining that a century or more from now, the years from 1914 to 1989 may be seen as a painful period in which Europe groped to rediscover the cooperative route it had begun to take before World War I. If this is true, we may be on the verge of a new era, and it may repay us well to understand the roots of the era that is ending.

INTEGRATION ITSELF CAN BE UNDERSTOOD as a series of ascending levels. On the lowest level, goods, raw materials, and capital flow more or less freely depending on tariffs, quotas, or financial restrictions. This kind of integration first took place in the nineteenth century among most industrialized countries and formed the basis on which the European Common Market tried to expand in the 1950s. A more complex level of integration allows businesses to move their operations between countries or to merge with firms in other countries. Likewise, it permits labor to cross borders relatively easily. Because the European Community found itself moving only tentatively toward this level of integration, it began the project known as "1992."[6]

To demonstrate that this higher level of economic integration had begun to emerge before 1914, this article will look particularly at German, Belgian, and French companies in the iron and steel industry and at the corresponding movements of immigrant workers. The iron and steel industry provides an excellent case study of integration because it had enormous importance in 1900, with its large labor force, huge capital investment, and crucial control over armaments. Furthermore, iron and steel had close links to the essential energy sector of coal, as well as to finance, shipping, machine building, and the electrical industry. The world of labor, as well as that of business, formed a critical part of

---

[6] A third level of integration would be monetary or economic union, in which countries internationalize control of the currency or economic policy. See Fritz Machlup, "A History of Thought on Economic Integration," in *Economic Integration: Worldwide, Regional, Sectoral; Proceedings of the Fourth Congress of the International Economic Association held at Budapest, Hungary,* Machlup, ed. (London, 1976), 61–85, as well as Robson and El-Agraa.

the story of these emerging multinationals. Heavy industrial firms that expanded across borders frequently employed immigrant workers, both at home and abroad. As in all industries, the decision to use immigrant workers was highly sensitive to both economic and political forces. As W. R. Böhning has remarked, "Demand [for immigrant workers] is caused economically, screened politically, and given effect to administratively."[7]

The traditional view of Europe before 1914 argues that a rising tide of aggressive nationalism forestalled cooperation between rival nation-states and led to war. One economic historian has stated, "In the forty years or so before the First World War, the tendencies that were breaking up the economic unity of Europe were getting stronger in relation to those that made for continuing integration."[8] Most Continental countries adopted higher tariff levels against foreign goods, thus abandoning the free trade policies of the mid-nineteenth century.[9] Coal-poor France, which had to import over a third of its coal, even imposed a duty on imported coal in order to keep prices up for domestic producers.[10] Behind this concern of protecting home markets lay a fear of foreigners. The reactionary Action Française writer Léon Daudet claimed that German goods and business investments in France represented "Jewish-German espionage."[11] Despite rapidly growing exports, many Germans were convinced that their economy's future in world markets was threatened by opposition from foreigners.[12] Even Britain, which clung to free trade, experienced campaigns against "Made in Germany."[13]

Tariffs not only buttressed xenophobia and dampened international trade, they also encouraged economic interest groups to coalesce around nationalist policies. In Germany, big agricultural landowners (Junkers) and heavy industry agreed to tariffs protecting each other. They later offered mutual support for a large army, which the Junkers officered, and a navy, which heavy industry built.[14] This "marriage of iron and rye" in Germany had its counterpart in the French "alliance of iron and wheat."[15] Arno Mayer has broadened this argument to suggest that conservative elites dominated politics over almost all of Europe.[16] These nationalist and protectionist policies often went hand-in-hand with imperialism. Colonies, it was believed, could buy goods and furnish raw materials that European countries might refuse to each other. Lenin was only one of the first of

[7] W. R. Böhning, *Studies in International Labour Migration* (London, 1984), 140.

[8] Sidney Pollard, *The Integration of the European Economy since 1815* (London, 1981), 59.

[9] P. A. Gourevitch, "International Trade, Domestic Coalitions, and Liberty: Comparative Responses to the Crisis of 1873–1896," *Journal of Interdisciplinary History*, 8 (1977): 281–313.

[10] François Crouzet, "Le charbon anglais en France au XIXe siècle," in *Charbon et sciences humaines*, Louis Trénard, ed. (Paris, 1966).

[11] Léon Daudet, *L'Avant-Guerre: Etudes et documents sur l'espionnage juif-allemand en France depuis l'affaire Dreyfus* (Paris, 1913).

[12] Maurice Ajam, *Le problème économique franco-allemand* (Paris, 1914).

[13] Ernest Edwin Williams, *"Made in Germany,"* 5th edn. (London, 1897).

[14] Alexander Gerschenkron, *Bread and Democracy in Germany* (Berkeley, Calif., 1943); Volker Berghahn, *Germany and the Approach of War in 1914* (London, 1973); Hans-Ulrich Wehler, *The German Empire, 1871–1918*, Kim Traynor, trans. (Dover, N.H., 1985). For a different view: Kenneth D. Barkin, *The Controversy over German Industrialization, 1890–1902* (Chicago, 1970).

[15] Herman Lebovics, *The Alliance of Iron and Wheat in the Third French Republic, 1860–1914* (Baton Rouge, La., 1988).

[16] Arno J. Mayer, *The Persistence of the Old Regime: Europe to the Great War* (New York, 1981).

1110   *Carl Strikwerda*

a long line of writers who saw imperialism leading to world war.[17] Meanwhile, the international labor union federations and the Socialist Second International failed to influence any diplomatic confrontation and, more devastating, had scant effect on popular nationalism.[18] It is hardly surprising that the dominant interpretation of the pre–World War I era emphasizes nationalism, imperialism, and militarism. Or, as Norman Stone concluded in an excellent recent textbook, "After 1911, the war had already broken out in people's minds."[19]

Despite this portrait of nationalism and antagonism, it is not necessarily clear that Europe, especially Western Europe, was moving inevitably before 1914 toward conflict. Tariffs, although they had risen since the low levels of the 1860s, still remained much lower than they had been historically and lower than they were to be in the 1920s and 1930s. German tariffs in 1927 were, on average, over a third higher than they had been in 1913; by 1931, they had more than doubled. French tariffs—which were already higher than most—went up only slightly by 1927 but went up approximately 30 percent more by 1931.[20] West European tariffs in 1913 were also much lower than those in Russia and the United States.[21] Nor did tariffs or nationalist agitation in Europe significantly dampen international trade: between France, Germany, Britain, and Russia, trade was at an all-time high and increased steadily in the last few years before World War I.[22] The very flourishing of nationalist agitation against foreign goods came, in part, as a reaction to the growth of international trade—a growth that nationalist agitators largely failed to curtail.[23]

Furthermore, the emphasis on nationalism and tariffs often overlooks the web of relationships between European states that certain activists created in order to *increase* internationalism. The French Ligue du Libre-Echange carried on a vigorous battle against protectionism, as did the Hansa-Bund in Germany.[24] The Comité Commercial Franco-Allemand and the Deutsch-Französischer Wirtschaftsverein worked actively with both countries' parliaments and consular officials for freer trade, lower railroad rates, and more uniform laws. In 1909, these two groups brought together members of the Chamber of Deputies and the Reichstag from Lorraine, mayors of towns on both sides of the border, and the

[17] V. I. Lenin, *Imperialism: The Highest Stage of Capitalism* [1917] (New York, 1939).
[18] Hans Mommsen, *Arbeiterbewegung und nationale Frage: Ausgewählte Aufsätze* (Göttingen, 1979); Milorad M. Drachkovitch, *Les socialismes français et allemand et le problème de la guerre, 1870–1914* (Geneva, 1953); Susan Milner, *The Dilemmas of Internationalism: French Syndicalism and the International Labour Movement, 1900–1914* (New York, 1990).
[19] Norman Stone, *Europe Transformed 1878–1919* (Cambridge, Mass., 1983), 153.
[20] H. Liepmann, *Tariff Levels and the Economic Unity of Europe: An Examination of Tariff Policy, Export Movements and the Economic Integration of Europe, 1913–1931* (London, 1938), 383–401.
[21] Gourevitch, "International Trade," 282–312; J. J. Pincus, "Tariffs," *Encyclopedia of American Economic History*, 2 vols., Glenn Porter, ed. (New York, 1980), 1: 439–49.
[22] W. Ashworth, "Industrialization and the Economic Integration of Nineteenth Century Europe," *European Studies Review*, 4 (1974): 291–314; Raymond Poidevin, *Les relations économiques et financières entre la France et l'Allemagne de 1898 à 1914* (Paris, 1969), 769–73, 885–86; Paul Bairoch, "European Trade Policy, 1815–1914," in *The Industrial Economies: The Development of Economic and Social Policies, Cambridge Economic History*, vol. 8, Peter Mathias and Sidney Pollard, eds. (Cambridge, 1989), 88–90.
[23] C. Buchheim, "Aspects of XIX Century Anglo-German Trade Rivalry Reconsidered," *Journal of European Economic History*, 10 (1981): 289.
[24] Yves Guyot, *La jalousie commerciale et les relations internationales* (Paris, 1911); Siegfried Mielke, *Der Hansa-Bund für Gewerbe, Handel und Industrie 1909–1914* (Göttingen, 1976).

two nations' railroad directors to plan a new railroad line between French and German Lorraine.[25] Despite opposition from the military, which delayed this project, the political and economic support for it is striking.

PERHAPS THE MOST SIGNIFICANT INDICATOR OF A PERSISTENT TREND toward international ties before 1914 is the rise of international business. Unilever, Royal Dutch Shell, and many U.S. multinationals had their roots in these years.[26] Many studies of multinational business imply that it is primarily a post–World War II phenomenon pioneered by U.S. corporations.[27] In terms of the businesses that existed across borders in the 1960s, there is some truth to this, but this notion overlooks the impressive growth up to 1914. Two world wars and the Great Depression destroyed the foreign holdings of so many European corporations that their growth after 1945 appears as virtually a new beginning. Many scholars have also argued that "finance capitalism" dominated this era. Large banks through indirect investments such as shares and loans are claimed to have controlled much of international business. Yet the level of direct foreign investment—that is, investment that carried significant management control as opposed to financial interest—was almost certainly higher in 1914 than at any time until the mid-1960s.[28] Direct investment by French and Belgians, for example, helped make Russia the world's fourth largest steel producer.[29] Britain was by far the greatest source of foreign investment; but, until recently, scholars have considered most of this investment as purely financial, that is, shares, bonds, and loans.[30] Much more of this investment, too, probably was direct.[31] Although international finance had expanded greatly, it was not new. Direct investment by multinational firms, because it could integrate whole economies, was genuinely a break with the past.

It is this cosmopolitan world of international business that can give us an insight into the trends that the world war abruptly destroyed. The creation of interna-

[25] Consular reports, Paris to Berlin, July 13, 1908, R 85/64, and April 14, 1910, R 85/65, Abteilung II, Auswärtiges Amt, Bundesarchiv, Koblenz; "La percée des Vosges," *Journal des Débats*, April 28, 1909; Poidevin, *Les relations économiques*, 784–90.

[26] Charles Henry Wilson, *The History of Unilever: A Study in Economic Growth and Social Change*, 2 vols. (London, 1954); Anthony Sampson, *The Seven Sisters: The Great Oil Companies and the World They Made* (New York, 1975); Mira Wilkins, *The Emergence of Multinational Enterprise: American Business Abroad from the Colonial Era to 1914* (Cambridge, Mass., 1970).

[27] See note 4.

[28] Peter Svedberg, "The Portfolio-Direct Composition of Private Foreign Investment in 1914 Revisited," *Economic Journal*, 88 (December 1978): 763–77; John H. Dunning, "Changes in the Level and Structure of International Production: The Last One Hundred Years," in *The Growth of International Business*, Mark Casson, ed. (London, 1983). Because Svedberg, on whom Dunning relies, concentrates on Asia, Africa, and Latin America, intra-European direct investment may have been even higher than these authors suspect.

[29] John P. McKay, *Pioneers for Profits: Foreign Entrepreneurship and Russian Industrialization, 1885–1913* (Chicago, 1970); René Girault, *Emprunts russes et investissements français en Russie, 1887–1914* (Paris, 1973).

[30] Herbert Feis, *Europe, the World's Banker, 1870–1914* [1930] (New York, 1968), 26–32.

[31] Mira Wilkins, "The Free-standing Company, 1870–1914: An Important Type of British Foreign Direct Investment," *Economic History Review*, 2d ser., 41 (1988): 259–82; John Stopford, "The Origins of British-Based Multinational Manufacturing Enterprises," *Business History Review*, 48 (Autumn 1974): 303–56.

tional business connections before World War I indicates the relative openness of the societies at the time. The reaction against such international ties and the failure of these ties to promote genuine cooperation, however, demonstrate the deep-rootedness of nationalism and the larger failure of the European political system to reconcile the power of nation-states with the need for economic integration.

The iron and steel industries on the West European continent—particularly Germany, France, Belgium, and Luxembourg—provide an interesting case study of international business before the war. Together, these were the most industrialized nations in the world after the United States and Britain. Iron and steel around 1900, more than at any other time, were the keys to economic and military power. Unlike Britain, the United States, or Russia, these nations lacked the right balance of iron ore and coal to be self-sufficient. France and Luxembourg had large reserves of iron but lacked coal. Germany and Belgium had coal reserves—Germany enormous ones—but needed to import iron.[32] These western Continental European states, because of their proximity to Britain, could more easily integrate their economies than could many other regions. Even though British business played little direct role in these countries, its indirect role was immense: London provided the foundation for international monetary stability, inexpensive British coal and shipping benefited all coastal areas, and Britain and its empire were the largest and most open market for international trade.[33]

Finally, the iron and steel industries in these countries became, along with those in nearby Italy and the Netherlands, the basis of today's European Community. In the 1950s, the European Coal and Steel Community and the European Economic Community partially re-created the relatively open Continental economy that had existed before 1914. Nevertheless, international business in pre-war heavy industry on the Continent has gone largely unexamined. There is a hardly a mention of it in any historical study of multinational business.[34] Studies of European economic integration treat trade, tariffs, labor migration, and international agreements on communications and transportation but largely ignore international business.[35] Even in the pre–World War I world, the importation of German goods drew more attention than did investment in foreign heavy

[32] Fernand Maurette, *Les grands marchés des matières premières* (Paris, 1922), 1–16, 153–61; Norman J. G. Pounds and William Parker, *Coal and Steel in Western Europe: The Influence of Resources and Techniques on Production* (Bloomington, Ind., 1957), 127–246. By 1910, Britain imported approximately 30 percent of its iron ore; but, earlier, imports had been much less, and Britain's large foreign investments and merchant marine made it easier to obtain ore. British ore reserves were actually quite ample and were only not being worked because available technology did not yet make them competitive vis-à-vis easily obtained foreign ores. Henry Louis, "The Iron Ore Resources of the United Kingdom," in *The Iron Ore Resources of the World*, 2 vols. (Stockholm, 1910), 2: 623–41.

[33] Britain's import surplus with most of Continental Europe helped fuel other economies, while its goods still helped set the standard for a European-wide economy; Ashworth, "Industrialization"; Derek H. Aldcroft, ed., *The Development of British Industry and Foreign Competition, 1875–1914* (Toronto, 1968).

[34] Lawrence G. Franko, *The European Multinationals: A Renewed Challenge to American and British Big Business* (Stamford, Conn., 1976), 26–54, treats pre–World War I Continental European multinationals as largely propelled by the search for raw materials.

[35] See Pollard, *Integration*, 42–60, for example.

industry.[36] Yet the sheer size of these corporations and their political and military importance offer material for a revealing case study of internationalism. In this era, capital could move freely across borders, foreigners enjoyed almost all rights of incorporation, and multinationals could employ large numbers of foreign workers in their international branches. In many ways, it was these freedoms, too, that were lost after 1914 and that the European Community sought to re-create in the 1950s.

One key to the movement of heavy industrial companies across West European borders was the need for raw materials, especially iron. Because coal was much more abundant and so much of it needed to be burned in smelting, the iron and steel industry in almost every country grew up near coal fields and imported iron ore. In the 1860s, the scarcity of usable iron ore drove the biggest German and Belgian metallurgical producers to obtain mining concessions in Spain. Both the Krupp company, based in the Ruhr, and the John Cockerill company, based near Liège, purchased iron mines near Bilboa, Spain, which they were to continue to work into the twentieth century. In the 1870s and 1880s, however, the invention of the Thomas and Siemans-Martin processes for making steel made it possible to use high-phosphorus iron ores. The largest deposits of these in Western Europe were in Lorraine, on both sides of the Franco-German border, in Luxembourg, and in Sweden.[37] The ability to use these reserves allowed for a vast expansion of the iron and steel industry, as well as an expansion of coal mining to provide fuel. Eventually, the most successful iron and steel firms became those that were vertically integrated, that is, those that controlled their own sources of fuel and ore and could both smelt iron and produce steel and finished products.

As a result of the new processes, iron and steel firms sought iron ore fields in German and French Lorraine, Luxembourg, and, eventually, as the demand for steel skyrocketed, Normandy, Russia, and Morocco. For decades, laws in France and Luxembourg allowed foreigners to purchase mining concessions freely. By 1910, German and Belgian interests owned perhaps as much as 35 percent of the iron ore fields in French Lorraine, the largest iron ore field in Europe, and probably 40 percent of those in Luxembourg.[38] Almost all the major Ruhr industrial firms participated, including Thyssen, Hugo Stinnes's Deutsch-Luxemburg, and Emil Kirdorf's Gelsenkirchener. With capitalizations of over 100 million marks and labor forces of some 40,000 workers each, these were among the largest companies in the world. The largest Belgian iron and steel producer,

[36] Paul de Mirecourt, *Le commerce français aux mains des Allemands* (Paris, [1912?]); Buchheim, "Aspects," 289.

[37] Maurette, *Les grands marchés*, 157; Pounds and Parker, *Coal and Steel*, 116–23; David S. Landes, *The Unbound Prometheus: Technological Change and Industrial Development in Western Europe from 1750 to the Present* (Cambridge, 1969), 249–69; M. P. Nicou, "Les ressources de la France en minerais de fer," 1: 3–20, and G. Einecke and W. Kohler, "Die Eisenerzvorräte des deutschen Reiches," 2: 671–716, both in *Iron Ore Resources of the World*.

[38] Estimates vary because many firms owned concessions jointly or through subsidiaries: Michel Ungeheueur, "Die wirtschaftliche Bedeutung der ostfranzösischen Erz- und Eisenindustrie," *Technik und Wirtschaft*, 5 (1912): 11–15; and "Die wirtschaftliche Bedeutung der luxemburgischen Erz- und Eisenindustrie," *Schmollers Jahrbuch*, 40 (1916): 211–73; Dr. Kohlmann, "Die neuere Entwicklung des lothringischen Eisenerzbergbaues," *Stahl und Eisen*, 31 (March 16, 1911): 413–24.

1114   *Carl Strikwerda*

Ougrée-Marihaye from Liège, bought numerous concessions in France, as did Cockerill, Espérance-Longdoz, and Providence.[39]

More revolutionary than the purchase of foreign iron ore concessions was these companies' decision to invest in iron and steel production in France and Luxembourg. In Luxembourg, laws compelled foreign owners of ore concessions to smelt iron within the duchy.[40] Also, it became more economical to bring coal to the iron mines and produce iron or steel there, rather than to bring iron ore to the coal fields. Technical advances dramatically lowered the amount of coal needed to smelt a ton of iron. Simultaneously, a "transportation revolution" occurred.[41] Steam-powered iron and steel ships lowered the costs of moving both coal and iron, and corporations began to consider the best location on the basis of not only raw materials but labor costs and access to markets as well.[42]

By 1912, German and Belgian heavy industry had taken over 90 percent of Luxembourg iron and steel and transformed itself in the process. Penetration by the Germans was facilitated because Luxembourg, although an independent state, belonged to the Zollverein, the German customs union. Deutsch-Luxemburg, the largest employer in the Ruhr after Krupp by 1913, was founded in 1901 when German companies combined with Belgian-owned Luxembourg firms.[43] Its close rival in the Ruhr, Kirdorf's Gelsenkirchener, produced even more iron in Luxembourg than did Deutsch-Luxemburg and nearly as much steel. The Belgian firm Ougrée-Marihaye purchased a Luxembourg plant in Rodange in 1905.[44] In 1911, Belgian investors created ARBED (Aciéries Réunies de Burbach, Eich, Dudelange) by combining three Luxembourg and German firms into one large corporation. Belgians controlled two-thirds of ARBED; the remaining capital was French, Luxembourgish, and German. ARBED also controlled iron ore fields in French Lorraine and iron and steel firms in the German Saar, making it larger than any other European heavy industrial concern except the largest Ruhr firms.[45] Luxembourg made an important contribution to German and Belgian industrial power; the tiny country was the world's sixth largest pig iron

[39] Claude Prêcheur, "Les liens financiers entre les industries des métaux de la France et de l'UEBL," in *Mélanges de géographie physique, humaine, économique, appliquée: Offerts à M. Omer Tulippe,* 2 vols. (Gembloux, 1967); Daniel Jacobs, "Gereguleerd Staal: Nationale en internationale economische regulering van de Westeuropese staalindustrie 1750–1950" (Ph.D. dissertation, Universiteit te Nijmegen, 1988), 210–15.
[40] Camille Wagner, *La sidérurgie luxembourgeoise* (Luxembourg, 1931), 20.
[41] E. Levasseur, "Ports et marine de la France," *Revue économique internationale* (July 1911): 8–46; Kurt Wiedenfeld, *Die nordwesteuropäischen Welthafen* . . . (Berlin, 1903); Tsunehiko Yui and Keiichiro Nakagawa, eds., *Business History of Shipping: Strategy and Structure* (International Conference on Business History 11, Fuji) (Tokyo, 1984).
[42] Wilhelm Pothmann, *Zur Frage der Eisen- und Manganerzversorgung der deutschen Industrie* (Jena, 1920), 22–24; Wilfried Feldenkirchen, *Die Eisen- und Stahlindustrie des Ruhrgebiets 1879–1914* (Wiesbaden, 1982), 84–85.
[43] *Recueil financier* (1910): 1115–16; Margareta Anna DeVos, *Kapitalverflechtungen in der Montanindustrie zwischen westlichen Deutschland und Belgien von etwa 1830 bis 1914* (Bonn, 1986), 207–10.
[44] Paul Spange, *Un siècle de hauts-fourneaux à Rodange 1872–1972* (Luxembourg, 1972).
[45] Félix Chomé, *Aciéries Réunies de Burbach-Eich-Dudelange: Un demi-siècle d'histoire industrielle, 1911–1964* (Luxembourg, 1964), 18–47; Prêcheur, "Les liens financiers," 78–79; Pounds and Parker, *Coal and Steel,* 368–70.

producer in 1913 and may have been the world's fourth largest exporter of steel.[46]

In France, Germans and Belgians went beyond investing in ore fields to taking over existing companies and changing the entire character of the French iron and steel industry. In 1903, Ougrée-Marihaye took control of the Chiers and Vireux-Molhain firms, while in 1908 Gelsenkirchener, with Belgian and Luxembourg investors, took over the Aubrives-Villerupt firm in the French Lorraine.[47] After 1900, Thyssen, Krupp, and the important Rotterdam merchant firms DePoorter and Muller opened up the Norman iron ore fields, which French capitalists had almost ignored.[48] Thyssen went further and, working with French companies, began building the largest steel mill in France in 1913 to process Norman iron ore. Thyssen's works near Caen took advantage of proximity to the ocean to bring in British, German, and French coal and to ship out finished steel.[49]

Comparison with Sweden and Spain shows just how innovative this investment in French iron and steel was. Sweden had huge reserves of iron ore, yet there was almost no foreign investment in its iron and steel industry. Swedish law made it difficult for foreigners to obtain mining concessions, and the distance from coal reserves and the scarcity of labor may have also kept out investors in iron and steel. In 1913, Sweden exported only 200,000 tons of pig iron but 6,500,000 tons of iron ore.[50] Despite Britain's long history of investment in Spanish iron mining, and available coal from both Spanish and British mines, there was little integration of British iron and steel with Spanish iron ore sources. One of the most successful and profitable of British firms, the Consett Iron Company, integrated its direct ownership of Spanish iron mines with its coal mining and iron and steel production in Britain. Consett, however, remained the exception.[51]

[46] Wagner, La sidérurgie luxembourgeoise, 24; B. R. Mitchell, European Historical Statistics 1750–1970 (New York, 1975), 224–25.

[47] Jean-Marie Moine, Les barons du fer: Les maîtres de forges en Lorraine du milieu du 19ᵉ siècle aux années trente (Nancy, 1989), 76–77, 130; François Roth, "La participation des intérêts belges à l'industrialisation de la Lorraine (1860–1914)," in Les relations franco-belges de 1830 à 1934 (Metz, 1975). In 1914, Aubrives-Villerupt had four French directors, three Belgians, three Luxemburgers, and one German—Heinrich Vehling, who served on the board (Vorstand) of Gelsenkirchener; Recueil financier (1915): 939, 848.

[48] Reports to Paul Reusch, 3001 93006/15, Historische Archiv der Gutehoffnungshütte, Oberhausen [hereafter, HA/GHH]; Jean de Maulde, Les mines de fer et l'industrie métallurgique dans le département du Calvados (Caen, 1916). Dutch capitalists invested in iron ore in order to have the flow of ore up the Rhine complement the shipment of coal down the river: H. P. H. Nusteling, De Rijnvaart in het Tijdperk van Stoom en Steenkool 1831–1914 (Amsterdam, 1974), 305; "Société Française de Mines de Fer," L'information (March 19, 1912): 2.

[49] M. Ungeheuer, "Die Industriellen Interessen Deutschlands in Frankreich vor Ausbruch des Krieges," Technik und Wirtschaft, 9 (1916): 38–42; Wilhelm Treue, Die Feuer verloschen nie: August Thyssen Hütte 1890–1926 (Düsseldorf, 1966), 153–59.

[50] B. Boethius, "Swedish Iron and Steel, 1600–1955," Scandinavian Economic History Review, 6 (1958): 143–75. Techniques in Swedish iron-making and bank financing in Sweden made foreign investment less promising: Theodor Sehmer, Die Eisenerversorgung Europas (Jena, 1911), 55–87; Kurt Samuelson, "Banks and the Financing of Industry in Sweden, c. 1900–1927," Scandinavian Economic History Review, 6 (1958): 176–90.

[51] M. W. Flinn, "British Steel and Spanish Ore: 1871–1914," Economic History Review, 2d ser., 8 (August 1955): 84–90; H. W. Richardson and J. M. Bass, "The Profitablity of Consett Iron Company before 1914," Business History, 7 (July 1965): 71–92. Kenneth Warren, Consett Iron, 1840 to 1980: A Study in Industrial Location (Oxford, 1990), unfortunately does almost nothing with Consett's activities outside of Britain.

1116   *Carl Strikwerda*

The German and Belgian investment in French and Luxembourg iron and
steel, in other words, was not just a response to scarce raw materials but a
contribution of managerial and entrepreneurial skills that raised the productive
capabilities of the entire European economy. In 1909, German and Belgian steel
production, for example, averaged 45,000 tons per blast furnace, the French
34,000, and the British 30,000.[52] Since the domestic French market grew slowly,
German and Belgian industrialists instead applied their expertise to the raw
materials, skilled labor, and transportation facilities in France in order to export
iron and steel products around Europe and the world.[53] Despite the arguments
for "finance capitalism," this was not simply an extension of international banking
or portfolio investment. France actually possessed more available capital than
Germany, and capital exports were one of the France's few successful weapons in
its economic competition with Germany.[54] French iron and steel firms, too, were
renowned for their large capital reserves. Yet only where industry and the state
took deliberate action to tie foreign loans to purchases of French goods did this
abundant capital help French industry.[55] Otherwise, French capital went into
government loans or was put at the disposal of foreign industry.[56] Even the ample
capital reserves of French iron and steel firms probably reflected their caution
rather than their success.[57] In Belgium and Germany, industrial firms and banks
worked much more closely than in France to target investment in mining and
manufacturing.[58] At the same time, in contrast to the "finance capitalism"
argument, the giant German industrial corporations often freed themselves in
these years from dependence on any one bank or group of banks.[59] Thus it was
the managerial skills of industrial capitalism, and not simply the abundant funds

[52] Robert C. Allen, "The Peculiar Productivity of American Blast Furnaces, 1840–1913," *Journal of Economic History*, 37 (1977): 625.
[53] Ann Wendy Mill, "French Steel and the Metal-Working Industries," *Social Science History*, 9 (1985): 307–38. Michael Jared Rust, "Business and Politics in the Third Republic: The Comité des Forges and the French Steel Industry, 1896–1914" (Ph.D. dissertaton, Princeton University, 1973), 158–60, describes how Ougrée-Marihaye's Gustave Trasenster nearly broke up the French rail cartel over obtaining an order to supply Tunisia.
[54] Poidevin, *Les relations économiques*, 723–26.
[55] This was particularly true in the armaments industry: Raymond Poidevin, "Fabricants d'armes et relations internationales au début du XIXᵉ siècle," *Relations internationales*, 1 (May 1974): 39–56.
[56] Karl Erich Born, *International Banking in the 19th and 20th Centuries* (Leamington Spa, 1983), 121–23.
[57] Maurice Vignes, "Le bassin de Briey et la politique de ses entreprises sidérurgiques ou minières," *Revue d'économie politique*, 27 (1913): 304–29.
[58] Hendricus Van der Valk, *De betrekkingen tussen banken en nijverheid in België* (Haarlem, 1932); Jacob Reisser, *The Great German Banks and Their Concentration* (Washington, D.C., 1911); Born, *International Banking*, 89–91.
[59] Gerald D. Feldman, *Iron and Steel in the German Inflation, 1916–1923* (Princeton, N.J., 1977), 19; Wilfried Feldenkirchen, "The Banks and the Steel Industry in the Ruhr: Developments in Relations from 1873 to 1914," *German Yearbook on Business History 1981*, 36–51. Germans and Belgians raised a good deal of French capital, often in Brussels or Alsace; Raymond Poidevin, "Weltpolitik allemande et capitaux français (1898–1914)," *Deutschland in der Weltpolitik des 19. und 20. Jahrhunderts*, Imanuel Geiss and Bernd Wendt, eds. (Düsseldorf, 1973); Born, *International Banking*, 123; Karl Strasser, *Die deutschen Banken im Ausland* (Munich, 1925), 12–90; R. Poidevin, "Les banques alsaciennes entre la France et l'Allemagne de 1871 à 1914," *Revue d'Allemagne*, 10 (1985): 479–89. The ability to raise French capital in Brussels, as well as the Latin Monetary Union, which put the Belgian and French francs at parity, may have encouraged Germans to work with Belgians.

of finance capitalism, that help to explain multinational investment in heavy industry.

BELGIAN AND GERMAN INVESTMENT IN LUXEMBOURG AND FRANCE began a process of internationalizing heavy industry in all four countries. ARBED, Ougrée-Marihaye's plant in Luxembourg, and Wendel—all Belgian and French firms—made up almost 20 percent of the German steel cartel, the Stahlwerksverband, while three of the six largest Ruhr members of the cartel—Gelsenkirchener, Deutsch-Luxemburg, and Thyssen—became heavily committed to investments in France, Belgium, or other countries.[60] Meanwhile, Belgian and German interests controlled perhaps 15 percent of the French iron and steel industry.[61] Thyssen, because of his Caen steel mill, belonged to the business association of the French iron steel industry, the Comité des Forges. Gustave Trasenster, president of Ougrée-Marihaye and head of the Belgian steel cartel, joined the French rail cartel. Not surprisingly, the French, Belgian, and German rail and steel cartels reached a number of price-fixing agreements.[62] By investing in French metallurgy, Belgians and Germans were even able to penetrate French cartels. The most important cartel in French iron and steel was the Comptoir Métallurgique de Longwy, which set prices and quotas for pig iron in the Meurthe-et-Moselle region. Since the region was the only one in France that produced a surplus of pig, it effectively controlled prices for all of France—as long as foreign importers cooperated. This cooperation arose, first, because Germans and Belgians invested in French firms and, second, because the French shared control of the Comptoir. In 1914, there were seventeen directors of the cartel: no less than eight represented firms either owned or associated with Germans or Belgians, even though these firms made up less than a quarter of the production of the cartel's members.[63]

In trying to match the Belgian and German interpenetration of coal and iron across borders, French firms further internationalized heavy industry. Between 1904 and 1913, France moved from supplying only 5 percent of Germany's iron ore imports to supplying one-third. Germany, meanwhile, provided 80 percent of

---

[60] Feldman, *Iron and Steel*, 34–35.

[61] If the production of Thyssen's new Caen works is considered at an annual rate, Chiers, Aubrives-Villerupt, Providence, Maizières-les-Metz, and Caen—all German or Belgian-owned—produced approximately 650,000 tons of pig iron, representing 12.5 percent of French production in 1913; while Providence and Caen produced over 10 percent of French steel. Calculated from Pounds and Parker, *Coal and Steel*, 368–70; Mitchell, *European Historical Statistics 1750–1970*, 217; "Die Werke von Caen," *Stahl und Eisen* (May 8, 1913): 784. There were a number of other foreign-owned firms.

[62] Rust, "Business and Politics," 157, 175.

[63] The Conseil of the Comptoir included the president, chairman, and two directors of Aciéries de Longwy, which had formed a partnership with Röchling, two managers of Aubrives-Villerupt owned by Gelsenkirchener, the chairman of Chiers owned by Ougrée-Marihaye, and the chairman of the Belgian-owned Providence firm. Louis Launay and Jean Sennac, *Les relations internationales des industries de guerre* (Paris, 1932), 41–43; P. Obrin, *Le Comptoir métallurgique de Longwy* (Paris, 1908), 39, 50–58. This suggests that German industrialists did not expand to escape the hold of domestic cartels.

the coke imported into France.[64] In 1906, Aciéries de Longwy gave 50 percent control of a major Lorraine iron mine to the Röchling firm of the Saar in Germany. In exchange, Röchling gave the French firm one-quarter participation in a coal mine that it owned near Aachen.[65] Wendel, whose two interlocked firms straddled the Franco-German border, and Schneider, the smaller French rival to Krupp in armaments, invested in coal mines in the Netherlands, Belgium, and Germany, as did Pont-à-Mousson and Marine-à-Homécourt. Breaking with French tradition, Wendel raised capital on public markets in Germany, rather than relying simply on internal funds.[66]

French investment in German, Belgian, and Dutch coal created a *de facto* alliance with the Ruhr-Westphalia coal and coke syndicates, which worked closely with the Belgian cartels and dominated the Dutch market.[67] Iron and steel was increasingly linked to the coal industry as more coal production came under the control of integrated works—metallurgical producers who owned or controlled their own coal sources. As the French Lorraine steel producer Aciéries de Micheville reported in 1910, "the German factory-mines [*mines-usines (Hütten-werke)*] have conquered the majority of the direction of the [Ruhr] coal syndicate of Essen, and Micheville, like other establishments in the Meurthe-et-Moselle, finds itself placed from the point of view of fuel, in a state of subjection all the more dangerous as the company exports an important share of its products."[68] Consequently, by 1913, Micheville, too, had invested in Belgian and German coal mines. Coal itself, however, was increasingly less important than coke—coal processed and hardened for use in smelting—and access to transportation between mines and blast furnaces. The Germans and Belgians had set up cokeries on the North Sea that could buy either British or German coal and ship coke to almost any iron and steel facility in Belgium, Luxembourg, or France.[69] Despite the concern of economic nationalists in France, who worried about industry's dependence on foreigners, in 1911, five French iron and steel firms from Lorraine, with Belgian backing, combined to set up a cokery on the Dutch coast, using English and German coal to provide some of the same advantages that the Germans and Belgians enjoyed.[70]

On the eve of the world war, the entire West European iron, coal, and steel

[64] Pothmann, *Zur frage der Eisen- und Manganerzversorgung,* 95, 157.

[65] Hermann Kellenbenz and Jurgen Schneider, "Les investissements allemands en France, 1854–1914," in *La position internationale de la France: Aspects économiques et financiers, XIXᵉ–XXᵉ siècles,* Maurice Lévy-Leboyer, ed. (Paris, 1977), 357.

[66] R. Poidevin, "Placements et investissements français en Allemagne, 1898–1914," in Lévy-Leboyer, *La position internationale de la France;* Claude Fohlen, "Entrepreneurship and Management in France," *Cambridge Economic History of Europe,* vol. 7 (Cambridge, 1978): 349–50; *François de Wendel 1874–1949* (n.p., [1949?]), 79; Claude Beaud, "La stratégie de l'investissement dans la société Schneider et Cie.," *Entreprises et Entrepreneurs XIX–XXᵉᵐᵉ siècles* (Paris, 1983), 118–24; J. Tribot-Laspière, *L'industrie de l'acier en France* (Paris, 1917), 224.

[67] Georges De Leener, *Le marché charbonnière belge* (Brussels, 1908), 67–76; Marcel Gillet, "Les charbonnages du Nord de la France face à la coalition germano-belge des producteurs de houille," in his *Histoire sociale du Nord et de l'Europe du Nord-Ouest* (Lille, 1984).

[68] *Recueil financier* (1915): 1658–59.

[69] De Leener, *Le marché charbonnière belge,* 74; Maurette, *Les grands marchés,* 13–14; "Rombacher Hüttenwerke," *Stahl und Eisen* (December 14, 1911): 2080–81.

[70] *A.C.Z.C.* (Sluiskuil, 1961); "Ein französisch-belgisches Kokerei-Unternehmen in Holland," *Stahl und Eisen* (February 23, 1911): 330.

industry was becoming interdependent among its member nations. Through integration, Europe had the potential to eliminate the advantage the United States supposedly held from its abundant natural resources. As Gavin Wright has pointed out, Europe considered as a continent was no less well endowed; the real U.S. advantage lay in the absence of political boundaries dividing different regions.[71] The multinational business connections that West European industrialists built up, both to obtain raw materials and to fill gaps left by firms that failed to innovate, had the potential to create an industrial economy as large as that of the United States.

Steel and iron was not exceptional in its degree of interpenetration. The growth of multinational oil and food-processing firms is relatively well known, but they may have done less to integrate Continental Western Europe than did firms in chemicals, metallurgy, and agriculture. In chemicals, Swiss and German firms, in addition to the Belgian firm Solvay, had operations throughout Europe.[72] The largest German zinc producer owned a large company in Belgium, while the Continent's largest zinc firm, the French-Belgian multinational Vieille-Montagne, had over 13,000 employees scattered in Germany, Belgium, France, Britain, Italy, Algeria, Tunisia, Spain, and Sweden.[73] In agriculture, by 1906 Germany had already become second only to Britain as an importer of grain. German companies in Antwerp and Rotterdam handled much of this importation, which also fed Switzerland.[74] One reason the younger count von Moltke, director of German strategy, altered the original Schlieffen plan of 1895 was to ensure that the Netherlands would remain neutral and thus able to trade with Germany: "She must be the windpipe that enables us to breathe."[75]

What made the international interpenetration of iron, coal, and steel doubly important was heavy industry's numerous links with other sectors. Because of its close links to electricity, mechanical construction, shipping, and chemicals, heavy industry could influence wide economic processes. Through its subsidiary Felten-Guilleaume, the German electrical giant AEG owned its own iron and steel plant in Luxembourg, and one of the largest mechanical construction firms in France was partly German-owned.[76] Norddeutscher Lloyd, the second largest shipping firm in Germany, invested in coal mines with Krupp, while Deutsch-Luxemburg invested heavily in steamship lines and ship building.[77] One of the major advantages that Belgian and German chemical firms had over French and British

---

[71] Gavin Wright, "The Origins of American Industrial Success, 1879–1940," *American Economic Review*, 80 (1990): 651–68.

[72] Paul M. Hohenberg, *Chemicals in Western Europe, 1850–1914: An Economic Study of Technical Change* (Baltimore, Md., 1967), 36–47; L. F. Haber, *The Chemical Industry during the Nineteenth Century* (Oxford, 1958), 9–35, 148–49, 170–80.

[73] *Recueil financier* (1915): 563–67, 852–54; Walter Hillman, *Die wirtschaftliche Entwicklung der deutschen Zinkindustrie* (Leipzig, 1911), 89–95, 112; Chambre Syndicale Française des Mines Métallurgiques, *Annuaire 1912–1913* (Paris, 1912), 188–96.

[74] Maurette, *Les grands marchés*, 62–63; Avner Offer, *The First World War: An Agrarian Interpretation* (Oxford, 1989), 86.

[75] L. C. F. Turner, "The Significance of the Schlieffen Plan," in *The War Plans of the Great Powers, 1880–1914*, P. Kennedy, ed. (London, 1979), 312.

[76] Wagner, *La sidérurgie luxembourgeoise*, 22, 181; Louis Bruneau, *L'Allemagne en France: Enquêtes économiques* (Paris, 1914), 236.

[77] Gaston Raphael, *Krupp et Thyssen* (Paris, 1925), 81; *Recueil financier* (1915): 1627.

competitors was the raw materials they obtained from the advanced coking processes used by Belgian and German heavy industry. Thyssen and Solvay even built a coking plant together, Thyssen to obtain coke for iron smelting, Solvay to acquire chemicals.[78] The need for iron and steel finally drove the German machine-building firm Mannesmann to purchase both a rolling mill and a coal mine, at the same time as it invested in countries all over Europe and tried to obtain iron ore concessions in Morocco.[79]

THE MOVEMENT OF IMMIGRANT WORKERS BEFORE WORLD WAR I was both a prerequisite for the growth of international business in heavy industry and a clear demonstration of the relative openness of the international economy before the war. Entrepreneurial investment across borders appears all the more intriguing given that German and Belgian industrialists often had to import a large part of the labor they employed in France. Thanks to a precociously declining birth rate, France had the slowest population growth in the industrial world. The persistence of artisanal labor and subsistence farming also kept labor out of the industrial sector. In 1912, immigrants made up 57 percent of the population in the industrial area of French Lorraine and an even larger part of the labor force. Two-thirds of the industrial work force was Italian.[80] When Thyssen built his blast furnaces in Normandy, his companies employed a polyglot work force that included Italians, Greeks, and Moroccans.[81] Nor was this foreign labor cheap, since during the economic boom before the war the United States and Argentina were often competing for the same workers. Germany itself employed approximately a million foreign workers.[82] French labor contractors were outraged when a trainload of Italians whom they had hired stopped en route in Metz, in German Lorraine, and German recruiters lured away the entire contingent.[83]

The dependence of multinational enterprise on an internationalized work force suggests interesting comparisons with firms in the late twentieth century that employ immigrant labor and move production to avoid high wages, strong unions, or generous welfare benefits. Wages in industrial areas in France and Luxembourg were generally higher than those in Belgium and only slightly lower than those in Germany. Many Belgians employed in French border towns lived in Belgium in order to take advantage of higher wages in France and lower costs in Belgium.[84] Unionization, too, was only slightly higher in Liège and the Ruhr than

[78] Hohenberg, *Chemicals in Western Europe*, 113, 126; DeVos, *Kapitalverflechtungen*, 239.

[79] Horst A. Wessel, *Kontinuität im Wandel: 100 Jahre Mannesmann, 1890–1990* (Düsseldorf, 1990), 144–48; Helmut Pogge v. Strandman, "Rathenau, die Gebrüder Mannesmann und die Vorgeschichte der Zweiten Marokkokrise," Geiss and Wendt, *Deutschland in der Weltpolitik des 19. und 20. Jahrhunderts.*

[80] Vignes, "Le bassin de Briey," 685–86.

[81] "Übersetzung einer der Briefe des Herrn Le Chatelier vom 29 Okt. 1913," 3001 93006/5, HA/GHH.

[82] Klaus Bade, "German Emigration to the United States and Continental Immigration to Germany in the Late Nineteenth and Early Twentieth Centuries," *Labor Migration in the Atlantic Economies: The European and North American Working Classes during the Period of Industrialization*, Dirk Hoerder, ed. (Westport, Conn., 1985), 133.

[83] Vignes, "Le bassin de Briey," 684.

[84] On wages: Hermann Aubin and Wolfgang Zorn, eds., *Handbuch der deutschen Wirtschafts- und*

in Luxembourg and the French Lorraine. Thus it seems unlikely that multinationals moved to avoid either high wages or unions. Although the German companies provided the most extensive system of welfare benefits, French and Belgian heavy industry also used costly benefits to recruit and control workers.[85]

Rather than fleeing from their native workers, Belgian and German industrialists may have used their long experience in employing immigrants and workers who spoke a different language to facilitate multinational expansion. As early as 1876, almost a quarter of the work force around Liège, the home base of Ougrée-Marihaye, was non-native: 9 percent were Germans, and 13 percent were Dutch-speaking Flemings from northern Belgium.[86] Ruhr industrialists began employing Polish miners in large numbers during the 1880s, almost all of them German citizens from east Prussia, Posen, or Silesia.[87] By 1910, at least one-quarter of Ruhr miners were Polish, either German citizens or foreigners from Austria-Hungary or Russia, while many others were Italian or Dutch.[88] Experience with this diverse and multi-lingual work force may have made it easier for Belgian and German firms to expand to Luxembourg and the French Lorraine, where a majority of the industrial workers were non-native. The same may have been true for French firms. Aciéries de Longwy, which later invested in German coal mines, in 1907 had a work force that was over 85 percent non-French—Belgians, Germans, Italians, and Swiss.[89] Thus multinational enterprise in iron, coal, and steel in Continental Europe went along with an internationalized work force.

A widespread perception exists that immigrants usually serve as an easily exploited "reserve army" of surplus labor.[90] Yet a significant number of foreign

---

Sozialgeschichte, vol. 2 (Stuttgart, 1976): 226–27; Jochen Krengel, *Die deutsche Roheisenindustrie 1871–1913* (Berlin, 1983), 91–101; "Reports of the British Board of Trade on Cost of Living in England and Wales, Germany, France, Belgium, and the United States," *Bulletin of the Bureau of Labor*, 93 (1911): 557–70; Ajam, *Le problème économique*, 35–37. On the border towns, Chambre des Députés, *Enquête sur l'état de l'industrie textile*, 5 vols. (Paris, 1906), 2: 184; Julian Thys and Olivier Vanneste, *Een analyse van de Grensarbeiders in Noord-Frankrijk* (Brugge, 1969), 36.

[85] E. Domansky-Davidsohn, "Der Grossbetrieb als Organisationsproblem des Deutschen Metallarbeiter-Verbandes vor dem Ersten Weltkrieg," *Arbeiterbewegung und industrieller Wandel*, Hans Mommsen, ed. (Wuppertal, 1978); Krengel, *Die deutsche Roheisenindustrie*, 32; C. Strikwerda, "Interest Group Politics and the International Economy: Mass Politics and Big Business Corporations in the Liège Coal Basin, 1870–1914," *Journal of Social History*, 25 (1991): 277–308; G. Noiriel, "Du 'patronage' au 'paternalisme': La restructuration des formes de domination de la main-d'oeuvre ouvrière dans l'industrie métallurgique française," *Le mouvement social*, 144 (1988): 17–36.

[86] J. M. Wautelet, "Accumulation et rentabilité du capital dans les charbonnages belges, 1850–1914," *Recherches économiques de Louvain*, 41 (1975): 79.

[87] Klaus Tenfelde, *Sozialgeschichte der Bergarbeiterschaft an der Ruhr im 19. Jahrhundert* (Bonn, 1977), 238–46.

[88] Christoph Klessmann, *Polnische Bergarbeiter im Ruhrgebiet 1870–1945* (Göttingen, 1978), 265–66; John J. Kulczycki, "Scapegoating the Foreign Workers: Job Turnover, Accidents, and Diseases among Polish Coal Miners in the German Ruhr," *The Politics of Immigrant Workers: Labor Activism and Migration in the World Economy since 1830*, Camille Guerin-Gonzales and Carl Strikwerda, eds. (New York, 1993), 133–54; Ulrich Herbert, *A History of Foreign Labor in Germany, 1880–1980: Seasonal Workers, Forced Laborers, Guest Workers*, William Templer, trans. (Ann Arbor, Mich., 1990), 21.

[89] Alphonse Merrheim, "L'Organisation patronale en France," *Le mouvement socialiste* (1908): 16.

[90] Gary S. Cross, *Immigrant Workers in Industrial France: The Making of a New Laboring Class* (Philadelphia, 1983), 10; Michael J. Piore, *Birds of Passage: Migrant Labor and Industrial Societies* (Cambridge, 1979); Stephen Castles and Godula Kosack, *Immigrant Workers and Class Structure in Western Europe* (London, 1973).

workers in this period were skilled, which suggests that, in the pre-1914 era, the labor market between West European countries functioned with some freedom. In 1913, the subprefect of Briey in Lorraine reported that the Marine-à-Homécourt firm recruited "a number of its engineers and the larger part of its foremen from the other side of the border"—Germany or Luxembourg.[91] Far from being exceptional in its employment of immigrants, heavy industry even modeled itself in some cases on other sectors, particularly agriculture. Poles and Italians worked the harvest in Germany, while French sugar-beet farmers depended on thousands of Flemish Belgian migratory workers, known as "Franschmans."[92] When the French iron and steel association, the Comité des Forges, wanted to systematize the recruitment of foreign labor, particularly Italians, it borrowed from the agreements made between Italy and the German government agency that coordinated the employment of agricultural workers, the Feldarbeitzentrale.[93]

Becoming multinational did not necessarily make firms more conciliatory toward labor; some may have used their diversified position against workers. In 1911, Stinnes's Deutsch-Luxemburg tried to break a strike in Dortmund by hiring workers in Essen, ostensibly for its establishments in Luxembourg, and then bringing them into the strike-bound mill in Dortmund.[94] Some multinationals hired disproportionate numbers of immigrant workers for their branches in foreign countries, perhaps because they preferred to hire their own country's workers or at least not to employ labor of the host country. At the Frederick-Heinrich coal mine near Aachen, Germany, owned by the French firm Wendel, an observer noted, "Very few of the workers are Germans; one finds a mélange of Poles, Hungarians, Belgians, Dutch, Italians, and Swiss."[95] In Luxembourg, Gelsenkirchener hired proportionately more Germans and Ougrée-Marihaye more Belgians than did other firms.[96] Because the Luxembourg and Lorraine mines and steel mills lay right on the French, German, and Luxembourg borders, and because all of these establishments relied on immigrant labor, a large pool of Italian, Belgian, German, and French workers moved back and forth. In 1906, French metallurgists charged that employers in all three countries conspired to break strikes on the border.[97]

The heavy demand for labor gave foreign workers bargaining power, however, and this may have encouraged some employers to improve conditions as an

[91] Sous-préfet to Préfet, July 19, 1913, 4M 219/2, Archives Départementales de Meurthe-et-Moselle, Nancy.

[92] M. Lair, "Les ouvriers étrangers dans l'agriculture française," *Revue économique internationale*, 4 (1907): 531–35; Luc Schepens, *Van Vlaskuter tot Franschman* (Brugge, 1973).

[93] Serge Bonnet, et al., "Les Italiens dans l'arrondissement de Briey avant 1914," *Annales de l'Est*, 5e série, 13 (1962): 83.

[94] David Crew, "Steel, Sabotage, and Socialism: The Strike at the Dortmund 'Union' Steel Works in 1911," *The German Working Class, 1888–1933: The Politics of Everyday Life*, Richard J. Evans, ed. (London, 1982), 129. Deutsch-Luxemburg had acquired Dortmund Union in 1910.

[95] Victor Cambon, *Les derniers progrès de l'Allemagne*, 3d edn. (Paris, 1914), 25.

[96] Deutsch-Luxemburg had the most heavily Italian work force. The Belgian-controlled but more locally managed ARBED employed the largest proportion of Luxemburgers; Ministère du Travail 52, Archives de l'Etat, Luxembourg; Serge Hoffmann, "L'immigration dans la tourmente de l'économie (1913/1940)," *Galerie*, 3 (1989): 339–43.

[97] "L'Alliance provisoire Franco-Allemande-Luxembourgeoise contre les grévistes métallurgistes de l'Est," *L'ouvrier métallurgiste* (May 1, 1906): 2.

alternative to repression. After 1905, French industrialists in Lorraine increased their wages and benefits and enticed a large number of Italian workers to move over the border from Germany.[98] Gelsenkirchener appears to have introduced welfare benefits that were standard in Germany into the Aubrives-Villerupt firm that it purchased in France.[99] The floating labor pool forced French, German, and Luxembourg firms to adopt similar wage scales and working conditions to attract workers. When implementation of the eight-hour day began to be discussed seriously, French, Belgian, and German representatives considered an international agreement to lower hours simultaneously.[100] Workers, furthermore, could in some cases use the international connections forged by multinationals and cartels to learn new techniques of labor organizing. When German metallurgists tried to organize workers in the Luxembourg plants of the multinationals, they worked with French and Italian unionists in order to reach Italians who drifted back and forth across the border. Union pamphlets sometimes came out in three languages—German, French, and Italian.[101] In 1911, the Belgian metallurgical unions in Liège reorganized themselves after sending a study group to learn German union methods.[102] The French metallurgist union leader Alphonse Merrheim repeatedly said that French iron and steel firms needed the challenge posed by the Germans to force them to modernize and, perhaps, to improve conditions for the workers.[103]

By 1914, then, there were significant signs of an emerging European economy, embracing both business and labor, in one of the world's most important industries. Despite the upsurge of nationalist feeling after the second Moroccan crisis of 1911 and the tensions in Germany over Lorraine created by the Zabern incident of 1913, the interpenetration of the border regions went on unabated. On the eve of the war, French, German, and Luxembourg authorities were planning the construction of a tramway system connecting the three countries, to aid both workers and consumers in crossing the border.[104] How far this integration would have proceeded if war had not broken out is impossible to say, but it certainly had the momentum on the eve of the war to bring nations much closer together. Rather than seeing nationalism and hostility as the wave of the future, it may be better to see European society as uneasily balancing two divergent trends: one toward economic integration, which had the potential at least to encourage further internationalism, and the other toward self-interested and destructive nationalism.[105]

[98] Bonnet, "Les Italiens," 87.
[99] Moine, *Les barons du fer*, 326.
[100] Rust, "Business and Politics," 240–42.
[101] J 76/70, Justice, Archives de l'Etat, Luxembourg.
[102] Centrale des Métallurgistes de Belgique, Province de Liège, Rapport du Comité Exécutif au Congrès du 2ème Semestre 1913, 8.
[103] Merrheim, "L'Organisation," 190–93.
[104] "Aktien-Gesellschaft für Bahn-Bau und Betrieb in Frankfurt/a/M. Elektr. Strassenbahn von Esch über Deutsch-Oth bei Villerupt," 15 AL 588, Archives Départementales de la Moselle, Metz; David Schoenbaum, *Zabern 1913: Consensus Politics in Imperial Germany* (London, 1982).
[105] John L. Gaddis has argued a similar case for the contemporary world; "Toward the Post-Cold War World: Structure, Strategy, and Security," *Foreign Affairs*, 70 (1991): 102–22.

1124   *Carl Strikwerda*

THE NATIONALISM PUSHING EUROPEANS TOWARD WAR and the reaction against
economic interdependence were closely woven together. In 1911, a French
newspaper claimed that a Belgian company was investing in the iron and steel
industry as part of Krupp's plot to weaken France.[106] The Wendel family, which
staunchly upheld their French identity after Germany annexed their establishments in Alsace-Lorraine, nonetheless tried to have France and Germany agree to
link the Wendel plants in the two countries via a new rail line. Nationalist and
military opinion doomed the project.[107] Thyssen's purchases of ore fields helped
to prompt a change in French mining law against foreign purchases.[108] Writing in
1912, the French law professor Maurice Vignes worried about the threat posed by
Italian labor in an industry that was critical for national defense and based right
on the border: "If a war breaks out with Germany, what will prevent Italy from
throwing this mass of workers against us?"[109] Reportedly, one reason Ruhr
industrialists hesitated to invest more in steel and iron-making in either French or
German Lorraine was the fear that the establishments would be directly in the
path of any war.[110]

German industrialists themselves undercut the logic of international economic
integration by playing a dangerous game of supporting, largely for domestic
reasons, militarists and reactionary nationalists like the Pan-Germans. Ruhr
businessmen wanted the support of the conservative elite and the Pan-Germans to
forestall the growing power of labor and Socialism; they failed to see that these
same groups could destroy Germany's international economic position.[111] The
alliance of German industry with conservative nationalism, however, should not
be taken out of context.[112] Despite their subsidies for the Pan-Germans and their
support for the imperial government, many industrialists in their day-to-day
business decisions were moving toward a Europe internationalized by contract,
not conquest. By 1914, this process of internationalization had not gone far
enough to force German industrialists to choose between national chauvinism and
international cooperation. But, had the war not broken out, such a decision almost
certainly would have been necessary in the near future.

The alliance between industrialists and radical nationalists in Germany was
especially dangerous, nonetheless, because it showed how little importance
industrialists attached to the need for a political alliance in favor of international

---

[106] Firmin Lentacker, *La frontière franco-belge* (Lille, 1974), 169.
[107] R 85/64, Auswärtiges Amt, Bundesarchiv, Koblenz; "Joeuf dans la vallée de l'Orne," Bib-
liothèque Municipale de Nancy, 142.
[108] "Décret du 14 janvier 1909 réglementant l'exploitation des mines," appendix to *Annuaire* 446;
Kellenbenz and Schneider, "Les investissements allemands," 358; Rust, "Business and Politics,"
215–16.
[109] Vignes, "Le bassin de Briey," 5. Italy was still nominally a member of the Triple Alliance with
Germany and Austria-Hungary.
[110] Feldenkirchen, *Die Eisen- und Stahlindustrie*, 86.
[111] Hartmut Kaelble, *Industrielle Interessenpolitik in der wilhelminischen Gesellschaft* (Berlin, 1967),
146–63; Elaine G. Spencer, *Management and Labor in Imperial Germany: Ruhr Industrialists as Employers,
1896–1914* (New Brunswick, N.J., 1984), 139–47; Roger Chickering, *We Men Who Feel Most German:
A Cultural Study of the Pan-German League, 1886–1914* (Boston, 1984), 227–30; John A. Leopold,
Alfred Hugenberg: The Radical Nationalist Campaign against the Weimar Republic (New Haven, Conn.,
1977), 2–11.
[112] Hans Jaeger, *Unternehmer in der deutschen Politik (1890–1918)* (Bonn, 1967), 132–42, points out
employers' ambivalence toward the Right.

integration. The arguments against imported goods, foreign investments, and multinational companies attracted the support of the lower middle class and farmers who already suffered from the downturns and harsh competition present in a capitalist system. Nationalist opposition to international economic integration was a convenient way for these groups to express their grievances against social and economic change under the banner of patriotism.[113] If the benefits of economic integration were eventually to be enjoyed, and, even more important, if economic justifications were not to be harnessed to the desire for war, their grievances would have to be addressed.

The tension between the two trends, one toward internationalization, the other toward nationalism and protectionism, inevitably raises questions about the origins of World War I. Which trend was growing stronger in the last years before July 1914: peaceful integration or nationalist militarism? Few writers have taken heavy industry's multinational ties into account in the debate on the war. Both the pre-war idealists who argued that finance capitalism would guarantee peace and the muckrakers who accused armaments manufacturers of causing the war seem to have been ignorant of how deeply heavy industry in Continental countries had become interdependent.[114] Nor have later historians addressed the awkward possibility that the captains of heavy industry and political leaders were moving in opposite directions, one toward interdependence and the other toward war. According to Fritz Fischer, Germany's leaders decided that war would not only solve the country's political difficulties but would also improve its long-run economic position. Germany's leaders, Fischer asserted, especially feared the shortage of iron ore, because the economic penetration of France had been set back by 1912 and Sweden since 1907 had put limits on the exports of ore.[115] But it seems doubtful that Germany's militarist leaders could justify a European war on these economic grounds. Many of the iron ore concessions that German industrialists had obtained in France had not yet even begun to be mined on the eve of the war. Sweden, meanwhile, had put only a percentage cap on iron ore exports to Germany: since the volume of iron ore production and exports rose enormously after 1907, the 80 percent that went to Germany increased from 2.5 to nearly 5 million tons between 1909 and 1913.[116] Indeed, Fischer's larger

---

[113] Wolfgang Mommsen, "Nationalism, Imperialism, and Official Press Policy in Wilhelmine Germany 1850–1914," *Opinion publique et politique extérieure: Colloque*, Vol. 1: *1870–1915* (Rome, 1981); Philip G. Nord, *Paris Shopkeepers and the Politics of Resentment* (Princeton, N.J., 1986); Michael Tracy, *Agriculture in Western Europe* (New York, 1964), 34–35.

[114] Norman Angell, *The Great Illusion* (London, 1913); Henry Noel Brailsford, *The War of Steel and Gold: A Study of the Armed Peace* (London, 1917). Contemporary opinion did focus on multinational iron ore concessions in North Africa and the manufacture of armor plate; Alphonse Merrheim, *L'Affaire de l'Ouenza* (Paris, 1910), and H. Robertson Murray, *Krupp and the International Armaments Ring* (London, 1915), 150–57.

[115] Fischer, *War of Illusions*, 322–26.

[116] Berthold Steinhoff, *Die schwedische Eisenerzproduktion und Eisenerzpolitik seit der Jahrhundertwende* (Berlin, 1937), 68. It had been difficult since 1900 for foreigners to purchase Swedish ore fields, but some continued to do so until foreign purchase was banned in 1916; Steinhoff, 88–93. Much of Fischer's evidence comes from Hermann Schumacher, "Die volks- und weltwirtschaftliche Bedeutung der Moselkanalisierung," *Technik und Wirtschaft*, 3 (1910): 705–25, which, though informative, is also a piece of special pleading, based on nationalism, for a Mosel canal that could better connect German Lorraine with the rest of Germany. Its pessimism about ore supplies was already questionable by 1913. Other writers were less pessimistic; Sehmer, *Die Eisenerversorgung Europas*,

argument, that the military elite drove Germany into war, is stronger if one sees the elite as ignoring economic interests and convincing itself that a quick war of conquest would have economic, as well political and military, advantages.[117] Nor is it clear that German industrialists' economic penetration of France and other countries before 1914 prefigured German annexationism during the war.[118] From the French point of view, Belgian industrialists such as Gustave Trasenster, head of Ougrée-Marihaye, acted little differently than did the Germans.[119] Industrialists pursued their multinational ventures, while taking for granted the maintenance of peace and an open, European-wide market that made these ventures possible. They little realized that political leaders valued their countries' military and diplomatic position most of all and had scant regard for how the international economy functioned.

World War I began a thirty-year process of destroying almost all economic integration in heavy industry between Continental European states—except for that which depended on force. West European leaders still recognized the need to link the iron and coal sectors across countries, but they rejected genuine economic integration. Although political leaders usually took the lead in this rejection, big business did little to defend international cooperation. Yet almost all the substitutes for integration were profoundly flawed. During World War I, the Germans' plans for annexing Belgium and creating an autarkical *Mitteleuropa* ignored Continental heavy industry's dependence on exports: Germany had exported 35 percent, and Belgium 80 percent, of its steel.[120] As shipping magnate Albert Ballin remarked ruefully, "If *Mitteleuropa* should be our future, then we will have to force half our population to emigrate."[121] French plans to displace Germany after the war hardly fared better. The project combining Luxembourg, Alsace-Lorraine, the Saar, and Belgium into a single coal and steel community with France floundered—and the Franco-Belgian attempt to add the Ruhr in 1923 did nothing to salvage it. Belgium and Luxembourg still needed to export, while France clung to protectionism, and there was almost no way to avoid trading French iron ore for German coal.[122] The European and International Steel Cartels finally gave Continental heavy industry a precarious stability, but they

---

354–56, and Einecke and Kohler, "Die Eiserzvorräte." Fischer admits that Poidevin, the foremost authority on Franco-German economic relations, disagrees with his interpretation of a breakdown before the war; Fischer, *War of Illusions*, 325–26.

[117] Fritz Fischer, *Germany's Aims in the First World War* (New York, 1967).

[118] "The industrialists in general demanded from the Government the annexation of Longwy-Briey, and also that of Belgium or at least its economic domination by Germany. They thus pursued the same tactics in war as in peace"; Arthur Rosenberg, *Imperial Germany: The Birth of the German Republic, 1871–1918* (Boston, 1964), 101. See also Hans Gatzke, *Germany's Drive to the West* (Baltimore, Md., 1966), 11–35.

[119] Rust, "Business and Politics," 158–62; Moine, *Les barons du fer*, 380, 422.

[120] Friedrich Naumann, *Central Europe* [1915] (London, 1917); Gatzke, *Germany's Drive*, 38–62, 105–71; Fischer, *Germany's Aims*, 108–11, 167, 591–98; Georges-Henri Soutou, *L'or et le sang: Les buts de guerre économiques de la Première Guerre mondiale* (Paris, 1989), 52–83; Henry Cord Meyer, *Mitteleuropa in German Thought and Action* (The Hague, 1955), 145–250.

[121] Lamar Cecil, *Albert Ballin: Business and Politics in Imperial Germany, 1888–1918* (Princeton, N.J., 1967), 317.

[122] Jacques Bariéty, *Les relations franco-allemandes après la Première-Guerre mondiale* (Paris, 1977), 121–92; Charles S. Maier, *Recasting Bourgeois Europe: Stabilization in France, Germany, and Italy in the Decade after World War I* (Princeton, N.J., 1975), 194–209, 272–304, 387–420.

were rarely more than truces between the various national cartels.[123] The lengths to which Germany went to obtain ore demonstrate the economic logic behind integration. During the Spanish Civil War, the Nazi regime forced Franco to shift iron ore exports from Britain to Germany, and, briefly, on the eve of World War II, Germany was dangerously dependent on Swedish ore.[124]

Despite the continuing advantages of interdependence, during the interwar years both international business in heavy industry and labor migration contracted. The Germans never revived the holdings they lost in Belgium, Luxembourg, and Alsace-Lorraine, the surviving multinationals like Ougrée-Marihaye nearly went bankrupt, and the French even ended up selling off some of the holdings they had acquired after the war in Luxembourg and the Saar.[125] Aside from some expansion in automobiles and food processing, multinational investment in Europe shrank in importance by comparison with investment in the rest of the world.[126] Although there were some large movements of immigrant workers during the interwar period, the relatively free movement of labor disappeared. Germany restricted still further the rights of foreign workers to enter that country.[127] By 1929, heavy industry in Luxembourg had increased its work force by half from the level of 1913, but native workers now filled 60 percent of the jobs as opposed to only 40 percent before the war.[128] France became more dependent than ever on immigrant workers, but immigration was now strictly controlled by nation-to-nation agreements—for example, between Mussolini's Italy and France.[129] During the Depression, France (and to a lesser extent, Belgium) pushed out immigrant workers as a way to export their unemployment.[130]

After the failure of Hitler's attempt at European empire, the only hope for prosperity in Continental heavy industry was a return to at least a degree of economic interdependence. France, Luxembourg, Belgium, Germany, and the Netherlands—those countries that had been moving toward interdependence in iron and steel in the pre–World War I era—founded the European Coal and Steel Community. The sixth member country was Italy, which had been the major

[123] Ulrich Nocken, "Das Internationale Stahlkartell und die deutsch-französischen Beziehungen 1924–1932," *Konstellationen internationaler Politik 1924–1932*, Gustav Schmidt, ed. (Bochum, 1983); Daniel Barbezat, "Cooperation and Rivalry in the International Steel Cartel, 1926–1933," *Journal of Economic History*, 49 (1989): 435–47.

[124] Robert H. Whealey, *Hitler and Spain: The Nazi Role in the Spanish Civil War, 1936–1939* (Lexington, Ky., 1989), 72–94; R. Karlbom, "Sweden's Iron Ore Exports to Germany, 1933–1944," *Scandinavian Economic History Review*, 13 (1965): 65–73; Alan Milward, "Could Sweden Have Stopped the Second World War?" *Scandinavian Economic History Review*, 15 (1967): 127–38.

[125] Bariéty, *Les relations franco-allemandes*, 144–71; Fritz Pflug, "Die Internationale ARBED," *Deutsche Volkswirt* (August 23, 1940): 1719–22; Eric Bussière, "La sidérurgie belge durant l'entre deux-guerres: Le cas d'Ougrée-Marihaye (1919–1939)," *Revue belge d'histoire contemporaine*, 15 (1984): 303–80.

[126] Dunning, "Changes in the Level and Structure," 85–93.

[127] Klaus J. Bade, "Labour, Migration, and the State," in Bade, ed., *Population, Labour, and Migration in 19th- and 20th-Century Germany* (New York, 1987), 81.

[128] Wagner, *La sidérurgie luxembourgeoise*, 189.

[129] Donald Reid, "The Politics of Immigrant Workers in Twentieth Century France," in Guerin-Gonzales and Strikwerda, *Politics of Immigrant Workers*, 245–78.

[130] Cross, *Immigrant Workers in Industrial France*, 203–07; Frank Caestecker, "Het Vreemdelingenbeleid in de Tussenoorlogse Period, 1922–1939 in Belgie," *Belgisch Tijdschrift voor Nieuwste Geschiedenis*, 15 (1984): 461–86.

1128 *Carl Strikwerda*

supplier of immigrant labor.[131] From a historical perspective, the Coal and Steel Community was a mixture of both the pre-1914 system and the interwar cartels. Prices and production were now strictly regulated, as though under cartels, but national cartels no longer had the power to struggle with each other behind the scenes. Prices and production levels were required to be public and under the scrutiny of an international institution.[132] The only way to stabilize the system was to encourage the movement of coal and iron across borders, fulfilling the old function of the international firms. And, just as they had found, the Coal and Steel Community soon saw that the freer movement of labor was a necessary complement of this interdependence. The deep involvement of government in heavy industry to protect employment made it difficult to re-create multinationals in iron and steel.[133] Yet, once the European Community was built on the foundation of the Coal and Steel Community, multinational manufacturers who expanded across Europe in a variety of other industries were able to follow the path first taken before 1914.

The new international economic institutions were only possible because the position of key interest groups and the relationship between governments and big business had changed greatly with the rise of the welfare state and social democracy. One aspect of this reorientation of European politics was that farmers and the lower middle class now had less temptation to respond to economic nationalism as a symbol for their discontent with capitalism and industrialization.[134] The European Community's Common Agricultural Policy and the myriad of regulations protecting small commerce helped ensure that a new Pan-German League or Action Française would arise only with difficulty. The existence of the European Community and the acceptance of the notion of social welfare—despite all its failings—meant that international integration would be seen differently than it was before 1914. At that time, it had been a natural process brought about by private interests but not necessarily one in which any group had a stake beyond its own immediate material benefit. Beginning in the 1950s, there was an attempt to establish the notion that regulated integration could conceivably support the common good.

A NUMBER OF LESSONS CAN BE DRAWN from Europe's troubled history of integration. First, the history of multinational business in heavy industry suggests a rethinking of the debate on the origins of World War I. The alliances historians have found between conservative, agrarian, or militarist elites and heavy industry

[131] Alan S. Milward, *The Reconstruction of Western Europe, 1945–51* (Berkeley, Calif., 1984), 126–67, 362–95; John Gillingham, *Coal, Steel, and the Rebirth of Europe, 1945–1955: The Germans and French from Ruhr Conflict to Economic Community* (Cambridge, 1991), 313–71.

[132] Jean-Paul Courthéoux, "Les pouvoirs économiques et sociaux dans un secteur industriel: La sidérurgie," *Revue d'histoire économique et sociale*, 38 (1960): 364; Dennis Swann, *The Economics of the Common Market*, 6th edn. (London, 1988), 4–7, 85.

[133] J. E. S. Hayward, "Steel," in *Big Business and the State: Changing Relations in Western Europe*, Raymond Vernon, ed. (Cambridge, Mass., 1974). The supply of raw materials has also changed enormously; Edmond Dourille, *La sidérurgie dans le monde depuis 1952* (Paris, 1981), 103–10, 131–41.

[134] Rudy Koshar, ed., *Splintered Classes: Politics and the Lower Middle Classes in Interwar Europe* (New York, 1990); Heinrich A. Winkler, *Mittelstand, Demokratie und Nationalsozialismus* (Cologne, 1972).

should perhaps be reinvestigated. Big business before the war does not seem to have had a clearly nationalist program, or at least its motives were much more complex and tension-ridden than we have thought.

Second, it seems clear that the integration that has occurred since the 1950s, in a purely business or economic sense, could have happened much earlier. The industrial corporations of 1913 were as advanced in their ability to organize multinational production as firms would be in the 1960s. Schemes of gradually evolving multinational firms or stages of financial and industrial capitalism thus do not apply very well. Labor migration, too, was almost as free as anyone can imagine it today. Theories of economic integration and business history hence are untenable without a heavy dose of political economy.

Third, the length of time it took for internationalism to attract support points directly to how powerfully political decisions act on economic trends. Industrialists, labor leaders, and politicians at various times recognized the value of international ties, but only rarely did they see internationalism itself as a value or work to institutionalize international cooperation. Yet without some such political agreement to protect or encourage connections between states, it was easy for opponents to argue that internationalism was harmful. How could France possibly benefit from German investment? What advantages did Germany gain by making concessions to France in return for connections across borders? In this battle over public opinion, the malleability of business is sobering. Industrialists saw the economic rationality of internationalism, but they cooperated just the same with nationalist programs. For all the continuities in European heavy industry from 1914 to the Coal and Steel Community, the changes were profound. European integration only succeeded when very broad coalitions of farmers, business, labor, commerce, and government could be brokered into supporting it. Despite the theoretical perspectives to the contrary, integration is never inevitable. Without political coalitions to distribute the benefits of integration and to ameliorate its disadvantages, internationalism cannot succeed, regardless of the economic logic behind it.

Recognizing the precociousness of early economic integration could lead, finally, to reformulating our chronology of the twentieth century. World War I, in short, was a true break in time. And the 1914 to 1989 era may yet be seen as a difficult journey back to the historical route that Europe was taking decades earlier. Our history may someday be seen as moving in ellipses, in which the "shorter twentieth century" of 1914 to 1989 lies as a detour between the long nineteenth century and the twenty-first century that lies ahead.

AHR Forum
Economic Integration and the European International System in the Era of World War I

PAUL W. SCHROEDER

NOT BEING AN EXPERT ON THE ECONOMIC ASPECTS of Carl Strikwerda's interesting and provocative article, I intend to comment chiefly on how it affects our general picture of nineteenth and twentieth-century European international relations. It seems to me to have important implications in three respects. First, the analysis it gives of the course of European economic integration, which I take to be basically sound, clearly deals with a major element in the overall picture. Second, Strikwerda offers a suggestive interpretation of the actual and potential effects of this economic integration on the subsequent course of twentieth-century international history. My reasons for disagreeing with this interpretation in certain respects will be the main focus of these comments. Finally, his article exemplifies a general approach to international history and a conception of it that I consider valuable not only for historiography but also for public education and policy.

As already indicated, I can add little to Strikwerda's main argument on the extent to which West European industry, especially coal, iron, and steel, was integrated by 1914. His account, to be sure, seems to confirm rather than drastically alter the prevailing picture of a European economy largely open and fairly well integrated in some major sectors. One might view the debate[1] over whether nationalist protection or internationalist integration was the dominant economic trend by 1914 as one in which either side could be right, depending on how one judged not merely the factual evidence but also the eventual outcome. An additional comment might be that any implied or explicit argument that further economic integration in the early twentieth century might have averted a general European war would have to take more than Western Europe into account. The issues, tensions, and rivalries that actually produced the war, including economic ones, lay more in Central, Eastern, and Southeastern Europe. And when Strikwerda argues that "the creation of international business connections before World War I indicates the relative openness of the societies at the time," while the reaction against these ties and their failure to lead to durable

This article was written while the author was a Jennings Randolph Peace Fellow at the United States Institute of Peace in Washington, D.C., whose support is here gratefully acknowledged.

[1] Summarized in Carl Strikwerda, "The Troubled Origins of European Economic Integration: International Iron and Steel and Labor Migration in the Era of World War I," *AHR*, 98 (October 1993): 1109–12.

cooperation indicates the strength of nationalism and the "failure of the European political system to reconcile the power of nation-states with the need for economic integration," few will disagree, but one might ask whether these are the only implications to be drawn or the most important ones.[2] Does not this also show how fragile that societal openness was, how shallow were the roots of integration and internationalism? Was the political failure to reconcile the power of nation-states with the need for economic integration perhaps a "failure" to do something impossible and almost inconceivable at the time?

Still, these are comments and questions, not criticisms. They do not detract from the strong case Strikwerda makes for the advanced state of the integration of key West European industries by 1914 and the persistence of this trend despite growing political, military, and nationalist rivalries. One can even accept that this trend offered possibilities for drawing nations together[3] (although, as political scientists sometimes point out, interdependence can produce greater friction as well as greater harmony) and agree with the author that Europe in 1914, rather than being borne inexorably toward war on a wave of nationalist hostility, was actually balanced uneasily between diverse trends and possibilities, including those of economic integration and nationalism.

WHEN IT COMES TO THE INTERPRETATION OF THESE TWO TRENDS and their relationship to each other, however, I find myself in important disagreement with him. He sees them as polar opposites, representing two divergent paths Europe could have taken: economic integration leading potentially toward further international cooperation and peace, or "self-interested and destructive nationalism" leading toward protectionism, militarism, and war.[4] Yet, while he notes that the forces promoting political and economic nationalism were in alliance, he recognizes correctly that there was no similar alliance between the industrialists who benefited from economic integration and those promoting the cause of international political cooperation. In fact, he writes, "German industrialists themselves undercut the logic of international economic integration" by an alliance with conservative military and nationalist forces against labor and the Socialists. This inconsistency, he argues, was the product of the industrialists' political immaturity (a failure to see their need for a political alliance in favor of economic internationalism) and of the immaturity of economic integration itself, which "had not gone far enough to force German industrialists to choose between national chauvinism and international cooperation."[5] While industrialists, as he insists (again, I think, largely correctly), were not pushing for war or annexations before 1914, they failed to understand the root requirements for their own security and prosperity in the international arena or to be sufficiently concerned about them:

[2] Strikwerda, "Troubled Origins," 1111–12.
[3] Strikwerda, "Troubled Origins," 1123.
[4] Strikwerda, "Troubled Origins," 1123.
[5] Strikwerda, "Troubled Origins," 1124.

1132   *Paul W. Schroeder*

Industrialists pursued their multinational ventures, while taking for granted the maintenance of peace and an open, European-wide market that made these ventures possible.
They little realized that political leaders valued their countries' military and diplomatic
position most of all and had scant regard for how the international economy functioned.[6]

In other words, Strikwerda sees economic integration and nationalism not merely
as two divergent trends leading toward two sharply different outcomes but also as
representing two opposed ways of thinking, two divergent collective mentalities,
each with its own set of blinders. The industrialist economic-integration mode of
thinking called for international economic and political cooperation but failed to
understand that this kind of cooperation would require a different set of rules for
the conduct of international politics generally. The political-military-nationalist
mode of thought operated on traditional assumptions of international rivalry,
coercion, and conflict and failed to understand or care about what this would do
to an increasingly integrated international economic system.

Leaving certain broader questions about the general character and sources of
pre-1914 nationalism aside,[7] this dichotomy does not seem to me the best way to
understand either the objective interrelationship between international politics
and economics in pre-1914 Europe or the way most European military, political,
and economic leaders thought about it. The problem and the main source of the
tragedy was not that leaders from different camps offered two divergent programs for achieving national security and prosperity, economic integration versus
nationalism, each involving mutually incompatible ideas and assumptions. It was
rather that leaders from all camps reached substantial agreement on one
program, differing only on details of emphasis and execution. By and large,
everyone assumed that the state, to ensure its citizens' security and prosperity, had
to succeed simultaneously in two fields of competition in the international arena,
both inextricably intertwined and mutually interdependent: politics and economics. The political and military strength and security of the state increasingly
required a strong, modern domestic economy to support it; a strong domestic
economy in turn increasingly required the state to develop and use adequate
diplomatic and military resources to ensure that its economic activity would enjoy
favorable or at least tolerable conditions in the world marketplace.

Naturally, there were important disagreements over just how to make this
mutual interdependence and support between international politics and economics work—disputes over protectionism versus free trade, autarky versus economic
integration and interdependence, security through armaments and military
alliances versus security through Concert diplomacy and multilateral agreements.
Of course, particular interests, ideologies, and outlooks played a powerful role in
these disputes. Yet no influential groups challenged the need for governments
and economic sectors to work closely together to guarantee the nation's security.

[6] Strikwerda, "Troubled Origins," 1126.
[7] Considerable scholarship on pre-war Germany, for example, pictures nationalism as radical
rather than conservative in character and arising from the middle class rather than being
manipulated from above by governmental, military, or economic leaders. See David Blackbourn,
Class, Religion, and Local Politics in Wilhelmine Germany (New Haven, Conn., 1980); Geoff Eley,
Reshaping the German Right (New Haven, 1980); and Blackbourn and Eley, *The Peculiarities of German
History* (Oxford, 1984).

In other words, no major groups in any state really abandoned nationalism in favor of international integration, either in politics or in economics. Even those interested in international economic integration wanted the national state to support them in it, to help ensure their safety and success. All the great trends and lessons of late nineteenth and early twentieth-century history reinforced this outlook. The lesson of German and, to a lesser extent, Italian unification was that national unity promoted success in the world economy, that it made commerce, both competitive and cooperative, more possible and beneficial. Imperialism, the great scramble for trade, colonies, and spheres of influence in the extra-European world, pressed the same point home. The real question was not whether Europe could best exploit its imperialist opportunities by international cooperation or by nationalist competition possibly leading to war. Instead, the reigning (and correct) assumption was that both cooperation and competition were possible and necessary in various circumstances but always on a fundamentally nationalist basis, between states striving to protect their national interests, political and economic. This seemed to work. Compared to the sixteenth, seventeenth, and eighteenth centuries, nineteenth and twentieth-century European overseas imperialism was remarkably peaceful, at least for the metropoles. The colonial scramble never led to war between European powers, and seldom seriously threatened to. Most issues were settled by mutual agreement, shares of the loot divided up more or less amicably, trade permitted with each other's colonies (the largest empire, the British, remained a free trade empire), and joint economic enterprises entered into. Nonetheless, everyone knew this to be an intensely competitive arena in which the government and various economic interests had to work together for success and in which states with governments and economies too weak, ill-organized, or distracted to do so (Italy, Austria-Hungary, Spain, Portugal) usually lost out.[8]

Even World War I did not destroy but confirmed the belief that to participate successfully in world politics and the world economy, including its vital aspects of international economic integration and cooperation, one had to have a strong state uniting and coordinating political, diplomatic, military, and economic strategies. Strikwerda's verdict that the war had a disastrous impact on international economic integration, and that postwar attempts to revive it were flawed, once again seems basically sound. Yet, as recent studies have shown, the pre-war liberal international order demonstrated a remarkable attractiveness and resiliency even during this cataclysmic conflict.[9] The various powers, including imperial Germany, rather than simply abandoning an international order once war began in favor of all-out protectionism or autarky, instead in various ways sought through military victory to maintain it, only changing it to ensure that they

[8] For an example of how this worked, see F. R. Bridge, "*Tarde venientibus ossa* [the latecomers get the bones]: Austro-Hungarian Colonial Aspirations in Asia Minor 1913–14," *Middle Eastern Studies*, 6 (1970): 319–30.

[9] Especially Georges-Henri Soutou, *L'or et le sang: Les buts de guerre économiques de la Première Guerre mondiale* (Paris, 1989); Horst Günther Linke, *Das zarische Russland und der erste Weltkrieg: Diplomatie und Kriegsziele, 1914–1917* (Munich, 1982); and Bernd Bonwetsch, *Kriegsallianz und Wirtschaftsinteressen: Russland in den Wirtschaftsplänen Englands und Frankreichs, 1914–1917* (Düsseldorf, 1973).

1134   *Paul W. Schroeder*

controlled it and enjoyed its advantages while their defeated foes bore its burdens—a goal not fundamentally different from the aim pursued in peacetime.

In other words, Strikwerda is right in perceiving a disjunction and ultimate contradiction between the world being gradually created by the trend toward economic integration before 1914 and the actual world of pre-war international politics and economics, governed by a competitive nationalist ethos and set of rules. He is wrong, however, in supposing that this disjunction could have been widely or clearly perceived before 1914 or that, had it been perceived, political and economic leaders could have done much to make the old international rules conform to the new emerging economic realities. The prevailing concept of how the international system worked, with political, military, and economic competition between national units forming part of a single interwoven complex, each strand within each national unit reinforcing the others, was too deep-rooted and universal. Strikwerda seems to imply that, had economic integration continued to develop without being derailed by nationalist pressures and war, Europe would eventually have insensibly reached the point where (as now in Western Europe) war between its various states would become a practical impossibility, too destructive of too many ties and interests to be seriously contemplated. Europe, in short, could have grown out of war through the process of economic integration, with realpolitik gradually giving way to international cooperation. Not only do the prevailing historical conditions and mindsets argue against any such hypothesis, one must add the consideration that no state or people involved in a high-stakes, fiercely competitive contest, even if it is losing badly, can risk dropping out and switching to a game based on cooperative rules without firm assurances either that all the other players will also simultaneously switch from conflict to cooperation or, failing that, that some other player will protect its interests in the current contest. Without those assurances, any such action simply makes one a sacrificial lamb.

The disaster in 1914 did not derive therefore from a failure by industrialists to understand the political logic and requirements of economic integration or even the failure or refusal of politicians, military men, various interest groups, and broad publics to appreciate the long-range advantages of peaceful international cooperation over unrestrained competition and conflict. It lay rather in the structure of international politics—the fact that its component individual states would not and could not, either separately or together, leap from a power-based competitive international system to a rule-based cooperative one. For governments and peoples effectively to realize that an international system dominated by power-political competition is in the long run incompatible with real, durable international economic integration and its benefits, and for them genuinely to opt for the latter rather than merely wish for it, they must first be convinced that the power-political game has become intolerably expensive and dangerous and must be abandoned and also persuaded that another more cooperative system is available, or at least possible, and that the other important players will try it as well or, if not, that some other player or players will protect them and their interests if they alone defect from the competition. None of these essential conditions prevailed before 1914.

All this affects Strikwerda's interesting argument about periodization. His suggestion that the West European economic integration launched after World War II under state direction represented a kind of reprise, a renewal of a long nineteenth-century process of economic integration interrupted by 1914, again seems to me broadly correct. Yet if real, durable economic integration logically requires first a discrediting and collective repudiation of power politics as the primary basis for international politics and economics alike, this affects how we periodize the nineteenth century (1815–1914) and the twentieth (1914–1989). Both need to be broken into smaller units. The early nineteenth century, lasting from 1815 to the early 1850s, was a period in which power politics was actually discredited and dethroned as the primary basis of European international relations. This same period also laid the foundations for early economic liberalism and international integration in much of Europe (Britain, Prussia, Germany, Belgium), which by the 1840s was beginning to spread elsewhere (France, northern Italy, even Austria). The last half of the nineteenth century, however, was dominated by two divergent trends in international relations: on the one hand, a rapid if uneven economic expansion and some real but limited international economic integration and interdependence; on the other, the revival and reaffirmation of power politics as the basis for international relations and the primary, almost exclusive, method of ensuring national security and prosperity.[10] Strikwerda's essay shows, among other things, how these two principles ultimately collided. The period 1914–1945 represents a more terrible reprise of the revolutionary and Napoleonic wars, in which once more, this time for good, both power politics and economic autarky were discredited as the bases for international life, at least in Europe. The period 1945–1989 represents in Western Europe a revival of the principles of 1815 on a far broader, more durable basis—the dethroning of power politics, the recognition of the ultimate futility and destructiveness of traditional "self-help" methods, and a deliberate movement toward political and economic integration and interdependence as not merely a better way but the only way to achieve security and prosperity.

I DO NOT WISH TO DWELL ON THESE DIFFERENCES of interpretation, however, or press my scheme of periodization, and still less to become mired in a sterile debate over which comes first and is more important in the transformation of international relations, politics or economics, the repudiation of power politics or the

---

[10] There is a striking historical irony here. The post-1815 period is regularly called the Age of Restoration and the period from 1848 to 1870 the Age of Liberalism and Nationalism. Yet the post-Vienna period, as I argue in a forthcoming book, was restorationist only to a limited degree even in domestic politics and not at all in international politics, where it produced much progressive change. As for 1848–1870, it undoubtedly brought a rise in liberalism and nationalism and some major instances of national unification. Yet, so far as international politics is concerned, this was clearly the Age of Restoration—a return to the reign of power politics. In domestic politics and economics, its greatest statesmen, Palmerston, Cavour, and Bismarck, were all more or less liberal or progressive; in international politics, however, they all consciously returned to eighteenth-century realpolitik as the norm for international conduct. See Paul Schroeder, *The Transformation of European Politics, 1763–1848* (Oxford, 1994), vii–ix, 575–82, and *passim*.

achievement of economic integration.[11] Far more important than any differences on these scores or others are the aspects of Strikwerda's picture of international relations on which we agree. His article clearly portrays it not as an arena of structurally determined competition and conflict but a sphere of human activity like many others, constantly changing and subject to transformation along with other aspects of society, especially as the result of economic developments. Still more important, it is a sphere not merely of change and development but also of collective learning. Peoples and states can and do learn over time how to order their international relations better, though with great difficulty and usually only under extreme pressure. They can and do adapt to new realities, find different and better ways to achieve their goals. This means that past failures, however tragic their consequences, are not simply failures but can and should be instructive preludes to new efforts.

These may sound like tedious bromides, Pollyannish sentiments. In fact, they have great current relevance. The most startling and important thing that has happened in world international relations since 1985 is not, in my view, the end to the Cold War, the disappearance of the Iron Curtain, the collapse of Communism, the unification of Germany, or even the dissolution of the Soviet Union. Dramatic, unexpected, and crucial though all these are, they have historical analogues and precedents. One great change does not. For the first time, a number of important states, including one superpower, territorially the largest and militarily the second most powerful state in the world, the USSR, chose to repudiate power politics and the balance of power as the prime basis for their security and prosperity, recognizing its counterproductive effects and ultimately intolerable consequences in the modern world, and to rely instead on achieving cooperative relationships with formerly bitter adversaries. In addition, they did this more or less voluntarily, without having experienced exhaustion or catastrophic defeat in a total war, as in 1815 and 1945.

Nothing could be a more dramatic proof of the possibilities for constructive change and learning in international politics than this development. Nothing is more vital for world peace and security than that this unique, courageous experiment be supported and carried through to the point of ultimate success. Every other desired end in Europe and the rest of the world—economic integration, the expansion of trade, the growth of liberal democracy, the protection of civil rights, the prevention of new ethnic and international conflict—depends to some degree on sustaining it, avoiding a reversion to power politics. What has happened and is happening in the former Yugoslavia is only a small reminder of the dangers of such a retrogression.

Yet within the American foreign policy community, and doubtless elsewhere, a vocal, influential group is proclaiming the message that none of this really happened; that the old power politics is not at all obsolete and has not been repudiated or that, if it has been, it was all a big mistake, and the sooner we

[11] If forced to state a view, I would say that power politics has to be dethroned and effectively curbed, though not wholly abolished, in order for any other changes to be secure, but that once this is done, both international political reform and economic integration can proceed side by side, and that of the two, economic integration is probably the more powerful agent in transforming international relations.

all—Americans, Russians, Germans, Japanese, West Europeans, Ukrainians, everybody—return to relying for ultimate security and prosperity on military strength and alliances, global and regional balances, mutual nuclear deterrence, and the other proved and solid devices of power politics, the better and safer we all shall be.[12]

This is not the place to argue against this (to me) recklessly unhistorical view. It may not be inappropriate, however, to use a little space in the official journal of the American Historical Association to plead for greater participation by historians, especially international historians, in vital current debates such as this. International politics is too important to be left solely to political scientists and journalists. The public and policy makers need to learn from us, through articles like Strikwerda's and in other ways, that there is a long view on international politics and that it is one of change, development, and learning; that we are not imprisoned in the fatal patterns of the past but can do better.

[12] The leading school in this kind of thinking (though by no means all members share it) is that of neorealism or structural realism, best expounded in Kenneth N. Waltz, *Theory of International Politics* (Reading, Mass., 1979), which sees power politics as at all times the central, structural determinant of international relations. For specific examples of the arguments I allude to, see John J. Mearsheimer, "Back to the Future: Instability in Europe after the Cold War," *International Security*, 15 (1990): 5–55; Christopher Layne, "The Unipolar Illusion: Why New Great Powers Will Rise," *International Security*, 17 (1993): 5–51; Mearsheimer, "The Case for a Ukrainian Nuclear Deterrent," *Foreign Affairs*, 72 (Summer 1993): 50–66.

[10]

AHR Forum
Response to "Economic Integration and the European International System in the Era of World War I"

CARL STRIKWERDA

IN HIS THOUGHTFUL COMMENT, PAUL SCHROEDER has pointed out that the debate over economic integration and the origins of World War I turns on one of the central questions of modern politics: the relationship between political and economic power. And, as he correctly points out, the way in which leaders and the public *believe* political and economic power are related is as important as how these two kinds of power actually do interact. Given the present momentous crossroads in the post–Cold War world, I can only second Schroeder's call for policy makers and the public to work for mutually beneficial economic and political relations between nations. In addition to the need to reach out to the former Soviet bloc, which Schroeder justly stresses, one could also argue that U.S.-Japanese relations, the North American Free Trade Agreement, and European integration are areas in which we need to remind ourselves that, in the long run, the advantages of cooperation and negotiation outweigh the dangers inherent in conflict and self-interested nationalism.

Although Schroeder's comment provides a number of important insights, I wonder whether we can perhaps draw a stronger lesson than he does from history. Schroeder argues that, despite the international cooperation in the economic sphere before 1914, a major war was still virtually inevitable. Leaders and most of the public believed, first, that international economic relations, just like great power politics, were necessarily rooted in conflict rather than cooperation and, second, that as a result states had to use political and military power to strengthen their international economic position. "By and large, everyone assumed that the state, to ensure its citizens' security and prosperity, had to succeed simultaneously in two fields of competition in the international arena, both inextricably intertwined and mutually interdependent: politics and economics."[1]

Yet, given that an enormous degree of economic integration did occur, perhaps we should also investigate whether all European leaders actually believed that political and military power were essential to economic success. Just because the assumption that international relations will always tend toward conflict has been so deeply rooted and because the results of that assumption can be so disastrous, historians would do well to question it. After all, if excellent scholars on the

[1] Paul W. Schroeder, "Economic Integration and the European International System in the Era of World War I," *AHR*, 98 (October 1993): 1132.

pre-war era like Sidney Pollard and Norman Stone could simply overlook economic integration, so the beliefs about political and economic power could also have been interpreted selectively.[2] Government action was often necessary to make economies more open and cooperative, and defense against a real military threat was a necessary consideration.[3] But these kinds of state action were quite different from militarism or imperialism. To put it another way, the existence of the various "means" that Schroeder sees as the only way in which Europeans differed on advancing their countries' power might in fact bring very different ends. "Free trade," "economic integration," and "Concert diplomacy" led in a direction different from "protectionism," "autarky," and "armaments and military alliances."[4] As Schroeder himself has suggested in an innovative article, by introducing consultative diplomacy, conservatives in the first half of the nineteenth century radically changed traditional great power politics.[5] Liberals then introduced international economic cooperation in the mid-nineteenth century, after which Bismarck's wars reasserted militarism.[6]

It is possible, then, that, rather than a consensus, leaders had at their disposal a set of conflicting interpretations on whether political and military power helped a state economically. Imperialist propaganda occupies such a huge place in historiography—in part, because of its sheer volume—that we may be misled. Perhaps its volume testifies to the need to convince the public and policy makers of colonialism's value when economic trends moved in other directions. Britain's wealth did not depend on imperialism.[7] Nor was it true that "the flag follows investment," or Britain would have tried to conquer Colorado.[8] France owed more to its trade and flows of labor and capital with tiny Belgium than it did to its empire.[9] In any case, as Schroeder reminds us, imperialism did not lead directly to war, since disputes were settled cooperatively.

We can also too easily read the pre-1914 era through the violence and polarization created by the world wars. For example, Germany's penetration of foreign economies before the war has frequently been linked to annexationism during the war. In what became one of modern European historiography's most-used quotations, the industrialist Hugo Stinnes declared in 1911, "three to four years of peace, and I can guarantee silent German dominance in Europe." But, as Hans Jaeger points out, Stinnes actually said this to Heinrich Class, leader of the Pan-Germans, to define the limits of the industrialists' support for

[2] Carl Strikwerda, "The Troubled Origins of European Economic Integration: International Iron and Steel and Labor Migration in the Era of World War I," *AHR*, 98 (October 1993): 1109–10.

[3] Charles Kindleberger, "The Rise of Free Trade in Western Europe 1820–1875," *Journal of Economic History*, 35 (1975): 20–55.

[4] Schroeder, "Economic Integration," 1132.

[5] Paul Schroeder, "Did the Vienna Settlement Rest on a Balance of Power?" *AHR*, 97 (June 1992): 683–706.

[6] Schroeder, "Economic Integration," 1135, and especially note 10.

[7] Instead, Britain's wealth allowed it to have an empire. India was the one important example of a colony that paid. Lance E. Davis and Robert A. Huttenback, *Mammon and the Pursuit of Empire: The Political Economy of British Imperialism, 1860–1912* (Cambridge, 1986); Patrick O'Brien, "The Costs and Benefits of British Imperialism 1846–1914," *Past and Present*, 120 (1988): 163–99.

[8] Henry Noel Brailsford, *The War of Steel and Gold: A Study of the Armed Peace* (London, 1917), 78.

[9] Robert Frank, "L'Allemagne dans le commerce français," in *France and Germany in an Age of Crisis, 1900–1960*, Haim Shamir, ed. (Leiden, 1990), 32; Raoul Blanchard, *La Flandre: Étude géographique de la pleine flamande en France, Belgique, et Hollande* (Dunkirk, 1906), 395–459.

aggressive nationalism. Stinnes saw no need for war since German industry was doing so well.[10]

In fact, one of the best examples of the confusion over the value of military power for economic success is the inability of Germany's leaders to explain what they hoped to gain from launching the most devastating war in modern history. As industrialists and economic advisers warned again and again during the war, unless the pre-war international economy was revived, even extravagant territorial gains in Continental Europe might leave Germany worse off economically.[11] Before the war, Britain and other trading partners had not been shutting out German goods, but they probably would have if Germany had tried to set up a Continental empire. Similarly, when the Prussian parliament discussed Germany annexing iron ore fields, the Socialist member Otto Hué reminded the government that German and French industrialists had simply cooperated in owning and shipping ore before the war. The only response was that the war itself had rendered cooperation no longer possible and necessitated annexations.[12] The confusion among the elite about how Germany could improve its economic position over the pre-war situation exemplifies how much more research we need to do on the relationship between economics and politics in European history.

It is true that Eastern Europe—relations between Germany, Austria-Hungary, Russia, and the Balkan states—provided the spark for the war itself, and the argument has been made that economic integration here had less effect than elsewhere. The enormous migration of labor, among other factors, however, was drawing these economies together.[13] The factors at work were similar. What we need to understand is why, just as in Western Europe, the political decisions to seek a supposedly stronger military position were made with so little reference to any real gains and with so little recourse to other solutions.

In many ways, this is a question for intellectual history or the social history of ideas as much as political history. Why did political leaders tend to believe in the end that international economic power needed to rest on political and military intervention? Schroeder suggests that players in a power-political game such as the pre-1914 world cannot change unless they believe "that another more cooperative system is available, or at least possible, and that the other important

[10] Heinrich Class, *Wider den Strom: Vom Werden und Wachsen der nationalen Opposition im alten Reich* (Leipzig, 1932), 217, my translation; Hans Jaeger, *Unternehmer in der deutschen Politik (1890–1918)* (Bonn, 1967), 137. Unfortunately, this is also one of the more easily misused quotations. Stinnes was actually summarizing his earlier statement: "Let us have three to four years of peaceful development, and Germany will be the undisputed economic master of Europe." Gatzke uses the summary, which drops the reference to "peaceful development" and makes it unclear whether the dominance is political or economic. Hans Gatzke, *Germany's Drive to the West* (Baltimore, Md., 1966), 34. Gillingham has Stinnes say this to "his former classmates," but the source is Gatzke; John Gillingham, *Coal, Steel, and the Rebirth of Europe, 1945–1955: The Germans and French from Ruhr Conflict to Economic Community* (Cambridge, 1991), 11.

[11] Egmont Zechlin, "Cabinet versus Economic Warfare in Germany," in *The Origins of the First World War*, H. W. Koch, ed., 2d edn. (London, 1984); Strikwerda, "Troubled Origins," 1126, note 120.

[12] Gatzke, *Germany's Drive*, 170–71. Gatzke accepts the annexationists' argument that German firms had had difficulties obtaining ore from France before the war, 245–47; I see little evidence for this.

[13] Lars Olsson, "Labor Migration as a Background to the First World War," paper delivered at the Eighth International Conference of Europeanists, Chicago, March 1992. Olsson argues, however, that the scramble for labor also increased tensions between Germany and its neighbors.

players will try it as well."[14] It is perhaps worth asking why leaders did not understand their own world as having the potential for this alternative, a cooperative system. It is surprising how few references there are in historical scholarship to the complicated web of international agreements that undergirded a world economy stretching from Australia to Russia. The International Postal Union, international telegraphic conventions, World Standard Time, the International Red Cross, and a host of other institutions connected states. Nor were these merely consultative; many had a direct impact on daily life and routine governmental activity. By one estimate, there were 119 new international organizations founded between 1900 and 1909 and an astonishing 112 more created between 1909 and 1914.[15] What is more, leaders of all states—including the insecure nationalists of Germany, Russia, and the new states of the Balkans—wanted their countries to participate in these agreements. One other aspect of pre–World War I Europe illuminates how much the nation-states of the era coexisted and even assumed a foundation of international cooperation. As surprising as it may seem, there were virtually no passports, and visa regulations were nonexistent or, by later twentieth-century standards, incredibly lax. Thousands of businesspeople and workers migrated or went to work temporarily in other countries without encountering governmental controls.[16] The pre-1914 era may suggest that international relations have not been as conflict-ridden as they appear and that cooperation has a basis in history just as the long history of human conflict does.

I agree with Schroeder that international relations are determined in a complex fashion by both changing social trends and shifting human activity. The critical question is why those who held power in Europe interpreted their world as they did. There is nothing inevitable about integration: it is a product of political decisions to allow economies to grow in that direction. For all their power in their own sphere, business leaders more often than not adapt to the political framework in which they find themselves, or, at most, they are one among a variety of interest groups trying to direct the way a political system changes. Political leaders, too, must choose to support integration by ameliorating its inevitable harmful effects. Just as integration is a product of political decisions, so the effect of economic integration on the political system depends on the lessons leaders and the public draw from it. Economic integration by itself cannot force political cooperation, although, as I argued, I believe that if it proceeds far enough, it can force the economic leaders carrying out integration to decide whether or not they wish to become advocates of international political cooperation as well. The German industrialists in 1914, I believe, were close to being faced with such a decision.[17]

[14] Schroeder, "Economic Integration," 1134.

[15] John McManners, *Lectures on European History, 1789–1914: Men, Machines and Freedom* (Oxford, 1966), 361–62; Stephen Kern, *The Culture of Time and Space 1880–1918* (Cambridge, Mass., 1983), 11–16, 230–31. These references are not representative of contemporary historiography: McManners's work is a textbook; Kern's study has had great impact as a piece of intellectual history; but the political import of his argument has not been widely recognized by historians.

[16] Kern, *Culture of Time and Space*, 194.

[17] Strikwerda, "Troubled Origins," 1124.

1142   *Carl Strikwerda*

Crises such as those encountered by Europe in the years before 1914 and by the Western world in the collapse of the Soviet bloc are, as Schroeder suggests, too important not to be seen in the long view as both political and economic turning points. Diplomatic historians and social and economic historians have too often pursued their research in isolation from each other. Even when this reflects the frequent disjuncture in society between political systems and social trends, that very disjuncture, I would argue, raises important and intriguing questions. We need all the insights and all the re-thinking of old questions scholars can give in order both to learn from history and to face the challenges of today.

[11]

THE LEGACY OF THE
FIRST WORLD WAR

2.1 The economics of 'total war'

It is impossible to understand the economic history of inter-war
Europe and, more specifically, that of its international economic
organization without considering the long-lasting effects of the First
World War. It was a war which was first bitterly fought, both on the
battlefield and on what came to be known as the economic front,
and then continued, more subtly, in post-war political and economic
policies.

The First World War marked the true watershed between the
nineteenth and twentieth centuries. This is particularly relevant
when we consider our central theme of international economic
organization. The late nineteenth century was characterized by a
relatively well-functioning international payment system, based on
the gold standard. London played a pivotal and stabilizing role, and
the leading central banks co-operated as necessary. In addition,
there was almost perfect mobility of factors of production, reflected
in large-scale movements of labour and capital from Europe to the
New World. This was the nineteenth-century international economic order.

The war itself was a major economic revolution. In pre-1914
peacetime economies the role of the state was extremely limited.
Governments provided for defence, foreign policy, domestic security, and, in some cases, for free universal elementary education;
they subsidized railways and built national roads. Total revenue,
and expenses, seldom exceeded 15 per cent of GDP in the final years

THE LEGACY OF THE FIRST WORLD WAR   19

of peace. This pattern was so firmly established in everybody's expectations that a 'short-war theorem' had developed among governments and chiefs of staff. It held that, given the limited resources available and the disruption wrought on economic and social life, any 'modern' war was bound to be brief.

As it turned out, the theorem was based on very shaky foundations. It disregarded both the flexibility of a modern economy and the exceptional adaptability of mankind to almost any situation. The revolutionary aspect of the war economy consisted mainly in the rapid shift of resources from consumption to arms production, and in the attendant reorganization of the entire economic life of the belligerent nations. In a relatively short period of time, nineteenth-century thrifty governments were turned into twentieth-century big spenders. In the United Kingdom, military expenditure rose from about 4 per cent of GDP in 1913 to 38 per cent in 1916–17, bringing total government expenditure close to half of national income. In Germany, military spending alone rose to 53 per cent of GDP by 1917 (see further Table 10.1 below). A colossal amount of labour had to be swiftly diverted from peacetime production to military service, and to rapidly expanding armament factories, chemical industries, shipyards, and the like. Female labour was widely used in the countryside. The capital needs for this enormous resource reallocation were met chiefly by borrowing or simply printing large quantities of bank notes.

As soon as the illusion of a short war had vanished, all the contenders organized for 'total war'. In Germany, the brilliant head of the AEG electrical combine—Rathenau—was put in charge of an agency set up to exercise control from above over military supplies. In Italy, capable industrialists and top generals were given similar jobs. Germany's central planning of the supply of raw materials, and their distribution to companies working for the government, turned out to be particularly effective. It was accompanied by an industrial reorganization that more often than not entailed compulsory cartelization. Small industry was sacrificed to the needs of industrial giants.

In Britain, the Ministry of Munitions was created in 1915 under Lloyd George. It slowly acquired most of the features of Germany's War Raw Material Office, supervising private business and, when necessary, supplementing their efforts with direct investment. At the end of the war, Britain had some 200 government-owned plants. In many areas this colossal productive effort was coupled with an

20 THE LEGACY OF THE FIRST WORLD WAR

acceleration of technical progress both in products and in production processes. Internal-combustion engine vehicles, surface ships, submarines, aeroplanes, and several other products were drastically improved during the war, most of them subsequently enjoying peacetime development. At the same time, plants became larger and more efficient; the workforce—subject to military discipline—was 'scientifically' organized.

With hindsight, one may say that perhaps the most revolutionary aspect of 'total war' was general conscription. Society, particularly in the countryside, was deeply changed by the departure of almost all acceptable men, and their replacement by women, children, and older workers. While serving in the trenches, men were exposed to mass propaganda of various kinds as never before. And some of them learned ways of organizing large numbers of people for political purposes. After the war, it was almost impossible for the ruling classes to ignore the reality of mass movements and revert to the old cosy ways of élite politics.

In the international economy—the matter that interests us here—the war brought about two major developments. First, the displacement of the agricultural sector in the belligerent countries led to the lifting of import duties in order to gain access to the cheapest overseas supplies. The production of grains and meat in the fertile regions of the United States, Canada, Argentina, and Australia expanded to exploit their comparative advantage in supplying European markets.

Secondly, financial co-operation was undertaken by the Entente powers in the form of inter-Allied loans. At first, Britain lent to its financially weaker allies: France, Italy, and Belgium. Later on, the United States provided war loans to all the European countries fighting against the central empires. As a result of this co-operation, exchange rates of the Allies could be pegged at politically acceptable levels, and hard currency was made available to buy overseas supplies, mostly in the home markets of the creditor countries themselves.

2.2 The economic consequences of the war

The most enduring legacy of the war was social and political instability, both domestic and international. It is not our aim here to

THE LEGACY OF THE FIRST WORLD WAR   21

discuss this issue. Suffice it to say that, on the various domestic fronts, its ultimate results took the names of Mussolini in Italy, Primo de Rivera in Spain, and Hitler in Germany. And, of course, it was the war that opened the way to the October Revolution in Russia. More stable democracies, such as France and Britain, suffered from immediate post-war instability and for a moment even they feared revolution.

In the international arena, the period between the Armistice of 11 November 1918, and the crisis of 1923–4 that led to some kind of 'stabilization', was one of great upheaval. The war left a permanent scar on international relations that made co-operation much more difficult for many years to come. In the Balkans, and in parts of the former Russian Empire, active fighting remained endemic for a long time after the official end of the war, often dragging European powers into costly and useless interventions. Even more damaging, in the long run, was the way in which the peace treaties, particularly the one with Germany, were drafted. The unnecessarily punitive nature of reparations, the military occupation of the Rhineland, and, eventually, the direct intervention in the Ruhr all carried momentous consequences, some of which are related in the coming chapters.

Though we are convinced that unsettled domestic and international conditions played a major role in generating an unstable international economic environment, we confine our attention to those consequences of the First World War which directly affected the post-war organization and activity of the Continental economies, individually and collectively. Some of these were an immediate effect of the war; others followed from the way in which the great powers dealt with the issues which had still to be resolved when the armies finally called a halt to the slaughter and destruction. We look first at four direct effects of the war.

The two exogenous shocks

As we have seen, the war caused a major disruption of the real economy, on both the demand and supply sides. In every belligerent country there were swift changes of great magnitude in production and consumption patterns, such as those briefly outlined above. In particular, heroic efforts were made to increase productive capacity

22 THE LEGACY OF THE FIRST WORLD WAR

in war-related industries such as engineering, iron and steel, and shipbuilding.

The second exogenous shock occurred when much of this capacity became superfluous once the war was over. It proved exceptionally difficult to adjust to the required patterns of peacetime production as swiftly as required by sudden changes in demand created by unfulfilled wartime needs. This was, to a certain extent, the consequence of the devastation of transport networks and of fields, houses, factories, and mines during the fighting. The destruction was worst in France, Belgium, Italy, and Poland, but many other countries had also endured considerable loss of fixed assets. Much more important proved to be the difficulties connected with the relocation of physical assets and of labour to peacetime production. For instance, huge investments were made in shipbuilding, a particularly asset-specific industry that found itself perennially saddled with excess capacity. We shall say more about these problems in Chapter 4.

Another difficulty in returning to pre-war patterns was created by the changes that had occurred in world markets. Competitors whose economic circumstances were relatively little affected by the war, notably the United States and Japan, had seized the opportunity created by the inability of European manufacturers to maintain their normal trading activity, and had successfully invaded their markets. Japan, in particular, rapidly increased her sales to many Asian countries which had previously looked mainly to Britain for their imports. Moreover, huge export capacity had been built by cheap primary producers. The war also stimulated domestic production in non-European countries in order to substitute for imports from Europe. This is what happened, for example, to cotton textiles and other light manufactures in India and Latin America, thereby reducing the markets on which the pre-war output of the exporting nations had depended.

A more rigid economic environment

Once the war was over, the greatest possible degree of flexibility in prices and practices would be required in order to adjust to these devastating domestic and external shocks, but in fact the prevailing trend was towards greater rigidity. A long-run tendency for the flexibility of price and wage structures to decrease is likely to be a

THE LEGACY OF THE FIRST WORLD WAR   23

feature of all advanced democratic economies which give high priority to the stability of incomes, prices, and employment, but the war considerably hastened this process. In the post-war labour market, wage flexibility was diminished as many more decisions were centrally negotiated in a greatly extended process of collective bargaining. Behind this change lay the growth of working-class militancy, and the dramatic rise in the membership and strength of the trade union movement.

In the goods market there was similarly a tendency to reduced flexibility of property incomes and of prices. The war contributed to this by an increase in government intervention in economic life, the formation or strengthening of trade associations and cartels, and the imposition of numerous controls; each of these features survived in varying degrees into the post-war period.

More fundamentally, the war accelerated the trend towards larger business units, and in the extremely difficult circumstances of the 1920s many firms looked to collusion, to cartels, and to the exercise of monopoly powers to escape the consequences of increasing competition for shrinking markets. In Germany, cartels and other forms of industrial combination were already well established before the war; the increase in their scope and strength during the 1920s enabled them to resist falling prices by restricting production. In Britain, a similar trend was strongly fostered by the government, which deliberately promoted legislation and other measures to reduce competition in industries such as cotton, shipbuilding, and coal mining.

A weaker financial structure

The financial sector was also greatly affected by the war, and by the extensive interference in the peacetime patterns of both domestic and international markets which it stimulated. Most obviously, the war and its aftermath gave rise to unprecedented needs for revenue: it is estimated that the direct cost of the war in constant pre-war prices was the equivalent of five times the worldwide national debt in 1914 (Woytinski and Woytinski 1955, quoted in Aldcroft 1977: 30).

In all countries note issues and bank credits were expanded by immense amounts. Little or no attempt was made either to raise taxes or to borrow from the public on the scale needed to offset the

24 THE LEGACY OF THE FIRST WORLD WAR

additional demand on resources generated by the enormous military expenditures. The United Kingdom did more than any other nation to impose additional taxes, but even this was sufficient to cover only one-third of its expenditure (Morgan 1952: 104). In France and Germany the proportion financed in this way was very much lower, although the precise figure for the latter is complicated by the role of local taxes.

After the war finance ministers faced the need to service these swollen internal public debts. Many of them were short-term, and threatened monetary stability. There were also external demands for payment of war debts and reparations, while at the same time, international financial co-operation had entirely vanished. The reduction of budget deficits was made more difficult by the need to provide for reconstruction, and by new demands from active trade unions for higher expenditure on social security and unemployment benefits.

A large body of literature exists on some aspects of international financial dislocation, especially on reparations, on inter-Allied debts (more generally on Europe becoming a net debtor) and on the new pattern of international lending. Less is known about changes in the web of international banking that provided the grass-roots connection for the international transfer of short- and long-term capital, as well as for the actual day-by-day functioning of an international payment system.

A fragile international monetary system

The classic gold standard was an early casualty of the conflict. Within a few months of the declaration of war, almost all European central banks, including those in countries that were to remain neutral, had unilaterally suspended gold payments. During the war, the powers of the Entente developed their own payment system, backed by the inter-Allied loans, as noted above. This co-operation was designed to allow the belligerent countries to sustain the level of imports required to achieve the maximum military contribution to the common cause.

Once the war was over, co-operation ceased almost overnight. Inter-Allied financial assistance was suspended, and creditor countries immediately made it clear that they expected reimbursement of their war loans. At the same time, the victorious powers insisted

THE LEGACY OF THE FIRST WORLD WAR 25

on extracting an unrealistic amount of reparations from those they had defeated. French retaliation for the terms which Germany had imposed on her after victory in 1870 was the dominant factor in preventing a more realistic settlement. A typical inter-war British view of the overall financial outcome is given in the following scathing comment by Lionel Robbins (1934: 6):

The inordinate claims of the victors, the crass financial incapacity of the vanquished, the utter budgetary disorder which everywhere in the belligerent countries was the legacy of the policies pursued during the war, led to a further period of monetary chaos.

We turn next to the developments which followed from the end of the war, including the shock to the domestic economies of the former belligerents, the signing of the peace treaties which settled relations between the former enemies, and the changes in the relations between the Allies. All these had further profound consequences for the financial and economic developments of the 1920s and beyond.

2.3 The economic consequences of the post-war settlements

The shock of economic restructuring and social unrest

During the war, as much as 30–40 per cent of the belligerents' GDP was directly or indirectly controlled by the state. While supplies to the army came to be the direct responsibility of governments, the rest of the economy was to a great extent subject to various forms of state supervision. Thus, forms of administrative controls were more often than not introduced on prices, wages, capital, and foreign exchange markets. The return to peacetime economic organization and production entailed a huge process of resource reallocation that, contrary to what is assumed in economics textbooks, not only required a long period of time, but also met with the resistance of the vested interests that had been created by the war.

Businessmen and industrialists were almost everywhere divided between those who favoured an immediate return to a *laissez-faire* economy and those—usually the suppliers to the army—who argued in favour of a slow 'return to normality', with strong state

26 THE LEGACY OF THE FIRST WORLD WAR

help in the process. While most proponents of the latter view only wanted the state to provide forms of financial support to ailing industries, and to guarantee the social peace, a militant minority in France, Germany, and Italy came to herald the birth of a 'technocrat' and 'corporatist' state that would actively support economic growth, particularly in the technologically more advanced sectors.

Whatever the pace was to be, industrial restructuring implied the closing of a number of plants (the case of shipyards is of particular relevance because of the magnitude of the supply cuts that were needed). Capital for the creation of factories that would meet consumers' demand was scarce at home and unlikely to come from foreign sources (see below). The result was unemployment. At the same time households were frustrated by the fall in the real value of the wartime savings they wanted to use to satisfy their pent-up demand for consumer goods. In several countries, the combination of these two conditions produced a short but deep recession between 1920 and 1921.

Social unrest was, however, the main post-war problem. Its discussion would lead us away from the particular economic focus of the present text, but the economic implications of the political developments must not be underrated. The almost universal explosion of working-class struggles and protests after the war can be primarily attributed to two factors.

The first was the powerful growth of their organization, strength, and solidarity. Workers had already formed increasingly successful unions in the years before the war, not only in Britain, where they dated back many decades, but on the Continent as well. The war provided a tremendous boost to these organizations. Maintaining the discipline and the morale of huge armies raised through compulsory conscription entailed both pressures and concessions, and the latter included promises of a better life for the masses as soon as hostilities were over. Life in the trenches also proved to be a tremendous catalyst for the emerging 'mass society': workers from various areas and occupations got to know each other's needs and local strengths while, at the same time, socialist propaganda could be much more effective in such huge concentrations of working-class people.

In addition, at home, the urgent need to increase production of military supplies, and overcome traditional restrictive practices, re-

THE LEGACY OF THE FIRST WORLD WAR   27

quired recognition of, and concessions to, the trade unions. From 1916 onward, trade union membership increased steeply in the United Kingdom, Germany, and France.

Secondly, the Russian Revolution exercised considerable influence on working-class movements, even though this influence was ambiguous: a model for a militant minority, but at the same time a highly divisive factor for those who did not share this ideology.

The economic impact of social developments differed according to the relative weakness of the economies and of the governments that emerged from the war. Thus, in Germany, the social democratic government undertook a number of social reforms, certainly out of its own political conviction, but also to undermine working-class support for the revolutionary movement. Mines and metal-making were 'socialized', trade unions fully recognized, the eight-hour week introduced. Deficit spending by the state followed, partly feeding into the price spiral. As a result, however, social unrest diminished considerably; by early 1920, hours lost in strikes were already half the number one year earlier.

Other defeated countries saw more dramatic developments that undoubtedly contributed to economic destabilization in central and eastern Europe. Thus, Bulgaria was swept by quasi-revolutionary winds, while Hungary was actually briefly governed in 1919 by the Communists in the so-called 'Councils' Republic'.

In Italy—socially and economically the weakest amongst the large countries on the winning side—workers took over the management of a number of companies during the so-called 'red biennium' (1920–1). The working-class movement was eventually weakened by the division resulting from the creation of a Communist Party in 1921, while reactionary forces gained sufficient strength to enable them to seize power violently by the March on Rome (1922) that inaugurated twenty years of fascist dictatorship. The latter, however, was mostly the result of the failure of the old 'liberal' politicians to provide viable solutions to the post-war problems, particularly the social issues.

In France and Britain too, the enormous number of strikes during 1919 affected both industrial output and investors' expectations. In both countries governments regained control of the situation during 1920, often by the adoption of rather harsh repressive measures. However, while in France the trade union movement suffered a serious set-back, in Britain the circumstances and the results of the

28 THE LEGACY OF THE FIRST WORLD WAR

social conflict were different, because the trade unions had already developed strong roots, and because the victory of Lloyd George in the 1918 elections brought in a relatively sympathetic government.

The economic consequences of the peace treaties

The war finally ended, and after much wrangling, peace treaties were signed in 1919 with Germany (at Versailles), Austria (at St-Germaine-en-Laye), and Bulgaria (at Neuilly), and in 1920 with Hungary (at the Trianon) and Turkey (at Sèvres). Various aspects of these treaties were to be a cause of severe disturbance to post-war trade and production. First, the way in which the political map of central and eastern Europe was redrawn disrupted long-standing economic relations and created new barriers to trade. Secondly, the attempt to hold Germany responsible for the war by imposing huge demands for reparations for the losses suffered by the victorious powers became a major cause of political antagonism and economic discord.

Pre-1914 trading patterns, communications, and financial relations had long been adjusted to the existing political boundaries. In the large central empires these had evolved to coincide with customs and monetary unions. These well-established arrangements were all disrupted when the formation of new nation states led to the creation of numerous smaller political units in the territories of the former Russian, German, Austro-Hungarian, and Ottoman empires.

The most extensive territorial changes came from the breaking up of the Habsburg Empire, leading to the loss of territory to Italy and the creation of six small nation states (Czechoslovakia, Poland, Romania, Yugoslavia, and a much-diminished Austria and Hungary) in place of a single large multi-ethnic geopolitical entity (see Map 2.1). Germany lost all her overseas colonies and some of her best industrial and agricultural land, including Alsace-Lorraine and the Saar coal-mines, to France; Upper Silesia and other territory to Poland; and smaller areas or towns to Denmark, Belgium, Lithuania, and Czechoslovakia. The Russian Empire also suffered major territorial losses, including four areas which became independent states (Finland, Estonia, Latvia, and Lithuania); Bulgaria was forced to cede territory to Greece; and there were substantial changes in the former Ottoman Empire, though the areas which Turkey lost

THE LEGACY OF THE FIRST WORLD WAR 29

Map 2.1. The new states of central Europe after the First World War

Source: Martin Gilbert (1970), *First World War Atlas*. London: Weidenfeld and Nicolson.
©Martin Gilbert. Reprinted by permission of Taylor and Francis Books Ltd.

30 THE LEGACY OF THE FIRST WORLD WAR

were outside Europe. The final outcome was that there were 38 independent nations in Europe in 1919, 12 more than in 1914.

In deciding on these changes to the map of central and eastern Europe, the victorious powers were primarily guided by the principle of national self-determination, not by economic considerations. This led to the creation of nation states: political entities encompassing people of the same language, culture, and tradition. This principle was perhaps consistent with the political needs and ideology of the time, but it did not necessarily respond to those of the economy. Foreign trade, in particular, was affected by the new frontiers, with significant consequences, both for the development of the region and for the overall performance of the international economy.

Furthermore, this huge process of border adjustments and state formation inevitably failed to reconcile and satisfy all the conflicting interests and aspirations involved, and so left behind a permanent residue of social and national resentments. In the view of one historian the territorial realignments may have created more problems than they removed (Thomson 1966: 633). The potential for further conflicts translated into the expectations of economic agents, particularly investors. In some cases endemic fighting continued well into the 1920s, increasing the overall sense of instability.

Each new state created its own currency, erected trade barriers to protect domestic industry, inaugurated independent fiscal and monetary policies. In particular, the imposition of tariffs (whether as a source of urgently needed revenue or as a means of protection), the loss of gold and exchange reserves, and the diminished possibilities for foreign borrowing by countries already over-burdened by debts and/or claims for reparations all helped further to restrict the scope for foreign trade. Even from a narrowly defined economic point of view—that is, without taking into account the adverse impact of political uncertainty on the expectations of economic agents— these developments had a deep effect on the international economy by distorting trade and capital flows relative to the pre-1914 situation.

By the last decade of the nineteenth century, the Habsburg Empire had become a well-functioning customs union; it was also a rather efficient, if not optimum, currency area. Each region within the empire tended to specialize in those industrial and agricultural products for which it enjoyed a comparative advantage. Vienna, and to a lesser extent Budapest, had developed into effective money and capital markets providing for the financial capital needs of the whole Dual Monarchy.

In the Danube region, where industrialization had hardly begun by 1914, the establishment of independent policy-maker regimes implied the encouragement of industrial development. Thus Romania, Yugoslavia, and Bulgaria tended to favour high-cost native firms by erecting tall tariff walls around them at a considerable cost to the consumer and to the large agricultural sector. In Hungary, a more industrially advanced country, this policy was less extreme but had none the less a negative impact on trade and growth.

The case of Czechoslovakia was different, in that the new state included the most highly industrialized parts of the former empire. Here the problem was that Czech industry was highly dependent on export markets which were severely affected by the new wave of protectionism. At the same time, the moderately protective agricultural policy of the Prague governments had serious effects on the export outlets of other former members of the empire, given the high income of Czech consumers.

Although less industrialized than Czechoslovakia, Poland had a similar problem. While it was not heavily dependent on the Danubian markets for its agricultural exports, its natural outlets for industrial trade were disturbed by the new frontiers. In the previous four decades the manufacturers of central Poland had developed 'as part of the wider Russian market in which, in certain branches, they had taken the technical lead . . . In the inter-war years this market vanished, and Polish trade was virtually nil' (Radice 1985: 34).

The international economy was also affected by the Bolshevik Revolution and by the civil war, which continued until the early 1920s. In the last part of the nineteenth century, the Russian Empire had been increasingly integrated into European trade and capital flows. After signing a separate peace treaty with Germany, the Bolsheviks effectively severed most of the country's pre-war links with the rest of the world. Trade was reduced to a fraction of its pre-1914 level, and western European capital was scared off by the repudiation of the Tsarist regime's foreign debt. True, new countries—Finland, Latvia, Estonia, and Lithuania—emerged at the edge of the former empire, but these were economically too small to compensate for the loss of trade with Russia.

To sum up: the dismemberment of the Dual Monarchy, the splitting off of parts of the German and Russian empires, and the latter's autarkic evolution all represented a major shock to the

32 THE LEGACY OF THE FIRST WORLD WAR

international economy. It was a cause of widespread resource misallocation, resulting in lower output and higher prices, particularly in central and eastern Europe. In the decades immediately
preceding the war, this large area had made significant progress
along the road of 'modern economic growth', and was thus
becoming ever more important to Europe's overall trade and production. In due time, of course, markets adjusted trade and capital
flows to the new situation, but this structure was less conducive
to economic efficiency than the one which had prevailed before
the war. Moreover, such adjustments were slow to come about—
the market process always takes far longer than economists are
ready to admit.

In the aftermath of the war, the adjustment was made even
slower by uncertainty as to the stability of the new regimes, by fear
of revolution, by the persistence of endemic conflicts, by lack of
information in western capitals about the new leaders, and by the
incompetence of some among the latter. It took, for instance, long
years of diplomatic effort and a number of international conferences
to re-establish more appropriate levels of trade with the Soviet
Union. And it was not until the mid-1920s that German exports
resumed their pre-war importance in the Reich's traditional central
European markets.

The end of financial solidarity among the Allies

The abrupt end to the system of inter-Allied loans which had been
put in place during the war delivered yet another shock to the
international economy. The system had implied a flow of financial
capital from the United Kingdom to the European members of the
Entente, and from the United States to the latter, as well as to
Britain. At the same time, part of this flow of capital was used
to stabilize the belligerents' exchange rates for both political and
economic reasons. If the downward trend in the currencies were too
steep, it might be interpreted as the expression of a pessimistic
assessment of the outcome of the war by the markets. And if the
fluctuations around the trend were too wide and erratic, this would
increase the cost of supplies in neutral markets.

Inevitably, however, the support for the European exchange rates
served to weaken the dollar on the Japanese and neutral markets.
While maintaining the domestic convertibility of the dollar,

Washington had to impose an embargo on the export of gold. All this was politically acceptable as long as it could be presented to American public opinion as part of an overall set of measures—military, economic, and diplomatic—aimed at maximizing a co-ordinated effort that would produce swift victory. Once the latter was achieved—in November 1918—few saw the necessity or even the possibility for a continuation of the wartime financial policy.

The war had been tremendously demanding on Europe's re-sources, both human and economic. In various parts of the Conti-nent, particularly in the defeated countries, food emergencies developed which could be met only with considerable difficulty, given the lack of foreign exchange to pay for agricultural imports. In other areas, particularly of France, Belgium, and, to a lesser extent, Italy, reconstruction required considerable amounts of capital. Fi-nance was needed all over Europe to carry on the reallocation of resources from war-related to peacetime production. In these cir-cumstances, the European countries, especially Britain and France, argued in favour of a 'soft landing'. This would have meant a con-tinuation of the financial assistance from the United States, and a slow relaxation of the wartime controls on exchange rates and, more generally, on the international economy.

At the same time, however, France invoked the imposition of very harsh conditions on the defeated powers, particularly on Ger-many. These required the payment of huge reparations to fund not only France's reconstruction and war pensions, but also her foreign debt. Indeed, the French insisted that the reimbursement of their debts to the United States and Great Britain must be linked to the actual receipt of reparations from Germany. The two sets of re-quests were not mutually consistent. If the aim was international solidarity to rebuild the European economy, then everyone should have been required to pay a price for the success of the co-operative effort; above all, those European countries that stood to benefit most from the Continent's swift recovery. If, on the other hand, the aim was justice—with everyone paying for the obligations incurred during the war—then there was no reason to establish a link be-tween debts and reparations.

While individual European countries, particularly those on the Continent, proved to be short-sighted in their narrow focus on their own immediate interests, it was the attitude of the United States which had by far the largest impact on subsequent developments. Its political weight was considerable, since it had to be reckoned that its

34 THE LEGACY OF THE FIRST WORLD WAR

intervention in the war had been decisive in tipping the scale in favour of the Entente; and, what mattered most, it was now the world's dominant financial power. However, America did not respond adequately to its newly acquired responsibility as world leader.

There were good political reasons—both domestic and international—for this attitude, but in retrospect it is evident that there was a cultural gap as well. The then leaders of the United States lacked the necessary insight to understand where the long-term interests of the country actually lay. The Victory Loan Act passed by Congress in March 1919 authorized the government to open credit to foreign countries only for the purchase of goods directly or indirectly belonging to the government, and of grains the price of which was guaranteed by the United States. Europe was thereby provided with a safety net against a fall in food consumption below subsistence levels, but it was denied US credit for reconstruction and for postwar industrial conversion to peacetime production. The pace of both was thus slower, and the economic and political impact of the post-war shock to the world economy more substantial, than they would otherwise have been.

One of the features—both cause and effect—of the post-war shock was immense turmoil in the world markets for foreign exchange. Before 1914 the most severe financial crises resulted in currency devaluations of only a few percentage points, even for those European countries that were forced out of gold. Nevertheless, they were considered a national disaster. With the end of the wartime financial support from the United States to Europe, and of the attendant pegging of the Entente currencies to the dollar, exchange rates were left to their own fate. The United States resumed gold payments in 1919. By 1920, the pound had lost about 25 per cent relative to its pre-war parity. The exchange rates of the other members of the Entente soon lost over 50 per cent of their 1914 value and continued to fall. As an average for 1920, the French franc stood at 36 per cent of its pre-war gold parity, the Italian lira at 25 per cent. In the defeated countries of central Europe colossal exchange rate devaluations ended up feeding into hyper-inflation (see Chapter 3.1). By 1920, the German mark was worth only 7 per cent of its 1914 value: in the following two years it disappeared as an international currency.

Of course, the blame for this cannot all be laid at the door of the United States. Wartime currency pegging was obviously untenable after the end of hostilities, and it was necessary for the exchange rate of each individual currency to adjust to changes in purchasing power parity driven by their respective rates of inflation. In so far as markets reacted to uncertainty, it must also be recognized that domestic circumstances were of paramount importance.

Nevertheless, errors of judgement and policy by the international leaders were an important additional factor. The retreat from wartime financial solidarity was too abrupt. The lack of international credit for reconstruction and industrial restructuring magnified the markets' unfavourable expectations about the pace of recovery in France, Belgium, and Britain. Uncertainty about the amount of reparations and the settlement of inter-Allied debt was also a major source of volatility in international markets. Finally, the idea of re-creating an international monetary system based on gold was not only highly ill-advised—as we shall see—but was also left to the initiative of central bankers, rather than being part of a larger political design springing from the world's leaders.

Reparations

In discussing the economic consequences of the war and the peace treaties we have several times mentioned reparations without actually discussing them. In fact they deserve specific treatment: they were by far the most controversial issue in the peace treaty with Germany, and are widely regarded as one of the critical elements underlying the political and economic failures of the inter-war period.

Article 231 of the Versailles Treaty held Germany responsible for the war, therefore establishing the legal ground for reparations. These were supposed to cover war-related material damages. To start with, the definition was ambiguous: while the cost of reconstruction was undoubtedly included, a controversy soon developed as to the inclusion of compensation for personal losses (mainly pensions to widows and disabled men).

Keynes was the first to condemn reparations on the scale proposed at Versailles as economically irrational and politically unwise. In a famous polemic (Keynes 1919) he argued that it was not sensible, indeed was ultimately against the best interests of the victorious powers, to cripple Germany economically, since much of Europe's pre-1914 welfare had depended on German economic growth.

36 THE LEGACY OF THE FIRST WORLD WAR

Moreover, Keynes envisaged difficulties in transferring real resources across borders, given the uncertainty as to how the post-war
international capital market would work. His overall view was
thus that reparations were 'vindictive', 'insane', and ultimately
'unworkable'.

Many modern historians regard Keynes's castigation of European
leaders on this issue as excessively harsh. Negotiators at Versailles
were aware that 'if the Weimar Republic was unduly hampered in
employing its skilled population and material resources produc-
tively, the continent as a whole would not easily recover its prosperity' (Schuker 1988: 14). However, they faced enormous budgetary
problems themselves as a result of the war, and public opinion could
not possibly be convinced to bear all the burden after the huge
sacrifices made during the conflict itself. 'La Boche payera' (The Hun
will pay) was a powerful political slogan in early post-war France.
Whatever the ultimate awareness by European leaders of the intricate web of problems bequecthed by the war, the fact remains that
the reparation issue injected a considerable additional amount of
uncertainty and acrimony into the volatile post-war economy.

A crucial feature of the Versailles Treaty was that no sum was
fixed by the treaty itself. Soon after the Armistice, Germany was
stripped of its gold reserves, most of its merchant navy, and whatever equipment (such as rolling stock) might have been of use to the
victors. Deliveries of coal were also required. In the following
months, preliminary reparation payments were required, pending a
final settlement. In March 1921 the German failure to fulfil part of
those preliminary requests prompted the occupation by Allied
troops of the towns of Dusseldorf, Duisberg, and Ruhrhort on the
east side of the River Rhine. Needless to say, this move did not
contribute to a stable international environment. Only one month
later, the so-called London Schedule of Payments for the first time
formally established Germany's reparation obligations. Germany,
however, dragged its feet so that the Allies again entered its territory
in 1923, this time occupying the mining district of the Ruhr.

It was not until 1924 that an agreement was reached, the Dawes
Loan, which created the pre-condition for a reasonably stable system of international payments which allowed private capital to flow
into Germany. This made it possible for reparations to be smoothly
transferred to France, which was due to receive the bulk of them (52
per cent), to the British Empire (22 per cent), to Italy (10 per cent),
to Belgium (8 per cent), and to the other minor Allies.

THE LEGACY OF THE FIRST WORLD WAR   37

The mechanism by which the post-war international payment system was allowed to work will be the subject of further discussion in the next chapter. Here we wanted to stress the immediate adverse repercussions of the post-war settlement on the world economy. While the sum finally agreed upon, and the schedule of payments, might not have been significantly above what Germany could reasonably have paid without crippling its economy, the manner in which the whole problem was dealt with between 1918 and 1924 added an enormous further element of uncertainty to an already volatile post-war international economy. At the same time, it made international relations difficult, acrimonious, and, eventually, full of damaging potential for revenge.

References

Aldcroft, Derek H. (1977), *From Versailles to Wall Street* (London: Allan Lane).

Keynes, John Maynard (1919), *The Economic Consequences of the Peace* (London: Macmillan), repr. as vol. 2 of Keynes (1971–89).

Morgan, E. Victor (1952), *Studies in British Financial Policy, 1914–1925* (London: Macmillan).

Radice, E. A. (1985), 'General Characteristics of the Region Between the Wars', in Kaser and Radice (1985), 23–65.

Robbins, Lionel (1934), *The Great Depression* (London: Macmillan).

Schuker, Stephen A. (1988), *American 'Reparations' to Germany, 1919–33: Implications for the Third World Debt Crisis*, Princeton Studies in International Finance, no. 61 (Princeton: International Finance Section).

Thomson, David (1966), *Europe since Napoleon* (Harmondsworth: Penguin).

Woytinsky, W. S., and Woytinsky E. S. (1955), *World Commerce and Government* (New York: Twentieth Century Fund).

Part III
Late Nineteenth-Century Backlash

[12]

GROUP BEHAVIOR AND INTERNATIONAL TRADE

C. P. KINDLEBERGER
Massachusetts Institute of Technology

I

THE primary tool of analysis in economics is the market. But Walker has expressed the opinion that an economics adequate for prediction and policy must include a theory of extra-market behavior.[1] Polanyi, further, has attempted to demonstrate that the emphasis on the market is likely to be misleading and that a rounded theory of social behavior would include economic drives as only one stand in a broad web of social motivation.[2] The present article is designed to suggest that, in certain situations in international trade, a useful tool of analysis may be found in a theory of group behavior at the national level. Unhappily, no such theory adequate for the task appears to have been developed. A few suggestions will be offered as to the types of variables with which such a theory should deal.

The method followed is to take the world decline in the price of wheat after 1870 and to indicate the responses to it in Great Britain, Germany, France, Italy, and Denmark. If a theory of market behavior were sufficient for prediction, it might be expected that the reduction in the price of wheat in Europe would lead to increased imports. Foreign sources of supply would be substituted for domestic. Resources engaged in the production of wheat would shift to less remunerative occupations. Some increase in wheat consumption would take place at the expense of other grains, to the extent that wheat would fall more in price than rye, oats, and barley would. Some of these changes did, in fact, occur, but the results were not uniformly of this character.

After the differences in response have been established, attention will be turned to a series of explanations dependent on nonmarket factors. None of these is completely satisfactory. What appears to be needed is a comprehensive theory of group behavior to deal with groups as large as nations—in particular, a theory which systematically makes allowances for variation in the relation among the subgroups which make up the larger entity.

I am conscious of the amateurish character of the economic history and sociology in what follows, and I am not inclined to apologize for this inevitable shortcoming. Interdisciplinary co-operation must begin with the utilization, however crude, of the products of other social sciences by practitioners in separate fields. I have greatly benefited from the assistance of experts in other fields;[3] but I have been obliged to restrict my use of their techniques, lest my special focus of interest be lost among a host of fine points.

[1] Ronald Walker, *From Economic Theory to Policy* (Chicago: University of Chicago Press, 1943), *passim*.

[2] K. Polanyi, *The Great Transformation* (New York: Rinehart, 1944), *passim*.

[3] Especially helpful have been Duncan Ballantine, John Blum, K. W. Deutsch, A. Gerschenkron, Bert F. Hoselitz, G. K. Krulee, E. E. Morison, W. W. Rostow, and J. E. Sawyer.

II

The main facts concerning the world decline in the price of wheat after the American Civil War and its causes are generally understood and accepted. The rapid spread of the American rail net work in the 1870's and 1880's made it possible to transport wheat to tidewater more cheaply and in far greater quantities than the canal system had been able to handle. A parallel development occurred in railroad construction from the Ukrainian wheat fields to Crimean ports. The technological shift from wooden to iron ships—another indirect effect of the Civil War—reduced trans-Atlantic freight rates and those to western Europe from the Crimea. The availability of demobilized manpower, untilled land, and wartime accumulations of money capital, coupled with the development of farm machinery for extensive cultivation, resulted in an expansion of the American supply, which passed the economies of production and distribution on to the consumer in Europe as cheaper wheat. In addition, the weather was favorable during the 1880's, and yields were high. The European peasant and landowner met increased competition in grain production from overseas.[4]

The difficulties of European wheat-growers were not solely caused by overseas competition. A series of bad seasons reduced yields and brought about a deterioration in quality. A Royal Commission of Inquiry, sitting from 1879 to 1882, reached the conclusion that the loss of British farm income was due primarily to untoward weather and only secondarily to foreign competition. The effects of the two causes were not unconnected. In a closed economy a short crop is at least partially compensated for, so far as farm income is concerned, by an increase in price. In an international, bi-hemispheric economy, an increase in the local price produced by a series of short crops is likely to be forestalled by imports from overseas.[5]

The view exists, however, that what hurt European agriculture was not overseas competition or any other factor peculiar to agriculture but over-all depression, lasting from 1873 to 1896. It is recognized that the price of wheat fell somewhat more than prices in general, and this is ascribed to the growth of production in the United States. This relative decline, given by one writer as only 10 per cent, is regarded as much less significant for the agricultural depression than was the general fall in prices.[6] The reasoning, however, is not persuasive in the light of price developments on, say, the Copenhagen market, which was unaffected by tariffs. Between 1873 and 1896 wheat fell in price by 53 per cent and rye by 48 per cent, as compared with a decline of 36 per cent in the *Statist*'s index of wholesale prices. And after 1873 American wheat appeared in European markets which had never before known it, including some cities, such as Trieste, which were known as export centers for European supplies.[7]

---

[4] See E. G. Nourse, *American Agriculture and the European Market* (New York: McGraw-Hill Book Co., 1924), Appendix A. An earlier and entirely orthodox account is furnished by Thorstein B. Veblen in "The Price of Wheat since 1867," *Journal of Political Economy*, I (December, 1892), 70–103.

[5] See Lord Ernle, *English Farming, Past and Present* (5th ed.; New York: Longmans, Green & Co., 1936), pp. 379–81; and R. C. K. Ensor, *England, 1870–1914* (Oxford: Oxford University Press, 1936), p. 116.

[6] See Einar Jensen, *Danish Agriculture: Its Economic Development* (Copenhagen: Munksgaard, 1937), pp. 192 ff. and esp. 212.

[7] *Ibid.*, statistical appendix. For a series of interesting contemporary European views see the *Report of the U.S. Commissioner of Agriculture* (1883), pp. 326–51 (quoted by Nourse, *op. cit.*, pp. 271 ff.).

32   C. P. KINDLEBERGER

The combination of weather and over-seas competition, then, produced potential economic distress for the farming community in the form of short crops and low prices. The remainder of this analysis, for convenience, treats this as a question solely of prices. In this connection, some importance attaches to the question of timing. The price of wheat fell from $1.70 to $0.66 a bushel in England from 1873 to 1894, and the sharpest decline was probably that from $1.31 in 1882 to $0.90 in 1886.[8] Action to meet the collapse in the price of wheat was taken, if at all, primarily in response to this pressure. But the nature of the response and the timing differed from country to country.

III

No action was taken in Britain. The issue had already been settled some years before, in 1846, with the repeal of the Corn Laws. The decline in the world price of wheat produced an improvement in the terms of trade for the rising industrial classes and a basis for lowering, or withholding increases in, the wages of the industrial labor force. The latter, in turn, received a new batch of recruits in the form of agricultural workers displaced from the farm by the unprofitability of wheat growing.

The repeal of the Corn Laws in 1846, fourteen years after the political settlement between the landed gentry and industry and commerce in the Reform Bill, produced no immediate economic effect.

The period of high farming in Britain continued uninterrupted. British agriculture in general was efficient and profitable from 1837, when the long period of distress after the Napoleonic Wars came to an end, until 1873. The American Civil War and the Crimean War had helped to postpone the effects of cheap wheat imports, but even in the 1850's there had been no significant effects of the repeal. Land under the plow in Britain reached a peak in 1872 never again attained, even in World War II.[9]

The bad summers from 1875 to 1879, the rinderpest attack of 1877, and the widespread loss of sheep to liver rot in 1879 may have convinced the farmers that their difficulties were due to the vindictiveness of nature rather than to a change in their position in the community. Landowners remained the richest class in the country for several years after the disaster of 1879. By 1886 their relative position had begun to slip.[10] No action was taken to halt the decline in farm prices or to assist the farming community.[11] The dominant group in the society—the rising industrial class—was content to have cheaper food and cheaper labor. Rents fell, young men left the farm for the town, land planted to crops shrank rapidly. The response to the

---

[8] Slight differences in range and timing existed in separate markets because of differing transfer costs and the accessibility of different sources of supply. In Sweden, for example, which is not covered below, the comparable decline was from $1.34 per bushel in 1881 to $0.78 in 1887. See Table II of the Appendix to the useful "Decline and Recovery of Wheat Prices," *Wheat Studies* (Food Research Institute), X, Nos. 8 and 9 (June and July, 1934), 347, which gives annual figures for a large number of countries.

[9] Roy Lewis and Angus Maude, *The English Middle Classes* (London: Phoenix House, 1949), p. 171.

[10] See Ensor, *op. cit.*, p. 117.

[11] This statement should perhaps be qualified by reference to the fair-trade agitation of the 1880's and the rise of protectionist sentiment in the 1890's under Joseph Chamberlain. Both these movements, however, were industrial in origin and sought to enlist rural support as an afterthought.

Some weight should perhaps also be given to the roles of bad weather and pestilence which delayed recognition of the importance of overseas competition. It is not certain that the reaction would have been equally passive had the country as a whole clearly understood the deep-seated nature of agriculture's troubles.

decline in the world price of wheat was to complete the liquidation of agriculture as the most powerful economic group in Britain.

IV

In Germany, France, and Italy the farmer was protected by the imposition of tariffs. In Germany the tariff on grain was enacted first in 1879, after fourteen years of free trade. Duties under this law were almost purely nominal, but rates were sharply raised in 1885 and again in 1887. The timing of tariff enactments in France and Italy was broadly similar, with the exception of the first step and with a significant difference in so far as Italy was concerned. Major increases in grain tariffs took place in Germany and France in 1885 and 1887. In Italy the first step was delayed until 1887, though the second followed more quickly in 1888.

The German situation is more properly analyzed in terms of the tariff on rye, which in the period to 1890 was identical with that on wheat. Gerschenkron makes clear that Bismarck's alliance ran not between industry and agriculture, as such, but between two powerful components of each, iron and rye.[12] Within industry the interests of the expanding steel industry were opposed to those of the fabricators of metal, who wanted cheap supplies. In this capital-intensive industry, moreover, the level of wages was relatively unimportant. In agriculture the large farms of the Junkers in eastern Germany produced rye as a cash crop for shipment to western Germany and for export. Their interest in high prices should have been opposed by the peasants of northern and western Ger-

many, who bought grain for animal feed and had an interest in low prices. Despite this interest, however, the peasants of Germany politically followed the leadership of the landed nobility and supported tariffs on grain. Gerschenkron claims that they were deluged with propaganda and deluded by the concurrent imposition of tariffs on pigs and other animals, which, however, afforded a much lower level of protection.[13] Even within the ranks of labor there were groups which appeared not to oppose the tariffs.

The enactment of the tariff on wheat in France required the repeal of the Le Chapelier Law of 1791 which forbade associations based upon economic interest. A modification of this law in 1865 had made it possible to establish associations for the improvement of agricultural techniques. Its final repeal in 1884 paved the way for agricultural syndicates, which began by acting as producer cooperatives in the buying of fertilizer and agricultural machinery and in establishing credit unions. Very shortly these groups began to agitate for higher tariffs. The owners of large farms, marketing a larger proportion of their crop for cash than did the owners of small farms, had a greater interest in the price of wheat; but all farmers were affected by it. In only 10 of 87 departments of France did grain occupy less than half the tillable land in 1882, and only in one, Corsica, did the percentage fall below 40.[14] There is some evidence that the leadership in the political drive for protection was taken by the cattle interests of Normandy and Brittany. But all parts of the country, from the northern wheat dis-

[12] See Alexander Gerschenkron, *Bread and Democracy in Germany* (Berkeley: University of California Press, 1943), p. 45.

[13] *Ibid.*, pp. 26–29 and 57–58.

[14] E. O. Golob, *The Méline Tariff: French Agriculture and Nationalist Economic Policy* (New York: Columbia University Press, 1944), pp. 81–82. I rely heavily on Golob's treatment.

tricts to the southern wine areas (suffering from the depredations of *Phylloxera*), were united in their zeal to raise the relative level of French farm prices.

The success of efforts to obtain protection for agriculture was aided by a compromise with industrial interests. Agriculture and industry had not always readily adjusted their conflicts of interest. In the time of Napoleon, French commercial policy had favored industrial exports at the same time that it forbade the export of wheat or of agricultural products used by industry. Agricultural interests thereafter tried on several occasions to secure protection on such industrial supplies as hides, wool, oil seeds, and silk. In 1881 the farm interests hoped that commerce and industry would agree to a tariff of 10 per cent on foodstuffs in exchange for the concession of freedom to import agricultural raw materials. The compromise of 5 per cent, which did not apply to wheat, produced little satisfaction. After the final repeal of the Le Chapelier Law in 1884 and more effective organization, the markedly higher rates on grain and animals of 1885 and 1887 were won with the assistance of threats of retaliation against industry.

Italian tariff policy in the 1870's and 1880's favored industry over agriculture. In 1864 wheat had been subjected to a duty of $\frac{1}{2}$ lira per quintal to raise revenue. This was increased to $\frac{3}{4}$ lira in 1866 to meet the costs of the war. The tariff revision of 1878, undertaken primarily to regularize the duties of the newly formed kingdom, increased the rate on wheat to 1.40 lire per quintal. These rates were low. In other directions there was no protection for agriculture. Imports of rice and barley, for example, were free of duty. Yet industry enjoyed a considerable measure of protection.

The question of taxes on food was widely discussed. An excise tax of 2 lire per quintal of wheat had been imposed internally in 1869 to improve governmental finances; and, although vigorously opposed by urban and industrial interests, it continued in effect for fourteen years. The experience with this tax appears to have given the Italian government pause when increasing imports of grain from overseas, encouraged by the appreciation of the lire, began in 1884. Three years later, in 1887, the tariff was raised to 3 lire, a full two years after similar action was taken in France and Germany. The rate was increased again to 5 lire in 1888, after the tariff war with France led to the loss of the French market for the wines of southern Italy, to compound the distress of the region.[15] But by this time it was too late. The Italian peasant had already begun to emigrate. Gross emigration across the Atlantic, primarily from agricultural regions of Italy, increased from an average of 25,000 annually in the period 1876–80 to 73,000 in 1885, 83,000 in 1886, 130,000 in 1887, and 205,000 in 1888.[16] The 1888 figure, which is presumed to reflect the period of nominal tariff rates before April, 1887, with a time lag, was to remain the peak for thirteen years. Recovery of wheat prices under the impact of the tariffs and other factors slowed down the pace of emigra-

[15] International Institute of Agriculture, *World Trade in Agricultural Products* (Rome, 1940), pp. 794–98.

[16] I. A. Hourwich (*Immigration and Labor* [New York: Huebsch, 1922], p. 201) notes for a somewhat later period that more than 70 per cent of Italian immigrants to the United States came from agricultural regions. Gross emigration rates differ from net, it may be observed, by rather sizable amounts because of the practice of trans-Atlantic migration on a seasonal basis for harvesting, particularly to Argentina, by so-called *golondrinos* ("swallows").

tion somewhat. The flow, once started, however, became cumulative and self-perpetuating. Early emigrants encouraged first their families and then their relatives and neighbors to follow.

The response of Germany, France, and Italy to the decline in the world price of wheat was to impose tariffs in an attempt to maintain the relative price of wheat and to protect grain producers. In Germany the movement was led by Bismarck as a step toward a new political alignment of Junkers and steelmakers, but it had the consent of many of those whose interests were adversely affected. In France agriculture, more or less as a whole, negotiated through the tariff in reaching a settlement with industry. The reluctance of Italian industry to agree to increased tariffs and the delay in imposing them meant that the Italian response to the decline in prices was to quit Europe.[17]

V

Like Britain, the Netherlands, and Belgium, Denmark did not impose a tariff on wheat. Instead, it gave up the attempt to compete in the world export market for wheat and became a wheat importer. This shift was incidental, however, to a revolution in Danish agriculture, which was converted from the growing of grain to animal husbandry.

[17] For lack of readily available secondary material, I have not investigated the course of events in Austria-Hungary, Sweden, Spain, and Portugal, which took action against new wheat imports, or in the Netherlands, Belgium, or Switzerland, which did not. A cursory examination of the tariff schedules (see "Decline and Recovery of Wheat Prices in the 'Nineties," Table VII, p. 350) and of annual figures for gross emigration overseas (*Annuaire statistique de France* [1914–15], Part III, p. 164) suggests that Austria-Hungary and Sweden were equally tardy in protecting agriculture and equally affected by emigration. Gerschenkron (*op. cit.*, pp. 40–41) gives an interpretation of the Swiss experience.

Denmark was assisted in responding thus by its proximity to the rapidly industrializing markets of England and Germany, with their expanding national incomes, and by the high income elasticity of demand for butter and bacon. Given the demand, however, there are certain remarkable features about the response of supply which merit investigation. Of particular importance are the middle-sized farm, which predominated in Danish agriculture, the agricultural school system, and the co-operative movement. The second of these, at least, and perhaps the whole response to the decline in wheat prices was deeply affected by the defeat of Denmark by Germany in 1864 and the loss of the province of Schleswig.

Of all the countries of Europe, only in Denmark has the size of the productive unit been stabilized at the medium-sized farm—around fifty acres.[18] In other countries, over considerable periods of time, farm size has been increasing or decreasing. Periodic reversals occur under the influence of such discontinuous events as land reform—primarily the distribution of church or noble lands and parcellation of peasant strips (or inclosures) when these became too many and too narrow to work (or extensive farming became more profitable than intensive). Aside from these turning points, however, farm size appears to have a tendency to increase, as in Hungary, East Prussia, and England up to World War I, or to decrease, as in France, Switzerland, and western Germany. In some countries, like Italy and Poland, the two processes take place side by side. Land purchases by the wealthy, primogeniture, high income taxes, poaching laws, veneration of blood sports in the

[18] See Jensen, *op. cit.*, p. 133.

36   C. P. KINDLEBERGER

culture, etc., tend to increase farm size. Equal inheritance and rapid population growth tend to reduce the size of the farm unit.[19]

In Denmark a variety of factors appears to have established and maintained the middle-sized farm. The principle of equal inheritance was offset by small family size, by a frontier of the sea to which extra sons could escape, and by easy credit, enabling farmer brothers to buy out their share of the patrimony. High land taxes made the maintenance of unproductive estates expensive. But the state intervened from an early date and continuously (1682, 1725, 1769, 1819) to prevent the landed aristocracy from adding peasant land to their holdings and to prevent undue subdivision as well. A policy of dividing large holdings into small, but not minuscule, units prevailed for several centuries and was reaffirmed in legislation providing for small holdings in 1899 and 1909. The institution of the middle-sized farm, which happens to be inefficient for grain production but is well suited to certain types of animal output, goes deep into Danish agricultural life.

The Folk School, or agricultural high school, was originated in 1844 by a remarkable man, Bishop N. F. S. Grundtvig, for the purpose of educating the rural population not in scientific agriculture but in "the Danish language and history and . . . its constitution and economic life." Classes are held in the five winter months for men and for three months in the summer for women, normally in some other part of the country than that in which the student lives. The schools attempt to provide the agricultural segment of the population with a unity of

background and an awareness of the life of the urban population of the country.

The first Folk School was founded in Schleswig. After the loss of the province to Germany, this school was moved to Danish territory. Thereafter the movement spread rapidly.[20] By 1870, before the collapse of wheat prices, there were sixty or seventy in the country.

The co-operative movements in Sweden and Denmark have been widely studied. For present purposes, therefore, it is sufficient to make a limited series of points. To sell butter in international trade required bringing the "peasant" butter of uneven taste and texture up to "manor" quality. This meant a standardized product. After the invention of the cream separator, the manufacture of butter could take place on a large scale, even though the labor-intensive production of milk still required the medium-sized farm. Economies of scale in marketing were available not only in butter but in eggs and bacon as well. In this situation the spread of the producers' co-operative movement in Danish agriculture was rapid after the establishment of the first co-operative dairy in Jutland in 1882.[21]

Denmark's response to the decline in world wheat prices, then, was to revolutionize her agriculture and to change from an exporter of grains to an importer. It may be observed that the acreage de-

[19] A more complete statement might attach importance to types of soil.

[20] Jensen, *op. cit.*, p. 101: "After the defeat in the war of 1864, the work which was already begun was taken up by able and enthusiastic men." See also Harald Westergaard, *Economic Developments in Denmark* (Oxford: Oxford University Press, 1922), p. 13: "For the economic life of Denmark, [the War of 1864] was of still greater importance in that it gave industry a strong impetus for attacking and solving the many problems which pressed upon it within the country's narrowed boundaries."

[21] For an account of forerunners see Harald Faber, *Co-operation in Danish Agriculture* (2d ed.; London: Longmans, Green & Co., 1931), pp. 25–30.

voted to cereal production in Denmark increased rather than declined after animal industry had developed.

VI

These differences in European responses to the decline in the world price of wheat in the 1870's and 1880's may be summarized as follows: In Britain agriculture was permitted to be liquidated. In Germany large-scale agriculture sought and obtained protection for itself. In France, where the demography, pattern of resources, and small scale of industrial enterprise favored farming, agriculture as a whole successfully defended its position with tariffs. In Italy the response was to emigrate. In Denmark grain production was converted to animal husbandry. What factors outside the market account for these national differences? A number of attempts have been made to explain at least some of these various responses. The present section undertakes to review and comment upon these efforts.

The most familiar contrast, perhaps, is between the free-trade ideas developed in Britain by Smith, Ricardo, and Mill and the theory of national economy propounded in Germany, especially by Friederich List. A variant of the List doctrine can be found in the "nationalist economics" of Paul-Louis Cauwès in France,[22] although it is difficult to make the case that Cauwès' ideas were more than an aberration in an intellectual atmosphere which was much more sympathetic to the doctrines of the Manchester School. The place of Smith and List in Denmark appears to have been taken by Bishop Grundtvig, whose métier was poetry and national mysticism rather than economics; and no particular figure rationalized the action taken in

Italy. It might be fair to say that the economists of Britain and the national economists of Germany provided the rationale for the action taken rather than its impetus.[23] And the relative unimportance of this function may be indicated by the action of France and Italy, taken in the absence of any distinctive rationale.

In its vulgar version the foregoing explanation is reduced to the single word "nationalism." Britain adhered to the international system; Germany and France were nationalistic in their responses. But this reasoning has evident weaknesses. Italy's solution was essentially international or one possible only in an international world, although the attempt was made to apply the "nationalist" solution of tariffs. It could be said that the Italian solution was more international than the British, where the displaced agricultural workers shifted into industry within their own country. The international solution, that is, may involve a shift in international trade or an international movement in factors. The explanation breaks down, further, on the side of nationalism. Leaving aside for the moment the subtle differences between the French and the German behavior, the Danish solution, like the French and the German, was a highly nationalistic one, taken without tariffs, to be sure, but in an atmosphere of nationalist emotion. Nationalism and internationalism in this context are compound variables of great complexity.

---

[22] See Golob, *op. cit.*, pp. 145 ff.

[23] I have discussed elsewhere the antithesis between the views of Keynes, who asserted that the world is ruled by little else than the theories of economists and political philosophers, and those of Arnold, who classes the economist with the lawyer and the scholar as performing a purely ceremonial role (see Lord Keynes, *The General Theory of Employment, Interest, and Money* [New York: Harcourt, Brace & Co., 1936], p. 383; and Thurman W. Arnold, *The Folklore of Capitalism* [New Haven: Yale University Press, 1937], esp. chap. iv).

38   C. P. KINDLEBERGER

They require, rather than furnish, explanation.

A more elaborate analysis, which fits the present case to a degree, though it makes no mention of it, is that developed by the Danish economist, Carl Major Wright, in his *Economic Adaptation to a Changing World Market.*[24] Wright observes that a country can respond to an adverse change in world market conditions by intervention to correct the world situation, by isolation from it, or by adaptation to it. His book contains a message for small countries like his own. These, he believes, are too weak to intervene in the world market and will not be allowed by the great powers to isolate themselves from it. In consequence, they have to adapt themselves to it. Toward this end he advocates increasing mobility of factors and competition among producers.

The contrast among intervention, isolation, and adaptation is suggestive as far as it goes, but it fails to canvass the alternatives fully or to explain the factors affecting choice among them. France and Germany isolated themselves from the world market, to the extent of the tariff. No country intervened to raise the world price of wheat, though this has been undertaken through international co-operation in the present century. England, Italy, and Denmark all adapted to the change, but in a variety of ways. Since a series of alternative adaptations was available and since adaptation was undertaken by large countries as well as by small, Wright's analysis fails to explain the differences in behavior which did occur. His emphasis on the necessity of small countries to adapt, however, suggests that larger countries are unable to adapt in the same way that is open to small countries. In Britain, for example,

some substitution of cattle for sheep occurred, and over a longer period animal husbandry expanded to fill part of the gap left by a decline in croplands.[25] But, on the whole, Britain was content to import its wheat and its high-value protein foods as well. British agriculture lacked the energy, the resources, and the ability to devise the institutions which would have been necessary for large-scale conversion from arable cropping to animal husbandry.

Several Continental writers have provided an illuminating framework of analysis against which to contrast the behavior of Italy (and southeastern Europe from Hungary to the Volga) with that of the other countries. In *Les deux Europes,*[26] for example, F. Delaisi distinguishes between Europe A, lying within a circle drawn through Stockholm, Vienna, Barcelona, Bilbao, and Glasgow, and Europe B, outside the circle. Europe A includes northern Italy, upper Austria, and Bohemia and Moravia but leaves out Ireland, northern Scotland, and most of Spain. In Europe A industrialization was possible because of the rise of the bourgeois and their insistence on the spread of education; even in agriculture there was established a basis for rural democracy as peasants acquired land. In Europe B, however, constitutions and parliaments had no roots, illiteracy prevailed, the bourgeois class was small and

---

[24] Copenhagen: Munksgaard, 1939.

[25] Ensor, *op. cit.*, p. 117. It may be observed that some protection was afforded to the cattle interests by the sanitary regulations, passed in the 1890's, forbidding the import of live animals from the Continent and overseas. The principal competition for home-grown meat, even at this time, however, was in meat imported from the Southern Hemisphere, a trade which developed with the innovation of refrigerated ships in the 1880's. Beef grazing, however, is far less labor-intensive than dairying and would have been, from the point of view of employment, a much less satisfactory adaptation.

[26] Paris: Payot, 1929.

timid, working with the aristocracy against the peasant and urban laborer rather than challenging the power of the feudal nobility.

When technological advance made industrialization possible, Europe A adopted it; Europe B gradually collapsed. After 1880 emigration rose sharply from Europe B, consisting particularly of Italy, Austria-Hungary, Spain, Portugal, and Finland, as far as Delaisi's statistics went, but including also Russia, Yugoslavia, and Greece. For the countries covered by Delaisi, emigration overseas in the decade 1881–90 amounted to 180,000 annually. In successive decades the annual average climbed to 265,000, 629,000, and 907,000 by 1901–13.[27] In Europe A, on the other hand, emigration to overseas areas declined, after hitting new peaks in 1881–85. This was because of the opportunities afforded by the expansion in industry.

But this explanation by no means covers the situation in its entirety. Britain was much further along in the urbanization process than was Germany or France. This may help to a degree to explain why industry was ready to permit the liquidation of agriculture and why emigrants from agriculture found their way into cities rather than abroad. After industrialization has started, however, and has reached a point where the process is self-generating and cumulative, the rate of growth should be more important than the existing level of industry. And this pace after 1870 was faster in Germany than in Britain. Nor was industrialization meaningless in France:

"While France accepted the new techniques and institutions of industry, and even played a significant role in developing them, she did not permit agriculture to be eclipsed, or to suffer revolutionary change."[28]

As between Italy and Denmark, the quality of agriculture was evidently more important than the proportions of population engaged in rural pursuits (which were of the same order of magnitude after adjustment for definitions of urban life). Delaisi's division of Europe into two and his discussion of the extent to which the collapsing feudal structure was replaced by modern industrial and national institutions are interesting. The fact of industrialization and the explanation of its concentration in northwestern Europe, however, fail to account for the differences among the responses of the several countries to the decline in the price of wheat.[28a]

VII

None of the foregoing explanations completely accounts for the differences in response to the market; and perhaps the differences should be approached from the standpoint of a theory of group behavior. To be adequate, such a theory

[27] *Ibid.*, p. 207. These sources are called "new," in contrast with Germany, Ireland, Britain, etc., in H. Jerome, *Migration and Business Cycles* (New York: National Bureau of Economic Research, 1926). It may be noted that emigration from Ireland fluctuated parallel to that of Europe A, though it lies in Europe B in Delaisi's scheme.

[28] Golob, *op. cit.*, p. 8.

[28a] W. Röpke (*The Social Crisis of Our Times*, [Chicago: University of Chicago Press, 1950]) finds the clue to the development of agriculture in the various countries of Europe in the existence or absence of a sturdy peasant body. Its absence accounts for the injury to British agriculture; its presence for the Danish success (pp. 245-46). The peasantry of Italy and "SE Europe lacked soundness" (p. 204). Wheat protection favors large estates and is detrimental to peasant agriculture (p. 247). But this analysis fails to cover the French case, where peasants gained from protection; and Röpke himself fatally damages the consistency of his position in the statement (p. 205): "Admittedly, agriculture is that part of the national economic system to which the principles of a free market economy could only be applied with broad reservations. . . ."

C. P. KINDLEBERGER

must include not only criteria for differentiating the responses of national groups as a unit but also a system of analysis for interrelations among the subgroups within the larger unit. The theory of group behavior appears not to have coped adequately with this sort of question. In the main, social psychologists, sociologists, anthropologists, etc., have concentrated their attention on the relation of the individual to the group, to the relative neglect of the structure of the very large group (the nation) and of functional groups within it.[29] Where intergroup relations have attracted attention, it has been focused on the problems posed by cultural minorities and the relations between groups differentiated by age, sex, etc., rather than on large functional groups. Lacking a foundation in scientific literature, the following notions on group behavior are general and tentative.

A group must exist in space and time. To be effective, a group must have a system of communications and a set of common values. The existence of the national group in *space* hardly merits discussion. It is an elementary principle of geography that mountain ridges make the best national boundaries—though they are disliked by the military interests charged with protecting the group—since they are the national barriers of language, culture, and commerce. Rivers provide a system of intercommunication rather than a barrier to it, and a country lying in a great plain, like Poland, has uncertain limits. Water in larger amounts is

[29] This statement is perhaps unfair to Talcott Parsons and Robert K. Merton and their structural-functional approach to sociology, with which I am inadequately acquainted. For an attempt to apply this to the French economy see the forthcoming essay by John E. Sawyer, "Strains in the Social Structure of Modern France," to be published in a volume on France by the Princeton University Press.

helpful in demarcating the national space. The existence of Britons as a homogeneous group has been assisted by their insular position, while subgroups are demarcated by highlands. Changes in the national space have an important reaction on national cohesion. The Danish "groupiness" or group consciousness was enhanced by the loss of Schleswig; the French by that of Alsace-Lorraine. Italy and Germany, at the same time, gained group solidarity from unification in space.

The existence of a group in *time* is connected with its *set of values*. This must be sufficiently attractive or forceful in the spiritual or emotional life of the group for its members to express their loyalty to the group by remaining a part of it through time and bringing their children up as members. The existence of the group in time suggests a difference between material things and social institutions. Matter can wear out evenly over time; when a functional group recognizes that it is doomed to extinction, however, it is difficult to let it decline slowly at the normal rate of depreciation by refusal to maintain it. When faith in the continuity of the organization or group is lost, the group is likely to disintegrate.

The importance of *communication* to the group is increasingly emphasized by social psychologists working with small functional groups, such as the personnel of factories, unions, etc. It is equally important in larger groups. Switzerland, where four languages are spoken, is cited as an illustration of its unimportance in certain situations. In this case space and a powerful set of values are sufficient to hold the group together. The subgroup of agriculture is typically weaker in cohesion than urban groups because of its dispersal in space and the resultant difficulty of communication among its members. The Folk Schools in Denmark and the formation of agricultural syndicates in France were requirements for the maintenance of the agricultural group in the face of the threat from reduced wheat prices.

An existence in space and a system of communication are not enough to constitute a functional group. The parts of the group must share a sense of identification and emotional involvement and a feeling of participation and purpose before the separate subgroups can be considered to make up a group. This sense of unity and purpose may be enhanced by the existence of an antithetical "out-group." If the sense is insufficiently developed to begin with, however, the development of an "out-group" may lead to the disintegration of the "in-group."

The major contrast lies between Denmark and Italy. In the former, national feeling was intense, as a result of territorial loss, and social cohesion was high. The rural population felt itself a unit and identified itself with the larger national unit. In Italy, despite the recent unification of 1871, the peasant's sense of belonging to the national group was feeble. A blow to his means of livelihood led to the disintegration of the national group, as far as he was concerned. He withdrew—the type of reaction which the classical economists thought was difficult because of cultural barriers and which, indeed, is today barred by the xenophobia of other national groups. Similar responses took place in the Balkans, the Iberian Peninsula, and throughout the rest of feudalistic Europe.

The weakness of the national group in Europe B, to use Delaisi's designation, was due to the failure of national unity to replace the disintegrated feudal group

structure. National groups lacked intercommunication and common values. Illiteracy, for example, ran from 10 per cent in the Po Valley in Italy to 30 per cent in Florence and Rome, 50 per cent in Naples, and 70 per cent in Calabria.[30] No new emotional attachment replaced the feudal ties which had bound the peasant to the latifundium. Group cohesion was too weak to meet the challenge, and the group, under pressure, collapsed.

The importance of the out-group to the cohesion and efficiency of the national group is illustrated effectively by the role played by German aggression and the loss of Schleswig in the Danish response to the decline in wheat prices. Other examples are not lacking in economic history. The French payment of the five-billion-mark indemnity in 1871 was an act of national dedication—and even immolation. To generalize from this experience as to the behavior of exports, imports, prices, and the banking system in similar situations where the group stimulus is absent is a familiar practice of economists,[31] but it is highly questionable.

VIII

The contrasting behavior of Britain, Germany, and France requires an understanding of more than the over-all degree of group cohesion at the national level. Attention must be given to the relations among the separate subgroups. This, to be sure, has a bearing on the over-all cohesiveness of the nation: a country in which the subgroups are not sharply differentiated and where a degree of social mobility between them exists is likely to

[30] Delaisi, *op. cit.*, pp. 46–47.

[31] See, e.g., F. Machlup, "Three Concepts, the Balance of Payments," *Economic Journal*, March, 1950, p. 59 n.

42   C. P. KINDLEBERGER

have greater cohesion. For the moment, however, our attention is restricted to the relations among the economic subgroups.[32]

E. R. Walker asks, "When do men accept the verdict of the market, and when do they attempt to alter it?"[33] A parallel question can be put for group behavior: When does an ascendant subgroup liquidate another subgroup within the large group, and when does it make adjustment with it? Under what circumstances do relationships among subgroups tend to stay in continuous equilibrium, and when do divergences of interest lead in cumulative fashion (as Marx predicted) to schism and clash? Why did industry allow the liquidation of agriculture in Britain, but not in Germany or France? The question appears not to be a simple one of relative strengths or even of more complex strategies of coalition, such as those suggested in *The Theory of Games*. There was no reason for the German steel manufacturer to accept coalition with an essentially backward[34] group of agriculturists or of French industry to make concessions to the pre-scientific peasant. The answer may be found in areas outside the normal province of the economic theorist or the economic historian. The decisive factors do not appear to lie in the field of economics at all but in that of sociology.

One clue to intergroup behavior may be found in the notion that not all group relations are competitive. Bateson, the anthropologist, has listed a series of stable interdependent subgroup relationships, which, to be sure, primarily apply to subgroups based on age and sex. These include bipolar relations, such as spectator-exhibitionist, dominance-submission, succoring-dependence, aggression-passivity, and the like, but may extend to more complex arrangements. Among the latter, Bateson distinguishes what he calls the "ternary relationship," which contains serial elements but includes face-to-face contact between the first and third elements. The function of the middle member in his illustrations—parent-nurse-child and officer-n.c.o.-enlisted man—is to discipline the third member in the forms of behavior which he should adopt toward the first.[35] The relations of the middle class to the wealthy and to the working classes may partake of this character in some political and social respects.[36]

This clue, by no means unambiguous, may assist in explaining what took place in Germany. Gerschenkron expresses the view that the Junkers deceived the peasants of western Germany, whose interest lay in cheaper grain prices, by provision for a tariff on animals and by other means. The reaction, however, may contain elements of submission of the peasant groups before the will of the Junker with higher status. Residual traces of the feudal relationship existed; probably more important were the battles won for the glory of the national group in 1864, 1866, and 1870. Part of labor and even the steel barons were content to main-

[32] An individual in the society, of course, will belong to a variety of subgroups based on his occupation, class, religion, avocations, age, sex, race, etc.

[33] *Op. cit.*, p. 109.

[34] This characterization is objected to as unfair to the Junkers, who, whatever their disagreeable attributes, were men of responsibility who energetically farmed their own land in the face of natural difficulties rather than live off the unearned increment *in absentia*. Yet they were backward in the sense that they clung to traditional crops farmed with traditional techniques. Perhaps a more appropriate adjective is "static."

[35] Gregory Bateson, "Morale and National Character," in G. Watson (ed.), *Civilian Morale* (Cambridge: At the University Press, 1942), pp. 71–81.

[36] See, e.g., Maude and Lewis, *op. cit.*, *passim*.

tain the economic position of the Junkers, in the face of opportunity to liquidate them, because of the element of status which in the former case outweighed class interest. The leadership and dominance exhibited by the Junker class probably explain the major part of its success in maintaining its position through the Caprivi tariff, World War I, the inflation, and the Nazi regime.

Another clue may lie in that most complex conception, the basic personality type of a culture or subculture. This notion, developed by the social psychologist with the help of anthropological data, denies that human nature is a constant in time or space but holds that the basic personality type of a culture will condition responses to external stimuli and, in turn, be altered by them. Of particular importance, it is held, is the way in which the society rears its children.[37]

This matter is far too complex and elusive to pursue here beyond the rough generalization that the basic personality type differs among England, France, and Germany, in putting primary emphasis in the culture, below the level of the national group, on, respectively, the individual, the family, and the class. If this be accepted, it may assist in explaining why Britain was willing to liquidate agriculture, while France and Germany were not.

Economic and political liberalism, born in Britain, required social mobility

to give importance to the individual at the level next below the national group. Mobility in space was provided for Britain, as for Scandinavia and the Netherlands, by the sea, which served as a frontier.[38] At home, despite the class structure, social mobility upward derived from the willingness of the aristocracy to admit successful commercial and industrial interests to the ownership of land and their sons to the public schools. Downward mobility was provided by primogeniture, which drew off the increase in the aristocracy into the middle class. Whatever the facts, the concept of class as a functional subgroup was not recognized in the culture. A blow to a broad economic interest was regarded as affecting not a class but a loose aggregation of individuals.[39] This may account for the passivity of the nation in watching unmoved the liquidation of agriculture in the thirty years after 1879.[40]

The opposition of industry and agri-

[37] See A. Kardiner, *The Psychological Frontiers of Society* (New York: Columbia University Press, 1945); Ruth Benedict, *Patterns of Culture* (Cambridge, Mass.: Houghton Mifflin Co., 1934); Clyde Kluckhohn, *Mirror for Man* (New York: Whittlesey House, 1949), etc. Given the emphasis on anthropological data, primary attention has been devoted to the personality types of cultures rather than subcultures, and Kardiner, for example, regards Western man as a homogeneous type. This notion is in process of correction at the hands of Meade, Bateson, Gorer, and others.

[38] See H. A. Innis, "Economic Significance of Cultural Factors," in his *Political Science in the Modern State* (Toronto: Toronto University Press, 1946), p. 87.

[39] A number of writers have referred to the alleged inability of the British farmer to co-operate because of his individualism. See, e.g., E. J. Russell, who states in the Foreword to Faber, *op. cit.*, pp. vii–viii: "The British method, in short, proved less capable of adaptation to new and adverse conditions than the Danish. Critics may argue . . . that the British farmer is so confirmed an individualist and so imbued with the idea of running his own farm in his own way that he cannot co-operate with his neighbor. It may or may not be so." See also H. Rider Haggard, *Rural Denmark and Its Lessons* (London: Longmans Green & Co., 1911), p. 273: "The Danes look upon their land as a principal means of livelihood . . .—in short, as a business proposition in which the Nation is most vitally concerned. In the main, although we [Britain] may not acknowledge it, we look upon our land, or much of it, as a pleasure proposition in which the individual only is concerned." Haggard also cites (pp. 192–93) the sad case of a Norfolk honorable secretary of a rat and sparrow club who was unable to enlist any co-operation from potential benefactees.

[40] See n. 11, above.

culture in France was more apparent than real; both were concerned not with economic interest as such but with economic interest in a context of the dominant social institution of the family. This has been studied in industry, where the conclusion has been reached that the size of firm which could be kept in the family from generation to generation limited the growth of industry.[41] The unwillingness of the French to emigrate is further evidence. And the continuity of the French farm in the family group from generation to generation is a commonplace.

In Germany the major subgroup, at least at the extremes, was the class. To the extent that the nobility was a farming group in occupation, group solidarity and economic interest were unified in the Junker portion of agriculture, while they were opposed among the peasants. Such conflict of group and economic interest is not, however, unusual: Walker has expressed surprise that the farmers of Australia support a program of land settlement contrary to their economic interest.[42] But these farmers gained more through the growth in numbers of their group than they lost through the increase of supply. The question was one of class and, within the total class structure, of dominance.

IX

The Danish response to the decline in the world price of wheat was by far the most satisfactory, whether in social and economic terms or in economic terms alone. It raised the level of real income for the producer group at the same time that it preserved the gain of cheaper bread for the consumer. Social upheaval was avoided. Was the whole episode an accident? Was this sort of solution possible for the other countries? To what extent is it possible to capitalize disaster in this fashion on a general scale?

The mind of the economist is likely to try to find a parallel in certain situations which occur when wage increases lead to expansion rather than to contraction of output because they provide the incentive to a recombination of factors in a more efficient fashion. The classic example is the elimination of the sweatshop through the efforts of union leaders, which increased incomes for both laborers and enterprisers and also reduced the cost of clothing. This was brought about by requiring firms in the garment industry to employ their newly expensive labor efficiently. The market opportunity for combining capital and labor in more efficient fashion had existed before the success of the union drive. Until the system was pushed off dead center, however, the path of least resistance was resistance to the demands of the union.

The parallel is not exact. A beginning of dairying to replace grain cultivation had been made in the 1860's before the decline in the price of wheat, primarily, however, on large estates.[43] The motive was only partly economic. In part it was observed that the soil was being impoverished by grain crops. There was still another difference. Although a market opportunity offered by the relative prices of grain and butter already existed, it was considerably increased by the decline in the price of wheat in the 1870's and 1880's and the rise in the demand for butter in the growing urban centers of

[41] David S. Landes, "French Entrepreneurship and Industrial Growth in the Nineteenth Century," *Journal of Economic History*, IX (1949), 45–61.

[42] Walker, *op. cit.*, pp. 123 and 222–23. Another case is probably that of the American Medical Association, which is unified in opposing expenditures on health by governmental bodies which would increase the incomes of the vast majority of its members.

[43] Faber, *op. cit.*, pp. 31–32.

GROUP BEHAVIOR AND INTERNATIONAL TRADE   45

England. A real impetus to the conversion came from the price decline. Particularly remarkable was the capacity of Danish economy, or polity, to develop the institutions which were necessary to complete the conversion on a large scale to take maximum advantage of the economic opportunity.

It may be contended that there was a marked degree of accident in the existence of the middle-sized farm, which was inefficient for wheat, and in the development of the agricultural high school, in response to the loss of Schleswig. The explanation for the prevalence of the middle-sized farm would appear to lie deep in the Danish basic personality type, which emphasizes stability rather than growth.[44] The development of the Folk School was perhaps partly an accident, but the Danish peasant had always shown a communicating tendency,[45] and this fact may be more important than the particular form of institution devised at the particular time.

The development of the co-operative in response to a technological need raises more fundamental problems. What factors govern the capacity of a society to develop institutions required to enable it to take advantage of economic, political, and social opportunities? Are these adaptations always accidental? Under certain conditions, are they made automatically; or can they be contrived through direction after conscious decision?

Most commentators on the co-operative believe that this development was the product of the prevalence of the freehold in Danish land tenure, together with the high degree of education in Danish farmers. "Tenant farmers will not co-operate because, co-operative accounts being open to inspection, they fear their landlords might raise the rents if it were found that they were prospering."[46] But the emphasis given to the form of land tenure goes deeper than this. The point is that co-operation in Denmark flourished, because of the social cohesion which enabled the farmers to create the necessary institutions, when the occasion demanded economies of scale in marketing along with labor-intensive production. The prevalence of freeholds bespeaks equality of status, which makes communication freer in all directions. Education increases the quantity and quality of communication. Together with a high degree of communication, a closely held set of values, and internal social mobility—all of which are interrelated—Denmark had social cohesion. It was this factor which enabled her to create institutions needed to take advantage of an economic opportunity. In the absence of the economic opportunity, however, the institutions would not have been devised.

In general, then, the suggestion is offered that the flexibility of a society in devising institutions to accomplish its purposes under changing conditions is a function of its social cohesion, which, in turn, depends upon its internal social mobility, system of communications, and set of values. If social cohesion is high, it may be possible to find a response

[44] See Benedict, *op. cit.*, pp. 53–56 and chap. iv for a discussion of the Spenglerian contrast between Apollonian and Faustian cultures and the description of a self-balancing society. Bateson has described another such primitive society in *Naven* (Cambridge: At the University Press, 1936). Franz Oppenheimer mentions other instances of the prevalence of small and medium-sized landholdings in Utah, Iowa, and New Zealand in "The Tendency of the Development of the State," in V. F. Calverton, *The Making of Society* (New York: Random House, 1937), pp. 40–42. Cf. H. Rider Haggard's literary description of the Danes as "tolerant-minded" (*op. cit.*, p. 212).

[45] See Faber, *op. cit.*, p. 7.

[46] Haggard, *op. cit.*, p. 190.

46   C. P. KINDLEBERGER

to external change which will bring about a new identification of the interests of the subgroups with those of the total group at an improved level of satisfaction for all. If the system of communication is sufficiently effective, moreover, it may be impossible to isolate the decision-making process so that the response of the society appears to be automatic.

X

What I have said can be reduced to some fairly elementary propositions. The response that will be made to an economic stimulus in international trade cannot always be predicted from the nature and extent of the stimulus. It may require a knowledge of the group situation within the separate countries affected. The response may be the disintegration of the group, leading to emigration if that is possible, or, if no such outlet is available, to pathological political behavior. The effect, on the other hand, may range from the liquidation of a particular subgroup in the society, for the benefit of others, as in Britain; through the protection of the affected group at the general expense, as in France and Germany; to an inspired act of readjustment undertaken by the group as a whole. Which of these actions will be taken lies deep in the structure of the society. For accurate prediction and policy-formation, an adequate theory of the behavior of large groups and their components is needed as an adjunct to the analytical tools of the market.

[13]

THE JOURNAL OF ECONOMIC HISTORY

VOLUME 57   DECEMBER 1997   NUMBER 4

————————••◦••————————

The European Grain Invasion, 1870–1913

KEVIN H. O'ROURKE

The article quantifies the impact of cheap grain on the European economy in the late nineteenth century. Falling transport costs led to dramatic declines in Anglo-American grain price gaps, but price convergence was less impressive between the U.S. and other European economies, and within Europe. Cheaper grain meant lower rents throughout Europe, and protection boosted rents, but the magnitudes involved differed between countries. Similarly, cheap grain increased real wages in Britain, but lowered them elsewhere. The grain invasion implied different shocks across countries, and this partly explains the varying trade policies pursued in Europe during this period.

The voyages of discovery were motivated by a desire for commodities that were scarce and therefore valuable. We know now that they were far more important economically than originally intended, precisely because they stumbled upon a resource so abundant that it was effectively free: New World land. The discoveries raised the endowment of land per European *capita* sixfold.[1] The long-run implications for European living standards are obvious. Less frequently remarked upon, but equally obvious, are the long-run implications for European income distribution. Such an increase in land endowments would inevitably spell disaster for European landowners. Over-all living standards might increase, but in the long run European rents would decline, with European labor or capital benefitting.

For these changes to occur, it was necessary that New World land be brought into cultivation. This required inputs of European labor and capital as well as the efficient transportation needed to make the produce of the land available to European consumers. Many of the great themes of the next four

The Journal of Economic History, Vol. 57, No. 4 (Dec. 1997). © The Economic History Association. All rights reserved. ISSN 0022-0507.

Kevin H. O'Rourke is Statutory Lecturer in Economics, Department of Economics, University College Dublin, Belfield, Dublin 4, Ireland.

All appendices are available upon request, from either the author or the offices of the *Journal of Economic History*. I am grateful to the following for help and advice: Beth Ann Bovino, Bill Collins, Mike Gavin, Chris Hanes, Joel Mokyr, Pierre Sicsic, and two anonymous referees; and to the following for sharing their data with me: Jean-Michel Chevet, Giovanni Federico, George Grantham, Ingrid Henriksen, Leandro Prados de la Escosura, Alan Taylor, and Jeffrey Williamson. Giovanni Federico, Avner Offer, Cormac Ó Gráda, Jeffrey Williamson and seminar participants at All Souls' College Oxford made extremely helpful comments on an earlier draft of the paper.

[1] Jones, *European Miracle*, p. 82; and Webb, *Great Frontier*.

O'Rourke

centuries—slavery, the extension of the frontier, voluntary mass migration—were part of the vast adjustment process that ensued.[2] By the late nineteenth century, this adjustment process was reaching a climax, as steamships and railroads linked New World land ever more closely to the European economy. One of the most visible results was the flood of New World grain, which lowered European grain prices from the mid-1870s. To what extent were the long-run distributional implications of Columbus fulfilled?

This article is primarily concerned with the effects of cheap grain on European wages, profits, and rents. It brings a quantitative focus to bear on the question, just as C. Knick Harley and others have examined the quantitative implications of the grain invasion for the New World.[3] It also hopes to address the vast political economy literature that asks: why did most of the Continent resort to protection during this episode, and why did Britain stick to free trade? Why did Denmark respond so successfully to the challenges posed by cheap wheat? What does this episode tell us about the difficulties involved in building and maintaining open international trading regimes?

Political scientists such as Peter Gourevitch, Ronald Rogowski, and Daniel Verdier have explored at length the ways in which price shocks in international commodity markets affect domestic politics.[4] What is missing from this work is a quantitative assessment of the impact of cheap grain in Europe. Did declining transport costs imply large or small declines in European grain prices, and did Continental protection overturn or merely mute these globalization forces? Protection meant that declining transatlantic transport costs may not have translated automatically into *intra*-European commodity market integration; a key task of the article will be to distinguish between transatlantic commodity market integration and intra-European developments.

The article plots the dimensions of the grain invasion in several European countries and explores the extent to which protection succeeded in insulating economies from this international commodity market shock. It explores the impact of cheap grain and tariff policies on resource allocation and income distribution in a number of countries, using both econometric and simulation techniques. The focus is comparative, in the tradition of Paul Bairoch, Charles Kindleberger, and others; and it is on northwestern Europe: France, Germany, Sweden, Denmark, and Britain.

BIG QUESTIONS, SIMPLE MODELS

When analyzing the political impact of the grain invasion, most authors implicitly rely on the sector-specific factors model of international trade

---

[2]Findlay, "International Trade."
[3]Harley, "Western Settlement" and "Transportation" and "Late Nineteenth Century Transportation."
[4]Gourevitch, *Politics*; Rogowski, *Commerce*; and Verdier, *Democracy*.

European Grain Invasion, 1870–1913   777

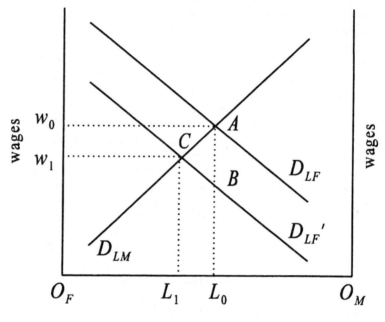

FIGURE 1
THE IMPACT OF CHEAP GRAIN

theory.[5] The model assumes two sectors, agriculture and industry. Agriculture produces food using land and labor; industry produces manufactures using capital and labor. Let food be the import good and manufactures the export good. Labor is mobile across sectors; the economy's labor endowment is given by the distance $O_F O_M$ in Figure 1. D_{LF} is the demand curve for agricultural labor, measured from O_F, D_{LM} is the industrial demand for labor curve, measured from O_M. Initially the equilibrium is at A, with nominal wages equal to w_0.

Now let the price of grain fall, as cheap New World cereals flood the domestic market. The demand for labor in agriculture contracts to D_{LF}', with AB being a measure of the decline in food prices. The equilibrium shifts to C: agriculture contracts, labor migrates to the towns, and industry expands. Nominal wages fall to w_1.

The distributional consequences of this shock are for the most part clear. Capitalists gain: as their wage costs fall, profits rise. On the other hand,

[5] The model is itself in part a gift to that field from cliometrics: see Temin, "Labor Scarcity"; and Jones, "Three-Factor Model." Rogowski, *Commerce*, is implicitly working with a model within which labor, capital, and land are all mobile between at least three sectors, but the model is never explicitly specified.

778   O'Rourke

landlords lose: the decline in output prices exceeds the decline in wage costs, and rents fall. The impact on workers is unclear: nominal wages have declined, but food prices have fallen by more. If food is a sufficiently important part of workers' budgets, then real wages increase; otherwise, they decline.

In the context of late nineteenth-century Europe, the model suggests that landlords should have favored agricultural tariffs, and that capitalists should have been free traders. The preferences of labor, the mobile factor, remain theoretically ambiguous; but this does not *a priori* preclude the possibility that workers were aware of where their interests actually lay, and lobbied accordingly.

The model's underlying intuition has frequently been drawn upon by contemporaries and historians discussing the political economy of late nineteenth-century trade policy. First, consider the impact of the grain invasion on labor, and the labor movement's attitude towards protection. In a simple Heckscher-Ohlin framework, European labor, as the abundant factor, should have favored trade, and this is what Rogowski assumes.[6] In a sector-specific factors framework, on the other hand, things are not so straightforward. The off-setting effects identified above—the cost-of-living effect on the one hand, and the labor-demand effect on the other—played a key role in the policy debates of the time. For example, Douglas Irwin has argued that Peel's decision to repeal the Corn Laws was due to his gradual realization that, contrary to classical wage theory, workers would benefit from low food prices.[7] On the other hand, Disraeli argued that "the price of wheat . . . is not a question of rent, but it is a question of displacing the labor of England that produces corn. . . . Will that displaced labor find new employment?"[8]

On the Continent, socialist groups tended towards free trade, although this was not universally the case (the picture in France is mixed).[9] Social Democrats in Germany, and socialist parties in Italy, Switzerland, and Belgium all took the view that cheap food was to be welcomed; in 1904 the British Labor Party adopted a free trade position to which it adhered for 30 years. This may seem paradoxical in light of Marx's view that free trade had hastened the depopulation of Ireland by provoking a switch from tillage to pasture; the fact that labor movements were largely urban may provide an explanation.[10] If labor were completely immobile between town and country, urban workers would only gain from cheap grain; even if rural-urban migration were possible (as it clearly was), unions might not have perceived the

[6]Rogowski, *Commerce.*
[7]Irwin, "Political Economy."
[8]Cited in Bairoch, "European Trade Policy," p. 129.
[9]The following discussion draws heavily on Bairoch, "European Trade Policy."
[10]Marx, *Capital*, p. 870.

full general equilibrium effects of the grain invasion; or alternatively, they might have correctly calculated that the cost-of-living effect dominated the labor-demand effect.

The sector-specific factors model also informs the discussion of how the two specific factors, land and capital, viewed tariff policy. In Britain, for example, a textbook analysis of the Repeal of the Corn Laws emphasizes the growing power of urban interests, symbolized by the Reform Act of 1832.[11] It was this shift in power from the countryside to the towns that made repeal inevitable. There is a problem with the analysis: in 1846, roughly 80 percent of MPs were still landowners.[12] One sophisticated response to the problem is given by Cheryl Schonhardt-Bailey, who argues that a rapidly developing internal British capital market led increasing numbers of landowners to invest their capital in nonagricultural sectors of the economy: free trade only damaged undiversified landowners.[13]

Similar puzzles have been debated in the context of Continental trade policy. The simple sector-specific factors model can easily account for the German debate of the 1890s, which pitted Agrarian economists such as Adolf Wagner, arguing for protection, against free-trading liberals such as Max Weber and Luigi Brentano; and agricultural lobby groups, such as the *Bund der Landwirte*, against the representatives of industry.[14] But what can explain the "marriage of iron and rye," which led to both agriculture *and* industry being protected in 1879? The model clearly predicts that the interests of capital and land were directly opposed; a combination of tariffs that benefited the one inevitably would have hurt the other. One response to this puzzle in the German historiography has been implicitly to argue that the model needs to be extended from two sectors to three or more sectors, each with its own specific factor; in such a context, the owners of two sector-specific factors (grain growers and heavy industry, for example) could combine to benefit themselves at the expense of politically weaker groups (peasants engaged in animal husbandry or light industry). Did agricultural protection hurt southern peasants, whose animals ate grain, or were they more than compensated by protection for animal products?[15] What were the effects of protection on light industry, or steel firms which were not vertically integrated? Once again, the debate has been largely conducted in a sector-specific factors framework.[16]

[11]Caves and Jones, *World Trade*, p. 106.
[12]The estimate is due to Aydelotte, "Country Gentlemen," cited in Schonhardt-Bailey, "Specific Factors," p. 547.
[13]Schonhardt-Bailey, "Specific Factors."
[14]Barkin, *Controversy*, gives a good account of late nineteenth-century German tariff controversies.
[15]Gerschenkron, *Bread*; Hunt, "Peasants"; and Webb, "Agricultural Protection."
[16]It is here that Rogowski's Heckscher-Ohlin framework provides the more elegant solution. Capital was still scarce in 1871, as was land, and so both were protectionist. By the 1890s capital was becoming abundant and becoming converted to free trade. This argument of course also assumes that

780   *O'Rourke*

Finally, note that opponents of free trade objected to the allocative consequences of the grain invasion, as well as to its implications for income distribution. In particular, the migration to the cities that would naturally result was seen by many as ethically and socially undesirable: this was a theme stressed by the German Agrarians, for example. Protectionism would help slow down this undesirable trend and was thus to be welcomed. Ireland's Eamon de Valera was to make similar cultural defenses of rural life in the twentieth century.[17] The Agrarian viewpoint in Germany was often characterized by anti-Semitism and racism, with the Slavicization of Prussia caused by the *Leutenot* (a scarcity of rural workers due to migration to the cities) being a frequent cause for concern. Even in liberal Britain, the dislike of urbanization occasionally surfaced in the debate, as the following quote from G.B. Longstaff indicates:

> the country life is more natural, and hence more desirable than the town life . . . the town life is not as healthy as the country life. . . . The narrow chest, the pale face, the weak eyes and bad teeth of the town-bred child are but too often apparent . . . long life in towns is accompanied by more or less degeneration of the race. The great military powers of the continent know this well enough, and it may be surmised that with them agricultural protection is but a device to keep up the supply of country-bred recruits.[18]

The sector-specific factors model can thus be used to shed light on many of the great debates surrounding tariff policy in late nineteenth-century Europe. Unhindered, the grain invasion would have reduced rents, boosted profits, and led to urban-rural migration. The question is by how much? And what was the net impact on labor: did the cost-of-living effect outweigh the labor-demand effect, or vice versa? What we need is some numerical flesh to hang on to the theoretical bones of the model. Moreover, the model needs to be generalized: capital can also be used in agriculture; land can be used in several agricultural sectors; some goods are nontraded; outputs from one sector can be used as inputs into others.[19]

The next section examines movements in grain prices in a number of economies between 1870 and 1913. The article then summarizes acreage, wage, and land price trends over the same period. Subsequent sections then attempt to make the analytical connection between commodity prices, on the

---

there was some third factor that would be hurt by protection—in this case, labor—and that there was a third, labor-intensive sector for policy makers to discriminate against.

[17]Although in Ireland's case, the protection that de Valera espoused would of course benefit industry and cities, at the expense of agriculture and the countryside. For an excellent analysis of the cultural contradictions at the heart of de Valera's economic policies, see Daly, *Industrial Development*.

[18]Longstaff, "Rural Depopulation," pp. 415-16. The strategic importance of grains at this time should also be kept in mind, as Offer, *First World War*, reminds us.

[19]See Fogel, "Specification Problem." A sensible response to Fogel's critique is to adopt a sufficiently general modeling structure so as to ensure that qualitative results are, as far as possible, not predetermined by the theoretical structure of the model.

European Grain Invasion, 1870–1913   781

one hand, and factor prices on the other. The article uses a computable general equilibrium (CGE) approach to tackle the question, and then uses an econometric approach. The conclusion draws some lessons for broader historical debates.

THE EUROPEAN GRAIN MARKET, 1870–1913

International Market Integration

This section compares grain prices in eight locations during this period: Britain, Denmark, Sweden, France, Bavaria, Prussia, Chicago, and Odessa. Price data for wheat, barley, oats, and rye were collected from a variety of sources, and transformed into common units (shillings per Imperial Quarter). Details are given in Appendix 1.

To see the full impact of declining transport costs, it is of course necessary to focus on commodity price gaps between exporting countries and an importing nation, like Britain, which adhered to free trade throughout the period. Panel A of Table 1 confirms what Harley and others have already found: there was dramatic transatlantic grain price convergence during the late nineteenth century.[20] The U.S. grain prices used here are not fully comparable with the European prices, implying that I may be incorrectly estimating price gap *levels*; but the *trends* in these price gaps are unmistakable.[21] The Anglo-American wheat price gap fell from 54 percent in 1870 to nothing in 1913; the barley price gap declined from 46 percent to 11 percent over the same period; and the oats price gap collapsed from 138 percent to 28 percent. These were enormous shocks to the international economy.[22]

Moreover, there was intra-European commodity market integration as well, at least between those countries that allowed it to take place. Britain was of course a net importer of all grains in this period, Denmark was a net exporter of barley, and Sweden was a net exporter of oats until 1899. Panel B of Table 1 shows extremely large declines in Anglo-Scandinavian price gaps for these two grains, confirming the findings of myself and Jeffrey G. Williamson.[23] For example, British barley prices were 42 percent higher than Danish prices in 1870, but the gap had vanished by the end of the period.

As an importing country, Britain's grain prices were higher than those both in the New World and in Scandinavia. Commodity market integration

---

[20]Harley, "Transportation."

[21]European prices are market averages; U.S. prices are for particular grades of grain. U.S. wheat prices were adjusted in an attempt to correct for this. Trends in transatlantic price gaps will be reliable unless average European wheat grades are changing over time. See Appendix 1 for details.

[22]The fact that wheat was a more expensive grain than oats may explain why price gaps were so much greater in percentage terms for the latter product.

[23]O'Rourke and Williamson, "Open Economy Forces."

782   *O'Rourke*

TABLE 1
INTERNATIONAL GRAIN PRICE SPREADS, 1870–1913
(percentages)

Grain	Countries	1870	1913
	Panel A. Transatlantic Price Gaps		
Wheat	Britain-United States	54.1	-0.8
Barley	Britain-United States	45.9	10.9
Oats	Britain-United States	138.1	28.1
	Panel B. Anglo-Scandinavian Price Gaps		
Barley	Britain-Denmark	42.0	-2.0
Oats	Britain-Sweden	55.3	5.0
Oats	Britain-Denmark	46.8	7.1
	Panel C. United States-Scandinavian Price Gaps		
Wheat	Denmark-United States	28.9	-4.6
Barley	Denmark-United States	0.4	11.4
Oats	Denmark-United States	60.1	19.4
Rye	Denmark-United States	44.7	5.3
Wheat	Sweden-United States	18.7	17.3
Barley	Sweden-United States	-6.0	17.6
Oats	Sweden-United States	53.4	22.3
Rye	Sweden-United States	39.2	26.1
	Panel D. Continental European-United States Price Gaps		
Wheat	France-United States	43.8	29.3
Barley	France-United States	6.1	15.4
Oats	France-United States	117.7	61.0
Rye	France-United States	61.1	16.9
Wheat	Bavaria-United States	44.0	37.1
Barley	Bavaria-United States	5.4	43.6
Oats	Bavaria-United States	82.6	106.3
Rye	Bavaria-United States	66.5	48.5
	Panel E. Western European-Odessa Price Gaps		
Wheat	Britain-Odessa	37.9	6.5
Wheat	Denmark-Odessa	15.7	4.9
Wheat	Sweden-Odessa	9.4	35.9
Wheat	France-Odessa	28.0	48.8
Wheat	Bavaria-Odessa	25.3	43.8
	Panel F. Intra-European Price Gaps		
Wheat	Britain-France	5.8	-23.5
Wheat	Denmark-France	-11.2	-26.2
Wheat	Sweden-France	-17.1	-9.2
Wheat	Bavaria-France	0.6	7.1

Source: Predicted values are from regressions of price gaps on time and time-squared. The underlying price data is as described in Appendix 1.

narrowed price gaps between Britain and both exporting markets. This price gradient, with Britain at the summit, can help explain the paradoxical finding that price gaps between the U.S. and Denmark, a free trader throughout the period, did not always decline (panel C of Table 1). The oats price gap fell from 60 percent to 19 percent over the period, a much smaller decline

European Grain Invasion, 1870–1913   783

TABLE 2
CEREAL PROTECTION, 1909–1913
(ad valorem equivalents, percentage)

Grain	France	Germany	Sweden
Wheat	38.1	37.2	32.0
Barley	21.0	35.5	42.2
Oats	16.9	45.1	0.0
Rye	20.6	42.9	39.9
Weighted geometric average	26.6	40.0	0.0
Weighted arithmetic average	28.4	40.1	24.0

Source: Tariff data for individual grains are given in Appendix 1. For weights used in computing average tariffs, see Appendix 5.

than in the Anglo-U.S. case; although the Danish-U.S. wheat price gap was eliminated by 1913, this was from a much smaller initial starting point than that of Anglo-America; and the Danish-U.S. barley price gap actually increased over the period.

What was true of Denmark was, not surprisingly, even more true of Sweden, which imposed tariffs on imports of wheat, barley, and rye. Table 2 gives average tariffs for the main grains in Germany, France, and Sweden for the five-year period 1909 to 1913.[24] The figures confirm what qualitative histories stress: the disproportionately high protection given to wheat in France and rye in Germany as well as the higher average level of protection in Germany than in France or Sweden.[25] As a traditional oats exporter, Sweden did not impose tariffs on imports of that grain.

As in the Danish case, the Swedish-U.S. barley price gap increased (and by somewhat more than in the Danish case); more significantly, the Swedish-U.S. rye price gap was only reduced by one-third, while the Danish-U.S. rye price gap was all but eliminated; and the Swedish-U.S. wheat price gap remained unchanged over the period.

France and Germany also succeeded in insulating themselves to a considerable extent from the impact of transatlantic transport cost declines (panel D of Table 1). France was of course a net grain importer. In this section I focus on Bavarian rather than Prussian prices since Prussia was a traditional grain exporter.[26] The Franco-U.S. wheat price gap fell by only one-third, and the Bavarian-U.S. gap by less than one-sixth; Bavarian oats and barley prices, and French barley prices, moved further from U.S. levels during the period; and the Bavarian-U.S. rye price gap fell by little more than one-

[24]Late nineteenth-century tariffs were specific; they are here converted to their *ad valorem* equivalents by dividing the specific tariff by a notional world price, set equal to the domestic price minus the specific tariff. This method of course produces alternative tariff estimates for Prussia and Bavaria (grain prices tended to be higher in the latter region). Prussian tariffs are given in Table 2.

[25]Note, however, the even higher protection for German oats.

[26]Bavarian grain prices were higher than Prussian grain prices during this period (except in the case of oats, early on). Of course, market integration was also occurring within Germany, with price-gap volatility declining sharply after German unification (except in the case of barley).

fourth. Average Bavarian cereal prices can hardly have moved much closer to U.S. levels during the period, while cereal prices converged far more strongly on U.S. levels in Britain and Denmark than in France and Sweden. A clear contrast thus emerges between free-trading Britain and Denmark, on the one hand, and protectionist countries on the other. This contrast is further born out when wheat prices in these five western European countries are compared with Odessa prices (panel E of Table 1). In the British and Danish cases, there was clear commodity price convergence, while wheat prices *diverged* between Odessa, on the one hand, and Sweden, Germany, and France on the other. Indeed, by 1913 British prices were closer to Odessa prices than were Swedish, French, or German prices, whereas the opposite had been true in 1870.[27]

Not only did Continental protection mute or overturn price convergence between western Europe and its U.S. and eastern granaries, it also hindered commodity market integration *within* western Europe. Panel F of Table 1 makes the point by focusing on wheat price gaps between France and other European countries. Surprisingly, *no* evidence of commodity market integration emerges here; in fact, for all four pairs of countries bar Sweden-France, price gaps actually *increased* over the period. An era in which the Old and New Worlds became much more economically integrated with each other was also an era in which grain markets *within* Continental Europe became more balkanized. Globalization was not a universal phenomenon, even during the comparatively liberal late nineteenth century.

Transport Costs, Protection, and Average Cereal Prices

Market integration raises prices in the exporting region and lowers prices in the importing region. The question now arising is whether the decline in transport costs documented above affected European or U.S. prices more. The answer depends, of course, on elasticities of supply and demand in the two regions. If these elasticities are taken to have been equal to 1.0 and −0.3, respectively, then a simple partial equilibrium model predicts that declining transport costs on their own would have led to a decline in British wheat prices of between 15 and 25 percent.[28]

By how much in real terms did wheat prices actually fall in Europe over this period? Table 3 gives real grain-price movements between 1870 to 1874

---

[27] Appendix 2 shows that these contrasts between free trading and protectionist countries can indeed be explained by protection. The appendix calculates Franco-British, Bavarian-British, Prussian-Danish, and Swedish-Danish grain price gaps. These price gaps were highly correlated with tariffs in the protectionist economies. This was particularly true in the case of wheat and in the case of Germany.

[28] This is based on O'Rourke and Williamson, "Late Nineteenth Century Anglo-American Factor Price Convergence" and "Erratum"; elasticities are from Harley, "Late Nineteenth Century Transportation," p. 604, and price gaps are documented above. Note that Harley himself estimates much larger price effects; his table 2 suggests wheat price declines in Britain of more than 50 percent.

European Grain Invasion, 1870–1913   785

TABLE 3
REAL GRAIN PRICE DECLINES, 1870–1874 TO 1909–1913
(percentage changes)

Grain	Britain	Denmark	Sweden	France	Germany
Wheat	35.3	33.3	23.2	22.5	21.2
Barley	25.5	3.6	9.9	12.6	8.3
Oats	18.7	-0.9	7.2	3.6	2.9
Rye	N/A	19.1	11.7	18.4	13.5

Note: A negative entry denotes a price increase. N/A indicates data were not available.
Source: For grain prices, see Appendix 1. For GDP deflators, see Appendix 6. German prices refer to Prussia.

and 1909 to 1913 for the five countries in my sample.[29] As can be seen, wheat prices fell by 35 percent in Britain, or by 10 to 20 percentage points more than the 15 to 25 percent warranted by the decline in transport costs alone. This large price decline reflects not only market integration but also agricultural supply shifts in the U.S. and elsewhere. Real wheat prices fell by a very similar amount in Denmark. What about France, Germany, and Sweden? In fact, avoiding wheat-price convergence on the U.S. was not enough to prevent wheat farmers from losing: wheat prices fell in real terms by roughly 20 percent in all three countries. Tariffs protected farmers from the impact of commodity market integration but did not protect them from the other supply-side forces lowering wheat prices during the period.

What about other cereal prices? Table 3 shows that other cereal prices fell by less in Britain; again, they fell by even less on the Continent; but again they did fall rather than increase. For example, oats prices fell by only 19 percent in Britain and by only 0 to 7 percent on the Continent. To repeat, tariffs muted or completely offset the impact of transatlantic commodity-market integration, but they did not offset the impact of mechanical reapers and all the other forces pushing down real grain prices during this period.

GRAIN ACREAGES AND FACTOR PRICES

Table 4 shows how the area under cereal cultivation changed in a number of European countries between 1871 and 1911. As can be seen, acreage expanded in Russia, an exporting country; it also expanded in Denmark (a barley exporter) and Sweden (an oats exporter before 1899) in the decades before 1891. Thereafter, the cereal acreage declined in Denmark but held steady in protectionist Sweden. The impact of protection also shows up clearly in the contrast between the dramatic declines in British and Irish cereal acreages, the very modest decline in France, and the slight increase in Germany.

Of course, it is the income distribution consequences of the grain invasion that were politically crucial, and Table 5 gives some basic facts. It reports

[29]Nominal grain prices are deflated by the relevant GDP deflator.

786   *O'Rourke*

TABLE 4
CEREAL ACREAGES, EUROPE 1871–1911
(1871 = 100)

Country	1871	1881	1891	1901	1911
Austria	100	97.2	103.9	101.8	106.0
Denmark	100	106.4	107.1	102.0	98.9[a]
France	100	101.7	97.7	98.6	95.1
Germany	100	100.2	101.4	103.8	106.3
Ireland	100	83.5	70.2	62.0	59.1
Italy	100[b]	96.0	96.5	N/A	100.7
Netherlands	100	107.6	105.3	105.5	107.2
Russia	100[b]	97.9	104.5[c]	121.3	162.5
Sweden	100	115.5	127.7	131.0	125.8
Britain	100	93.9	84.4	76.8	75.1

[a]1912
[b]1872
[c]1892
Note: N/A indicates data were not available.
Source: Figures are calculated from the data given in Mitchell *European Historical Statistics*, table D1.

data on wages and land prices, collected in collaboration with Alan Taylor and Jeffrey G. Williamson.[30] The data, deflated by the relevant consumer price indices, are for five European countries—Britain, Germany, France, Denmark, and Sweden—and for two New World countries—the United States and Australia—and are given as five-year averages between 1875 and 1913. Table 5 confirms the dramatic real wage growth in Scandinavia that was the focus of O'Rourke and Williamson, but it is the data on agricultural land prices that are chiefly of interest here.[31] British land prices collapsed, declining by over 40 percent; they declined more modestly in France and Sweden and not at all in protectionist Germany or in the free-trading but cooperating Denmark.[32] By contrast, land prices tripled in the New World, where wage-rental ratios fell by a half; wage-rental ratios more than doubled in free-trading Britain and Denmark but increased by less than 50 percent in protectionist France and Germany.[33]

It looks as if there may be a link between trade policies and income distribution: land prices fell by a lot more in free-trading than in protectionist countries, and wage-rental ratios moved exactly as standard trade theory

[30]O'Rourke, Taylor and Williamson, "Factor Price Convergence." Data on rents would of course be preferable, but they are unavailable. If Offer, "Farm Tenures," is right, and the "positional advantages of ownership" were declining in late nineteenth-century Britain, then British land rents would have declined more slowly than land values; this appears to have been the case. The results in the following two sections refer to the impact of grain prices on land *rents*.

[31]O'Rourke and Williamson, "Education."

[32]These national figures disguise much regional variation; for example, in Britain rents would have held up well around urban centers, which demanded growing amounts of milk and other relatively nontraded products.

[33]The Swedish figure is not such an anomaly; Sweden adopted protection relatively late, and average protection levels were slightly lower than in France or Germany (Table 2).

European Grain Invasion, 1870–1913   787

TABLE 5
FACTOR PRICES, 1875–1913

Year	Australia	United States	France	Germany	Great Britain	Denmark	Sweden
		Panel A. Real Wages, 1875–1913					
1877	100.0	100.0	100.0	100.0	100.0	100.0	100.0
1882	95.5	104.7	105.2	96.5	104.0	112.1	99.3
1887	102.4	116.4	113.9	110.0	113.9	126.6	110.4
1892	109.9	121.1	116.9	110.2	118.8	138.1	120.0
1897	133.9	127.2	123.1	124.6	127.6	180.7	138.6
1902	123.4	135.5	132.2	131.2	121.6	204.0	151.6
1907	123.5	142.9	142.3	132.9	128.6	224.8	168.3
1912	126.3	142.3	122.2	135.1	125.9	252.2	180.8
		Panel B. Real Land Prices, 1875–1913					
1877	100.0	100.0	100.0	100.0	100.0	100.0	100.0
1882	99.9	108.2	95.6	94.0	77.3	108.9	86.1
1887	121.0	124.7	82.9	102.4	76.1	97.5	83.7
1892	201.3	136.0	89.2	90.1	76.7	90.0	80.9
1897	226.4	141.7	84.5	92.1	82.2	89.3	77.5
1902	240.8	153.8	81.8	97.8	69.8	85.3	76.2
1907	313.6	212.9	89.8	101.8	68.3	97.8	80.1
1912	307.8	274.5	84.7	108.0	58.2	111.2	80.6
		Panel C Wage-Rental Ratios, 1875–1913					
1877	100.0	100.0	100.0	100.0	100.0	100.0	100.0
1882	95.6	96.7	110.1	102.7	134.5	103.0	115.4
1887	84.7	93.4	137.3	107.4	149.7	130.2	131.9
1892	54.6	89.0	131.1	122.3	154.9	153.3	148.3
1897	59.2	89.8	145.7	135.2	155.2	202.2	178.9
1902	51.2	88.1	161.6	134.2	174.1	238.8	198.9
1907	39.4	67.1	158.3	130.6	188.2	229.4	210.1
1912	41.0	51.9	144.2	125.0	216.3	223.6	224.4

Source: For factor prices, see O'Rourke et al.,"Factor Price Convergence," app. 1; for consumer price indices, see Appendix 6.

would predict. However, there were many other forces at work influencing income distribution during this period, notably factor accumulation and technical progress. The following two sections thus make more explicitly the connection between commodity prices and factor prices.

GRAIN PRICES AND INCOME DISTRIBUTION: CGE ANALYSIS

Model Specification

This section uses CGE models for Britain, France, and Sweden that have identical theoretical specifications but whose parameters reflect different country characteristics. The purpose of the article is comparative, and it is therefore important that results do not differ between countries because of different model specifications. Adopting a uniform theoretical framework shifts the focus towards the calibration of individual country models; different results will reflect different factor endowments, sectoral factor intensities, and other fundamental economic parameters that emerge from the data. Calibration requires information on all relevant input-output relationships and trade flows in the three countries in a base year. Appendix 3 describes in full the procedures used.[34]

There are five sectors in the model, three agricultural and two nonagricultural: pasture P, grain G, nongrain vegetable production NG, manufacturing M and services S.[35] Services are nontraded; all other goods are traded. Since the price shocks being imposed are large, so-called Armington assumptions are made on both the export and the import side. These assumptions are standard in the CGE literature; their purpose is to insulate domestic sectors from world price shocks to some extent, thus ensuring that economies do not entirely stop producing particular commodities. The way this is done is to assume that each traded goods sector produces two goods: a domestic good D destined for local consumption and an export good X. Imported goods M substitute imperfectly with domestic goods in producing aggregate goods, which are then consumed or used as intermediate inputs.

Allowing domestic goods, exported goods, and imported goods to be perfect substitutes would imply grain production (unrealistically) ceasing entirely in several experiments. A further advantage of this article's Armington-style treatment of international trade is that it allows for the reality of two-way trade in all commodities, a possibility that would be ruled out *a priori* by assuming that domestic and foreign goods were perfect substitutes.[36]

The second set of assumptions that are important in determining the final results have to do with the mobility of factors across sectors. Capital is assumed to be fully mobile across all sectors. Labor is imperfectly mobile between agricultural and urban sectors; that is, the economy is endowed with raw labor, which is then transformed into agricultural (L_A) and nonagricultural (L_{NA}) labor via a constant elasticity of transformation production function.[37] Land is only used in agriculture. In some experiments, it is fully mobile between all three agricultural sectors; this assumption is relevant when exploring the long-run impact of price shocks on average rents. In other experiments, land is assumed to be specific to either tillage (both grains and nongrains) or pasture. This assumption is relevant to the shorter

---

[34]The British and Swedish models are substantially revised versions of the models used in O'Rourke and Williamson, "Late Nineteenth Century Anglo-American Factor Price Convergence," "Open Economy Forces."

[35]Appendix 4 provides some rudimentary sensitivity analysis, establishing that changing the specification of the French and Swedish models in particular directions does not affect the results of the article.

[36]Harley, "Antebellum American Tariff," has a good discussion of the Armington approach.

[37]The benchmark elasticity of transformation is set equal to 10.

European Grain Invasion, 1870–1913   789

run, and is useful for exploring the initial impact of price shocks on the relative fortunes of grain producers and farmers engaged in animal husbandry. Production takes place in all three countries according to

$$(P_D, P_X) = P(L_A, K, R, \{I\}) \tag{1}$$
$$(G_D, G_X) = G(L_A, K, R, \{I\}) \tag{2}$$
$$(NG_D, NG_X) = NG(L_A, K, R, \{I\}) \tag{3}$$
$$(M_D, M_X) = M(L_{NA}, K, \{I\}) \tag{4}$$
$$S = S(L_{NA}, K, \{I\}) \tag{5}$$

where K denotes capital, R denotes land, and $\{I\}$ is a vector of intermediate inputs.[38] The production functions in equations 1 through 4 are constant elasticity of transformation, with benchmark elasticities of transformation equal to 10. Similarly, the Armington elasticity of substitution between imported and domestic goods is set equal to 10 in the benchmark case. All production functions are nested (Figure 2), with intermediate inputs being combined with value-added aggregates in a Leontief fashion; at a lower level, primary factors of production produce the value-added aggregate via CES production functions. The benchmark elasticity of substitution is 1 for agricultural sectors and 0.5 for nonagricultural sectors. All production functions exhibit constant returns to scale.

There is a single representative consumer in the model, endowed with all factors of production, whose function it is to generate demands for final commodities. The consumer's endowment of foreign exchange, the *numeraire* good, is sufficient to enable the economy to run the benchmark trade deficit.

The Impact of Cheap Grain

The CGE models used here incorporate an aggregate grain sector, rather than distinguishing between individual grains. Appendix 5 thus calculates aggregate price shocks affecting this sector, which involves taking account of the different crop mixes in the three countries. Between 1870 to 1874 and 1909 to 1913, British cereal prices fell by 28.9 percent in real terms (when divided by the GDP deflator). In France they fell by 16.1 percent, reflecting a world price decline of 33.7 percent and a tariff of 26.5 percent. Finally, in Sweden average cereal prices fell by 10.4 percent, reflecting a world price decline of 26.8 percent and an average tariff of 22.4 percent.

---

[38]This is not equivalent to assuming identical technologies in the three countries. The parameters that define these production functions vary from country to country, reflecting the different economic structures in each. See Appendix 3.

790   *O'Rourke*

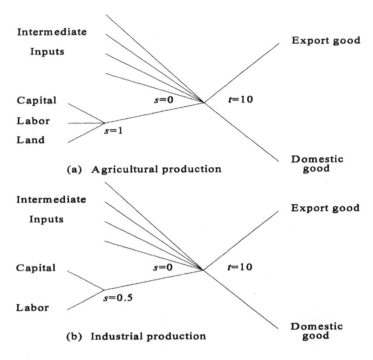

FIGURE 2
THE STRUCTURE OF PRODUCTION

Note: *s* denotes elasticity of substitution; *t* denotes elasticity of transformation.

I start by asking what would have happened in the three countries if cereal prices had declined by 28.9 percent, as in Britain. Since the three models are theoretically identical, and the same shock is being imposed on them, any differences in results can only reflect differences in the underlying economic structures in the three countries. Table 6 gives some key facts.

Table 7 gives the results obtained when cereal prices are allowed to fall by 28.9 percent in all three economies. As outlined above, about half to two-thirds of this actual British price decline may be attributed to declining transport costs, while the remainder was due to other supply-side forces reducing grain prices worldwide. Several key features stand out from the table.

First, these price shocks had a *big* impact on land rents. In the short run, tillage farmers would have seen their rents decline by 8.8 percent in France, 20.6 percent in Sweden, and a massive 38.1 percent in Britain.[39] These

---

[39]Throughout, factor returns are deflated by country-specific consumer price indices, reflecting the budget weights of urban workers. See Appendix 3.

European Grain Invasion, 1870–1913   791

TABLE 6
ECONOMIC STRUCTURE, 1871
(percentage)

Sector	Britain	France	Sweden
Panel A. Sectoral Output Shares within Agriculture			
Pasture	56.5	40.7	27.8
Grain	27.2	23.7	39.4
Nongrains	16.3	35.6	32.8
Panel B. Sectoral Output Shares within Tillage			
Grain	62.5	40.0	54.5
Nongrains	37.5	60.0	45.5
Panel C. Sectoral Output Shares			
Agriculture	19.2	40.7	36.9
Manufacturing	44.6	38.5	30.3
Services	36.2	20.8	32.8
Panel D. Sectoral Value Added Shares			
Agriculture	14.9	35.9	40.1
Manufacturing	39.8	38.2	11.4
Services	45.4	25.9	48.5
Share of labor force in agriculture	22.6	50.5	67.6
Net grain imports/production	54.7	4.3	13.9

Note: Percentage totals do not always add up to 100, due to rounding.
Source: See Appendix 3. For the agricultural labor share, see Appendix 3; and O'Rourke and Williamson, "Open Economy Forces," app. 5, p. 10 and "Were Hecksher and Ohlin Right," app. 3, p. 5. The British figure only counts nondefense employment.

different magnitudes are partly explained by the different shares of grains and nongrains in total tillage output: cereals accounted for 63 percent of tillage output in Britain but only 55 percent of Swedish tillage output and 40 percent of French tillage output (Table 6).

Second, as Gerschenkron emphasized, farmers engaged in animal husbandry stood to gain from the grain invasion, at least in the short run. Cheap grain meant cheap fodder, and this boosted pasture rents in all three countries, particularly in Britain.[40]

Third, and in qualification to the second point, the relative fortunes of tillage and pasture areas depended crucially on the ease with which land could be switched between crops and pasture. To take an extreme case, if land were fully mobile between all agricultural sectors, all farmers would see their rents move in a similar fashion. Table 7 indicates that in this extreme case, average rents would have fallen by 4 percent in France, 9.4 percent in Britain, and 14.4 percent in Sweden.[41] Again, these differing mag

[40] Williamson, "Impact," found the same in the context of the Repeal of the Corn Laws.
[41] These declines in average land rents are much smaller than those reported for Britain in O'Rourke and Williamson, "Late Nineteenth Century Anglo-American Factor Price Convergence," "Erratum," who were exploring the impact of declining price gaps for meat and manufactures, as well as grains.

O'Rourke

TABLE 7
EFFECTS OF A 28.9 PERCENT DECLINE IN CEREAL PRICES
(percentage changes)

Variable	Britain		France		Sweden	
	Fixed	Mobile	Fixed	Mobile	Fixed	Mobile
P	+7.2	+21.3	+3.0	+11.4	+2.2	+5.4
G	-74.5	-85.1	-47.1	-48.5	-20.6	-21.6
NG	+42.7	+20.9	+22.5	+19.4	+8.6	+8.4
M	+5.7	+6.0	+3.1	+2.9	+13.9	+14.1
S	-0.3	-0.2	-1.3	-1.4	+1.4	+1.5
WA	+2.5	+3.0	-4.5	-4.4	-1.7	-1.0
WNA	+5.0	+5.7	-3.7	-3.6	-0.4	+0.4
K	+5.3	+6.0	+5.3	+6.7	+6.0	+6.3
R		-9.4		-4.0		-14.4
RT	-38.1		-8.8		-20.6	
RP	+14.1		+8.4		+7.4	
LA	-19.2	-20.6	-4.8	-4.9	-6.2	-6.2

Note: Fixed experiments assume land specific to either pasture or tillage; mobile experiments assume land mobile between all agricultural sectors. *P, G, NG, M, S* are outputs in pasture, grains, nongrains, manufacturing, and services. *WA, WNA, K, R, RT, RP* are real returns to agricultural and nonagricultural labor, capital, land, and land in tillage and pasture. *LA* is agricultural employment.
Source: See the text.

nitudes can be explained by the varying shares of grain in *total* agricultural output; grain accounted for only 24 percent of agricultural output in France but for 39 percent of Swedish agricultural output.

Fourth, the impact of cheap grain on real wages was indeed different in different countries. In the British context, it appears that Peel was right and Disraeli was wrong; that is, the positive cost-of-living effect of cheap grain outweighed the negative labor-demand effect. Urban real wages increased by 5 to 6 percent as a result of the grain invasion, and even agricultural workers benefitted.[42] The story was rather different on the Continent, where agriculture accounted for a far larger share of total employment. The same price shock would have *reduced* wages by 3.5 to 4.5 percent in France and would have had little effect on Swedish real wages.[43] This makes sense. By 1871, only 22.6 percent of the British labor force was in agriculture, as opposed to 67.6 percent in Sweden and 50.5 percent in France.[44] Table 7 shows the grain invasion having a relatively bigger impact on agricultural employment in Britain than elsewhere; but even a large decline in employment in such a small sector translated into only a minor fall in aggregate labor demand and thus led to only a small decline in nominal wages.

These real-wage findings have implications for recent debates about trade and real-wage convergence. Transatlantic transport cost declines implied

[42]This is also the finding of Williamson, "Impact"; and O'Rourke and Williamson, "Late Nineteenth Century Anglo-American Factor Price Convergence."
[43]This is consistent with the findings in O'Rourke and Williamson, "Open Economy Forces."
[44]Note that a relatively large amount of Swedish agricultural labor was engaged in forestry.

European Grain Invasion, 1870–1913 793

factor-price convergence between the Old and New Worlds but may also have implied factor-price divergence, or at least real-wage divergence, within Europe, leading British real wages to pull further ahead of real wages in the European periphery.[45] This in turn may have stimulated intra-European migration, corresponding to a reshuffling of resources from European agriculture to European industry: certainly Irish migration to Britain can be partly understood in this context.[46] Globalization, and in particular international factor flows, did offer peripheral European countries the chance to converge on Britain; free trade in grain may have worked in the opposite direction.

Finally, Table 7 shows that cheap grain had a substantial impact on agricultural employment in Britain, if not elsewhere. A 28.9 percent decline in cereal prices would have led to a 20 percent fall in British agricultural employment, compared with a 5 percent fall in France, and a 6 percent fall in Sweden. This discrepancy makes sense. The migration of labor to the towns in response to a negative agricultural shock would depress urban wages, lowering the incentive to move. In Britain, where agriculture accounted only for a small proportion of total employment, nonagricultural wages would have been largely immune from such an effect, which in France and Sweden would have muted the migration response to the grain invasion.

The potential impact of the grain invasion was significant in all three countries, especially for tillage farmers. To what extent did tariffs succeed in protecting this constituency?

The Impact of French and Swedish Protection

Tables 8 and 9 explore the impact of protection in France and Sweden. In each case I impose a counterfactual "free-trade" price shock (grain prices falling by 33.7 percent in France and 26.8 percent in Sweden), followed by the same world price shock, combined with a domestic tariff on grains (26.5 percent in France, implying the actual domestic price decline of 16.1 percent; and 22.4 percent in Sweden, implying the actual domestic price decline of 10.4 percent).

If the primary aim of protection was to mute the impact of the grain invasion on agricultural incomes, it succeeded. Protection cut the declines in rent associated with cheap grain by one-third in Sweden and by one half in France: big effects indeed. French grain output was twice what it would have been in the absence of protection; protection raised Swedish grain output by a much more modest 8 percent. As expected, protection was bad for capital in both countries, but it helped French labor (while leaving Swedish labor basically unaffected).

[45]O'Rourke and Williamson, "Late Nineteenth Century Anglo-American Factor Price Convergence"; and O'Rourke, Taylor and Williamson, "Factor Price Convergence."

[46]O'Rourke, "Repeal."

794

O'Rourke

TABLE 8
THE IMPACT OF PROTECTION IN FRANCE
(percentage changes)

Variable	Sector-Specific Land			Mobile Land		
	Free Trade	Protection	Tariff Impact	Free Trade	Protection	Tariff Impact
P	+3.9	+1.0	−2.7	+15.0	+4.3	−9.3
G	−60.1	−20.0	+100.3	−61.6	−20.6	+107.2
NG	+29.2	+9.1	−15.5	+24.9	+7.9	−13.6
M	+3.6	+1.2	−2.3	+3.3	+1.1	−2.1
S	−1.6	0.0	+1.6	−1.7	0.0	+1.7
WA	−5.2	−2.3	+3.1	−5.2	−2.2	+3.2
WNA	−4.3	−1.9	+2.5	−4.2	−1.8	+2.6
K	+6.9	+2.2	−4.4	+8.8	+2.7	−5.6
R				−4.3	−2.3	+2.1
RT	−10.3	−4.5	+6.5			
RP	+11.1	+3.1	−7.2			
LA	−5.7	−2.3	+3.6	−6.0	−2.4	+3.9

Note: Sector-specific experiments assume land specific to either pasture or tillage; mobile experiments assume land mobile between all agricultural sectors. The free-trade scenario imposes a 33.7 percent decline in the price of grain, whereas the protection scenario imposes a 33.7 percent decline in the world price of grain and a 26.5 percent tariff on grain imports. The tariff-impact column simply compares the previous two columns. P, G, NG, M, S are outputs in pasture, grains, nongrains, manufacturing, and services. WA, WNA, K, R, RT, RP are real returns to agricultural and nonagricultural labor, capital, land, and land in tillage and pasture. LA is agricultural employment.
Source: See the text.

TABLE 9
THE IMPACT OF PROTECTION IN SWEDEN
(percentage changes)

Variable	Sector-Specific Land			Mobile Land		
	Free Trade	Protection	Tariff Impact	Free Trade	Protection	Tariff Impact
P	+1.9	+0.9	−1.0	+4.7	+2.4	−2.2
G	−18.7	−12.2	+8.0	−19.5	−12.3	+8.9
NG	+7.9	+5.3	−2.4	+7.6	+5.0	−2.4
M	+12.7	+8.3	−3.9	+12.8	+8.1	−4.2
S	+1.2	+0.8	−0.4	+1.4	+0.9	−0.5
WA	−1.7	−1.5	+0.2	−1.0	−1.1	−0.1
WNA	−0.4	−0.7	−0.3	+0.2	−0.3	−0.5
K	+5.3	+2.9	−2.2	+5.6	+2.9	−2.5
R				−13.2	−8.9	+4.9
RT	−18.9	−12.8	+7.5			
RP	+6.4	+3.0	−3.2			
LA	−5.6	−3.6	+2.1	−5.6	−3.5	+2.2

Note: Sector-specific experiments assume land specific to either pasture or tillage; mobile experiments assume land mobile between all agricultural sectors. The free-trade scenario imposes a 26.8 percent decline in the price of grain, whereas the protection scenario imposes a 26.8 percent decline in the world price of grain and a 22.4 percent tariff on grain imports. The tariff-impact column simply compares the previous two columns. P, G, NG, M, S are outputs in pasture, grains, nongrains, manufacturing, and services. WA, WNA, K, R, RT, RP are real returns to agricultural and nonagricultural labor, capital, land, and land in tillage and pasture. LA is agricultural employment.
Source: See the text.

European Grain Invasion, 1870–1913   795

GRAIN PRICES AND INCOME DISTRIBUTION: ECONOMETRIC ANALYSIS

An alternative way of estimating the impact of commodity price shocks on income distribution is to obtain data on a panel of countries and proceed econometrically. O'Rourke, Taylor and Williamson did precisely this; their focus was on the effects of relative agricultural prices on the wage-rental ratio.[47] This section asks a more narrowly focused question: how did movements in grain prices affect landowners?

To answer this question, some theoretical structure is needed, and the sector-specific factors model seems the natural place to start. What exogenous parameters affect income distribution in such a framework? Endowments clearly do. An increase in the land-labor ratio will lower rents; an increase in the capital-labor ratio will pull workers into industry, increasing wages and again lowering rents. Aggregate technological progress has ambiguous effects on income distribution, depending on whether it is labor- or land-saving, and on which sector it occurs in. Goods prices will also clearly influence factor prices. An increase in agricultural prices will increase rents; an increase in manufactured goods prices, on the other hand, will pull workers out of agriculture, raising nominal wages and lowering rents.

O'Rourke, Taylor, and Williamson collected data on endowments, manufactured goods prices, and outputs in a sample of seven countries— Australia, the United States, France, Germany, Britain, Denmark, and Sweden—over eight five-yearly time periods from 1875 to 1913. They also collected data on average agricultural prices; since I am interested in grains, I use wheat prices instead. Furthermore, I want to control for movements in other agricultural prices, and collected meat prices for this purpose. I estimate equations of the form

$$DREAL_{it} = \alpha_{i0} + \alpha_1 CAPLAB_{it} + \alpha_2 LANDLAB_{it} + \alpha_3 OLDPROD_{it} + \\ \alpha_4 NEWPROD_{it} + \alpha_5 PM_{it} + \alpha_6 PW_{it} + \alpha_7 PMFG_{it} + e_{it} \qquad (6)$$

$$DREAL_{it} = \alpha_{i0} + \alpha_1 CAPLAB_{it} + \alpha_2 LANDLAB_{it} + \alpha_3 OLDPROD_{it} + \\ \alpha_4 NEWPROD_{it} + \alpha_5 PM_{it} + \alpha_6 PW_{it} + \alpha_7 PMFG_{it} + d_t + e_{it} \qquad (7)$$

where the variables are defined as follows:

$DREAL$ = log(nominal land price/CPI)[48]
$CAPLAB$ = log(K/L)
$LANDLAB$ = log($Land/L$)
$PROD$ = Solovian residual, share of K = 0.4, share of land = 0.1
$OLDPROD$ = $PROD$ if country is in Europe, 0 otherwise

---

[47]O'Rourke, Taylor and Williamson, "Factor Price Convergence."
[48]Land rents would of course be preferable but the data are unavailable. See note 30.

796   *O'Rourke*

TABLE 10.
THE DETERMINANTS OF REAL LAND PRICES, 1875–1913

Regression	No Time Dummies	Time Dummies Included
CAPLAB	-1.53	-1.46
	(-6.71)	(-5.42)
LANDLAB	-1.39	-1.73
	(-8.60)	(-4.92)
OLDPROD	0.23	0.52
	(1.10)	(1.57)
NEWPROD	1.94	2.26
	(6.09)	(5.29)
PM	0.49	0.58
	(2.54)	(2.68)
PW	0.46	0.52
	(2.08)	(1.35)
PMFG	-0.95	-0.84
	(-2.78)	(-2.12)
Mean of dependent variable	0.210	0.210
Standard deviation of dependent variable	0.360	0.360
Standard error of regression	0.115	0.121
R-squared	0.922	0.928
Adjusted R-squared	0.897	0.887
Log of likelihood function	49.592	51.949
Durbin–Watson statistic	1.380	1.382
Number of observations	56	56

Notes: The dependent variable equals agricultural land prices divided by CPI. All variables are in log form. Estimation is OLS with fixed effects (country dummies). Fixed effects are not reported. *t*-statistics are in parentheses. Dependent variables are defined in text.

TABLE 11
CHEAP GRAIN AND PROTECTION, 1871–1913
(percentage changes in real land values)

Scenario	Model	Britain	France	Sweden	Germany	Denmark
Free trade	CGE	-9.4	-4.3	-13.2	N/A	N/A
Protection	CGE	N/A	-2.3	-8.9	N/A	N/A
Tariff impact	CGE	N/A	2.1	5.0	N/A	N/A
Free trade	MIN	-13.3	-15.5	-12.3	-15.7	-4.5
Protection	MIN	N/A	-7.4	-4.8	-5.2	N/A
Tariff impact	MIN	N/A	9.6	8.6	12.5	N/A
Free trade	MAX	-15.0	-17.5	-13.9	-17.8	-5.1
Protection	MAX	N/A	-8.4	-4.8	-5.9	N/A
Tariff impact	MAX	N/A	11.1	10.6	14.5	N/A

Note: CGE results are based on Tables 7, 8 and 9. MIN results are based on the estimate without time dummies in Table 10. MAX results are based on the estimate with time dummies in Table 10. For France and Sweden, the free-trade, protection, and tariff-impact scenarios are as described in Tables 8 and 9. The free-trade scenarios for Britain and Denmark involve grain prices falling by 28.9 percent and 9.8 percent, respectively (Appendix Table 5.2). For Germany, the focus is on Bavarian price movements; grain prices fall by 34.2 percent in the free-trade scenario and by 11.4 percent in the protection scenario, reflecting a tariff of 34.7 percent (Appendix 5). N/A means either not available or not applicable.
Source: See the text.

European Grain Invasion, 1870–1913   797

NEWPROD = PROD if country is in New World, 0 otherwise
PM = log(price of meat/GDP deflator); beef prices where possible
PW = log(price of wheat/GDP deflator)
PMFG = log(manufacturing price index/GDP deflator)
d_t = time dummy

and CPI is the consumer price index, K is capital stock, L is labor force, and *Land* is the agricultural land area.

Details on the data sources used are given in Appendix 6. The estimated equations are given in Table 10. The results are good. The coefficients on the endowment variables have the expected sign and are large and strongly significant. As expected, agricultural prices have a positive effect on land prices, and manufactured goods prices have a negative effect. Introducing time dummies has only a minor impact on the coefficients of interest (although *PW* becomes insignificant at conventional levels).[49] The results indicate that the long-run elasticity of land prices with respect to wheat prices lay between 0.46 and 0.52.

Table 11 summarizes the impact both of cheap grain and of protection on land rents in Europe. It uses both the econometric and the CGE results so that these can be compared with each other. First it details what would have happened to land rents if countries had maintained free trade in grain. By then asking what declining world grain prices combined with actual grain tariffs implied, it derives the impact of grain tariffs alone on land rents. The table repeats the earlier CGE results for Britain, France, and Sweden, taking the long-run case when land is fully mobile between sectors (as is appropriate when thinking about average rents). It also uses the elasticities estimated in Table 10 (0.46 and 0.52) to estimate the effects of these price shocks on land values.[50]

Cheap grain on its own would have led to British rents declining by between 9 and 15 percent, and to Swedish rents falling by between 12 and 14 percent. In France cheap grain could have reduced rents by as little as 4 percent, or by as much as 18 percent. In Germany free trade in grain would have led to average rents falling by an enormous 16 to 18 percent, and grain-price movements in Denmark only led to rents there declining by 4 to 5 percent.

Compared with this hypothetical free-trade scenario, protection boosted land rents by 2 to 11 percent in France, by 5 to 11 percent in Sweden, and by 13 to 15 percent in Germany (the "tariff impact" rows in Table 11). On

---

[49]Coefficients on the time dummies are insignificant; they decline steadily over time. Coefficients on the country dummies are very large and positive for Australia and the U.S.; positive for Denmark and Britain; and quite large and negative for Sweden, France, and Germany.

[50]The (counterfactual) free-trade price shocks and the actual price shocks, given protection, are as reported in Appendix Table 5.2.

the other hand, in all three countries, the combined impact of the grain invasion and protection on rents was negative (the "protection" rows in Table 11). Protection did offset the impact of declining transatlantic transport costs on grain prices; and it did mute the negative impact of cheap grain on land rents. However, real grain prices still fell in all these countries, and this shock was reducing land rents everywhere, *ceteris paribus*.

The econometric ('MIN' and 'MAX') and CGE results are very similar for both Britain and Sweden, which is reassuring. On the other hand, in the French case the elasticity of rents with respect to grain prices is much lower if the CGE results are to be believed than if the econometric results are correct. There is in fact a plausible explanation for this. The econometric results are based on an average elasticity derived from a cross-section of Old World and New World countries. In France, however, grain accounted for a smaller share of agricultural output than was true elsewhere (Table 6); grain prices could therefore be expected to have had a smaller impact on French rents than on Swedish rents, say. The CGE models take account of this difference in agricultural structures, whereas the econometric results impose a uniform elasticity on all countries. This discrepancy thus highlights an important potential advantage of CGE over econometric methods.

CONCLUSION

By 1913 the world economy had settled into an equilibrium that well reflected the original promise of the voyages of discovery. The New World exported food and raw materials, feeding European factories and people. European capital and labor had sought employment on the frontier and pushed it back; by 1890, the U.S. frontier was officially declared closed. On the other side of the Atlantic, the distributional implications of Christopher Columbus were finally being realized as steamships and railroads exported New World land to Europe, embodied in New World food.

The article has calculated that cheap grain, by itself, implied rent reductions of between 10 and 20 percent in Britain, France, and Germany. Refrigeration would eventually remove the protection afforded animal husbandry. In the free-trading U.K., rents collapsed. In Ireland the grain invasion triggered a struggle between landlords and tenants regarding who should carry the burden of adjustment. The landlords were eventually dispossessed, although British subsidies softened the blow. In other economies, landowners sought and received protection, as they continue to do to this day; nevertheless, the age of the great landowning aristocracy was coming to an end.

The grain invasion provoked different political responses across the Continent. Whereas the Danes and the British adhered to free trade, the French and the Germans protected their agriculture, abandoning a free-trade

European Grain Invasion, 1870–1913   799

policy dating from the 1860s. In an oft-cited article, Charles Kindleberger used these differing reactions as a peg on which to hang a general discussion of how nations vary in their responses to common shocks.[51]

To what extent do these differing political responses reflect different political institutions, or different political and social cultures? In fact, closer examination reveals that the grain invasion implied different shocks in different economies. First, it implied different price shocks. Grain prices clearly fell less in traditional grain-exporting countries, like Denmark, than they did in traditional grain-importing countries, like Britain. Second, even identical price shocks could have very different effects on income distribution across countries, reflecting the different roles of grain production and agriculture more generally in each.

The results of this article may help in understanding different political responses to the grain invasion. The grain invasion did not lower grain prices in Denmark as much as elsewhere and only lowered Danish rents by 4 to 5 percent. This surely helps explain Denmark's willingness to stick to free trade as does the fact that Denmark had a comparative advantage in many agricultural commodities that were largely (intercontinentally) nontraded. Similarly, the grain invasion benefitted British capital *and* labor, whereas in Continental economies like France it *hurt* labor as well as land. Such differences may well have mattered for political outcomes.

It is true that simplistic models involving economic interest alone are unlikely to fully explain the differing political responses to the grain invasion. Institutions and ideas clearly matter for trade policy too. However, the fact that the grain invasion implied different shocks in different countries makes it less necessary to appeal to different mediating institutions in each. The results of the article are thus consistent with an interest-based account of trade policy formation in late nineteenth-century Europe.

[51]Kindleberger, "Group Behavior."

REFERENCES

Aydelotte, W. O. "The Country Gentlemen and the Repeal of the Corn Laws." *English Historical Review* 82, no. 322 (1967): 47–60.
Bairoch, Paul. "European Trade Policy, 1815–1914." In *The Cambridge Economic History of Europe*, Vol. 8, edited by Peter Mathias and Sidney Pollard, 1–160. Cambridge: Cambridge University Press, 1989.
Barkin, Kenneth D. *The Controversy over German Industrialization 1890–1902.* Chicago: University of Chicago Press, 1970.
Caves, Richard E. and Ronald W. Jones. *World Trade and Payments: An Introduction.* Third edition. Boston: Little, Brown and Co., 1981.
Daly, Mary E. *Industrial Development and Irish National Identity, 1922–1939.* Syracuse: Syracuse University Press, 1992.

800   *O'Rourke*

Findlay, Ronald. "International Trade and Factor Mobility with an Endogenous Land Frontier: Some General Equilibrium Implications of Christopher Columbus." In *Theory, Policy and Dynamics in International Trade: Essays in Honor of Ronald W. Jones*, edited by Wilfred J. Ethier, Elhanan Helpman and J. Peter Neary, 38–54. Cambridge: Cambridge University Press, 1993.

Fogel, Robert W. "The Specification Problem in Economic History." this JOURNAL 27, no. 3 (1967): 283–308.

Gerschenkron, Alexander. *Bread and Democracy in Germany*. Berkeley: University of California Press, 1943.

Gourevitch, Peter. *Politics in Hard Times: Comparative Responses to International Economic Crises*. Ithaca: Cornell University Press, 1986.

Harley, C. Knick. "Western Settlement and the Price of Wheat, 1872–1913." this JOURNAL 38, no. 4 (1978): 865–78.

_____. "Transportation, the World Wheat Trade, and the Kuznets Cycle, 1850–1913." *Explorations in Economic History* 17, no. 3 (1980): 218–50.

_____. "Late Nineteenth Century Transportation, Trade and Settlement." In *The Emergence of a World Economy 1500–1914, Part II: 1850–1914*, edited by Wolfram Fischer, R. Marvin McInnis and Jürgen Schneider, 593–617. Stuttgart: Franz Steiner Verlag, 1986.

_____. "The Antebellum American Tariff: Food Exports and Manufacturing." *Explorations in Economic History* 29, no. 4 (1992): 375–400.

Hunt, James C. "Peasants, Grain Tariffs, and Meat Quotas: Imperial German Protectionism Reexamined." *Central European History* 7, no. 4 (1974): 311–31.

Irwin, Douglas A. "Political Economy and Peel's Repeal of the Corn Laws." *Economics and Politics* 1, no. 1 (1989): 41–59.

Jones, E. L. *The European Miracle: Environments, Economies and Geopolitics in the History of Europe and Asia*. Second edition. Cambridge: Cambridge University Press, 1981.

Jones, Ronald W. "A Three-Factor Model in Theory, Trade, and History." In *Trade, Balance of Payments and Growth: Papers in International Economics in Honor of Charles P. Kindleberger*, edited by Jagdish N. Bhagwati, Ronald W. Jones, Robert A. Mundell and Jaroslav Vanek, 3–21. Amsterdam: North-Holland, 1971.

Kindleberger, Charles P. "Group Behavior and International Trade." *Journal of Political Economy* 59, no. 1 (1951): 30–47.

Longstaff, G. B. "Rural Depopulation." *Journal of the Royal Statistical Society* 56 (September 1893): 380–433.

Marx, Karl. *Capital*. Vol. 1. New York: Vintage Books, 1977.

Mitchell, B. R. *European Historical Statistics 1750–1975*. Second revised edition. New York: Facts on File, 1981.

Offer, Avner. *The First World War: An Agrarian Interpretation*. Oxford: Oxford University Press, 1989.

_____. "Farm Tenures and Land Values in England, c. 1750–1950." *Economic History Review* 44, no. 1 (1991): 1–20.

O'Rourke, Kevin H. "The Repeal of the Corn Laws and Irish Emigration." *Explorations in Economic History* 31, no. 1 (1994): 120–138.

O'Rourke, Kevin H., Alan M. Taylor and Jeffrey G. Williamson. "Factor Price Convergence in the Late 19th Century." *International Economic Review* 37, no. 3 (1996): 499–530.

European Grain Invasion, 1870–1913   801

O'Rourke, Kevin H. and Jeffrey G. Williamson. "Were Heckscher and Ohlin Right? Putting History Back Into the Factor-Price-Equalization Theorem." *HIER Discussion Paper* no. 1593. Cambridge, Massachusetts (May 1992).

_____. "Late 19th Century Anglo-American Factor Price Convergence: Were Heckscher and Ohlin Right?" this JOURNAL 54, no. 4 (1994): 892–916.

_____. "Open Economy Forces and Late 19th Century Swedish Catch-Up." *Scandinavian Economic History Review* 43, no. 2 (1995): 171–203.

_____. "Erratum." this JOURNAL 55, no. 4 (1995): 921–22.

_____. "Education, Globalization and Catch-Up: Scandinavia in the Swedish Mirror." *Scandinavian Economic History Review* 43, no. 3 (1995): 287–309.

_____. "Open Economy Forces and Late 19th Century Scandinavian Catch-Up." *HIER Discussion Paper* no. 1709. Cambridge, Massachusetts (January, 1995).

Rogowski, Ronald. *Commerce and Coalitions: How Trade Affects Domestic Political Arrangements.* Princeton, NJ: Princeton University Press, 1989.

Schonhardt-Bailey, Cheryl. "Specific Factors, Capital Markets, Portfolio Diversification, and Free Trade: Domestic Determinants of the Repeal of the Corn Laws." *World Politics* 43, no. 4 (1991): 545–69.

Temin, Peter. "Labor Scarcity and the Problem of American Industrial Efficiency in the 1850's." this JOURNAL 26, no. 3 (1966): 277–98.

Verdier, Daniel. *Democracy and International Trade: Britain, France, and the United States, 1860–1990.* Princeton: Princeton University Press, 1994.

Webb, Steven B. "Agricultural Protection in Wilhelminian Germany: Forging an Empire with Pork and Rye." this JOURNAL 42, no. 2 (1982): 309–26.

Webb, Walter Prescott. *The Great Frontier.* Austin, Texas: University of Texas Press, 1952.

Williamson, Jeffrey G. "The Impact of the Corn Laws Just Prior to Repeal." *Explorations in Economic History* 27, no. 2 (1990): 123–56.

[14]

Immigration Policy Prior to the 1930s: Labor Markets, Policy Interactions, and Globalization Backlash

ASHLEY S. TIMMER
JEFFREY G. WILLIAMSON

AFTER THE 1870s, New World doors gradually closed to immigrants. Although much of the literature has focused on the drastic policy changes in the period just after World War I, the doors did not suddenly slam shut on American immigrants when the United States Congress overrode President Woodrow Wilson's veto of the immigrant literacy test in February 1917 or when it passed the Emergency Quota Act of May 1921. A half-century before the Literacy Act, the United States started imposing restrictions on what had been free immigration, and the United States was not the only country becoming less receptive to immigrants. Argentina, Australia, Brazil, and Canada enacted new measures, although the timing varied, and the policies often took the form of a large drop in or even disappearance of immigrant subsidies rather than outright exclusion of immigrants. Immigration policy varied considerably across these five countries over the period from 1860 to 1930, the conventional portrayal of one big policy switch around World War I to the contrary.

What was true of immigration policy was also true of trade policy. Globalization proceeded in fits and starts after 1846 when Britain repealed the Corn Laws and started a liberal trend toward free trade. It took the form of mass migrations, a trade surge, and international capital flows at (relative) levels never reached before or since.[1] The liberal trend did not last long, however, in the face of a globalization backlash. Tariffs started to rise on the European continent. Restrictions on immigration and trade started to rise in the New World. With the end of World War I, the world economy plunged into a dark age of de-globalization and policy antagonism toward factor and goods mobility.

What explains the globalization backlash? A number of candidates have been nominated in the case of immigration policy. Economists have suggested that immigrants crowded out native unskilled workers and contributed to rising inequality in labor-scarce economies, as did free trade. The policy reaction may also have reflected the greater voting power in the hands of those hurt most—the working poor. Possible noneconomic factors include increasing racism, xenophobia, and widening ethnicity gaps between the population stock and the current immigrant flow. The increase in immigrant flows, "lower-quality" immigrants, and the threat of even lower-quality immigrants may have provided further impetus to close the doors.

There have been few attempts to introduce these factors into explicit models of immigration policy formation.[2] This article uses what little theory exists to identify the fundamental factors that underlie changes in immigration policy and to clarify the differences between market and nonmarket influences. In addition, the article explores the extent to which policy responded to the impact of immigrants on labor markets, and the extent to which it tried instead to anticipate those impacts by reacting to the quantity and quality of immigrants.

Finally, the article assesses the impact of policies abroad on policies at home. Which countries were most sensitive to immigration policies elsewhere in the New World, and to what extent did the largest among them, the United States, set the pace for the rest? Trade policy over this period was clearly an interactive game, as countries sought to respond to escalating tariffs elsewhere. But little has been said about how other New World destinations reacted to increasing immigration restrictions by the United States, or, for that matter, how they responded to the push of emigrants out of the United Kingdom. We seek to examine the degree to which one country's immigration policy may have been influenced by the policies of others.

Measuring immigration policy

Having set a goal to calibrate the determinants of immigration policy, we must construct a measure that can quantify the policy in the New World. Such a measure is necessary if we hope to assess the extent to which globalization backlash was at work and to identify the form that it took. We have designed an index of immigration (and in one case, emigration) policy that will be used to confront a set of competing hypotheses. The index is likely to be subject to the same criticism as those used to measure trade openness (Anderson and Neary 1994; Sachs and Warner 1995). We recognize that a subjective component to the index remains, but we have tried to use a consistent algorithm.

The index ranges over a scale of +5 to −5. A positive score denotes a pro-immigration policy, possibly including comprehensive subsidies for passage and for support upon arrival. A negative score denotes anti-immigration policy, possibly including quotas, literacy tests, and legal discriminatory treatment after arrival. A zero denotes policy neutrality, or a neutral outcome between conflicting pro- and anti-immigration policies. A policy can have two functions: first, to signal to groups that their interests are being tended to and second, to change the status quo. Clearly, political agents were trying to affect the flow of immigrants and to respond to their constituencies. Policies were not always effective, but the goal here is to capture the intention, or political signal. The following algorithm was the basis for our assigning scores, and we use it consistently across countries and over time:

5   Active worker recruitment abroad with advertising and labor offices, free land or subsidized land purchase, subsidized or assisted passage, temporary lodging, free transport inland from port of arrival, easy naturalization, legal property ownership.

4   Free or subsidized land, immigration treaties or contracts with shipping companies, lodging, worker recruitment, easy naturalization, legal property ownership.

3   Overseas immigration offices, debarkation coordination, land designated for settlement, easy naturalization, legal property ownership.

2   Overseas immigration offices, debarkation coordination, easy naturalization, legal property ownership.

1   Modest advertising, easy naturalization, legal property ownership.

0   Open doors, no encouragement, no discouragement. Or, a balance of pro-immigration and anti-immigrant policies.

−1   Regulations on shipping companies and/or contracts for assisted passage.

−2   Class restrictions on immigration (no paupers, potential wards of the state, criminals) or selective source-country bans (e.g., no Asians).

−3   The above restrictions plus laws for registration, deportation provisions, laws restricting property ownership, unenforced selectivity laws (such as literacy tests).

−4   Restrictive quotas, enforced literacy tests, or other measures designed to reduce immigration volume significantly.

−5   Closed (or only slightly ajar) doors, enforced.

Several complications repeatedly arose in assigning scores to policy. Canada, Australia, and the United States all enacted legislation against Asian immigration, even while encouraging (or at least not discouraging) immigration from Europe. At some points, all three countries had a set of policies that sent a mixed message to both potential immigrants and constituents. Whenever we found a mix of pro-immigration and anti-immigration policies, we simply added up the positive and negative attributes to get an overall score. Since a source-country ban on immigration was generally scored –2, and subsidy and recruitment programs were generally scored +3, Canada received a net score of +1 around the turn of the century. Similarly, in the early twentieth century, Australia recruited and subsidized immigration but also required a dictation test on demand, and we scored this mix a 0 for several years. Because of the mix of policies, we allowed half-steps in the scoring. Appendix B uses United States experience to illustrate the scoring, but the full details for all countries can be found elsewhere (Timmer and Williamson 1996: Appendix C). To assess the impact of Empire settlement plans, we also scored the emigration policy of the United Kingdom, using a parallel algorithm.

These policy indexes, plotted in Figure 1, confirm that whereas immigration in the 1860s was generally unrestricted, the doors to the New World were effectively closed by 1930. But in the intervening decades, the trends were less clear. Argentina started on a path of increasing openness and pro-immigration subsidies, but reversed the policy in the 1880s, and the index dropped from +4.5 to –2.5 by the 1920s. Brazil's index underwent a similar path, although the anti-immigrant legislation all came in a rush at the end of the period. Australia's index fell from +3 in the mid-1860s to –1 shortly after the turn of the century, and to –2 in 1930, but exhibited short episodes of more open policies, especially in the 1920s. Canada's index behaved similarly. The United States index fell from 0 in the early 1860s to –5 by 1930, and it was the only country never to have a major policy reversal over the period. Thus, while the United States exhibited a steady drift away from free immigration, the others closed their doors in fits and starts.

Although there are some cases of substantial short-term variance, as in Australia between 1890 and 1930, strong policy persistence is the norm. Policy was slow to change, sometimes constant over a decade or more, even though intensive political debate often accompanied the apparent quiescence. The best examples of this stability are Brazil over the three decades from 1890 to 1920, a period that ended in 1921 when immigration restrictions were imposed, and the United States from 1888 to 1916, a period that ended with the override of President Wilson's veto of the legislation introducing an immigrant literacy test in 1917.

The literature offers several explanations of the evolution of immigration policy from the middle of the nineteenth century to the Great Depression.

Models of immigration policy

Formal models of immigration policy are few, but there is a general consensus that immigration policy has always been sensitive to labor market

ASHLEY S. TIMMER / JEFFREY G. WILLIAMSON **743**

FIGURE 1 POLICY: An immigration policy index

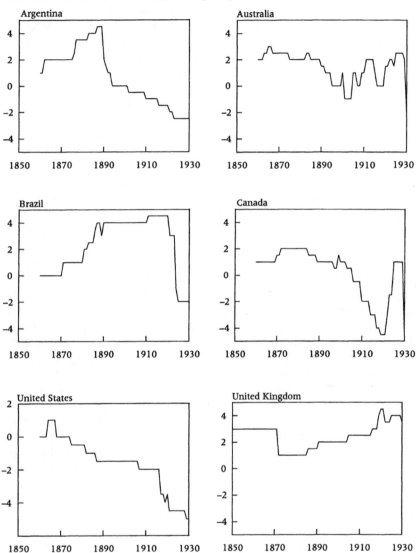

NOTE: The index ranges over a scale of +5 to –5. A positive score denotes a pro-immigration policy, a negative score an anti-immigration policy. See text for further explanation.

conditions,[3] and that immigration itself has always been sensitive to wage and unemployment rate differentials between countries. For example, Claudia Goldin (1994) notes that in the United States in the late 1890s, during a time of economic recession and high unemployment, there was a new push for immigration restrictions. At that time, however, the rate of immigration slowed markedly, reaching a low in 1897, the same year that the first vote on immigration restriction was taken in the House of Representatives. Similarly, Australian inflows dropped sharply in the recession of the 1890s when attitudes inimical to immigrant subsidies hardened (Pope and Withers 1994). These observations suggest that the impetus to restrict immigration was far more sensitive to labor market conditions than to immigration levels.

To complicate matters, the ethnic composition of immigrants was clearly a factor in the politics of restriction. Australia maintained a strict policy aimed at keeping the country one of British and Irish descent, while avoiding persons of "yellow" skin (Pope and Withers 1994). The United States completely banned immigrants from China in 1882 and immigrants from all of Asia in 1917 (Green 1995). Increasing demands for restriction in the 1880s and 1900s paralleled an increase in the relative numbers of immigrants from southern, central, and eastern Europe, the so-called new immigrants. It is difficult to sort out whether these policies were a result of racism and xenophobia or whether ethnic origin merely served to signal, however imperfectly, the human capital content or "quality" of the immigrants (Foreman-Peck 1992).[4] If countries were sensitive to the source of immigrants, this further suggests that there might be competition among them for those of higher quality, or competition to keep out those of lower quality. Did Argentina, for example, have to subsidize immigration in order to attract better immigrants? Were they successful in doing so?

As James Foreman-Peck (1992) notes, the two central questions for any model of immigration policy formation are: Who gains and who loses? Who decides the policy? Consensus is clear regarding the first question. Wage earners—unskilled workers in particular—lose with immigration, as the labor pool swells and wages sag. Owners of other factors of production—land, capital, and perhaps even skills—gain from the more abundant unskilled labor supply that makes these other factors more productive. We hasten to add two caveats. While most attempts to measure the impact of mass migration on wages prior to 1914 have found that wages were downwardly sensitive to immigration (Williamson 1974; Taylor and Williamson 1997; Green 1994; Goldin 1994; Hatton and Williamson 1995; Williamson 1996), a study of Australia found that wages actually increased with immigration, if only marginally (Pope and Withers 1994). The Australian result could be explained if immigrants augmented labor demand enough to offset their impact on increased labor supply (for example, by working previously unsettled land or by inducing an accumulation response as capital from the home country chased after labor). If labor demand keeps pace with labor supply, then native labor is not hurt by immigration.

The second caveat concerns disequilibriums in the labor market, when the impact of immigration on wages is unclear. The issue of unemployment has not really been examined in the context of immigration policy, but suppose wages are sticky downward and unrelated to the size of the unemployment pool, perhaps for efficiency reasons or "fairness."[5] In such a situation, immigration will not have any effect on wages, but it will add to the numbers unemployed. No one benefits from immigration: capitalists do not gain by a fall in wages, and the number of unemployed increases. Eventually, both sides might unite in favor of immigration restrictions. Goldin (1994) suggests that this aligning of interests occurred in the United States during the 1890s. Note, however, that the impact of an economic downturn on native unemployment should have been partially muted by immigrant behavior, as recent (but now jobless) immigrants returned home—that is, immigrants themselves did voluntarily what a policy of immigrant restriction would have done.[6] This they did in great numbers, but not great enough to make the "guestworker effect" operate with much quantitative muscle, even during that critical depression decade of the 1890s (Hatton and Williamson 1995); while the US unemployment rate was reduced a bit by return migration in the 1890s, the reduction was a modest share of the total unemployment rate.

These two caveats aside, most discussions of the politics of immigration assume that the interests of capital and labor are divided. As such, the immigration literature should be closely aligned with theories of long-run interest groups in trade policy. The parallels between trade and immigration policy are discussed at length in our previous article (Timmer and Williamson 1995) so here we focus only on immigration policy.

In addition to the capital–labor divide, Foreman-Peck (1992) argues that land ownership might have mattered, especially in the late nineteenth century when agriculture was still a large sector of the economy.[7] He takes the following approach. Assume that individuals receive their incomes from one of the following three sources: wages, profits, or land rents. Depending on the franchise, the government maximizes a weighted objective function that includes rents, profits, and wages of native labor. The critical question is whether immigrant and native labor are complements or substitutes in production: if they are substitutes, then immigration hurts wages of the natives. Estimating a production function, Foreman-Peck concludes that they were substitutes in the late-nineteenth-century US economy. Thus, the larger the weight on labor interests, the more restrictive the immigration policy. The reverse is true as the political system attaches larger weights to the interest of capital or land.

Foreman-Peck allows for the possibility of two types of immigrants: skilled and unskilled. It might be that skilled immigrant labor was a complement to domestic labor, whereas unskilled immigrant labor was a substitute. We would then expect to see a policy that encouraged the immigration of skilled and discouraged the immigration of unskilled workers. Foreman-Peck argues that this concern about unskilled labor, and not racism or xenophobia, was responsible for policies in the Americas that restricted Asian immigration and for policies in South Africa that restricted African immigration.

Although Foreman-Peck does not implement a formal empirical test, his discussion of Argentina, Britain, South Africa, and the United States indicates that some of the historical facts are consistent with his theory. For example, landed interests were largely in control of immigration policy in Argentina and the government offered generous subsidies to attract farm laborers from the Mediterranean Basin. In contrast, the United States had a more universal voting franchise, rejected subsidies, and gradually closed the door as the frontier itself was closed (by 1890, or so said the Census Commissioner at that time).

Goldin (1994) takes a different approach. Following a long tradition in American historiography that has focused on sectional interests, she looks at regional splits and rural–urban differences. Although she does not model the relationship formally, she assumes that individual US Senators and Representatives advocate policies that favor their constituents, in proportion to the numbers represented by each urban, rural, and regional interest group. The passage of the literacy test, which was first attempted in 1897 and was finally successful in 1917, seems to have been the result of two (often opposing) forces: demographic changes and changes of heart. The changes of heart were many. Goldin suggests that capitalists were for the first time aligned with labor in opposing immigration during the recessionary years of the 1890s when unemployment was high. Later, during times of full employment and rising wages, capital shifted back to its more traditional pro-immigration stance, but the South adopted an anti-immigration stance, a change of heart probably motivated by the urge to protect its relative population share and voting clout. Finally, the northern Midwest, fairly pro-immigration in the 1890s, underwent an anti-immigration switch following World War I. Goldin argues that this was mostly a change of heart by older immigrant groups, pushed to patriotism by the war.

The political impact of the change in North–South demographic composition was offset by the changing composition of the cities. Goldin finds that the probability that a legislator would vote for immigration restrictions was negatively related to the proportion of foreign-born in the district and was also negatively related to the level of urbanization. This relationship suggests that efforts of what we might now call family reunification were operating in the cities, and since cities were on the rise pro-immigration interests increasingly made themselves heard.

More important than either of these nonmarket influences, however, was the impact of increasing immigration on wages and the subsequent effect on votes. Especially after the turn of the century, Goldin finds a significant negative impact of immigration on wages, a result consistent with other historical studies (Hatton and Williamson 1998). The change in real wages is, in turn, a significant explanatory variable in accounting for the Congressional vote to override the presidential veto of the literacy test in 1915. The higher the growth in wages, the less likely was the Representative to vote for an override (and thus for restriction).

These two findings of Goldin's research—that wages influenced US immigration policy and that immigrants influenced wages in American labor markets—are useful in our comparative assessment of immigration policy in the New World. However, we only require that politicians and their constituents *believed* that immigration retarded wage advance. It appears that they did.

William Shughart, Robert Tollison, and Mwangi Kimenyi (1986) look at shifting degrees of enforcement of immigration restrictions. Workers want high wages, and they pressure politicians to enforce immigration restrictions. Capitalists and landowners want lower wages, and they try to reduce enforcement. Their model predicts that as the economy goes through business cycles, the ideal policy mix shifts, resulting in changes in the degree of enforcement against immigration. The authors test the model using data from the United States from 1900 to 1982, and the results are supportive. Even taking into account official changes in immigration policy, the size of the enforcement budget, and the political party in the White House, the degree of enforcement is significantly, and negatively, related to real GNP. Unemployment and the real wage were also significant explanatory variables, but not so consistently as real GNP. Had the authors looked at US policy toward indentured labor contracts prior to 1900, they would have seen the same correlation: harsh policy during slumps; soft policy during booms.

The three studies discussed above are the only ones to offer empirical support for theories of immigration policy.[8] All three address the role of labor markets, but they limit their attention to absolute gains and losses resulting from immigration, ignoring the relative effects. Recently, a renewed interest in distributional questions has developed among those studying the consequences of migration. Immigrants can create more inequality in the country of destination and less inequality in the country of origin. The empirical literature on this issue has grown voluminous in a short time, perhaps because the consequences of immigration have gained prominence on the American political scene. The debate began over the impact of immigration in the United States (Borjas 1994), expanded to consider European immigration (Freeman 1995), and spilled over into the issue of outmigration from developing countries (Wood 1994). The distributional impact of migration has even been confirmed for the late nineteenth cen-

tury, with the demonstration that inequality increased in the receiving countries and decreased in the sending countries (Williamson 1997).

There is not yet consensus (or much theory) on how these distributional consequences will affect immigration policy. Consider the impact of
immigration on future economic growth. It is true that a labor-scarce country will do better to allow immigration than to allow the export of capital,
thus becoming more populous rather than less so (Cheng and Wong 1990).
But if immigration induces falling wages or greater inequality, and if, as a
consequence, the median voter becomes too poor, then citizens might vote
for distortionary redistributive policies that can slow growth. Inequality
may also lead to political instability, which can slow growth. While all of
these assertions may sound plausible, economists have yet to identify un-
ambiguously the impact of inequality on growth.[9]

There are other models of income distribution and policy formation
that do not depend on a link to economic optimization. For example, citizens might vote for restriction on immigration simply because they dislike
increased inequality and the lower living standards of their unskilled neighbors (Luttmer 1997). Or, changes in income distribution might tip the balance of political power among competing interest groups, leading to changes
in immigration policy (Timmer 1996). Jess Benhabib (1996) suggests that
the distribution of capital and labor among voters will, from the perspective of the median voter, affect the skill mix of an ideal immigrant. A relatively capital-rich median voter will prefer a less-skilled immigrant; a relatively labor-rich voter prefers a capital-rich, skilled immigrant.

A menu of hypotheses

This brief review of the literature offers several promising hypotheses that
we organize here around a set of explanatory variables. Details of the variables and their sources can be found in Appendix A.

First, immigration policy might respond to either the quantity or the
quality of immigration, or both. The size of the immigrant flow as a share
of the native labor force is one obvious variable, although the experience
of the 1890s has already suggested that labor market conditions might have
mattered far more than size of flow. The quality of the immigrants is another candidate, measured in comparison with the native labor force. The
vast majority of immigrants came from and entered unskilled jobs. Some
had good health, high levels of literacy, numeracy, on-the-job training,
and considerable exposure to work discipline. Other immigrants did not.
Quality and quantity were highly correlated prior to World War I: the switch
of emigrant source from higher-wage to lower-wage areas of Europe correlated with the rise in immigration rates. It is likely that these two effects
reinforced each other in their impact on policy. A variable that combines

the rising quantity of immigration with the falling quality might do better than the two measures of quantity and quality in competition with each other.

Second, immigration policy might respond to labor market conditions. This possibility can be sharpened by distinguishing between short-run timing and long-run fundamentals of policy. Unemployment, wage growth, and other macro indicators should serve to isolate the role of business cycles, trade crises, world price shocks, and other short-run events that might affect the timing of changes in immigration policy. In addition, the use of lagged dependent variables should help to ascertain how slowly policy responds to long-run labor market fundamentals.

We expect labor market fundamentals to be captured by unskilled real wages—a measure of absolute performance—or by unskilled wages relative to income of the average citizen—a measure of relative performance. The latter is a measure that gauges the unskilled worker's economic performance against that of the average: it is a measure of inequality that politicians and voters could easily see and understand. The validity of these variables does not require that immigration was the key force driving the living standards of the working poor in the New World. It requires only that politicians and voters believed that immigration was a powerful influence on living standards. Whether it was the absolute or the relative performance that mattered is an empirical issue, but Figure 2 suggests that the inequality variable is likely to do well, especially in the cases of Argentina, Canada, and the United States.

Third, a country's immigration policy may have been influenced by the immigration policies of other countries, either directly or indirectly. If the country anticipates the influence of immigration policies abroad on immigration inflows at home, the effect is direct. Since the labor market in the United States was so large relative to the rest of the New World, and since so many European emigrants went there,[10] it is unlikely that the United States paid much attention to immigration policies being introduced elsewhere. Australia may have been more concerned with British Empire settlement policy than with United States policy. Argentina and Brazil, meanwhile, must have paid close attention to United States policy since they could reasonably expect the marginal European emigrant (for example, southern Italian emigrants) to be pulled from or pushed toward Latin America in response to less or more restrictive policy in the United States. Authorities might have moderated those changes by mimicking United States policy before being confronted with the actual migrant response. The same might have been true of Canada, which, in spite of British Empire settlement policy, had to accommodate a long porous border with its big neighbor to the south.

Fourth, nonmarket forces probably remain after these market forces have been allowed to have their impact. After controlling for immigrant

FIGURE 2   The inequality and immigration policy correlation

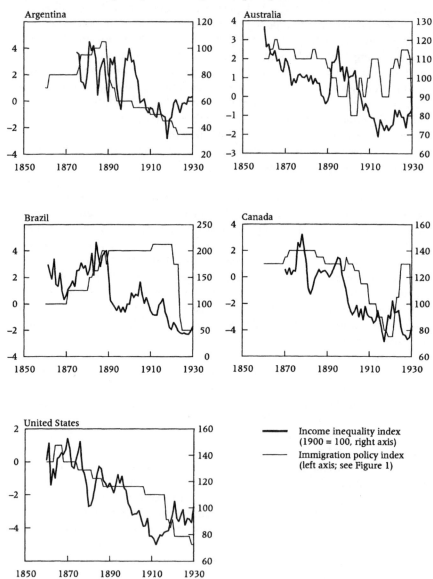

NOTE: Higher inequality index indicates less inequality.

quality, did racism have an independent influence? Did differences in ethnicity matter? Did the political response to market events change as the
working poor found their political power increasing?

Empirical tests

Since our interest is in long-run fundamentals, we smooth the policy index exponentially, and call the converted index *polism*.[11] The converted index should do better in isolating the underlying fundamentals affecting policy in contrast with the timing of policy change. We estimate policy equations to identify the impact of market and nonmarket forces. Was policy driven by labor market conditions or by ethnic concerns? Was the reaction to a rising immigrant flood everywhere the same in the New World? With the policy equations estimated, we then use them to identify the sources of policy change.

Time series results

Overall, the empirical findings are quite satisfying. Table 1 reports results using a lagged dependent variable (that is, a lagged policy index for the country in question), while Table 2 reports results where the policies of other countries replace the lagged dependent variable.

There are no variables in the tables that measure political environment. We cannot find evidence that changing political institutions and franchises systematically affected the degree and direction of policy change. We tried two measures of political openness: an index of democratic characteristics and a measure of competitiveness in political participation, both constructed by Ted Gurr (1990). Although these variables might be significant in explaining policy differences across countries, they are not important in explaining policy shifts within countries.[12] This result is probably due to the fact that significant political change was minor in our time series.

The most consistent effect emerging from Table 1 is that immigration policy is slow to change. The lagged dependent variable is highly significant in all countries. This is especially true of Brazil and the United States, but the result is driven by the 1888-1916 period in the United States and by the 1890–1920 period in Brazil. These two episodes of persistence were followed by a major switch in policy, from open to closed. Big policy switches often required long periods of debate. This was not always true, however, as can be seen by the major switch in Argentina's policy over only five years, 1889–94.

We have introduced variables with differing lags. Labor market and immigration variables were usually lagged two periods—an indicator of legislative delay—while economic conditions were taken as current. These measures of current macroeconomic conditions—growth in real GDP per capita (*ypcgrr*) and unemployment (*unemp2*)—did not prove consistently useful in accounting for policy change: macroeconomic conditions mattered in Australia, but not in Canada and the United States, and they took the wrong sign in Brazil. Thus, Australia offers the only evidence that these

TABLE 1   Explaining immigration policy using lagged dependent variables: Ordinary least squares; dependent variable is immigration policy, POLISM

	Argentina	Brazil	Australia	Canada	United States
Labor market effects					
Nominal wages/ GDP per capita WTOY(−1)	0.003 (0.547)				
Nominal wages/ GDP per capita WTOY(−2)		0.005* (1.773)			
Nominal wages/ GDP per capita WTOY(−4)				0.015** (2.460)	0.005* (1.973)
Nominal wages WAGEN(−2)			0.004* (1.903)		
Real wages WAGER(−2)		0.007* (1.698)			
Change in real wage growth D(WGRR(−2))					1.407* (1.677)
Economic conditions					
Growth in real GDP per capita YPCGRR	−1.044* (−1.913)	3.452** (2.565)			
Unemployment rate UNEMP2		−0.034*** (−3.104)			
Immigrant effects					
% foreign population FORPOP(−2)	−4.740** (−2.425)				
Change in % foreign population D(FORPOP(−2))			−18.405* (−1.741)		
Average wages at immigrant origin IMWAGE(−2)				0.031** (2.468)	
Change in immigrant wages D(IMWAGE(−2))			0.028** (2.379)		0.015** (2.005)
Brazilian relative wages BRWTOY(−1)	0.011** (2.291)				
Brazilian real wage growth BRWGRR	0.862** (2.341)				
Lagged dependent variable					
POLISM(−1)	0.677*** (4.413)	0.953*** (24.592)	0.761*** (9.842)	0.874*** (17.582)	0.957*** (29.839)
Constant	−0.327 (−0.530)	−1.116* (−1.686)	−0.341 (−1.088)	−4.018*** (−2.958)	−0.704** (−2.138)
No. of observations	54	68	70	57	70
Mean dependent variable	0.362	2.385	1.485	0.050	−1.649
R-squared	0.971	0.924	0.809	0.909	0.972
Adjusted R-squared	0.967	0.919	0.791	0.904	0.970
Log likelihood	−27.430	−63.164	−52.495	−55.548	−6.249
Durbin–Watson	1.691	1.589	1.948	2.098	1.386
F-statistic	316.527	192.143	44.570	176.309	555.669

(t-statistics in parentheses; White-corrected standard errors) (*** significant at the .01 level; ** at the .05 level; * at the .1 level)
NOTE: POLISM is the POLICY variable smoothed using exponential weights selected by TSP software.

macroeconomic conditions were critical in shaping the timing of policy change.

Did labor market conditions have a consistent influence on immigration policy? And if so, was it the absolute or relative income performance of unskilled workers that mattered? It appears to have been both. The change in real wage growth of the urban unskilled (*dwgrr*) mattered most in the United States, nominal wages (*wagen*) mattered most in Australia, while real wage levels (*wager*) mattered most in Brazil.[13] But apart from the lagged dependent variable, the most significant influence on policy is the ratio of the unskilled wage to per capita income, or of income near the bottom of the distribution to the average (*wtoy*). This measure of unskilled labor's relative economic position stands up as an important influence on policy in the United States, Canada, and Brazil, regardless of what else is included in the equation—including real wage growth, real wage levels, unemployment, and attributes of the immigrants. The variable is not significant for Argentina and Australia. But for the other countries, high unskilled wages relative to average income correlate with more open immigration policies, and the correlation is significant; greater relative scarcity of unskilled labor encouraged less restrictive policy; declining relative scarcity of unskilled labor encouraged more restrictive policy.

So far, we have looked at the indirect impact of immigration on policy by exploring labor market performance.[14] Perhaps the size and character of the current and expected future immigrant flow precipitated policy change, the latter serving to anticipate the labor market impact. Two variables measure these direct immigration effects. First, the quality, or human capital content, of the immigrants is proxied by the real wage of unskilled urban workers in the source countries (*imwage*). Changes in that proxy were important for Australia. Second, we use measures of both the current flow—the immigration rate (*imrate*)—and the cumulative stock—the share of foreign-born within the total population (*forpop*). The immigration rate never proved to be a helpful explanatory variable, but the share of foreign-born did matter for Argentina and Australia. Higher immigrant quality or rising immigrant quality tended to precipitate more open immigrant policy in Australia, Canada, and the United States. More to the point, low and falling immigrant quality precipitated immigrant restriction, even after controlling for other forces. To some extent, therefore, policy in these countries anticipated the impact of low-quality immigrants on unskilled wages and moved to eliminate such immigration. In addition, Argentina seems to have looked to the north across the Rio de la Plata to watch labor market conditions in Brazil, acting as if they knew those conditions could divert immigrants to or from Argentina's borders, either by immigrant responses to these relative labor market conditions or by their responses to likely policy changes in Brazil. Thus, rising relative unskilled wages and rising absolute wages in Brazil tended to produce more open policy in Argentina. This result is consistent with the estimated policy spillovers reported in Table 2, results that we discuss below.

We also explored the impact of a variable that measured the difference in ethnic composition between the current immigration flow and the population stock (*gap*), but it was never significant. The literature had led us to expect that a rising gap between the ethnic origins of the population stock and the new immigrants would erode commitments to free immigration. In Table 2 Brazil offers some weak support for this view, but the effect does not appear elsewhere.

To what extent was a change in a country's policy a reaction to policy changes abroad? The results appear in Table 2, where the lagged dependent variable is replaced by migration policy changes abroad. As expected, the United States—the New World immigration leader—was not responsive to competitors' policies. Nor, for that matter, was Canada, a surprising result that seems to confirm Canadian success in shielding its labor market from the eastern and southern European exodus to North America. For the other countries, policy abroad mattered greatly. For Argentina, it was the combined impact of Australian, Canadian, and Brazilian policy that mattered, more restrictive policy abroad inducing more restrictive policy at home. Brazil tended to mimic the policies followed in Argentina and the United States, although it also exhibited that puzzling inverse response to policy change found in Australia and Canada.[15] Australia, in turn, was more likely to favor open immigration policies when the United Kingdom offered more generous subsidies to its emigrants, and also when the United States was more open.

While the size of the immigrant flow did not have any consistent impact on New World policy up to 1930, its low and declining quality certainly did, provoking restriction. Racism or xenophobia does not seem to have been at work. Rather, immigrant quality, labor market conditions, and policies abroad—especially those set by the economic leaders, Britain and the United States—mattered most. New World countries acted in an effort to defend the economic interests of domestic unskilled labor.

Policy spillovers on immigrant destination by quantity and quality

Table 3 elaborates on the issues already raised in Table 2, namely, how policies adopted in one part of the New World influenced immigrant flows to other parts of the New World. The dependent variable in Table 3 is a given country's share of that year's five-country immigration flow. As we might have expected from Table 2, policies abroad hardly mattered at all for the United States. That is, the US share of immigration did not depend

TABLE 2 Explaining immigration policy using cross-country policy responses: Ordinary least squares; dependent variable is immigration policy, POLISM

	Argentina	Brazil	Australia	Canada	United States
Labor market effects					
Real wages WAGER(-2)	-0.034*** (-4.246)	0.059*** (10.260)			
Nominal wages WAGEN(-2)			0.031*** (5.618)		
Nominal wages/GDP per capita WTOY(-2)	0.017* (1.941)	-0.024*** (-3.940)			
Nominal wages/GDP per capita WTOY(-4)				0.051*** (3.447)	0.031*** (3.810)
Real wage growth WGRR					4.730 (1.390)
Economic conditions					
Unemployment UNEMP2			-0.061*** (-4.738)	-0.045*** (-2.885)	
Growth in GDP per capita YPCGRR			2.720* (1.797)		
Immigrant effects					
% foreign population FORPOP(-2)	-19.447*** (-6.476)				
Immigrant–native ethnicity gap GAP(-2)		-4.146 (-1.626)			
Skill-weighted immigration rate THREAT(-2)				-0.649* (-1.687)	
Policy spillovers					
Argentine policy ARPOLISM(-2)		1.038*** (8.301)		0.002 (0.017)	0.213* (1.711)
Australian policy AUPOLISM(-2)	0.480*** (4.773)	-0.960*** (-7.583)		-0.022 (-0.105)	-0.050 (-0.327)
Brazilian policy BRPOLISM(-2)	0.401*** (4.153)				0.068 (0.654)
Canadian policy CAPOLISM(-2)	0.328*** (5.369)	-0.635*** (-9.728)	-0.002 (-0.032)		0.120 (1.055)
US policy USPOLISM(-2)		0.531*** (3.743)	0.681*** (5.614)	-0.120 (-0.360)	
British policy UKPOLISM(-2)			0.186* (1.848)	-0.395 (-0.891)	-0.107 (-0.475)
Constant	4.262*** (6.484)	1.499 (1.626)	-1.828*** (-3.714)	-3.649* (-1.916)	-5.285*** (-4.963)
No. of observations	54	68	69	57	69
Mean dependent variable	0.278	2.385	1.480	0.050	-1.673
R-squared	0.913	0.815	0.626	0.769	0.635
Adjusted R-squared	0.901	0.794	0.590	0.731	0.593
Log likelihood	-57.300	-93.498	-75.422	-82.013	-94.225
Durbin–Watson	0.991	0.943	0.877	0.878	0.242
F-statistic	81.735	37.790	17.309	20.029	15.129

(t-statistics in parentheses; White-corrected standard errors) (*** significant at the .01 level; ** at the .05 level; * at the .1 level)

TABLE 3   Policy spillovers on immigrant destination: Ordinary least squares; dependent variable is the share of immigrants arriving at destination (IMMPCT)

	Argentina	Brazil	Canada	Australia	United States
Policy spillovers					
Argentine policy					0.011
ARPOLISM					(1.497)
Australian policy			−0.007*		0.005
AUPOLISM			(−1.726)		(0.390)
Brazilian policy			−0.003	−0.005**	0.004
BRPOLISM			(−1.413)	(−2.387)	(0.491)
Canadian policy				−0.004*	0.004
CAPOLISM				(−1.984)	(0.516)
US policy	−0.010***	−0.005	−0.004	−0.003	
USPOLISM	(−2.991)	(−1.422)	(−1.150)	(−1.493)	
Lagged dependent variable					
Immigrant share	0.537***	0.711***	0.744***	0.638***	0.632***
IMMPCT(−1)	(5.443)	(8.391)	(8.125)	(7.256)	(6.469)
Constant	0.033***	0.017*	0.043***	0.031***	0.207***
	(3.557)	(1.808)	(3.184)	(2.911)	(2.959)
No. of observations	69	69	69	69	69
Mean dependent variable	0.102	0.086	0.108	0.065	0.639
R-squared	0.562	0.556	0.643	0.725	0.597
Adjusted R-squared	0.549	0.542	0.620	0.708	0.565
Log likelihood	134.302	119.532	140.170	166.176	78.201
Durbin–Watson	1.886	2.396	1.613	1.607	1.846
F-statistic	42.406	41.314	28.767	42.138	18.660

(t-statistics in parentheses) (*** significant at the .01 level; ** at the .05 level; * at the .1 level)

on the policies elsewhere. But for the other destinations, more open immigration policies abroad reduced one's share of arrivals. For example, Australia's openness decreased flows to Canada, Brazil's pro-immigrant subsidies reduced flows to Australia, and Argentina saw an increased share of the immigrant pie as the United States closed its doors. The impact of policy spillovers is significant but small, due to the stickiness of both policy and immigration patterns.

Table 3 explores the impact of policy abroad on the distribution of immigrant destinations, while Table 4 explores the impact on immigrant quality. The quality proxy is a weighted average of (urban) unskilled wages prevailing in the sending regions at various points in time. Table 4 shows that the lagged dependent variable and policy choices in other countries account for more than 80 percent of the variance in the quality measure. When US policy became more restrictive, immigrant quality rose everywhere else. Immigrants favored the United States, so that when the United

TABLE 4 Policy spillovers on immigrant quality: Ordinary least squares; dependent variable is the quality of immigrants (IMWAGE)

	Argentina	Brazil	Canada	Australia	United States
Policy spillovers					
Argentine policy		0.256	0.691		
ARPOLICY		(0.657)	(1.645)		
Brazilian policy	0.435*		0.008		-1.114***
BRPOLICY	(1.814)		(0.030)		(-2.955)
Canadian policy	-0.891**	-1.125***		0.135	-0.667**
CAPOLICY	(-2.977)	(-2.948)		(0.344)	(-2.351)
US policy	-1.729***	-1.632**	-3.123***	-1.251**	
USPOLICY	(-3.071)	(-2.536)	(-3.734)	(-2.007)	
Lagged dependent variable					
Average wages at immigrant origin	0.564***	0.655***	0.673***	0.845***	0.790***
IMWAGE(-1)	(6.672)	(7.679)	(8.047)	(14.548)	(10.963)
Constant	17.917***	14.024***	18.674***	10.512***	17.194***
	(5.428)	(3.901)	(3.699)	(2.645)	(3.070)
No. of observations	71	-69	71	71	71
Mean dependent variable	46.907	48.932	72.799	77.987	68.313
R-squared	0.891	0.888	0.867	0.883	0.853
Adjusted R-squared	0.885	0.881	0.859	0.878	0.847
Log likelihood	-186.894	-191.023	-207.621	-213.240	-201.135
Durbin–Watson	1.754	1.881	1.573	1.683	2.082

(t-statistics in parentheses) (*** significant at the .01 level; ** at the .05 level; * at the .1 level)

States became more restrictive, the other countries got rejects of higher quality than they would have received otherwise. The same was true of restrictive Canadian policy, for Argentina, Brazil, and the United States. Even the United States found its immigrant quality falling as Brazil subsidized immigration more heavily: that is, as Brazil increased subsidies, the United States lost some high-quality immigrants. Similarly, the United States seemed to benefit from more restrictive Canadian policy (often taking the form of lower subsidies), just as Canada benefited from more restrictive US policy. Interestingly, Argentina may have benefited from aggressive subsidy programs in Brazil. Perhaps higher-quality immigrants, arriving in Brazil under subsidy plans, found conditions unsatisfactory and moved over the border to Argentina.

Quantifying the sources of policy change

Using the estimates from Table 1, Table 5 reports how much each variable contributed to closing the immigrant door. We identified for each country

TABLE 5 Decomposing the sources of policy change

	Argentina		Australia		Brazil		Canada		United States			
Time period	1888–98		1926–30		1917–27		1899–1919		1865–85		1885–1917	
Policy	4.5 to 0		2.5 to −2		4.5 to −2		1.5 to −4.5		1 to −1		−1 to −3.5	
Total change	−4.5	100%	−4.5	100%	−6.5	100%	−6	100%	−2	100%	−2.5	100%
Attributable to:												
Labor market effects												
Nominal wages/GDP per capita WTOY(−1)	−0.196	4.4%										
Nominal wages/GDP per capita WTOY(−2)					−1.676	25.8%						
Nominal wages/GDP per capita WTOY(−4)							−4.024	67.1%	−1.298	64.9%	−0.312	12.5%
Real wages WAGER(−2)					−2.330	35.8%						
Nominal wages WAGEN(−2)			+0.115	−2.6%								
Change in real wage growth D(WGRR(−2))									−0.646	32.3%	+0.292	−11.7%
Economic conditions												
Growth in GDP per capita YPCGRR			−0.737	16.4%	−0.357	5.5%						
Unemployment UNEMP2			−0.457	10.2%								
Immigrant effects												
% foreign population FORPOP(−2)	−1.182	26.3%										
Change in foreign population D(FORPOP(−2))			−0.004	0.09%								
Wages at immigrant origin IMWAGE(−2)							−0.681	11.4%				
Change in wages at immigrant origin D(IMWAGE(−2))			+0.111	−2.5%					−1.719	86.0%	−1.020	40.8%
Brazilian relative wages BRWTOY(−1)	−3.292	73.2%										
Growth in Brazilian real wages BRWGRR	−0.115	2.6%										
Residual	+0.285	−6.3%	−3.528	78.4%	−2.137	32.9%	−1.295	21.6%	+1.663	−83.2%	−1.46	58.4%

a period of major change toward more restrictive immigration policy. How much of the change was attributable to general economic conditions, to indirect labor market effects, to direct immigrant effects, and to other factors?[16]

When Brazil's door slammed shut in the 1920s, over 60 percent of the 6.5-point drop in the policy index was attributable to deteriorating labor market conditions, a good share of which was rising inequality. Although the residual is large (over 30 percent), labor market forces still account for nearly two-thirds of this major policy switch from an open immigration policy with generous subsidies in 1917, to a restrictive policy in 1927.

Canada offers even stronger evidence in support of the view that labor markets mattered. During the Prairie Boom from 1899 to 1919, the policy index dropped 6 points. Two-thirds of this drop can be attributed to rising inequality over those two decades (67 percent), and another tenth or so (11 percent) to diminished immigrant quality. The residual is only 22 percent.

Between 1888 and 1898, the policy index for Argentina fell by 4.5 points. Indirect labor market effects at home apparently made only a modest contribution to this big policy change (4 percent). However, it could be argued that Argentina anticipated the likely labor market effects at home by watching labor market developments in Brazil. Rising inequality and deteriorating wage growth in Brazil account for three-quarters of Argentina's policy switch. Increasing foreign presence in Argentina accounts for an additional quarter of the policy switch (26 percent).

Between 1865 and 1885, the immigration policy index for the United States dropped by 2 points. Almost all of that drop can be attributed to labor market effects and deteriorating income conditions of the unskilled. Direct immigrant effects mattered almost as much, captured here by declining quality. We have no explanation for the offsetting residual. In contrast with the powerful labor market effects apparent between 1865 and 1885, almost none of the 2.5-point drop between 1885 and 1917 can be assigned to labor market conditions (1 percent). Thus, Goldin (1994) was right in attributing the passage of the immigrant literacy test largely to nonmarket factors. That is, the residual is very large during this period, confirming the views of American historians who stress nonmarket forces. Note, however, that deteriorating immigrant quality accounts for four-tenths of the move to restriction in the United States during the period (41 percent).

The estimated equations do not explain nearly as much of the Australian switch to more restrictive policy during the late 1920s. The Australian residual is by far the largest in Table 5 (78 percent). We can offer no explanation for the finding, except to argue that many of the variables may have already been affecting the political scene even though policy remained unchanged prior to 1926. The time period is the shortest in the table.

Conclusions

Our results point to long-run fundamentals driving immigration policy that are very different from the short-term influences on timing about which so much has been written. We find little support for the conventional wisdom that current macroeconomic conditions, as measured by growth and unemployment, had a consistent influence on policy change. Although there is some evidence that policy was sensitive to the "quality" of immigrants—especially in the non-Latin countries, there is no evidence of the influence of racism or xenophobia, once underlying economic variables are taken into account.

Income distribution trends seem to have been especially important for the United States and Canada, both of which tried to protect the economic position of their unskilled workers. Labor became relatively more abundant when immigrants poured in; and governments sought to stop any absolute decline in the wages of the domestic unskilled with whom the immigrants competed, and often even a decline in their wages relative to the average income recipient. The greater the perceived threat to these wages from more immigrants or from lower-quality immigrants, the more restrictive policy became. Meanwhile, Australia was paying attention to unemployment, growth, and nominal wages, and may have reacted to protect the relative position of workers vis-à-vis landed interests (Timmer and Williamson 1996).

Immigration policy seems to have been influenced indirectly by labor market conditions, and directly by immigration forces that, if left to run their course, would have had their impact on labor market conditions. The switch to more restrictive policies was less the result of rising immigrant presence and more the result of falling immigrant quality. But countries did not act in isolation. Domestic policy was correlated with policy elsewhere, and rationally so: except for the United States, countries saw both the quantity and quality of immigration respond to the policies of others, so it is hardly surprising that the door-closing was reactive. (Likewise, it is not surprising that the United States did not react to policy changes by others.) These policy correlations may well have to do more with the change in immigration flows than with any preemptive policy measure.

These results offer lessons for contemporary debates about immigration. The parallels are clear. Inequality has been on the rise in the European economies since the early 1970s, manifested especially by a rising income gap between unskilled and skilled workers, just as it was in the New World economies in the late nineteenth century. We should therefore not be surprised by the renewed interest, in both the United States and Europe, in reducing the migrant flow. Labor-scarce economies have been sensitive in the past to inequality trends in their midst, using restrictive immigration policy to offset, or at least to dampen, those trends. If history repeats itself, policies will become increasingly anti-immigrant, at least as long as the relative position of unskilled workers lags behind that of other economic groups.

Appendix A: Independent variables

Economic variables

Variables are lowercased and italicized when used in text. Sources can be found in Timmer and Williamson (1996: Appendix A).

Population (POP)	Reported as actual estimated population.
Nominal GDP (GDPN)	All series have been converted to indexes, with 1900=100.
Real GDP (GDPR)	All series have been converted to indexes, with 1900=100.
Nominal wages (WAGEN)	All series have been converted to indexes, with 1900=100. Unless otherwise noted, the series are wage rates for urban unskilled workers.
Real wages (WAGER)	All series have been converted to indexes, with 1900=100. Unless otherwise noted, the series are real wage rates for urban unskilled workers.
Land values (LANDV)	Nominal estimates. Missing years are estimated by linear interpolation.
Export (X) and import (M) values	Current-dollar estimates of merchandise export and import values.
Growth in real wages (WGRR)	Calculated as $(WAGER_{t+1} - WAGER_t)/(WAGER_t)$
Wages relative to income (WTOY)	Calculated as WAGEN/GDPN/POP, indexed to 1900=100.
Wages relative to land values (WTOR)	WAGEN/LANDV, indexed to 1901=100.
Per capita growth in real GDP (YPCGRR)	Calculated as $(GDPR_{t+1}/POP_{t+1} - GDPR_t/POP_t)/(GDPR_t/POP_t)$
Unemployment (UNEMP)	Estimated by regressing GDPN on time and time squared, and taking the negative of the residuals.
Unemployment (UNEMP2)	Estimated by regressing GDPR on time and time squared, and taking the negative of the residuals.
Trade share of GDP (XMTOY)	Calculated as the total nominal value of exports plus imports, divided by nominal GDP.

Immigration variables

Most of the immigration data were assembled from: Ferenczi and Willcox (1929, 1930); more detailed sources defending our revision of these data are found in Timmer and Williamson (1996: Appendix A).

The following regional geographic groupings were used:

Southern Europe	Greece, Italy, Portugal, Spain
Northern Europe	Belgium, Denmark, Finland, France, Germany, Netherlands, Norway, Sweden, Switzerland
United Kingdom	England, Ireland, Scotland, Wales
Eastern Europe	Albania, Austria, Bulgaria, Czechoslovakia, Estonia, Hungary, Latvia, Lithuania, Poland, Romania, Russia, Turkey, Yugoslavia
Asia	China, Hong Kong, India, Japan, and others in present-day East Asia, South Asia, Southeast Asia, and the Pacific Islands

Immigration rate (IMRATE): Calculated as total immigration divided by total population.

Average wages at origin (IMWAGE): Measures the average quality of the immigrant, at least as implied by the unskilled wages prevailing in sending countries. For each country, immigration flows were grouped into regions of origin, and the percentage of immigration from each region was calculated. For each region, an annual series of wages was constructed using Williamson's (1995) internationally comparable series, which are purchasing-power-parity adjusted: United Kingdom uses the wage series for Great Britain; Northern Europe uses the series for the Netherlands; Southern Europe uses the wages for Portugal from 1850 to 1870, and, from 1870 to 1930, Italian wages were used but scaled such that the 1870 level of purchasing power matched that of Portugal for the same year (a correction of less than 10 percent); Eastern Europe and "other miscellaneous origin" wages were estimated to be two-thirds of those in Southern Europe; Asian wages were estimated to be half the level of Southern Europe. The variable simply calculates a weighted average of these wages, using the percentage of immigration from each region as the weight.

The following groupings were used:

Australia	United Kingdom, Northern Europe, Southern Europe, Eastern Europe, Asia, and other
Argentina	United Kingdom, Northern Europe, Southern Europe, Eastern Europe, and other
Brazil	Northern Europe (includes in this case United Kingdom), Southern Europe, Eastern Europe, and other
Canada	United Kingdom, Northern Europe, United States (assigned UK wages), Eastern Europe, and other
United States	United Kingdom, Northern Europe, Southern Europe, Eastern Europe, Asia, and other

Immigrant wages relative to destination (IMWREL): Like IMWAGE, this variable also captures immigrant quality, but in this case relative to the receiving region. It was calculated in much the same way as IMWAGE, except that, in addition, it measures wages in regions of emigration relative to wages in the country of destination.

Wage threat from immigration (THREAT): This variable was calculated to measure the extent to which immigration reflected "unfair competition from cheap foreign labor," that is, a threat to unskilled resident labor. Calculated to interact immigration rates with relative immigrant quality: THREAT = (100 − IMWREL)*IMRATE. Low IMWREL and high IMRATE implies big threat and large positive THREAT.

Percent foreign population (FORPOP): For most countries, the foreign-born population is counted every ten years in the census. Using immigration data cited above, and in some cases emigration data, the between-census years are estimated. These estimates are divided by the total population estimates to calculate the percent who are foreign.

Difference in regional stocks and flows (GAP): Using the annual composition of immigration (grouped as in FORPOP) and the annual composition of the foreign population (as estimated for FORPOP), an index was constructed to measure a shift in the composition of immigration relative to the current foreign-born population. For each year and for each group the difference between the percentage of immigrants and the percentage of foreign born was squared, and all groups except "other" were then summed. The index has a minimum value of zero, if the immigration flow looks just like the current foreign population. The theoretical maximum value is 1.

Appendix B: On constructing the dependent variable: The example of the United States

The text described how the index of immigration policy is constructed, the index or score (POLICY) ranging from +5, a policy of generous subsidy and non-discrimination upon arrival, to −5, a policy of serious immigration restriction, effectively enforced. This appendix illustrates the index for the United States between 1860 and 1930. The dependent variable for other countries is described at length in Timmer and Williamson (1996, Appendix C). The value of POLICY is reported only for years when it changed.

United States immigration policy, 1860–1930[17]

Pre-1860	Prior to 1840, most policy was set by individual states. Some restricted the entrance of paupers and criminals, or imposed head taxes to pay for immigrant services. Naturalization was allowed after five years of residence. From 1847 to 1849, the first effective legislation regulating passenger ships was enacted, requiring 14 square feet of clear deck space per passenger and adequate ventilation and food supplies. In 1849, the Supreme Court ruled that the state policies of head taxes and bonding were unconstitutional, leaving no funds to pay for lodging and health services provided to immigrants. In 1855, the individual passenger acts were consolidated and recodified to strengthen the health and safety regulations. Also in 1855, wives and foreign-born children of citizens were granted automatic citizenship.
1860	Passenger Acts are amended to protect female passengers from "seduction by ship personnel." POLICY=0
1862	Congress bans trade by US vessels in coolie, or indentured, labor.

1864   Commission of Immigration Office is established with a budget of $20,000/year for publishing and distributing recruiting literature. Congress legalizes indentured labor contracts of less than one year for payment of passage. POLICY=+1.0

1865   Congress fine-tunes the steamship regulations.

1866   Congress issues a formal protest to European governments against the deportation of criminals to the United States.

1868   Congress repeals the labor-contract provision of the 1864 act. POLICY=0

1869   Laws against the coolie trade are strengthened, notably making it illegal to transport individuals under fraudulent claims to induce emigration.

1870   Responding to concern that there were insufficient safeguards in the naturalization process, Congress tightens the regulations and puts checks into place. The act extends the right of naturalization to those of African descent.

1871   Recognizing deficiencies in the law, Congress reworks the passenger acts, without substantive change.

1875   The Immigration Act establishes the notion of "excludable" classes. The Act prohibits the importation of Chinese women for "immoral purposes" (prostitution) and bringing in persons without their consent; makes contracting to supply coolie labor a felony; designates criminals as an excludable class, but specifies that this does not include political offenses or those who received pardons in return for leaving their country of origin. POLICY=−0.5

1876   Congress requires a "declaration of intent" prior to naturalization (i.e., filling out paperwork.)

1880   The United States negotiates a treaty with China, recognizing the right of the United States to regulate, limit, or suspend Chinese immigration, but not the right to prohibit it.

1882   The Passenger Acts are completely revised, detailing the required deck space, food portions, water, and ventilation. New classes are added to the list of excludables: paupers, convicts, persons suffering from "mental alienation," lunatics, and idiots. A head tax of $0.50/immigrant is imposed to defray the costs of administration. Congress establishes the first legal terms for deportation, by legislating that convicts will be returned to their country of origin. Chinese immigration is suspended for ten years, with a provision to deport illegal Chinese residents. Congress instructs the courts that they are to disallow citizenship for the Chinese. POLICY=−1.0

1884   Congress amends the Chinese immigration suspension law to require evidence from legal entrants of belonging to an allowed group (merchants and travelers). Congress clarifies that the law applies to all

Chinese, regardless of country of origin. Carriers between the United States and Mexico or Canada are exempted from the head tax, while the tax is imposed on those who come by land as well as by ship.

1885   The Alien Contract Labor Act makes it illegal to prepay an individual's voyage in return for labor services; voids all existing contracts made prior to immigration; establishes penalties for violators. The Act exempts diplomats and other foreigners temporarily in the United States who bring over staff, specialty labor, domestic servants, and certain professional groups.

1887   The Contract Labor Law clarifies the enforcement mechanism of the 1885 Act, and provides that prohibited workers would be sent home. Congress passes a law banning any noncitizen from owning real estate and prohibiting more than 20 percent foreign-held ownership of a corporation, unless the individuals had properly declared their intent to become citizens. POLICY=−1.5

1888   The Chinese Exclusion Act suspends all Chinese immigration for 20 years (with student/diplomatic exemptions) and establishes the rules of deportation and fines for violators. For the first time, the law allows for the imprisonment of those who are in the United States unlawfully. (The suspension part of the Act was later found null after failure to ratify the treaty, although the 1882 ban remains in effect.) Congress makes it illegal for Chinese residents to return to the United States if they leave (even if here legally), and stops issuing identity certificates, which had functioned as passports. Alien land-ownership laws are amended to allow governments to set up their attachés in Washington, DC. Congress authorizes funds for finding and deporting illegal contract labor.

1891   The Immigration Act adds new groups to the list of excludable classes: those "likely to become public charges," polygamists, those suffering from contagious and dangerous diseases, and anyone "assisted" in passage. The Act bans all advertising for the purpose of encouraging immigration, except by offices of the states. Also, the Act extends the exemptions from the contract labor law to include professors, professionals, and ministers, while adding to those prohibited contracts with family or friends.

1892   The Chinese Exclusion Act extends the ban on immigration for another ten years, requires legal Chinese to file for a residency certificate within one year, and provides for the deportation of those who do not have their certificates within that year, unless "at least one credible white witness" can attest to their difficulty in obtaining the certificate.

1893   Quarantine act allows the President to restrict or suspend immigration in response to contagious disease threats in foreign countries. Congress reworks some of the procedures to help enforce existing laws. The Chinese Exclusion Act is amended to strengthen its enforcement, and to allow any non-Chinese witness in place of the white witness.

1895   Head tax is raised to $1/immigrant

1898   Congress sets up a commission to examine the effects of immigration on labor and industry, to report back to Congress with advice for handling immigration.

1902   The Chinese Exclusion Act extends the ban for another ten years. Essentially, it is the 1892 law reissued.

1903   The Immigration Act raises the head tax to $2. It also adds to the list of excludable classes: professional beggars, epileptics, the insane, prostitutes, and anarchists or others endorsing the overthrow of foreign governments. The Act also extends the period of deportability to two years from admission.

1904   Immigrants from Newfoundland are exempted from the head tax. Congress extends the ban on Chinese immigration to all US islands and territories.

1907   The Immigration Act raises the head tax to $4, except for arrivals from Mexico, Canada, Newfoundland, and Cuba. It also restricts entry of those who were granted a passport for a different destination. The Act adds more classes to the list of excludables: unaccompanied minors, "induced" immigrants, and the disabled. The Act establishes a financial test, so that each individual must have $25, or $50 per family, the first such requirement on immigrants. Congress sets up another commission to study immigration. POLICY=–2.0

1909   Canada and Mexico are exempted from having to produce manifests of their alien arrivals.

1910   The White Slave Traffic Act expands deportation statutes and laws on prostitution offenses to include any alien (i.e., any foreign men involved can be prosecuted as well as women), and to extend the period of deportability indefinitely.

1917   The Immigration Act establishes a literacy test for immigrants, to be given in any language. Failure to demonstrate literacy will be grounds for denial of admission, although certain groups are exempted. Act adds to the classes of excludables those of "constitutional psychopathic inferiority," a jargon phrase that was also used in Canadian legislation. It is interpreted to mean those who will fail to assimilate. The Act also defines a zone in Asia (actually most of Asia) from which individuals would be ineligible for citizenship through naturalization. Immigration is banned for those who would not be eligible for citizenship through naturalization. Thus, all immigration of Asians is effectively banned. The Act also doubles the head tax to $8. POLICY=–3.5

1918   Congress strengthens the ban on anarchists and other political troublemakers, and also agrees to readmit certain aliens who served in the military for the United States or its allies during World War I.

1919   Congress gives the President temporary powers to make any necessary rules/prohibitions on alien entry in order to protect the public safety. (Power expired on 4 March 1921.) POLICY=–4.0

1920   Congress establishes a five-year window of opportunity to allow admission to those who cannot read, if they are going to marry someone who fought in the war, even if he is an alien (war brides). Congress passes rules to deal with alien activists. It allows the deportation of those "interned as dangerous but not actually convicted of any crime." It also extends the definition of anarchist to include those associated with antigovernment groups, publications, or organizations affiliated with the publications. POLICY=–3.5

1921   Quotas are established to restrict the quantity of immigration from any one country to 3 percent of its population in the United States in 1910, for one year. The ban on all Asian immigration remains in effect, while all immigration from the Western Hemisphere is free from restriction. To keep Canada and Mexico from being throughways to the United States, immigrants from the Western Hemisphere have to have been in those countries for one year before qualifying for quota-free admission. This law, the Emergency Quota Act, was originally a temporary measure, expired in 1922. POLICY=–4.5

1922   Act extends the 1921 Act until 1924, and extends the Western Hemisphere residency period to five years. Establishes a $200 fine for bringing an illegal immigrant, and allows certain aliens brought in over quota to remain.

1924   1921 Act is amended to use quotas of 2 percent of a country's population, using 1890 as the base year (thus further restricting the "new" immigrants). Establishes that, as of July 1927, the quota will be 150,000 total, in the same proportion as the "national origin" of the US population in 1920, excluding from the count immigrants brought against their will (i.e., former slaves do not count toward Africa's quota). The Act establishes that wives and children under 18 have non-quota status, as do natives of the Western Hemisphere, ministers, professors, and students. Quota preference is given to children of citizens under 21, parents, spouses, and those trained in agriculture.

1926   Congress admits wives and children under 18, and professors, who were in the United States prior to 1924. The use of a "national origins" system is postponed until 1928.

1928   "National origins" system is postponed until 1929. Women who were US citizens but who gave up such status by marrying a foreigner are admitted if they are unmarried. Congress establishes that one-half of the quotas will be reserved for the preferred classes—wives and children, parents, agricultural workers. Clarifies that American Indians may travel freely across borders without immigration restrictions, as long as they are not part of a tribe by adoption.

1929   The Deportations Act makes it a felony to return to the United States if deported and a felony or misdemeanor to enter the country at an unauthorized point. Also establishes that those punishable will first be imprisoned, then deported after serving their sentence. National Origins Act takes effect 1 July. POLICY=–5.0

Appendix C: Decomposing policy changes

We use the estimated equations from Table 1 to construct the decomposition in Table 5. After the change in each of the right-hand side variables is calculated, it is multiplied by the estimated coefficient. Then we calculate their multiplicative impact through the lagged dependent variable. Consider the following example. We have a six year period, 1925–30. Each variable contributes contemporaneously, but also will have its share in the lagged dependent variable. Suppose we have the following equation:

$$\text{POLICY} = C_0 + C_1 * \text{POLICY} (-1) + C_2 * \text{WTOY}(-2)$$

The change in policy is the difference in the index from 1925 to 1930. Then we calculate how much of that change is due to changes in WTOY(–2) from 1925 to 1930 as the sum of all the following components:

$A = \{\text{WTOY}(1924) - \text{WTOY}(1923)\} * C_2$
$B = \{\text{WTOY}(1925) - \text{WTOY}(1924)\} * C_2, \quad A * C_1$
$C = \{\text{WTOY}(1926) - \text{WTOY}(1925)\} * C_2, \quad B * C_1, \quad A * C_1 * C_1$
$D = \{\text{WTOY}(1927) - \text{WTOY}(1926)\} * C_2, \quad C * C_1, \quad B * C_1 * C_1, \quad A * C_1 * C_1 * C_1$
$E = \{\text{WTOY}(1928) - \text{WTOY}(1927)\} * C_2, \quad D * C_1, \quad C * C_1 * C_1, \quad B * C_1 * C_1 * C_1, \quad A * C_1 * C_1 * C_1 * C_1$

Note that this method does not consider the impact of previous changes to WTOY that are still playing themselves out slowly through the lagged dependent variable. It is not clear whether this means we are underestimating the effects, since the equations themselves omit variables that may have been significant for certain time periods, but were not statistically significant in the regressions using the entire time series.

Notes

This is a much-revised version of "Racism, xenophobia or markets? The political economy of immigration policy prior to the Thirties," NBER Working Paper No. 5867, National Bureau of Economic Research, Cambridge, MA (December 1996). The authors gratefully acknowledge the support of the National Science Foundation (grants SES 92-23002 and SBR 9505656), the technical help of Timothy Hatton and Alan Taylor, and the research assistance of Spyros Poulios. In addition, the authors have benefited by comments from William Collins, James Foreman-Peck, Timothy Hatton, Dani Rodrik,

Peter Timmer, and the participants in the Harvard Economic History lunch seminar, the Harvard Economic History Workshop, the Harvard–MIT Research Training Group in Positive Political Economy, and the MIT Seminar on Migration.

1 Liberalization also helped induce economic convergence within the greater Atlantic economy (Williamson 1996).

2 The exceptions are surveyed in our previous article (Timmer and Williamson 1995).

3 After World War II, a focus on human rights developed; most Western countries changed their immigration policies to provide special consideration for political and economic refugees. Prior to the 1930s, such classifications did not exist.

4 The world labor market was by 1890 almost completely segmented into what economists today would call "North" and "South" (Lewis 1978; Taylor 1994; Hatton and Williamson 1994b), and these new immigrant flows were from the "South."

5 This, it turns out, is a reasonable assumption by the 1890s, at least for United States manufacturing (Hanes 1993, 1996).

6 Immigrants did it even better, of course. A policy of immigrant exclusion would have done no better than to reduce the net inflow to zero. Voluntary return migration drove up out-migration rates to levels high enough to make net inflows negative.

7 The same is true in many developing countries today, where agriculture is a fifth, a quarter, or even a third of the economy. In such countries, rural wage employment is important and landed interests are powerful.

8 Jess Benhabib (1996) takes the median-voter approach, allowing individuals to earn both labor and capital income in the spirit of the growth model of Alesina and Rodrik (1994); voters determine the amount of capital that immigrants must bring with them in order to be admitted. The model, an attempt to look at the dynamics of policy implications, gets very complicated. Perhaps for

that reason, Benhabib does not test the model empirically.

9 See, however, Perotti (1996) for a comprehensive review of the competing hypotheses.

10 About 60 percent of the total emigration out of Europe was to the United States (Hatton and Williamson 1998: Ch. 2), and about 70 percent of the total emigration to our five-country New World sample was to the United States.

11 The smoothing function uses exponentially decreasing weights, as selected by TSP software.

12 In Timmer and Williamson (1996), we constructed a panel data set and used the political variables to help explain policy levels. However, only fixed-effect estimation was possible since the economic data are presented in a form where they are indexed to 1900.

13 These results do not, of course, speak to the issue of whether immigration had an impact on wages. Indeed, we know that it did (Taylor and Williamson 1997; Hatton and Williamson 1998). However, policy changes usually did not have a large enough impact on immigration to matter much for wages.

14 We also constructed a variable that attempted to measure the threat to native wages, by dividing the immigration rate by the average wages in the countries of origin (THREAT). Thus, the variable increases with the volume of immigration and with declining immigrant skills. It was found not significant.

15 This inverse response may well be due to collinearity among the policy indexes.

16 We do not measure the impact of *past* performance on the lagged dependent variable, although we do multiply through the changes in the explanatory variables as they play out slowly *within* the period. Appendix C details the methodology of the calculations.

17 See E. P. Hutchinson, *Legislative History of American Immigration Policy, 1798–1965* (Philadelphia: University of Pennsylvania Press, 1981).

References

Alesina, Alberto and Dani Rodrik. 1994. "Distributive politics and economic growth," *Quarterly Journal of Economics* 109, no. 2: 465–490.

Anderson, James and J. Peter Neary. 1994. "Measuring the restrictiveness of trade policy," *The World Bank Economic Review* 8, no. 2: 151–169.

Benhabib, Jess. 1996. "On the political economy of immigration," *European Economic Review* 40, no. 9: 1737–1743.

Black, Duncan. 1948. "On the rationale of group decision making," *Journal of Political Economy* 56, no. 1: 23–34.

Borjas, George. 1994. "The economics of immigration," *Journal of Economic Literature* 32, no. 4: 1667–1717.

Cheng, Leonard K. and Kar-Yiu Wong. 1990. "On the strategic choice between capital and labor mobility," *Journal of International Economics* 28, nos. 3/4: 291–314.

Collins, William J., Kevin H. O'Rourke, and Jeffrey G. Williamson. 1997. "Trade and factor mobility: Complements or substitutes in history?" Paper presented at the Council on Economic Policy Reform Conference on Trade and Factor Mobility, Venice, 23–26 January.

Ferenczi, Imre and Walter Willcox. 1929. *International Migrations: Volume I—Statistics*. New York: National Bureau of Economic Research.

———. 1930. *International Migrations: Volume II—Interpretations*. New York: National Bureau of Economic Research.

Flam, Henry and M. June Flanders. 1991. *Heckscher-Ohlin Trade Theory*. Cambridge: MIT Press.

Foreman-Peck, James. 1992. "A political economy model of international migration, 1815–1914," *The Manchester School* 60, no. 4: 359–376.

Freeman, Gary P. 1992. "Migration policy and politics in the receiving states," *International Migration Review* 26, no. 4: 1144–1167.

Freeman, Richard. 1995. "Are your wages set in Beijing?" *Journal of Economic Perspectives* 9, no. 3: 15–32.

Goldin, Claudia. 1994. "The political economy of immigration restriction in the U.S., 1890 to 1921," in Claudia Goldin and Gary Libecap (eds.), *The Regulated Economy: A Historical Approach to Political Economy*. Chicago: University of Chicago Press.

Green, Alan G. 1994. "International migration and the evolution of prairie labor markets in Canada, 1900–1930," in Hatton and Williamson 1994a.

———. 1995. "A comparison of Canadian and US immigration policy in the twentieth century," in Don J. DeVoretz (ed.), *Diminishing Returns: The Economics of Canada's Recent Immigration Policy*. Toronto: C. D. Howe Institute.

Gurr, Ted R. 1990. *Polity II: Political Structures and Regime Change, 1800–1986*, Inter-university Consortium for Political and Social Research, data set #9263. Ann Arbor: ICPSR.

Hanes, Christopher. 1993. "The development of nominal wage rigidity in the late nineteenth century," *American Economic Review* 83, no. 4: 732–756.

———. 1996. "Changes in the cyclical behavior of real wage rates, 1870–1990," *Journal of Economic History* 56, no. 4: 837–861.

Hatton, Timothy J. and Jeffrey G. Williamson (eds.). 1994a. *Migration and the International Labor Market, 1850–1939*. London: Routledge.

———. 1994b. "Late-comers to mass emigration: The Latin experience," in Hatton and Williamson 1994a.

———. 1995. "The impact of immigration on American labor markets prior to the quotas," NBER Working Paper No. 5185. National Bureau of Economic Research, Cambridge, MA.

———. 1998. *The Age of Mass Migration*. New York: Oxford University Press.

Hillman, Arye L. 1989. *The Political Economy of Protection*. New York: Harwood Academic Publishers.

Lewis, W. Arthur. 1978. *The Evolution of the International Economic Order*. Princeton: Princeton University Press.

Luttmer, Erzo. 1997. "Group loyalty and the taste for redistribution," mimeo., Harvard University.

Markusen, James R. 1983. "Factor movements and commodity trade as complements," *Journal of International Economics* 14, nos. 3/4: 341–356.

Perotti, Roberto. 1992. "Income distribution, politics, and growth," *American Economic Review* 82, no. 2: 311–316.

———. 1993. "Political equilibrium, income distribution, and growth," *Review of Economic Studies* 60, no. 205: 755–776.

———. 1996. "Growth, income distribution, and democracy: What the data say," *Journal of Economic Growth* 1, no. 2: 149–187.

Pope, David and Glenn Withers. 1994. "Wage effects of immigration in late-nineteenth-century Australia," in Hatton and Williamson 1994a.

Sachs, Jeffrey D. and Andrew Warner. 1995. "Economic reform and the process of global integration," *Brookings Papers on Economic Activity* 1.

Shughart, William, Robert Tollison, and Mwangi Kimenyi. 1986. "The political economy of immigration restrictions," *Yale Journal on Regulation* 51, no. 4.

Stolper, Wolfgang and Paul A. Samuelson. 1941. "Protection and real wages," *Review of Economic Studies* 9, no. 1: 58–73.

Taylor, Alan M. 1994. "Mass migration to distant southern shores," in Hatton and Williamson 1994a.

Taylor, Alan M. and Jeffrey G. Williamson. 1997. "Convergence in the age of mass migration," *European Review of Economic History* 1, no. 1: 27–63.

Timmer, Ashley S. 1996. "Using politics to keep up with the Joneses: United States immigration policy and relative incomes," paper presented to the Research Training Group in Positive Political Economy, Harvard University, April.

Timmer, Ashley S. and Jeffrey G. Williamson. 1995. "The political economy of migration policies," mimeo., Harvard University.

———. 1996. "Racism, xenophobia or markets? The political economy of immigration policy prior to the Thirties," NBER Working Paper No. 5867, National Bureau of Economic Research, Cambridge, MA.

Venables, Anthony J. 1997. "Trade liberalization and factor mobility: An overview," paper presented at the Council on Economic Policy Reform Conference on Trade and Factor Mobility, Venice, 23–26 January.

Verdier, Thierry. 1994. "Models of political economy of growth: A short survey," *European Economic Review* 38, nos. 3/4: 757–763.

Williamson, Jeffrey G. 1974. "Migration to the New World: Long term influences and impact," *Explorations in Economic History* 11, no. 4: 357–389.

———. 1990. *Coping with City Growth During the British Industrial Revolution*. Cambridge: Cambridge University Press.

———. 1995. "The evolution of global labor markets since 1830: Background evidence and hypotheses," *Explorations in Economic History* 32, no. 2: 141–196.

———. 1996. "Globalization, convergence and history," *Journal of Economic History* 56, no. 2: 277–306.

———. 1997. "Globalization and inequality, past and present," *The World Bank Research Observer* 12, no. 2: 117–135.

Wood, Adrian. 1994. *North-South Trade, Employment and Inequality: Changing Fortunes in a Skill-Driven World*. Oxford: Clarendon Press.

Wong, Kar-Yiu. 1983. "On choosing among trade in goods and international capital and labor mobility: A theoretical analysis," *Journal of International Economics* 14, nos. 3/4: 223–250.

Journal of Economic Perspectives—Volume 12, Number 4—Fall 1998—Pages 51–72

Globalization, Labor Markets and Policy Backlash in the Past

Jeffrey G. Williamson

Two important features of the world economy since 1970 also characterized the economy in the late 19th century. First, the earlier period was one of rapid globalization: capital and labor flowed across national frontiers in unprecedented quantities, and commodity trade boomed as transport costs dropped sharply. Second, the late 19th century underwent an impressive convergence in living standards, at least within most of what we would now call the OECD club, but what historians call the Atlantic economy. Poor countries at the European periphery tended to grow faster than the rich industrial leaders at the European center, and often even faster than the richer countries overseas in the New World. This club excluded, of course, most of the third world and eastern Europe, and even around this limited periphery there were some who failed to catch up.

A recent literature has developed which argues that most of the convergence between 1850 and 1914 was due to the open economy forces of trade and mass migration. By inference, it also suggests that convergence stopped between 1914 and 1950 because of de-globalization and implosion into autarchy. These facts are directly relevant to debates over globalization today.[1] The new historical research shows that these forces of globalization had a significant distributional impact within participating countries. It also suggests that these distributional events helped create a globalization backlash which caused a drift towards more restrictive immigration and tariff policy prior to World War I.

---

[1] For an overview of the rapidly expanding literature which argues that open economy forces were central in driving convergence prior to 1914, see Williamson (1996), Hatton and Williamson (1998), and O'Rourke and Williamson (1997a).

■ *Jeffrey G. Williamson is Laird Bell Professor of Economics, Harvard University, Cambridge, Massachusetts.*

This essay starts with a brief review of the convergence evidence. It focuses on factor prices—like real wages—rather than GDP per capita or GDP per worker, since factor prices provide a more revealing way of discussing the connections between economic forces and political reactions than do GDP aggregates. It then documents inequality trends around the Atlantic economy, a systematic rise in the labor-scarce economies and a systematic decline in the labor-abundant economies. The essay then turns to immigration policy responses in the labor-scarce New World, since it was mass migration which was doing most of the work driving convergence, and observers then thought it was also mass migration which was doing most of the work driving inequality. Next, the essay explores tariff responses in land-scarce Europe to the invasion of foodstuffs from the New World. The impact of these globalizing price shocks on land rents and landed wealth appear to have been the central ingredients of rising tariffs. I conclude with some reasons why these powerful lessons of history need to be qualified.

Late 19th Century Convergence

Convergence of What?

Most economists who have written about the comparative growth of nations have used GDP per capita or per worker-hour to measure catching up and convergence.[2] This essay favors instead real wage rates—purchasing-power-parity adjusted, and typically for urban unskilled workers. I can think of at least four good reasons why it is a mistake for the convergence debate to have ignored wages and other factor prices.

First, the pre-World War II real wage data are probably of better quality than the GDP data, and they are certainly available for a wider sample of 19th century economies. The bigger sample reduces the risk of selection bias identified by De Long (1988) and others. Second, income distribution matters, and wage rates with other factor prices offer a window to look in on distribution issues. Real people earn wages or profits or rents, not that statistical artifact known as GDP per capita. GDP per worker-hour is a sound measure of aggregate productivity, but I would argue that the living standards of ordinary workers as captured by real wages are a better indicator of the economic well-being of a society. By averaging all incomes, we throw away valuable information. Third, factor price movements help in understanding the sources of convergence. For example, rapid technological catch-up in a poor country is more likely to increase all factor prices equally than is mass emigration or an export boom in labor-intensive manufactures. The open economy mechanisms which were important in driving late 19th century convergence—

---

[2] The literature is enormous, but it has been led by Abramovitz (1986), Barro (1991, 1996, 1997), Barro and Sala-i-Matin (1992, 1995), Baumol (1986), Bloom and Williamson (1997), Mankiw, Romer and Weil (1992), Sachs, Radelet and Lee (1997) and Sachs and Warner (1995). See also the recent surveys in this journal by Pritchett (1997) and Jones (1997).

trade, migration and capital flows—operated directly on factor prices, and thus only indirectly on GDP per capita. A focus on GDP per capita misses a large part of this story. Fourth, and possibly most important, economic change nearly always involves winners and losers, a fact which is crucial in accounting for the evolution of policy. Changes that would increase GDP per capita but would also cause losses to some politically powerful are often successfully resisted, and examining the behavior of factor prices is the first step in understanding such political resistance.

Divergence Shocks and Convergence Responses: 1830–1870

The Atlantic economy in the first half of the 19th century was characterized by high tariffs (even in Britain where the Corn Laws were repealed only in 1846), modest commodity trade, very little mass migration (the famine-induced Irish flood was not released until the late 1840s), and an underdeveloped global capital market. Two profound shocks occurred in this environment still hostile to liberal globalization policy: early industrialization in Britain which then spread to a few countries on the European continent; and resource "discovery" in the New World, set in motion by sharply declining transport costs linking overseas suppliers to European markets, so much so that real freight rates fell by 1.5 percent per annum between 1840 and 1910 (O'Rourke and Williamson, 1998, ch. 3). These two shocks triggered a divergence in wages across countries that can be documented as starting at least as early as 1830 and lasting until the middle of the century.

Figure 1 documents real wage dispersion between 1830 and 1869. The summary statistic plotted there, C(N), is the variance divided by the square of the mean for a sample size, N, of either eight (line with diamonds) or 13 (line with squares) countries.[3] Based on the eight Atlantic countries for which data are available in the early part of this period—Brazil, France, Great Britain, Ireland, the Netherlands, Spain, Sweden and the United States, C rises from 0.143 in 1830 to 0.402 in 1846, a near-tripling in the dispersion of real wages, and, presumably, in the dispersion of living standards. While we do not have similar real wage data this early in the century for, say, Canada or Australia, the U.S. evidence suggests that the global labor market disequilibrium was being driven primarily by rising wage gaps between Europe and the English-speaking New World. Does it follow that there were no industrial-leader and latecomer-follower dynamics which served first to augment wage gaps in Europe before catching up eroded them? No. We must remember an inherent selectivity bias underlying this small sample, which includes only six European economies. Since the sample excludes many poorly-documented latecomers, real wage dispersion within Europe is likely to have risen even more than these figures suggest.

---

[3] Dispersion statistics like C have been used extensively in the convergence debate, and it is our measure of what has come to be called σ-convergence. C is equivalent to the coefficient of variation, but easier to decompose.

Figure 1
International Real Wage Dispersion, 1830–1869

Source: Williamson (1995, Table A2.1; revised in O'Rourke and Williamson, 1997).

Late 19th Century Convergence

According to Figure 1, the years between 1846 and 1854 denote a secular turning point toward convergence of real wages. This convergence appears in both the eight-country sample (line with diamonds) and an expanded 13-country sample (line with squares). The five countries added to the broader sample are Australia, Belgium, Germany, Norway and Portugal. Figure 2 shows that the striking convergence which started in mid-century continued up to 1913. The line on the upper left of Figure 2 is a continuation of the 13-country sample from Figure 1. The dashed line in Figure 2 shows an expanded 17-country sample, now including in addition Argentina, Canada, Denmark and Italy. This measure shows the convergence tide ebbing around 1900. If we exclude Canada and the United States, two "exceptional" rich countries which bucked the convergence tide, convergence continues rapidly up to 1913. If we exclude in addition Portugal and Spain, two countries that failed to play the globalization game, convergence up to 1913 is faster still. In the full sample of 17 countries, the measure of wage divergence drops by more than a third over the three decades 1870–1900 (falling from 0.313 to 0.200), and divergence drops by perhaps two-thirds over the half century following 1854.

Figure 2
International Real Wage Dispersion, 1854–1913

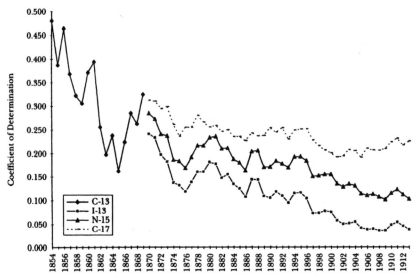

Source: Williamson (1995, Table A2.1; revised in O'Rourke and Williamson, 1997).

The wage dispersion evidence suggests that the middle of the 19th century is an appropriate date for the start of modern convergence in the Atlantic economy. One might view this convergence as one of transition toward globally-integrated Atlantic factor markets. The convergence in wages from about 1854 to the end of the 19th century was the most extensive that the Atlantic economy has seen since 1830, including the better-known convergence of the post-World War II era, although the "speed" per decade wasn't as fast as during the spectacular post-World War II epoch (Crafts and Toniolo, 1996). Most of the convergence was complete by the turn of the century.

Convergence wasn't limited to real wages and living standards of the working poor: GDP per capita converged as well (O'Rourke and Williamson, 1998, ch. 2). However, real wage convergence was much faster than convergence of GDP per capita, and the globalization arguments which follow offer some reasons why.

Our measure of Atlantic economy wage dispersion can be decomposed into three additive parts: wage dispersion within the New World; wage dispersion within the Old World; and the wage gap between the Old World and the new (Williamson, 1996). On average, the wage gap between the New World and the old accounted for about 60 percent of the real wage variance across these 17 countries over the four decades prior to 1913. The remaining 40 percent of the real wage variance was explained equally by the variance within Europe and within the New World. Thus, real wage variance among the European countries in our sample was a modest part of real wage variance in the Atlantic economy as a whole (although as already confessed, the absence of poor east European nations from the sample probably accounts for much of this result). Finally, about 60 percent of the convergence between 1870 and 1900 is explained by the collapse in the wage gap between Europe and the New World, although that gap did not disappear altogether.

In the late 19th century, wage convergence was mostly a story about Europe catching up with the New World, and of Argentina and Canada catching up with Australia and the United States. It was less a story about European latecomers catching up to European leaders. Convergence *did* take place within Europe, but it was a modest affair in the aggregate since the spectacular catching-up successes on the continent were offset by some equally spectacular failures. This European experience deserves a closer look.

Given the great debate about Britain's loss of industrial leadership (Crafts, 1998), there is a tendency to seek evidence of convergence by looking at German or U.S. catching up on (and overtaking of) Britain. But that's the wrong place to look for general lessons, since it deals only with who was at the top among the rich countries. What mattered far more for convergence was whether the really poor agrarian countries in Europe were catching up on the rich industrial ones. The well-to-do European economies of that time included the Netherlands, Belgium, France and Germany, as well as Britain. In contrast, the nine members of the European periphery at this time were Austria, Denmark, Finland, Ireland, Italy, Norway, Portugal, Spain and Sweden. (Austria and Denmark can be viewed as straddling the margin between core and periphery.) The industrial core countries had levels of GDP per head 67 percent higher than the poor European periphery (O'Rourke and Williamson, 1997, Table 1.1), and their real wages were 86 percent higher than the periphery. Note again that the sample excludes east and southeast Europe simply because the late 19th century data are inadequate for those regions. We do know, however, that these countries were relatively poor even compared with our sample European periphery of nine countries. Bairoch's (1976, Table 6, p. 286) rough estimates suggest that Bulgaria, Greece, Romania, Russia, and Serbia all had levels of GDP per head that were just 40–50 percent of the core. Thus, this essay ignores the poorest parts of Europe, with the exception of Portugal. As better historical data emerge from east and southeast Europe they can be used to test the assertions which follow.

The narrative begins with a spectacular Scandinavian catch-up to the leaders. The first column of Table 1 shows comparatively rapid growth of wages in Sweden, Denmark, Norway and Finland. Real wages in Scandinavia grew at rates almost three times those prevailing in the European core. In fact, no other country in Europe underwent real wage growth even close to that of Sweden, Denmark or Norway.

Table 1 (column 2) also documents trends in the wage/rental ratio. These relative factor price movements are an important analytical component of the open economy impact and policy response. While the ratio of wage rates per worker to farm land values per acre fell everywhere in the New World by an average rate of

Table 1

Relative Economic Performance of the European Periphery in the Late 19th Century: Growth Per Annum *(percent)*

Country	(1) Real Wage per Urban Worker 1870–1913	(2) Wage/Rental Ratio 1870–1910	(3) Real GDP Per Capita 1870–1913	(4) Real GDP Per Worker Hour 1870–1913	(5) Impact of Migration 1870–1910 on 1910 Labor Force (%)
The European Periphery					
Denmark	2.63	2.85	1.57	1.90	−14
Finland	na	na	1.44	1.80	na
Norway	2.43	na	1.31	1.65	−24
Sweden	2.73	2.45	1.46	1.74	−20
Scandinavia	2.60	2.65	1.45	1.77	−19
Italy	1.74	na	1.28	1.33	−39
Portugal	0.37	na	0.69	1.10	−5
Spain	0.44	−0.43	1.11	1.52	−6
Austria	na	na	1.46	1.76	na
Ireland	1.79	4.39	na	na	−45
Periphery	1.73	2.32	1.29	1.60	−22
The European Industrial Core					
Belgium	0.92	na	1.05	1.24	9
France	0.91	1.80	1.30	1.58	−1
Germany	1.02	0.87	1.63	1.88	−4
Great Britain	1.03	2.54	1.01	1.23	−11
The Netherlands	0.64	na	1.01	1.34	−3
Switzerland	na	na	1.20	1.46	na
Industrial Core	0.09	1.74	1.20	1.46	−2
Europe	1.39	2.10	1.25	1.54	−13
The New World					
Argentina	1.74	−4.06	na	na	86
Australia	0.14	−3.30	0.87	1.08	42
Canada	1.65	na	2.29	2.31	44
USA	1.04	−1.72	1.81	1.93	24
New World	1.14	−3.03	1.66	1.77	49

Notes and Sources: All averages are unweighted. Columns 1–4 from O'Rourke and Williamson (1997b, Table 2). Column (5) from Taylor and Williamson (1997, Table 1). See appendix for description of the data.

about 3 percent per year over the period 1870–1910, it rose everywhere in Europe (with the exception of Spain). These events reflect the invasion of grains from the New World (and Russia) which lowered farm rents and land values in Europe and raised them in the American Midwest, the Australian outback, the Argentine pampas, and the Ukraine. Note that this relative factor price index converges fast too, just like real wages and absolute factor prices. For example, the Scandinavian wage/ rental ratio rose half again faster than that of the European core (2.65 percent versus 1.74 percent per annum).

Aggregate measures using gross domestic product per worker also confirm the impressive Scandinavian catch-up, as shown in columns 3 and 4 of Table 1, although the differences are less spectacular than those for relative or absolute factor prices. Consistent with the fact that Scandinavian emigrants were economically active, leaving behind young and old dependents, the superiority of Scandinavian GDP per capita growth over that of the industrial core (1.45 versus 1.2 percent per annum) is even smaller than that of GDP per worker-hour, but it is still superior.

Scandinavia outperformed the rest of Europe (and probably the rest of the world) in the late 19th century, of that there can be little doubt. They were over-achievers even by catching up standards,[4] and we know the reasons why: three-quarters of the Swedish catch-up on the U.S. wage was due to mass migration and capital inflows, a tenth to trade, and the small remainder to schooling and to other as yet unidentified "new growth theory" forces (O'Rourke and Williamson, 1997, Table 10). What about the rest of the periphery? Based on Maddison's (1994, 1995) data, Austria seems to have done about as well as Scandinavia: GDP per capita and GDP per worker-hour grew almost exactly as fast (1.46 versus 1.45 and 1.76 versus 1.77). In contrast, while Ireland obeyed the laws of convergence, it was no over-achiever. Irish real wages grew twice as fast as they did in the industrial core (1.79 versus 0.90 per annum), but they grew about as fast as the periphery average, and they recorded only three-quarters of the Scandinavia growth rate. On the other hand, the Irish wage/rental ratio rose faster.

The western Mediterranean basin did very badly. Spain and Portugal fell far behind the growth rates recorded in the rest of the periphery. Real wages crawled upwards at only about 0.4 percent a year in those countries. Thus, Spain and Portugal missed out on the first great globalization boom—with small emigration rates and big trade restrictions, as did Egypt, Turkey and Serbia at the other end of the Mediterranean Basin (Williamson, 1998).[5] While the wage/rental ratio soared at 3.23 percent a year elsewhere around the periphery, it *fell* by 0.43 percent a year in Spain. The same wide gap appears for GDP per capita growth, which averaged 0.9 percent per annum for Spain and Portugal and 1.42 percent per annum elsewhere around the periphery. Maddison's real GDP per worker-hour data also confirm the poor performance for Spain and Portugal, but the gap is not quite so great. Italy does somewhat better, but even she—except for real wages—falls below the average for the periphery. The importance of the Iberian failure to overall Atlantic economy

---

[4] All of the assertions here and in the next paragraph have been successfully tested with conditional convergence models (O'Rourke and Williamson 1997; 1998, ch. 1).

[5] The appendix indicates that an "Atlantic economy" real wage data base for 17 countries between 1820 and 1940 is available upon request. The author will also have available a similar data base for Latin America and Asia, like that for the Mediterranean Basin cited in the text (for example, Williamson, 1998).

convergence has already been seen in Figure 2; remember, convergence after 1854 was steeper for the line where Spain and Portugal are removed.

Four countries can be used to illustrate the convergence process best: Ireland and Sweden (with heavy emigrations from the late 1840s onwards); the United States (with heavy immigrations from the late 1840s onwards); and Britain (the industrial leader, but losing its leadership). In 1856, unskilled real wages in urban Sweden were only 49 percent of Britain, while in 1913 they were at parity, an impressive doubling in Sweden's wage relative over 57 years. Relative to the United States, Sweden's real wages rose from 24 percent to 58 percent over the same period. In 1852, and shortly after the famine, unskilled real wages in urban Ireland were only 61 percent of Britain. Real wages in Ireland started a dramatic convergence with Britain during the 1850s (and did so largely in the absence of Irish industrialization) so that they were 73 percent of British levels by 1870, and 92 percent by 1913. Irish convergence with the booming U.S. economy was less dramatic, but Irish real wages did increase from 43 percent to 53 percent of U.S. real wages between 1855 and 1913.

What a Difference Factor Prices Make

The forces of convergence which seem to be so pronounced in the real wage data, adjusted for purchasing power parity, lead to different conclusions from those often reached by prominent studies that have focused on GDP per capita or per worker-hour. For example, in the words of Moses Abramovitz (1986, pp. 385, 395): "the rate of convergence . . . showed marked strength only during the first quarter-century following World War II"; and "in the years of relative peace before 1913 . . . the process [of convergence] left a weak mark on the record." We have already seen how the convergence behavior of these measures differed in the past, with real wages and other factor prices converging far faster than the GDP aggregates. Now consider three reasons why this was so.

First, GDP per worker can be thought of as a sum of per unit factor returns weighted by factor endowments per worker. Factor price convergence does not imply that all factor prices in the rich country fall relative to the poor. Some may rise. Suppose the initially rich countries are land-abundant and labor-scarce, while the initially poor countries are land-scarce and labor-abundant. While factor price convergence implies that low wages in poor countries catch up to high wages in rich countries, it also implies that low land rents in the rich catch up to high land rents in the poor. A similar argument applies to skill premia. Thus, wage convergence is likely to be more dramatic than convergence in GDP per worker, and relative factor price convergence, as measured here by the wage/rental ratio, should be most dramatic. This was typically the case.

Second, the GDP and wage deflators differ. In a world of very incomplete commodity price equalization, the difference may matter, especially since laborers heavily consume wage goods which are expensive to move internationally like dwelling space and foodstuffs. The truth of this statement is especially easy to defend for the previous century, when declining transport costs edged the global economy closer to commodity price equalization, especially in the grain market, but also for butter, cheese and meats. Thus, the price of food, relative to the implicit GDP price deflator, fell in much of Europe, but rose in North America.

Third, there may be a wedge between per capita and per worker indices, created partly by differences in labor force participation rates across countries over time, combined with different migration environments and differential rates of population growth. If the forces of demographic transition (higher fertility and lower infant mortality) are strongest for richer countries, causing population growth to exceed labor force growth, then per capita convergence will be faster than per worker convergence. If the forces of mass migration dominate instead, then the opposite would be true, since migrants were disproportionately young adult males. It turns out that the latter dominated the Atlantic economy during the age of mass migration (Williamson, 1997b).

In short, factor prices like wages, and aggregate productivity measured through GDP, *should* exhibit different convergence properties. However, factor prices will be far more helpful in identifying winners and losers, and thus in understanding policy responses.

Globalization and Inequality

Eli Heckscher and Bertil Ohlin (translated in Flam and Flanders, 1991) argued that integration of global commodity markets would lead to convergence of international factor prices, as countries everywhere expanded the production and export of commodities which used their abundant (and cheap) factor intensively. Table 1 is consistent with Heckscher and Ohlin: the trade boom led to rising wage/rental ratios in Europe, and falling wage/rental ratios in the New World; as a consequence, conditions improved for the poor unskilled worker relative to the rich landlord in much of Europe, while the opposite was true of the New World.

Migration helped the process of factor convergence along. The poorest European countries tended to have the highest emigration rates while the richest New World countries tended to have the highest immigration rates. The correlation wasn't perfect, since potential emigrants from poor countries often found the cost of the move too high, and some New World countries restricted the inflow from certain countries along the poor European periphery (and Asia). But the correlation is still very strong (Hatton and Williamson, 1998, ch. 3). Furthermore, the last column of Table 1 shows that the labor force impact was very big: mass migration after 1870 had augmented the 1910 New World labor force (in the four countries listed) by 49 percent, reduced the 1910 labor force in the emigrant countries around the European periphery (in the eight countries listed) by 22 percent, and reduced the 1910 labor force in the European industrial core (in the five countries listed) by 2 percent. Mass migration by itself may explain about 70 percent of the real wage convergence in the late 19th century Atlantic economy (Williamson, 1996; Taylor and Williamson, 1997; O'Rourke and Williamson, 1998, ch. 8).

Since the migrants tended to be unskilled, and became increasingly so as the late 19th century unfolded (much like the U.S. experience in recent decades), they tended to flood labor markets at the bottom in destination countries, thus lowering the unskilled wage relative to the skilled wage, as well as relative to white collar incomes, entrepreneurial returns and land rents. Mass migration implied rising inequality in labor-scarce, resource rich countries. Emigration implied falling inequality in labor-abundant, resource poor countries.

Complete income distributions at various benchmarks between the mid-19th century and World War II are available only for a few countries and dates,[6] but even if fuller data were available, it is not obvious that they would be the best way to explore the underlying causes and impact of globalization. Our interest here is factor prices: wages, rents and the structure of pay. How did the typical unskilled worker near the bottom of the distribution do relative to the typical landowner or capitalist near the top, or even relative to the typical skilled blue collar worker or educated white collar employee near the middle of the distribution? The modern debate over inequality has a fixation on wages, but since land and landed interests were far more important to late 19th century inequality trends, we need to add them to our distribution inquiry.[7] In any case, we have two kinds of evidence available to document late 19th century inequality trends: changes in the ratio of the unskilled wage to farm land values per acre, and changes in the ratio of the unskilled wage to GDP per worker-hour.

Recall from Table 1 that relative factor price convergence *did* characterize the four decades prior to World War I. The wage/rental ratio plunged in the New World, where it had been initially high. One study has it that the Australian ratio had fallen to one-quarter of its 1870 level by 1913, the Argentine ratio had fallen to one-fifth of its mid-1880 level, and the U.S. ratio had fallen to less than half of its 1870 level (O'Rourke, Taylor and Williamson, 1996). In Europe, the (initially low) wage/rental ratio surged up to World War I. The British ratio increased by a factor of 2.7 over its 1870 level, while the Irish ratio increased by even more. The Swedish and Danish ratios both increased by a factor of 2.3. Not surprisingly, the surge was more pronounced in free trade than in protectionist countries. As examples of protectionist countries, the ratio increased by a factor of 1.8 in France, 1.4 in Germany, and not at all in Spain.

---

[6] Some evidence on late 19th century inequality trends has been collected by economic historians since Simon Kuznets published his presidential address to the American Economic Association in 1955. For a recent survey, see Lindert (1997). These data seem to offer support for the view that inequality was on the rise in the United States before World War I while it had been falling in Britain since the 1860s. But the Atlantic economy coverage is not sufficiently comprehensive to be used in the pre-1914 discussion which follows.

[7] Recent studies of the impact of globalization on inequality in the third world also tend to focus on wage inequality, and sometimes even only *urban* wage inequality. This is a big mistake for countries where rural wage employment is significant and where landed interests are powerful. Surely, the economic positions of the landlord and the rural laborer matter in economies where agriculture is one-fifth, one-quarter or even one-third of the economy.

Landowners tended to be near the top of the distribution, although this was certainly more true of Europe, Argentina and the American South, and less true for the American Midwest and Canada, where the family farm dominated. The evidence that the wage/rental ratio was dropping in the rich, labor-scarce New World is consistent with the hypothesis that inequality rose there, while the rising wage/rental ratio was consistent with the belief that inequality was falling in poor, labor-abundant Europe. There is also some evidence that globalization mattered: European countries staying open to trade absorbed the biggest distributional hit; European countries retreating behind tariff walls absorbed the smallest distributional hit (Williamson, 1997a).

What about the ratio of the unskilled worker's wage (w) to the returns on *all* factors per laborer as measured by Maddison's (1995) estimates of GDP per worker-hour (y)? Changes in this ratio measure changes in the economic distance between the working poor near the bottom of the distribution and the average citizen in the middle of the distribution. It turns out that this statistic is highly correlated with more comprehensive inequality measures in the few cases where both are available.[8]

The 14 countries in our sample (all mentioned in this paragraph) exhibited *very* different inequality trends over the four decades prior to the Great War. When the index of unskilled wages/GDP per worker is normalized to 100 in 1870, we get the following for 1913: the index is at about 153 for Denmark and Sweden, and at 53 or 58 for Australia and the United States. An alternative way to standardize these distributional trends up to 1913 is to compute the annual percentage change in the index for each country relative to its 1870 base: the per annum rates range from +0.97 and +0.98 for Denmark and Sweden, to −1.22 and −1.45 for Australia and the United States. This measure of inequality change is plotted against the 1870 real wage in Figure 3, and it offers strong confirmation of the globalization hypothesis: between 1870 and 1913, inequality rose dramatically in rich, land-abundant, labor-scarce New World countries like Australia, Canada and the United States; inequality fell dramatically in poor, land-scarce, labor-abundant, newly industrializing countries like Norway, Sweden, Denmark and Italy; inequality was more stable in the European industrial economies like Belgium, France, Germany, the Netherlands and the United Kingdom; and inequality was also more stable in the poor European economies which failed to play the globalization game, like Portugal and Spain.

Globalization Backlash: Immigration Restrictions

Measuring Immigration Policy

The American doors did not suddenly and without warning slam shut on European emigrants when the U.S. Congress overrode President Wilson's veto of the im-

---

[8] Some countries do have time series for more comprehensive inequality indicators. Between 1870 and 1929, we have both the top 10 percent income share and w/y for Denmark, Germany, the Netherlands, Norway, Sweden and the United Kingdom: for these, $R^2 = -.944$ (Williamson, 1997b). The w/y data are reported at length in Williamson (1997a).

Figure 3
Initial Real Wage vs Equality Trends, 1870–1913

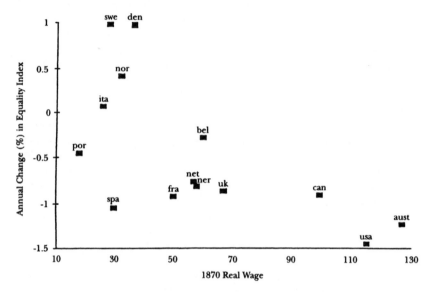

migrant literacy test in February 1917, or when it passed the Emergency Quota Act of May 1921. Over the half-century prior to the Literacy Act, the United States had been imposing restrictions on what had been free immigration—including contract labor laws, Chinese exclusion acts, excludable classes, head taxes, and so on—and had long been debating more severe restrictions. The Quota Act of 1921 was preceded by 25 years of active Congressional debate, and the first vote in 1897 had 86 percent of the Congressmen favoring more restriction in the form of a literacy requirement (Goldin, 1994, Table 7.1). The United States was hardly alone in this trend. Argentina, Australia, Brazil, and Canada enacted similar measures, although the timing was sometimes different, and the policies in these countries more often took the form of an enormous drop in or even disappearance of immigrant subsidies, rather than of outright exclusion. Contrary to the conventional wisdom, therefore, the United States did not make an abrupt regime switch around World War I away from free immigration to quotas, but rather evolved toward a more restrictive immigration policy. One important goal of these policies was to segment the international labor market into two parts, what we would now call North and South (Lewis, 1978, ch. 3).

In two recent papers, Timmer and Williamson (1996, 1997) constructed an immigration policy index which ranges over a scale of +5 to −5. A positive score denotes a pro-immigration or open policy, typically including comprehensive subsidies for passage and support upon arrival. A negative score denotes anti-literacy tests and discriminatory treatment upon arrival. A zero denotes policy neutrality.[9] The immigration policy indices constructed for Argentina, Australia, Brazil, Canada and the United States reveal that despite universal openness to immigration in the 1860s, the New World doors were effectively closed by 1930. With some exceptions, immigration policy was typically slow to change, sometimes remaining constant over a decade or more, even though there was almost always intensive political debate underlying that apparent quiescence. The best examples of this stability are Brazil over the three decades from 1890 to 1920, a period which ended in 1921 when tough immigration restrictions were imposed, and the United States from 1888 to 1916, a period which ended with the override of President Wilson's veto in 1917 and the quotas in 1921. However, the policy evolution varied widely over those seven decades: Argentina and the United States exhibited a relatively steady drift away from free immigration; Brazil remained open much longer, suddenly slamming the door shut in the 1920s; and Canada actually reversed the trend in the 1920s, while Australia did it more than once over the period.

Immigration Policy: Searching for Hypotheses

There is a general consensus in the historical literature that immigration policy has been sensitive to labor market conditions, and also that immigration flows have been sensitive to wage and unemployment differentials between countries. For example, Goldin (1994) notes that there was a strong push for immigration restrictions in the United States in the late 1890s, a time of economic recession and high unemployment. At that time, however, the rate of immigration slowed dramatically, reaching a secular low in 1897, the same year that the first vote on immigration restriction was taken in the House of Representatives. Similarly, Australian inflows dropped sharply in the recession of the 1890s, even as attitudes towards immigrant subsidies hardened (Pope and Withers, 1994). These events suggest that the political impetus to restrict immigration was far more sensitive to labor market conditions than to immigration levels. Inequality is one manifestation of these labor market conditions, and the living standard of the working poor is another.

Presumably, the policy response to immigration should take a far-sighted view. That is, immigration may induce falling wages for unskilled workers and greater inequality in the short run, but the key question for some voters might be whether it augments or inhibits economic growth in the longer run. The traditional Smithian view had it that the rising inequality would place relatively more income in the hands of those who save, thus raising the investment rate and growth. Modern political economists tend to take a different view, arguing that if a country lets its poorest voters become too poor, richer voters might join poorer voters to pass distortionary redistributive policies that can slow growth (Alesina and Perotti, 1994; Perotti, 1996). Economists do not yet have a clear answer to this question, especially

---

[9] It takes some doing to summarize these policies with a score for each year, but applied economists struggle with the same problem when trying to summarize just how open a country's trade policy is at any point in time (Anderson and Neary, 1994; Sachs and Warner, 1995).

for a century ago when government redistributive intervention was modest. But citizens might also vote for immigration restriction for other reasons: they may simply dislike seeing a deterioration in the living standards of their unskilled neighbors, or they may fear that these events might provoke some sort of political rebellion from below. Furthermore, since the stronger economic position of unskilled labor was manifested by stronger political voice in the labor-scarce immigration countries, their economic condition was more likely to be translated into a restrictive policy response.

Immigration Policy: Some Evidence

The empirical literature on the determinants of immigration policy is very new, so that much of what follows is still speculative. But some outlines are beginning to emerge (Timmer and Williamson, 1996, 1997).

The most consistent pattern is that immigration policy has been slow to change. This was especially true of Brazil and the United States, but it is worth noting that these two countries with the strongest historical persistence also exhibited the biggest policy switch at the end of the period of quiescence, from wide open to tightly closed. Big policy switches usually required long periods of debate. Thus, measures of current macroeconomic conditions—like unemployment rates—are unlikely to help account for long-run policy changes.

Labor market conditions have also had a consistent influence on immigration policy, and it appears that both the absolute and relative income performance of unskilled workers mattered. Poor wage performance was associated with more restrictive policy in Australia, Brazil and the United States. However, the most consistently significant variable reported by Timmer and Williamson (1996, 1997) is the ratio of the unskilled wage to per capita GDP, or of income near the bottom of the distribution to income in the middle. Rising inequality was associated with increasingly restrictive immigration policy. It is well known that (new) immigrants were unskilled and tended to cluster at the bottom of the distribution, at least initially, and that this was increasingly true as the late 19th century unfolded (Hatton and Williamson, 1998, ch. 7). Regardless of what else is included in the regression, this measure of unskilled labor's relative economic performance stands out as an important influence on immigration policy. Rising relative unskilled labor scarcity encouraged more open immigration policies; declining relative unskilled labor scarcity encouraged more restrictive immigration policies.[10]

The evidence just summarized speaks to the indirect impact of immigration on policy by looking at absolute and relative wage performance in labor markets. What about the direct impact of immigration on policy? To measure these direct immigration effects, one might use some proxy for the quality, or human-capital content, of the immigrants and the change in that quality proxy; one such proxy

---

[10] Furthermore, this effect is likely to be biased downwards since open immigration policy implies more immigrants and lower ratio of unskilled wages to per capita GDP, as I argued above.

that has been effective is the real wage of unskilled urban workers in the source countries. Alternatively, one might measure immigrant quantity by the foreign-born population share. It does appear that low and falling immigrant quality precipitated more restrictive immigrant policy, even after controlling for other forces. To some extent, therefore, New World policy anticipated the impact of low quality immigrants on unskilled wages and moved to shut it down. The other measure of immigration's attributes—the difference in ethnic composition between the current immigration flow and the foreign population stock—seems to have had little bearing on policy.

To what extent was a change in a country's policy in part a reaction to changes in immigration policy elsewhere? The United States—the immigrant leader of the New World—was completely unresponsive to competitors' policies. For most other countries, policy elsewhere mattered a great deal. For Argentina, it was the combined impact of Australian, Canadian and Brazilian policy that mattered, with more restrictive policy abroad inducing more restrictive policy at home. Brazil tended to mimic the policies followed by Argentina and the United States. Australia tended to favor open immigration policies when the United Kingdom offered more generous subsidies to its emigrants, and also, to some extent, when Canada adopted more open policies.

To summarize, while the absolute size of the immigrant flow did not seem to have any consistent impact on New World policy up to 1930, its low and declining quality certainly did, provoking restriction. Policies adopted by one's global competitors mattered even more. Labor market conditions mattered most, with deteriorating conditions provoking a restrictive policy reaction, as New World countries acted to defend the economic interests of unskilled labor.

Globalization Backlash: European Tariffs

Land-abundant New World economies became increasingly integrated with labor-abundant European economies in the late 19th century. While the distributional impact of this shock varied from country to country, there is broad support for the Heckscher-Ohlin prediction that European land and American labor suffered. Not surprisingly, European agricultural interests lobbied for protection. Landowners were successful in some countries, such as France and Germany, and tariffs were introduced. These tariffs can be viewed as the precursors of today's European Common Agricultural Policy (Tracy, 1989). Other countries, like Britain, Ireland and Denmark, stuck to their free trade guns, forcing agriculture to adapt or decline.

What explains the differing European political responses to the grain invasion? While this question has become canonical in the comparative political economy literature, only recently has it been decomposed into the relevant component parts: the size of the globalization shock experienced by each country, the distributional impact within each country, and, only then, the policy response (O'Rourke, 1997; O'Rourke and Williamson, 1998, ch. 5).

O'Rourke (1997) explores these issues by looking primarily at the grain market. He finds that where tariffs were raised, they were high enough to insulate continental Europe from the globalizing impact of steamships, railroads and international canals: German grain prices did not converge on American prices at all; French and Swedish prices converged only modestly; but British and Danish prices converged dramatically. The contrast between free-trading Europe (Britain and Denmark) and protectionist Europe (Germany, France and Sweden) is also born out when European prices are compared with those of the Ukraine. There is no evidence of grain market integration on the continent during the 40 years prior to World War I. An era when Europe and the New World became globally integrated was also one when grain markets *within* Europe became more balkanized. In this sense, globalization was not a universal phenomenon, even during the comparatively liberal late 19th century.

The literature which seeks to explain tariff responses to grain invasions begins with Charles Kindleberger (1951) and Ronald Rogowski (1989). Oddly enough, Rogowski the political scientist uses a conventional Heckscher-Ohlin model to sort the problem out, while Kindleberger the economist uses sociology and political science. Yet, both authors implicitly assume that the grain invasion generated the same shock to all economies, and that identical price shocks had the same impact on income distribution! O'Rourke (1997) shows that neither assumption held.

Consider the assumption that the grain invasion generated the same shock to all economies. Denmark was a free trader, but while real cereal prices fell by 29 percent in Britain between 1870 and 1913, they fell by only 10 percent in Denmark (O'Rourke, 1997, app. 5). Without protection, French and German cereal prices would have declined by an estimated 34 percent under free trade, and Swedish prices would have declined by 27 percent. If the grain invasion lowered cereal prices by less in Denmark than in the rest of Europe, then the grain invasion lowered Danish rents by less as well. If the elasticity of land prices with respect to grain prices was around 0.5, as O'Rourke estimates, then the cost to French, German and Swedish landowners of maintaining free trade in the face of the grain invasion would have been a 12 to 18 percent reduction in land values, while cheap grain lowered Danish land values by only 4 or 5 percent. Moreover, globalization raised the prices of Danish animal products exported to British markets. Armed with this new evidence, the Danish decision not to protect agriculture seems less surprising.

The second assumption was that identical price shocks had the same effects on income distribution, but depending on the structure of production, the effects could have been very different. Agriculture was a relatively small sector in capital-abundant Britain, an early industrial leader. Therefore, the 29 percent decline in real grain prices that Britain absorbed *increased* real wages in free trade Britain, while in the absence of tariffs a similar price shock would have *reduced* real wages in more agriculture-dependent France, and in the absence of tariffs it would have lowered real wages only modestly in Sweden, according to computable general equilibrium calculations (O'Rourke, 1997). These differences can be easily interpreted in the context of the sector-specific factors model: Cheap grain lowered workers' cost of living economy-wide, but reduced the demand for agricultural labor. Where agriculture was a big employer, nominal wages fell economy-wide. Where agriculture was a small employer, nominal wages did not fall economy-wide. Only 23 percent of the British labor force worked in agriculture in 1871, while the corresponding figure for France was 51 percent. Thus, a negative shock to agricultural labor demand had a much bigger impact on French nominal wages, while the impact on workers' cost of living was about the same. One key reason why Britain maintained free trade while the continent protected agriculture was that agriculture was a lot less important to the Britain than to the continental economies. Not only did this imply that cheap grain was better for British than for continental workers, but it also meant that the assets of the landowning rich declined by less (land was a smaller share of total assets), and that agricultural interests had less political clout.

The Lessons of History

Factor prices converged in the Atlantic economy up to 1914. This was true of absolutes, like real wages and farm rents, and it was true of relatives, like wage/rental ratios. The post-World War II decades have exhibited the same convergence, although economists have tended to measure it by use of aggregates like GDP per capita and GDP per worker. Convergence of relative factor prices implies something about inequality trends too. Where unskilled wages rise relative to farm rents and skilled wages, inequality falls; where unskilled wages fall relative to farm rents and skilled wages, inequality rises. The evidence from the late 19th century confirms that prediction, since inequality was on the rise in labor-scarce New World countries, while it was on the decline in labor-abundant Old World countries. The United States, and to some extent Europe as well, has exhibited the same inequality rise since the early 1970s.

Recent work by economic historians suggests that a large share of these trends in factor prices and inequality everywhere around the late 19th century Atlantic economy can be explained by globalization forces. Not all, but a large share. Is the same likely to be true of the late 20th century? Probably not. After all, it looks like mass migration played the central globalization role a century ago, not the indirect effects of trade, and migration has never returned to "mass" levels since the quotas were imposed after World War I.

There was a de-globalization implosion after 1914, coinciding with two world wars, two periods of fragile peace, a great depression and a cold war. The last few decades of the 20th century have marked a successful struggle to reconstruct that pre-World War I global economy. The standard view of history has treated these spectacular changes in global policy largely as switches in regime that were pretty much independent of economic events and thus can be taken as exogenous (Sachs and Warner, 1995).

This view ignores the evidence of factor price convergence and trends in income distribution cited a moment ago. It also ignores the fact that immigration policy in labor-scarce parts of the global economy became increasingly less generous and more restrictive prior to 1914, and that much of this retreat from open immigration policies was driven by a defense of the deteriorating relative economic position of the working poor. In addition, it fails to note the fact that liberal attitudes towards trade were brief, and that protection rose sharply almost everywhere on the European continent from the 1870s onwards. Much of this retreat from free trade was manifested by protection of domestic agriculture from the negative price shocks associated with globalization. And most of this retreat from free trade was driven by a defense of the trade-induced deterioration in the relative economic position of both the landed rich and the landless poor.

Thus, a more accurate narrative of globalization experience in the decades prior to World War I would read like this: A spreading technology revolution and a transportation breakthrough led first to a divergence of real wages and living standards between countries. The evolution of well-functioning global markets in goods and labor eventually brought about a convergence between nations. This factor price convergence planted, however, seeds for its own destruction since it created rising inequality in labor-scarce economies (like the United States) and falling inequality in labor-abundant economies (like those around the poor European periphery). Obviously, most gained by the globalization process, but the improved economic conditions of now-less-abundant European stayers and of the recently-moved new immigrants were not relevant to restrictionist debates in destination countries, nor were the improved economic conditions of labor and capital in growing export sectors well represented in protectionist debates on the European continent. The voices of powerful interest groups who were hit hard by these globalization events *were* heard, however, and these were in particular the ordinary worker in labor-scarce economies and the landlord in the labor-abundant economies. These interest groups generated a political backlash against immigration and trade, and this backlash, which had been building up for decades, was brought to a head by events around World War I.

A late 19th century globalization backlash made a powerful contribution to interwar de-globalization. Is this history likely to repeat? Maybe not. After all, wealth and employment are not nearly as concentrated in the tradable sector today as they were a century ago, thus insulating OECD economies from the kind of trade backlash seen in the past. And while restrictions on farm imports are still prominent in Europe today, OECD farm sectors are far too small to matter economy-wide to the extent that they did a century ago. Furthermore, the migrations from poor to rich countries today are pretty trivial affairs compared with the mass migrations up to World War I. Today, only the U.S. has across-the-border migration rates anything like those recorded *all over* the converging Atlantic economy prior to the quotas. And governments today have far more sophisticated ways to compensate losers than they had a century ago.

All of these qualifications may suggest that a move towards de-globalization is unlikely to repeat. Yet history does supply that warning: if a globalization backlash can be found in our past, it may reappear in our future.

Data Appendix

Real Wages: These are urban male unskilled wage rates, typically weekly and for construction work. They are deflated by cost of living indices. These real wage time series are projected from purchasing-power-parity benchmarks constructed for the period 1905–1914 by the author. Sources, methods and the data are elaborated in Williamson (1995), but the data have been revised in O'Rourke and Williamson (1997). This revised "Atlantic economy" data base will be made available on diskette upon request from the author at ⟨jwilliam@kuznets. fas.harvard.edu⟩, along with a detailed appendix describing its construction and sources.

Wage/Rental Ratio: The nominal wage rates under "real wages" above are divided by nominal per unit farm land values, and indexed 1901=100. The data are described and defended at length in O'Rourke, Taylor and Williamson (1996, pp. 521–4).

Equality Index: The nominal wage rates under "real wages" above are divided by nominal GDP per worker-hour, the latter taken from Maddison (1995). The ratio (w/y) is indexed 1870=100. The data are described and defended at length in Williamson (1997a).

GDP per capita and per worker: These data, nominal and real, are mainly from Maddison (1994, 1995) as revised and augmented in O'Rourke and Williamson (1997).

POLICY: The New World immigration policy index described in the text ranges from −5 (restrictive) to +5 (open with subsidies) and it measures political message rather than impact. The index is described at length in Timmer and Williamson (1996).

Net migration impact: Net migration between 1870 and 1910 is converted from population to labor force equivalents, and then expressed as a share of the sending or receiving 1910 labor force. The figures are taken from Taylor and Williamson (1997, Table 1).

■ *This paper has been supported by NSF grant SBR-9505656, and it has benefited enormously by collaborations with Kevin O'Rourke of University College Dublin and Ashley Timmer of Harvard University. I want to thank both of them for allowing me to draw freely on our as yet unpublished work. Bill Collins and Asim Khwaja were also helpful in solving some technical problems. In addition, I would like to thank Alan Krueger, Brad De Long, Dani Rodrik and Timothy Taylor for comments that improved the paper.*

References

Abramovitz, M., "Catching Up, Forging Ahead, and Falling Behind," *Journal of Economic History,* June 1986, *46,* 385–406.

Alesina, A., and R. Perotti, "The Political Economy of Growth: A Critical Survey of the Recent Literature," *World Bank Economic Review,* September 1994, *8,* 351–71.

Anderson, J. E., and J. P. Neary, "Measuring the Restrictiveness of Trade Policy," *World Bank Economic Review,* May 1994, *8,* 151–69.

Bairoch, P., "Europe's Gross National Product: 1800–1975," *Journal of European Economic History,* May-August 1976, *5,* 273–340.

Barro, R. J., "Economic Growth in a Cross Section of Countries," *Journal of Political Economy,* May 1991, *106,* 407–43.

Barro, R.J., "The Determinants of Economic Growth," *Lionel Robbins Lecture,* London School of Economics, February 20–22, 1996.

Barro, R.J., *Determinants of Economic Growth.* Cambridge, Mass.: MIT Press, 1997.

Barro, R. J., and X. Sala-i-Martin, "Convergence," *Journal of Political Economy,* April 1992, *100,* 223–52.

Barro, R. J., and X. Sala-i-Martin, *Economic Growth.* New York: McGraw-Hill, 1995.

Baumol, W., "Productivity Growth, Convergence and Welfare: What the Long-Run Data Show," *American Economic Review,* December 1986, *76,* 1072–85.

Bloom, D., and J. G. Williamson, "Demographic Transitions and Economic Miracles in Emerging Asia," NBER Working Paper 6268, National Bureau of Economic Research, Cambridge, MA, November 1997.

Crafts, N. F. R., "Forging Ahead and Falling Behind: The Rise and Relative Decline of the First Industrial Nation," *Journal of Economic Perspectives,* Spring 1998, *12.2,* 193–211.

Crafts, N. F. R., and G. Toniolo, *Economic Growth in Europe Since 1945.* Cambridge: Cambridge University Press, 1996.

De Long, J. B., "Productivity Growth, Convergence and Welfare: Comment," *American Economic Review,* December 1988, *78,* 1138–54.

Flam, H., and M. J. Flanders, *Heckscher-Ohlin Trade Theory.* Cambridge, MA: MIT Press, 1991.

Goldin, C., "The Political Economy of Immigration Restriction in the United States, 1890 to 1921." In C. Goldin and G. D. Libecap, eds., *The Regulated Economy: A Historical Approach to Political Economy.* Chicago: University of Chicago Press, 1994.

Hatton, T. J., and J. G. Williamson, *The Age of Mass Migration: An Economic Analysis,* New York: Oxford University Press, 1998.

Jones, C., "On the Evolution of the World Income Distribution," *Journal of Economic Perspectives,* Summer 1997, *11,* 19–36.

Kindleberger, C. P., "Group Behavior and International Trade," *Journal of Political Economy,* February 1951, *59,* 30–46.

Lewis, W. A., *The Evolution of the International Economic Order.* Princeton, NJ: Princeton University Press, 1978.

Lindert, P. H., "Three Centuries of Inequality in Britain and America." In A. B. Atkinson and F. Bourguignon, eds., *Handbook of Income Distribution,* Amsterdam: North-Holland, 1997.

Maddison, A., *Phases of Capitalist Development.* Oxford: Oxford University Press, 1982.

Maddison, A., "Explaining the Economic Performance of Nations." In W. J. Baumol, R. Nelson, and E. N. Wolff, eds., *Convergence of Productivity: Cross-National Studies and Historical Evidence.* New York: Oxford University Press, 1994.

Maddison, A., *Monitoring the World Economy 1820–1992.* Paris: OECD Development Centre Studies, 1995.

Mankiw, N. G., D. Romer, and D. N. Weil, "A Contribution to the Empirics of Economic Growth," *Quarterly Journal of Economics,* May 1992, *107,* 407–37.

O'Rourke, K. H., "The European Grain Invasion, 1870–1913," *Journal of Economic History,* December 1997, *57,* 775–801.

O'Rourke, K. H., A. M. Taylor, and J. G. Williamson, "Factor Price Convergence in the Late Nineteenth Century," *International Economic Review,* August 1996, *37,* 499–530.

O'Rourke, K. H., and J. G. Williamson, "Around the European Periphery 1870–1913: Globalization, Schooling and Growth," *European Review of Economic History,* August 1997, *1,* 153–90.

O'Rourke, K. H., and J. G. Williamson, *Globalization and History: The Evolution of a 19th Century Atlantic Economy.* Cambridge, MA: MIT Press, 1998, forthcoming.

Perotti, R., "Growth, Income Distribution and Democracy," *Journal of Economic Growth,* June 1996, *1,* 149–87.

Pope, D., and G. Withers, "Wage Effects of Immigration in Late-Nineteenth-Century Australia." In Timothy J. Hatton and Jeffrey G. Williamson, eds., *Migration and the International Labor Market, 1850–1939.* London: Routledge, 1994.

Pritchett, L., "Divergence, Big Time," *Journal of Economic Perspectives,* Spring 1997, *11,* 3–17.

Rogowski, R., *Commerce and Coalitions: How Trade Affects Domestic Political Arrangements.* Princeton, NJ: Princeton University Press, 1989.

Sachs, J. D., S. Radelet, and J-W Lee, "Economic Growth in Asia," ch. 2 in *Emerging Asia.* Manila: Asian Development Bank, 1997.

Sachs, J. D., and A. Warner, "Economic Reform and the Process of Global Integration," *Brookings Papers on Economic Activity,* Washington, D.C.: Brookings Institution, 1995.

Taylor, A. M., and J. G. Williamson, "Convergence in the Age of Mass Migration," *European Review of Economic History,* April 1997, *1,* 27–63.

Timmer, A., and J. G. Williamson, "Racism, Xenophobia or Markets? The Political Economy of Immigration Policy Prior to the Thirties," NBER Working Paper 5867, National Bureau of Economic Research, Cambridge, MA, December 1996.

Timmer, A., and J. G. Williamson, "Immigration Policy Prior to the Thirties: Labor Markets, Policy Interactions and Globalization Backlash," Department of Economics, Harvard University, March 1997.

Tracy, M., *Government and Agriculture in Western Europe 1880–1988,* 3rd ed. New York: Harvester Wheatsheaf, 1989.

Williamson, J. G., "The Evolution of Global Labor Markets Since 1830: Background Evidence and Hypotheses," *Explorations in Economic History,* April 1995, *32,* 141–96.

Williamson, J. G., "Globalization, Convergence and History," *Journal of Economic History,* June 1996, *56,* 1–30.

Williamson, J. G., "Globalization and Inequality, Past and Present," *World Bank Research Observer,* August 1997a, *12,* 117–35.

Williamson, J. G., "Growth, Distribution and Demography: Some Lessons From History," NBER Working Paper 6244, National Bureau of Economic Research, Cambridge, MA, October 1997b.

Williamson, J. G., "Real Wages and Relative Factor Prices Around the Mediterranean Basin 1500–1940," paper presented to the *Conference on Long Run Economic Change in the Mediterranean Basin,* Istanbul, Turkey, June 4–6, 1998.

Part IV
Contemporary Views of Interwar Disintegration

[16]

PART II
AN ANALYSIS OF THE REASONS FOR THE SUCCESS
OR FAILURE OF INTERNATIONAL PROPOSALS

In Part I of this study, the commercial policy pursued by States in the inter-war period was compared with the recommendations on the subject made by international conferences, committees, and other authoritative bodies. In regard to the crucial issues, there emerged from that comparison a striking paradox: the international conferences unanimously recommended, and the great majority of Governments repeatedly proclaimed their intention to pursue, policies designed to bring about conditions of "freer and more equal trade"; yet never before in history were trade barriers raised so rapidly or discrimination so generally practised. In spite of this paradox, however, a great deal was accomplished by these various international bodies in the field of commercial policy during the inter-war period.

The objects of this second part of the study are:

(a) to consider the reasons for the success, the partial success, or the failure of the recommendations of the conferences, and

(b) to draw lessons from those successes and failures.

We shall have to examine not only the reasons why commercial policy followed the course we know it to have followed, but also why the recommendations took the form they did. We shall have to examine whether the procedures adopted were suited to their purpose and to consider the varying fortunes of each group of proposals at different periods. Only thus will we be in a position to draw lessons from the experience presented.

The great international conferences of the first post-Armistice decade aimed at the following main objects:

(a) the extension of the code of international commercial law, the extension of international commercial arbitration, the general application of administrative principles tending to facilitate trade and the removal of various legal, fiscal and administrative obstructions to trade;

— 102 —

(b) the abolition of war-time trade prohibitions and controls and, later, the removal of the hard core of prohibitions and restrictions that remained in a number of countries;

(c) the restoration of pre-war tariff practices involving

(i) the suppression of fighting tariffs and measures of tariff warfare;

(ii) the re-establishment of the system of long-term commercial treaties which had been shattered during the war;

(iii) the restoration of multilateral trade by the removal of all forms of discrimination and the widest possible application of the most-favored-nation principle;

(iv) greater stability in tariff rates and classifications.

(d) the elimination of "excessive" or "artificial" rates and, later, the general reduction of tariff levels;

(e) special agreements between some of the small countries of Central and Eastern Europe for the purpose of achieving (b), (c) and (d).

Substantial progress was made in regard to (a)—relatively minor matters not affecting the central issues of policy—throughout the inter-war period, but more especially up to 1930 or 1931. On (b) and the various problems falling under (c), the heritage of the Great War was partly liquidated and some progress made towards a restoration of "normal" practices; but such progress was limited and, by and large, all that had been gained—and more—was lost after 1929. In regard to (d), the reduction of tariff levels—the central recommendation of the World Economic Conference of 1927, an objective proclaimed by business and labour opinion in almost all countries and to the realization of which the States Members of the League of Nations pledged themselves in no uncertain terms—nothing whatever was achieved, unless one counts as an achievement the temporary lull in the protectionist hurricane that occurred in 1927 and 1928. The efforts to bring about (e) failed almost completely.

After 1929, as the Great Depression deepened, measures of quantitative restriction on trade, exchange controls and open and concealed discriminatory practices, again made their ap-

— 103 —

pearance, especially in Europe. The International Monetary and Economic Conference of 1933 and a long series of lesser gatherings, official and unofficial, world-wide and continental, reaffirmed the basic doctrines set forth at Brussels, at Genoa, and at Geneva in the 1920's. By one plan after another—the Oslo Pact of 1930, the Ouchy Convention and the Stresa plan of 1932, the Tripartite Agreement of 1936, the Van Zeeland proposals of 1938—Governments sought to find some practical means of applying those doctrines or of creating conditions which would facilitate their application. All those efforts failed; the recommendations were practically without effect.

CHAPTER II

INTERNATIONAL COMMERCIAL AND FISCAL LEGISLATION

1. Proposals and Achievements

Before taking up the problems of commercial policy proper, we may deal very briefly with the group of problems in regard to which substantial success was achieved. These problems were, as stated above, of four kinds:

(a) the development of an international code of commercial law;

(b) the extension of international commercial arbitration;

(c) the general acceptance of certain administrative principles tending to facilitate trade;

(d) the removal of certain legal, fiscal and administrative obstructions to international trade.

They may be considered together and in roughly chronological order:[1]

(i) *Simplification of Customs Formalities.*

"The removal of obstacles to trade created by instability in administrative and legal measures and the publication of tariffs in easily accessible form," which the Genoa Conference had recommended, was substantially achieved by the International Convention of 1923. This Convention also provided for the simplification of regulations and procedure, for greater expedition and non-discrimination in the application of regulations, for appropriate means of redress, for greater facilities to commercial travellers and for the simplification of formalities regarding "certificates of origin".

The Economic Committee was able to record in 1927 that "striking progress" had been achieved as a result of the Convention, which was brought into force in some 35 countries.

[1] For a fuller description, see Part I, Chapters II (§2 and 3), V (§2,c) and VII (§2,ii.).

— 105 —

(ii) *The Prevention of Unfair Competition.*

Before the last War, certain international Conventions relating to the suppression of unfair competition had been entered into, but the protection thus afforded was inadequate because many important States were not Parties, because the practices to be repressed were not clearly defined and because the procedure for obtaining redress was defective.

These difficulties were partly met by the International Convention for the Protection of Industrial Property of 1925—based on drafts worked out by the League Economic Committee—which was brought into force in some 25 States and territories, and by the supplementary international agreement concluded in 1934.

Of greater importance was the development of

(iii) *International Commercial Arbitration.*

It was essential to the efficient functioning of a system of arbitration, such as was being built up by the International Chamber of Commerce, that the validity of arbitration clauses in commercial contracts between parties in different countries should be recognized by national courts. At the instance of the Genoa Conference, the League Economic Committee worked out an international protocol for this purpose. This Protocol, which was opened for signature in 1923, provided for the enforcement of arbitral awards made within the territory in which execution was sought; it was completed in 1927 by a Convention binding the Parties—which included all important European trading countries—to ensure the execution of awards given outside their territories. The Protocol received over 30, the Convention some 25, ratifications and accessions.

(iv) *Assimilation of Laws regarding Bills of Lading and Bills of Exchange.*

Following the recommendation of the Brussels Conference in 1920 on this subject, the Hague rules relating to bills of lading, drawn up by the International Law Association, were incorporated in an International Convention concluded at Conferences held at Brussels in 1922 and 1923.

— 106 —

A considerable advance towards the assimilation of laws relating not only to Bills of Exchange but also to Promissory Notes and Cheques was made by a series of six international Conventions concluded under the auspices of the League in 1930 and 1931. These Conventions were brought into force in the course of 1933 and 1934 by some 20 States.

(v) *The Unification and Simplification of Customs Nomenclature.*

The League's draft Standard Nomenclature and Classification, the outcome of recommendations by the World Economic Conference of 1927 as well as the Genoa Conference, was published in first draft in 1931 and in revised form in 1937. It has been applied in many countries as and when tariff revisions have taken place and is under study in others.

Among the questions falling under group (d) above, the removal of double taxation and also, perhaps, the standardisation of veterinary police measures, remain to be mentioned:

(vi) *Double Taxation.*

The work taken up in 1921 by the League in conjunction with the International Chamber of Commerce, led, in 1928, to the formulation of a series of model treaties, each dealing with a distinct group of taxes. Between 1929 and 1939, some hundred new bilateral agreements for the elimination of double taxation, based very largely on these League models, were concluded.

(vii) *Veterinary Police Measures.*

The World Economic Conferences of 1927 and 1933 recommended that a code of sanitary regulations should be established by international convention which would prevent the spread of animal and plant diseases without unnecessarily obstructing the trade in animal and agricultural products. The three Conventions concluded in Geneva in 1934 and 1935—relating to measures against contagious diseases of animals, to the transit of animals, meat and other animal products and to the import and export of certain animal products—went some way towards realising those

— 107 —

objectives. But the Conventions were brought into force in only a very limited number of countries—most of them of minor importance in this trade.

2. REASONS FOR SUCCESS ACHIEVED.

Now, what were the reasons why success was attained on the above questions—at any rate as regards (i) to (vi) and not on tariff questions and the more serious issues connected with commercial policy? Let us attempt to answer the first part of this question and leave the second till later. Most of these matters related to the legal conditions under which the individual trader operated. National laws on these questions had been gradually and independently evolved and substantial differences existed from country to country which were definitely disadvantageous to those engaged in international trade. There was, therefore, a strong support for this work of assimilation, and, more important, little opposition. Traders as a class wanted this work done, and other business interests either wanted it too or were not concerned. That was the first reason.

The second was the widespread desire of governments to restore some reason and order into international affairs. Administrations were ready to co-operate in promoting "freer and more equal trade" provided no "sacrifice of national interests"—and no substantial sacrifice of private vested interests—was involved. This desire was strong enough to induce governments to modify their own conduct up to a point, as is exemplified by the Convention on Customs Formalities. Governments were prepared to modify their administrative practices but not the principles of their commercial policy.

All the questions dealt with above had exercised national administrations and business circles before 1914. Several of them had been the subject of conferences which yielded little or no result; others, for lack of any prospect of international agreement, had not advanced beyond the stage of study. They were taken up after the War under conditions of intensified economic nationalism and of acute economic dislocation. That substantial progress was made must be ascribed in very large measure to a third factor, namely, the creation of a suitable international machinery for joint discussion, study and negotiation in the Economic and Financial Organization of the League. The existence of this international machinery served a further purpose. Several of the international agreements mentioned above were "elastic" and subject to numerous reservations. Their positive effect accordingly depended largely on the spirit in which they were applied. The goodwill between responsible officials, brought together periodically at League Conferences or Committee meetings, and the informal supervision exercised by the Economic Committee, were important elements in determining the real advance that was registered.

The success of the double taxation draft conventions cannot be explained by the above considerations alone. Not only was government policy involved, but also government receipts. It is worth noting that the hundred odd bilateral treaties for the reduction of double taxation were negotiated between 1929 and 1939—a period, that is, during which finance ministers in all countries were more than usually reluctant to make concessions.

The support of the business world for relief from taxation was, of course, assured. But the most important factor may well have been the procedure adopted. The Fiscal Committee of the League was world-wide in its composition; consisting as it did of revenue officials, it was assured of the co-operation of the fiscal authorities of all important countries, including the United States of America; and by framing conventions intended to be used as the basis, not of multilateral negotiations, but of such bilateral agreements as might be concluded, it achieved that measure of uniformity which was compatible with differences in national economic structures and financial practices and provided a standard to which countries could gradually conform.

Mention has been made, perhaps improperly, of the draft veterinary regulations—perhaps improperly, because it is doubtful whether this work can be classed as a success. But it is convenient to consider this case here to illustrate two points. The London Conference had recommended a general multilateral convention. That proved impossible. Why? Because the time for multilateral conventions had passed. After the failure of the London Conference, the breaking up of the world into more or less antagonistic if shifting currency groups and the gradual drift

— 109 —

through quantitative restrictions on trade to autarky, the will
to conclude such conventions even on questions of minor importance was sapped.

But it is not certain that this was the only cause, for these
veterinary problems were very close to major issues of commercial policy. The improper application of regulations concerning
contagious diseases or the proper application of obstructive regulations were one weapon of protection in the armoury of governments. In all important countries, some agricultural interests
would oppose the surrender of these weapons.

Why, then, did governments recommend their abolition if
they were not prepared to abolish them in fact? Here we return
to the central problem regarding commercial policy as a whole
in this period, a problem which requires to be considered in connection with issues more important than the diseases of plants
and animals and the use of these maladies for purposes of protection.

CHAPTER III

COMMERCIAL POLICY PROPER, 1919-1929

1. PROPOSALS AND THE COURSE OF POLICY.

It will be convenient to deal first with the vital problems of commercial policy in the first post-war decade only. After 1929, forces were set in motion which had previously exercised little or no influence and the nature of the problem was radically changed. For a few years after 1925, moreover, non-tariff impediments to trade were overshadowed by rising tariffs; after 1930, the tariff question was complicated by the emergence of new forms of trade regulation and finally overshadowed by them.

The early post-war Conferences aimed, as we have seen, at the following main objectives;

(a) the abolition of prohibitions and restrictions, exchange controls and excessive export duties on raw materials;

(b) the restoration of pre-war tariff practices—the suspension of fighting tariffs, the conclusion of long-term commercial treaties, non-discrimination and the extension of M.F.N., greater stability in tariff rates and classifications;

(c) the elimination of excessive duties and the general reduction of tariff levels.

Let us briefly recapitulate the main conclusions of Part I regarding the degree of success or failure attending those proposals.

(a) *Prohibitions, etc.*

Outside Europe and in several European countries, e.g. Great Britain, the Netherlands, Belgium and the Scandinavian countries, such restrictions had almost entirely disappeared by 1920. In other European countries, their removal was a slower and less continuous process; several countries which abolished their war-time measures of quantitative trade restrictions and exchange control soon after the Armistice felt obliged to re-impose them

— 111 —

later; in Central and South Eastern Europe, where trade had practically ceased by the end of the World War and was only gradually resumed first on the basis of intergovernmental barter, then on that of general prohibitions modified by licence, it was not until the middle 'twenties that something approaching a regime of unrestricted trading was restored.

There remained, however, in many countries—and especially in Central and Eastern Europe—a hard core of prohibitions and quantitative restrictions and it was against this that the efforts of the Prohibitions Conferences of 1927-1929 were directed. An international Convention was concluded in 1927 under which the 29 Parties undertook, subject to various reservations, "to abolish within a period of six months all import and export prohibitions or restrictions and not thereafter to impose any such restrictions". A supplementary agreement for the removal of prohibitions and restrictions on exports of (and the limitation of export duties on) hides, skins and bones, was concluded and brought into force among the States principally concerned. But the main Convention—by far the most elaborate and delicately balanced multilateral commercial agreement ever concluded— finally failed, owing to the absence of one essential ratification— that of Poland, which considered that certain reservations made by Germany jeopardised her economic life. The Convention was in fact brought into force in 1930 for a short period by seven States, not including any from Central and Eastern Europe.

But even in that region, the process of whittling down prohibitions and restrictions continued, by and large, up to 1930 or 1931. It may therefore be said that in spite of the very limited direct results of intergovernmental action, there was no striking contrast between the recommendations of international conferences on this subject and the results achieved in the first postwar decade.

(b) *Tariff Practices.*

The instability which was a feature of post-war tariff regimes— as reflected in the surtaxes and "coefficients of increase" to meet currency depreciation which many governments were empowered to introduce and modify without reference to Parliament, as well as in frequent changes in schedules—became less marked after

— 112 —

1922 or 1923; but nothing approaching the pre-war tariff stability was ever regained, even after 1927. That failure was one aspect of the failure to rebuild the system of long-term treaties.

The commercial agreements concluded in the early 'twenties were few and, without exception, of short duration. From about 1925, and more especially in the years immediately following the World Economic Conference, treaty-making was speeded up—though serious gaps remained—and the treaties more frequently provided for the consolidation or reduction of duties. Although the numerous treaties concluded in 1927 and 1928 continued to be denounceable at short notice, denunciation became less frequent. The Franco-German Agreement of August 1927 seemed to have laid the basis for a stable system of commercial relationships. The consolidation movement was, however, arrested in 1928 and reversed in 1929.

The attempt to rebuild the commercial treaty system was closely bound up with the fortunes of the M.F.N. Clause. The re-establishment of the Clause as the basis of the commercial relationships between States was one of the few real successes of the first post-war decade in the sphere of commercial policy proper. The United States adopted the unconditional form of the Clause in 1922; Italy became its advocate in 1921, joining forces with the United Kingdom and other traditional upholders of the Clause, together with Germany and her ex-allies, to break down the opposition of France and Spain. France returned to the Clause in her agreement with Germany in 1927 and Spain adopted it in 1928.

The generalisation of the M.F.N. Clause was, however, not accompanied by any general extension of 'National treatment' to foreign traders and firms, as was the case before the war; and efforts, culminating in the International Conference on the Treatment of Foreigners in 1929, to secure the recognition of a body of liberal principles to be observed in this connection, met with little success. Nor did the Clause in fact go far towards meeting the problem of discrimination, which was effectively practised by means of tariff specifications so detailed that only the Parties to a bilateral negotiation were likely to benefit from the tariff reductions agreed upon. Anti-dumping and countervailing duties were further sources of alleged discrimination, but these factors declined in importance as the decade advanced.

— 113 —

The really fundamental issue in the efforts to restore pre-war tariff practices centered around the problem of tariff bargaining. 'Tarifs de combat' were a far more serious obstacle to trade than before the war owing to the increased margin allowed for bargaining and the hitherto almost unheard of practice of enforcing the inflated bargaining tariffs first and negotiating afterwards.

Such changes in methods reflected the increase in the intensity of tariff bargaining. Never had there been such general reluctance to grant the smallest concession without a more than compensatory counter-concession, never were concessions in tariff treaties so limited in number, small in degree and difficult to secure at any price.

On the whole, neither the methods of tariff bargaining nor the spirit in which it was conducted were substantially modified throughout the inter-war period, though, as mentioned in Part I[1], the German and French Governments officially stated that their treaty of August 1927 would have been much more difficult to conclude "if the Parties had not been able to rely upon the principles laid down by the World Economic Conference and to benefit by the atmosphere created by its discussions."

(c) *Tariff Levels.*

In the early post-war years in Europe, the level of duties was a preoccupation quite secondary to other forms of trade restriction and the tendency towards increased protectionism was in many cases concealed by currency depreciation which temporarily reduced the effective height of duties. But within a few years—and more especially after the stabilization of most of the European currencies—it became clear that Europe was following the road that had been taken by the United States in 1921 (emergency duties on agricultural products) and 1922 (Fordney-McCumber Tariff). The new tariffs worked out all over Europe were not only higher than their predecessors; they were also—as we have seen—far less frequently and less substantially reduced by negotiation. Indeed, there was a continuing tendency towards tariff increases, effected by means of successive partial revisions.

[1] Chapter V.

— 114 —

Up to about 1925, the main increases in tariffs referred to industrial products; after 1925, agricultural duties in Italy, Germany and France led the upward movement. For two years following the World Economic Conference, the general upward
tendency was checked, though not arrested. Proposed increases
in a few countries (France, Norway) were moderated and in a
few others some actual reductions in duties were effected by
bilateral treaties and by autonomous action (Czechoslovakia,
Canada); but these reductions were outweighed by increases
elsewhere, especially on agricultural products. From the middle
of 1929, a wave of agricultural protectionism swept over Europe
and the interlude during which the issue of greater world integration or greater national isolation had seemed to hang in the balance was past.

The storm centre of the high protectionist movement in Europe
lay in the Danubian region. The Peace Treaties provided that
Austria, Hungary, and Czechoslovakia might form a preferential
customs 'bloc'. This remained a dead letter. Equally ineffective
were the recommendations of the Supreme Economic Council, the
Brussels Conference and the Portorose Conference and the protracted efforts of the Economic Committee which have been described in Part I.

2. Reasons for Success and Failure in regard to the aboli-
   lition of prohibitions and restrictions, exchange controls, etc.

The bulk of the war-time prohibitions and restrictions on imports and exports were removed in the United States, the United
Kingdom and certain other countries shortly after the Armistice,
because there was a clamour for their removal. In other countries, as we have seen, they were removed or gradually whittled
down in the course of the following 10 years. The efficient cause
of this demobilization of quantitative restrictions lay in the fact
that most governments, reflecting public opinion, did not desire
to maintain quantitative control of trade as a permanent system.
They postulated that the pre-war system was the normal and
natural system and their opinion was reinforced by the declarations of International Conferences and Committees. Exchange
control, widely enforced in the post-armistice years by European

— 115 —

countries in a weak financial position, was likewise generally condemned.   The restoration of financial stability in Europe—towards which the League of Nations made a noteworthy contribution—enabled one country after another to decontrol foreign exchange operations.

Why was the demobilization of quantitative restrictions a slow and uneven process in many countries?

In many parts of Europe, scarcity of raw materials and foodstuffs made governments reluctant to abandon export controls in the immediate post-war years, while currency fluctuations rendered the abolition of import controls difficult.   Countries with depreciating or weak currencies maintained, and in several cases (e.g. France in 1922, Poland in 1925) re-imposed import controls in order to strengthen their balance of payments.   They believed that this could be more easily done by checking imports than by allowing the depreciation of currency to stimulate exports, especially as currency depreciation was liable to become cumulative and "self-inflammatory" owing to its effects on confidence. Moreover, they wished to avoid the rise in domestic prices consequent upon depreciation.   Various countries with stable or relatively stable currencies maintained or re-imposed controls to protect their own industries against "exchange-dumping".   In every European country, the United Kingdom not excepted, certain prohibitions were maintained in order to foster industry or conserve resources considered necessary for national security; and in certain cases, such controls were used as an instrument of commercial warfare aimed at weakening the position of potential enemies.

It must not be forgotten that actual fighting continued in parts of Europe until 1922 and that it was only after 1925 that the danger of fresh conflicts receded into the background.   The Locarno Agreements of October 1925 opened a more hopeful prospect for Western European relationships; but in the same month, war between Greece and Bulgaria was only averted by a hair's breadth.

The passing of the conditions of scarcity, the restoration of political and monetary stability and the introduction, in one country after another, of new and higher Customs tariffs rendered possible the gradual removal of the bulk of prohibitions and restrictions on the European continent.   In the restoration of stability, the financial reconstruction of Austria marks an important date. The Hungarian reconstruction scheme likewise contributed. At the Geneva Customs Conference of 1923, the representative of Hungary stated that his Government "might be obliged to maintain the system of prohibitions owing to economic and currency reasons". Early the following year, in accordance with a recommendation of the League Financial Committee, Hungary abolished her whole system of export prohibitions and licences and, with the introduction of the new tariff later in the same year, also abolished her import prohibitions lists. More important still for its effect on European commercial policies was the stabilization of the mark in 1924; the German import licence system was, moreover, abolished in 1925 when Germany regained her tariff freedom.

But why was the process of demobilising prohibitions never completed? The clue may be found in a sentence from the resolution of the League Assembly of 1924 governing the League's efforts to secure an international agreement on the subject. The Assembly decided that "provisions relating to the vital interests of States shall not be affected". The interpretation given to this phrase 'vital interests' was largely determined by two fundamental factors in the political situation at that time: doubts about the maintenance of peace and mutual mistrust. Governments were prepared to advocate collectively policies which implied trust to some limited extent. But when each government severally was faced with the need for formulating its own individual policy and taking sovereign action, it felt unable to act on the assumption that the political risks of which it felt conscious did not exist. Hence, at no stage of the negotiations between 1927 and 1929 were the majority of European Governments prepared to forego their control over the export of certain products essential for their own national defense and important for the purpose of bargaining with other governments.[1] Nor were the majority of governments prepared to guarantee that the removal of import prohibitions would not be neutralized by prohibitive tariffs, by arbitrary veterinary regulations or other weapons of "indirect protectionism". They were not prepared altogether to abandon their power of direct control over the

---

[1] Reservations regarding export prohibitions on scrap metal were maintained by 10 continental governments, including all the principal metal producers.

— 117 —

most important lines of trade with each and every country or to renounce completely the most convenient instruments for exercising that control.

In addition to the political causes mentioned above, there were profound economic causes of the unwillingness of governments to accept, in their commercial policies, the logic of the resolutions to which they had subscribed. These economic causes may be more conveniently considered in connection with tariffs, which gradually replaced prohibitions to a very large extent as an instrument of protection.

The 1927 Convention, for all the reservations maintained by many of its signatories, would have involved the removal of a very wide range of prohibitions and it must not be forgotten that this Convention nearly succeeded. The whole course of the multilateral negotiations for the purpose of bringing the Convention into force would have been facilitated and the specific hitch which was the immediate cause of the breakdown—namely, the commercial war between Germany and Poland—possibly avoided had the hopes of general tariff reductions entertained in 1927 been, even in small measure, fulfilled. General agreement regarding both the partial removal of prohibitions and some reduction or at least stabilization of tariffs might conceivably have been achieved had inter-governmental negotiations for the latter purpose been begun in 1927 instead of 1930.

3. Reasons for General Failure—and Specific Successes— of Proposals aiming at the Restoration of "normal" Tariff Practices and the Commercial Treaty System.

The slow and very incomplete response to the recommendations of Conferences that pre-war tariff practices and tariff relationships should be restored was due partly to special and temporary, partly to general and more permanent, causes.

Long-term treaties and the consolidation of rates were impossible when

(a) specific rates were employed, as in Europe, and the future of most currencies was highly speculative;

(b) new States, and States which had been enlarged or truncated, did not know how their economy would work out;

— 118 —

(c) new tariffs were almost everywhere in preparation;

(d) there were grave political risks and uncertainties;

(e) many governments were faced with pressing social problems—unemployment or low standards of living among certain
economic groups—the solution of which might require, *inter alia,*
some manipulation of tariff rates;

(f) prices on world markets—as distinct from prices expressed
in fluctuating national currencies—were violently oscillating.

The same factors rendered the acute instability of rates and
classifications in the early post-war years inevitable. It should
be added that the paucity of even short-term agreements in the
five or six years following the Armistice was largely due to the
attempts vainly made by France in this period to withhold
M.F.N. treatment.

By the time the World Economic Conference met in 1927, this
last factor as well as (a), (b) and (c) had ceased to operate.
Factor (d) was less prominent but, like (e) and (f), still of
importance. There remained a condition of uncertainty, political as well as economic, which made governments hesitate to
take the risk of binding themselves for more than a very short
more than possible that governments would have been prepared
to enter into longer term commitments. Under the leadership of
Mr. Hull, many governments actually did so after 1934, despite
the effects of the depression.

The vicissitudes of the M.F.N. clause can be broadly explained
in a few words. All countries feel a certain reluctance to extend
to third parties "concessions" which are made as a result of a
bilateral bargain. This feeling is likely to be enhanced (1) at
a time of international tension and ill-feeling, (2) if one or more
of the potential beneficiaries under the operation of the clause
has raised insuperable barriers against the exports of the country
granting the tariff reduction, and (3) if one or more of those
beneficiaries employs not only non-negotiable but high rates of
duty. The tension in Europe and the tariff policy of the United
States (as well as the introduction of prohibition in that country, damaging the wine-producing countries) explain the attitude

— 119 —

towards M.F.N. and the effective discrimination practised by other means in a large number of European countries in this period.

Nevertheless, most of these countries—including the small countries in a weak bargaining position—found that on balance their interests lay in a general adoption of the clause. A guarantee of equality of treatment for their exports in foreign markets was indispensable even if of limited value, and the only hope of obtaining it lay in guaranteeing equality in their own markets. A general reduction in trade barriers was also desired and it was assumed—at any rate in the early 'twenties—that the most hopeful method of achieving this lay in creating a network of treaties containing the clause. France and Spain ultimately adopted M.F.N. after their experience of the difficulties of negotiating on a basis of pure reciprocity.

If the recommendations of the Conferences regarding M.F.N. were formally fulfilled, effective discrimination by methods which did not violate the letter of the clause continued to be widely practised. The art of specifying individual positions in the tariff was developed to an extent that frequently rendered tariff concessions of little or no value to third parties. For other reasons, too, the clause itself became increasingly discredited. It was felt that instead of facilitating, the clause tended to obstruct the reduction of tariffs by means of bilateral or multilateral agreement, owing to the reluctance of governments to make concessions which would be generalized by it. This was the result, mainly, of two causes: first, the refusal of the United States to reduce its own very high tariff by negotiation while claiming to benefit from any tariff reduction negotiated between European countries; secondly, the opposition of certain countries—notably the United Kingdom, the United States and the British Dominions—to derogations from strict M.F.N. practice permitting the conclusion of regional or similar agreements for tariff reduction, the benefits of which would be limited to the participants. This second point was important—for when it became apparent that multilateral negotiations on an almost universal scale were not likely to succeed, certain groups, especially the Oslo group of countries, were anxious to achieve the general objects advocated in international conference within a more restricted area. Had general support of such endeavours been forthcoming, it is possible that the practice of reduction through group agreements might have spread and the groups gradually have extended their size. Such a procedure might have been less favourable to world trade as a whole than the rapid conclusion between a large number of countries of bilateral treaties embracing the M.F.N. clause, but not less favourable than the failure to grant concessions owing to the quasi-universal implications of M.F.N.

The causes of the persistence of tariff warfare are extremely complex. Political tensions provide a partial explanation; so does the accident that at the time that many of the new European tariffs were published, negotiations were impossible and the tariffs had consequently to be enforced before they could be reduced by agreement; so, again, does the fact that, if used by one, fighting tariffs tend to be used by all, in self-defence.

But all this does not really explain why trade was consistently regarded as a form of warfare, as a vast game of beggar-my-neighbour, rather than as a co-operative activity from the extension of which all stood to benefit. The latter was the premise on which the post-war conferences based their recommendations —a premise accepted by all in theory but repudiated by almost all in practice. It was repudiated in practice because, as the issue presented itself on one occasion after another, it seemed only too evident that a Government that did not use its bargaining power would always come off second-best. In the inter-war period, States were taking over the competitive struggle from individual manufacturers and traders, between whom competition was being attenuated by the rapid growth of trusts and cartels and the extension of Government control in various forms.

4. CAUSES OF FAILURE TO ACHIEVE A REDUCTION IN TARIFF LEVELS.

(i) *Causes of the Post-war rise in Tariff levels.*

To understand the causes of the rise in tariffs in Europe, it must be remembered that in the early post-armistice days, tariffs scarcely counted and trade was controlled by quantitative restrictions. These restrictions, together with the currency chaos, meant or produced great disequilibrium in national price levels, and governments were afraid of jumping into the cold water of

— 121 —

an extremely tumultuous world price ocean. They therefore tended not to jump but to impose tariffs more or less equivalent to prohibitions, with the intention of reducing them through negotiations. This, indeed, was the course recommended by the Genoa Conference.

Many of these countries were new or had acquired new or lost old territories and had to create or reorganize their administrative systems. They were afraid to take risks. They had to nurture new populations. They did not know how the industrial organization of their territories was going to hang together, and felt incapable of elaborating a carefully thought-out commercial policy. The safest thing to do seemed to be to impose high tariffs all around and protect everybody.

They were ignorant of world markets and those markets themselves were disorganized. Their old trade connections had been severed and to many of the small new states the cost of creating an export market, of appointing consuls, sending salesmen, etc., was prohibitive. Nor had they the capital necessary to reorganize their industrial life. Inevitably, their primary concern was to secure at least the home market to their existing industries. Inevitably, their attitude towards foreign trade was defensive.

So, for somewhat different reasons, was the attitude of the majority of the larger European countries. These countries, owing to changes in the economic structure of the world, had in many cases permanently lost foreign markets and certain industries which previously, as dynamic exporters, had upheld free trade principles, now demanded protection. Governments were under pressure to protect war-expanded industries in order to keep in employment some part of the plant and labour which had become excessive.

Economic re-adjustment, particularly in the older industrial countries, was rendered extremely difficult by the increased rigidity of their economic structures, a rigidity arising not only from the normal conditions of large-scale industrial economies— heavy capital investment and a high degree of labour specialization—but also from the resistance of organized labour to wage reductions. Readjustment, again, was discouraged by the uncertain future of world markets. There was thus every inducement to buttress up existing industries by all appropriate means, including tariff protection. Where new and more promising lines of production were attempted, tariff protection was likewise required.

In countries with stable or relatively stable currencies, currency depreciations elsewhere reinforced the demands for protection by industries threatened by "exchange-dumping". German dumping had similar effects. Either straight tariff increases or special "anti-dumping" duties were introduced in one country after another to meet such "abnormal" foreign competition.

In the primary-producing countries outside Europe, the process of industrialization had been accelerated during the war owing to the curtailment of supplies of manufactures from the old industrial countries. Tariffs were raised—in some countries, for example Australia, to very high levels—for the purpose of safeguarding the existence of the newly established industries against the revival of foreign competition. In other words, the war had created a high measure of protection all around and governments were afraid of undergoing the deflationary process incidental to its reduction.

The immediate causes of the steep rise in the United States tariff in 1921 and 1922 are set out by the United States Tariff Commission in the following words:[1] "After the World War, there arose a demand for tariff revision which was intensified by currency depreciation in European countries, particularly in Germany. Industries which had grown up or expanded during the war were fearful of the increased foreign competition, and a severe decline in agricultural prices in 1920 caused the farmers also to advocate increases in tariff rates. In response to this demand, the Congress enacted the Emergency Tariff of 1921 and later the Tariff Act of 1922. These acts raised the general level of tariff rates to a position approximating to that which prevailed prior to 1913."

In fact, the fears of foreign competition entertained by the American producers—agriculturists as well as manufacturers—would scarcely have withstood the test of objective analysis. The real explanation of post-war tariff policy in the United States lay in the widespread belief in the desirability of high tariffs as such.

---

[1] U. S. Tariff Commission. Trade Agreement between the United States and the United Kingdom, Washington, 1938. Vol. I, p. 30.

— 123 —

This point will be dealt with more fully in connection with the further strengthening of United States tariff protection in 1930.[1]

One effect of United States tariff policy on European policies, namely the reluctance to grant tariff reductions from which the United States would benefit under M.F.N., has already been noted. Another, of still greater importance, was the development of a position of highly unstable equilibrium under which the constant deficit in the payments position of European debtor countries vis-à-vis the United States was covered, and could only be covered, by a flow of United States capital to Europe on a vast scale. This precarious situation broke down when the net outward movement of United States capital ceased in the middle of 1928.[2] Thenceforward, European countries were under increasingly severe pressure to curtail imports in order to adjust their foreign payments position.

While this specific factor did not make itself seriously felt until 1929, pressure on balances of payments had exercised an influence several years earlier on the new tariffs of weak-currency countries in Europe. This pressure on national currencies provides one explanation of the high duties on luxury and unessential imports invariably found in Central and Eastern Europe; another factor was the need for revenue. Of all taxes, customs duties are the easiest to impose and to collect. The Ministries of Finance of those impoverished countries—in which, on the one hand, indirect taxation was responsible for a high proportion of national revenue and, on the other, military preparations, subsidies and social services, as well as debt obligations, called for very heavy expenditures—were insistent that the duties on luxury articles should be high. High duties on such goods also reflected a widespread and natural desire in countries lacking capital to endeavour to prevent luxury expenditure and promote saving.

Let us return to consider the forces and the arguments favouring increased protection for national industry. We have mentioned the grounds on which industries claimed such increased protection and some of the reasons why those demands were met. But there were others of no less importance. It was considered desirable, in almost every country, to build up certain lines of production of importance for national defence, and to assist that

[1] See page 126.
[2] There was a short temporary revival of U. S. Capital exports to Europe in 1930.

— 124 —

development by preventing foreign competition. Even the United Kingdom protected "key industries"; but it was on the European Continent that the memories of the blockade were most vivid and the lessons of that war-time experience most fully drawn. The industrial States fostered their agriculture, the agricultural States their industry, in pursuit of a greater measure of self-sufficiency and security.

In the new, mainly agricultural, States, there were, it is true, special politico-strategic reasons for rapid industrialization. Each of those States desired to consolidate its hardly won political independence by economic independence; each was suspicious of one or more of its neighbours and conscious of the precariousness of its own position; each knew that military power depended in large measure on national industrial production. But the main reasons leading to policies of industrialization in the agricultural countries were undoubtedly social and economic. Throughout the greater part of the period under consideration, many of those countries had a surplus agricultural population. Most of them, as well as their larger neighbours with a more mixed economy, had sent a steady stream of surplus labour overseas before the war and were seriously affected by the new restrictions on immigration, more especially in the United States. The agricultural unemployed could only be absorbed by industry; industry had therefore to be built up and for that purpose tariff protection seemed to be indispensable. Protection was made general in many cases because the plans for industrialization were amorphous.

The position of agricultural countries became more difficult and the need to protect industry more pressing when the great industrial countries increased their agricultural protection. The movement was ushered in by the "Battle of Wheat" in Italy and the new agricultural duties in Germany in 1925. Like the industrialization movement which we have just discussed, it was conditioned partly by the wish to utilize to the full the resources available at home when emigration was checked and export markets difficult to penetrate, partly by the desire for self-sufficiency, partly by other considerations, social as well as economic. It was held to be desirable, in terms of social stability, to maintain a prosperous and numerous peasantry, to check the long-continued drift to the towns. As a result, in part, of the expan-

— 125 —

sion of overseas production which the war had stimulated, a wide margin had developed between the trends in agricultural and industrial prices (the "scissors"); farmers had a grievance and were sufficiently powerful politically to enforce acceptance of their demands.

In Germany and in England, there was a deep-lying (though still but half recognised) economic reason for protecting and fostering agriculture. Both these great industrial States had reached a stage in economic evolution at which a large proportion of their exports took the form of capital goods, a form of trade peculiarly sensitive to economic fluctuations. When this stage is reached, insurance against fluctuations may become more important than maximum income in the optimum year. That insurance can be effected by diverting productive activities to agriculture and to industrial consumption goods. It was so effected in both countries.

Thus the highly industrialized countries at the one end of the scale and agricultural countries at the other endeavoured to secure a better balance by developing miscellaneous consumption goods industries—while in one agriculture waxed and in the other it waned. Between these two extremes, lay the truncated industrial States, Czechoslovakia and Austria, in which the labour mobility factor took a special form. These States protected industry to secure at least their home market, and agriculture, in part for rural-political reasons, in part in the hope of re-absorbing some of the surplus industrial population. Had they regained their old markets in Danubia, that surplus would not have existed. Two alternative policies lay before them—the one which they adopted (and possibly carried too far), the other that of constructing customs unions or some form of preferential customs regime with the other succession States. A customs union would have saved their industry and lessened their need for agricultural protection. But for it to have been economically sound (or acceptable to the other States), labour mobility would have been indispensable. The surplus agricultural labour from all parts of the customs union would have had to be granted the right to move to the industrial centres anywhere within its frontiers. That solution was incompatible with young nationalism. Partly for that reason, partly because of the conflicting interests of other Powers, it was never pressed by conferences. Nor was the estab-

— 126 —

lishment of a preferential regime seriously advocated, owing to the rigid M.F.N. ideas that were current, particularly in Anglo-Saxon countries. As we have seen in Part I, Chapter IV, Austria almost succeeded in negotiating preferential arrangements with Czechoslovakia and Italy in 1925; but the attempt failed owing to Italian insistence that all Czechoslovak concessions to Austria should be extended to Italian products.

Between 1922 and 1929 the United States enjoyed a period of great and increasing prosperity. In this prosperity agriculture shared, though it benefited less than industry. Foreign competition was scarcely a serious factor in any section of economic activity. Yet before the collapse of 1929, even before the end of 1928, it was clear that the United States tariff was going to be raised above the formidable level of 1922.

The explanation has frequently been given in terms of political pressure exercised first by the farming and later by the industrial groups—the sort of pressure which has been important in all countries and constitutes indeed a major problem of government.[1] But this explanation is insufficient, for it begs the question why those sectional groups thought that they would benefit from still higher tariffs all round. Nor is it sufficient to point out that those who knew they would benefit pressed for higher protection while the others were content to follow their lead, for it would still be necessary to explain that amenability. The real explanation of the United States tariff of 1930, as well as that of 1922, would seem to lie in the existence of a deep suspicion of import trade as an element of disturbance and depression and a belief in the beneficial effects of economic isolation, a belief based on the experience of the preceding half century or more, during which the United States had grown to be the greatest and most prosperous industrial country in the world under a system of high tariffs. The Fordney-McCumber Tariff was a development of that trend, which persisted in spite of the fundamentally changed position of the United States when she ceased to be a debtor country and became the world's greatest creditor.

---

[1] The present commercial policies of the world constitute a kind of bastard socialism, conceived not in the public interest but pressed upon Governments by strong sectional organizations." Sir Arthur Salter: *The Framework of an Ordered Society,* Cambridge, 1933, p. 17.

— 127 —

ii) *Now near was Europe to accepting conference doctrine in 1927-1929?*

For some two years after the meeting of the World Economic Conference, the rise in tariffs, which had hitherto been both steep and continuous, was checked, though not entirely arrested. The hopes of gradual tariff demobilization aroused by the Conference were wrecked in 1929. It is important, however, to consider how near the world was to accepting the doctrine of the Conference in 1927-29. Was the failure due to accidental causes? How far did errors and omissions in procedure contribute? Was it the inevitable result of certain of the factors considered above?

At the Conference, it was realized that a general demobilization of tariffs would at best be a slow process. Any substantial reduction in tariffs, to which, by and large, national industrial structures had adapted themselves, would have involved particular sacrifices and general deflationary consequences which no government could lightly accept. Little immediate result was therefore expected from autonomous action. States were recommended to begin by removing barriers "that gravely hamper trade" and had been imposed "to counteract the effect of disturbances arising out of the war".

Greater hopes were placed in bilateral action for the conclusion of arrangements under which, on balance, both parties should benefit. But here, too, it was clear that progress would be slow and difficult owing not only to the high tariff of the United States and the opposition to European preferential agreements, but also to the non-negotiable character of the tariffs of some of the principal trading countries of the world. The last factor was of considerable importance. It was not so much the level of the United States tariff as the fact that it could not be reduced by negotiation that made countries with negotiable tariffs reluctant to enter into agreements among themselves for tariff reductions, since such reductions would constitute a non-compensated concession to the world's greatest exporter. The United Kingdom and the Netherlands, the two countries which had not introduced a high protective system and were particularly interested in general tariff demobilization, were likewise unable to take part in negotiations for reciprocal tariff reductions. Since their duties were at that time not subject to reduction by agreement, they were unable to offer tariff concessions against the concessions they sought to obtain from others.

Various delegations to the World Economic Conference desired the Conference to enter a forthright recommendation in favour of negotiable tariffs and the matter was subsequently considered at length by the Economic Committee. But, whatever advantages negotiable tariffs offered for the purpose of bilateral or multilateral agreements, it was impossible to disregard the fact that the principal European countries with the non-negotiable system were those whose tariffs were the lowest. It would have been patently ridiculous to denounce the low- (or no-) tariff countries for their abstention from tariff bargaining. The position was, of course, changed in the early 30's, when those countries abandoned their traditional free-trade or quasi free-trade position.

The relatively small results achieved by autonomous and bilateral action in 1927 and 1928 do not by themselves afford any evidence that further results might not have been gradually achieved had the depression not occurred and had United States tariff policy followed a different course. That the manner in which the problem of collective action was approached was open to question is argued in Chapter V below; but it is possible that more could have been achieved in those two years had the idea of collective action been taken up with greater enthusiasm. During the whole of that period, indeed, no direct negotiations between Governments for the purpose of collective tariff agreements were attempted and the Economic Committee, which had been instructed by the League Council to explore the possibilities of agreement, found itself thwarted at every point by technical difficulties and conflicts of private interest—factors which, had Governments been generally and genuinely determined to secure such agreement, might well have been overcome. The Committee reported in March 1928 that there appeared to be no prospect of achieving general tariff reduction by means of standard percentage reductions or the fixing of maximum scales. As with national armaments some years later, so with national tariffs, it proved impossible to find an acceptable general principle on which reductions by different States, with widely varying systems and degrees of protection, might be based. The Committee then proposed to make a start with groups of commodities—semi-manu-

— 129 —

factures, such as cement and aluminium—in regard to which the prospects of general agreed tariff reduction seemed least dim. After more than a year of negotiations with the representatives of the national industries concerned, it reported that no progress could be made. The main technical reasons for this failure appear to have been as follows: a) each national tariff being adapted—in theory at least—to the national economic structure, action restricted to one group of products tended to upset the balance of the tariff as a whole; b) since a reduction in the protection afforded to semi-manufactures would constitute an increase in the protection afforded to the finished goods made from them, it was difficult to confine action to the first class of commodities; and c) the essence of international trade being the exchange of different kinds of goods, it was far from easy "to find within a single group of commodities that compensatory factor, which ultimately underlies every commercial agreement".[1]

It was not until the autumn of 1929, when the post-Conference lull was over and the danger of a renewal of active tariff warfare acute, that the governments decided to attempt direct collective negotiations for a general reduction of tariffs. But by the time the Tariff Truce Conference met in February 1930, the opportunity had passed. Had the opportunity been seized in 1927 or even in 1928 when the fate of the Prohibitions Convention hung in the balance, it is possible that a tariff truce might have been concluded and some tariff reductions agreed between countries most directly affected by the prevailing tendencies, which might have been followed by bilateral and group negotiations for more permanent stabilization and further reductions. The fact that the necessary stimulus to intergovernmental action was lacking in those fateful years reflects the fear that each country felt when faced by the practical implications of applying the policies all or almost all advocated. For the application of those policies would inevitably have involved an initial shock, a reduction in prices, unemployment in some industries, not offset at once, perhaps, by increasing employment in others, the protests of those adversely affected and the political dangers of these protests. It also reflects the absence of any clear popular conception, even in the countries that were leaders in the movement, of the ultimate

[1] Report of the Economic Consultative Committee: Second Session, Geneva, 1929. League of Nations document C.192.M.73. 1929. II.

goal of freer trade policies and the consequent failure of the World Economic Conference to evoke strong popular support for its recommendations. The idea of freer trade was not effectively linked to that of increased welfare in the public mind, nor the idea of greater economic isolation with that of diminished welfare and increasing dangers of international friction.

Had a greater measure of popular support been forthcoming, had Governments acted with greater resolution, had opportunities been fully exploited, some advance in the direction of tariff demobilization might clearly have been expected. But it is important to bear in mind the limitations to which any such move would have been subject. Fundamental problems would have remained and deep-lying tendencies and forces continued to operate which make it scarcely conceivable that the broad lines—as distinct from the accidental features—of policy pursued in most European countries could have been very different from what they were. To make this point clear it may be well to pick up again the thread of the argument contained in the preceding section.

Some of the factors contributing to higher tariffs which we have indicated were temporary phenomena arising out of the Great War; they made an early post-war rise in tariffs inevitable but they had largely worked themselves out by the end of our period. Some, of more enduring influence, sprang from what it is now generally agreed were errors in human judgment and policy. Amongst such may be ranged the whole familiar catena of mistakes from the endeavour of certain governments to protect an incompetent or unfavourably situated industry at one end of the scale to the two major volitional causes of the distortion of trade and commercial policy in the period; the endeavour to extract large-scale reparations from Germany while restricting imports from that country and the failure of the United States to adapt her commercial policy to the fundamental change in her balance of payments. The pressure by the debtors to meet their obligations led to an unstable balance which ultimately collapsed and the general feeling of economic insecurity was one of the most pervasive causes both of the desire of governments to isolate their countries behind high tariffs and of their reluctance to move out of that isolation and incur the hazards of a world economy.

— 131 —

But the really fundamental factors were those arising out of the stage of economic evolution reached and the precarious economic situation of many European countries, and the impact on those basic economic conditions of the ferment of nationalism and the instability of the post-war world. These phenomena were interdependent; the course of policies was determined by a combination of the forces they produced. But their respective influences can be distinguished.

We have noted with what circumspection and with what scant results autonomous tariff reduction was recommended. This was due to the fact that, while each country believed that the tariffs imposed by others were damaging to it, it believed that its own were an asset not readily, certainly not gratuitously, to be sacrificed. There was, that is, no general belief that each extension of the division of labour would bring about an economy in production and hence an increase in welfare, or that each country must gain, even if the degree of gain varied, from a general reduction in trade barriers.

The economy in the more highly industrialized States had become so rigid that the advantages of lower tariffs were seriously questioned. When the factors of production could be shifted with relative ease from one occupation to another and full employment of resources might reasonably be expected, a lowering of tariffs should, it was argued, lead to an international specialization from which all would benefit, without creating too much disturbance in the process. But in the post-war world, full employment of resources was quite generally not attained in industrial states. Labour had become highly specialized and immobile; wage and price adjustments were extremely difficult to effect. The lowering of tariffs would have involved an inrush of foreign goods, forcing down certain prices in a highly rigid productive and price structure, and increasing unemployment in certain industries without any manifest certainty of increasing employment elsewhere.

In the face of this situation, which was more generally felt in the bones of the politician and the business man than expounded by the pen of the economist (though gradually it was quite fully expounded), the recommendations of the various conferences we have considered appear at first sight paradoxical. But in fact the paradox may have been more apparent than real. The lesson

— 132 —

to be drawn is rather that the possibility of achieving tariff reductions at any moment was dependent on the phase of the trade cycle reached at that moment, than that no reduction was possible or desirable. No reduction could be attained save under conditions of general prosperity, relatively full employment and, preferably, rising prices. The date for the 1927 Conference was thus well chosen, though the slump came too quickly.

But the influence of the trade cycle on commercial policy was more profound and more positive than this. It did not simply determine the timing of action, it directly affected the attitude of the business world and of Governments to the whole problem of foreign trade. This point is one which will need further consideration in connection with the policies pursued after 1929, but it requires to be stated briefly here. As observed above, the richer industrial States had reached a stage of economic development and of wealth at which consumers' demand had become more erratic, more susceptible to sudden contraction, than in areas and periods in which a very large proportion of demand consisted of the bare necessities of existence. Throughout the whole inter-war period Governments were becoming more conscious of the risks inherent in this unstable demand, the risks of depressions and unemployment, and of the obligations which those risks imposed on them. With this growing sense of responsibility developed the fear that, if the economy of a country were largely dependent on uncontrollable foreign supplies and demands, the government's power to influence economic activity, to avoid or overcome a depression, would prove inadequate.

This factor was perhaps not of major importance during the 'twenties; it became of dominant importance after 1930; but it resulted directly from secular changes in economic and demographic structure, certain of which had been greatly accelerated by the war of 1914-1918. By the later 'thirties, a stage had been reached in the whole process of economic evolution at which it was becoming obvious that, were Governments only willing to cooperate, the solution to these difficulties lay not in isolation and contraction, but in joint efforts to overcome the trade cycle itself. Indeed a Delegation of the League of Nations appointed to report on this subject was in the middle of its labours at the outbreak of the present war. In reviewing the development of

— 133 —

policy during this period, it is important to remember that the war itself broke off the work in hand.

While the highly industrial and richer States had reached a stage of economic development which rendered them peculiarly sensitive to depressions, many agricultural States were eager to develop their industry both in order to absorb surplus agricultural population and as an insurance against the risk of violent changes in the prices of their agricultural exports and in their balances of payments. It was inevitable that they should demand a high degree of protection for their new industries and find it difficult to reduce that protection later. It is not so obvious why they should have been unwilling to reduce duties on the wide range of industrial articles which they did not produce and had no immediate prospect of producing. The purpose of the duties on such goods was threefold: to produce revenue, to encourage the establishment of foreign industries within the country and to restrict the volume of non-essential imports in order to safeguard the national balance of payments and currency. These countries were poor, they were greatly in need of foreign capital, they were apprehensive of any action that might compromise their currencies or render them unable to meet their heavy foreign obligations. How could they be expected to apply the recommendations of the 1927 Conference until and unless those problems were at least in the way to finding a solution? Nor would the application of the Conference recommendations by the industrial countries have greatly assisted them, for agrarian protectionism was only in its early stages in 1927-1929 and the tariffs attacked by the Conference were the industrial tariffs by which the agricultural countries were, as exporters, only indirectly affected.

The problem constituted by the multiplicity of small and poor economic units in Central and Eastern Europe, heavily indebted to the Western World, was extremely complex and purely economic measures could only have made a partial contribution to its solution. Among such economic measures, however, the primary need was for a constructive plan to facilitate the development of their industries and for help in the execution of that plan. Since no action along these lines was initiated, it is understandable that the agricultural countries were unwilling to take the risks involved in any liberalization of their tariff policies.

— 134 —

So far, we have discussed the instability and insecurity of the post-war world mainly in terms of internal economic and social conditions; but the effects of external elements of insecurity on commercial policies were no less fateful. The extent to which the international commercial relationships existing before the first World War depended upon confidence in political stability, in the stability of foreign currencies and in the contractual honesty of States is perhaps insufficiently appreciated. Such conditions provided the framework essential to long-term commercial agreements and stable tariff policies. That framework, shattered by the war, was never fully restored. It is true that currencies were gradually stabilized and the memories of the Russian debt repudiation and the indirect defaults resulting from the depreciation of currencies partly forgotten by the later 20's. It is true that the years immediately following the World Economic Conference were the heyday of international political co-operation in the inter-war period; they were also the heyday of international economic co-operation. But one must not overestimate the extent of the return of confidence, especially in the political world. Reporting in 1931, the Sub-Committee of Economic Experts set up by the Commission of Enquiry for European Union expressed the opinion that "the economic development of which Europe stands so much in need is dependent upon an assurance of lasting peace; in the absence of this assurance, the nations are not content to become dependent upon one another for food, raw materials, or the basic products of industry".[1]

That chronic lack of confidence in permanent peace in Europe was really of fundamental importance. It was fundamental because European Governments inevitably tended to approach the problem of commercial policy primarily from the angle of national defence and national power; if they endeavoured to enhance the economic welfare of their peoples, to find solutions for economic and social problems, they sought to combine these ends with the overriding political end and to refrain from policies incompatible with the latter; inevitably, their commercial relationships with other countries, and more especially those directly feared, were imbued with the spirit of conflict rather than of co-operation.

[1] League of Nations document C.510.M.125. 1931. VII.

— 135 —

Accentuating the instability and insecurity which we have discussed, and in turn aggravated by them, nationalism was a force
consistently resisting the forces making for greater world integration. In the violent forms which it assumed in certain countries
of Central and Eastern Europe, it was the product of the Great
War, the result of the enhanced sense of national unity and of
the xenophobia aroused in the gigantic struggle of peoples and
nationalities, the result of the history preceding the liberation of
subject peoples.

CHAPTER IV

COMMERCIAL POLICY, 1930-1939

1. SUMMARY OF PROPOSALS AND THE COURSE OF POLICY.

The evolution of commercial policy in the inter-war period falls into two phases of almost equal duration. From 1920 to 1929, in spite of an almost constant rise in tariff barriers, the general trend of policy was, as we have seen, towards a return to something like the pattern of pre-war commercial relationships; from 1930 to 1939, in spite of the momentous change in United States policy after 1934, in spite, too, of the temporary relaxation of restrictions in many countries, as post-depression recovery reached its zenith, the general trend was set with increasing force towards greater national economic isolation and new forms of inter-State economic relationships.

The prospect, gradually confirmed in the course of the year 1929, of a further strengthening of protection in the United States on the one hand, and the deepening of the economic depression in the primary producing countries and its spread to the United States and other industrial countries, on the other, marked the turning point. The immediate effect of the first factor on policies elsewhere was very marked; and when the Hawley-Smoot tariff finally passed into law in June 1930, numerous countries promptly raised their tariffs. But its direct effect on the course of world policy in the years that followed became of secondary importance compared with its indirect effect in deepening the world economic depression, each phase and aspect of which brought its own baleful consequences.

The characteristic developments in commercial policy under the stress of the depression may be very briefly recapitulated:

(i) The collapse of markets and the fall of prices led each country to endeavour to protect its price structure and to maintain, as far as it could, both the level of domestic employment and the stability of its currency by keeping out foreign goods and seizing for its own exports the largest possible share of the

— 137 —

dwindling foreign market. Recourse was had almost everywhere to the classical method of economic defence, namely the raising of tariffs.

(ii) The financial crisis of the summer of 1931, involving the breakdown of the structure of multilateral settlements and accordingly an increased pressure on the balances of payments of many countries, was followed by currency depreciation in many countries and a welter of new and more formidable trade restrictions.

New tariffs were introduced (for example, in the United Kingdom) and existing tariffs raised, and other forms of restriction, exchange control, quotas, etc., made their appearance and soon came to overshadow tariffs as obstacles to trade. The speed with which this movement spread to almost all countries of the world is explained by the intricate manner in which the active and passive trade balances of each country depend upon one another and dovetail into those of other countries.

(iii) Most of the countries which abandoned the gold standard or further depreciated their currencies following the lead of the United Kingdom—the British Dominions, the Scandinavian countries and numerous other countries in Europe, Latin America and Asia—linked their currencies to sterling. The United States dollar was allowed to depreciate in April 1933.

Four currency groupings thus emerged: (1) the gold bloc—France, Switzerland, the Netherlands, Italy (until 1934), Belgium and Luxemburg (until 1935)—maintaining the parity of their currencies and full convertibility; (2) countries maintaining an artificial parity by means of exchange control (Germany, Italy (after 1934), in varying degrees certain of the primary producing countries of Europe); (3) countries with depreciated and controlled exchanges (most Latin-American countries and some European countries such as Greece and Czechoslovakia); (4) countries with depreciated and free exchanges.

These currency developments had profound effects on the course of international trade and on commercial policies.

(iv) The countries of the fourth—and to some extent, American countries of the third—group were in a position to pursue policies of domestic reflation, without recourse to extreme measures of trade restriction. The fair degree of currency stability

— 138 —

within the sterling area facilitated an expansion of trade between the members of that group.

The devaluation acted as an added barrier to imports from and stimulated exports to the countries with over-valued exchanges. These countries, whose position was thus seriously aggravated, resorted to increasingly stringent measures to restrict imports and encourage exports.

(v) Recourse to import quotas on a large scale was characteristic of the defensive measures adopted by countries of the "gold bloc." In France, there was a special reason for quotas, in that numerous items of her tariff had been consolidated for long periods.

(vi) In the countries practising exchange-control, quotas were supplemented by the rationing of foreign exchange for the purchase of imports. Exchange-control was rapidly developed into an instrument for the purpose of minimizing the need for, and maximizing the acquisition of, free foreign exchange. This purpose was achieved mainly through the use of bilateral clearings.

(vii) Clearings were first established in order to enable certain free-currency countries to collect the service of debts from and continue some trading with, countries with controlled currencies—particularly Germany, which declared a moratorium on the transfer of debt payments in 1934. The countries with controlled currencies established clearings in order to trade among themselves.

(viii) The closing of the established channels of trade and the breakdown of the world-wide multilateral system of settlements provoked attempts by many countries to develop their exchanges of goods and realize a system of settlement within restricted areas. Thus, the United Kingdom and France expanded their imperial trade. Germany sought new outlets and sources of supply in Central and South Eastern Europe and in Latin America. Certain of the smaller European countries endeavoured—though on the whole with small success—to expand their mutual trade by means of regional trade agreements.

The acute difficulties of settlement experienced by many debtor countries gave rise to the problem of "commercial access to raw materials."

(ix) With certain notable exceptions (for example, the efforts of the Oslo group), the above developments were accompanied

— 139 —

by the creation of new or the extension of existing preferential systems and the emergence of new forms of commercial discrimination. By the Ottawa Agreements of 1932, and the Import Duties Act adopted in the United Kingdom the same year, a general preferential system within the British Commonwealth and the Colonial Empire was established. The German trading methods were frankly and flagrantly discriminatory. Through the use of exchange-control and quantitative restrictions, the M.F.N. clause lost much of its value in European commercial relationships.

The lowest point in the depression was reached in most countries around 1932/33. The four or five years that followed were a period of recovery, slow and uneven at first, rapid and general in 1936 and the earlier part of 1937. After a recession in 1937/38, the year preceding the outbreak of war was, in general, one of renewed economic recovery.

As we have seen, after the economic and monetary dislocation of the early 20's, emergency trade restrictions had been gradually relaxed and the old pattern of commercial relationships in part restored. The course of post-depression policy in Europe in the thirties was fundamentally different. Except during a short interval between 1935 and 1937—more especially after the devaluation of the "gold bloc" currencies in the autumn of 1936—the general tendency was towards the extension and consolidation of trade restrictions. Measures that had been adopted for defensive purposes became permanent instruments of offensive policy. Germany and Italy pursued autarky as a primary objective and exerted political pressure to bring the smaller countries of Eastern and South Eastern Europe within their economic orbit. In Germany and Italy and to a lesser degree their satellites, state control over foreign trade was extended to cover individual commercial transactions, and a centralized system of state regulated trading superseded the system of competitive trading by individual merchants.

A restraining influence on the spread of these tendencies was exercised by the United States under the Reciprocal Tariff Agreements programme of 1934. The United Kingdom, though not unaffected by the trend towards bilateral trade regulation, also threw her weight into the balance in favour of the maintenance of the basic institutions of an international trading system.

— 140 —

The new tendencies towards intensified trade restrictions and discriminations were denounced, as is related in Part I, by every important international gathering held between 1930 and 1939. Among the measures proposed as means to the desired ends, some related directly to commercial policies, others to the removal of the conditions underlying those policies. Proposals of the first kind were largely concerned with tariffs. The most important were:

(i) The Tariff Truce, as a first step to multilateral or simultaneous bilateral negotiations. This was rejected at the Geneva Conference of 1930, but, under strong representations from the United States Government, accepted by almost all countries for the period of the Monetary and Economic Conference of 1933. The "Oslo Group" in 1930 adopted a procedure for notification of, and appeal against, tariff increases within the group. It proved impossible to extend this practice or even (as proposed by the League Council in 1935) to obtain a general agreement providing for one month's notification of changes in tariffs or other restrictions.

(ii) The allowance of permanent exceptions to M.F.N. in case of agreements between groups of States for the purpose of reducing tariffs, urged by the Commission of Enquiry for European Union (1931) and the Preparatory Committee for the London Conference of 1933, as well as by the Montevideo Conference of American States (December 1933), and frequently taken up later, for instance, as part of the van Zeeland plan of 1938. The Ouchy Convention of July 1932, concluded between the Netherlands, Belgium and Luxemburg, was the test case. It failed, owing primarily to the refusal of the United Kingdom either to become a party or to forego its rights to benefit by the proposed tariff reductions.

(iii) Bilateral agreements, based on M.F.N., for the reduction of tariffs. These received the special commendation of the Montevideo Conference and, after the re-orientation of United States policy in 1934, found a prominent place in subsequent Conference recommendations as a practical and hopeful approach to the tariff problem.

In the latter part of this period, the Hull agreements brought about a reduction in tariffs affecting a substantial volume of world trade as well as an extension of the principle of equal trading opportunity.

(iv) As regards quotas, a gradual enlargement of industrial quotas with a view to their ultimate removal and improvements in the quota system so as to avoid discrimination were recommended (e.g. by the Economic Committee, 1933 and 1937). The replacement of industrial quotas by "tariff quotas" and the enlargement of agricultural quotas were likewise proposed (van Zeeland, 1938). A direct attack on quotas was made by the Oslo Group in 1937 under the short-lived Hague Convention.

(v) Payments agreements were recommended in preference to clearings agreements, so long as the retention of exchange-control made such arrangements necessary. As regards the method of decontrol, the League Committee on Clearings (1935) proposed that commercial transactions should first be liberated, private compensation encouraged and the free rate of exchange allowed to prevail in a gradually expanding field of operations. Between 1935 and 1937, there was a fairly widespread movement towards a simplification and relaxation of control measures along the lines adumbrated by the League Committee.

There were obvious limitations to what could be achieved by means of a direct attack on the problems of high tariffs, quotas and exchange-control. The really central problem was how to remove or attenuate the force of those depression factors that were considered by Governments—rightly or wrongly—to make the retention of such measures inevitable.

One important factor, it is true, was the severity of those very restrictions on the world's principal import markets. Conferences and Committees consistently emphasized the special responsibility of the richer and the creditor countries *vis-a-vis* those that were impoverished and indebted. An element in every programme, from Stresa in 1932 to the van Zeeland plan in 1938, aiming at the restoration of free exchanges in Central and Eastern Europe was the opening of the Western, and particularly of Western European, markets. Very little was done in this direction.

But no less vital were the problems of indebtedness, of the cessation of long-term capital movements, of "hot money", of currency uncertainties, of discrepancies between national price-levels and last, but not least, of low commodity prices. In very

— 142 —

rough outline, the main recommendations of Conferences on these financial issues were as follows:

1) Currency stabilization was held to be of primary importance. The proposals in this sense put forward by the Preparatory Committee of the Monetary and Economic Conference failed when the United States was unwilling to enter into any undertaking regarding the future value of the dollar, but virtual dollar-sterling stability was achieved in 1934. Thenceforward, the best hope of extending the area of stable currencies was seen to lie in bringing about an orderly devaluation of the "gold bloc" and as many as possible of the controlled currencies. The attempt made under the Tripartite Agreement in 1936 to achieve this result was only partially successful owing to the subsequent decline in the French franc.

2) If an alignment of over-valued currencies was a condition of stabilization, it was also urged as a condition of removing the wide discrepancies between national price-levels which had arisen partly owing to differences in currency policy and domestic economic policies, partly owing to trade restrictions. While such discrepancies remained, the retention of controls to bolster up artificially high price-levels was clearly inevitable.

3) The raising of commodity prices was considered no less essential. This task was approached from various angles. In the early years of the depression, the most urgent problem facing the European Conferences appeared to be the collapse of the export prices of European agricultural products and various schemes for the revalorization of such products were proposed. These schemes came to nothing, although some help was forthcoming through the negotiation of bilateral agreements of different kinds between those countries and European importers. A more general approach was through international commodity controls, as proposed by the Preparatory Committee and a Commission of the Monetary and Economic Conference of 1933. The Wheat and Sugar Agreements of 1933 and 1937 respectively were the somewhat limited results of these efforts. The most important of the Preparatory Committee proposals, however, was to raise commodity prices through the reflationary effects of a cheap money policy. This policy, though not open to the "gold bloc" countries, was successfully pursued within the dollar-sterling area.

— 143 —

4) Debt settlement, with financial assistance to countries anxious to abandon exchange control and align their price structure by an orderly devaluation, was recommended by successive conferences. None of the general schemes of which such proposals formed a part came to anything; but outside support for the purpose of facilitating decontrol was forthcoming in the case of Austria and a few countries which relaxed their controls between 1935 and 1937, while a large number of provisional arrangements between debtors and creditors were made under the general pressure of events.

2. REASONS FOR THE COMPARATIVE INEFFECTIVENESS OF CONFERENCE PROPOSALS.

The restraining influence exercised by international Conferences and Committees and the aid which they afforded to those anxious to promote more liberal policies must not be overlooked. Among the developments in line with their recommendations, the most important were the historic reversal of United States tariff policy in 1934 and the drive for lower tariffs and M.F.N. undertaken by the United States in the years that followed. The League Economic Committee's defence of M.F.N. as the essential basis of peaceful international trading and the last barrier against all-out trade warfare may be described as a successful "rear-guard action". Tariff discrimination was throughout held in check even in Europe and although quantitative restrictions are inherently incompatible with M.F.N. and were indeed normally applied on the basis of reciprocity, there was a constant pressure on Governments to apportion quotas and foreign exchange on some basis of at least historical equity.

Other achievements to which international action contributed were: the Tariff Truce of 1933 and the agreements for consultation in regard to tariffs and other restrictions concluded between the Oslo countries; the reflation based on cheap money and depreciated exchanges carried out within the whole sterling area under the leadership of the United Kingdom, which was of the greatest importance in checking the trend towards further restrictions in those countries; the currency alignment of the "gold bloc" in 1936, followed by temporary relaxation of trade restrictions; the substantial improvements in the administration of quotas and exchange-control and finally the actual measures of decontrol taken by several countries between 1935 and 1937.

The influence of the inter-American Conferences, the Congresses of the International Chamber of Commerce and the League Assembly and Committees, was clearly salutary; that of certain other gatherings (notably the London Conference of 1933) was, as stated below, probably on the whole unfavourable.

The partial achievements of international action, however, only serve to qualify the failure to prevent the disintegration of the world trading system. The proposals of the Conferences either remained a dead letter or were applied on too small a scale or within too narrow an area to offset the opposing trends. In spite of the gradual recovery in economic conditions after 1933 and the removal or attenuation of many of the economic factors which had led to the imposition of quantitative restrictions, no substantial or permanent relaxation of such restrictions ensued. The political, centrifugal forces prevailed.

There was little hope of reversing economic tendencies once those political forces had gained momentum. But why did the efforts made in the early thirties to arrest the trend towards economic isolation fail?

The first answer to this question is that at the beginning of the depression there was a quite inadequate knowledge of the concerted measures between countries, or even within each country, by which recovery from a major depression might be brought about. The pressure of the social problems to which the depression gave rise forced governments to take some action, however piecemeal, at least to relieve distress. To eliminate as far as possible influences coming from abroad seemed to diminish for a time, at any rate, the economic dangers so obscure and so threatening. The proposals put forward with international authority for maintaining some measure of freedom in trade relations were directed rather against one of the secondary effects of the depression, namely the drift towards isolationism, than against the depression itself. And when constructive proposals for restoring economic activity—for instance, the cheap money policy recommended by the London Conference Preparatory Committee— were made, agreement on them could not be reached.

There was indeed in those early days no plan for concerted action to relieve the depression; the machinery for executing a

— 145 —

plan, had there been one, was embryonic; there was no accepted corpus of doctrines for national action. *Sauve qui peut.*

The momentum of the depression was such that it could only have been arrested by courageous and constructive policies carefully timed and unhesitatingly applied by at least the major industrial countries acting in unison. But the momentum was uneven, and, as the League Economic Committee observed, "the situations which the crisis created in the several countries were so different that a concerted—or even analogous—policy was impossible."[1] It is clear from the context that reference is made here to political possibility and, in this sense, the weight of the argument can be appreciated if one contrasts, for example, the favoured position of France in the early years of the depression with that of the debtor countries who were desperately struggling with the transfer problem created by the reversal of the flow of foreign capital and the steep fall in the prices of primary products. Concerted action might have saved the situation if governments had known what action to concert; but it is at least improbable that they would have agreed on a programme of concerted action at a time when the shadow of the depression had scarcely crossed the frontiers of some of the most important of them.

Can we assume that concerted action might have been achieved, had the depression been less acute, had situations been more similar, had different countries not been hit at different times and in different ways, had the impossibility of escaping by purely national measures of defence been more fully understood? Clearly not. In the absence of any real knowledge of or unanimity of opinion regarding methods of combating depression, individual and cut-throat measures were to be expected. France, the United Kingdom and the United States of America pursued divergent policies on the basis of different and incompatible theories. In the United Kingdom, the new tariff became a vital element in a recovery based on cheap money and the abandonment of the gold standard; currency depreciation was conceived as an instrument of reflation in the United States; while French policy pursued the then orthodox deflationary course.

[1] Remarks on the Present Phase of International Economic Relations, Geneva, 1935.

— 146 —

If successful concerted action postulated agreement on questions of economic policy, at least between the leading Powers, it also postulated a degree of international solidarity far greater than at any time showed signs of developing—a willingness on the part of all countries, and especially the richer and more powerful, to abstain from defensive or discriminatory measures harmful to others, a willingness on the part of creditors to accept goods in payment of debt obligations, whatever the effect on their price levels and employment situation. But there were two other factors of steadily increasing importance working against the acceptance of the recommendations made in favour of more liberal trade policies during the depression: (a) the obstructions imposed by what were in fact the semi-concealed military policies of certain states; and (b) the inhibitions caused by recent experience which rendered many of the recommendations unacceptable. Of these inhibitions, by far the most important was the fear of inflation which was deeply imbedded in the minds of the public in all those countries that had passed through a period of hyper-inflation in the 20's. This fear, coupled with a widespread misunderstanding of the nature and causes of inflation led the governments of many of those countries to reject immutably all proposals in favour of devaluation.

The new restrictions were thus a consequence of the various forces brought into play by the depression (above all the political effects of mass unemployment), of the revival of old fears and of the lack of any agreed policy for dealing with the depression. They became entrenched as part of national recovery programmes and political systems and thus persisted in spite of the attenuation of many of the economic conditions that had produced them.

The breakdown of the Monetary and Economic Conference of 1933 (when some constructive proposals were put forward) was of fateful consequence for the subsequent course of economic policies. The world's hopes of finding a basis on which international trade could be revived were turned to that Conference. The very magnitude of those hopes served to enhance the psychological effect of the Conference's failure, which helped to confirm every country in the belief that it must solve its depression problems and plan for recovery itself, as best it could. But while recognizing the adverse psychological effects of that failure, it

— 147 —

remains of course true that neither currency measures alone (in the narrow sense of that term) nor the reduction of trade barriers would have sufficed to restore economic activity or to put the international financial mechanism into working order. Indeed, no proposals which failed to deal with, for instance, the problem of short-term capital movements and the breakdown of the world system of multilateral settlements, could have proved more than a temporary palliative. To some extent it is true to say that the disequilibria in international trade were the cause of the trade barriers rather than caused by them and that to deal with the barriers alone would have meant mistaking effect for cause.

The economic aims of most national recovery programmes, elaborated and perfected in the years following the London Conference, were to find work for the unemployed and prevent a further fall in prices. The pursuit of these aims—which were held to require national insulation from outside economic influences—and the gradual aberration from them in certain countries under the influence of political motives provide the broad explanation of the new protectionism that developed in Europe in those years—the transformation of emergency defensive measures into permanent instruments of offensive economic policy, the emergence of autarky as a principal objective of policy, and the extension and consolidation of state control over trade. Quotas came to be used both as a means of stabilizing the domestic market and as bargaining counters in the struggle for foreign markets. Upon exchange-control, Germany and her imitators began to build up an entirely new system of regulated foreign trade, essential features of which were over-valuation of national currencies and bilateral clearings. The breakdown of the system of multilateral world trade following the breakdown of the world monetary system had started the movement toward bilateralism. The opportunity was seized by Germany to expand and stabilize her markets by imposing a system of rigid bilateralism on her weaker neighbours. To a limited extent, other economically powerful States also used their bargaining position to secure specially favourable terms and thus an advantage over third parties.

The movement towards autarky, particularly in Germany, Italy and Japan was at once a reaction to the repression and a preparation for war. The failure of concerted action had paved

the way for militant nationalism. In the 'twenties, political uncertainty and instability impeded the advance in economic welfare which was desired by all; in the middle 'thirties preparation
for war rather than economic welfare became the prime objective
of the policy of certain governments. Under the threat of war,
considerations of defence perforce assumed increasing importance
even in the most peace-loving countries.

National "planning" and the regulation of foreign trade are
interdependent. While every new restriction on imports encourages the "regulation" of the industry concerned, industrial
or agricultural regulation is impracticable without a control of
competition, domestic and foreign. Thus, the extension of national planning—a snowball process, each industrial plan postulating for its success the control of other industries—was inevitably accompanied by an extension of centralized control over
foreign trade.

At an early stage in that process, direct quantitative restrictions and exchange control are found to be a useful adjunct to
tariffs. At a later stage, such as that reached by Germany and
Italy in the later 'thirties, when not only the character, the
prices, the quantities, the destination and the provenance of
goods crossing national frontiers but also all individual trading
operations are brought under state control, such measures are
essential.

The postulate of the conferences, that there was a general desire to abandon quantitative restrictions and exchange-control
and to return to a system of relatively free and unregulated trading and to an international monetary standard, thus gradually
ceased to apply. Many small countries, it is true, found the new
tendencies not only immediately damaging to them but ominous
for both their economic and political future. Several of them,
as we have seen, made great efforts to relax quantitative restrictions in the period 1935-1937. But the growing preponderance
of Germany in the foreign trade of Eastern and South-Eastern
European countries and the German trading methods which
raised their prices and thus reduced their competitive capacity
in the free markets, made it well-nigh impossible for them not
to accept their place in the German system. Moreover, the
darkening prospects of war enhanced the danger of a flight of

— 149 —

capital if controls were removed and discouraged the foreign credits that might have facilitated orderly devaluation and de-control.

In the later 'thirties, the commercial policies of Europe were entirely dominated by the anticipation or fear of war. The rigid control of trade and of capital movements in Germany were an integral part of the mobilization of all national resources for military purposes. Clearings had likewise become an essential instrument for the economic and political control of dependent countries. The proposals that continued to be put forward by international bodies for the abatement of controls and a restoration of the international monetary system in Europe were part of the political endeavour to avert war.

In the years of depression and of recovery, what had been required to prevent the disintegration of the world trading system was a co-ordination of national economic policies and whole-hearted co-operation between the administrations of the more important countries in the financial as well as the strictly economic sphere. The Tripartite Agreement of September 1936 was a step along the road of such co-operation; thereafter, further progress under the influence of the United States or the United Kingdom was still possible over a large part of the world. But in Europe and in the Far East, the political foundations for any liberalization of commercial policy had been shattered and the tendencies towards closed economies and rigid state regulation gained impetus from year to year under the exigencies of a near-war economy.

CHAPTER V

WERE THE RECOMMENDATIONS OF THE CONFERENCES MISDIRECTED?

The early post-war conferences contributed to the partial restoration of pre-war commercial practices; to a limited extent, they achieved their purpose. The recommendations of the World Economic Conference of 1927 regarding tariff policy exercised an immediate—though, as we have seen, very temporary—influence; they had the further merit of bringing home to Governments and peoples the fact, hitherto contested, that "tariffs, though within the sovereign jurisdiction of the separate States, are not a matter of purely domestic interest"; they called attention to a grave pathological development in the relationships between States.

But, if the analysis given in the foregoing chapters is correct, the 1927 Conference, in insisting on tariff reduction and in reiterating the demand for long-term agreements, tariff stability and the abandonment of the practices of commercial warfare, took too narrow a view of a highly complex problem. Had the Conference been held ten years later, there can be little doubt that it would have placed the need for joint anti-depression policies in the forefront of its programme. That could not have been expected in 1927. But in that year and throughout the earlier post-war years, commercial policy tended to be considered as a problem distinct and apart and not as an aspect of economic policy as a whole. That inherent defect in procedure and outlook was due no doubt very largely to the fact that international bodies were reluctant to interfere with issues which were considered essentially domestic and that the part of economic policy which was most clearly international in its effects was that dealing with foreign trade (but it is noticeable that less hesitation was shown in making recommendations on financial matters of a strictly domestic character).

This unwillingness to interfere with national economic problems accounts, in part, for the very general nature of the recom-

— 151 —

mendations made. There was no endeavour to consider in detail
the tariff rates or the general commercial policy of particular
countries; there was no attempt to work out for any country a
careful plan of industrial development. It is difficult to escape
the conclusion, in the light of subsequent evidence, that much
greater progress might have been made towards freer trade had
more courage been shown. If international help had been offered
to countries in the elaboration of a carefully thought-out plan of
industrial development, if technicians, machinery and equipment
on credit and possibly other capital assistance had been put at
the disposal of governments, and the need for high tariffs on
products of the new industries recognized, it should have been
possible to incorporate in the whole constructive scheme an
undertaking by the beneficiary governments to reduce tariffs on
the products of other industries.

Such action as was taken to aid individual governments was
confined almost exclusively to financial reconstruction. It is
true that until monetary stabilisation had been achieved, all
recommendations in favour of long-term commercial treaties
were premature and were generally accepted as being rather
ideological than practical. By 1927, monetary stability had
been generally attained. How unstable the equilibrium was, was
perhaps not fully recognized; but if there was a failure to insist
sufficiently on the major causes of instability (reparations, the
large French liquid balances abroad, United States tariff policy)
that failure was one rather of degree of emphasis than of understanding.

The disastrous effects of uncontrolled budget deficits and inflation were manifest. The effects of loss of markets to industries
in the Succession States or of demographic pressure were perhaps
no less obvious though far less dramatic, and the need for international action to overcome these problems—as distinct from
sympathy or exhortation—was no less vital.

There was again, in that period, a misunderstanding of the
profundity of the changes which the war had caused or accelerated—the changes in economic structure and perhaps also the
changes in the spirit in which policy was formulated and applied.
The tendency to look back to 1913 still persisted. The doctrines
advocated were inherited from a time when labour and prices
were more mobile and economic fluctuations less violent, before

the emergence of the new problems posed, for example, by the "Balkanisation" of Europe. During the course of the depression in the 'thirties, it became increasingly apparent that the expansion of trade would not have sufficed to secure economic progress —that indeed some solution of the problem of economic stability was a prerequisite of both the growth of trade and the promotion of economic welfare. The traditional doctrines, which continued to be preached with only minor qualifications and amplifications, were comfortably worn but not visibly threadbare. They implied through their generalization no special criticism of any single State. They were conservative, but cloaked with liberalism. They demanded little prior work and study.

The last point is of great importance. Neither the League of Nations, nor the International Chamber of Commerce, was adequately equipped to deal with the problems of commercial policy. No Conference or Committee could alone have considered the detailed rates or the special conditions governing the policy of particular countries, nor could it have worked out for each country with others co-ordinated plans of economic development which, by improving internal economic conditions and stabilizing prices and markets, might have provided the basis for a reduction and stabilization of tariffs. The headquarters staff in Geneva was altogether too small to undertake the detailed and constant spadework that would have been required. The need for such a staff was never clearly appreciated and indeed so long as it was assumed that, given good will and understanding, trade barriers would fall like the walls of Jericho, this was natural.

That assumption was based on the belief that tariff policy could be separated from economic policy as a whole, and that, since a general reduction in tariffs was in the economic interest of all countries, governments, when brought to realise this fact, would draw the necessary consequences. None of these postulates was valid. It was perhaps unfortunate that so little was done until the later 'thirties—when the opportunity for successful international action had passed—either to re-interpret such free-trade doctrines as may have become obsolete and therefore unconvincing or to bring home to the public in intelligible terms the importance of an expansion of international trade within the framework of a world trading system as a means to achieving

— 153 —

an advance in economic and social welfare under conditions of international peace.

At the World Economic Conferences of 1927 and 1933, the aim of concerted action was conceived as being the conclusion of broad multilateral agreements. General multilateral conventions yielded positive, though limited results in achieving a greater measure of uniformity in national administrative practices or national laws or tax systems and in removing certain specific obstacles to international trade. But tariff barriers could only have been reduced by international convention if countries with wholly different tariff systems and levels had been prepared—as they not unnaturally never were—to apply some uniform system of pruning, such for instance as a given percentage reduction all round. In fact, the tariff concessions that might have been expected—and were desired—differed from country to country and for the purpose of achieving such concessions, negotiation between pairs and small groups of countries was the first essential step. It is of course true that, owing to the complex nature of multilateral trade, such negotiation would have greatly benefited from central direction and co-ordination.

Conference recommendations, especially in the 'twenties, had further weaknesses which require to be noted. They were frequently little more than formulae representing a compromise between divergent or ever conflicting opinions; they frequently concealed fundamentally incompatible aims and irreconcilable interests of the principal economic Powers in the matters of tariff policy; they were accepted by delegates and governments with every variety of mental reservation as to their practical applicability. They did not bind governments to specific acts of policy[1] nor were the Governments which endorsed them always competent to take the necessary decisions.

The proposals made after the middle 'thirties may, at first sight, appear unrealistic in the sense that they were based on the postulate that all countries desired, or could be induced by suitable concessions, to return to a free price economy and the pursuit of economic welfare. This fact, however, reflects nothing more

[1] Cf. in this connection, the vague drafting of the majority of the "Declarations concerning the Recommendations of the International Economic Conference," League of Nations document C.E.1. 45. Geneva, 1928.

than the inevitable dilemma confronting all whose role is to promote co-operation and dissipate conflict.

Let us now attempt a broad explanation of the paradox which constitutes the theme of the present study. The discrepancy between the recommendations of Conferences and the policies actually pursued, between the professions and the actions of Governments, was due largely to the fact that neither were entirely suited to the circumstances and neither were based on a clear or fully informed conception of the issues involved. In regard to policy, sectional pressures rather than impartial judgement, sectional interests rather than the public interest were too often paramount. Policy was misdirected as a result of such pressures, as a result of the immediate impact of a persistent series of external events—the depreciation of currencies, the threat of political trouble—and as a result of the inescapable ignorance of the form that economic forces, which only slowly revealed themselves, would take. National economic policies in consequence tended to be concerned with the determination of immediate tactics rather than with the formulation of a broad strategy. The recommendations put forward at international meetings, on the other hand, tended to ignore the tactical issues and concentrate on strategy, a strategy which was based on the principles and conditions of the first rather than the third or fourth decades of the century. Viewed from the angle of many European countries, they appeared rather as pious hopes than as serious recommendations in regard to immediate policy and they bore the stigma attaching to propositions stated in absolute terms but postulating conditions unlikely of fulfillment. Because they seemed to disregard the problems which national commercial policies were designed, however crudely and shortsightedly, to meet, they were so frequently ignored.

This explains why Governments and individual experts often behaved with apparent inconsistency, why the same people who recommended one line of policy at Geneva or elsewhere were often responsible for pursuing the opposite policy at home. Ministers, officials, economists and business men alike continued to think about the broad issues of commercial policy in the light of the economic and political conditions obtaining in the spacious pre-war era and desired the general re-adoption of long-run policies appropriate to those conditions. But they were obliged

— 155 —

to act from day to day in the light of the pressing social and economic exigencies of the unstable post-war world. Mental adjustment to revolutionary change is inevitably a slow process; the real magnitude and scope of the differences between the pre- and the post-war world were concealed by many deceptive appearances of a return to normality in the 'twenties.

CHAPTER VI

CONCLUSIONS

The final purpose of this study is not simply to portray a facet of the history of commercial policy during the inter-war period nor to analyze the factors influencing that history; it is rather to consider the lessons for the future that may be drawn from that description and that analysis. These lessons are of two quite distinct orders: first, the broad conclusions that may be drawn regarding the practicability and desirability of alternative policies and secondly, more specific conclusions regarding the suitability of possible procedures for attaining the objects in view. It is convenient to treat those two classes of deduction in this order.

1. Conclusions Regarding Policy.

(a) The first obvious lesson resulting from both studies is that the chances of getting generally adopted a commercial policy designed to promote rather than to restrict international relations as a whole may be jeopardized in the first post-war months if governments fail to agree in advance upon some orderly process of decontrol and some financially and economically sane system of reviving the economic life of countries impoverished by the war. Commercial policy was distorted at the outset after the last war by the violent reaction to the danger of exchange dumping. The depreciation in exchanges was due very largely to the failure to appreciate that relief and the restarting of the machinery of production were a single problem or to consider the effect of the relief policies actually adopted on the power of States to obtain what was required for industrial revival.

There was indeed a general failure to take any concerted international action to achieve an orderly transition from war to peace economy. But this is the first problem that arises and cannot be considered in terms of commercial policy alone.

(b) Another of the two or three major causes of the failure to get more liberal commercial policies adopted was the continu-

— 157 —

ance of political insecurity—caused in large part by war-bred political passions. It is clearly not possible to prevent—though something may be done by governments to allay and much to promote—international mistrust. It follows that the first essential for the achievement of commercial policies designed to promote trade, is the establishment of a mechanism for the preservation of peace so adequate and sure as to create confidence despite antipathies or mistrust. Until this is done, governments are likely again to shun the world and seek a wholly insecure security in isolation.

(c) But after the experience of the 30's, apprehensions resulting from economic insecurity have become at least as important as fear of the risk of the recurrence of war. Governments faced by the social pressures caused by sudden and serious unemployment or rapidly shrinking farmers' income endeavoured to secure freedom of action for themselves by rendering their national economies as immune as possible from external economic influences. Commercial policy cannot be considered by itself therefore. It must be considered as a part of the more general, constructive policies agreed among governments for the prevention (or mitigation) of economic depressions and assurance of social stability.

(d) Failure to concert such policies will involve the risk of the revival of the type of autarkic commercial policies which developed during the 30's and the replacement of a commercial system by a mechanism for economic warfare.

(e) The dependence of commercial policy on

(1) An orderly transition from war to peace economy
(2) Political security
(3) Economic security

are perhaps the three major lessons to be deduced from the commercial history of the inter-war period, but there are others of a somewhat different order that may clearly be ranked as of almost equal importance. Of these the first is the absolute necessity of adapting commercial policies to the circumstances influencing national balances of payments. Great wars inevitably affect many items in those balances, and the changes brought about may require a rapid and radical modification of commercial policies in order to allow the flow of goods to adapt itself to the new conditions. If creditor countries impede the import of goods with which their debts can be paid, if new obligations are created and no commodity provision made for their service, if debtor countries obstruct the export of the goods with which they may meet the service of their debts, disequilibrium must be caused which will influence the commercial policy of almost all states. In such a state of disequilibrium long-term commercial treaties cannot be concluded, and high tariff rates or quotas are likely to be employed with which to negotiate short-term bargains.

(f) The tendency after the last war for international bodies to take a restricted view of their right to concern themselves with the economic policies of States resulted in an arbitrary line being drawn between commercial policy and other aspects of economic policy and in the failure to consider the whole catena of problems—relief reconstruction, surplus capacity resulting from the specialization of industries working for the war, etc.— which arose immediately after the Armistice. It led to a failure also to put forward constructive proposals later to meet the need of countries anxious to promote industrial development. Adaptation to the longer term economic or demographic forces, some of which may be accelerated by war, cannot be accomplished by measures of commercial policy alone. To consider such measures independently of other measures necessary for economic adjustment, as was frequently done especially in the 20's, is almost certain to fail to produce any useful results. Thus, planning for industrial development requires more than the imposition of high tariff rates; the execution of such plans may require external aid, technical or financial, and may afford an occasion for a careful revision of the aided countries' tariff schedules. Such a revision may necessitate the raising of certain duties to protect the new industries and the lowering of many others to reduce costs. Trade is more likely to be promoted if the economic structure and economic needs of each country are carefully considered, than by general declarations regarding commercial policy alone.

(g) During the 30's, the fact that commercial policy was an integral and inseparable part of economic policy as a whole gradually became self-evident. Indeed, there was a certain tendency towards the end of this decade for those responsible for commercial policy to claim that trade could not be released from its

— 159 —

shackles until the international credit and money mechanism had been restored, until the difficulties arising from international indebtedness had been solved, and for those responsible for financial policy to maintain that no monetary reform or satisfactory debt arrangements could be made while quantitative restrictions on trade continued in force. This apparent logical *impasse* was in fact a phase in the process of understanding the essential unity of the economic and financial issues; and the failure to abolish the restrictions was in the end not due to a lack of understanding of the technical issues at stake, which were very thoroughly studied, but to the unwillingness of certain States to promote political security or to abandon the new system by which they exercised commercial pressure. The essential lessons to be learned from the experience of the 30's would seem then to be not the difficulty of emerging from the sort of *impasse* that was created— granted good will—but

(a) that the pursuit of uncoordinated recovery programmes by great States is likely to involve a disruption of the whole mechanism of trade and economic relations in general and must inevitably do so if severe quantitative restrictions on trade are an integral part of such programmes;

(b) that any important market can, if it desires to do so, create price disequilibria between not only itself and the rest of the world but between markets largely dependent on it and the rest of the world, such as to set limits to the scope of multilateral trade; but

(c) that these limits do not necessarily preclude the maintenance of a free price economy in international trade (such, for instance, as that of the Sterling Bloc) among countries not within the orbit of the determinate influence of any country pursuing an opposed policy.

(h) The growing appreciation of the need to consider commercial policy in a wider setting resulted in two, in a sense contradictory, types of recommendation concerning agriculture—the first in favour of restricting the output of certain agricultural products, the second in favour of expanding the demand for foodstuffs by raising national standards of living and of nutrition. Though to some limited extent both types of policy were

— 160 —

applied, the problem of agricultural excess remained unsolved, and the friction caused by the growth of agricultural protectionism was but slightly mitigated. But there is no evidence to show that had peace been preserved and time been available for the development of these policies, agriculture would not have been materially assisted by them and the incentive to protect weakened. The first line of policy, however, is essentially restrictive, undynamic and unconstructive, while the second postulates and endeavours to promote a dynamic society and general welfare. The success of the second naturally lessens the need, if need there be, for the first.

(i) The M.F.N. clause, which should have been a means for spreading the benefits granted under trade agreements, tended to some extent at any rate, to check the granting of such benefits. This seems to have been due mainly to three distinct causes: (a) the half-hearted belief in the assumptions underlying the clause and the greater freedom of trade that it was intended to promote; (b) the reluctance of Governments to grant any benefits, even indirectly, to countries which enforced a non-negotiable tariff and high rates or to countries with which political relations were strained; (c) the employment of M.F.N. rights to prevent the formation of customs unions, or the formation of preferential areas in Europe, especially when preferences were being increased elsewhere.

A repetition of conditions in the future similar to those which obtained in the period under review is likely to have similar results. A whole-hearted belief in the beneficial effects of the clause is clearly once more likely to be dependent on the degree to which political security and economic security and activity are assured and on the removal of the other objections to the clause. The complete abolition of non-negotiable tariffs would no doubt go far to overcome the second of the objections mentioned; but so long as basic rates in any important markets are out of line with those of other countries or with the logic of a balance of payments situation, objections to the clause are likely to be raised.

The third group of objections, that connected with customs unions, raises still more complex issues.

A greater freedom of trade in the aggregate may be attained either by a given degree of universal tariff reductions or by a

— 161 —

given degree (or varying degrees) of reduction within specific areas. But the effects of these two alternatives may be widely dissimilar. The Peace Treaties, by increasing the number, decreased the size of the free trade areas and gave some rather restricted scope for their subsequent enlargement. The opportunity offered was not seized, and gradually vested interests within the areas to which that opportunity was offered and external opposition acquired sufficient influence to prevent agreements being reached. One result of this fact was the growth of the scepticism about the M.F.N. clause just mentioned; but the lessons of major importance to be drawn from this experience are (a) that if wider free trade areas are to be established, they should be created before peace-time vested interests have time to develop, and (b) that if either complete customs unions or preferential areas are to be given a chance of developing later, it would seem to be necessary to get certain safeguarding principles agreed upon in advance. The first of these two lessons is obvious and requires no exposition. Certain principles concerning the latter were discussed about 1930 but never formulated in an authoritative statement. The suggestions under consideration were that preferential unions between contiguous States or States having close economic affiliations might be recognized if (a) these states formed them in order to reduce rates of duty *inter se* and did not raise the rates against other countries, and (b) any other (such) country whose rates of duty did not average demonstrably higher than those of the contracting parties, could join the union by making concessions to those parties comparable to those which they had made to each other.

Were some such doctrine accepted as a generally recognized derogation from M. F. N., one of the grounds of objection against that clause would be removed. The acceptance of any such general derogation would not, of course, in any way preclude more radical derogations in specific cases.

(j) The last important point that falls to be mentioned here is one which forms a natural link between lessons regarding policy and lessons regarding procedure. The increased rigidity of the economic system in all industrial or semi-industrialized States results in any reduction in tariffs causing a greater shock and one more slowly absorbed than was the case fifty years ago. Consequently the opposition to changes is greater, and indeed

— 162 —

the benefit that may be derived from a change must be greater than heretofore if it is to offset the increased disadvantages resulting from it. Those disadvantages are greatest in times of falling prices and unemployment. Hence the timing of tariff changes has acquired special importance and the procedure adopted is likely to affect not only the chances of success of any change in policy, but also the justification for success, to a greater extent than previously.

There was some tendency during the last twenty years to confuse the "young countries" argument with the "young industries" argument, and to assume that the latter only applied to "young countries." The actual force of circumstances went to show that highly industrialized countries were tending to reach a stage of economic evolution in which their dependence on capital goods industries made them peculiarly sensitive to economic depressions. These countries felt the need for protecting various forms of consumers' industries—"the light industries"—as an insurance against that risk. This tendency to seek greater stability in increased diversification may well make itself felt again and is indeed likely to make itself felt immediately after the war owing to the almost universal over-expansion of engineering and heavy industries.

II. CONCLUSIONS REGARDING PROCEDURE.

(a) When applied to complex questions, which affected different countries in different ways and to varying degrees, and to problems affecting the central issues of national economic policies, the method of general diplomatic conference and convention revealed serious limitations. A lesson may be drawn from the experience of certain modifications of this method attempted by the League:

(1) The limitation of such conferences to States especially concerned in a particular problem and anxious to secure immediate results through concerted action and agreements limited to those States. The Wheat Agreement of 1933 and the Sugar Agreement of 1937 resulted from limited conferences of this kind.

(2) The framing of conventions which were not intended to be signed and ratified but to be accepted by Governments as models or standards in negotiating and drafting subsequent bi-

— 163 —

lateral agreements. Where such a system can be applied, it has great advantages.. Not only does it achieve exactly that measure of uniformity which is compatible with national peculiarities and differences in economic and financial structure, but it is also dynamic: as one country or another develops, it is able—and, *ex hypothesi*, likely to find it expedient—to apply to an increasing extent the common principles laid down. This method has been used with remarkable success in the matter of double taxation.

(3) The establishment of standards or norms for adoption, as and when changes in national legislation were undertaken, or merely to serve as a guide for the formulation of policy in the future. This method was used, for example, in the case of Tariff Nomenclature.

(b) For the purpose of achieving tariff reduction, negotiations between pairs or groups of countries were clearly shown to be more efficacious than general multilateral negotiations, and an extension of the bilateral method may be found appropriate in the future. This might take the form of simultaneous negotiations between numerous pairs or small groups of countries, directed and co-ordinated by an international authority and facilitated both by multilateral consultations and, as occasion required, by multilateral agreements on specific subjects.

(c) Diplomatic conferences on complex subjects cannot themselves work out solutions or produce agreement but can only adopt solutions the general lines of which have already been worked out and agreed upon between all—or, at any rate, the principal—parties concerned.

(d) The existence of non-negotiable tariffs in certain important countries was an obstacle to the realization of the programme of tariff reduction laid down by the Economic Conference of 1927. The adoption of freely negotiable tariffs by all countries would mark a useful advance.

(e) Under the system of specific tariffs commonly employed on the continent of Europe, the burden of duties is reduced in times of rising prices and increased in times of falling prices. That system thus tends to aggravate every depression and contribute to the forces making for greater commercial restriction.

(f) Another fact that is perhaps not quite immediately apparent from what has been said above relates to the international equipment for the preparation of Committee meetings, Conferences, etc. Each national administration had at its disposal an elaborate administrative machine at home and consular officers and commercial attaches abroad, whose function it was to study trading conditions with the object of promoting national trade interests. But there was no similar international organization. Trade and trading policy continued in fact to be regarded wholly in terms of rivalry.

The officials of the League dealing with commercial policy never numbered more than half a dozen; there was no attempt at—indeed no possibility of—studying in detail the position of different countries on the spot or of keeping, as was required, in constant touch with national administrations throughout the world. There was only a very limited possibility of following the development of trade as a whole and quite inadequate equipment for following the trade in different commodities. The tendency of international bodies to generalize reflected in part the inability of Headquarters in these circumstances to make, in advance, detailed studies of the real issues, broken down into their component parts. That failure in turn reflected a persistent underestimation by governments of the magnitude of the task involved in any attempt to view world trade as a world problem.

[17]

THE HUNDRED YEARS' PEACE

NINETEENTH CENTURY civilization has collapsed. This book is concerned with the political and economic origins of this event, as well as with the great transformation which it ushered in.

Nineteenth century civilization rested on four institutions. The first was the balance-of-power system which for a century prevented the occurrence of any long and devastating war between the Great Powers. The second was the international gold standard which symbolized a unique organization of world economy. The third was the self-regulating market which produced an unheard-of material welfare. The fourth was the liberal state. Classified in one way, two of these institutions were economic, two political. Classified in another way, two of them were national, two international. Between them they determined the characteristic outlines of the history of our civilization.

Of these institutions the gold standard proved crucial; its fall was the proximate cause of the catastrophe. By the time it failed most of the other institutions had been sacrificed in a vain effort to save it.

But the fount and matrix of the system was the self-regulating market. It was this innovation which gave rise to a specific civilization. The gold standard was merely an attempt to extend the domestic market system to the international field; the balance-of-power system was a superstructure erected upon and, partly, worked through the gold standard; the liberal state was itself a creation of the self-regulating market. The key to the institutional system of the nineteenth century lay in the laws governing market economy.

Our thesis is that the idea of a self-adjusting market implied a stark utopia. Such an institution could not exist for any length of time without annihilating the human and natural substance of society; it would have physically destroyed man and transformed his surroundings into a wilderness. Inevitably, society took measures to protect itself, but whatever measures it took impaired the self-regulation of the market, disorganized industrial life, and thus endangered society in yet another

3

way. It was this dilemma which forced the development of the market system into a definite groove and finally disrupted the social organization based upon it.

Such an explanation of one of the deepest crises in man's history must appear all too simple. Nothing could seem more inept than the attempt to reduce a civilization, its substance and ethos, to a hard and fast number of institutions; to select one of them as fundamental and proceed to argue the inevitable self-destruction of civilization on account of some technical quality of its economic organization. Civilizations, like life itself, spring from the interaction of a great number of independent factors which are not, as a rule, reducible to circumscribed institutions. To trace the institutional mechanism of the downfall of a civilization may well appear as a hopeless endeavor.

Yet it is this we are undertaking. In doing so we are consciously adjusting our aim to the extreme singularity of the subject matter. For the civilization of the nineteenth century was unique precisely in that it centered on a definite institutional mechanism.

No explanation can satisfy which does not account for the suddenness of the cataclysm. As if the forces of change had been pent up for a century, a torrent of events is pouring down on mankind. A social transformation of planetary range is being topped by wars of an unprecedented type in which a score of states crashed, and the contours of new empires are emerging out of a sea of blood. But this fact of demoniac violence is merely superimposed on a swift, silent current of change which swallows up the past often without so much as a ripple on the surface! A reasoned analysis of the catastrophe must account both for the tempestuous action and the quiet dissolution.

Ours is not a historical work; what we are searching for is not a convincing sequence of outstanding events, but an explanation of their trend in terms of human institutions. We shall feel free to dwell on scenes of the past with the sole object of throwing light on matters of the present; we shall make detailed analyses of critical periods and almost completely disregard the connecting stretches of time; we shall encroach upon the field of several disciplines in the pursuit of this single aim.

First we shall deal with the collapse of the international system. We shall try to show that the balance-of-power system could not ensure peace once the world economy on which it rested had failed. This accounts for the abruptness with which the break occurred, the inconceivable rapidity of the dissolution.

But if the breakdown of our civilization was timed by the failure of world economy, it was certainly not caused by it. Its origins lay more than a hundred years back in that social and technological upheaval from which the idea of a self-regulating market sprang in Western Europe. The end of this venture has come in our time; it closes a distinct stage in the history of industrial civilization.

In the final part of the book we shall deal with the mechanism which governed social and national change in our time. Broadly, we believe that the present condition of man is to be defined in terms of the institutional origins of the crisis.

The nineteenth century produced a phenomenon unheard of in the annals of Western civilization, namely, a hundred years' peace—1815–1914. Apart from the Crimean War—a more or less colonial event—England, France, Prussia, Austria, Italy, and Russia were engaged in war among each other for altogether only eighteen months. A computation of comparable figures for the two preceding centuries gives an average of sixty to seventy years of major wars in each. But even the fiercest of nineteenth century conflagrations, the Franco-Prussian War of 1870–71, ended after less than a year's duration with the defeated nation being able to pay over an unprecedented sum as an indemnity without any disturbance of the currencies concerned.

This triumph of a pragmatic pacifism was certainly not the result of an absence of grave causes for conflict. Almost continuous shifts in the internal and external conditions of powerful nations and great empires accompanied this irenic pageant. During the first part of the century civil wars, revolutionary and anti-revolutionary interventions were the order of the day. In Spain a hundred thousand troops under the Duc d'Angoulème stormed Cadiz; in Hungary the Magyar revolution threatened to defeat the Emperor himself in pitched battle and was ultimately suppressed only by a Russian army fighting on Hungarian soil. Armed interventions in the Germanies, in Belgium, Poland, Switzerland, Denmark, and Venice marked the omnipresence of the Holy Alliance. During the second half of the century the dynamics of progress was released; the Ottoman, Egyptian, and the Sheriffian empires broke up or were dismembered; China was forced by invading armies to open her door to the foreigner and in one gigantic haul the continent of Africa was partitioned. Simultaneously, two powers rose to world importance: the United States and Russia. National unity was achieved by Germany and Italy; Belgium, Greece, Roumania,

6   THE INTERNATIONAL SYSTEM   [Ch. 1

Bulgaria, Serbia, and Hungary assumed, or reassumed, their places as
sovereign states on the map of Europe. An almost incessant series of
open wars accompanied the march of industrial civilization into the
domains of outworn cultures or primitive peoples. Russia's military
conquests in Central Asia, England's numberless Indian and African
wars, France's exploits in Egypt, Algiers, Tunis, Syria, Madagascar,
Indo-China, and Siam raised issues between the Powers which, as a
rule, only force can arbitrate. Yet every single one of these conflicts
was localized, and numberless other occasions for violent change were
either met by joint action or smothered into compromise by the Great
Powers. Regardless of how the methods changed, the result was the
same. While in the first part of the century constitutionalism was
banned and the Holy Alliance suppressed freedom in the name of
peace, during the other half—and again in the name of peace—constitutions were foisted upon turbulent despots by business-minded
bankers. Thus under varying forms and ever-shifting ideologies—
sometimes in the name of progress and liberty, sometimes by the authority of the throne and the altar, sometimes by grace of the stock exchange
and the checkbook, sometimes by corruption and bribery, sometimes by
moral argument and enlightened appeal, sometimes by the broadside
and the bayonet—one and the same result was attained: peace was
preserved.

This almost miraculous performance was due to the working of the
balance of power, which here produced a result which is normally
foreign to it. By its nature that balance effects an entirely different
result, namely, the survival of the power units involved; in fact, it
merely postulates that three or more units capable of exerting power will
always behave in such a way as to combine the power of the weaker
units against any increase in power of the strongest. In the realm of
universal history balance of power was concerned with states whose
independence it served to maintain. But it attained this end only by
continuous war between changing partners. The practice of the ancient
Greek or the Northern Italian city-states was such an instance; wars
between shifting groups of combatants maintained the independence
of those states over long stretches of time. The action of the same principle safeguarded for over two hundred years the sovereignty of the
states forming Europe at the time of the Treaty of Münster and Westphalia (1648). When, seventy-five years later, in the Treaty of
Utrecht, the signatories declared their formal adherence to this principle, they thereby embodied it in a *system*, and thus established mutual

guarantees of survival for the strong and the weak alike through the medium of war. The fact that in the nineteenth century the same mechanism resulted in peace rather than war is a problem to challenge the historian.

The entirely new factor, we submit, was the emergence of an acute peace interest. Traditionally, such an interest was regarded as outside the scope of the state system. Peace with its corollaries of crafts and arts ranked among the mere adornments of life. The Church might pray for peace as for a bountiful harvest, but in the realm of state action it would nevertheless advocate armed intervention; governments subordinated peace to security and sovereignty, that is, to intents that could not be achieved otherwise than by recourse to the ultimate means. Few things were regarded as more detrimental to a community than the existence of an organized peace interest in its midst. As late as the second half of the eighteenth century, J. J. Rousseau arraigned trades people for their lack of patriotism because they were suspected of preferring peace to liberty.

After 1815 the change is sudden and complete. The backwash of the French Revolution reinforced the rising tide of the Industrial Revolution in establishing peaceful business as a universal interest. Metternich proclaimed that what the people of Europe wanted was not liberty but peace. Gentz called patriots the new barbarians. Church and throne started out on the denationalization of Europe. Their arguments found support both in the ferocity of the recent popular forms of warfare and in the tremendously enhanced value of peace under the nascent economies.

The bearers of the new "peace interest" were, as usual, those who chiefly benefited by it, namely, that cartel of dynasts and feudalists whose patrimonial positions were threatened by the revolutionary wave of patriotism that was sweeping the Continent. Thus, for approximately a third of a century the Holy Alliance provided the coercive force and the ideological impetus for an active peace policy; its armies were roaming up and down Europe putting down minorities and repressing majorities. From 1846 to about 1871—"one of the most confused and crowded quarter centuries of European history" [1]—peace was less safely established, the ebbing strength of reaction meeting the growing strength of industrialism. In the quarter century following the Franco-Prussian War we find the revived peace interest represented by that new powerful entity, the Concert of Europe.

[1] Sontag, R. J., *European Diplomatic History, 1871–1932*, 1933.

8   THE INTERNATIONAL SYSTEM   [Ch. 1

Interests, however, like intents, necessarily remain platonic unless
they are translated into politics by the means of some social instrumentality. Superficially, such a vehicle of realization was lacking; both the
Holy Alliance and the Concert of Europe were, ultimately, mere groupings of independent sovereign states, and thus subject to the balance of
power and its mechanism of war. How then was peace maintained?

True, any balance-of-power system will tend to prevent such wars
as spring from one nation's failure to foresee the realignment of powers
which will result from its attempt to alter the *status quo*. Famous
instances were Bismarck's calling off of the press campaign against
France, in 1875, on Russian and British intervention (Austria's aid to
France was taken for granted). This time the Concert of Europe
worked against Germany who found herself isolated. In 1877–78
Germany was unable to prevent a Russo-Turkish War, but succeeded
in localizing it by backing up England's jealousy of a Russian move
towards the Dardanelles; Germany and England supported Turkey
against Russia—thus saving the peace. At the Congress of Berlin a
long-term plan for the liquidation of the European possessions of the
Ottoman Empire was launched; this resulted in averting wars between
the Great Powers in spite of all subsequent changes in the *status quo,*
as the parties concerned could be practically certain in advance of the
forces they would have to meet in battle. Peace in these instances was
a welcome by-product of the balance-of-power system.

Also, wars were sometimes avoided by deliberately removing their
causes, if the fate of small powers only was involved. Small nations
were checked and prevented from disturbing the *status quo* in any way
which might precipitate war. The Dutch invasion of Belgium in 1831
eventually led to the neutralization of that country. In 1855 Norway
was neutralized. In 1867 Luxembourg was sold by Holland to France;
Germany protested and Luxembourg was neutralized. In 1856 the
integrity of the Ottoman Empire was declared essential to the equilibrium of Europe, and the Concert of Europe endeavored to maintain that
empire; after 1878, when its disintegration was deemed essential to that
equilibrium, its dismemberment was provided for in a similarly orderly
manner, though in both cases the decision meant life and death to several
small peoples. Between 1852 and 1863 Denmark, between 1851 and
1856 the Germanies threatened to disturb the balance; each time the
small states were forced by the Great Powers to conform. In these
instances, the liberty of action offered to them by the system was used by
the Powers to achieve a joint interest—which happened to be peace.

But it is a far cry from the occasional averting of wars either by a timely clarification of the power situation or by the coercing of small states to the massive fact of the Hundred Years' Peace. International disequilibrium may occur for innumerable reasons—from a dynastic love affair to the silting of an estuary, from a theological controversy to a technological invention. The mere growth of wealth and population, or, eventually, their decrease, is bound to set political forces in motion; and the external balance will invariably reflect the internal. Even an organized balance-of-power system can ensure peace without the permanent threat of war only if it is able to act upon these internal factors directly and prevent imbalance *in statu nascendi*. Once the imbalance has gathered momentum only force can set it right. It is a commonplace that to insure peace one must eliminate the causes of war; but it is not generally realized that to do so the flow of life must be controlled at its source.

The Holy Alliance contrived to achieve this with the help of instruments peculiar to it. The kings and aristocracies of Europe formed an international of kinship; and the Roman Church provided them with a voluntary civil service ranging from the highest to the lowest rung of the social ladder in Southern and Central Europe. The hierarchies of blood and grace were fused into an instrument of locally effective rule which needed only to be supplemented by force to ensure continental peace.

But the Concert of Europe, which succeeded it, lacked the feudal as well as the clerical tentacles; it amounted at the best to a loose federation not comparable in coherence to Metternich's masterpiece. Only on rare occasions could a meeting of the Powers be called, and their jealousies allowed a wide latitude to intrigue, crosscurrents, and diplomatic sabotage; joint military action became rare. And yet what the Holy Alliance, with its complete unity of thought and purpose, could achieve in Europe only with the help of frequent armed interventions was here accomplished on a world scale by the shadowy entity called the Concert of Europe with the help of a very much less frequent and oppressive use of force. For an explanation of this amazing feat, we must seek for some undisclosed powerful social instrumentality at work in the new setting, which could play the role of dynasties and episcopacies under the old and make the peace interest effective. This anonymous factor was *haute finance*.

No all-around inquiry into the nature of international banking in the nineteenth century has yet been undertaken; this mysterious institution has hardly emerged from the chiaroscuro of politico-economic mythology.[2] Some contended that it was merely the tool of governments; others, that the governments were the instruments of its unquenchable thirst for gain; some, that it was the sower of international discord; others, that it was the vehicle of an effeminate cosmopolitanism sapping the strength of virile nations. None was quite mistaken. *Haute finance*, an institution *sui generis*, peculiar to the last third of the nineteenth and the first third of the twentieth century, functioned as the main link between the political and the economic organization of the world in this period. It supplied the instruments for an international peace system, which was worked with the help of the Powers, but which the Powers themselves could neither have established nor maintained. While the Concert of Europe acted only at intervals, *haute finance* functioned as a permanent agency of the most elastic kind. Independent of single governments, even of the most powerful, it was in touch with all; independent of the central banks, even of the Bank of England, it was closely connected with them. There was intimate contact between finance and diplomacy; neither would consider any long-range plan, whether peaceful or warlike, without making sure of the other's good will. Yet the secret of the successful maintenance of general peace lay undoubtedly in the position, organization, and techniques of international finance.

Both the personnel and the motives of this singular body invested it with a status the roots of which were securely grounded in the private sphere of strictly business interest. The Rothschilds were subject to no *one* government; as a family they embodied the abstract principle of internationalism; their loyalty was to a firm, the credit of which had become the only supranational link between political government and industrial effort in a swiftly growing world economy. In the last resort, their independence sprang from the needs of the time which demanded a sovereign agent commanding the confidence of national statesmen and of the international investor alike; it was to this vital need that the metaphysical extraterritoriality of a Jewish bankers' dynasty domiciled in the capitals of Europe provided an almost perfect solution. They were anything but pacifists; they had made their fortune in the financing of wars; they were impervious to moral consideration; they had no objection to any number of minor, short, or localized wars. But their business would be impaired if a general war between the Great Powers

---

[2] Feis, H., *Europe, the World's Banker, 1870–1914*, 1930, a work we have often textually followed.

should interfere with the monetary foundations of the system. By the logic of facts it fell to them to maintain the requisites of general peace in the midst of the revolutionary transformation to which the peoples of the planet were subject.

Organizationally, *haute finance* was the nucleus of one of the most complex institutions the history of man has produced. Transitory though it was, it compared in catholicity, in the profusion of forms and instruments, only with the whole of human pursuits in industry and trade of which it became in some sort the mirror and counterpart. Besides the international center, *haute finance* proper, there were some half dozen national centers hiving around their banks of issue and stock exchanges. Also, international banking was not restricted to the financing of governments, their adventures in war and peace; it comprised foreign investment in industry, public utilities, and banks, as well as long-term loans to public and private corporations abroad. National finance again was a microcosm. England alone counted half a hundred different types of banks; France's and Germany's banking organization, too, was specific; and in each of these countries the practices of the Treasury and its relations to private finance varied in the most striking, and, often, as to detail, most subtle way. The money market dealt with a multitude of commercial bills, overseas acceptances, pure financial bills, as well as call money and other stockbrokers' facilities. The pattern was checkered by an infinite variety of national groups and personalities, each with its peculiar type of prestige and standing, authority and loyalty, its assets of money and contact, of patronage and social aura.

Haute finance was not designed as an instrument of peace; this function fell to it by accident, as historians would say, while the sociologist might prefer to call it the law of availability. The motive of *haute finance* was gain; to attain it, it was necessary to keep in with the governments whose end was power and conquest. We may safely neglect at this stage the distinction between political and economic power, between economic and political purposes on the part of the governments; in effect, it was the characteristic of the nation-states in this period that such a distinction had but little reality, for whatever their aims, the governments strove to achieve them through the use and increase of national power. The organization and personnel of *haute finance*, on the other hand, was international, yet not, therefore, altogether independent of national organization. For *haute finance* as an activating center of bankers' participation in syndicates and consortia,

investment groups, foreign loans, financial controls, or other transactions of an ambitious scope, was bound to seek the co-operation of
national banking, national capital, national finance. Though national
finance, as a rule, was less subservient to government than national
industry, it was still sufficiently so to make international finance eager
to keep in touch with the governments themselves. Yet to the degree to
which—in virtue of its position and personnel, its private fortune and
affiliations—it was actually independent of any single government, it
was able to serve a new interest, which had no specific organ of its own,
for the service of which no other institution happened to be available,
and which was nevertheless of vital importance to the community:
namely, peace. Not peace at all cost, not even peace at the price of any
ingredient of independence, sovereignty, vested glory, or future aspirations of the powers concerned, but nevertheless peace, if it was possible
to attain it without such sacrifice.

Not otherwise. Power had precedence over profit. However closely
their realms interpenetrated, ultimately it was war that laid down the
law to business. Since 1870 France and Germany, for example, were
enemies. This did not exclude noncommittal transactions between
them. Occasional banking syndicates were formed for transitory purposes; there was private participation by German investment banks in
enterprises over the border, which did not appear in the balance sheets;
in the short-term loan market there was a discounting of bills of exchange and a granting of short-term loans on collateral and commercial
papers on the part of French banks; there was direct investment as in
the case of the marriage of iron and coke, or of Thyssen's plant in
Normandy, but such investments were restricted to definite areas in
France and were under a permanent fire of criticism from both the
nationalists and the socialists; direct investment was more frequent in
the colonies, as exemplified by Germany's tenacious efforts to secure
high-grade ore in Algeria, or by the involved story of participations in
Morocco. Yet it remains a stern fact that at no time after 1870 was the
official though tacit ban on German securities at the Bourse of Paris
lifted. France simply "chose not to risk having the force of loaned
capital" [3] turned upon herself. Austria also was suspect; in the Moroccan crisis of 1905–06 the ban was extended to Hungary. Financial
circles in Paris pleaded for the admission of Hungarian securities, but
industrial circles supported the government in its staunch opposition to
any concession to a possible military antagonist. Politico-diplomatic

[3] Feis, H., *op. cit.*, p. 201.

rivalry continued unabated. Any move that might increase the presumptive enemy's potential was vetoed by the governments. Superficially, it more than once appeared as if the conflict had been quashed, but the inside circles were aware that it had been merely shifted to points even more deeply hidden under the amicable surface.

Or take Germany's Eastern ambitions. Here also politics and finance intermingled, yet politics was supreme. After a quarter of a century of perilous bickering, Germany and England signed a comprehensive agreement on the Baghdad railway, in June, 1914—too late to prevent the Great War, it was often said. Others argued that, on the contrary, the signing of the agreement proved conclusively that the war between England and Germany was *not* caused by a clash of economic expansionism. Neither view is borne out by the facts. The agreement actually left the main issue undecided. The German railway line was still not to be carried on beyond Basra without the consent of the British government, and the economic zones of the treaty were bound to lead to a head-on collision at a future time. Meanwhile, the Powers would continue to prepare for The Day, which was even nearer than they reckoned.[4]

International finance had to cope with the conflicting ambitions and intrigues of the great and small powers; its plans were thwarted by diplomatic maneuvers, its long-term investments jeopardized, its constructive efforts hampered by political sabotage and backstairs obstruction. The national banking organizations without which it was helpless often acted as the accomplices of their respective governments, and no plan was safe which did not carve out in advance the booty of each participant. However, *power finance* just as often was not the victim, but the beneficiary of *Dollar diplomacy* which provided the steel ribs to the velvet glove of finance. For business success involved the ruthless use of force against weaker countries, wholesale bribing of backward administrations, and the use of all the underhand means of gaining ends familiar to the colonial and semicolonial jungle. And yet by functional determination it fell to *haute finance* to avert general wars. The vast majority of the holders of government securities, as well as other investors and traders, were bound to be the first losers in such wars, especially if the currencies were affected. The influence that *haute finance* exerted on the Powers was consistently favorable to European peace. And this influence was effective to the degree to which the governments themselves depended upon its co-operation in more than one

[4] Cf. Notes on Sources, page 264.

direction. Consequently, there was never a time when the peace interest was unrepresented in the councils of the Concert of Europe. If we add to this the growing peace interest inside every nation where the investment habit had taken root, we shall begin to see why the awful innovation of an armed peace of dozens of practically mobilized states could hover over Europe from 1871 to 1914 without bursting forth in a shattering conflagration.

Finance—this was one of its channels of influence—acted as a powerful moderator in the councils and policies of a number of smaller sovereign states. Loans, and the renewal of loans, hinged upon credit, and credit upon good behavior. Since, under constitutional government (unconstitutional ones were severely frowned upon), behavior is reflected in the budget and the external value of the currency cannot be detached from the appreciation of the budget, debtor governments were well advised to watch their exchanges carefully and to avoid policies which might reflect upon the soundness of the budgetary position. This useful maxim became a cogent rule of conduct once a country had adopted the gold standard, which limited permissible fluctuations to a minimum. Gold standard and constitutionalism were the instruments which made the voice of the City of London heard in many smaller countries which had adopted these symbols of adherence to the new international order. The Pax Britannica held its sway sometimes by the ominous poise of heavy ship's cannon, but more frequently it prevailed by the timely pull of a thread in the international monetary network.

The influence of *haute finance* was ensured also through its unofficial administration of the finances of vast semicolonial regions of the world, including the decaying empires of Islam in the highly inflammable zone of the Near East and North Africa. It was here that the day's work of financiers touched upon the subtle factors underlying internal order, and provided a *de facto* administration for those troubled regions where peace was most vulnerable. That is how the numerous prerequisites of long-term capital investments in these areas could often be secured in the face of almost insuperable obstacles. The epic of the building of railways in the Balkans, in Anatolia, Syria, Persia, Egypt, Morocco, and China is a story of endurance and of breathtaking turns reminiscent of a similar feat on the North American Continent. The chief danger, however, which stalked the capitalists of Europe was not technological or financial failure, but war—not a war between small countries (which could be easily isolated) nor war upon a small country by a Great Power (a frequent and often convenient occurrence), but a general war between the Great Powers themselves. Europe was not an empty continent, but the home of teeming millions of ancient and new peoples; every new railroad had to thread its way across boundaries of varying solidity, some of which might be fatally weakened, others vitally reinforced, by the contact. Only the iron grip of finance on the prostrate governments of backward regions could avert catastrophe. When Turkey defaulted on its financial obligations in 1875, military conflagrations immediately broke out, lasting from 1876 to 1878 when the Treaty of Berlin was signed. For thirty-six years thereafter peace was maintained. .That astounding peace was implemented by the Decree of Muharrem of 1881, which set up the Dette Ottomane in Constantinople. The representatives of *haute finance* were charged with the administration of the bulk of Turkish finance. In numerous cases they engineered compromises between the Powers; in others, they prevented Turkey from creating difficulties on her own; in others again, they acted simply as the political agents of the Powers; in all, they served the money interests of the creditors, and, if at all possible, of the capitalists who tried to make profits in that country. This task was greatly complicated by the fact that the Debt Commission was *not* a body representative of the private creditors, but an organ of Europe's public law on which *haute finance* was only unofficially represented. But it was precisely in this amphibious capacity that it was able to bridge the gap between the political and the economic organization of the age.

Trade had become linked with peace. In the past the organization of trade had been military and warlike; it was an adjunct of the pirate, the rover, the armed caravan, the hunter and trapper, the sword-bearing merchant, the armed burgesses of the towns, the adventurers and explorers, the planters and conquistadores, the manhunters and slave traders, the colonial armies of the chartered companies. Now all this was forgotten. Trade was now dependent upon an international monetary system which could not function in a general war. It demanded peace, and the Great Powers were striving to maintain it. But the balance-of-power system, as we have seen, could not by itself ensure peace. This was done by international finance, the very existence of which embodied the principle of the new dependence of trade upon peace.

We have become too much accustomed to think of the spread of capitalism as a process which is anything but peaceful, and of finance capital as the chief instigator of innumerable colonial crimes and expansionist aggressions. Its intimate affiliation with heavy industries made Lenin assert that finance capital was responsible for imperialism, notably for the struggle for spheres of influence, concessions, extraterritorial rights, and the innumerable forms in which the Western Powers got a stranglehold on backward regions, in order to invest in railways, public utilities, ports, and other permanent establishments on which their heavy industries made profits. Actually, business and finance were responsible for many colonial wars, but also for the fact that a general conflagration was avoided. Their affiliations with heavy industry, though really close only in Germany, accounted for both. Finance capital as the roof organization of heavy industry was affiliated with the various branches of industry in too many ways to allow one group to determine its policy. For every one interest that was furthered by war, there were a dozen that would be adversely affected. International capital, of course, was bound to be the loser in case of war; but even national finance could gain only exceptionally, though frequently enough to account for dozens of colonial wars, as long as they remained isolated. Every war, almost, was organized by financiers; but peace also was organized by them.

The precise nature of this strictly pragmatic system, which guarded with extreme rigor against a general war while providing for peaceful business amidst an endless sequence of minor ones, is best demonstrated by the changes it brought about in international law. While nationalism and industry distinctly tended to make wars more ferocious and total, effective safeguards were erected for the continuance of peaceful business in wartime. Frederick the Great is on record for having "by reprisal" refused, in 1752, to honor the Silesian loan due to British subjects.[5] "No attempt of this sort has been made since," says Hershey. "The wars of the French Revolution furnish us with the last important examples of the confiscation of the private property of enemy subjects found in belligerent territory upon the outbreak of hostilities." After the outbreak of the Crimean War enemy merchantmen were allowed to leave port, a practice which was adhered to by Prussia, France, Russia, Turkey, Spain, Japan, and the United States during the fifty following years. Since the beginning of that war a very large indulgence in commerce between belligerents was allowed. Thus, in the Spanish-American War, neutral vessels, laden with American-owned cargoes

[5] Hershey, A. S., *Essentials of International Public Law and Organization,* 1927, pp. 565–69.

other than contraband of war, cleared for Spanish ports. The view that eighteenth century wars were in *all* respects less destructive than nineteenth century ones is a prejudice. In respect to the status of enemy aliens, the service of loans held by enemy citizens, enemy property, or the right of enemy merchantmen to leave port, the nineteenth century showed a decisive turn in favor of measures to safeguard the economic system in wartime. Only the twentieth century reversed this trend.

Thus the new organization of economic life provided the background of the Hundred Years' Peace. In the first period, the nascent middle classes were mainly a revolutionary force endangering peace as witnessed in the Napoleonic upheaval; it was against this new factor of national disturbance that the Holy Alliance organized its reactionary peace. In the second period, the new economy was victorious. The middle classes were now themselves the bearers of a peace interest, much more powerful than that of their reactionary predecessors had been, and nurtured by the national-international character of the new economy. But in both instances the peace interest became effective only because it was able to make the balance-of-power system serve its cause by providing that system with social organs capable of dealing directly with the internal forces active in the area of peace. Under the Holy Alliance these organs were feudalism and the thrones, supported by the spiritual and material power of the Church; under the Concert of Europe they were international finance and the national banking systems allied to it. There is no need to overdo the distinction. During the Thirty Years' Peace, 1816–46, Great Britain was already pressing for peace and business, nor did the Holy Alliance disdain the help of the Rothschilds. Under the Concert of Europe, again, international finance had often to rely on its dynastic and aristocratic affiliations. But such facts merely tend to strengthen our argument that in every case peace was maintained not simply through the chancelleries of the Great Powers but with the help of concrete organized agencies acting in the service of general interests. In other words, only on the background of the new economy could the balance-of-power system make general conflagrations avoidable. But the achievement of the Concert of Europe was incomparably greater than that of the Holy Alliance; for the latter maintained peace in a limited region in an unchanging Continent, while the former succeeded in the same task on a world scale while social and economic progress was revolutionizing the map of the globe. This great political feat was the result of the emergence of a specific entity, *haute finance*, which was the given link between the political and the economic organization of international life.

It must be clear by this time that the peace organization rested upon economic organization. Yet the two were of very different consistency. Only in the widest sense of the term was it possible to speak of a political peace organization of the world, for the Concert of Europe was essentially not a system of peace but merely of independent sovereignties protected by the mechanism of war. The contrary is true of the economic organization of the world. Unless we defer to the uncritical practice of restricting the term "organization" to centrally directed bodies acting through functionaries of their own, we must concede that nothing could be more definite than the universally accepted principles upon which this organization rested and nothing more concrete than its factual elements. Budgets and armaments, foreign trade and raw material supplies, national independence and sovereignty were now the functions of currency and credit. By the fourth quarter of the nineteenth century, world commodity prices were the central reality in the lives of millions of Continental peasants; the repercussions of the London money market were daily noted by businessmen all over the world; and governments discussed plans for the future in light of the situation on the world capital markets. Only a madman would have doubted that the international economic system was the axis of the material existence of the race. Because this system needed peace in order to function, the balance of power was made to serve it. Take this economic system away and the peace interest would disappear from politics. Apart from it, there was neither sufficient cause for such an interest, nor a possibility of safeguarding it, in so far as it existed. The success of the Concert of Europe sprang from the needs of the new international organization of economy, and would inevitably end with its dissolution.

The era of Bismarck (1861–90) saw the Concert of Europe at its best. In two decades immediately following Germany's rise to the status of a Great Power, she was the chief beneficiary of the peace interest. She had forced her way into the front ranks at the cost of Austria and France; it was to her advantage to maintain the *status quo* and to prevent a war which could be only a war of revenge against herself. Bismarck deliberately fostered the notion of peace as a common venture of the Powers, and avoided commitments which might force Germany out of the position of a peace power. He opposed expansionist ambitions in the Balkans or overseas; he used the free trade weapon consistently against Austria, and even against France; he thwarted Russia's and

Austria's Balkan ambitions with the help of the balance-of-power game, thus keeping in with potential allies and averting situations which might involve Germany in war. The scheming aggressor of 1863–70 turned into the honest broker of 1878, and the deprecator of colonial adventures. He consciously took the lead in what he felt to be the peaceful trend of the time in order to serve Germany's national interests.

However, by the end of the seventies the free trade episode (1846–79) was at an end; the actual use of the gold standard by Germany marked the beginnings of an era of protectionism and colonial expansion.[6] Germany was now reinforcing her position by making a hard and fast alliance with Austria-Hungary and Italy; not much later Bismarck lost control of Reich policy. From then onward Great Britain was the leader of the peace interest in a Europe which still remained a group of independent sovereign states and thus subject to the balance of power. In the nineties *haute finance* was at its peak and peace seemed more secure than ever. British and French interests differed in Africa; the British and the Russians were competing with one another in Asia; the Concert, though limpingly, continued to function; in spite of the Triple Alliance, there were still more than two independent powers to watch one another jealously. Not for long. In 1904, Britain made a sweeping deal with France over Morocco and Egypt; a couple of years later she compromised with Russia over Persia, and the counter-alliance was formed. The Concert of Europe, that loose federation of independent powers, was finally replaced by two hostile power groupings; the balance of power as a system had now come to an end. With only two competing power groups left its mechanism ceased to function. There was no longer a third group which would unite with one of the other two to thwart whichever one sought to increase its power. About the same time the symptoms of the dissolution of the existing forms of world economy—colonial rivalry and competition for exotic markets—became acute. The ability of *haute finance* to avert the spread of wars was diminishing rapidly. For another seven years peace dragged on but it was only a question of time before the dissolution of nineteenth century economic organization would bring the Hundred Years' Peace to a close.

In the light of this recognition the true nature of the highly artificial economic organization on which peace rested becomes of utmost significance to the historian.

[6] Eulenburg, F., *Aussenhandel und Aussenhandelspolitik*. In "Grundriss der Sozialökonomik," Abt. VIII, 1929, p. 209.

CONSERVATIVE TWENTIES, REVOLUTIONARY
THIRTIES

THE BREAKDOWN of the international gold standard was the invisible link between the disintegration of world economy since the turn of the century and the transformation of a whole civilization in the thirties. Unless the vital importance of this factor is realized, it is not possible to see rightly either the mechanism which railroaded Europe to its doom, or the circumstances which accounted for the astounding fact that the forms and contents of a civilization should rest on so precarious foundations.

The true nature of the international system under which we were living was not realized until it failed. Hardly anyone understood the political function of the international monetary system; the awful suddenness of the transformation thus took the world completely by surprise. And yet the gold standard was the only remaining pillar of the traditional world economy; when it broke, the effect was bound to be instantaneous. To liberal economists the gold standard was a purely economic institution; they refused even to consider it as a part of a social mechanism. Thus it happened that the democratic countries were the last to realize the true nature of the catastrophe and the slowest to counter its effects. Not even when the cataclysm was already upon them did their leaders see that behind the collapse of the international system there stood a long development within the most advanced countries which made that system anachronistic; in other words, the failure of market economy itself still escaped them.

The transformation came on even more abruptly than is usually realized. World War I and the postwar revolutions still formed part of the nineteenth century. The conflict of 1914–18 merely precipitated and immeasurably aggravated a crisis that it did not create. But the roots of the dilemma could not be discerned at the time; and the horrors and devastations of the Great War seemed to the survivors the obvious source of the obstacles to international organization that had

20

so unexpectedly emerged. For suddenly neither the economic nor the political system of the world would function, and the terrible injuries inflicted on the substance of the race by World War I appeared to offer an explanation. In reality, the postwar obstacles to peace and stability derived from the same sources from which the Great War itself had sprung. The dissolution of the system of world economy which had been in progress since 1900 was responsible for the political tension that exploded in 1914; the outcome of the War and the Treaties had eased that tension superficially by eliminating German competition while aggravating the causes of tension and thereby vastly increasing the political and economic impediments to peace.

Politically, the Treaties harbored a fatal contradiction. Through the unilateral disarmament of the defeated nations they forestalled any reconstruction of the balance-of-power system, since power is an indispensable requisite of such a system. In vain did Geneva look towards the restoration of such a system in an enlarged and improved Concert of Europe called the League of Nations; in vain were facilities for consultation and joint action provided in the Covenant of the League, for the essential precondition of independent power units was now lacking. The League could never be really established; neither Article 16 on the enforcement of Treaties, nor Article 19 on their peaceful revision was ever implemented. The only viable solution of the burning problem of peace—the restoration of the balance-of-power system —was thus completely out of reach; so much so that the true aim of the most constructive statesmen of the twenties was not even understood by the public, which continued to exist in an almost indescribable state of confusion. Faced by the appalling fact of the disarmament of one group of nations, while the other group remained armed—a situation which precluded any constructive step towards the organization of peace—the emotional attitude prevailed that the League was in some mysterious way the harbinger of an era of peace which needed only frequent verbal encouragement to become permanent. In America there was a widespread idea that if only America had joined the League, matters would have turned out quite differently. No better proof than this could be adduced for the lack of understanding of the organic weaknesses of the so-called postwar system—so-called, because, if words have a meaning, Europe was now without any political system whatever. A bare *status quo* such as this can last only as long as the physical exhaustion of the parties lasts; no wonder that a return to the nineteenth century system appeared as the only way out. In the meantime the League Council might have at least functioned as a kind of European directorium, very much as the Concert of Europe did at its zenith, but for the fatal unanimity rule which set up the obstreperous small state as the arbiter of world peace. The absurd device of the permanent disarmament of the defeated countries ruled out any constructive solution. The only alternative to this disastrous condition of affairs was the establishment of an international order endowed with an organized power which would transcend national sovereignty. Such a course, however, was entirely beyond the horizon of the time. No country in Europe, not to mention the United States, would have submitted to such a system.

Economically, the policy of Geneva was much more consistent in pressing for the restoration of world economy as a second line of defense for peace. For even a successfully re-established balance-of-power system would have worked for peace only if the international monetary system was restored. In the absence of stable exchanges and freedom of trade the governments of the various nations, as in the past, would regard peace as a minor interest, for which they would strive only as long as it did not interfere with any of their major interests. First among the statesmen of the time, Woodrow Wilson appears to have realized the interdependence of peace and trade, not only as a guarantee of trade, *but also of peace*. No wonder that the League persistently strove to reconstruct the international currency and credit organization as the only possible safeguard of peace among sovereign states, and that the world relied as never before on *haute finance*. J. P. Morgan had replaced N. M. Rothschild as the demiurge of a rejuvenated nineteenth century.

According to the standards of that century the first postwar decade appeared as a revolutionary era; in the light of our own recent experience it was precisely the contrary. The intent of that decade was deeply conservative and expressed the almost universal conviction that only the re-establishment of the pre-1914 system, "this time on solid foundations," could restore peace and prosperity. Indeed, it was out of the failure of this effort to return to the past that the transformation of the thirties sprang. Spectacular though the revolutions and counter-revolutions of the post-war decade were, they represented either mere mechanical reactions to military defeat or, at most, a re-enacting of the familiar liberal and constitutionalist drama of Western civilization on the Central and Eastern European scene; it was only in the thirties that entirely new elements entered the pattern of Western history.

The Central and Eastern European upheavals and counterup-
heavals of 1917–20 in spite of their scenario were merely roundabout
ways of recasting the regimes that had succumbed on the battlefields.
When the counterrevolutionary smoke dissolved, the political systems
in Budapest, Vienna, and Berlin were found to be not very far different
from what they had been before the War. This was true, roughly, of
Finland, the Baltic states, Poland, Austria, Hungary, Bulgaria, and
even Italy and Germany, up to the middle of the twenties. In some
countries a great advance was made in national freedom and land
reform—achievements which had been common to Western Europe
since 1789. Russia, in this respect, formed no exception. The tendency
of the times was simply to establish (or re-establish) the system commonly associated with the ideals of the English, the American, and the
French revolutions. Not only Hindenburg and Wilson, but also Lenin
and Trotzky were, in this broad sense, in the line of Western tradition.

In the early thirties, change set in with abruptness. Its landmarks
were the abandonment of the gold standard by Great Britain; the
Five-Year Plans in Russia; the launching of the New Deal; the
National Socialist Revolution in Germany; the collapse of the League
in favor of autarchist empires. While at the end of the Great War
nineteenth century ideals were paramount, and their influence dominated the following decade, by 1940 every vestige of the international
system had disappeared and, apart from a few enclaves, the nations
were living in an entirely new international setting.

The root cause of the crisis, we submit, was the threatening collapse
of the international economic system. It had only haltingly functioned
since the turn of the century, and the Great War and the Treaties
had wrecked it finally. This became apparent in the twenties when
there was hardly an internal crisis in Europe that did not reach its
climax on an issue of external economy. Students of politics now
grouped the various countries, not according to continents, but according to the degree of their adherence to a sound currency. Russia had
astonished the world by the destruction of the rouble, the value of
which was reduced to nothing by the simple means of inflation. Germany repeated this desperate feat in order to give the lie to the Treaty;
the expropriation of the rentier class, which followed in its wake, laid
the foundation for the Nazi revolution. The prestige of Geneva rested
on its success in helping Austria and Hungary to restore their currencies,
and Vienna became the Mecca of liberal economists on account of a
brilliantly successful operation on Austria's *krone* which the patient,

unfortunately, did not survive. In Bulgaria, Greece, Finland, Latvia, Lithuania, Esthonia, Poland, and Roumania the restoration of the currency provided counterrevolution with a claim to power. In Belgium, France, and England the Left was thrown out of office in the name of sound monetary standards. An almost unbroken sequence of currency crises linked the indigent Balkans with the affluent United States through the elastic band of an international credit system, which transmitted the strain of the imperfectly restored currencies, first, from Eastern Europe to Western Europe, then from Western Europe to the United States. Ultimately, the United States itself was engulfed by the effects of the premature stabilization of European currencies. The final breakdown had begun.

The first shock occurred within the national spheres. Some currencies, such as the Russian, the German, the Austrian, the Hungarian, were wiped out within a year. Apart from the unprecedented rate of change in the value of currencies there was the circumstance that this change happened in a completely monetarized economy. A cellular process was introduced into human society, the effects of which were outside the range of experience. Internally and externally alike, dwindling currencies spelled disruption. Nations found themselves separated from their neighbors, as by a chasm, while at the same time the various strata of the population were affected in entirely different and often opposite ways. The intellectual middle class was literally pauperized; financial sharks heaped up revolting fortunes. A factor of incalculable integrating and disintegrating force had entered the scene.

"Flight of capital" was a *novum*. Neither in 1848, nor in 1866, nor even in 1871 was such an event recorded. And yet, its vital role in the overthrow of the liberal governments of France in 1925, and again in 1938, as well as in the development of a fascist movement in Germany in 1930, was patent.

Currency had become the pivot of national politics. Under a modern money economy nobody could fail to experience daily the shrinking or expanding of the financial yardstick; populations became currency-conscious; the effect of inflation on real income was discounted in advance by the masses; men and women everywhere appeared to regard stable money as the supreme need of human society. But such awareness was inseparable from the recognition that the foundations of the currency might depend upon political factors outside the national boundaries. Thus the social *bouleversement* which shook confidence in the inherent stability of the monetary medium shattered also the naïve concept of financial sovereignty in an interdependent economy. Henceforth, internal crises associated with the currency would tend to raise grave external issues.

Belief in the gold standard was the faith of the age. With some it was a naïve, with some a critical, with others a satanistic creed implying acceptance in the flesh and rejection in the spirit. Yet the belief itself was the same, namely, that bank notes have value because they represent gold. Whether the gold itself has value for the reason that it embodies labor, as the socialists held, or for the reason that it is useful and scarce, as the orthodox doctrine ran, made for once no difference. The war between heaven and hell ignored the money issue, leaving capitalists and socialists miraculously united. Where Ricardo and Marx were at one, the nineteenth century knew not doubt. Bismarck and Lassalle, John Stuart Mill and Henry George, Philip Snowden and Calvin Coolidge, Mises and Trotzky equally accepted the faith. Karl Marx had gone to great pains to show up Proudhon's utopian labor notes (which were to replace currency) as based on self-delusion; and *Das Kapital* implied the commodity theory of money, in its Ricardian form. The Russian Bolshevik Sokolnikoff was the first postwar statesman to restore the value of his country's currency in terms of gold; the German Social Democrat Hilferding imperiled his party by his staunch advocacy of sound currency principles; the Austrian Social Democrat Otto Bauer supported the monetary principles underlying the restoration of the *krone* attempted by his bitter opponent Seipel; the English Socialist, Philip Snowden, turned against Labor when he believed the pound sterling not to be safe at their hands; and the Duce had the gold value of the lira at 90 carved in stone, and pledged himself to die in its defense. It would be hard to find any divergence between utterances of Hoover and Lenin, Churchill and Mussolini, on this point. Indeed, the essentiality of the gold standard to the functioning of the international economic system of the time was the one and only tenet common to men of all nations and all classes, religious denominations, and social philosophies. It was the invisible reality to which the will to live could cling, when mankind braced itself to the task of restoring its crumbling existence.

The effort, which failed, was the most comprehensive the world had ever seen. The stabilization of the all-but-destroyed currencies in Austria, Hungary, Bulgaria, Finland, Roumania, or Greece was not only an act of faith on the part of these small and weak countries, which literally starved themselves to reach the golden shores, but it also put their powerful and wealthy sponsors—the Western European victors—to a severe test. As long as the currencies of the victors fluctuated, the strain did not become apparent; they continued to lend abroad as before the War and thereby helped to maintain the economies of the defeated nations. But when Great Britain and France reverted to gold, the burden on their stabilized exchanges began to tell. Eventually, a silent concern for the safety of the pound entered into the position of the leading gold country, the United States. This preoccupation which spanned the Atlantic brought America unexpectedly into the danger zone. The point seems technical, but must be clearly understood. American support of the pound sterling in 1927 implied low rates of interest in New York in order to avert big movements of capital from London to New York. The Federal Reserve Board accordingly promised the Bank of England to keep its rate low; but presently America herself was in need of high rates as her own price system began to be perilously inflated (this fact was obscured by the existence of a stable price level, maintained in spite of tremendously diminished costs). When the usual swing of the pendulum after seven years of prosperity brought on the long overdue slump in 1929, matters were immeasurably aggravated by the existing state of cryptoinflation. Debtors, emaciated by deflation, lived to see the inflated creditor collapse. It was a portent. America, by an instinctive gesture of liberation, went off gold in 1933, and the last vestige of the traditional world economy vanished. Although hardly anybody discerned the deeper meaning of the event at the time, history almost at once reversed its trend.

For over a decade the restoration of the gold standard had been the symbol of world solidarity. Innumerable conferences from Brussels to Spa and Geneva, from London to Locarno and Lausanne met in order to achieve the political preconditions of stable currencies. The League of Nations itself had been supplemented by the International Labor Office partly in order to equalize conditions of competition amongst the nations so that trade might be liberated without danger to standards of living. Currency was at the heart of the campaigns launched by Wall Street to overcome the transfer problem and, first, to commercialize, then, to mobilize reparations; Geneva acted as the sponsor of a process of rehabilitation in which the combined pressure of the City of London and of the neo-classical monetary purists of Vienna was put into the service of the gold standard; every international endeavor was ultimately directed to this end, while national governments, as a rule, accommodated their policies to the need of safeguarding the currency, particularly those policies which were concerned with foreign trade, loans, banking, and exchange. Although everybody agreed that stable currencies ultimately depended upon the freeing of trade, all except dogmatic free traders knew that measures had to be taken immediately which would inevitably restrict foreign trade and foreign payments. Import quotas, moratoria and stand-still agreements, clearing systems and bilateral trade treaties, barter arrangements, embargoes on capital exports, foreign trade control, and exchange equalization funds developed in most countries to meet the same set of circumstances. Yet the incubus of self-sufficiency haunted the steps taken in protection of the currency. While the intent was the freeing of trade, the effect was its strangulation. Instead of gaining access to the markets of the world, the governments, by their own acts, were barring their countries from any international nexus, and ever-increasing sacrifices were needed to keep even a trickle of trade flowing. The frantic efforts to protect the external value of the currency as a medium of foreign trade drove the peoples, against their will, into an autarchized economy. The whole arsenal of restrictive measures, which formed a radical departure from traditional economics, was actually the outcome of conservative free trade purposes.

This trend was abruptly reversed with the final fall of the gold standard. The sacrifices that were made to restore it had now to be made once more in order that we might live without it. The same institutions which were designed to constrict life and trade in order to maintain a system of stable currencies were now used to adjust industrial life to the permanent absence of such a system. Perhaps that is why the mechanical and technological structure of modern industry survived the impact of the collapse of the gold standard. For in the struggle to retain it, the world had been unconsciously preparing for the kind of efforts and the type of organizations necessary to adapt itself to its loss. Yet the intent was now the opposite; in the countries that had suffered most during the long-drawn fight for the unattainable, titanic forces were released on the rebound. Neither the League of Nations nor international *haute finance* outlasted the gold standard; with its disappearance both the organized peace interest of the League and its chief instruments of enforcement—the Rothschilds and Morgans—vanished from politics. The snapping of the golden thread was the signal for a world revolution.

But the failure of the gold standard did hardly more than set the date of an event which was too big to have been caused by it. No less than a complete destruction of the national institutions of nineteenth century society accompanied the crisis in a great part of the world, and everywhere these institutions were changed and re-formed almost out of recognition. The liberal state was in many countries replaced by totalitarian dictatorships, and the central institution of the century—production based on free markets—was superseded by new forms of economy. While great nations recast the very mold of their thought and hurled themselves into wars to enslave the world in the name of unheard-of conceptions of the nature of the universe, 'even greater nations rushed to the defense of freedom which acquired an equally unheard-of meaning at their hands. The failure of the international system, though it triggered the transformation, could certainly not have accounted for its depth and content. Even though we may know why that which happened happened suddenly, we may still be in the dark about why it happened at all.

It was not by accident that the transformation was accompanied by wars on an unprecedented scale. History was geared to social change; the fate of nations was linked to their role in an institutional transformation. Such a symbiosis is no exception in history; though national groups and social institutions have origins of their own, they tend to hitch on to one another in their struggle for survival. A famous instance of such a symbiosis linked capitalism and the seaboard nations of the Atlantic. The Commercial Revolution, so closely connected with the rise of capitalism, became the vehicle to power for Portugal, Spain, Holland, France, England and the United States, each of them benefiting from the chances offered by that broad and deep-seated movement, while, on the other hand, capitalism itself was spreading over the planet through the instrumentality of these rising Powers.

The law applied also in the reverse. A nation may be handicapped in its struggle for survival by the fact that its institutions, or some of them, belong to a type that happens to be on the down grade—the gold standard in World War II was an instance of such an antiquated outfit. Countries, on the other hand, which, for reasons of their own, are opposed to the *status quo,* would be quick to discover the weaknesses of the existing institutional order and to anticipate the creation of institutions better adapted to their interests. Such groups are pushing that which is falling and holding on to that which, under its own steam, is moving their way. It may then seem as if they had originated the process of social change, while actually they were merely its beneficiaries, and may be even perverting the trend to make it serve their own aims.

Thus Germany, once defeated, was in the position to recognize the hidden shortcomings of the nineteenth century order, and to employ this knowledge to speed the destruction of that order. A kind of sinister intellectual superiority accrued to those of her statesmen in the thirties who turned their minds to this task of disruption, which often extended to the development of new methods of finance, trade, war, and social organization, in the course of their attempt to force matters into the trend of their policies. However, these problems themselves were emphatically not created by the governments which turned them to their advantage; they were real—objectively given—and will remain with us whatever be the fate of the individual countries. Again, the distinction between World Wars I and II is apparent: the former was still true to nineteenth century type—a simple conflict of powers, released by the lapse of the balance-of-power system; the latter already is part of the world upheaval.

This should allow us to detach the poignant national histories of the period from the social transformation that was in progress. It will then be easy to see in what manner Germany and Russia, Great Britain and the United States, as power units, were helped or hampered by their relation to the underlying social process. But the same is true of the social process itself: fascism and socialism found a vehicle in the rise of individual Powers which helped to spread their creed. Germany and Russia respectively became the representatives of fascism and socialism in the world at large. The true scope of these social movements can be gauged only if, for good or evil, their transcendant character is recognized and viewed as detached from the national interests enlisted in their service.

The roles which Germany or Russia, or for that matter, Italy or Japan, Great Britain or the United States, are playing in World War II, though forming part of universal history, are no direct concern of this book; fascism and socialism, however, were live forces in the institutional transformation which is its subject. The *élan vital* which produced the inscrutable urge in the German and Russian people to claim a greater share in the record of the race must be taken as factual data of the conditions under which our story unfolds, while the purport of Fascism and Socialism or New Deal is part of the story itself.

This leads up to our thesis which still remains to be proven: that the origins of the cataclysm lay in the utopian endeavor of economic liberalism to set up a self-regulating market system. Such a thesis seems to invest that system with almost mythical powers; it implies no less than that the balance of power, the gold standard, and the liberal state, those fundamentals of the civilization of the nineteenth century, were, in the last resort, all shaped by one common matrix, the self-regulating market.

The assertion appears extreme, if not shocking in its crass materialism. But the peculiarity of the civilization the collapse of which we have witnessed was precisely that it rested on economic foundations. Other societies and other civilizations, too, were limited by the material conditions of their existence—this is a common trait of all human life, indeed, of all life, whether religious or nonreligious, materialist or spiritualist. All types of societies are limited by economic factors. Nineteenth century civilization alone was economic in a different and distinctive sense, for it chose to base itself on a motive only rarely acknowledged as valid in the history of human societies, and certainly never before raised to the level of a justification of action and behavior in everyday life, namely, gain. The self-regulating market system was uniquely derived from this principle.

The mechanism which the motive of gain set in motion was comparable in effectiveness only to the most violent outburst of religious fervor in history. Within a generation the whole human world was subjected to its undiluted influence. As everybody knows, it grew to maturity in England, in the wake of the Industrial Revolution, during the first half of the nineteenth century. It reached the Continent and America about fifty years later. Eventually in England, on the Continent, and even in America, similar alternatives shaped daily issues into a pattern the main traits of which were identical in all countries of Western civilization. For the origins of the cataclysm we must turn to the rise and fall of market economy.

Market society was born in England—yet it was on the Continent that its weaknesses engendered the most tragic complications. In order to comprehend German fascism, we must revert to Ricardian England. The nineteenth century, as cannot be overemphasized, was England's century. The Industrial Revolution was an English event. Market economy, free trade, and the gold standard were English inventions. These institutions broke down in the twenties everywhere—in Germany, Italy, or Austria the event was merely more political and more dramatic. But whatever the scenery and the temperature of the final episodes, the long-run factors which wrecked that civilization should be studied in the birthplace of the Industrial Revolution, England.

Name Index

Abramovitz, M. 344
Aldcroft, D.H. 241
Alesina, A. 333, 349
Alexander I of Russia 182, 187, 196
Andersen, F.N. 105
Anderson, J.E. 50, 306, 349
Angoulème, duc d' 427
Arnold, T.W. 19, 266
Ashton, T. 16

Babbage, C. 13
Bairoch, P. 41, 53, 56, 277, 341
Bandini, S. 6, 7
Barber, C.L. 95
Baring 10
Bastiat 6, 21
Bateson, G. 271–2, 274
Bauer, O. 447
Bauwens, L. 162
Benedict, R. 274
Benhabib, J. 312, 333
Benham, F.C. 108
Bennett, R.B. 99
Bergsten, C.F. 89
Bernstorff 176
Beveridge, W.H. 99
Bevin, E. 99
Bhagwati, J. 55, 144
Bidwell, P.W. 113, 119
Bismarck, O. 28–30, 34, 179–80, 182, 228, 232, 262, 430, 440–41, 447
Bloom, D.E. 56
Böhning, W.R. 202
Borjas, G. 311
Bowring, J. 16, 17, 26
Boyer, F. 139
Brading, C.W. 64
Brebner, J.B. 10
Bretano, L. 280
Brigden, J.B. 94–5
Bright, J. 14
Brown, W.A. 91
Brüning, H. 98, 105, 111
Buckingham, Duke of 15
Bullit 107
Bulmer-Thomas, V. 60, 66, 84–5

Caird, J. 16
Canning 11
Cappellarsi 31
Caprivi, G. 46
Carey, H. 21
Carteret, J. 176
Castlereagh 196
Catherine the Great 182–3, 187
Cauwés, P.-L. 266
Cavour, Count C. 7, 11, 30, 178–90, 228
Centeno, M.A. 59
Chamberlain, J. 14, 261
Charles V 183
Charles VI 175
Chatham 183
Cheng, L.K. 312
Cherbuliez 30
Chevalier, M. 11, 21–2, 30, 31
Churchill, W. 447
Class, H. 232
Clemens, M.A. 49, 56, 78, 83–4
Clough, S.B. 32
Coatsworth, J.H. 50, 75
Cobden, R. 5, 14, 15, 22, 24, 30
Cockerill, W. 162
Condliffe, J.B. 92, 100, 116, 121
Coolidge, C. 93, 447
Copland, D.B. 95
Crafts, N.F.R. 340–41
Curzon, G. 137
Czatoryski, Prince A. 196

Daudet, L. 202
Davis, J.S. 96
De Cérenville, B. 168
De Long, J.B. 337
De Tocqueville, A. 30
De Valera, E. 281
Dehio, L. 182
Delaisi, F. 267–8, 270
Detering, H. 93
Diaz-Alejandro, C. 52
Diebold, W. 129, 133
Disraeli, B. 279
Dohan, M. 109
Dollar, D. 55–6